Rathbun and Monica M. Grecu (1987)

60 *Canadian Writers Since 1960, Second Series,* edited by W. H. New (1987)

61 *American Writers for Children Since 1960: Poets, Illustrators, and Nonfiction Authors,* edited by Glenn E. Estes (1987)

62 *Elizabethan Dramatists,* edited by Fredson Bowers (1987)

63 *Modern American Critics, 1920-1955,* edited by Gregory S. Jay (1988)

64 *American Literary Critics and Scholars, 1850-1880,* edited by John W. Rathbun and Monica M. Grecu (1988)

65 *French Novelists, 1900-1930,* edited by Catharine Savage Brosman (1988)

66 *German Fiction Writers, 1885-1913,* 2 parts, edited by James Hardin (1988)

67 *Modern American Critics Since 1955,* edited by Gregory S. Jay (1988)

68 *Canadian Writers, 1920-1959, First Series,* edited by W. H. New (1988)

69 *Contemporary German Fiction Writers, First Series,* edited by Wolfgang D. Elfe and James Hardin (1988)

70 *British Mystery Writers, 1860-1919,* edited by Bernard Benstock and Thomas F. Staley (1988)

71 *American Literary Critics and Scholars, 1880-1900,* edited by John W. Rathbun and Monica M. Grecu (1988)

72 *French Novelists, 1930-1960,* edited by Catharine Savage Brosman (1988)

73 *American Magazine Journalists, 1741-1850,* edited by Sam G. Riley (1988)

74 *American Short-Story Writers Before 1880,* edited by Bobby Ellen Kimbel, with the assistance of William E. Grant (1988)

75 *Contemporary German Fiction Writers, Second Series,* edited by Wolfgang D. Elfe and James Hardin (1988)

76 *Afro-American Writers, 1940-1955,* edited by Trudier Harris (1988)

77 *British Mystery Writers, 1920-1939,* edited by Bernard Benstock and Thomas F. Staley (1988)

78 *American Short-Story Writers, 1880-1910,* edited by Bobby Ellen Kimbel, with the assistance of William E. Grant (1988)

79 *American Magazine Journalists, 1850-1900,* edited by Sam G. Riley (1988)

80 *Restoration and Eighteenth-Century Dramatists, First Series,* edited by Paula R. Backscheider (1989)

81 *Austrian Fiction Writers, 1875-1913,* edited by James Hardin and Donald G. Daviau (1989)

82 *Chicano Writers, First Series,* edited by Francisco A. Lomelí and Carl R. Shirley (1989)

83 *French Novelists Since 1960,* edited by Catharine Savage Brosman (1989)

84 *Restoration and Eighteenth-Century Dramatists, Second Series,* edited by Paula R. Backscheider (1989)

85 *Austrian Fiction Writers After 1914,* edited by James Hardin and Donald G. Daviau (1989)

86 *American Short-Story Writers, 1910-1945, First Series,* edited by Bobby Ellen Kimbel (1989)

87 *British Mystery and Thriller Writers Since 1940, First Series,* edited by Bernard Benstock and Thomas F. Staley (1989)

88 *Canadian Writers, 1920-1959, Second Series,* edited by W. H. New (1989)

89 *Restoration and Eighteenth-Century Dramatists, Third Series,* edited by Paula R. Backscheider (1989)

90 *German Writers in the Age of Goethe, 1789-1832,* edited by James Hardin and Christoph E. Schweitzer (1989)

91 *American Magazine Journalists, 1900-1960, First Series,* edited by Sam G. Riley (1990)

92 *Canadian Writers, 1890-1920,* edited by W. H. New (1990)

93 *British Romantic Poets, 1789-1832, First Series,* edited by John R. Greenfield (1990)

94 *German Writers in the Age of Goethe: Sturm und Drang to Classicism,* edited by James Hardin and Christoph E. Schweitzer (1990)

95 *Eighteenth-Century British Poets, First Series,* edited by John Sitter (1990)

96 *British Romantic Poets, 1789-1832, Second Series,* edited by John R. Greenfield (1990)

97 *German Writers from the Enlightenment to Sturm und Drang, 1720-1764,* edited by James Hardin and Christoph E. Schweitzer (1990)

98 *Modern British Essayists, First Series,* edited by Robert Beum (1990)

99 *Canadian Writers Before 1890,* edited by W. H. New (1990)

100 *Modern British Essayists, Second Series,* edited by Robert Beum (1990)

101 *British Prose Writers, 1660-1800, First Series,* edited by Donald T. Siebert (1991)

102 *American Short-Story Writers, 1910-1945, Second Series,* edited by Bobby Ellen Kimbel (1991

103 *American Literary Biographers, First Series,* edited by Steven Serafin (1991)

104 *British Prose Writers, 1660-1800, Second Series,* edited by Donald T. Siebert (1991)

105 *American Poets Since World War II, Second Series,* edited by R. S. Gwynn (1991)

106 *British Literary Publishing Houses, 1820-1880,* edited by Patricia J. Anderson and Jonathan Rose (1991)

107 *British Romantic Prose Writers, 1789-1832, First Series,* edited by John R. Greenfield (1991)

108 *Twentieth-Century Spanish Poets, First Series,* edited by Michael L. Perna (1991)

109 *Eighteenth-Century British Poets, Second Series,* edited by John Sitter (1991)

110 *British Romantic Prose Writers, 1789-1832, Second Series,* edited by John R. Greenfield (1991)

111 *American Literary Biographers, Second Series,* edited by Steven Serafin (1991)

112 *British Literary Publishing Houses, 1881-1965,* edited by Jonathan Rose and Patricia J. Anderson (1991)

113 *Modern Latin-American Fiction Writers, First Series,* edited by William Luis (1992)

114 *Twentieth-Century Italian Poets, First Series,* edited by Giovanna Wedel De Stasio, Glauco Cambon, and Antonio Illiano (1992)

115 *Medieval Philosophers,* edited by Jeremiah Hackett (1992)

116 *British Romantic Novelists, 1789-1832,* edited by Bradford K. Mudge (1992)

117 *Twentieth-Century Caribbean and Black African Writers, First Series,* edited by Bernth Lindfors and Reinhard Sander (1992)

118 *Twentieth-Century German Dramatists, 1889-1918,* edited by Wolfgang D. Elfe and James Hardin (1992)

119 *Nineteenth-Century French Fiction Writers: Romanticism and Realism, 1800-1860,* edited by Catharine Savage Brosman (1992)

(Continued on back endsheets)

Twentieth-Century Caribbean and Black African Writers

Second Series

Dictionary of Literary Biography® • Volume One Hundred Twenty-Five

Twentieth-Century Caribbean and Black African Writers

Second Series

9939

Edited by
Bernth Lindfors and Reinhard Sander

A Bruccoli Clark Layman Book
Gale Research Inc.
Detroit, London

Printed in the United States of America

Published simultaneously in the United Kingdom
by Gale Research International Limited
(An affiliated company of Gale Research Inc.)

The paper used in this publication meets the minimum requirements
of American National Standard for Information Sciences–Permanence
Paper for Printed Library Materials, ANSI Z39.48-1984. ⊚ ™

Table of Contents

Plan of the Series vii

Introduction ix

Acknowledgments xiv

Michael Anthony (1932–) 3
    Harold Barratt

Edward Kamau Brathwaite (1930–) 8
    Laurence A. Breiner

Austin C. Clarke (1934–) 29
    Victor J. Ramraj

Nuruddin Farah (1945–) 35
    Jacqueline Bardolph

C. L. R. James (1901–1989) 41
    Reinhard Sander

Ismith Khan (1925–) 48
    Ketu H. Katrak

George Lamming (1927–) 54
    Sandra Pouchet Paquet

Earl Lovelace (1935–) 70
    Chezia Thompson-Cager

Roger Mais (1905–1955) 78
    Kamau Brathwaite

Ali A. Mazrui (1933–) 82
    Omari H. Kokole

Es'kia (Ezekiel) Mphahlele (1919–) 89
    Ursula A. Barnett

Oswald Mbuyiseni Mtshali (1940–) 109
    Cecily Lockett

Meja Mwangi (1948–) 114
    Simon Gikandi

V. S. Naipaul (1932–) 121
    John Thieme

Ngugi wa Thiong'o (1938–) 145
    David Maughan-Brown

Arthur Nortje (1942–) 170
    David Bunn

Flora Nwapa (1931–) 178
    Gay Wilentz

Grace Ogot (1930–) 184
    Brenda F. Berrian

Gabriel Okara (1921–) 188
    Bruce King

Christopher Okigbo (1930–) 200
    Donatus Ibe Nwoga

Okot p'Bitek (1931–1982) 225
    Bernth Lindfors

Kole Omotoso (1943–) 238
    F. Odun Balogun

Femi Osofisan (1946–) 243
    Sandra L. Richards

Sol T. Plaatje (1876–) 251
    Brian P. Willan

V. S. (Vic) Reid (1913–) 256
    Michael G. Cooke

Richard Rive (1931–) 261
    Martin Trump

Ola Rotimi (1938–) 265
    Joel Adedeji

Andrew Salkey (1928–) 270
    Anthony Boxill

Dennis Scott (1939–1991) 276
    Al Creighton

Sam Selvon (1923–) 281
    Harold Barratt

Mongane Wally Serote (1944–) 291
    David Attwell

Wole Soyinka (1934–) 298
    James Gibbs

Taban lo Liyong (1939?–) 327
    Peter Nazareth

Amos Tutuola (1920–) 332
    Bernth Lindfors

Books for Further Reading 347

Contributors 350

Cumulative Index 353

Plan of the Series

. . . Almost the most prodigious asset of a country, and perhaps its most precious possession, is its native literary product — when that product is fine and noble and enduring.

Mark Twain*

The advisory board, the editors, and the publisher of the *Dictionary of Literary Biography* are joined in endorsing Mark Twain's declaration. The literature of a nation provides an inexhaustible resource of permanent worth. We intend to make literature and its creators better understood and more accessible to students and the reading public, while satisfying the standards of teachers and scholars.

To meet these requirements, *literary biography* has been construed in terms of the author's achievement. The most important thing about a writer is his writing. Accordingly, the entries in *DLB* are career biographies, tracing the development of the author's canon and the evolution of his reputation.

The purpose of *DLB* is not only to provide reliable information in a convenient format but also to place the figures in the larger perspective of literary history and to offer appraisals of their accomplishments by qualified scholars.

The publication plan for *DLB* resulted from two years of preparation. The project was proposed to Bruccoli Clark by Frederick C. Ruffner, president of the Gale Research Company, in November 1975. After specimen entries were prepared and typeset, an advisory board was formed to refine the entry format and develop the series rationale. In meetings held during 1976, the publisher, series editors, and advisory board approved the scheme for a comprehensive biographical dictionary of persons who contributed to North American literature. Editorial work on the first volume began in January 1977, and it was published in 1978. In order to make *DLB* more than a reference tool and to compile volumes that individually have claim to status

*From an unpublished section of Mark Twain's autobiography, copyright by the Mark Twain Company

as literary history, it was decided to organize volumes by topic, period, or genre. Each of these freestanding volumes provides a biographical-bibliographical guide and overview for a particular area of literature. We are convinced that this organization — as opposed to a single alphabet method — constitutes a valuable innovation in the presentation of reference material. The volume plan necessarily requires many decisions for the placement and treatment of authors who might properly be included in two or three volumes. In some instances a major figure will be included in separate volumes, but with different entries emphasizing the aspect of his career appropriate to each volume. Ernest Hemingway, for example, is represented in *American Writers in Paris, 1920-1939* by an entry focusing on his expatriate apprenticeship; he is also in *American Novelists, 1910-1945* with an entry surveying his entire career. Each volume includes a cumulative index of the subject authors and articles. Comprehensive indexes to the entire series are planned.

With volume ten in 1982 it was decided to enlarge the scope of *DLB*. By the end of 1986 twenty-one volumes treating British literature had been published, and volumes for Commonwealth and Modern European literature were in progress. The series has been further augmented by the *DLB Yearbooks* (since 1981) which update published entries and add new entries to keep the *DLB* current with contemporary activity. There have also been *DLB Documentary Series* volumes which provide biographical and critical source materials for figures whose work is judged to have particular interest for students. One of these companion volumes is entirely devoted to Tennessee Williams.

We define literature as the *intellectual commerce of a nation:* not merely as belles lettres but as that ample and complex process by which ideas are generated, shaped, and transmitted. *DLB* entries are not limited to "creative writers" but extend to other figures who in their time and in their way influenced the mind of a people. Thus the series encompasses historians, journalists, publishers, and screenwriters. By this means readers of *DLB* may be aided to perceive literature not as cult scripture in the keeping of intellectual high priests but firmly positioned at the center of a nation's life.

DLB includes the major writers appropriate to each volume and those standing in the ranks immediately behind them. Scholarly and critical counsel has been sought in deciding which minor figures to include and how full their entries should be. Wherever possible, useful references are made to figures who do not warrant separate entries.

Each *DLB* volume has a volume editor responsible for planning the volume, selecting the figures for inclusion, and assigning the entries. Volume editors are also responsible for preparing, where appropriate, appendices surveying the major periodicals and literary and intellectual movements for their volumes, as well as lists of further readings. Work on the series as a whole is coordinated at the Bruccoli Clark Layman editorial center in Columbia, South Carolina, where the editorial staff is responsible for accuracy of the published volumes.

One feature that distinguishes *DLB* is the illustration policy – its concern with the iconography of literature. Just as an author is influenced by his surroundings, so is the reader's understanding of the author enhanced by a knowledge of his environment. Therefore *DLB* volumes include not only drawings, paintings, and photographs of authors, often depicting them at various stages in their careers, but also illustrations of their families and places where they lived. Title pages are regularly reproduced in facsimile along with dust jackets for modern authors. The dust jackets are a special feature of *DLB* because they often document better than anything else the way in which an author's work was perceived in its own time. Specimens of the writers' manuscripts are included when feasible.

Samuel Johnson rightly decreed that "The chief glory of every people arises from its authors." The purpose of the *Dictionary of Literary Biography* is to compile literary history in the surest way available to us – by accurate and comprehensive treatment of the lives and work of those who contributed to it.

The *DLB* Advisory Board

Introduction

Since the mid 1980s scholarly interest in postcolonial (including Caribbean and African) writing has grown considerably in most literature departments at colleges and universities in the United States and elsewhere. In recent years many high-school students have been exposed to works such as *Things Fall Apart* (1958) by Nigerian novelist Chinua Achebe, which appear on new multicultural reading lists. In 1986 another Nigerian writer, Wole Soyinka, was the first African to receive the Nobel Prize for literature – followed in 1992 by Derek Walcott, the first Caribbean recipient. Therefore it seems timely for the *DLB* to publish volumes of biobibliographical critical essays on major anglophone writers from Africa and the Caribbean. These volumes are meant as research and reference tools for teachers, students, and general readers; it is hoped that they will also contribute to the realization – to quote the Caribbean writer George Lamming – "that the English language does not belong to the Englishman. It belongs to a lot of people who do a lot of things with it; it is really a tree that has now grown innumerable branches, and you cannot any longer be alarmed by the size or quality of the branch" (in *Kas-Kas: Interviews with Three Caribbean Writers in Texas*, 1972).

The evolution of such branches has a long history. When Christopher Columbus and other mariners embarked on their voyages half a millennium ago, they set in motion a process that led to Europe's military, economic, and cultural domination of much of the rest of the world. Spain and Portugal, soon challenged by Great Britain and other European powers, carved out colonial possessions for settlement or exploitation around the globe. The colonizers' treatment of the indigenous peoples they encountered ranged from genocide – as committed in parts of the Americas – to various forms of direct and indirect rule, as practiced throughout Africa. The process also led to vast movements of people within the colonized countries and between continents. The enslavement and transportation of millions of Africans across the Atlantic during the early phase of colonialism set the stage for subsequent developments in the Caribbean – where people of Af-

rican descent were to outnumber all others – that closely paralleled those on the African continent. This connection is evident in the chronology of the decolonization process that began after World War I and in the cross-fertilization of ideas concerning the anticolonial struggle. African and Caribbean nationalists developed similar political and cultural strategies for achieving independence.

Europeans differed widely in their attitudes toward the peoples and cultures they colonized, but their policies invariably facilitated the imposition and dissemination of European languages. European immigration to North and South America and Australia, and the establishment of smaller European enclaves in parts of Africa and Asia, accelerated the process of linguistic unification and domination.

The internationalization of English during the period of colonialism has had interesting literary consequences, for it has led to the creation of new literatures in English all over the world. These literatures emerged first in areas of European settlement such as the United States, Canada, and Australia, where English was the native language of many immigrants. But such a development also has occurred more recently in parts of South Asia, East Asia, and Africa, where English gained a foothold mainly as a second language spoken by an educated elite. In the British Caribbean, English-based creole languages eclipsed African languages such as Igbo, Yoruba, Kikongo, and Wolof and were used by all sections of the society, including postemancipation Asian indentured laborers and the offspring of the original colonizers. However, the plantation system and various debilitating socioeconomic factors delayed the spread of English as a written language – and thus delayed the creation of a written regional literature.

Some of the earliest black authors to express themselves in English were African-born former slaves or servants writing in Great Britain or North America at the end of the eighteenth century. Phillis Wheatley wrote religious and moral poetry, publishing her first elegy in Boston in 1770, when she was seventeen years old. Between 1770 and 1789

Ukawsaw Gronniosaw, Ottobah Cugoano, and Olaudah Equiano published autobiographical narratives telling of their capture, sale, suffering, and emancipation, and arguing forcefully for the abolition of slavery. Ignatius Sancho, who had been born on a slave ship, also contributed significantly to abolitionist literature: his collected letters were published posthumously in London in 1782. But these earliest anglophone African authors, writing at a time when few blacks in the Western world had access to formal schooling, tended to be regarded in the literary world of their day as remarkable curiosities and possibly even frauds. Some commentators, including Thomas Jefferson, believed that their works must have been ghostwritten by others. Such readers found it difficult to credit the notion that blacks could write so well.

However, in the nineteenth century, slave narratives continued to appear, some of them written by talented women from the New World such as Mary Prince and Harriet Jacobs. There were also books by Africans and West Indians resident in the British Isles: *The Life, History and Unparalleled Sufferings of John Jea, the African Preacher* (1815), Robert Wedderburn's *The Horrors of Slavery* (1824), *The Wonderful Adventures of Mrs. [Mary] Seacole in Many Lands* (1857), James Africanus Horton's *West African Countries and Peoples* (1868), Edward Wilmot Blyden's *Christianity, Islam and the Negro Race* (1887), and J. J. Thomas's *Froudacity* (1889). These books did much to dispel the idea that blacks were incapable of independent authorship.

Literary works from Africa itself were slower to appear. The first novel to be published in English by an African author was *Guanya Pau* (1891) by J. J. Walters, a Liberian graduate of Oberlin College. This was followed nearly two decades later by a pair of Ghanaian works, O. Dazi Ako's *The Seductive Coast: Poems, Lyrical and Descriptive, from West Africa* (1909) and J. E. Casely Hayford's nationalistic allegory *Ethiopia Unbound* (1911), the subtitle of which is *Studies in Race Emancipation*. During the next quarter of a century a second novel emerged from Liberia — Charles Edward Cooper's *Love in Ebony: A West African Romance* (1932), written under the pseudonym Varfelli Karlee — and a trio of brief works were published in South Africa: R. R. R. Dhlomo's novella *An African Tragedy* (1926), Sol T. Plaatje's novel *Mhudi: An Epic of South African Life a Hundred Years Ago* (1930), and H. I. E. Dhlomo's play *The Girl Who Killed to Save* (1935). H. I. E. Dhlomo went on to write *Valley of a Thousand Hills: A Poem* (1941); and the first collections of poetry and short stories by Peter Abrahams were published in the early 1940s,

during World War II, as were the maiden works of three Ghanaian writers: J. B. Danquah's play *The Third Woman* (1943), R. E. Obeng's novel *Eighteenpence* (1943), and George Awoonor-Renner's volume of poems *This Africa* (1943). This small output suggests that colonial conditions were not conducive to the development of anglophone African literatures. In this half century of European rule (from the 1890s to the 1940s) scarcely more than a dozen book-length literary works were published in English by African authors. During the same period more literature was produced in African languages, much of it published at mission stations or by colonial educational agencies.

In the Caribbean, at the beginning of the twentieth century, a recognizable West Indian literary movement finally began to form. In this respect Jamaica clearly emerged as the center of literary activity during the first three decades of the twentieth century. As early as 1929 the president of the Jamaica Poetry League, J. E. Clare McFarlane, was able to produce a wide-ranging anthology of local poetry, and some twenty years before that an attempt had been made by Thomas MacDermot to establish an indigenous publishing house. His All Jamaica Library published four works of fiction: MacDermot's *Becka's Buckra Baby* (1904) and *One Brown Girl And —* (1909); E. A. Dodd's *Maroon Medicine* (1905); and W. A. Campbell's *Marguerite: A Story of the Earthquake* (1907). Overshadowing all other Jamaican writers and dominating the cultural scene well into the 1930s was H. G. de Lisser. He was talented and intelligent but consistently defended the position of the colonial ruling class and was opposed to any moves to give political rights to the black majority. De Lisser put forward his views in novels that made clever use of familiar features of Jamaican life. His first novel, *Jane: A Story of Jamaica* (1913; republished as *Jane's Career*, 1914), is an early precursor of the barrack-yard story (a subgenre based on lower-class urban life) and is as entertaining and realistic as any fiction C. L. R. James, Alfred H. Mendes, or Ralph de Boissière wrote during the 1920s and 1930s in Trinidad. Although later works by de Lisser, such as *Triumphant Squalitone* (1916), *Revenge* (1919), and *Under the Sun* (1937), are more overtly conservative, they are thematically the natural ancestors of the West Indian historical novel and the sociopolitical satire. V. S. (Vic) Reid's *New Day* (1949), in which he attempts to reinterpret the Morant Bay Rebellion in Jamaica in 1865, may even have been conceived as an attempt to counter de Lisser's unfavorable interpretation of the rebellion in *Revenge*. The poet and novelist Claude

McKay left Jamaica when he was in his early twenties. His poetry collections *Songs of Jamaica* and *Constab Ballads*, both published in 1912, represent a completely different line of development to that encouraged by the Jamaican literary establishment. McKay never returned to Jamaica and became instead one of the foremost writers associated with the Harlem Renaissance in the United States.

After World War II there was a spurt of indigenous literary activity in various corners of the British Empire. Literatures written in English by non-European speakers of the language developed contemporaneously with the movements for political independence and generally supported them. As England increasingly lost its direct grip on colonial territories, these literatures grew prodigiously, especially in Africa and the Caribbean. Independence accelerated their growth to the extent that it is now possible to speak of distinct national literatures in English having emerged in such countries as India, Nigeria, Ghana, Kenya, Zimbabwe, and the various Caribbean islands. Not all this vigorous, new anglophone writing comes from former British colonies. One also finds it, for example, in Puerto Rico and the Philippines, where English was introduced by the United States.

The writers included in the first two volumes of *Twentieth-Century Caribbean and Black African Writers* were at the forefront of indigenous literary movements in English in Africa and the Caribbean. The Guyanese writer Edgar Mittelholzer, who wrote and published more than twenty novels in rapid succession, set the example and pace for the Caribbean novelists of the 1950s and 1960s. The quality of the Barbadian George Lamming's anticolonial fiction, the Guyanese Wilson Harris's New World modernist novels, and the Trinidadian V. S. Naipaul's controversial fictional explorations of the postcolonial world remains unsurpassed by any other trio of postcolonial novelists writing in the English language. The careers of such Caribbean novelists were paralleled by those of major poets and dramatists – among them the poet Edward Kamau Brathwaite of Barbados, with his focus on Africa in the Caribbean; and Derek Walcott of Saint Lucia, who in his poetry and plays draws on both rural and metropolitan styles and traditions. In South Africa, pioneers such as Plaatje, Abrahams, and Es'kia (Ezekiel) Mphahlele started writing without models from their own culture to emulate. The latter two, and many others after them, found they had to leave their country in order to continue writing, so an extensive black South African literature was produced in exile, supplemented in more recent years

by vigorous protest literature in South Africa. In Nigeria, Amos Tutuola and Cyprian Ekwensi, authors without a university education, led the way, the first by writing folk fantasies based on local oral narratives, the other by producing zesty imitations of Western popular fiction set in recognizable Nigerian environments – the bustling city, the farmland village, and the peripatetic nomadic settlement. Skilled artists with a fuller knowledge of world literature soon followed, the best being Achebe, Soyinka, and the poet Christopher Okigbo – a trio whose remarkable command of language and originality in handling topical African themes rapidly earned them international recognition. In East Africa, Ngugi wa Thiong'o and Okot p'Bitek developed into the most powerful voices, Ngugi by writing politically charged fiction and drama, Okot by composing amusing satirical verse commenting on cultural confusion in modern Africa. The success of such forerunners encouraged many others to express themselves creatively in a former colonial language. Today there are hundreds of black African and Caribbean authors who have published novels, plays, and volumes of verse in English. In the coming years there are bound to be thousands more.

The sixty-five writers included in the first two volumes of *Twentieth-Century Caribbean and Black African Writers* are drawn from fourteen nations in Africa and the Caribbean, with the greatest number coming from Nigeria (16), South Africa (11), Jamaica (8), Trinidad and Tobago (6), Guyana (5), Ghana (5), and Kenya (4). There are many reasons for the numerical imbalance of writers from various nations in Africa, the foremost being the availability of Western education in the countries concerned. Nigeria, Africa's most heavily populated nation, may have more university graduates than the rest of anglophone Africa combined. South Africa, Ghana, and Kenya also have a relatively high percentage of people with a Western education. In some nations – particularly Nigeria and South Africa – local publishers of books, journals, and popular magazines have provided indigenous outlets for new writing. Of special importance have been *Drum*, *Black Orpheus*, *Okike*, and *Nigeria Magazine*. There have also been active writers' groups, such as the Mbari Clubs in Nigeria, that have sponsored literary competitions, staged plays, organized cultural festivals and book fairs, encouraged the production of children's literature, and sought to protect the financial interests of authors. Such activities have helped to launch and sustain strong anglophone literary movements in areas of the world where English is a language learned at school.

In the British Caribbean, where a distinct variety of English is spoken by the educated sections of the society, some of the same social and institutional forces have been at work. Education was not available to the majority of the population until the last quarter of the nineteenth century, but by the middle of the twentieth century the Caribbean possessed some of the best secondary schools in the British Empire. Furthermore, the foundations had been laid for the establishment of the University of the West Indies, whose campuses in Jamaica, Barbados, and Trinidad boast several published writers among their former students and current faculties. The Caribbean has produced many writers, a lot of whom – like tens of thousands of their countrymen – have left the Caribbean to seek their fortunes elsewhere, especially in Great Britain, Canada, and the United States. However, the indigenous publishing industries that have begun to flourish in the Caribbean and Africa are much in evidence in this *DLB* volume, as more than one-third of the authors represented here published their first book in their native area, ten of them in Africa (primarily Nigeria and South Africa) and two in the Caribbean. The other twenty-two authors saw their first book published in Great Britain or the United States, but several of those also later published in their home countries or regions. It is, however, two British firms, Heinemann and Longman, that continue to dominate the publishing of African and Caribbean writing through their paperback series aimed at secondary-school and college students.

Nearly all the African writers in this *DLB* volume are bilingual, and some are fluent in three or more languages as well as in a local pidgin. Recently some have switched from writing in English to publishing first in African languages and then translating their books into English. Caribbean authors express themselves mainly in English. However, their published work often also draws on the patois or creole languages of the particular islands on which they grew up. In Africa and the Caribbean, ready access to other languages and dialects has led to adventurous stylistic innovations, as authors seek to capture the complex verbal texture of the pluralistic environment they and their characters inhabit. By bending and twisting the English language, they are able to evoke the complexity of African and West Indian social realities. They are forcing an old language to tell new truths.

While many African and Caribbean writers of the 1950s and 1960s tended to explore the colonial past and the colonial experience in their writings, more-recent writers have turned to probing postcolonial life. In carrying out this task, African writers in particular have frequently attracted the censure of their governments and have been imprisoned or forced into exile. Those able to continue writing in such circumstances have developed fresh perspectives on the vulnerability of their societies to economic and political pressures exerted by the outside world; these viewpoints have resulted in writings that examine the black experience in the context of global power struggles. Close linkages of thought and feeling unite politically committed African, Caribbean, and African-American authors. Their novels, plays, and poems increasingly transcend parochial, domestic concerns and address wider, international issues that have an impact on all blacks. Since black African and Caribbean writers are citizens of societies that share a common set of postcolonial problems, they often seek answers to the same vexing sociopolitical questions. They are drawn together by history and geography as well as by race.

One of the authors, Equiano, who is discussed in the appendix to the First Series (*DLB 117*), wrote in the eighteenth century. All the rest – in this and the first volume – are men and women who began to have their work published in the twentieth century, though four (de Lisser, McKay, Plaatje, and Jean Rhys) were born in the late nineteenth century. The selection was based entirely on influence and reputation: those writers most written about, most widely studied in schools and universities, and most frequently read for pleasure were the ones chosen for inclusion. While we considered it appropriate to include a Caribbean writer of European descent (Rhys – in the First Series), white South African writers were excluded because they belong to a different literary tradition, one shaped by a peculiar set of social, cultural, and historical experiences not shared by other African writers or by writers from the Caribbean. (They will be covered in a future *DLB*.)

In the interest of providing a balanced mix of talents from Africa and the Caribbean in each volume, we have included the writers from Gambia, Ghana, Guyana, Saint Lucia, and Dominica in the First Series, and those from Kenya, Uganda, Sudan, Somalia, Barbados, and Trinidad and Tobago in the Second Series. The many authors from Nigeria, South Africa, and Jamaica have been divided between the two volumes.

It is our intention to prepare a third volume of *Twentieth-Century Caribbean and Black African Writers* that will focus on some of the younger writers who have earned reputations for themselves in recent years. That compilation will also include several significant older authors we did not have enough space to cover in the first two volumes. Africa and the Caribbean, though young literary cultures, have already produced so many important writers that it is difficult to fit them all into synoptic surveys that range so widely over the globe. In the future it may be necessary for the *DLB* to devote individual volumes to each of the new national literatures from Africa and the Caribbean that have enriched the expressive culture of the English-speaking world.

— Bernth Lindfors and Reinhard Sander

Acknowledgments

This book was produced by Bruccoli Clark Layman, Inc. Karen L. Rood is senior editor for the *Dictionary of Literary Biography* series. Jack Turner was the in-house editor.

Production coordinator is James W. Hipp. Projects manager is Charles D. Brower. Photography editors are Edward Scott and Timothy C. Lundy. Layout and graphics supervisor is Penney L. Haughton. Copyediting supervisor is Bill Adams. Typesetting supervisor is Kathleen M. Flanagan. Mary Scott Dye is editorial associate. Systems manager is George F. Dodge. The production staff includes Rowena Betts, Steve Borsanyi, Barbara Brannon, Joseph Matthew Bruccoli, Teresa Chaney, Patricia Coate, Rebecca Crawford, Margaret McGinty Cureton, Denise Edwards, Sarah A. Estes, Joyce Fowler, Robert Fowler, Brenda A. Gillie, Bonita Graham, Jolyon M. Helterman, Ellen McCracken, Kathy Lawler Merlette, John Myrick, Pamela D. Norton, Thomas J. Pickett, Patricia Salisbury, Maxine K. Smalls, Deborah P. Stokes, and Wilma Weant.

Walter W. Ross and Samuel Bruce did library research. They were assisted by the following librarians at the Thomas Cooper Library of the University of South Carolina: Jens Holley and the inter-library-loan staff; reference librarians Gwen Baxter, Daniel Boice, Faye Chadwell, Cathy Eckman, Rhonda Felder, Gary Geer, Jackie Kinder, Laurie Preston, Jean Rhyne, Carol Tobin, Virginia Weathers, and Connie Widney; circulation-department head Thomas Marcil; and acquisitions-searching supervisor David Haggard.

The volume editors would like to thank Rhonda Cobham, Margaret Groesbeck, Nuhad Jamal, and Michael Kasper – all of Amherst College – for their substantial help with this project.

Dictionary of Literary Biography® • Volume One Hundred Twenty-Five

Twentieth-Century Caribbean and Black African Writers

Second Series

Dictionary of Literary Biography

Michael Anthony

(10 February 1932 –)

Harold Barratt
University College of Cape Breton

BOOKS: *The Games Were Coming* (London: Deutsch, 1963; Boston: Houghton Mifflin, 1968);
The Year in San Fernando (London: Deutsch, 1965);
Green Days by the River (London: Deutsch, 1967; Boston: Houghton Mifflin, 1967);
Cricket in the Road, and Other Stories (London: Deutsch, 1973);
Sandra Street, and Other Stories (London: Heinemann, 1973);
Glimpses of Trinidad and Tobago: With a Glance at the West Indies (Port of Spain: Columbus, 1974);
King of the Masquerade (London: Nelson, 1974);
Profile Trinidad: A Historical Survey from the Discovery to 1900 (London: Macmillan, 1975);
Folk Tales and Fantasies (Port of Spain: Columbus, 1976);
Streets of Conflict (London: Deutsch, 1976);
The Making of Port of Spain (Port of Spain: Key Caribbean, 1978);
All That Glitters (London: Deutsch, 1981);
Bright Road to El Dorado (Walton-on-Thames, U.K.: Nelson Caribbean, 1982);
Port of Spain in a World at War, 1939–1945 (Port of Spain: Ministry of Sports, Culture & Youth Affairs, 1983);
First in Trinidad (Port of Spain: Circle, 1985);
Heroes of the People of Trinidad and Tobago (Port of Spain: Circle, 1986);
A Better and Brighter Day (Port of Spain: Circle, 1987);
Towns and Villages of Trinidad and Tobago (Port of Spain: Circle, 1988);

Michael Anthony (photograph copyright by Erich Malter)

Parade of the Carvinals of Trinidad, 1839–1989 (Port of Spain: Circle, 1989).

OTHER: "In a South-Eastern Village," in *David Frost Introduces Trinidad and Tobago*, edited by

3

Dust jacket for Anthony's 1963 novel, the story of a dedicated cyclist who learns that self-discipline is a vital part of success and happiness

Anthony and Andrew Carr (London: Deutsch, 1975), pp. 48–56;

"Thoughts on a Dawning Sunset," in *Studies in Commonwealth Literature*, edited by Eckhard Breitinger and Reinhard Sander (Tübingen, Germany: Gunter Narr, 1985), pp. 15–18;

Gaylord Kelshall, *The History of Aviation in Trinidad and Tobago, 1913–1962*, edited and indexed by Anthony (Port of Spain: Paria, 1987).

SELECTED PERIODICAL PUBLICATION –
UNCOLLECTED: "Growing up with Writing: A Particular Experience," *Journal of Commonwealth Literature*, 7 (July 1969): 80–87.

Michael Anthony has written five novels, numerous short stories, books for children, and assorted histories of Trinidad and Tobago. His fiction is widely read as prescribed texts at all levels of education, and he has made a major contribution to the remarkable emergence of a distinctive and vibrant West Indian literature. Examining the lives of those who survive in poverty and hopelessness, he shows candor and a sensitive understanding of their silent desperation, and he explores areas sometimes considered too banal for serious literary treatment.

Anthony's best work shows a finely tuned understanding of his native society.

Born to Nathaniel (a farmer) and Eva Jones Anthony in Mayaro, Trinidad, on 10 February 1932, Michael Anthony was educated in San Fernando. In 1954 he quit his job at a foundry in Pointe à Pierre and set out for England, where he worked in factories, then for Reuter's News Agency. However, he disliked the class-oriented social and racial climate there, and he eventually returned to Trinidad in 1970 – after a two-year sojourn in Brazil, where he served in the Trinidad diplomatic corps. He has lived in Trinidad ever since and works closely with the National Cultural Council. On 8 February 1958 he married; he and his wife, Yvette, a typist, have two sons and two daughters.

Mayaro, a seaside village on the southeastern coast of Trinidad, has a tenacious hold on Anthony's imagination. Mayaro is his spiritual home, and it provides much more than a pallid setting for the action in his novels; it seems as tangible as the sweaty runnels on the gleaming torsos of the fishermen he describes. In *Green Days by the River* (1967) the beauty of the Mayaro landscape is a palpable presence in the developing consciousness of

Shellie, the young hero. Cedar Grove (near Mayaro), where much of the plot takes place, is a paradise of flowers, fruit, and songbirds. In this resplendent Eden, Shellie journeys toward adult responsibility. Mayaro is for Anthony an emblem of idealized existence. One notices this symbolism also in the short story "Hibiscus" (in *Sandra Street*, 1973) when the boy-narrator, on returning to his native Mayaro from a bleak sojourn in London, discovers a recuperative freshness at the heart of the village. The 1981 novel *All That Glitters* also unfolds against this idyllic setting. Anthony successfully blends background, theme, and characterization in his characteristically terse prose.

One of Anthony's most important contributions to the continuing development of West Indian fiction is his emphasis on strong, dour personalities. The abused or abandoned wives and mothers are particularly tenacious, and many of these women are their families' only bulwark against destitution. One or two are worth noting. In spite of her husband's brutalities, the wife in "Drunkard of the River" (in *Cricket in the Road*, 1973) courageously awaits his arrival every Saturday night. Like the work-crippled mother in *The Year in San Fernando* (1965), the drunkard's wife ages prematurely, but she stoically resists the injustices of her harassed life. Her intransigence is rooted in her love for a man who, she says with characteristic resignation, "had only turned out badly." A similar fortitude is noticeable in "The Girl and the River" (also in *Cricket in the Road*). This story bears an interesting resemblance to William Wordsworth's "Resolution and Independence" (1807). In both poem and story the central figure resists the hardships of a tedious livelihood with a doggedness that stuns the narrators, both of whom, seeking solitude and respite from troublesome thoughts, accidentally encounter the central figures in isolated and austerely beautiful settings. Anthony draws one's attention to the girl's poverty, but he also emphasizes her silent perseverance and a stoicism uncommon in such a young woman. There is an understated heroism in the girl's strenuous life.

For Anthony's men and women the world is "blood and sweat and pressure," as the pragmatic businessman puts it in "The Patch of Guava" (in *Cricket in the Road*). The world offers only unrelieved pressure for Leon Seal, the obsessed cyclist of *The Games Were Coming* (1963), one of Anthony's most artistically controlled pieces of fiction. Victory in the fifteen-mile Blue Riband race at the prestigious Southern Games is Leon's all-consuming passion. The austerity and self-denial this passion produces are called up in the severe sparseness of Leon's room. Leon's rigid discipline sometimes turns him into a callous, rather rebarbative young man; yet there is something admirable about Leon's unswerving commitment to the rigors of his training. Anthony keeps the sensual allure of the annual carnival and the demanding rigors of Guaracara Park, site of the games, in the foreground. The juxtaposition between park and carnival is the hub around which all the novel's major issues turn. Anthony sets Leon's ascetic regimen against the unbridled sensuality of the coming carnival and the equally compelling charms of the nubile Sylvia, Leon's rejected girlfriend. Sylvia eventually turns to the randy Mohansingh, who arouses in her a dormant sensuality she both despises and enjoys; and the bond between Leon and his regimen is close enough to elicit from Sylvia a bitter comment: "Bicycle is his woman!"

But the race is considerably more than just a strenuous event; the games are a test of Leon's moral fiber. Anthony describes the race as if it were a battle and Leon's competitors his enemies, one of whom is "killed off." Metaphorically, the "giants" in the race, all of whom have demonstrated their prowess, are overwhelmed by Leon's inexorable pursuit of excellence, part of which has involved a denial of the flesh. Self-discipline, the novel implies, is essential for the achievement of excellence. Dolphus, Leon's mischievous younger brother, can easily shift between the two worlds of the park and the carnival; for Leon, however, they are incompatible.

In *The Year in San Fernando* and *Green Days by the River* Anthony's skill in exploring a youngster's maturation can be seen at its most consummate. Anthony's successful effacing of the authorial voice in *The Year in San Fernando* is one of his finest achievements. Francis, through whose shifting perceptions the story is told, is an affectionate boy suddenly wrenched from his family in Mayaro and placed as a servant in the turbulent Chandles household, where a difficult initiation into life begins immediately upon his arrival. He acquires the art of deception as a survival tactic, and his understanding of adult behavior slowly grows — for instance, during his ambivalent relationship with Julia, the attractive woman with whom Mr. Chandles is having a secret liaison. Francis's puppy love for Julia has a strong sexual component, as his disquieting dreams show. However, he soon discovers that Julia is a complex person, and he begins to adopt a protective, even patronizing, attitude toward her.

Francis's relationship with Chandles is equally

instructive. When the isolation of the interminable rainy season brings them together, there is a significant improvement in their abrasive relationship. The boy realizes that his hate for Chandles might have been precipitate, and, a week before the Christmas holidays, their earlier efforts to understand each other are rewarded as Francis comes to share Chandles's fears and anxieties. Anthony presents the growing camaraderie of boy and man against the backdrop of the brilliant renewal in nature: healthy trees grow toward the sky in places arid before the rains. Finally Francis and Chandles are drawn together by the shared experience of Mrs. Chandles's death. Their closeness is emphasized in a passage that demonstrates Anthony's ability to convey Francis's growing sensibilities:

> It was coming home to me that at this hour we were becoming friends. I could feel it there between us. I could feel it strong and real. . . . I wondered how come he felt he could talk to me like this and be friends with me. I knew he was no tyrant now and I was feeling easy with him. I looked down at the sweetbroom and at the love-birds and inside me I was feeling new.

By the end of the novel Francis's psychological dependence on others has been replaced by a more adult understanding of human interdependence.

In *Green Days by the River* Anthony shows that an ennobling pertinacity can be found in the humblest of places. Even though her family is in desperate need, Mrs. Lammy permits young Shellie to accept his friend Mr. Gidharee's generosity only grudgingly: her resistance is of a piece with the family's determination to maintain its integrity in the face of Mr. Lammy's recurrent illness. The powerful scenes in which the family's fortitude is presented are juxtaposed with the adolescent joys of Shellie and Joan strolling along a dark, romantic beach. Writing sparse but emotionally charged prose, Anthony quietly draws readers into the remarkable strength of an unremarkable man (Mr. Lammy) as he faces death.

Anthony is particularly interested in the growing consciousness of sensitive youngsters, and he has created several. Dolphus in *The Games Were Coming*, for instance, is a precursor of the type that Shellie in *Green Days by the River* more fully embodies. Dolphus is hypersensitive to the throbbing life around him, and Anthony conveys the excitement of the carnival and the coming games largely through Dolphus's sensibilities and resourceful imagination. At one point Dolphus recognizes that one must "suffer to become pure." An equally imaginative youngster, Alan, son of staid parents, appears in Anthony's *King of the Masquerade* (1974), which, although written for children, is a trenchant defense of the carnival and an attack on the pretensions of Trinidad's middle class.

Like Francis in *The Year in San Fernando*, Shellie in *Green Days by the River* is also receptive to the changing rhythms of his world. The most important catalyst in Shellie's development is Mr. Gidharee, his surrogate father. In the first phase of his education, Shellie discovers that his Edenic world is ephemeral. His journey to the hospital where his father lies wasting away is a symbolic journey toward adult responsibility. In the hospital Shellie's innocence is shattered by the disconcerting and perplexing reality of human suffering. He can no longer comprehend the vagaries of justice, rewards, and punishments. Meanwhile his ambivalent and tormenting relationships with Rosalie (Gidharee's daughter) and the sophisticated Joan culminate in his seduction of Rosalie.

The second phase of Shellie's development is his growing realization that maturity involves accepting the consequences of one's decisions and actions. Gidharee brings this home to him with brutal directness amid the quiet isolation of woods and river, which Anthony skillfully uses as an ironic setting for the protagonist's "baptism of blood." When Gidharee turns his vicious dogs on the defenseless boy, he is emphasizing the supreme importance of Rosalie's integrity. The savage attack leaves Shellie alone, exhausted, and seriously wounded, but the ferocious rain that drenches him immediately after the attack seems to confirm his purification.

In *Streets of Conflict* (1976) Anthony draws heavily on his sojourn in Brazil. The novelist chooses the bristling streets of Rio on the eve of the turbulent 1970s as the setting for exploring the contradictions in the life of an idealistic but rash Trinidadian. Anthony uses parallels between paired sets of characters to launch a discussion about the merits of political and moral commitment in the unstable Brazilian society. But the discussion is not substantial, and the characters are not compelling. Marisa, the central female character, is frigid, and the vexing problems of society are not sufficiently urgent to disturb the even tenor of her unruffled personality. The system against which Mac, the fervid revolutionary, struggles is given marginal treatment. Mac's vociferous commitment to the black cause is compromised by his white wife, his white mistress, and his sexual indifference toward Marisa, but this problem is not fully developed. In *Streets of Conflict* commitment ironically leads to futility and despair, both of which are effectively mirrored in the unrelenting bleakness of the Praca Saens Pena area, in which much of the action takes place.

Several reviewers adopted severe and patronizing attitudes toward Anthony's work in the mid 1960s. Since then more perceptive critics have noted the quality of his uncluttered prose and his valuable explorations of the physical and metaphysical contours of his society. Anthony continues to produce a substantial oeuvre for future scholars and students.

Interviews:

Ian Munro and Reinhard Sander, "The Return of a West Indian Writer," *Bim*, 14 (January–June 1973): 212–218;

Sander, "The Caribbean Writer at Home," *World Literature Written in English*, forthcoming.

References:

Harold Barratt, "The Committed Individual in Selvon, Lovelace, Anthony and Coetzee," in *Literature and Commitment*, edited by Govind Sharma (Toronto: TSAR, 1988), pp. 26–33;

Barratt, "Michael Anthony: A Critical Assessment," *Bim*, 17 (June 1983): 157–164;

Barratt, "Michael Anthony and Earl Lovelace: The Search for Selfhood," *ACLALS Bulletin*, 5 (December 1980): 62–73;

Wolfgang Binder, " 'The Quality of Fact in Fiction': Mayaro and Childhood Experience in Michael Anthony's Short Stories," in *The Story Must Be Told*, edited by Peter O. Stummer (Würzburg, Germany: Könighausen & Neumann, 1986), pp. 67–76;

Steven R. Carter, "Michael Anthony's *All That Glitters*: A Golden West Indian Experimental Mystery," *Journal of West Indian Literature*, 2 (December 1987): 41–54;

Paul Edwards and Kenneth Ramchand, "The Art of Memory: Michael Anthony's *The Year in San Fernando*," *Journal of Commonwealth Literature*, 7 (July 1969): 59–72;

Gareth Griffiths, Introduction to Anthony's *Green Days by the River* (London: Heinemann, 1973), pp. vii–xviii;

Steve Harney, "Nation Time: Earl Lovelace and Michael Anthony Nationfy Trinidad," *Commonwealth Essays and Studies*, 13 (Spring 1991): 31–41;

Eric King, "*The Year in San Fernando*," *Caribbean Quarterly*, 16 (December 1970): 87–91;

Anthony Luengo, "Growing up in San Fernando: Change and Growth in Michael Anthony's *The Year in San Fernando*," *Ariel*, 6 (April 1975): 81–95;

Frank McGuinness, "West Indian Windfall," *London Magazine* (April 1967): 117–120;

Alastair Niven, " 'My Sympathies Enlarged': The Novels of Michael Anthony," *Commonwealth Essays and Studies*, 2 (1976): 45–62;

Kenneth Ramchand, "The Games Were Coming," in his *An Introduction to the Study of West Indian Literature* (Sunbury-on-Thames, U.K.: Nelson Caribbean, 1976), pp. 143–154;

Reinhard Sander, "The Homesickness of Michael Anthony," *Literary Half-Yearly*, 16 (January 1975): 95–125;

Richard I. Smyer, "Enchantment and Violence in the Fiction of Michael Anthony," *World Literature Written in English*, 21 (Spring 1982): 148–159.

Papers:

The Michael Anthony Papers (1957–1984), in the New York Public Library Schomburg Center for Research in Black Culture, include correspondence with family, friends, and publishers – especially with André Deutsch – as well as manuscripts and typescripts of Anthony's literary and historical works.

Edward Kamau Brathwaite

(11 May 1930 –)

Laurence A. Breiner
Boston University

BOOKS: *Four Plays for Primary Schools* (London: Longmans, 1964);

Odale's Choice (London: Evans, 1967);

Rights of Passage (London & New York: Oxford University Press, 1967);

Masks (London & New York: Oxford University Press, 1968);

Islands (London & New York: Oxford University Press, 1969);

Folk Culture of the Slaves in Jamaica (London & Port of Spain: New Beacon, 1970; revised, 1981);

The Development of Creole Society in Jamaica, 1770–1820 (Oxford: Clarendon, 1971);

Caribbean Man in Space and Time (Mona, Jamaica: Savacou, 1974);

Contradictory Omens: Cultural Diversity and Integration in the Caribbean (Mona, Jamaica: Savacou, 1974);

Days & Nights (Mona, Jamaica: Caldwell, 1975);

Other Exiles (London & New York: Oxford University Press, 1975);

Black + Blues (Havana: Casa de las Américas, 1976; Benin City, Nigeria: Ethiope, 1978);

Mother Poem (Oxford & New York: Oxford University Press, 1977);

Our Ancestral Heritage: A Bibliography of the English-Speaking Caribbean (Mona, Jamaica: Savacou, 1977);

Wars of Respect: Nanny, Sam Sharpe and the Struggle for People's Liberation (Kingston, Jamaica: Agency for Public Information, 1977);

Soweto (Mona, Jamaica: Savacou, 1979);

Word Making Man: A Poem for Nicolás Guillén (Mona, Jamaica: Savacou, 1979);

Barbados Poetry, 1661–1979 (Mona, Jamaica: Savacou, 1979);

Jamaica Poetry: A Checklist (Kingston: Jamaica Library Service, 1979);

Afternoon of the Status Crow (Mona, Jamaica: Savacou, 1982);

Sun Poem (Oxford: Oxford University Press, 1982);

Gods of the Middle Passage (Mona, Jamaica: Brathwaite/Savacou, 1982);

Kumina (Mona, Jamaica: Savacou, 1982);

Third World Poems (Harlow, U.K.: Longman, 1983);

Colonial Encounter: Language (Mysore, India: University of Mysore, 1984);

History of the Voice: The Development of Nation Language in Anglophone Caribbean Poetry (London & Port of Spain: New Beacon, 1984);

Roots: Literary Criticism (Havana: Casa de las Américas, 1986);

Jah Music (Mona, Jamaica: Savacou, 1986);

Visibility Trigger / Le détonateur de visibilité (Belgium: Cahiers de Louvain, 1986);

X/Self (Oxford & New York: Oxford University Press, 1987);

Sappho Sakyi's Meditations (Mona, Jamaica: Savacou, 1989);

Shar (Mona, Jamaica: Savacou, 1992);

Middle Passages (Newcastle upon Tyne, U.K.: Bloodaxe, 1992).

Collection: *The Arrivants: A New World Trilogy* (London & New York: Oxford University Press, 1973) – comprises *Rights of Passage*, *Masks*, and *Islands*.

PLAY PRODUCTIONS: *Four Plays*, Anglican Primary School, Saltpond, Ghana, December 1961;

Odale's Choice, Mfantsiman Secondary School, Saltpond, Ghana, June 1962.

RECORDINGS: *The Arrivants: Rights of Passage*, Argo, DA 101–102, 1969; reissued, PLP 1110–1111, 1972;

Masks, Argo, PLP 1183, 1972;

Islands, Argo, PLP 1184–1185, 1973;

Poemas, Havana, Casa de las Américas, LD-CA-L-12, 1976.

OTHER: *Iouanaloa: Recent Writing from St. Lucia*, edited, with contributions, by Brathwaite (Castries, Saint Lucia: UWI, Department of Extra-Mural Studies, 1963);

Edward Kamau Brathwaite (photograph copyright 1986 by Dr. Peter Stummer)

"Cricket," in *Caribbean Prose*, edited by Andrew Salkey (London: Evans, 1967);

"Art and Society: Kapoa Context," in *Jamaican Folk Art* (Kingston: Institute of Jamaica, 1971), pp. 4–6;

Melville J. Herskovits, *Life in a Haitian Valley*, introduction by Brathwaite (Garden City, N.Y.: Doubleday/Anchor, 1971), pp. v–viii;

Roger Mais, *Brother Man*, introduction by Brathwaite (London: Heinemann, 1974), pp. v–xxi;

"The Love Axe/1: Developing a Caribbean Aesthetic 1962–1974," in *Reading Black: Essays in the Criticism of African, Caribbean and Black American Literature*, edited by Houston A. Baker, Jr. (Ithaca, N.Y.: Cornell University, Africana Studies and Research Center, 1976), pp. 20–36;

"Caliban, Ariel, and Unprospero in the Conflict of Creolization: A Study of the Slave Revolt in Jamaica in 1831–32," in *Comparative Perspectives on Slavery in New World Plantation Societies*, edited by Vera Ruben and Arthur Tuden (New York: New York Academy of Sciences, 1977), pp. 41–62;

New Poets from Jamaica: An Anthology, edited, with an introduction, by Brathwaite (Mona, Jamaica: Savacou, 1979);

"Caribbean Culture: Two Paradigms," in *Missile and Capsule*, edited by Jürgen Martini (Bremen, Germany: University of Bremen, 1983), pp. 9–54;

Rex Nettleford, *Dance Jamaica*, introduction by Brathwaite (New York: Grove, 1985), pp. 7–11;

Dream Rock: A Collection of Poems, edited by Brathwaite (Kingston: Jamaica Information Service, 1987);

"History, the Caribbean Writer, and *X/Self*," in *Crisis and Creativity in the New Literatures in English*, edited by Geoffrey Davis and Hena Maes-Jelinek (Amsterdam & Atlanta: Rodopi, 1990).

SELECTED PERIODICAL PUBLICATIONS – UNCOLLECTED: "A West Indian Culture?," *Harrisonian* (1949);

"The Controversial Tree of Time," *Bim*, 8 (January–June 1960): 104–114;

"The New West Indian Novelists," *Bim*, 8 (July–December 1960): 199–210; (January–June 1961): 271–280;

"Roots," *Bim*, 10 (July–December 1963): 10–21;

"*Kyk-over-al* and the Radicals," *New World: Guyana Independence Issue* (1966): 55–57;

"Jazz and the West Indian Novel," *Bim*, 11 (January–June 1967): 275–284; 12 (July–December 1967): 39–51; (January–June 1968): 115–126;

"West Indian Prose Fiction in the Sixties," *Critical Survey* (Winter 1967): 169–174; revised in *Black World*, 31 (September 1971): 15–29; revised again in *Caribbean Quarterly*, 16 (December 1970): 5–17;

"The Caribbean Artists Movement," *Caribbean Quarterly*, 14 (March–June 1968): 57–59;

"Caribbean Critics," *New World Quarterly*, 5 ("Dead Season–Crop Time" 1969): 5–12;

"Creative Literature of the British West Indies during the Period of Slavery," *Savacou*, 1 (June 1970): 46–73;

"Rehabilitations," *Bim*, 13 (July–December 1970): 174–184;

"Timehri," *Savacou*, 2 (September 1970): 34–44;

"Foreward," *Savacou*, 3/4 (December 1970–March 1971): 5–9;

"Race and the Divided Self," *Frontier*, 14 (November 1971): 202–210; revised and expanded in *Black World*, 32 (July 1972): 54–68;

"The African Presence in Caribbean Literature," *Daedalus*, 103 (Spring 1974): 73–109;

"Caribbean Man in Space and Time," *Savacou*, 11/12 (September 1975): 1–17;

"Submerged Mothers," *Jamaica Journal*, 9, nos. 2–3 (1975) 48–49;

"Houses in the West Indian Novel," *Literary Half-Yearly*, 17 (January 1976): 111–121; revised as "Houses: A Note on West Indian Literature," *First World*, 1 (March–April 1977): 46–49;

"Resistance Poems: The Voice of Martin Carter," *Caribbean Quarterly*, 23 (June–September 1977): 7–23;

"Kumina: The Spirit of African Survival in Jamaica," *Jamaica Journal*, 42 (1978): 44–63;

"Introduction," *Savacou*, 14/15 (1979): 3–5;

"Martin Carter's Poetry of the Negative Yes," *Caliban*, 4 (Fall–Winter 1981): 30–47;

"Gods of the Middle Passage," *Caribbean Review*, 11 (Fall 1982): 18–19, 42–44;

"Helen & the Tempest-Nègre: René Depestre's *A Rainbow for the Christian West*," *Caribbean Quarterly*, 30, 1 (1984): 33–47;

"Metaphors of Underdevelopment," *New England Review/Bread Loaf Quarterly*, 7, no. 4 (1984): 453–476;

"World Order Models – A Caribbean Perspective," *Caribbean Quarterly*, 31 (March 1985): 53–63;

"The Unborn Body of the Life of Fiction: Roger Mais' Aesthetics with Special Reference to *Black Lightning*," *Journal of West Indian Literature*, 2 (December 1987): 11–36; (October 1988): 33–35;

"The 4th Traveller," *Callaloo*, 38 (1989): 184–191;

"Ala(r)ms of God – Konnu and Carnival in the Caribbean," *Caribbean Quarterly*, 36 (December 1990): 77–107.

Within the English-speaking Caribbean, Edward Kamau Brathwaite is widely regarded as the most important West Indian poet, though his work is not so well known abroad as that of Derek Walcott. Brathwaite's reputation rests on several volumes of verse, including two trilogies; on his electrifying performances of his own work; and on his charismatic presence: like Pablo Neruda or Nicolás Guillén, he is often perceived as the voice of his region's reflections about itself. At the same time, he has pursued an impressive academic career of scholarship (both historical and literary/historical). His essays on history and culture, his commentaries and chronicles of West Indian life, and his extensive writing on other Caribbean authors merit attention in their own right. They are also particularly important for the understanding of his poetry, whose central metaphors the essays often provide or explicate.

Born on 11 May 1930 and christened Lawson Edward Brathwaite, he was the son of Hilton and Beryl Gill Brathwaite; he grew up in Bridgetown, Barbados, and attended Harrison College. With friends he started a school newspaper there in the late 1940s and wrote a column himself on jazz – a lifelong interest that has affected both the substance and the technique of his poetry. Several poems of his appeared in that paper, the *Harrisonian*, in 1949 and 1950. His first major publication was in *Bim*, the pioneering literary journal Frank Collymore had been publishing in Barbados since 1942. *Bim* was respected and read throughout the West Indies; George Lamming, Edgar Mittelholzer, A. J. Seymour, and Derek Walcott, among others, had published work in its pages by 1950, when Brathwaite's "Shadow Suite" was published (soon to be followed in *Bim* by "Fantasie in Blue and Silver," a sequence first printed in the *Harrisonian*).

"Shadow Suite" is typical of Brathwaite's early poetry. Most of his earliest work is in sequences of eight or ten lyrics, often quite different in form but integrated by diction or theme. The overwhelming influence in these poems is T. S. Eliot. In the case of "Shadow Suite," the shadows themselves, the High

Church liturgical diction and decor, even the cats,
all seem to come from Eliot. By contrast, only two
of the poem's eight sections include recognizably
Caribbean details, and these are stereotypical palm
trees, sand, and surf. From such beginnings Brathwaite grows toward trilogies that pursue Eliot's interest in complex rhythms of structure, in the architectural possibilities (and problems) involved in
making large poems of free-standing lyrics.
Brathwaite himself has written that "The only 'European influence' I can detect and will acknowledge
is that of T. S. Eliot. The tone, the cadence, and
above all the *organization* of my long poems . . . owe
a great deal to him" (quoted by Gordon Rohlehr in
Pathfinder, 1981).

Perhaps more importantly Brathwaite drew inspiration from a side of Eliot almost forgotten: the
jazz poet, the explorer of the whole gamut of American voices and their rhythms, whose phonograph
recordings of his work inspired Caribbean poets to
shape their own speech into poetry. That model
stands behind Brathwaite's early interest in recording his own work, often with musical accompaniment. His performance of his first trilogy, *The
Arrivants* (1973), was released commercially between 1969 and 1973, and his criticism often reverts
to the subject of preserving the voice in written
verse. What a jazzman does with the old standards
is for Brathwaite also a model for what the West Indian poet, indeed any postcolonial poet, can do with
standard English. In *The Development of Creole Society
in Jamaica, 1770–1820* (1971), Brathwaite histori-
cizes the insight: "It was in language that the slave
was perhaps most successfully imprisoned by his
master, and it was in his (mis-)use of it that he perhaps most effectively rebelled." But as early as in
"Shadow Suite" expressions such as "dyawning"
and "splashtered" are the first isolated signs of what
Brathwaite later called "calibanisms."

Like his taste for jazz, this aesthetic reveals the
roots of Brathwaite's long search for an alternative
to the undiluted British tradition so strong in the
West Indies of his youth and especially in Barbados. He once described his goal in these revealing
terms: "I'm trying to outline an alternative to the
English Romantic/Victorian cultural tradition
which still operates among us and on us, despite the
'colonial' breakthrough already achieved by Eliot,
[Ezra] Pound, and [James] Joyce; and despite the
presence among us of a folk tradition which in itself,
it seems to me, is the basis of an alternative" ("Jazz
and the West Indian Novel," *Bim*, July–December
1967).

At Harrison College in 1949 Brathwaite won

Dust jacket for the second volume in Brathwaite's The Arrivants, *a
trilogy that comprises his best-known poetry*

the coveted Barbados Island Scholarship to Cambridge, in those days one of the few tickets to a metropolitan education. He read history and English at
Pembroke College, earning an honors degree (a
B.A.) in history in 1953 and a certificate in education the following year. He also continued to write.
Brathwaite remembers his first snowstorm as the
moment when he felt he was mentally possessing
the English landscape, but his poem on the subject,
"The Day the First Snow Fell" (*Bim*, 1951), despite
traces of the style of Dylan Thomas, is a poem resolutely in black and white, incorporating signs of
alienation. The Barbados Island Scholarship un-
avoidably linked recognition of intellectual prowess
and promise with departure, even escape, from the
Caribbean. Like many other West Indians, however, Brathwaite discovered that England was not
home but a place of exile, that he was perceived as
an alien, not a native son. Even at Cambridge he
found that the magazines were interested only in his

exotically "West Indian" work. This experience planted the seeds of Brathwaite's masterpiece, *The Arrivants*. The earliest poem in the first volume, *Rights of Passage* (1967), is "A Caribbean Theme" (originally in the anthology *Poetry from Cambridge 1947–50* [1951]) – pointedly identified by its title as one of the poems that met the expectations at Cambridge.

Brathwaite continued to produce sequences, too, during this period. Some were published in local magazines at Cambridge, but most were sent back home to appear in *Bim*. In May 1953 Brathwaite found a particularly congenial outlet for his work: between 1953 and 1958 more than fifty of his poems, some of them still not published, were broadcast by the BBC's *Caribbean Voices* program. In the mid 1950s *Bim* and the BBC between them also presented several of his stories. These might be called experimental; at least they suggest that Brathwaite was still searching for his medium. "The Professor" (BBC, 1954) is a fictionalized portrait of the critic F. R. Leavis. "The Black Angel" (*Bim*, June 1955) is a mysterious story about a camp of outcasts in which the characters have the names of Greek letters, and the "black angel" is a leather jacket. With two exceptions Brathwaite published no further fiction after that brief burst of activity until "The 4th Traveller" (*Callaloo*, 1989), a hallucinatory representation of grief, whose sinister atmosphere recalls the world of the Haitian painter Wilfredo Lam, or that of Franz Kafka. One exception is trivial: the story "Cricket" (in *Caribbean Prose*, 1967) is virtually identical to the poem "Rites," in *Islands* (1969). The other exception, however, reveals an important dimension of Brathwaite's development. "Christine" (*Bim*, January–June 1961) is a chapter from "The Boy and the Sea," an unpublished novel dating from Brathwaite's Cambridge days. This story, two decades later, was transformed into poetry as "Return of the Sun" in *Sun Poem* (1982).

Brathwaite's alienation from England might plausibly have inspired him to undertake a novel or autobiography that could confirm for him his rootedness in Barbados. His turn away from fiction and the very long dormancy of this Barbadian material reflect the impact of a profoundly formative event: the publication in 1953 of *In the Castle of My Skin*, the autobiographical novel by his slightly older compatriot George Lamming. Brathwaite recounts his response to this novel: "everything was transformed. Here breathing to me from every pore of line and page was the Barbados I had lived" ("Timehri," *Savacou*, September 1970). Brathwaite's

commitment as a writer owes much to the publication of *In the Castle*, and while critics routinely compare him with Walcott, his continuing rivalry with Lamming has been much more important for the shaping of Brathwaite's career. Lamming began as a poet, and the authority of his voice as a successful reader of his own work in England impressed Brathwaite very much, as Eliot's recorded voice had. Lamming's example as a novelist seems nearly to have deflected Brathwaite from the prose medium altogether and from any sustained attention to Barbadian subject matter until the writing of *Mother Poem* (1977). Much of Brathwaite's cultural criticism took its initial cue from Lamming's *Pleasures of Exile* (1960), in which the analysis of William Shakespeare's *Tempest* shaped Brathwaite's account of the "personality types" to be found in creole culture.

After graduating from Cambridge, Brathwaite worked from 1955 to 1962 in various capacities for the Ministry of Education in what is now Ghana, during the period of the country's transition to independence. The BBC continued to air Brathwaite's poems, including new sequences, such as "Poems from the Gold Coast" (1956), "Sappho Sakyi's Meditations" (1957), and "The Hopeful Journey" (1958). Gordon Rohlehr, the scholar to whom all the other readers of the poet's work are indebted, singles out "Sappho Sakyi's Meditations" as the first emergence of "the distinctive Brathwaite style and sound," and the work was printed as a book in 1989.

Henry Swanzy, founding editor of the *Caribbean Voices* program and a great supporter of Brathwaite's work, had also come to the Gold Coast in 1955 and had initiated for the Ghana Broadcasting System a program titled *The Singing Net*, based on the successful model of *Caribbean Voices*. Material from these broadcasts was duly published as *Voices of Ghana* (1958), and Brathwaite's review of the collection for *Bim* (January-June 1960) is revealing. It presents Brathwaite as a careful observer reporting back to the Caribbean with firsthand knowledge of Africa, and more specifically it identifies some explicit sources for his *Masks* (1968): Andrew Opoku's poem "Afram" and Joseph Nketia's essay "Poetry of Drums." He had not gone to Africa out of nostalgia but, as he sometimes puts it, "by accident," and through his work he came to know it at its most prosaic. But as he recounts in "Timehri," the experience of rural Africa is crucial to his sense of himself as an artist ("I was no longer a lonely individual talent") and to his subsequent understanding of West Indian culture. In a sense Africa made it possible for

Brathwaite to recognize the Caribbean as home. So the moving poem "South" (*Bim*, January–June 1959), which was to mark a structurally important transition in *Rights of Passage*, preserves his first nostalgic look back from Africa to the Caribbean ("We who were born of the ocean can never seek solace / in rivers"). In 1960 Brathwaite began directing a children's theater group in Ghana. Several of the plays he wrote for this group were published; others – including "Pageant of Ghana" and "Edina" – later provided material for *Masks*. Also in 1960, while in Barbados on a long leave, Brathwaite met and married Doris Monica Welcome, a teacher and librarian. They had one child, Michael Kwesi Brathwaite.

It was during his years in Africa that Edward Kamau Brathwaite came to be recognized in the West Indies as an important critic, thanks again to *Bim*, which remained his sole line of print communication until the late 1960s. These early essays demonstrate his extensive knowledge of a wide range of West Indian writing, and in them his special authority as a critic takes shape, grounded in his close attention to details and his forthright judgment. Brathwaite's essays typically combine encouragement with critique, but they are most valuable for their extrapolation of trends, avenues of development, and occasional dead ends for individual authors or for West Indian literature as a whole. In short, Brathwaite used the critical survey as an occasion for shaping his thoughts about what he would come to call a West Indian aesthetic, about the function of the writer in the West Indies, and about his own objectives – and obligations – as a writer. Certainly one objective in these early essays is to establish a beachhead for his own reentry into the West Indian literary scene.

In "Sir Galahad and the Islands" (*Bim*, July–December 1957; collected in *Iouanaloa*, 1963), Brathwaite's theme is exile – "the desire (even the need) to migrate is at the heart of West Indian sensibility: whether that migration is in fact or by metaphor." There are the "Emigrants" (novelists such as Sam Selvon, Wilson Harris, and Lamming, who were living in England), but even among the "Islanders" there is the danger of withdrawal into "brilliant loneliness" because of the shortage in the islands of "material on which the spirit is sustained." Brathwaite sees this withdrawal as a problem particularly for middle-class writers (Roger Mais, Walcott), but even for the "folk" writer, "individual talent is not enough. . . . If he is to develop the richness and the promise which is his, he needs not 'luck,' but a whole living tradition." So the ques-

tion is "can our [West Indian] society produce *enough* writers with the talent and *insight* to use folk material creatively; not as 'reporters,' but with a sufficient sweetness of maturity to establish a tradition?" Brathwaite's tentative answer lays out the terms for much of his criticism published in the 1960s and 1970s: "If [West Indian] society is in good health, our 'central' writers (those based on the 'folk') will continue to find nourishment from their soil. What is more, greater social intercommunication, and the understanding that would have to go with it, would give the 'middle class' writer (and possibly the majority of our writers are middle class) easier access not only into folk society, but would open up the surely untapped riches of their own environment."

"Sir Galahad" shows Brathwaite identifying writers as "middle class" or "folk" on the basis of their origins; four years later (in *Bim*, January–June 1961) in reviewing the West Indian issue of the *Tamarack Review*, Brathwaite initiated a distinction based more on a sense of audience, a distinction between what he calls "humanist" and "folk" artists, on the basis of for whom they write. This interest in the relationship between artist and audience was already developing in "The New West Indian Novelists" (*Bim*, July–December 1960). Mirroring his account of the impact of Lamming's *In the Castle*, he identifies the successful novelist as one "who names and seeks to give significance to our old familiar actions and thoughts." But perhaps in anticipation of Brathwaite's own return to the Caribbean, there is a new emphasis on the special relationship between the writer and his native public, on the principle that together they create the work: "We, the special audience . . . have a special concern and responsibility in the matter." Such a statement takes on urgency, even pathos, in the light of his own situation: one of the most prominent West Indian readers of West Indian literature was then in Africa reading books that came from England.

Brathwaite's growing interest in the artist's relation to his social environment, to the people who provide both his subject matter and his audience, led to his many wide-ranging essays on rootedness and deracination. It is also a facet of his broader concern with how West Indians fit into their physical and metaphysical environment – what he sometimes calls the "geo-psychic environment." So, for example, he criticized Wilson Harris's early poetry because characters present in the landscape are not engaged with it.

Reflecting on his own return to West Indian society and landscape, Brathwaite in "Roots" (*Bim*,

July–December 1963; in *Roots*, 1986) elaborates the ideas set forth in "Sir Galahad." For him the impulse to migrate is not just economic but psychic. Writers at home who wrote of the islands but wished for exile, no less than writers in exile who embraced then recoiled from their foreign status, manifested a characteristic West Indian restlessness, which Brathwaite sees as an African heritage. Brathwaite writes that this feeling "expresses itself in the West Indian through a certain psychic tension, an excitability, a definite feeling of having no past, of not really belonging . . . and finds relief in laughter and (more seriously) in movement – dance, cricket, carnival, emigration." He sees this characteristic enacted in both the form and the language of West Indian fiction, in the structure of novels that offer "the vernacular description of a world through which the writer moves unerringly to his inevitable 'escape,' " and in the poetic or picturesque vernacular typical of such fiction. (He has in mind *In the Castle* again and V. S. Naipaul's *Miguel Street*, 1959.) On the positive side, he notes that the inherent health of West Indian culture has produced Naipaul, whose work set new standards for fiction and so made significant progress toward establishing the kind of tradition Brathwaite had hoped for in "Sir Galahad." Brathwaite, who had just recently achieved for himself a Caribbean home and a family, particularly praises *A House for Mr. Biswas* (1961) as the first West Indian novel whose basic theme is not rootlessness and the search for social identity; the first novel with a clearly defined character who is trying to get in, not out; and the first novel with clearly defined boundaries: a house, a district, and a family.

While Brathwaite was in Africa, the West Indian Federation had collapsed, opening the way to independence for Jamaica and Trinidad in 1962. In conjunction with these political events, the University of the West Indies (UWI) was established as an independent, degree-granting institution in April of that year. Brathwaite returned to the Caribbean in 1962 and served for a year as a resident tutor in Saint Lucia, also broadcasting and producing for the Windward Islands Broadcasting Service. In 1963 he took an appointment as a lecturer in history at the Jamaican campus of UWI at Mona.

During his year in Saint Lucia he wrote "The Role of the University in Developing Society" (in *Iouanaloa*), which argues strenuously that independence calls for greater intellectual investment in the region: "Is it not significant that the very purest forms of our self-expression – the poets – Walcott, Telemaque, Roach – have not written outside the Caribbean area?" The essay is also a kind of official announcement of his interest in "things African": "To say that things African are equal to things European and Asian is a more than reasonable premise, and needs to be stressed. To suggest that things African are probably *better*, is leaving the sphere of University thought for temporal propaganda." The creole context of Brathwaite's first statement of this theme is noteworthy because he was repeatedly criticized, especially during the 1970s, as a partisan Africanist.

Brathwaite's trilogy *The Arrivants*, which made his international reputation, incorporates some earlier poetry, but it is impressive, perhaps above all, because of the breadth and unity of its conception, and that conception, with all its implications for method and style throughout his career, took shape during 1964 and 1965 – so quickly that when Brathwaite departed for graduate study in England in late summer 1965, the first volume, *Rights of Passage*, was already complete. *Rights* is a sustained poem of some eighty pages and at the same time a collection of nineteen discrete poems, gathered in a loosely narrative structure. There are four sections: "Work Song and Blues," "The Spades," "Islands and Exiles," and "The Return." The opening "Prelude" presents an evocative, lyric view of "the long story . . . of the migrant African moving from the lower Nile across the desert to the Western ocean only to meet the Portuguese and a History that was to mean the middle passage, America, and a rootless sojourn in the Caribbean Sea." Thus Brathwaite sets the mythical/historical context for the entire trilogy. The central figure of the volume is Tom, the representative survivor of "the middle passage," who is at once the last African and the first "New World Negro" – a conduit of memory, blood, and soul. For the purposes of the poem he has one single cultural possession, a memory of the golden age of the Ashanti Empire under Osei Tutu, but it is a painful and apparently useless story he cannot pass on to his children. In "Didn't He Ramble," named for the traditional funeral tune, Tom, now dead, grieves over the rootlessness of his descendants – literally from the grave, where roots transfix his body. The two central sections, "The Spades" and "Islands and Exiles," present the diaspora as a series of masks, the stereotypical identities donned by those sons of Tom in response to the pressures of the world.

The fourth section turns to unmasked Caribbean realities, grounded in the lives of the common folk. Significantly readers first hear sustained female voices when in "The Dust" a group of women meeting in a shop try to understand the inexplicable blighting of their world by volcanic dust from a neighboring island. These are unmediated Caribbean identities, and Brathwaite gives glimpses of the obscured history that leads back to Tom, whose decaying cabin (the allusion to Harriet Beecher Stowe's *Uncle Tom's Cabin* [1852] is intentional and provocative) "is all that's left of hopes, of hurt, of history . . . " while around it the Caribbean is being transformed into a cheap imitation of the metropolises in steel and concrete.

The closing "Epilogue" repeats, sometimes literally, the opening poem of cyclical migration, but it also introduces a new figure, "Old Negro Noah," who, like Tom, steps into a new world, like him lives to be mocked by his own sons, and like him bears the responsibility to make choices for the descendants whose survival he has just assured: "Should you . . . walk in the morning fully aware of the future to come?"

Rights functions as a prelude to the entire trilogy; it amounts to the elaborate articulation of a single question – which Brathwaite states as "Where then is the nigger's home?" – through a mythologized history. That was not yet apparent when the volume first appeared in isolation, but the critical response to *Rights* set the terms for subsequent reactions to the trilogy as a whole, and indeed to all of Brathwaite's work. Early critics noted his affinities with Eliot, Walt Whitman, and Hart Crane, as well as with Lamming and Mais, though North American critics tended to view the book as yet another articulation of black rage. But Edward Baugh, like several other Caribbean critics, was more impressed by the innovations of form and technique than by the subject, about which he concluded the poem says "nothing new" (*Bim*, July–December 1967). That the poem demanded public performance was clear from the start; Baugh also thought it "better heard than read." Derek Walcott, in his insightful review in the *Sunday Guardian Magazine* (19 March 1967), concurred: "the poem, read aloud, subdues and arrests the onrush of its subject, by the closely packed rhythms, by the tautness of its short stresses." Mervyn Morris, the critic who was the most attentive to the technical details in the poem, praised the varying rhythms set off against each other and the effectiveness of the puns and half-rhymes, though he voiced what would become a recurrent complaint when he confessed that Brathwaite's lineation presents "a puzzlement and an occasional irritation" (*New World Quarterly*, 1967). While some called the poem plain or thin, Walcott praised Brathwaite's economy and "mod-

Brathwaite circa 1968

esty": "everything has been honed down to a sliver-thin essential" by "a refined, anguished sensibility bent on achieving not power, but grace, not grandeur but sharp, piercing truths." All the critics who were themselves poets (Walcott, Baugh, and Velma Pollard) concurred with Morris's judgment that "The Dust" is "the most notable achievement in *Rights*," and in general nothing was more admired than the variety and immediacy of the voices in the poem, the successful use of colloquial Caribbean rhythms. Baugh is unequivocal: "no West Indian . . . has used dialect more subtly, probingly, or suggestively."

The seventy pages of *Masks* include twenty-three poems, divided into six sections. The first three parts trace a migratory tribal history, while the latter three recount a modern poet's journey to Africa: his pilgrimage and visions, his disillusionment and its resolution. *Masks* starts again with the sun, but the image now represents the leavening heat of rhythm, not the whiplash of *Rights*. A prayer for fruitful harvest establishes the African setting. By the end of the first section, "Libation," which recounts the making of the drum and its accompanying instruments (and the making of the drummer), the scene is fully in Africa. Half the text of "Atumpan" is in Akan, and from this point on the rhythms of the verse are markedly different from those in *Rights* – steadier, more premeditated, and more "African," as the traditional drummer salutes his god and prays for success in his performance. In the next section, "Pathfinders," is the voice of the griot, who sings a series of relatively tight, nearly stanzaic, poems in very high diction, a series that depicts the emblematic migration from East to West Africa. This sequence of poems provides a focused, integral, even redemptive counterpart to the fragmented voices, faces, and places of the section of *Rights* titled "The Spades."

The third section of *Masks*, "Limits," traces the migration of a desert people across the savannas to their "final" settlement in the forests of West Africa. Brathwaite emphasizes the transformation of culture that results from the adjustment to radically new conditions, especially the transformation of religion from the monotheistic response to the sun in the desert to animism in the dense forest, where "leaf eyes shift, twigs creak, buds flutter, the stick becomes a snake." But the shore of the western ocean was, in spite of appearances, not the final destination; instead (as readers know from the early parts of *Rights*) it was the setting for the fateful encounter with Europe, slavery, and the forced migration of "the middle passage."

The second half of *Masks* begins with "The Return," the moment in the present when the speaker, reversing the Atlantic voyage, arrives for the first time in West Africa. But this journey is not like that in Alex Haley's *Roots* (1976); the traveler returns as a stranger, amid fear and mistrust. The poems of this section are unexpectedly dark, disappointing readers who expect a return to Africa that somehow fixes everything.

In "Crossing the River," the next section, the speaker begins his pilgrimage up-country to Kumasi (the old imperial capital of the Ashanti), which culminates in a vision of Osei Tutu and his court. Readers see enacted the events that Tom in *Rights* has compressed into a memory: Tutu's consolidation of the Ashanti Empire through the unifying symbol of the "Golden Stool," its heavenly origin attested to by the priest and adviser Anokye. But the vision discloses not only the glory of the imaginative victory but the expedient sacrifices; unexpectedly, the speaker sees his own people brought as captives to "this red town" and sold to slavers. Tom's treasured memory is revealed as a slave's memory of his master. African glory is itself a mask:

"I wear this past I borrowed; history bleeds behind my hollowed eyes." As Rohlehr explained in his review of *Islands* (*Caribbean Quarterly*, December 1970), the powerful mask of Africa, "part of a process of personal incarnation and self-discovery, becomes for the New World Negro a shabby disguise to hide the fact that he lacks a true face," so it must be taken off, and home must be looked at unmasked.

Orphaned and alone, cut off from ancestry both in Africa and the Americas, the speaker travels along with the river god Tano into the night. From this low point, with the support of the god, the speaker, like a successful limbo dancer, rises again to his feet. In this night dry seeds split to sprout, the drums begin again, and, enlivened by the rhythm, dancers rise into motion like trees from split seeds. Like the possessed believer, the dancer and the drummer, too, are envisioned as conductors that ground the lightning of the god, and from that contact with the earth they produce music and movement for the community. The final poem of the volume, "The Awakening," is thus named after a traditional drummer's prelude. The poem ties together the major threads of *Masks*. The context is so dense that at this point the resonances of four very plain lines – "so slowly slowly / ever so slowly / I will rise / and stand on my feet" – associate the chastened, purified speaker with the rising dancer of "Tano," the drummer of "Atumpan," and Osei Tutu himself. Brathwaite ends *Masks* by personalizing the invocation first seen in "Atumpan": "let us succeed" has become "let me succeed." The poet explicitly identifies himself with the African drummer.

At the center of *Masks* is the oldest memory of the New World Negro Tom: his ideal vision of African kingship. But in his vision the speaker, a descendant of Tom, is imaginatively present at the event and sees not just the central ritual but its grimmer context. He is forced to accept the totality of African experience, not just the ideal, and to accept in addition the West Indian's severance from all that to which he can return only as a tourist or dreamer. The volume ends as the orphaned speaker returns to basics, to the earth, meaning not the African earth but the Caribbean. And the poet cannot be an African drummer. What he can aim to be is whatever in his West Indian society corresponds to the role of the drummer in African traditional society (and while the image is of a drummer, the concept for Brathwaite includes the functions of drummer, praise singer, and griot/historian). Every mask is an alienation from self that paradoxically allows participation in the activity of the group; for Brathwaite this mask of the drummer offers a point of entry into an integrated society, whereas the masks of "The Spades" are enforced constraints within which invisible men can function.

To date, two of the three critical books on Brathwaite are commentaries on *Masks*. This situation is interesting, since the book is his most "masked," most self-consciously written in a voice other than his own, and most unlike his other work; its unusually self-contained and "classical" form reflects the coherence of the traditional African culture that provides both its subject and its formal models. Indeed it was one of the first West Indian texts to present an accurate (because firsthand) view of Africa, and probably for that reason it has earned praise from African critics: Ama Ata Aidoo noted that *Masks* succeeds better than any previous work in "acceptance of Africa – our shame, our glories, past and present – not in defense or aggression, but quietly." In the Caribbean both Baugh and Jean D'Costa praised the unity of tone and conception, and Baugh added, "one is now better able to appreciate how the more strident tone of that book [*Rights*], the greater looseness of structure, the more violent shifts of tone express the dislocation, rootlessness and fragmentation of the New World Negro" (*Bim*, July-December 1968).

Islands is the longest of the three volumes in the trilogy, twenty-nine poems amounting to over one hundred pages. *Rights* asks its central question, "Where is the nigger's home?" And *Masks* seems to offer the predictable answer: "Africa" – until the speaker discovers what lies behind that answer. *Islands* then ventures another answer: "his home is where he is." "New World," the first of five sections, returns to the Caribbean, where "the gods have been forgotten or hidden." Bereft of mythology or native language, objects have no meanings, or remain the property of the European who names them. For that reason, "clinks of dew in the grass is the nearest we will get to god," and the choice of words calls to mind at once the vision of Africa that Tom glimpses in the dew in *Rights*. With eyes freshened by the experience of Africa, Brathwaite surveys the Caribbean for its repressed culture, its survivals from Africa, and its indigenous innovations – the psychic furniture that might make it a comfortable home. So in *Islands* he recognizes the gods who (sometimes disguised or distorted) have made the middle passage: Anansi, Legba, Ogun, and the rest. Eventually the speaker sees continuities in his own relatives, so in his uncle he recognizes Ogun, and out of the background Tom begins to emerge again. Brathwaite is equally concerned with acknowledging the living rites that the Caribbean has forged for

itself out of its creole heritage: rituals as various in function and origin as "pocomania" (a Jamaican religion), limbo, cricket, and the carnival. The poem "Shepherd," for example, dramatizes the act of spirit possession in pocomania and contextualizes it in the trilogy by means of verbal echoes of the arrival of Osei Tutu, of the "Atumpan" drumbeat, and of the orphan's lament, all these traces of Africa (that is, of *Masks*) now audible in the Caribbean.

Most of *Islands* is taken up with various investigations of and reflections on the matters of cultural continuity, survival, recovery, and reconstruction. Throughout the book Brathwaite's faith in the Caribbean is figured in a group of paradoxical images – seed, egg, pebble, coral, fetus, and closed fist – all of which combine apparent imperviousness and sterility with growth.

Characteristically the final section of the entire trilogy is entitled "Beginning," and in the poem "Vévé," as so often in the trilogy, Brathwaite ends with a moment on the brink of vision – just before the carefully crafted net of the fisherman imposes its patterned order on the sea, just before the god is invited to walk among us in the body of the living, just before the poem itself effects the goal of transformation. After all, this poem exemplifies the active cultural role of poetry in a living society, and it ends with the empowering of its readers. By the success of his poem's articulation Brathwaite clearly hopes to make the idiom of his people admirable to them and at the same time to inspire West Indians to see and shape their own culture. As *Islands* concludes, he looks forward to a communal effort at making "here . . . on his broken ground . . . something torn and new."

Critics praised the final volume of the trilogy for its lucidity of construction and of imagery, though Kenneth Ramchand (in *Tapia*, 2 January 1977) rather curiously criticized *Islands* for its "rhetorical precision, the crafty appropriateness of writing with palpable designs upon us." As usual Morris spoke for many readers: "the fact is, the author of *Islands* is a better poet than the author of *Rights of Passage*" (*New World Quarterly*, 1969). With the publication of *Islands*, it was possible to address the trilogy as a whole, even before it appeared in a single volume as *The Arrivants*. Attention focused on the technical innovations, on the contribution to the exploration of Caribbean identity, and on the deft harmonization of personal and public objectives.

That last point was particularly prominent in Jamaica, where as Morris said, Brathwaite was seen as "a public figure arguing for particular kinds of social and cultural change," a highly visible cultural hero of such personal presence and authority that he was sometimes called a "guru." When critic Marina Maxwell (*New World Quarterly*, 1971) characterized him as "the central drum sounding the way home," she indicated how much the regional success of the poem and its author depended on its immediate, popular impact through live performances, beginning with a historic reading for the Jamaican P.E.N. Club in 1968 and continuing through recordings and radio presentations. Unlike much of Brathwaite's later work, *The Arrivants* is not difficult poetry, there is no great density of expression, and its apparent obscurities are more often cleared up by information than by interpretive skill. Indeed one of the effects, and perhaps one of the conscious objectives, of the trilogy is to make readers aware of African and Caribbean history, West Indian folk culture, and more – just as Eliot's *The Waste Land* (1922) made its first generation of readers aware of metaphysical poetry and Jacobean drama.

Many critics, of course, attempt to place Brathwaite's book according to the various literary traditions it evokes, and the significance of Eliot in particular is much disputed. Bruce King (in *The New English Literatures*, 1980) proposed a very close affinity: "Brathwaite's desire to establish a cultural tradition grounded in communal ritual and his concern with individual moments of escaping from the fragmented, chaotic present into an experience of oneness, in which the artist becomes the voice of a culture and its beliefs, show that he has profoundly understood Eliot." But in context King was arguing that Brathwaite's techniques are not so much revolutionary innovations as they are already "part of the accepted modern repertoire." At the other extreme Hayden Carruth, maintaining Brathwaite's originality, saw the influence of Eliot "almost entirely limited to matters of organization and structure . . . and perhaps . . . rhyming. . . . In texture, in verbal technique, in almost everything, nothing could be further from Eliot's poetry than Brathwaite's."

There is a similar critical dispute about the relation between Brathwaite and Walcott, which sometimes devolves into a quarrel about which is more politically correct, and there is a continuing debate, notably between Rohlehr and Ramchand, about the claims Brathwaite makes for "orature" – reliance on oral literature as a norm for West Indian poetry. A more rarified dispute, related to Marxist discussions about the role of voodoo in contemporary Haitian culture, centers on whether the upshot of the trilogy is the rebirth of African gods in the Caribbean, or a refusal of transcen-

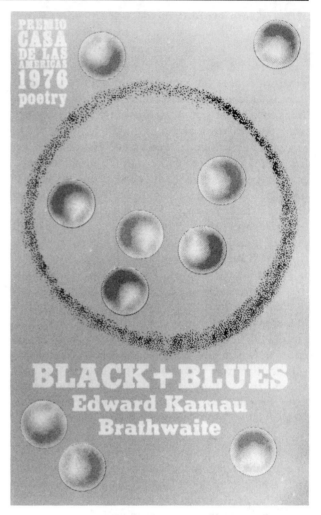

Dust jacket for the collection of poems that served as a springboard for Brathwaite's second trilogy by focusing on the themes of resurrection, revolution, and optimism regarding the future of the Caribbean islands

dence, a grounding in human society in the face of the failure of one's gods.

Generally, however, critics tend to address either the themes or the technical aspects of the poem. Morris, in a close and detailed reading of the poem, is the first to make good use of critical sources on African literature and culture, and while Rohlehr is the first critic to emphasize the need to read Brathwaite's poetry in the context of his historical research and cultural criticism, he has also established himself as Brathwaite's most devoted reader.

During the years when the volumes of *The Arrivants* were being published, Brathwaite was at the University of Sussex in England pursuing historical research that eventually resulted in a Ph.D. thesis, later published as *The Development of Creole Society in Jamaica, 1770–1820*. Beginning in 1966 he served as an editor of *Bim* and as founding secretary of the Caribbean Artists Movement (CAM) – positions in which he encouraged the work of other West Indian writers and artists. In 1968 he obtained his Ph.D. Two important and lengthy essays by him came out of this period, both wide-ranging surveys of the state of West Indian fiction. Emerging from Brathwaite's increasingly articulate interest in the relations between writers and their society, "West Indian Prose Fiction in the Sixties" (*Critical Survey*, Winter 1967) emphasizes such encouraging developments as the return of writers from exile to an imaginative base in the islands and the new interest in indigenous Caribbean language and culture. It includes praise for Naipaul's *A House for Mr. Biswas* as "a novel that has come out of the structure and cultural awareness of a specific community."

"Jazz and the West Indian Novel" (presented at a CAM meeting and subsequently published in *Bim*, 1967–1968) records Brathwaite's own attempts (reflected in *Islands*) to identify the features of a Caribbean aesthetic. Rohlehr (*Caribbean Quarterly*, December 1970) describes this essay as seeking "a new and more relevant aesthetic for the assessment of West Indian writing," and that evaluative, even judgmental, element in Brathwaite's criticism has continued to generate opposition to what are perceived as ex cathedra pronouncements on West Indian literature. For that reason his extreme tentativeness at this early stage is noteworthy: "I am asking here whether we can, and if it is worthwhile attempting to, sketch out some kind of aesthetic whereby we may be helped to see West Indian literature in its (it seems to me) proper context of an expression both European and African at the same time. And if in this essay I stress the African aspects of this literature, it is not, I submit, because I am not aware of the other, but because in most of the critical work so far available on this subject 'Africa' has been neglected. . . ." Though "there is no West Indian jazz," Brathwaite wants to treat jazz as the archetype of "the general movement of New World creative protest": unlike the blues and spirituals, jazz is not slave music at all but the music of the emancipated Negro – that is, of the rootless, truly expatriate Negro. To Brathwaite jazz was a good model because of its apparent bridging of the gap between artist and society, which preoccupied him at this time: "each successful improvisation is a true creation and is an expression not only of the individual artist or artists, but of the group of which the artists are part." Brathwaite, of course, thinks like a poet; for him word, image, and rhythm are the basic elements of a jazz aesthetic. But he defines a jazz novel as one that expresses the essence of a folk community through its form.

In the light of these observations, part 3 of his essay discusses Roger Mais's *Brother Man* (1954) and Andrew Salkey's *A Quality of Violence* (1959) – by Brathwaite's criteria, the only extant West Indian jazz novels. His account of *Brother Man* is a forerunner of the detailed analysis of the novel's "musical structure" in the essay "Brother Mais," his introduction to a 1974 edition of it. Brathwaite's admiration for the originality of this novel found expression again more than a dozen years later in "The Unborn Body of the Life of Fiction" (December 1987), where he argues that in *Brother Man* "the traditional social realism narrative form of the West Indian ghetto/yard novel has been transformed into a remarkable & careful pattern, based on . . . jazz principles . . . and over-all, informing the form, as it were, a strong sense, as in jazz, especially in 'small group' jazz, of the individual-within-the-community."

Brathwaite returned from England to his teaching job in Jamaica amid political turmoil on and off campus (which he later chronicled in "The Love Axe/1," 1976). His return was the beginning for him of an enormous project of cultural study, a great unearthing of Caribbean resources, which has been Brathwaite's primary mission ever since. The project grew most immediately out of the objectives in *The Arrivants*, but its roots are deep; in some sense it can be traced back to a brief student essay titled "A West Indian Culture?" in the *Harrisonian* in 1949. The direct recovery of submerged elements of the Caribbean past has been carried out during Brathwaite's work as a professional historian, in essays such as *Folk Culture of the Slaves in Jamaica* (1970) and "Creative Literature of the British West Indies during the Period of Slavery" (June 1970), as well as in *The Development of Creole Society*. Brathwaite was equally concerned with the recognition and dissemination of contemporary Caribbean culture, and, in his position as one of the founding editors of *Savacou*, from 1970 on he devoted considerable energy to the publication of West Indian writers while he continued to write criticism.

The early 1970s also saw the further formulation of the fundamental themes of Brathwaite's criticism and, to a considerable extent, of his poetry. His effort to trace the lineaments of a "West Indian aesthetic" continued, nearly always in close conjunction with the search for "alternatives" to the European tradition – that is, for elements in Caribbean culture, high or low, that might serve as growing points for an indigenous aesthetic. Brathwaite's earliest essays touch on the relations between an artist and his society. The most compelling vision of the poet's place in society came to him in Ghana; having seen that model, he considered how to bring it about in Caribbean terms. Hence the function of the writer in Caribbean society became a central concern to him. In part because of his own public role as a performing artist in Jamaican society, this interest came into great prominence in the early 1970s, first in his objection that too much criticism of Caribbean literature treated each writer as an isolated individual and not as the "agent of his society." At the Association of Commonwealth Literature and Language Studies (ACLALS) conference of 1971, with its theme of "the function of the writer," Brathwaite had the opportunity to develop his ideas in a confrontational atmosphere. While he was willing to grant, in the abstract, that some writers draw on the resources of self while others reveal the consciousness of the people, he insisted that West Indian writers "inhabit the fulcrum of our consciousness . . . creating a continuum between elite and folk." In this insistence that the artist must forge a regional identity out of the fragments and buried resources of alternative traditions, Brathwaite was, of course, his own model for the West Indian writer. As he says in "Timehri," "In the Caribbean . . . the recognition of an ancestral relationship with the folk or aboriginal culture involves the artist and participant in a journey into the past and hinterland which is at the same time a movement of possession into present and future. Through this movement of possession we become ourselves. . . ." In his essay "Foreward" (*Savacou*, December 1970–March 1971) he claims, "We write out of – some of us as a result of – a fragmented society. True. But every artist's work tries to create a world and he writes towards what he conceives to be a common future of wholeness."

Brathwaite often discusses these issues by way of environmental or architectural analogies. Sometimes he develops these ideas on the largest possible scale, what he calls the "geo-psychic" scale, as is the case throughout his second trilogy but also in contemporaneous essays (such as "Caribbean Man in Space and Time," September 1975), when he speaks of the fragmentary Caribbean islands and the drowned sierra that is their "submarine unity," or alternatively when he speaks of "the inner plantation," "the outer plantation," and the isolation of escape or rebellion.

A problematic relation between house building and migration or diaspora is recurrent in *The Arrivants*, and Brathwaite from early in his career has commented on the rarity of established houses in West Indian fiction. Brathwaite himself seems to reject the comforts of the private house for the vitality of the barrack yard and balm yard. He ulti-

mately identifies one particular exterior space, the vodun *hounfort*, as "the heart and signal of the African experience in the Caribbean/New World," the ideal space for the manifestation of what he calls *nam* – which he has defined as "the African 'phenomenon,' continuously present, like a bomb, in the New World since the abduction of the first slaves . . . [that] triggers itself into visibility at each moment of crisis in the hemisphere" ("The African Presence in Caribbean Literature," *Daedalus*, Spring 1974). *Nam*, a mysterious, multivalent concept, has become increasingly central to his thought, particularly in the second trilogy and in his essays of the early 1980s, where it is presented as an untheological way of conceiving a divine presence akin to the African *orisha* or the Haitian *loa*; it is generalized as the "atomic core" of a culture, the germ or seed of the group's identity.

Such a line of thought arises out of Brathwaite's lifelong study of the African cultural presence in the Caribbean, and since Caribbean culture is not "pure" African but "an adaptation carried out mainly in terms of African tradition," to study "Africa-in-the-Caribbean" is to study creolization. For Brathwaite this study began with his Sussex thesis, and he has repeatedly striven to define the concept more carefully in subsequent essays, notably *Contradictory Omens* (1974), which examines creolization up to the postemancipation period, *Kumina* (1982), "a sociological and linguistic study of Afrocreolization," and especially "Caliban, Ariel, and Unprospero in the Conflict of Creolization" (1977), in which he significantly develops and modifies his theory of the mechanisms of creolization. On the one hand, he concludes that "the idea of creolization as an a/culturative, even an interculturative process between 'black' and 'white,' with the (subordinate) black absorbing progressive ideas and technology from the white, has to be modified into a more complex vision in which appears the notion of *negative or regressive creolization*: a self-conscious refusal to borrow or be influenced by the Other, and a coincident desire to fall back upon, unearth, recognize elements in the maroon or ancestral culture that will preserve or apparently preserve the unique identity of the group." On the other hand, he also seeks to account for the ways in which blackness (for example) can, as a result of creolization, become a *cultural* element for all West Indians, regardless of race – a process most evident in Cuba and Puerto Rico, where white and mulatto writers turned to black-based literary expression as a form of protest, thereby remaking themselves as "authentic alter/natives."

For Brathwaite the mid 1970s were a period of self-fashioning, of both personal and cultural retrospection. The bibliography *Our Ancestral Heritage* (1977) assembles the results of years of research and constitutes an important resource for Caribbean studies, even though it amounts only to half of a projected bibliography documenting European, African, and other contributions to creole Caribbean culture. During the same period, Brathwaite was circulating the manuscript of his comprehensive "Bibliography of Caribbean Poetry in English," which amounts to a literary history; the complete text of this enormously valuable work has never been published, though compressed versions of the sections on Barbados and Jamaica were printed as pamphlets in 1979. The essay "The Love Axe/1," like much of Brathwaite's work since the 1970s, combines elements of chronicle, bibliography, and autobiography in a kind of grass-roots literary history. It looks back on the formative events of the late 1960s, which in Jamaica at least were closely associated with UWI in Mona (notably the expulsion of historian Walter Rodney and the student occupation of the Creative Arts Centre). The essay links those events to literary production: "perhaps for the first time in our history, our native protest movements had a considerable measure of organization, and their artistic/literary output was large and significant." In 1976 Brathwaite began regularly using a name given to him in Africa, so that his title pages thereafter identify him as Edward *Kamau* Brathwaite. (He had initially signed himself "L. E. Brathwaite," then occasionally "L. Edward"; "Edward Brathwaite" was the norm from the late 1960s until 1976.)

The mid 1970s was also a transitional period for Brathwaite's poetry. *Other Exiles* (1975), a collection of thirty poems from the years 1950 to 1975, presents personal poetry, in contrast to the public poetry of *The Arrivants*: there are several unusually intimate poems; portraits sketched from his travels as a student in Europe; and explorations of voices in West Indian "folk" poems as well as in poems that have jazz and the blues as either their subjects or their models. Pollard, in the best review of the collection (*Caribbean Quarterly*, 1977), characterizes the early poetry as a training ground for the first trilogy, though she notes that the 1975 book lacks the balancing hope for the future that is a feature of *The Arrivants*. "Conqueror," the most overtly political and complex poem in *Other Exiles*, anticipates the subjects and techniques of the second trilogy, but that forward-looking perspective is more characteristic of the complementary volume *Black + Blues* (1976), published after winning the Casa de las Américas prize for poetry. This set of twenty-three

Edward Kamau Brathwaite

poems is an exploration of material that generated the second trilogy, and it also carries on Brathwaite's continuing study of the dramatic representation of Caribbean voices. The titles of the various sections — "Fragments," "Drought," and "Flowers" — reveal the central movements of the collection, sketching an argument that fragments can flower, that "out of the ruins / grass still presses," that drought in the West Indies is a season of flowers. As part of Brathwaite's search for submerged unities, *Black + Blues* shows him preoccupied with relics, totems, fetishes, ruins, and shards. There is a strong sense that these fragments are "survivals," the past alive in the present, though damaged or broken, and that attention to them can bring them to life. Both *resurrection* and *revolution* are key terms, sometimes as alternatives to one another. In the poem "Starvation" a revolutionary Jamaican voice hopes the high rises will "resurrect dem self back down to gravel." While there are desperate, revolutionary even incendiary voices in the book, the characteristic feeling is a kind of metaphysical optimism, familiar because of its appearance in *The Arrivants*. This optimism is clearest in "Harbour," with its movement from "islands floating" to a "cool harbour." The concluding image of the dried coconut making its own "middle passage," to take root and flourish in the Caribbean, contrasts eloquently with Brathwaite's first evocation of this image in "Shadow Suite": "The isolated islands / exchange only adventurous sea-coconuts / Antilles without tradition."

Brathwaite began concerted work on his second trilogy under the auspices of a Guggenheim Fellowship during 1972 and 1973. The first two volumes of this trilogy (with no collective title) gradually delineate a vast, mythic frame conceived on the scale of geologic time and inhabited by characters who have, in effect, both human and geologic (or astronomical) aspects. Thus *Mother Poem* focuses on women, beginning with the mother who is at the same time the speaker's native island, Barbados, set apart in the mothering sea. In contrast, *Sun Poem* elaborates on the linear career of the father, figured variously as the trajectory of the sun from dawn to dark, the sequential colors of the rainbow, and an African spirit swept westward from home to be cast up on the island's Atlantic shore. The mythic apparatus of the first two volumes becomes itself the subject of *X/Self* (1987), whose multiform eponymous hero is the "child" of that sun and mother.

The scale and organization of *Mother Poem* recall those of the earlier trilogy; there are twenty-five poems arranged in four sections. "My Mother, Barbados" is both the setting and the central character. She is a pool, but also the cloud that evaporates from the pool, and the porous limestone through which the falling rain "percolates"; she is the island, a stone shaped like a tear. In much the same way that *Rights* shows Brathwaite meditating on Tom by turning attention to his children, *Mother Poem* depicts the central figure by showing her relations with the men in her life (husband, parson, teacher, debt collector, and others). All of them are broken or distorted by the heritage of colonialism, so that she must somehow find ways to support them at the same time that she resists their demands on her. The bulk of the volume is occupied with this depiction and with glimpses of the risky expedients by which she survives. Even as it celebrates her strength, the book condemns the social conditions past and present that constrain her. As often happens in *The Arrivants*, the momentum leads to a final "beginning" through spirit possession, which is at once an escape, a grounding, an empowerment, and an act of resistance. Finally, through the "birth" that is her death, she is metamorphosed from natural to mythic mother. When the volume concludes, readers have learned how she became the pool/rain

cloud of the opening: the flow of her words, which have dominated the book, fills the island's watercourses that had been dry so long, "travelling inwards under the limestone / widening outwards into the sunlight / towards the breaking of her flesh with foam."

The thirty-three poems in *Sun Poem* are arranged in twelve sections, the sequence of which maps a spectrum of light from infrared ("Red Rising") through ultraviolet ("Indigone") to full darkness. Further, in keeping with its title, the work as a whole is notable for extraordinary descriptions of light and its various effects. This volume complements the female landscape of its predecessor with the corresponding male history; the sun that rises and sets over the island, alternately warming and then abandoning it, enacts the male life cycle from child to husband to grandfather. The central character is a boy called Adam – whose name signals the allegorical dimensions of the work. Like *Masks*, the central volume of the first trilogy, *Sun Poem* has a relatively strong narrative thread. In the course of the story Adam moves from the west coast of Barbados to the east coast, measuring himself against beach boys on the more "public," tourist (west) side and against "Cattlewash boys" on the eastern shore, which is both wilder and more private. Within the symbolic framework of the poem the boy's eastward movement, contrary to the progress of the sun, is a movement back to origins. (Similarly Brathwaite's own notes to the poem describe the fifth section, "The Crossing," as "the Middle Passage in reverse.") Thus the book's visionary center (section 6, "Noom") recounts the story of how the African *loa* Legba once emerged from the Atlantic, at the end of his own "middle passage," on this coast of Barbados. As Brathwaite often reminds readers, it is the part of the Caribbean closest to Africa – and incidentally a part of the island particularly associated with Lamming.

Two other characters play significant roles in the poem: one is Bussa, leader of a nineteenth-century slave rebellion on the east coast, and the other is Batto, the beach bully of the west coast, who is mythologized by the admiration and fear of boys such as Adam. *Sun Poem* ends away from both coasts in the center of the island, at the country house where Adam witnesses his grandfather's funeral and as a result becomes conscious of the cycle of manhood, perceived in a cosmic context. The cycle of the poem ends in night, but it is a night full of stars, and the volume concludes with an extraordinary creation song that envisions a "nameless dark horse of devouring morning" arriving out of the

East to bring the dawn: "out of that brass / that was beating its genesis genesis genesis genesis / out of the stammering world / . . . my thrill- / dren are coming up coming up coming up coming up / and the sun / new."

The broad movement of *The Arrivants* is historical and dialectical, going back from the Caribbean to Africa, not in hopes of reentering a dream but in order to bring a meaningful Africa to bear on the experience of the Americas. The setting of *Mother Poem* and *Sun Poem* is again Caribbean, but *X/Self* stages a coup and turns to "Rome" – for once, Europe is treated as myth. If *The Arrivants* can be described as investigating the realities under the familiar myths of Africa as the "dark continent," symbolized by the jungle, *X/Self* correspondingly proposes that readers consider Europe using the figure of the Alps. Thus Mont Blanc is the center and central image of Europe, its hub and holy mountain. Its counterpart is Kilimanjaro, the African hub of histories. The human imitation of the first one is the Roman Empire and its successors; of the other, the kraal and the village compound. One is an industrial furnace, while the other is an agrarian center, surrounded by the diverse life of the savanna. *X/Self* presents an impressive array of such oppositions – male and female, aggressive and patient, stable and unstable, linear and circular, the continuing city versus the apocalyptic missile, and cultures of the "projectile" and of the circular "target." Brathwaite envisions history as a cycle of changing relations between these opposites – the kind of cycle he elsewhere calls "tidalectics," an ebb and flow of antithetical ideas or processes.

Midway between the two symbolic mountains, in the bowl of the Sahara, is Lake Chad. The lake is emotionally (though not structurally) significant in *Masks*, but in *X/Self* it functions as the source of dynamism for the entire figurative system. It is a manifestation of *nam*, and its effect is represented by the harmattan, the dry wind out of the desert that affects the weather even of the Caribbean. Yet, like other manifestations of *nam*, it is inherently ambivalent: the harmattan contributes to the trade winds that made possible the slave trade; and it is also associated with hurricanes, which since "The Cracked Mother" in *Islands* have symbolized European cultural aggression in Brathwaite's poetry. This symbolic system is one of many indications that Brathwaite is particularly interested in the complexities of revolution, creolization, and similar historical processes. *The Arrivants* shows a careful questioning of assumptions behind the idealization of Africa; the book is an exhaustive investigation of issues of

Dust jacket for the second book (1982) in Brathwaite's second trilogy. Set in Barbados, Sun Poem *focuses on a boy named Adam, who discovers the cosmic cycle of life.*

origin. The pointed and provocative repositioning of Uncle Tom and the similar reevaluation of Tutu and glorified Africa have their counterparts, for example, in the complex rehabilitation of "Rome" – for the purposes of *X/Self*, in the vacuum left when Rome burns, slavery begins.

There is also ambivalence inherent in the central character of the volume. Altogether, this second trilogy focuses on ancestral/mythic figures; after mother/island and father/sun, the third volume presents X/Self as a crossing point of the others, a blend of the heroic/unheroic sons of those parents. The result is a small but intensely resonant pantheon. Some of its avatars are Prospero, Sycorax, and Caliban/Ariel. X/Self is, in a way, a tribe: all the resistant selves on the margins of the empire who together carry the multiple masks and "calibanizing" voices of *The Arrivants* beyond the American context of "The Spades" and "All God's

Chillun" and out into the global village. They represent the creole presence both within and against the empire. Thus the volume starts with a letter from an inconsequential nephew of the emperor. But the emperor is Severus, and that choice initiates the play of centrality and marginality: he is the first African to become emperor, thereby bringing his marginality to the utmost center of Rome but in the end bringing his centrality to the margins, to die at York, a place that was then on the edge of the world. X/Self is the name for Severus, and his nephew, and all the obscure populations at the margins of the empire who were perceived as monkeys or savages, gorillas or guerrillas. Not surprisingly X/Self is a poem of things misheard, misspoken, and twisted to advantage. It is virtually about transmission, noise, and distortion. While the entire second trilogy is engaged in radically experimental play with language, X/Self especially shows Brathwaite in the exploration of "calibanisms" – Joycean wordplay forged under the pressure of exile and colonialism, the blue notes of language, the black-and-blue notes of people who have been battered by colonialism.

There have been several useful studies of the second trilogy's subversive language, but generally this trilogy has not received extensive critical response. It is not so vividly the long poem of a specific historical moment as The Arrivants is, and since it is more personal, more complex, and less public in expression, it may also be less immediately accessible. Sun Poem in particular has attracted surprisingly little attention, apart from Rohlehr's magisterial account of its themes and their interplay (Jamaica Journal, 1983). X/Self has fared better. Anthony Kellman, for example (in Callaloo, Summer 1988), considered it in conjunction with Harris's Palace of the Peacock (1960); Laurence A. Breiner discussed the conceptual framework (Partisan Review, 1989); and Edward Chamberlin (Carib, 1989) read the volume quite successfully as a spiritual autobiography (with illuminating comments on the meanings of X). Mother Poem, perhaps because it is the first of the series, has elicited more commentary, but some critics voice disappointment. King, focusing on the political dimension, concluded that "the protest style of Mother Poem is less interesting than the earlier poetry." Mark McWatt, approaching the work from a different angle, wrote: "The ring of authority and the sureness of rhythm and diction are missing from this poem, although the level of intellectual appreciation and involvement remains high" (Bim, 1978). To date only one aspect of the volume has generated significant controversy. Provocative feminist views presented by Bev E. L. Brown and

Sue Thomas inspired an energetic response from Rohlehr, who asserted that Mother Poem constitutes "perhaps the most varied kaleidoscope of female experience that yet exists in West Indian literature" (from an unpublished paper he read at UWI, Mona, 1988).

Paradoxically the finest available commentaries on this trilogy are probably Brathwaite's own contemporaneous essays, particularly those that elaborate his thinking on metahistorical and "geopsychic" subjects: "Gods of the Middle Passage," "Metaphors of Underdevelopment,'' and "World Order Models – A Caribbean Perspective." These essays offer detailed accounts of his most essential terms, such as nam, missile, and capsule as metaphors for different kinds of cultures; at the same time, the essays explicate his fundamental ideas about the relation of individual and group to environment, and about the many facets of creolization, including the subtle interaction he calls "interculturation" – the process by which "the conquerors are conquered and the colonized colonize."

In the years coinciding with the publication of the second trilogy, Brathwaite was honored both abroad (winning Fulbright fellowships in 1982 and 1987) and in Jamaica, where in 1983 he was appointed professor of social and cultural history at the University of the West Indies. In the same year another volume of his poems was published. The twenty-three works in Third World Poems are nearly all reprinted from other published books, though "Kingston" and "Poem for Walter Rodney" are notable exceptions. Some variants in the details of the poems will be of interest to scholars: lineation and even spelling sometimes differ from other printed versions; and there is a tendency to reduce punctuation, as elsewhere in Brathwaite's work of the 1980s. The subtle implications and effects of this particular organization of the poems will be of interest to close readers of Brathwaite's work, but for most this collection functions merely as a convenient "selected poems."

During the 1980s Brathwaite continued to produce important literary criticism. In addition to studies of works by Roger Mais and René Depestre, his essays on the Guyanese poet Martin Carter are especially significant: they offer a revelatory account of the poet but at the same time register Brathwaite's fascination with a figure in whom he sees himself reflected. In "Martin Carter's Poetry of the Negative Yes" Brathwaite delineates the phases of Carter's poetic career in a way that strongly invites comparison with his own development. The same seems true in "Resistance Poems," when he

*Brathwaite reading from his work during the Caribbean Literature
Conference at the Commonwealth Institute in London, 1986
(photograph by Fabian Becker)*

writes that, in Carter's early poetry, one encounters "the voice of Revolution without the Revolution" and when he calls Carter "one of the few authentically optimistic English-writing Caribbean poets." The difference he emphasizes is also revealing: "My guess is . . . that Carter's work has dealt little (directly) with his landscape: physical and socio-cultural. In formal terms there is no **nation language** (dialect), no 'nancy forms.' " Unlike Carter, Brathwaite has increasingly devoted his energy and authority to the recovery of indigenous linguistic and formal resources as media for poetry. In fact even his criticism since the mid 1970s often contains passages written in "nation language." He explains the practice in the following terms (in *Contradictory Omens*, 1974): "the Caribbean environment demands its own style, vocab, its own norms; and I'm saying that these demands (should) challenge the

scholar/intellectual as deeply as they do the artist, and that this creole aesthetic cannot be adequately developed outside the Caribbean; not even by Caribbeans themselves." This concern with making the Caribbean voice audible is expressed in several articles, particularly "Creative Literature of the British West Indies during the Period of Slavery" and "The African Presence in Caribbean Literature," but it receives its fullest statement in *History of the Voice* (1984). In all of these instances Brathwaite links literary history directly with his cultural and anthropological concerns; he conceives the essential development of Caribbean literature as a progression from objective depiction of the "native" to subjective voicing, which approximates a kind of incarnation of the native in the text, analogous to the real presence of the *loa* in the possessed worshiper. Curiously Brathwaite has also been recasting the visual form of his reissued poetry, even as he insists on its oral basis.

The death of Brathwaite's wife, Doris, in 1986 marked a critical juncture in his career. The shock came in the midst of a series of publications that year: a retrospective collection of essays (*Roots*); a retrospective collection of poems (*Jah Music*); and Doris's own labor of love, the bibliography *EKB: His Published Prose & Poetry 1948–1986*. There is an unavoidable sense of finality in that coincidence of events. Another blow came in 1988, when Hurricane Gilbert virtually destroyed Brathwaite's house and buried most of his library in mud, entombing an unequaled collection of Caribbean writing as well as Brathwaite's own papers.

In 1991 he left Jamaica to take a position at New York University. There have been rumors of a third trilogy in progress. Certainly Brathwaite has continued to write, and critical attention to his work has continued to increase – two recent studies have initiated the task of considering his literary and cultural essays in their own right. His influence on younger West Indian writers, both through the example of his work and through his personal support, continues to have a measurable effect on the literature of the entire region. As poet, critic, and historian, Brathwaite continues to pursue the objectives he described in 1977 in *Wars of Respect*, when he wrote that West Indians need poets and novelists "to restore our sense of an intimate, emotional connection with our past; to restore, in fact, our folk myths. But we also need to have a sense of connection and continuity – a sense of historicity – so that we may come to believe, in ourselves, in the credentials of our past. This is where our historians (should) come in; not with the practice, only, of Euro-classical archival 'discipline'; but with the kind of vision (the ability of the muse) which makes it possible to leap our discontinuities and connect our fragments."

Interviews:

Nii Laryea Korley, "Brathwaite: Home Again," *West Africa*, no. 3627 (16 March 1987): 514–515;

Stewart Brown, "Interview with Edward Kamau Brathwaite," *Kyk-over-al*, 40 (December 1989): 84–93.

Bibliographies:

Doris Monica Brathwaite, *EKB: His Published Prose & Poetry 1948–1986: A Checklist* (Mona, Jamaica: Savacou, 1986);

Brathwaite, *A Descriptive and Chronological Bibliography (1950–1982) of the Work of Edward Kamau Brathwaite* (London & Port of Spain: New Beacon, 1988).

References:

Ama Ata Aidoo, "Akan and English," *West Africa*, no. 2677 (21 September 1968): 1099;

Funso Aiyejina, "The Death and Rebirth of African Deities in Edward Brathwaite's *Islands*," *World Literature Written in English*, 23 (Spring 1984): 397–404;

Samuel O. Asein, "The Concept of Form: A Study of Some Ancestral Elements in Brathwaite's Trilogy," *ASAWI Bulletin*, 4 (December 1971): 9–38;

Asein, "Symbol and Meaning in the Poetry of Edward Brathwaite," *World Literature Written in English*, 20 (Spring 1981): 96–104;

Bill Ashcroft, Gareth Griffiths, and Helen Tiffin, *The Empire Writes Back* (London & New York: Routledge, 1989);

Edward Baugh, "Edward Brathwaite as Critic: Some Preliminary Observations," *Caribbean Quarterly*, 28, nos. 1–2 (1982): 66–75;

Laurence A. Breiner, "The Other West Indian Poet," *Partisan Review*, 56, no. 2 (1989): 316–320;

Breiner, "Tradition, Society, the Figure of the Poet," *Caribbean Quarterly*, 26, nos. 1–2: (1980): 1–12;

Bev E. L. Brown, "Mansong and Matrix: A Radical Experiment," in *A Double Colonization: Colonial and Post-Colonial Women's Writing*, edited by K. Petersen and A. Rutherford (Aarhus, Denmark: Dangaroo, 1986), pp. 68–79;

Lloyd Brown, "The Cyclical Vision of Edward Brathwaite," in his *West Indian Poetry* (Boston: Twayne, 1978), pp. 139–158;

Angus Calder, "Walcott's 'The Schooner Flight' and Brathwaite's 'Nametracks': Two Short Verse Narratives," in *Short Fiction in the New Literatures in English*, edited by Jacqueline Bardolph (Nice, France: Faculté des Lettres & Sciences Humaines, 1989), pp. 109–119;

Hayden Carruth, "Poetry Chronicle," *Hudson Review*, 27 (Summer 1974): 308–320;

Edward Chamberlin, "Myself Made Otherwise: Edward Kamau Brathwaite's *X/Self*," *Carib*, 5 (1989): 19–32;

G. R. Coulthard, "Edward Brathwaite y el neoafricanismo antillano," *Cuadernos Americanos*, 31 (September–October 1972): 170–177;

Michael Dash, "Edward Brathwaite," in *West Indian*

Literature, edited by Bruce King (London: Macmillan, 1979), pp. 210–227;

Jean D'Costa, "The Poetry of Edward Brathwaite," *Jamaica Journal*, 2 (September 1968): 24–28;

Robert Fraser, *A Critical View on Edward Brathwaite's Masks*, edited by Yolande Cantù (London: Collings, 1981);

Damian Grant, "Emerging Image: The Poetry of Edward Brathwaite," *Critical Quarterly*, 12 (Summer 1970): 186–193;

Patricia Ismond, "Walcott versus Brathwaite," *Caribbean Quarterly*, 17 (September–December 1971): 54–71;

Louis James, "A Caribbean Poet Questing," *Third World Quarterly*, 10 (March 1988): 334–337;

James, "Caribbean Poetry in English – Some Problems," *Savacou*, 2 (1970): 78–86;

Anthony Kellman, "Projective Verse as a Mode of Socio-Linguist Protest," *Ariel*, 21 (April 1990): 45–57;

Kellman, "A Rich Plural Heritage as a Tool for Survival," *Callaloo*, 11 (Summer 1988): 645–648;

Arthur Kemoli, "The Theme of 'The Past' in Caribbean Literature," *World Literature Written in English*, 12 (November 1973): 304–325;

Bruce King, "Walcott, Brathwaite, and Authenticity," in his *The New English Literatures* (London: Macmillan, 1980; New York: St. Martin's Press, 1980);

Maureen Warner Lewis, "Image and Idiom in Nationalist Literature: Achebe, Ngugi, and Brathwaite," in *Studies in Commonwealth Literature*, edited by Eckhard Breitinger and Reinhard Sander (Tübingen, Germany: Narr, 1985), pp. 105–114;

Lewis, *Notes to Masks* (Benin City, Nigeria: Ethiope, 1977);

Lewis, "Odomankoma Kyerema Se," *Caribbean Quarterly*, 19 (June 1973): 51–99;

Nathaniel Mackey, "Edward Brathwaite's New World Trilogy," *Caliban*, 3 (Spring–Summer 1979): 58–88;

Jürgen Martini, "Literary Criticism and Aesthetics in the Caribbean, I: E. K. Brathwaite," *World Literature Written in English*, 24 (Autumn 1984): 373–383;

Marina Maxwell, "The Awakening of the Drum," *New World Quarterly*, 5, no. 4 (1971): 39–45;

Maxwell, "Towards a Revolution in the Arts," *Savacou*, 2 (1970): 19–32;

Russell McDougall, " 'Something Rich and Strange' in the Poetry of Edward Kamau Brathwaite's *The Arrivants*," in *(Un)Common Ground: Essays in Literatures in English*, edited by Andrew Taylor

Dust jacket for the final volume in Brathwaite's second trilogy. X/Self, which sets up a series of oppositions, including Europe versus Africa and male versus female, has been called Brathwaite's spiritual autobiography.

and McDougall (Adelaide, Australia: CRNLE, 1990), pp. 63–74;

Gerald Moore, "Confident Achievement," *Journal of Commonwealth Literature*, 7 (July 1969): 122–124;

Moore, "West Indian Poet," *Transition*, 7 (August–September 1967): 62–63;

Pamela Mordecai, "The Image of the Pebble in Brathwaite's *Arrivants*," *Carib*, 5 (1989): 60–78;

Mervyn Morris, "Niggers Everywhere," *New World Quarterly*, 3, no. 4 (1967): 61–65;

Morris, "This Broken Ground: Edward Brathwaite's Trilogy of Poems," *New World Quarterly*, 5, no. 3 (1969): 14–26;

Chandrabhanu Pattanayak, "Brathwaite: Metaphors of Emergence," *Literary Criterion*, 17, no. 3 (1982): 60–68;

Velma Pollard, "The Dust – Tribute to the Folk,"

Caribbean Quarterly, 26 (March–June 1980): 41–48;

Pollard, "Language in the Poetry of Edward Brathwaite," *World Literature Written in English*, 19 (Spring 1980): 62–73;

John Povey, "The Search for Identity in Edward Brathwaite's *The Arrivants*," *World Literature Written in English*, 27 (Autumn 1987): 275–289;

Kenneth Ramchand, "Edward Brathwaite," in his *An Introduction to the Study of West Indian Literature* (London: Nelson Caribbean, 1976), pp. 127–142;

Ramchand, "The Pounding in His Dark: Edward Brathwaite's Other Poetry," *Tapia*, 7 (2 January 1977): 5–7;

Gordon Rohlehr, "Afterthoughts," *Tapia* (26 December 1971): 8, 13;

Rohlehr, "The Carrion Time," *Tapia*, 4 (June 1974): 5–8, 11;

Rohlehr, *Pathfinder: Black Awakening in* The Arrivants *of Edward Kamau Brathwaite* (Tunapuna, Trinidad: Rohlehr, 1981);

Rohlehr, "West Indian Poetry: Some Problems of Assessment," *Tapia* (29 August 1971): 11–14;

K. E. Senanu, "Brathwaite's Song of Dispossession," *Universitas*, 1 (March 1969): 59–63;

Sue Thomas, "Sexual Politics in Edward Brathwaite's *Mother Poem* and *Sun Poem*," *Kunapipi*, 9, no. 1 (1987): 33–43;

Derek Walcott, "Tribal Flutes," *Sunday Guardian Magazine* (Trinidad), 19 March 1967, pp. 2–3;

Anne Walmsey, "Dimensions of Song: A Comment on the Poetry of Derek Walcott and Edward Brathwaite," *Bim*, 13 (July–December 1970): 152–167.

Austin C. Clarke

(26 July 1934 –)

Victor J. Ramraj
University of Calgary

See also the Clarke entry in *DLB 53: Canadian Writers Since 1960*, First Series.

BOOKS: *The Survivors of the Crossing* (London: Heinemann, 1964; Toronto: McClelland & Stewart, 1964);

Amongst Thistles and Thorns (London: Heinemann, 1965; Toronto: McClelland & Stewart, 1965);

The Meeting Point (London: Heinemann, 1967; Toronto: Macmillan, 1967; Boston: Little, Brown, 1972);

When He Was Free and Young and He Used to Wear Silks (Toronto: Anansi, 1971; revised and enlarged edition, Boston: Little, Brown, 1973);

Storm of Fortune (Boston: Little, Brown, 1973);

The Bigger Light (Boston: Little, Brown, 1975);

The Prime Minister (Don Mills, Ont.: General Publishing, 1977; London: Routledge & Kegan Paul, 1978);

Growing Up Stupid Under the Union Jack (Toronto: McClelland & Stewart, 1980; Havana, Cuba: Casa de las Américas, 1980);

When Women Rule (Toronto: McClelland & Stewart, 1985);

Nine Men Who Laughed (Markham, Ont. & New York: Penguin, 1986);

Proud Empires (London: Gollancz, 1986; Markham, Ont.: Viking-Penguin, 1988).

OTHER: "Some Speculations as to the Absence of Racialistic Vindictiveness in West Indian Literature," in *The Black Writer in Africa and the Americas*, edited by Lloyd W. Brown (Los Angeles: Hennessey & Ingalls, 1973), pp. 165–194.

SELECTED PERIODICAL PUBLICATIONS – UNCOLLECTED: "Harrison College and Me," *New World: Barbados Independence Issue* (1966–1967): 31–34;

"Cultural-Political Origins of Black Student Anti-

Austin C. Clarke (photograph by Rolf Kalman)

Intellectualism," *Studies in Black Literature*, 1 (Spring 1970): 69–82;

"In the Semi-Colon of the North," *Canadian Literature*, 95 (Winter 1982): 30–37.

Among West Indian writers, Austin C. Clarke occupies a special position. While many other writers migrated to Great Britain and the United States, Clarke made Canada his adopted home and became the foremost recounter of the black West Indian immigrants' experience in Canada. Of his generation of West Indian novelists he is perhaps the most outspoken and bitter in depicting the experience of the poor black when confronted with the establishment, whether it is that of the white majority in Canada, the colonial expatriate, or the postcolonial ruling black middle class in Barbados. Clarke is perhaps better known for his Toronto novels and stories: the trilogy comprising *The Meeting Point* (1967), *Storm of Fortune* (1973), and *The Bigger Light* (1975); and his short-story collections *When He Was Free and Young and He Used to Wear Silks* (1971), *When Women Rule* (1985), and *Nine Men Who Laughed* (1986). However, he has written as many works set in Barbados – more, in fact, than his fellow Barbadian novelist George Lamming – *The Survivors of the Crossing* (1964), *Amongst Thistles and Thorns* (1965), *The Prime Minister* (1977), *Growing Up Stupid Under the Union Jack* (1980), *Proud Empires* (1986), and some short stories scattered in his collections.

Austin Chesterfield Clarke was born on 26 July 1934 in Saint James, Barbados, and was the son of Kenneth Trotman, an artist, and Gladys Clarke, a hotel maid. He attended Combermere High School, where he won a scholarship to Harrison College. His school days and other boyhood and adolescent experiences are vividly portrayed in his memoirs, *Growing Up Stupid Under the Union Jack*. After graduating from Harrison College, Clarke taught at the Coleridge-Parry Primary School in Saint Peter for three years before leaving Barbados in 1955 to study economics and political science at the University of Toronto. When Clarke was in high school, Frank Collymore, the editor of the influential Caribbean literary magazine *Bim*, encouraged him to write. Clarke initially wrote poetry, and during his first year at the University of Toronto he entered some of his poems written in Barbados in a poetry competition and won an undergraduate prize. He preferred fiction, however, for which he began preparing himself by writing for newspapers, first as a reporter in Timmins and Kirkland Lake in northern Canada for two years and later as a free-lance journalist for the *Toronto Globe and Mail* and the Canadian Broadcasting Corporation.

During these years, he wrote two novels but was not satisfied enough with them to submit them for publication. He published his first novel, *The Survivors of the Crossing*, about a decade after he immigrated to Canada. Clarke set it and his second novel, *Amongst Thistles and Thorns*, in Barbados, exploring in his first book the exploitation of sugar-plantation laborers and in his second the unhappy

experiences of a poor boy who seeks, in ways that echo Clarke's own life, to escape his suffocating environment. These two novels were received as apprenticeship pieces. They portray vividly the world of Clarke's childhood in colonial Barbados and reveal his immense talent for capturing the feel and flow of Barbadian speech and his adeptness at creating hilariously comic scenes. But they are weakly structured and lack aesthetic distancing and tonal discipline.

In *The Survivors of the Crossing* Rufus, a sugar-plantation laborer, attempts to challenge the powerful white plantation owners by calling a strike. He is unsuccessful, however, not just because of the repressive power of the owners, who control the government and the police force, but because of the sycophantic, conservative black middle class who are contemptuous of the working class and ally themselves with the whites. When the strike fails, Rufus resorts to violence and alienates the poor, who now perceive him as an outlaw. Even his girlfriend abandons him for a while. The reader, too, tends to stand apart from Rufus. One of the characteristics of Clarke's novels is that his protagonists seldom enlist the reader's unqualified sympathy, despite their unfortunate and unjust circumstances. In this first novel Clarke conveys convincingly the exploitation of the poor but often finds it difficult to keep his anger under artistic control. He manipulates the plot too obviously. But the novel shows his evident facility at using the Barbados dialect and creating exuberantly comic scenes.

The narrator in *Amongst Thistles and Thorns* is nine-year-old Milton Sobers, an illegitimate child who runs away from his uncaring mother and her boyfriend and finds his father, whom he has never known. His rebellion lasts for just a weekend, but when he returns home, he has a vague sense of pride and independence, instilled in him by his father's embellished stories of blacks in Harlem. Milton is still alienated from his home and yearns to escape its emotional sterility. The novel marks an improvement on *The Survivors of the Crossing*. Although the structure is awkward and the nine-year-old's point of view is not sustained, the narrative is less improbable, and the characterization achieves some psychological depth and complexity.

In both these novels North America beckons the protagonists. Rufus is inspired to lead the revolt against the whites because of a letter he receives from Canada telling him about the rights of the workers there. And Milton's father holds Harlem out to him as a world of opportunities. What North America, in particular Canada, actually holds for

Dust jacket for the first volume of Clarke's memoirs, which tells of his childhood in Saint James, Barbados, and ends with him entering high school

the black migrant is not so pleasant, however, which is the concern of Clarke's next three novels, the Toronto trilogy.

In these novels Clarke examines the black working-class immigrants' struggles in an inhospitable white society. He shows them living bleak lives, the victims of racial prejudice, and he captures well their intense feelings of alienation. His unerringly sharp ear for Barbadian speech patterns and rhythms contributes much to the richness of his characterization. Some critics feel, however, that he depends too much on this talent in portraying his characters and that his dialogues often become indiscriminate tape recordings of his characters' conversations. Clarke's strident anger against the unaccommodating white society, his overt plot manipulation to support his stand, and his inability to keep sufficient authorial distance from protagonists, who are often undeserving of sympathy, work against the Toronto novels being unqualified successes.

In *The Meeting Point*, for example, the protagonist, Bernice Leach, is a black Barbadian immigrant who works as a maid in the home of a Jewish family in Toronto. She and her fellow Barbadian maids feel threatened by the exclusive whiteness of the environment, symbolized by the recurring snow imagery. Perceiving herself as a twentieth-century slave and never comfortable in her adopted home, she is nevertheless hesitant to return to her impoverished peasant life in Barbados. Her male Barbadian friends, chronically unemployed, attempt futilely to achieve acceptance through sexual relationships with white women. These characters have to contend with inner as well as outer conflicts as they try to retain their black pride and identity and come to grips with self-hatred and beckoning materialism.

In *Storm of Fortune* the same group of Barbadian immigrants reappears. No longer fresh immigrants, they still feel alienated and unaccommodated. Some are managing to improve their fortunes, although the ways by which they are doing so often strain the reader's credulity. The characters who have achieved a measure of economic success and feel they deserve acceptance into the system now have to cope with more sharply felt social alienation that heightens their self-doubt and self-hatred. Clarke introduces some new white characters in this novel, the most memorable of whom is Gloria Macmillan. She is exceptionally well portrayed, unlike Clarke's other white characters, who seldom come alive or achieve psychological credibility.

The Bigger Light, the concluding volume of the Toronto trilogy, focuses on the experiences of Boysie, one of the immigrants who has achieved financial success. His social life is wanting, however, and he suffers from intense depression, which is pointed up by recurring death imagery. Boysie's is the most probing psychological portrait that Clarke has undertaken. Desperate to belong in Canada, Boysie gradually becomes estranged from his wife and his West Indian identity as he attempts whatever tenuous assimilation is afforded him. He writes letters to prestigious Toronto newspapers, wears three-piece suits, avoids West Indian parties, and rejects calypsos for Judy Collins's songs. The novel ends with Boysie driving his car across the Canadian-American border, but there is little to suggest that he can rally himself and arrest his malaise. Clarke puts Boysie and his fellow immigrants in a less ugly physical setting in this novel, and though they continue to struggle in an alien society, their lives are shown to be not as oppressive and debilitating as those portrayed in the earlier novels of the trilogy. Of the three novels, this last one is the least-dismal depiction of the Barbadian immigrants' lives in Toronto.

Boysie's self-doubt, his quest for acceptance in the white society, his shunning of his fellow West Indians and of West Indian culture are reflected in the main character of Clarke's story "Four Stations in His Circle" (in *When He Was Free and Young and He Used to Wear Silks*), where the protagonist isolates himself in a mansion he has purchased in a white neighborhood. Ironically his neighbors assume that he is just the caretaker. All the stories in *When He Was Free* similarly have themes and narrative styles that echo the novels. In fact some are germinations and close versions of episodes in the novels. Many are characteristically loose and rambling, but a few, such as "Four Stations in His Circle" and "Griff," are skillfully written and confirm Clarke's ability to create consummately written episodes in his novels. There are two versions of this collection of stories. The later version, published in 1973, omits a few

stories and includes four that are set in the United States. These four portray the lot of American blacks, whom Clarke considers to be worse off than West Indian blacks.

For these American stories Clarke was drawing on his visits to the United States during the late 1960s and early 1970s. The publication of *The Meeting Point* had established him as a significant talent, and he was offered several appointments as creative writer and visiting professor at Yale, Duke, and Texas. He was also appointed Barbados's cultural attaché in Washington for 1974 and 1975.

In 1975 he became general manager of the Caribbean Broadcasting Company in Barbados, a post he left prematurely when he ran afoul of the prime minister. On returning to Canada, Clarke, piqued, began writing *The Prime Minister*, a novel based on his frustrating experience with the Barbados government. Like Clarke, the protagonist of the novel, an artist, returns to Barbados to take up an important cultural position with the government. Resented by several individuals who see him as an opportunistic intruder, he is framed as a conspirator, and, fearing for his life, he flees the island. The novel has the pace, suspense, and intrigue of a thriller. The island politicians are unmitigatingly portrayed as corrupt, amoral, and capable of murder. Several West Indian reviewers pounced on the book as an indulgence in vindictiveness and urged unsuccessfully that it be banned in Barbados.

Writing this novel, however, was not Clarke's only preoccupation on his return to Canada. Somewhat surprisingly, after his unhappy experience with Barbados politics, he plunged into Canadian politics, running unsuccessfully in the 1977 Ontario provincial election as a Progressive Conservative candidate in the Toronto riding of York South. Asked by interviewer Graeme Gibson why he, an advocate of socialism, should run as a Conservative, he pleaded that Clarke the man should be kept apart from Clarke the novelist, adding, however, that the Conservative party does not bar the "radical."

After the publication of *The Prime Minister*, Clarke turned his hand to what he perceives to be the first volume of his memoirs, *Growing Up Stupid Under the Union Jack*, in which he recounts his early experiences in rural Barbados, concluding with his leaving Combermere School for Harrison College, Barbados's prestigious senior high school. The many dramatic scenes, the lively dialogue, and the narrative pace invite the reader to parallel this memoir with Clarke's novels. Clarke renders vividly details of time, place, customs, and habits. And he evokes, not just recalls, his moods and feelings. The work points up how much *Amongst Thistles and Thorns* issued from Clarke's own boyhood experiences.

After a gap of five years, Clarke published in quick succession two volumes of stories: *When Women Rule* and *Nine Men Who Laughed*. Of the eight stories in *When Women Rule*, five have the familiar working-class West Indian protagonist struggling to find his place in Canadian society. These stories are about men rendered impotent as much by their inhospitable environment as by wives, friends, and their own self-hatred. The other three are about working-class white Canadians, who, like the protagonist of "The Collector," resent the incursion of immigrants, yearning for a time when Canada was "pure."

In his introduction to *Nine Men Who Laughed* Clarke rails against the Canadian system that perpetually perceives the West Indian immigrant as an outsider, but Clarke is equally annoyed with the immigrant who, on achieving a measure of material success, becomes tolerant of abuses and indulges in feeble, amnesiac laughter. Such laughter, Clarke insists, is the response of fools, of those too lazy to think, and of those "morally dead." The stories show the dire consequences of laughter. The protagonists all meet dismal ends: they either lock themselves away, go mad, commit suicide, or are raped and murdered. One of the nine stories, "A Funeral," clearly belongs with *The Prime Minister*. Set in Barbados, it unremittingly ridicules the corrupt politician. These later volumes of stories show Clarke honing his skills as a short-story writer. Most of the stories achieve an ironic control, discipline, and aesthetic distance not evident in the earlier work. Clarke appears capable of relatively probing studies of his protagonists' psyches.

Clarke's novel *Proud Empires* looks back at the Barbados politics of the 1950s. Boy, a thirteen-year-old high-school student, prepares for a scholarship examination in the middle of a national election, which proves to be a rite of passage for him. It opens his eyes to the corruption and treachery of island politics. But Clarke is less concerned with Boy's development than with the reprehensible conduct of the politicians and the distorted values of the middle class. At the end of the novel Boy, who had gone to study in Toronto (where inevitably, like Clarke's other immigrant characters, he experiences racism), returns to the island and allows himself to be persuaded to enter politics. But Boy's experiences are so cursorily given and his character so sketchily portrayed that it is not clear exactly what

he has learned about politics and what he can contribute politically. Characteristically *Proud Empires* has many fine episodes and scintillating dialogue, employing the rhythm and idiom of Barbados English, which helps considerably to bring the characters to life. The novel confirms that Clarke's strength as a novelist lies not so much in his probing the psyche and inner development of his protagonists as in capturing the subtleties of the social and political behavior of his Barbadian characters whether at home or abroad.

Clarke resides in Toronto with his wife, Betty Joyce Reynolds Clarke, and their three children: Janice, Loretta, and Mphahlele. Clarke seems a writer at mid career, whose creativity is undiminished, having produced between 1985 and 1987 *When Women Rule*, *Nine Men Who Laughed*, and *Proud Empires*. He is currently working on his second volume of memoirs and a sequel to *Proud Empires*.

There are evident shortcomings in Clarke's fiction, but they do not eclipse his just-as-evident talent as a writer. He is a significant name in West Indian literature and deserves his reputation as Canada's most distinguished black writer. He has won several literary awards, including in 1965 the University of Western Ontario Medal for best story, the Belmont Short Story Award, three Canada Council Arts Fellowships, and in 1980 the Cuban Casa de las Américas Literary Prize.

Interviews:

Graeme Gibson, "Interview with Austin Clarke," in his *Eleven Canadian Novelists Interviewed by Graeme Gibson* (Toronto: Anansi, 1973), pp. 33–54;

Terrence Craig, "Interview with Austin Clarke," *World Literature Written in English*, 26 (Spring 1986): 115–127.

References:

Edward Baugh, "Education and Politics in West Indian Fiction: Austin Clarke's *Proud Empires*," *Sargasso* (1988): 166–174;

Baugh, "Friday in Crusoe's City: The Question of Language in Two West Indian Novels of Exile," *ACLALS Bulletin*, 5 (December 1980): 1–12;

Frank Birbalsingh, "West Indians in Canada: The Toronto Novels of Austin Clarke," *Journal of Caribbean Studies*, 5 (Fall 1985–Spring 1986): 71–78;

Anthony Boxill, "The Novels of Austin Clarke," *Fiddlehead*, 75 (Spring 1968): 68–72;

Lloyd W. Brown, *El Dorado and Paradise: Canada and*

the Caribbean in Austin Clarke's Fiction (London, Ont.: Centre for Social and Humanistic Studies, University of Western Ontario, 1989);

Brown, "The West Indian Novel in North America: A Study of Austin Clarke," *Journal of Commonwealth Literature*, 9 (July 1970): 89–105;

Brown, "West Indian Writers and the Canadian Mosaic," *World Literature Written in English*, 21 (Summer 1982): 374–385;

Cyril Dabydeen, "Outside El Dorado: Themes and Problems of West Indian Writing in Canada," *Journal of Caribbean Studies*, 5 (Fall 1985–Spring 1986): 79–90;

Horace Goddard, "The Immigrants' Pain: The Socio-Literary Context of Austin Clarke's Trilogy," *ACLALS Bulletin*, 8, no. 1 (1989): 39–57;

Keith S. Henry, "An Assessment of Austin Clarke, West Indian-Canadian Novelist," *College Language Association Journal*, 29 (September 1985): 9–32;

Horace I. Ishmael, "The Psychology of Fear and Hate in Austin Clarke's Trilogy," *Chimo: CACLALS Journal*, 10 (1985): 10–13;

Arnold Itwaru, "Being and Non-Being and the Production of the Subject in Austin Clarke," in *Perspectives theoriques sur les littératures africaines et caribéennes*, edited by Suzanne Crosta and others (Toronto: University of Toronto, 1987), pp. 39–58;

Clare MacCulloch, "Look Homeward, Bajan: A Look at the Work of Austin Clarke," *Bim*, 14 (July–December 1972): 179–182;

Victor J. Ramraj, "Temporizing Laughter: The Later Stories of Austin Clarke," in *Short Fiction in the New Literatures in English*, edited by Jacqueline Bardolph (Nice, France, 1989), pp. 127–132;

Miriam Waddington, "No Meeting Points," *Canadian Literature*, 35 (Winter 1968): 74–78.

Papers:

The Austin Clarke Collection in the Mills Memorial Library of McMaster University, Hamilton, Ontario, is substantial. It includes Clarke's correspondence and manuscripts of his published and unpublished work, as well as contracts, newspaper clippings, and reviews.

Nuruddin Farah

(1945 –)

Jacqueline Bardolph
University of Nice

BOOKS: *Why Die so Soon?* (Mogadishu: Somali News, 1965);
From a Crooked Rib (London: Heinemann, 1970);
A Naked Needle (London: Heinemann, 1976);
Sweet and Sour Milk (London: Allison & Busby, 1979; London & Exeter, N.H.: Heinemann, 1980);
Sardines (London: Allison & Busby, 1981);
Close Sesame (London & New York: Allison & Busby, 1983);
Maps (London: Pan, 1986; New York: Pantheon, 1986);
Gåvor (Stockholm: Bonniers, 1990).

PLAY PRODUCTIONS: *A Dagger in Vacuum*, Mogadishu, Somalia, 1969;
Yussuf and His Brothers, Jos, Nigeria, University Theatre, 2 July 1982.

RADIO: *A Spread of Butter*, BBC, 1978.

SELECTED PERIODICAL PUBLICATIONS – UNCOLLECTED: "Do You Speak German?!," *Okike*, 22 (September 1982): 33–38;
"The Creative Writer and the African Politician," *Guardian* (Lagos), 7 September 1983, p. 11;
"In Praise of Exile," *Third World Affairs* (1988);
"Why I Write," *Third World Quarterly*, 10 (October 1988): 1591–1599;
"Childhood of My Schizophrenia," *Times Literary Supplement*, 23–29 November 1990, p. 1264.

Nuruddin Farah, 1988 (photograph by Horst Tappe)

Nuruddin Farah's novels are an important contribution to African literature. He writes about his country, Somalia, a nation in the Horn of Africa with apparently no connection with the Commonwealth or the English-speaking world, so his books introduce readers to the political turmoil in a new state and to a culture new to English fiction. But the interest is more than regional: the books present the theme of individual freedom in the face of arbitrary power in a way that is relevant outside Africa as well, and they do so with an intellectual and poetic control that makes him one of the most stimulating prose writers in Africa today.

Born in 1945 in Baidoa to Hassan Farah (a merchant) and Aleeli Faduma Farah (a poet), Nuruddin Farah was educated at first in the Ogaden, the Somali-populated area now in Ethiopia. His first languages as a child were Somali, Amharic, and Arabic, followed by Italian and English. From these early years one can see two important features that were to dominate his writing life. First, he was brought up in a tradition with a rich oral culture, in which poetry is a craft that takes years to master. Poetry enters political debates in a sophisticated manner, epic or satirical but also oblique and allusive, and plays an important social function. Some of Farah's relatives, including his mother, are known masters of the genre. Second, the history of colonization and borders gave him early access to a wide range of cultures: his travels and readings made him a cosmopolitan writer, a world nomad who was to write from a distance about Somalia, "my country in my mind," as he once called it.

In 1965 his novella *Why Die so Soon?* brought him to public attention in his country and into contact with the Canadian writer Margaret Laurence, then in Somalia. While a student at the University of Chandigarh in India (1966-1970) he wrote – in two months – *From a Crooked Rib* (1970), published in the Heinemann African Writers Series. In this slim novel a young Somali woman, Ebla, leaves her nomad community to avoid an arranged marriage, and in her quest for independence she finally finds a kind of stability in the capital, Mogadishu, living with two men of her choice. The journey to freedom can be read as an allegory of the birth of Somalia as a new nation. But the attraction of the book lies in the sensitive portrayal of a young peasant woman, illiterate but not naive, aware of her low status in society but always clear-eyed and resourceful. It came as a surprise to readers to realize how well the young writer, male and Muslim, could represent a woman's perception of herself, her body, and the world. This feat of characterization allows for great empathy as well as a discreet measure of irony, a light humor. One is spared all the moralizing clichés about the innocent young woman in the corrupting city. Hailed as one of the first feminist books to come out of Africa, this simple, attractive story has remained popular, and curiously, although never reviewed, it has remained available and is widely translated.

In 1969 a coup gave power to the military regime of Siad Barre. In 1970 Farah went back to Somalia with his Indian wife, Chitra Muliyil Farah, and their son, Koschin (born in 1969). Farah then taught at a secondary school and finished his second novel, *A Naked Needle*. The publisher accepted it but agreed to hold it, until 1976, due to political uncertainty in Somalia. It describes the debates among the elite in the capital, the "privilegentzia," and the tentative hopes in the new "revolution." As its mood is questioning and skeptical, it was thought the novel might bring trouble to the writer. The

text, being as intellectual and modernist as *From a Crooked Rib* was straightforward and understated, shows the young author had been reading works by Samuel Beckett, James Joyce, and Virginia Woolf. A completely different facet of Farah's talent appears. Later he rejected this early book as irrelevant and refused to have it reprinted: "It was not the answer to the tremendous challenge the tyrannical regime posed," he says in "Why I Write" (1988).

In 1972 the Somali language was given an official transcription and dictionary; what was spoken by the whole nation could become a national literary language. It was for Farah the long-awaited opportunity to write fiction in his mother tongue and thereby speak directly to his people. In 1973 he started the serialization of a novel titled "Tolow Waa Talee Ma . . . !" in *Somali News*, but the series was interrupted by censorship. Farah, then on a trip to the U.S.S.R., was advised not to run any more risks. Thus he began a long exile from his country.

The following years saw him, like his nomadic forebears, traveling light and never staying long in any place. He lived in the United States and in various countries in Europe and Africa, occasionally teaching or being resident writer on a campus but most of the time concentrating on his writing, with the ambition of living from his pen, independent of institutions or regimes – a position most African writers find difficult to achieve.

His visit to the U.S.S.R. extended to a trip through Hungary, Egypt, and Greece in the days of the military regime. From this contact with various types of political power came his first major novel, *Sweet and Sour Milk* (1979). It had to be written in English, since Farah could no longer be published at home. But this imposed language, implicitly creating an international readership, extended the scope of his fictional exploration of political themes. With this novel Farah started a trilogy he calls "Variations on the Theme of an African Dictatorship," which has much relevance inside and outside Africa.

Sweet and Sour Milk is both simple in its outline and complex in its realization. A young intellectual, Soyaan, dies in the prologue, maybe poisoned by a milk drink. His twin brother, Loyaan, embarks on a sort of detective quest among friends and relatives to discover whether it was murder and whether family feuds or the Special Police were behind it. The plot is spun out of this determined questioning by Loyaan, in a society where most would like the matter to lie undisturbed: Soyaan has been described officially as a national hero. Following Loyaan's footsteps, the reader discovers the mechanisms of fear in a country where everything is hushed up in case the "Dionysian ear," the ear of the tyrant, might overhear. The rumors, hints, false news, and sudden silences create an uncertain web in the narrative. Truth seems to be more and more elusive, all the more so in a mostly nonliterate society, where bureaucratic measures and arrests leave no traces. The patriarchal power inside the family and the power of the "Father of the Nation" reinforce each other. As Loyaan contacts the friends of his dead brother, who are apparently involved in some kind of conspiracy against the president, he can never ascertain who is a friend, who is an informer, and who is a torturer. He seems to be getting to an elusive underground movement when he is suddenly forced by the president to leave for a country in the Eastern bloc. Loyaan does not know if the order is a promotion or a threat.

As a thriller, the novel creates a distinctive menacing atmosphere, reminding one of works by Franz Kafka in its silent, absurd system of oppression. Farah denounces tyrannical power of any kind and the mixture of cowardice and vested interests on which it feeds. His application of the theories of Wilhelm Reich to a society deeply penetrated by Islam is new and stimulating. But Farah is also writing in the tradition of Somali poetry, which has always been political and prompt to attack and satirize but also ornate and rich in layers of meaning. Each chapter of *Sweet and Sour Milk* is headed by a short prose poem, which sets the mood and establishes a thematic pattern that connects family circles and cosmic cycles. Some strong metaphors about the national father, or the state as a devouring mother, are centered on feeding and poisoning; the pastoral, coherent vision of the nomad is made significant in modern terms. This type of metaphorical writing allows an exploration of the ambiguities around the themes of power, fear, freedom, and identity, and all this is a counterpoint to the more explicit analysis provided by the main characters. Altogether the book made a great impact, being noted by critics both for the vigor of its message and the originality of its format. It received the English Speaking Union Literary Award in 1980.

After living in England and in Italy, Farah finished his next novel in the trilogy at the University of Bayreuth in West Germany. *Sardines* (1981) is another of Farah's strikingly feminist novels. Its characters are connected in some ways to those of *Sweet and Sour Milk*, but the story focuses on the world of women hemmed in together in their houses, women who are like children hiding in closets when they play the game "sardines." Medina, a journalist, has

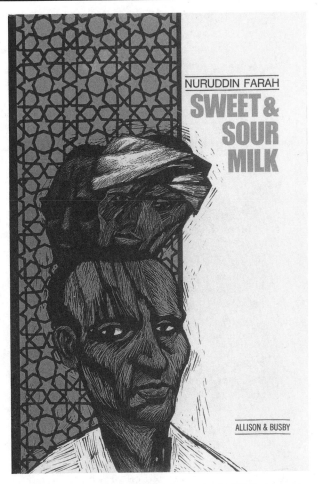

Dust jacket for the first novel in a trilogy Farah calls "Variations on the Theme of an African Dictatorship." The second and third books in this trilogy are Sardines and Close Sesame.

decided that her daughter, Ubax, aged eight, is not going to go through the ritual clitoral excision and infibulation performed on all Somali women according to custom. Medina is pitted against her ineffectual husband and the power of her mother and mother-in-law. The novel presents a wide range of women of all conditions and ages, a few of them trying to invent new roles in a new state still bound by tradition. For Medina no immediate solution is forthcoming, but the many dialogues show active, articulate women coming to a better consciousness: they are not fighting against men but for the future of their children. *Sardines* once more shows Farah's nearly uncanny sensitivity in the portrayal of women together and of mother-daughter relationships. Although ideological debates play an important part in the story, the main weight of the meaning is again carried by a dense metaphorical network: natural images – fire, water, and birds – show how the balance in the fertility cycles is bro-

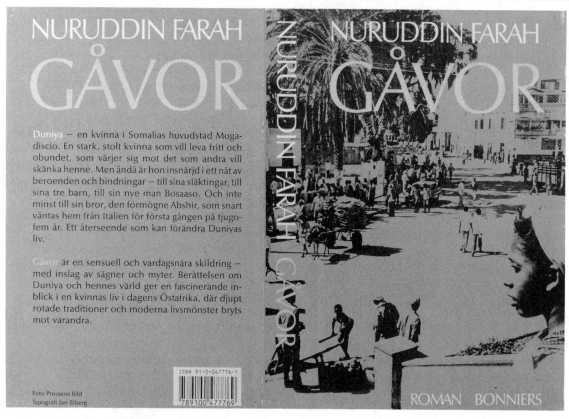

Duniya — en kvinna i Somalias huvudstad Moga-
discio. En stark, stolt kvinna som vill leva fritt och
obundet, som värjer sig mot det som andra vill
skänka henne. Men ändå är hon insnärjd i ett nät av
beroenden och bindningar — till sina släktingar, till
sina tre barn, till sin nye man Bosaaso. Och inte
minst till sin bror, den förmögne Abshir, som snart
väntas hem från Italien för första gången på tjugo-
fem år. Ett återseende som kan förändra Duniyas
liv.

Gåvor är en sensuell och vardagsnära skildring —
med inslag av sägner och myter. Berättelsen om
Duniya och hennes värld ger en fascinerande in-
blick i en kvinnas liv i dagens Östafrika, där djupt
rotade traditioner och moderna livsmönster bryts
mot varandra.

Dust jacket for the Swedish translation of Farah's "Gifts," not yet published in English. The novel is the first part of a planned trilogy.

ken by the socially enforced clitoral circumcision, seen by Farah as a deliberate maiming of women. Again the issue is not merely feminism; it is connected with overall political oppression: "Like all good Somali poets," Farah told Julie Kitchener, "I used women as a symbol for Somalia. Because when the women are free, then and only then can we talk about a free Somalia." In *Sardines* Farah touches a taboo subject as a warning to his compatriots, but also to all nations where, according to him, the subjection of women paves the way for the establishment of tyranny. The novel is more static than *Sweet and Sour Milk*. It attracted attention by the way it deals with a burning issue in a moving and restrained manner and from a Somali point of view and sensitivity.

For eight months in 1976 Farah had been resident writer at the Royal Court Theatre in London and had written plays for the BBC. In 1982, while teaching at the University of Jos in Nigeria, Farah wrote a play, *Yussuf and His Brothers*, which was produced on campus later that year. The play deals with the problems of exile and the value of heroic acts. The next year saw the publication of *Close Sesame*, the third novel in Farah's trilogy. This time the

reader enters the consciousness of an old man, Deeriye, a pious Muslim who was jailed in the 1940s for his rebellion against Italian colonizers. As he meditates on the Koran and recites Somali epic poetry, he remembers the nationalist struggles of his people but also the many failures and betrayals. The small group of intellectuals now opposed to the regime is of the same generation as his children, and the group seems to be dwindling, as one after the other disappears because of death, prison, or exile. The old man wonders whether violent action would be morally justified to avenge his son's unexplained death and eliminate an unjust ruler. But Deeriye's pathetic personal gesture proves ineffectual: the gun meant to shoot the president remains entangled in Deeriye's prayer beads. *Close Sesame* has a great unity, achieved through intense concentration on the protagonist. This pious, kind patriarch, seen with great empathy through his musings, memories, and prayers, is an unusual character in fiction. A tragic dimension is given to the novel by his attempt to find political and spiritual coherence, in vision and deeds, in a violently perturbed society. *Close Sesame* is a mature book in which the old man's outlook seems close to the pessimistic yet passionately involved stance of the exiled writer.

In the following years Farah attended several international conferences, where he aired his views on human rights, dictatorships, and the plight of women. "My novels," he says in the essay "In Praise of Exile" (1988), "are about states of exile: about women shivering in the cruel cold in a world ruled by men; about the commoner denied justice; about a torturer tortured by guilt, his own conscience; about a traitor betrayed." These topics are explored in his first trilogy.

After living in Gambia, Europe, and the Sudan, he started working on a new trilogy. The first volume, *Maps*, published in England and America in 1986, breaks new ground in many ways: *Close Sesame* began with the morning prayers to Allah of the old Deeriye; *Maps* opens with the first perceptions and emotions of a newborn baby. The novel takes a young man, Askar ("Soldier"), through three stages: his first years in the Ogaden with his foster mother, the servant Misra; then his circumcision and the discovery both of writing and of the border war between Ethiopia and Somalia; and finally his adolescence in a middle-class home in Mogadishu, where he is riddled with indecision — will he join the Liberation Front in this protracted war? The title, *Maps*, obviously raises the question of Somali identity. But the questioning goes beyond the obvious political debate on frontiers and nationalism. With the plot of a thriller, the novel explores the uncertain bond between Askar, with his new national fervor, and Misra, born an Oromo (a Somali-speaking person in the Ogaden) and perhaps a traitor to the fighters of the Liberation Front. Identity is examined — not only the social identity defined by territory, blood, and language but also the tension it creates when it is opposed to a personal, emotive sense of self. *Maps* is an ambitious novel with a complex time construction and a dense weaving of violent metaphors connecting blood, wounds, and earth as the child discovers "the territory of pain." An allegorical reading is an obvious dimension, with Somalia as the mutilated Misra at the end — a great distance from the hopeful Ebla in *From a Crooked Rib. Maps* is also remarkable for the intimate, sensuous reconstruction of the early bond between mother and child, which constitutes a relationship that for Farah is both the basis of identity and the limit to individual freedom.

Farah's complex novels are constructed like thrillers and describe to the English-speaking world a little-known country, Somalia, but they are in no way escapist, popular fiction. The complex structures and rich metaphorical textures demand, and

deserve, attention. He is held in high regard by other writers: Doris Lessing, writing for *New Society* (November 1983), found in him "the same compassionate rage as [in] Solzhenitsyn," and Salman Rushdie has praised him for charting "the chasms of the soul." Farah's talent is rich and singular. Whether he will move even further into more demanding forms and a more limited readership remains to be seen.

Having been divorced from his first wife, Farah married Dr. Amina Mama, a Nigerian, on 21 July 1992. They now reside, for at least part of each year, in Kaduna, Nigeria. But he will remain, as always, emotionally tied to Somalia.

Interviews:

Julie Kitchener, "Author in Search of an Identity," *New African* (December 1981);

H. O. Nazareth, "In the Land of the General," *City Limits* (11 November 1983);

Funsho Aiyejina and Bob Fox, "Nuruddin Farah in Conversation," *Ife Studies in African Literature and the Arts*, 2 (1984): 24–37;

Robert Moss, "Mapping the Psyche," *West Africa* (1 September 1986): 1827–1828;

"Just Talking: Chinua Achebe and Nuruddin Farah," *Artrage*, 14 (Autumn 1986): 4–8.

References:

Ian Adam, "The Murder of Soyaan Keynaan," *World Literature Written in English*, 26 (Autumn 1986): 203–211;

Adam, "Nuruddin Farah and James Joyce: Some Issues of Intertextuality," *World Literature Written in English*, 24 (Summer 1984): 34–42;

François Balogun, "Promenade à travers les romans de Nuruddin Farah," *Présence Africaine*, 145 (1988): 157–164;

Jacqueline Bardolph, "L'Evolution de l'écriture dans la trilogie de Nourredine Farah: Variations sur le thème dictature africaine," *Nouvelles du Sud*, 6 (1986–1987): 79–92;

Bardolph, "Idéologie et fiction chez Ngugi wa Thiong'o et Nuruddin Farah," *Notre Librairie*, 98 (July–September 1989): 88–93;

Bardolph, "The Literary Treatment of History in Nuruddin Farah's *Close Sesame*," in *Proceedings of the Third International Congress of Somali Studies*, edited by Annarita Publieli (Rome: Pensiero Scientifico, 1988), pp. 133–138;

Bardolph, "Un Cas singulier: Nuruddin Farah, écrivain somalien," *Notre Librairie*, 85 (1986): 61–64;

Bardolph, "Time and History in *Close Sesame*," *Jour-*

nal of Commonwealth Literature, 24, no. 1 (1989): 193–206;

Bardolph, "Women and Metaphors in Nuruddin Farah's *Sweet and Sour Milk* and *Sardines*," in *Proceedings of the Second International Congress of Somali Studies, University of Hamburg, August 1–6, 1983*, edited by Thomas Labahn (Hamburg: Buske, 1984), I: 429–444;

Bardolph, "*Yussuf and His Brothers* by Nuruddin Farah," in *L'Islam et les littératures africaines* (Paris: Silex, 1987), pp. 79–91;

Rhonda Cobham, "Misgendering the Nation: African Nationalist Fictions and Nuruddin Farah's *Maps*," in *Nationalisms and Sexualities*, edited by Andrew Parker and others (New York & London: Routledge, 1992), pp. 42–59;

Judith Cochrane, "The Theme of Sacrifice in the Novels of Nuruddin Farah," *World Literature Written in English*, 18 (April 1979): 69–77;

Jean-Pierre Durix, "Nuruddin Farah, ou l'énigme de la liberté," *L'Afrique Littéraire*, 67 (Spring 1983): 175–189;

D. R. Ewen, "Nuruddin Farah," in *The Writings of East and Central Africa*, edited by G. D. Killam (London: Heinemann, 1984), pp. 192–210;

Josef Gugler, "African Literary Comment on Dictators: Wole Soyinka's Plays and Nuruddin Farah's Novels," *Journal of Modern African Studies*, 26 (March 1988): 171–177;

Hilarie Kelly, "A Somali Tragedy of Political and Sexual Confusion: A Critical Analysis of Nuruddin Farah's *Maps*," *Ufahamu*, 16, no. 2 (1988): 21–37;

Shuaib Ahmed Kidwai, "The Two Novels of Nuruddin Farah," in *Somalia and the World: Proceedings of the International Symposium Held in Mogadishu, October 15–21, 1979*, edited by Hussein M. Adam (Mogadishu, Somalia: State Printing Press, 1980), I: 191–201;

Wendy Kindred, "Ethiopia and Somalia: Factions and Fiction," *Maine Scholar*, 2 (1989): 47–54;

Felix Mnthali, "Autocracy and the Limits of Identity: A Reading of the Novels of Nuruddin Farah," *Ufahamu*, 17, no. 2 (1989): 53–69;

G. H. Moore, "Nomads and Feminists: The Novels of Nuruddin Farah," *International Fiction Re-*

view, 11 (Winter 1984): 3–12;

Juliet I. Okonkwo, "Literature and Politics in Somalia Today: The Case of Nuruddin Farah," *Africa Today*, 32, no. 3 (1985): 57–65;

Okonkwo, "Nuruddin Farah and the Changing Roles of Women," *World Literature Today*, 58 (Spring 1984): 215–221;

Kirsten Holst Petersen, "The Personal and the Political: The Case of Nuruddin Farah," *Ariel*, 12 (July 1981): 93–101;

János Riesz, "Ein Kosmopolit aus Somalia: Das Werk des Schriftstellers Nuruddin Farah," *Baobab*, 2 (1982): 14–21;

Salman Rushdie, "Nuruddin Farah," in his *Imaginary Homelands* (London: Granta, 1991), p. 201–202;

Fiona Sparrow, "Telling the Story Yet Again: Oral Traditions in Nuruddin Farah's Fiction," *Journal of Commonwealth Literature*, 24, no. 1 (1989): 164–172;

Florence Stratton, "The Novels of Nuruddin Farah," *World Literature Written in English*, 25 (Spring 1985): 16–30;

Barbara Turfan, "Opposing Dictatorship: A Comment on Nuruddin Farah's Variations on the Theme of an African Dictatorship," *Journal of Commonwealth Literature*, 24, no. 1 (1989): 173–184;

Itala Vivan, "Nuruddin Farah: Il primo romanziere somalo," in her *Tessere per un mosaico africano: Cinque scrittori neri dall'esilio* (Verona, Italy: Morelli, 1984), pp. 40–67;

Anne Walmsley, "Nuruddin Farah and Somalia," *Index on Censorship*, 10 (April 1981): 17–19;

Derek Wright, "Parents and Power in Nuruddin Farah's Dictatorship Trilogy," *Kunapipi*, 11, no. 2 (1989): 94–106;

Wright, "Requiems for Revolutions: Race-Sex Archetypes in Two African Novels," *Modern Fiction Studies*, 35 (Spring 1989): 55–68;

Wright, "Unwritable Realities: The Orality of Power in Nuruddin Farah's *Sweet and Sour Milk*," *Journal of Commonwealth Literature*, 24, no. 1 (1989): 185–192;

Wright, "Zero Zones: Nuruddin Farah's Fiction," *Ariel*, 21 (April 1990): 21–42.

C. L. R. James
(4 January 1901 – 31 May 1989)

Reinhard Sander
Amherst College

BOOKS: *The Life of Captain Cipriani: An Account of British Government in the West Indies* (Nelson, U.K.: Coulton, 1932);

Minty Alley (London: Secker & Warburg, 1936; London & Port of Spain: New Beacon, 1971);

World Revolution, 1917–1936: The Rise and Fall of the Communist International (London: Secker & Warburg, 1937; New York: Pioneer, 1937);

The Black Jacobins: Toussaint L'Ouverture and the San Domingo Revolution (London: Secker & Warburg, 1938; New York: Dial, 1938; revised edition, New York: Vintage, 1963; revised again, London: Allison & Busby, 1980);

A History of Negro Revolt (London: Fact, 1938; New York: Haskell House, 1967); revised as *A History of Pan-African Revolt* (Washington, D.C.: Drum & Spear, 1969);

Mariners, Renegades and Castaways: The Story of Herman Melville and the World We Live In (New York: Privately published, 1953; Detroit: Bewick, 1978; London: Allison & Busby, 1985);

Facing Reality, by James as J. R. Johnson, with Grace C. Lee and Pierre Chaulieu (Detroit: Correspondence, 1958);

Modern Politics (Port of Spain: PNM, 1960; Detroit: Bewick, 1973);

Party Politics in the West Indies (Port of Spain: Vedic, 1962);

Beyond a Boundary (London: Stanley Paul/Hutchinson, 1963; New York: Pantheon, 1984);

State Capitalism and World Revolution (Detroit: Facing Reality, 1969);

Notes on Dialectics: Hegel, Marx, Lenin (Detroit: Friends of Facing Reality, 1971; London: Allison & Busby, 1980);

Nkrumah and the Ghana Revolution (London: Allison & Busby, 1977; Westport, Conn.: Hill, 1977);

The Future in the Present (London: Allison & Busby, 1977; Westport, Conn.: Hill, 1977);

Spheres of Existence (London: Allison & Busby, 1980; Westport, Conn.: Hill, 1980);

Cover for the third volume (1984) of James's selected writings, including fiction and nonfiction

At the Rendezvous of Victory (London: Allison & Busby, 1984);

C. L. R. James's 80th Birthday Lectures, edited by Margaret Busby and Darcus Howe (London: Race Today, 1984);

Cricket (London & New York: Allison & Busby, 1986);

The C. L. R. James Reader, edited by Anna

Grimshaw (Oxford, U.K. & Cambridge, Mass.: Blackwell, 1992).

PLAY PRODUCTIONS: *Toussaint L'Ouverture*, London, Westminster Theatre, 1936; revised as *The Black Jacobins*, Ibadan, University of Ibadan, 1967.

RECORDINGS: *Black Jacobins and Black Reconstruction*, Atlanta, Institute of the Black World, 1974;
How I Would Re-write Black Jacobins, Atlanta, Institute of the Black World, 1974;
How I Wrote Black Jacobins, Atlanta, Institute of the Black World, 1974;
Nkrumah, Padmore and the Ghanaian Revolution, Atlanta, Institute of the Black World, 1974;
On Oliver Cox's Caste, Class, and Race, Atlanta, Institute of the Black World, 1974;
The Role of the Black Scholar in the Struggles of the Black Community, Atlanta, Institute of the Black World, 1974.

OTHER: *The Black Jacobins* [play], in *A Time . . . and a Season: 8 Caribbean Plays*, edited by Errol Hill (Port of Spain: University of the West Indies, Extra-Mural Studies, 1976), pp. 355–420.

After the publication of the three volumes of his selected writings – *The Future in the Present* (1977), *Spheres of Existence* (1980), and *At the Rendezvous of Victory* (1984) – reviewers across the political spectrum were unanimous in their praise of C. L. R. James. They rated the Caribbean intellectual and man of letters "among the greats of the twentieth century," called him "the black Plato of our generation," and found it "remarkable how far ahead of his time he was on so many issues." In London the reviewer for the *Sunday Times* wrote, "C. L. R. James has had an extraordinary life. He has arguably had a greater influence on the underlying thinking of independence movements in the West Indies and Africa than any living man." James's contributions as a historian, political theorist/activist, and cultural/literary critic have attracted international attention for several decades. However, as the author of a novel, a play, and several short stories, all written in the 1920s and 1930s, he was also one of the early pioneers of West Indian creative writing.

Cyril Lionel Robert James was born on 4 January 1901 in Tunapuna, Trinidad. The son of a schoolteacher, James, at the age of nine, won a scholarship to Queen's Royal College in Port of Spain. After graduating in 1918, he taught at the college and then at the Government Training College for Teachers. In 1932 he left Trinidad for England, where he lived until 1938, working first as a sports correspondent for the *Manchester Guardian* and later as editor of the journal of the International African Service Bureau, the organ of George Padmore's Pan-African movement. Between 1938 and 1952 James lectured widely in the United States. After internment during the McCarthy era and deportation from America, he returned to Trinidad and had a short-lived association with the People's National Movement as editor of the party's official newspaper, the *Nation*. During the 1960s and 1970s he continued to write and lecture in Europe, America, and the Third World. From 1981 until his death on 31 May 1989 he lived and wrote in the Brixton area of London.

In the early 1920s James, then a junior master at Queen's Royal College, and Alfred H. Mendes, a Trinidad Creole of Portuguese descent, became the focal point of a group of liberal British expatriates and young Trinidadian intellectuals of various ethnic backgrounds. Mendes provided the others with books from his "collective library" of about five or six thousand volumes, and James became their literary doyen after the British *Saturday Review of Literature*, on 15 October 1927, published his short story "La Divina Pastora" (collected in *Spheres of Existence*). James's success – Mendes has referred to it as "a sensation in Trinidad amongst those of us who were really interested in the arts" – gave a tremendous boost to the group's creative endeavors. The group published the literary magazine *Trinidad*, which appeared twice: at Christmas 1929 and at Easter 1930. At about this time another Portuguese Creole, Albert M. Gomes, returned from New York to Trinidad and was introduced to the group. The *Beacon* magazine was launched under Gomes's editorship in 1931, and over the next three years twenty-eight issues of the magazine appeared.

Trinidad and the *Beacon* marked the emergence of West Indian short fiction. In choosing the subjects for their short fiction, the writers put into practice their theoretical demands that West Indian writing utilize West Indian settings, speech, characters, and conflicts. Many of their stories explored the life-style and culture of lower-class Trinidadians, and the writers paid particular attention to the independence and vitality of the women who were part of this class. The short fiction published in these magazines initiated the tradition of "barrack-yard stories," still very much alive among present-day writers.

*James in the United States during the 1940s (C. L. R. James
Institute, New York, New York)*

James published some of his best stories in the pages of *Trinidad* and the *Beacon*. They range from cautionary tales of middle-class greed and materialism, such as "Turner's Prosperity" (*Trinidad,* 1929; collected in *Spheres of Existence*) – in which a clerk who lives beyond his means tries to dupe his employer into giving him an unnecessary loan – to stories about rural superstition, and exuberant comedies of barrack-yard life. Two of James's shorter tales in the *Beacon* provide a possible insight into James's methods of collecting material for his fiction. Both stories take the form of interviews, and in both the narrator's curiosity draws the full details of the recounted experience from the informant. The first piece, "Revolution" (May 1931; collected in *At the Rendezvous of Victory*), reproduces an encounter with a Venezuelan exile living in Trinidad who had participated in a revolution in his native country. In the second piece, "The Star That Would Not Shine" (June 1931; collected in the same book), a chance meeting with a stranger gives

the narrator an opportunity to hear a bizarre tale about the stranger's son, who had passed up a career in the movies because he had been asked to play the role of a character called "Fatty Arbuckle," the hated nickname with which he had been taunted by his schoolmates. Neither piece is fully developed, but both give an indication of James's lively curiosity about the people he encountered.

Both "La Divina Pastora" and "Triumph" (*Trinidad,* 1929; collected in *The Future in the Present*) are successful short stories framed by narrative devices of a similar nature. "La Divina Pastora" is narrated by a reporter who opens with a disclaimer: "Of my own belief in this story I shall say nothing. What I have done is to put it down as far as possible just as it was told me, in my own style, but with no addition to or subtraction from the essential facts." The plot revolves around an attempt by a cocoa worker, Anita Perez, to invoke the aid of the saint La Divina Pastora in bringing her hesitant suitor Sebastian up to scratch. When Anita's plans begin to succeed and she expresses regret about her gift of a treasured gold chain to the saint, the gift mysteriously reappears in her room. The reader is left to speculate as to whether Anita's neglect of her patron saint is the cause of the reversal that follows in her relationship to Sebastian and whether the reappearance of her chain is a psychological illusion or a miracle.

James made a clear distinction between the settled pattern of a rural existence and the turbulent, competitive life of the urban poor, and indeed "La Divina Pastora" is one of the few early Trinidadian stories to deal with peasant characters in a rural setting. Mamitz's flamboyant independence in "Triumph" is a far cry from Anita's approach to life. "Triumph" is probably the most entertaining of the barrack-yard stories. In it a flashy and expansive cab driver and a hardworking butcher compete for the affections of the placid and amply endowed creole beauty, Mamitz. Mamitz plays her suitors off against each other successfully until a jealous neighbor attempts to arouse the suspicions of the butcher, who is paying Mamitz's rent. With the aid of her shrewish friend and adviser Celestine, Mamitz is able to placate the butcher. Instead of starting a fight, he apologizes and gives Mamitz all the money he has made over the Easter weekend. Celestine and Mamitz pin the dollar bills all over Mamitz's door so that the whole yard can see how Mamitz has triumphed over her jealous neighbor.

"Triumph" is a comic story, and its tone is appropriately lighthearted. Like many early barrack-yard stories, it plays down the misery and violence. James goes as far as implying in his opening remarks that barrack-yard violence is a rare occurrence or a thing of the past, but there seems to be little justification for this statement.

James's social background is typical of the class of educated black West Indians that began to emerge at the turn of the century. This faction had little direct social contact with lower-class black Trinidadians and only a superficial knowledge of their African-derived culture. These intellectuals saw the mass of ignorant, uneducated people around them as deserving of their sympathy and guidance but would hardly have considered such people capable of teaching them anything in the way of moral or cultural values. When as a young writer James began to look more closely at the lifestyle and values of the lower class, he had to deal with this social alienation. The relationship between the educated black man and the uneducated black masses is a recurring preoccupation in his early writing.

Minty Alley (1936) explores this theme of social ambivalence. A middle-class young man's temporary financial difficulties force him to seek lodging in a yard that is only slightly more respectable than the one described in "Triumph." The narrative pretext allows the reader to observe with young Haynes the life of the yard and to follow his initiation into manhood by its inhabitants. James has acknowledged (in his interview in *Kas-Kas,* 1972) an autobiographical link with this work: "I was about 27 or 28 at the time when I went to live in that household described in the novel . . . the people fascinated me, and I wrote about them from the point of view of an educated youthful member of the black middle class. . . . Many of the things that took place in the story actually took place in life."

Apart from a focus on the meeting of the classes, the pioneering achievement of James's novel lies in its presentation of lower-class life itself. The length of the work gave James the scope to explore some of the less exotic features of barrack-yard life, such as the activities of children in the yard and the details of everyday existence, which his short stories often leave out. In *Minty Alley*, as in "Triumph," James is particularly successful in his portrayal of lower-class women. He emphasizes their humanity rather than their colorful or exotic features. Maisie, the hotheaded young beauty who initiates Haynes into sexual maturity, is idealized. However, she is also presented as susceptible to the racial prejudices of the rest of the society – she hates the Indian maid – and her rudeness and sarcasm to her aunt are at times inexcusable. At the same time, she is the most ambitious member of the household, and James makes her a symbol of all that he considered progressive in the lower classes. She is too spirited to accept the poor working conditions and wages that have broken other women around her and is not afraid to abandon the relative security of life with her aunt in order to better her standard of living: "For staying at home she had no plans. But she wanted to go to America to work for good money. In America you worked hard but you got good food and pay and had a fine time. Why the hell should she starve and slave to get a few shillings a week from some employer in the town?"

Maisie's rebelliousness and self-imposed exile seem to indicate the limits of James's evaluation and understanding of the mood of the Trinidad working class in the late 1920s. He was preoccupied with cultural matters and saw the lower class as a fitting subject around which to build an indigenous literature. James recalls that he and Mendes "didn't interfere with politics," and so he makes no attempt to exploit the potential of Maisie's rebelliousness as a symbol of political protest. Like Maisie's, James's response at the time to the limitations of his society was a personal rather than a political one — an escape rather than an attempt to fight the system. His political awakening was a result of his exposure to radical new ideas in England, and when he turned his pen to the attack of the old order he did so as a historian and polemicist rather than as a creative writer. As he explains in *Beyond a Boundary* (1963): "Fiction-writing drained out of me and was replaced by politics. I became a Marxist, a Trotskyist. I published large books and small articles on these and kindred subjects. I wrote and spoke. Like many others, I expected war, and during or after the war social revolution."

In England, James wrote one further literary work, the play *Toussaint L'Ouverture*, which was written in 1936 and presented in the same year by the London Stage Society in a special performance with Paul Robeson in the lead role. The play was revised and published as *The Black Jacobins* in *A Time . . . and a Season* (1976). *Toussaint L'Ouverture* is a literary precursor to James's major historical study *The Black Jacobins: Toussaint L'Ouverture and the San Domingo Revolution* (1938). The play was written at a time when the African nationalist movement, which coalesced around Padmore's International African Service Bureau in London, had just begun to attract attention. James probably saw his play as a contribution to the quest for an intellectual framework through which to conceptualize the struggle against colonialism.

James's play does not concentrate on celebrating the military feats of the slaves who took part in the Haitian revolution. Instead his concern is to reveal and examine the strengths and weaknesses of the revolution's black leadership. The play advances the view that Haiti's independence, although in itself a significant achievement, did not result in freedom for the Haitian people but ushered in a despotic regime that was in many ways as vicious as the earlier French colonial system: white masters were exchanged for black ones; slavery, though abolished in name, persisted; and the dream of liberty, equality, and fraternity was dissipated.

James bases most of the major male characters in *Toussaint L'Ouverture* on actual historical personalities, and the speeches are often taken word for word from personal letters and other historical records. Apart from Toussaint, Jean-Jacques Dessalines, and Napoléon Bonaparte, the characters include two other Haitian leaders — Henri Christophe and Moïse; several French, Spanish, and En-

Drawing of James by Margaret Glover (C. L. R. James Institute, New York, New York)

glish military figures; and the American consul in French San Domingo. James makes little effort at individual characterization. Instead each character becomes a mouthpiece for a particular ideological position, and, with a few exceptions, their positions are portrayed through speeches rather than action.

James blames the disastrous outcome of the revolution on the decline of Toussaint's power as a leader, which creates weaknesses in the Haitian line of command that are easily exploited by Dessalines. From the start of the play these two leaders are contrasted. They are first encountered in the prologue when news reaches San Domingo of the slave uprising in Martinique and Guadeloupe. Dessalines, watching the street crier who carries the news, "looks up with determination and hate on his face. He raises a fist to the sky and shouts, 'We will kill them all. Every one.'" Toussaint on the other hand is engrossed in the reading of Abbé Raynal's *Philosophical and Political History of the Establishments and Commerce of the Europeans in the Two Indies*, which was published in 1770 and includes passages severely critical of European colonialism and the practice of slavery. However, unlike Dessalines, Toussaint wavers for months before finally deciding to join the slave uprising in 1791.

James presents Moïse as the only Haitian leader with an intellectual capacity equal to that of Toussaint. Like Toussaint, he is a committed Republican and an admirer of French revolutionary thought, but these beliefs do not cloud his judgment when it comes to choosing the policies he considers best suited to Haiti's interests. Early in the play he tells Toussaint, "We want to be free and equal; make San Domingo independent, the people will come with us." Shortly before Moïse's execution he urges Toussaint again to abandon his half-measures, and he voices the play's most convincing arguments against Toussaint's policies: "The country does not know where it stands. Is slavery abolished forever? Or is a French expedition coming to restore slavery? The ex-slaves don't know, the ex-slave owners don't know. I have told you to declare the island independent. Expel all those who do not want to accept it. Assure the ex-slaves that slavery is gone forever. That is what they want to know. Break up those accursed big plantations. As long as they remain, freedom is a mockery. Distribute the lands carefully among the best cultivators in the country. Let everybody see that there is a new regime."

Toussaint is presented in the play as an intellectual concerned with the ultimate future of his country. However, his awareness of the limitations of his society blind him to its potential self-sufficiency and make it impossible for him to conceive of severing ties with France. His idealism leads him to attempt the impossible, and that, as James points out in his documentary, gives Toussaint's career a tragic dimension. James's play presents no easy answers. It leaves the audience to assess the relative virtues of the conflicting attitudes to nationalism epitomized in the positions held by Toussaint, Moïse, and Dessalines, and in the context of the 1930s nationalist debate this ending must have stimulated a great deal of discussion.

Toussaint L'Ouverture was written while James was beginning to utilize his understanding of Marxist ideology to examine the problems of alienation and imitation that hampered the development of the colonial intellectual. This new awareness is reflected in his treatment of Toussaint, who for all his heroic stature is implicitly criticized because he consistently underestimates the intelligence of his followers and the strength of their commitment to the ideal of liberty. Moïse by contrast is presented as a colonial intellectual who is able to establish and maintain contact with the lower classes. Unfortunately the audience is not given an opportunity to see Moïse's ideas in action; he functions only as a foil to Toussaint. James's play is full of undigested theoretical material, and this material makes it less successful as a work of art than the earlier, more politically naive novel *Minty Alley*. Perhaps his failure to combine political insight with artistic talents in a work of fiction influenced James to abandon creative writing for history and polemic. However, he transferred much of the wit and flair for anecdote that characterize his early creative work to his consideration of topics as diverse as the social role of cricket in *Beyond a Boundary* and the politics of the Haitian revolution in the historical book *The Black Jacobins*.

Regarding his private life, James had an unsuccessful first marriage, which ended in divorce but produced one child. In 1955 he married Selma Weinstein. C. L. R. James died on 31 May 1989.

Interviews:

Ian Munro and Reinhard Sander, "Interview with C. L. R. James," in their *Kas-Kas: Interviews with Three Caribbean Writers in Texas* (Austin: University of Texas, African and Afro-American Research Institute, 1972), pp. 22–41;

"*Afras Review* Talks to C. L. R. James," *Afras Review*, 2 (1976): 4–8.

Bibliography:

"C. L. R. James: Bibliography," in James's *At the Rendezvous of Victory* (London: Allison & Busby, 1984), pp. 275–299.

Biography:

Paul Buhle, *C. L. R. James: The Artist as Revolutionary* (London & New York: Verso, 1988).

References:

Frank Birbalsingh, "The Literary Achievement of C. L. R. James," *Journal of Commonwealth Literature*, 19, no. 1 (1984): 108–121;

Paul Buhle, ed., *C. L. R. James: His Life and Work* (London & New York: Allison & Busby, 1986);

Buhle and Paget Henry, eds., *C. L. R. James's Caribbean* (Durham, N.C.: Duke University Press, 1992);

Hazel V. Carby, "Proletarian or Revolutionary Literature: C. L. R. James and the Politics of the Trinidadian Renaissance," *South Atlantic Quarterly*, 87 (Winter 1988): 39–52;

Michael Gilkes, "C. L. R. James: *Minty Alley*," in his *The West Indian Novel* (Boston: Twayne, 1981), pp. 28–35;

Albert M. Gomes, *Through a Maze of Colour* (Port of Spain: Key Caribbean, 1974), pp. 15–35;

Robert Hamner, "The Measure of the 'Yard Novel': From Mendes to Lovelace," *Commonwealth Essays and Studies*, 9 (Autumn 1986): 98–105;

Merle Hodge, "Peeping Tom in the Nigger Yard," *Tapia*, 25 (2 April 1972): 11–12;

Leota S. Lawrence, "Three West Indian Heroines: An Analysis," *College Language Association Journal*, 21 (December 1977): 238–250;

Alfred H. Mendes, "Talking about the Thirties," *Voices*, 1, no. 5 (1965): 3–7;

Kole Omotoso, *The Theatrical into Theatre: A Study of the Drama and Theatre of the English-Speaking Caribbean* (London: New Beacon, 1982), pp. 131–134;

Kenneth Ramchand, Introduction to James's *Minty Alley* (London & Port of Spain: New Beacon, 1971), pp. 5–15;

Amon Saba Saakana, *The Colonial Legacy in Caribbean Literature* (London: Karnak House, 1987; Trenton, N.J.: Africa World, 1987), pp. 71–75;

Reinhard W. Sander, "The Thirties and Forties," in *West Indian Literature*, edited by Bruce King (London: Macmillan, 1979; Hamden, Conn.: Anchor/Doubleday, 1979), pp. 45–62, 231;

Sander, *The Trinidad Awakening: West Indian Literature of the Nineteen-Thirties* (New York, London & Westport, Conn.: Greenwood, 1988);

Sander, ed., *From Trinidad: An Anthology of Early West Indian Writing* (London: Hodder & Stoughton, 1978; New York: Holmes & Meier, 1978);

Sander, ed., "The Turbulent Thirties in Trinidad: An Interview with Alfred H. Mendes," *World Literature Written in English*, 12 (April 1973): 66–79;

K. T. Sunitha, "C. L. R. James (1901–1989): A Tribute," *Literary Half-Yearly*, 30 (July 1989): 145–149;

Gillian Whitlock, "The Bush, the Barrack-Yard and the Clearing: 'Colonial Realism' in the Sketches and Stories of Susanna Moodie, C. L. R. James and Henry Lawson," *Journal of Commonwealth Literature*, 20, no. 1 (1985): 36–48.

Papers:

Anna Grimshaw, in *The C. L. R. James Archive: A Reader's Guide* (New York: C. L. R. James Institute, 1991), gives details of the available collection.

Ismith Khan

(16 March 1925 –   )

Ketu H. Katrak
University of Massachusetts – Amherst

BOOKS: *The Jumbie Bird* (London: MacGibbon & Kee, 1961; New York: Obolensky, 1963; Port of Spain: Longman Caribbean, 1974);
The Obeah Man (London: Hutchinson, 1964);
The Crucifixion (Leeds, U.K.: Peepal Tree, 1987);
A Day in the Country and Other Stories (Leeds, U.K.: Peepal Tree, 1990).

RADIO: *The Obeah Man* [play], BBC, 1970.

OTHER: "Dialect in West Indian Literature," in *The Black Writer in Africa and the Americas*, edited by Lloyd W. Brown (Los Angeles: Hennessey & Ingalls, 1973), pp. 141–164;
"Image and Self-Image in West Indian Writing," in *Indians in the Caribbean*, edited by I. J. Bahadur Singh (New Delhi: Sterling, 1987), pp. 45–62.

Ismith Khan is a Trinidadian writer descended from the Pathan people, originally of India, whom Khan described in his interview with Daryl C. Dance as "this group of people who are in the hills of Afghanistan right now fighting with the Russians. . . . They are an unconquered people – the British never made it into those hills." A common, though unfortunate, tendency in most critical assessments of Caribbean writers of Indian origin is to focus almost exclusively on V. S. Naipaul. Unlike Naipaul, who comes from an orthodox Brahman family, Khan, a third-generation Trinidadian, has a Muslim background. Though not as accomplished a craftsman as Naipaul, Khan presents a sympathetic and evocative portrait of the plight of his community. Khan's significance in Caribbean literary tradition lies in his literary explorations of issues of identity – "the double consciousness," to borrow W. E. B. Du Bois's phrase – of being a Pathan from India, in terms of his ethnic origins, and a Trinidadian, in terms of his upbringing in that country.

Ismith Khan was born to Faiez and Zinab Khan on 16 March 1925 in Port of Spain, Trinidad. The strongest influence on his early life was his pa-

ternal grandfather, Kale Khan: "My grandfather was ever involved in all things anti-British . . . his life was one of dissent, he ridiculed the Raj [and] chastised fellow Indians for being run over roughshod by Sahibs." Kale Khan's opposition to the British was in line with the historical reality of Pathan resistance against colonial power: "During one of the uprisings [in India], when Indians were called upon to shoot Indians, he fired at the British, chucked the military, and took off with his family." Unlike most Indians who were brought to Trinidad as indentured laborers, Kale Khan migrated as a free man with his family.

Though deeply influenced by Kale Khan's fierce fighting spirit and sense of pride in his Pathan roots, Ismith Khan's mature identity is rooted in the culture of Trinidad rather than any nostalgic hope of return to his grandfather's home, India. In his first novel, *The Jumbie Bird* (1961), Khan explores his boyhood and treats his Indian past. This past is not rejected or denied but recognized as part of his heritage. Having accomplished that personal/spiritual journey, Khan proceeds, in *The Obeah Man* (1964), to explore the Trinidadian culture in which he grew up. All his subsequent work is set in and focused on Trinidad.

Khan was educated at an Anglican church school and at Queen's Royal College in Port of Spain. His entry into creative writing was spurred by his experience as a journalist for the *Trinidad Guardian*, which "sharpen[ed] [his] interests, not only in the Indian community, but the island as a whole, all of its peoples, its direction." Like many Caribbean writers before and after him, Khan became established as a writer after leaving Trinidad. He attended the New School for Social Research in New York, where he earned a B.A. in sociology. Later he received his M.A. in creative writing at Johns Hopkins University. His novel *The Crucifixion* (1987) was begun as part of his M.A. thesis.

Since the mid 1950s Khan has lived in the United States – on the East Coast in the 1950s and

Ismith Khan (photograph by Farida Khan)

1960s, in California in the 1970s, and since 1983 in New York. He taught creative writing at the New School from 1959 to 1969; was visiting professor at the University of California, Berkeley, during the academic year 1970–1971; and then lectured in Caribbean and comparative literature at the University of California, San Diego (1971–1974), the University of Southern California (1977), and California State University, Long Beach (1978–1981). Since 1986 he has taught at Medgar Evers College in Brooklyn, New York.

Although Khan has spent more than half his life in the United States, none of his published work so far is set there. The themes and characters that provide his imaginative inspiration are still firmly grounded in Trinidad – a literary and social phenomenon not uncommon among expatriate writers, who are perhaps satisfying a need to come to terms with the very reality of being expatriates. Khan's success as a novelist lies in his accurate use of Trinidad dialect and his ear for dialogue; he can echo speech patterns as they would occur on streets, in shops, in the yard, or in the marketplace.

The Jumbie Bird traces the individual and family history of three generations of Pathans – Kale Khan, his son Rahim, and his grandson Jamini. The search for identity, explored against the larger historical backdrop of British colonialism (in Trinidad and India), is particularly poignant for the second and third generations of Pathans in Trinidad. For Kale Khan identity is not an agonizing issue: not only does he know who he is but the dream of repatriation is real to him and his generation. However, Ismith Khan skillfully depicts the dangers of a naive sentimentalism and the inability of men of Kale Khan's generation to face the harsh realities of India's own colonial history and its aftermath. They share a tendency to idealize what they consider home and a desire to return home, even though that home no longer welcomes them. Attitudes to repatriation dramatize the generational difference and conflict in the novel. The old man's dominant personality makes him unable even to hear an argument different from his own, and he merely asserts his dream of returning to India. For Rahim and his son, Jamini, however, the idea of repatriation offers only an illusory escape from the real problems around them, as they struggle to create a life and means of livelihood in the country where they have grown up.

Ismith Khan's male-centered vision reflects Pathan culture, which grants a marginal status to women. Khan uncritically describes the self-reliance of men such as Kale Khan who think they can dispense with their wives after they have served their purpose as child bearers: Khan deserts his wife, Binti, and lives in his son's household. Binti's experience as wife and mother has been dark indeed.

Significantly, instead of the "bright spot of color, usually red" worn in the center of their foreheads by married women, Binti "had hers tattooed in blue-black. It faded and worked into her skin." Moreover, Kale Khan suffers no qualms about "giving away his own daughter to a total stranger in the Cawnpore Railway Station" and only bringing his son Rahim with him to Trinidad.

Kale Khan's rejection of Binti is doubly poignant. Binti had "disobeyed her parents and run away one night to keep an appointment with a young Pathan of Her Majesty's regiments . . . and never saw her parents again." Marooned in Trinidad, her anguish and bitterness are turned against herself rather than against Kale Khan. She cannot even express her sorrow. All she registers is "the tightening of the throat that swallows hard, but not a time for tears . . . she wept without a tear, without a sigh, without a rise and fall of her bosom." Binti is presented, at best, as survivor and, at worst, as victim.

Although Ismith Khan does not explore or develop the imbalance in sexual and social power between males and females in *The Jumbie Bird*, readers need to recognize Binti's strength and her impact on her son and grandson. Further, Kale Khan's variety of self-reliance and deliberate exclusion of women from his life are the underlying causes for the breakdown of his particular community.

The sensitive and observant Jamini finds his grandfather's overbearing personality captivating. Kale Khan attempts to pass on his ideals and family pride to his grandson: "You listen to Dada. You not come here like the rest of these low-class coolies in bond, you hear!" For Jamini his grandfather is living history — not only of his own family but of all Indians in Trinidad. "You ain't go learn all that in history book," Khan tells him. "Listen good so you know what you come from."

As Jamini matures, he grows away from his grandfather's dreams. His youthful naiveté (expressed in the question "an' we goin' to Hindustan Dada?") is overtaken by the reality of creating a life for himself in Trinidad. Rahim's words of advice at the end of the novel express one piece in the vast jigsaw of Jamini's life, his identity, and his place in history: "Day by day, if you look hard enough you will find that work that made for you. It ain't have nothing else in this world to make a man feel happy like that."

Rahim's crisis in the novel is twofold: personal estrangement ("We ain't belong to Hindustan," he remarks, "we ain't belong to England, we ain't belong to Trinidad"); and professional disillu-sionment, when, as a jeweler, he painfully recognizes his marginal status. Young people "preferred costume jewellery, coarse, gaudy, flashy." When Rahim is tricked and loses his shop, he reaches a point of futility. "You ain't only lose the shop Rahim," says his wife, Meena, "you lose yourself." From the depths of his despair it is his mother, Binti, who literally lights the way out of the darkness in his house. Once he is emotionally comforted, she deals with him severely for "giving up" and for wallowing in self-pity.

The main achievement of Khan's first novel is his interweaving of history into a fictional world. The process of history, of identity within postcolonial societies, is dealt with successfully. One of the most poignant depictions of Khan's novel is that of the life and activity around Woodford Square, particularly the portraits of those "lost souls," those "old derelicts" of Kale Khan's generation. These poor, aged men who have spent their youth and energy are dispossessed; they sleep on old newspapers spread out on the benches and wait for festival days when the poor are fed. Ismith Khan draws a humane portrait of the socioeconomic marginalization and spiritual impoverishment of these men:

> Many of them had left the sugar plantations long ago and come to the city. They had lost their trade, their ways of ploughing and sowing, they had come to the city to wander, to spend the rainy nights under the Town Hall, curled into the stoops of buildings across from the Square . . . only to be awakened by boys of Jamini's age . . . or the steel-helmeted policemen.

These men hold to their impossible dream of returning to India, and they seek out Kale Khan as their spokesman. As they sit together in the early morning light around Khan, all dwelling on "an old, old yearning," they bitterly reminisce on the false hopes with which they had come to Trinidad. The disillusionment had begun even as they got on the ship leaving the Indian shore.

Ismith Khan's second novel, *The Obeah Man*, as the title indicates, probes the heart of Caribbean culture. In hypothesizing about possible reasons for Khan's interest in obeah and the psychology of those who practice it, Kenneth Ramchand's general explanation of obeah is useful. Ramchand regards the person who practices obeah as one who must come to "accept alienation as the painful condition of art." The theme of alienation is certainly related to the crisis of identity experienced by East Indians in Trinidad. Moreover, the ending of *The Jumbie Bird* makes it clear that for the second and third generations of Indians there is no possibility of a return to India. Both Rahim and Jamini acknowledge Trinidad as their home, which is not to deny that a deep sense of alienation, of "unbelonging," may persist. But this alienation is of a kind that belongs in the present and has much in common with a sense of alienation that some blacks feel in relation to their African origins.

In this second novel, then, Khan uses the concept and practice of obeah as a possible avenue by means of which his characters can come to grips with alienation. Built into the practice of obeah are elements that may be particularly suited to those who, by race, by inclination, or by occupation, can only belong on the fringes of society. For example, as an obeah man, Khan's protagonist, Zampi, lives a culturally legitimized life, although he is removed from the trials and tribulations of daily existence. The practice of obeah gives Zampi a sense of having a useful place within the community whenever he emerges from his isolation and goes into the city. Since obeah helps people, particularly in crises, it provides the obeah man a more meaningful way of belonging than a "traditional" trade. Paradoxically Zampi's physical location outside the city facilitates a "centeredness" in terms of his role and status within the community, which Rahim's struggle to retain his trade in the city, in *The Jumbie Bird*, does not ensure.

Two interrelated themes are introduced from the novel's inception: Zampi's identity as obeah man and his relationship with Zolda. The obeah aspect of the story and the romantic/jealousy theme unfold side by side. In fact, Khan tends to sexualize his portrayal of obeah. As Zampi works obeah on the character Massahoud's war stick, he remarks, "If you fight clean you bound to win! Remember that! Don't have nothing to do with woman until the sun go to sleep, otherwise you get your head bust open." And this prophetic warning comes true in the conclusion of the novel when the sexual intrigues come together in violent struggle.

Zampi's relationship with Zolda revolves around the issues of sexual desire and possession. In his newfound obeah power Zampi is too arrogant, self-seeking, and dogmatic to recognize or respect any of Zolda's needs. Her personality and actions are determined by the fact that she is recognized both by herself and by the community, notably by the other men, as the obeah man's woman. Hence, Massahoud's desire for Zolda involves "a complexity of motives." He wants her not for herself but as a symbol of his conquest over Zampi. Moreover, Zampi's obeah power is perversely connected to the idea of sexually possessing Zolda. So

Cover for the 1974 Longman edition of Khan's autobiographical novel about three generations of Pathans who live in Trinidad while clinging to their Indian heritage

Massahoud "knew that if he could once have the obeah man's woman he would no longer have to go to him." Zolda's sexuality itself is equated with obeah power. The violent resolution, in which Massahoud is killed, unfolds on the sordid level of "getting the woman."

The end of *The Obeah Man* seems contrived: Zolda, understandably upset by the violent turn of events, begs to be taken away from the city, and Zampi triumphs. Not only has he "won" Zolda, but he has conveniently disposed of all his male rivals. The narrator's rationale for Zampi's exercise of power over Zolda is love. That power is used to dominate her will and her body: "She wished to throw herself in his arms, to have him possess her with thrusts like lightning bolts that would scorch her loins." This passage is "another of the lurid patches of writing," comments Ramchand, "that mars the work." Zampi's sexual power is fully realized in the woman's "asking for" her own subjugation.

Khan's latest novel, *The Crucifixion* (1987), is described on the dust jacket as "an ironic fable of tragic self-deception." It presents a male protagonist, Manko, a self-declared priest, who, convinced he is in "communion with God," sets out to save the sinners in Port of Spain. As in *The Jumbie Bird* Khan deals with the transition from adolescence to adulthood; and there are continuities with *The Obeah Man*. Like Zampi, Manko is isolated from the community, and his mission can be compared to Zampi's practice of obeah. In *The Crucifixion* Khan explores the propensity of religious practitioners to deceive people. Manko, at age fourteen, is impressed by the preacher's "power" over human beings, the ability to "read their minds." The spell that the preacher could cast over his listeners through the power of both the Word and of words makes a lasting impact on young Manko. As an impressionable child, then, he recognizes, perhaps subconsciously, the integral connection between power and knowledge.

The novel delineates the ironies inherent in the profession of preaching. When Manko takes the preacher's place, despite the fact that he has no training as a preacher but has "heard the call," Khan indirectly raises a question: what makes a true "man of God"? How can one distinguish that person from the fakes? In some ways "following the call" seems to be one of the easiest professions for the displaced and the dispossessed. If, like Manko, one can win over a crowd, even turn them against the "real," trained preacher, then one has indeed succeeded.

As in *The Obeah Man*, where Zampi's personal conflict of identity as obeah man was conflated with his desires and need to possess Zolda, Manko's self-doubts about being a "man of God" are problematized through his sexual desires for Miss Violet. The theme is not satisfactorily dealt with, nor is it well resolved, mainly because of the male narrator's sexist stance toward female characters. Manko's dream that "his ears were cut off, and he held them, one in each of his hands like the open Bible" suggests a crisis of faith, and Violet is quick to put his subconscious fears into words: "You playing holy," she shouts, "but you like women . . . I know . . . and you like rum . . . it have something bad in your eyes. You think I don't know what goes on in you mind?" Toward the end of the novel Manko is reassured that "God had not abandoned him," and when he dreams once again that his ears have been cut off, "this time he was able to replace them and they clung to his head easily." Since Violet has been condemned and cast out by the community, her earlier challenge of Manko loses its power: "You hate me because men love me and all of you who only playin' decent, don't know the first thing bout what decent mean. . . . You rotten . . . all of you . . . you all rotten from inside to outside." The final scene where Violet and a cripple are in a sexual embrace is Khan's typical way of resolving many more difficult issues: "They bodies move and writhe, they know that this was some kind of primitive understandin', some way of sayin' to each other that this is not use or abuse, but still they couldn't call it love . . . they didn't feel so much appeased, but relieved, discovered. They satisfy each other."

In *The Crucifixion* Khan includes segments of his short stories, particularly the ones in dialect. The short story "The Red Ball," for instance, is included almost in its entirety, with only minor changes. The stories are set off from the main text, both by italics and by the use of dialect instead of standard English. Their insertion serves no apparent purpose as they interrupt the main story line, detracting from the cohesiveness of the novel as a whole.

Khan's short stories collected in *A Day in the Country and Other Stories* (1990) explore aspects of childhood, particularly the father-son relationship. In "Shaving" the relationship involves a grown-up son who lives in New York and has taken to certain American ways different from those of his father — one example is that he uses an electric razor. "Why can't we do things like Americans?" asks the somewhat alienated, returned son. "Is it because for more than a century we have been told, 'You can't . . . ?' " Notable in all the stories in the collection is Khan's ability to bring characters to life. In "Shaving" he presents the vivid image of the barber Sookoo, who has lovingly nicknamed the narrator Clark Gable.

"A Day in the Country" evokes a happy boyhood amid a close, loving community, peopled by such folks as Uncle Rajo and his wife; the young narrator; and his cousin, Kemal. Uncle Rajo could not go abroad and study engineering because the narrator's grandfather "felt that some of this great tribe should remain always close to the soil, the people." Hence Rajo had had to move "out of the family house into his own, equipped with everything: wife, furniture, all the way down to the safety pins and the alarm clock on the shelf of the shop. No one disappointed the old tyrant, and Rajo, just as was predicted, soon got used to shopkeeping."

The shop itself, described through the young,

sensitive, observant boy's eyes, is rich in local color, right down to the wonderful aromas of various spices:

> A strange silence would then fall across the shop as we ate our dinner that evening in the midst of all those bags of flour, rice, and all those pins and hair clips from all the world . . . soaps, perfumes, candles, and now and then a quick waft of new white bolt-cotton, in which people would bury their dead . . . and spices from India in dozens of jars, each one filled with its own aroma . . . and the smell of onions and garlic drying on the string suspended from the ceiling.

Ismith Khan's achievement as a Caribbean writer of Indian descent lies in his exploration of the themes of boyhood, of identity, and of self-knowledge as his protagonists attempt to find their place in the world. His most noteworthy contribution to West Indian letters is his ability to reproduce the speech heard in the yards, the streets, and the bars of Trinidad.

Interview:

Daryl C. Dance, *New World Adams: Conversations with Contemporary West Indian Writers* (Leeds, U.K.: Peepal Tree, 1992).

References:

W. Lloyd Brown, "The Calypso Tradition in West Indian Literature," *Modern Black Literature*, 2 (Spring/Summer 1971): 127–143;

Stewart Brown, Introduction to Khan's *The Jumbie Bird* (Harlow, U.K.: Longman, 1985), pp. iii–xvi;

Rhonda Cobham, "*The Jumbie Bird* by Ismith Khan: A New Assessment," *Journal of Commonwealth Literature*, 21, no. 1 (1986): 240–249;

Barrie Davies, "The Personal Sense of a Society – Minority Views: Aspects of the 'East Indian' Novel in the West Indies," *Studies in the Novel*, 4 (Summer 1972): 284–295;

Renu Juneva, "Representing History in *The Jumbie Bird*," *World Literature Written in English*, 30 (Spring 1990): 17–28;

R. M. Lacovia, "Ismith Khan and the Theory of Rasa," *Black Images*, 1 (Autumn/Winter 1972): 23–27;

Kenneth Ramchand, "Obeah and the Supernatural in West Indian Literature," *Jamaica Journal*, 3, no. 2 (1971): 127–143.

George Lamming

(8 June 1927 –)

Sandra Pouchet Paquet
University of Miami

BOOKS: *In the Castle of My Skin* (London: Joseph, 1953; New York: McGraw-Hill, 1953; Trinidad & Jamaica: Longman Caribbean, 1970); republished with an introduction by Lamming (New York: Schocken, 1983);

The Emigrants (London: Joseph, 1954; New York: McGraw-Hill, 1955);

Of Age and Innocence (London: Joseph, 1958);

Season of Adventure (London: Joseph, 1960);

The Pleasures of Exile (London: Joseph, 1960); republished with an introduction by Lamming (London & New York: Allison & Busby, 1984; Ann Arbor: University of Michigan Press, 1992);

Water with Berries (London & Port of Spain: Longman, 1971; revised edition, New York: Holt, Rinehart & Winston, 1972);

Natives of My Person (London & Port of Spain: Longman, 1972; New York: Holt, Rinehart & Winston, 1972);

Conversations. George Lamming: Essays, Addresses and Interviews, 1953–1990 (London: Karia, 1992).

OTHER: "Of Thorns and Thistles," in *West Indian Stories*, edited by Andrew Salkey (London: Faber & Faber, 1960);

New World Quarterly: Guyana Independence Issue (1965), edited by Lamming and Martin Carter;

New World Quarterly: Barbados Independence Issue (1966–1967), edited by Lamming and Edward Baugh;

"Dedication from Afar: A Song for Marian" and "Swans," in *Caribbean Verse*, edited by O. R. Dathorne (London: Heinemann, 1967), pp. 41–44;

"Birthday Poem for Clifford Sealy," in *Caribbean Voices*, volume 2, edited by John Figueroa (London: Evans, 1970), pp. 119–121;

"The Indian People," in *Caribbean Essays*, edited by Salkey (London: Evans, 1973), pp. 5–16;

Cannon Shot and Glass Beads: Modern Black Writing, ed-

ited, with an introduction, by Lamming (London: Pan/Picador, 1974);

"The Indian Presence as a Caribbean Reality," in *Indenture and Exile: The Indo-Caribbean Experience*, edited by Frank Birbalsingh (Toronto: TSAR, 1989), pp. 45–54.

SELECTED PERIODICAL PUBLICATIONS– UNCOLLECTED: "David's Walk," "For the People of Trinidad," and "The Fishermen," *Life and Letters*, 59 (November 1948): 116–123, 145;

"February 1949," *Bim*, 3 (June 1949): 111;

"The Illumined Graves" and "Birthday Weather," *Bim*, 4 (December 1951): 165–166, 183–187;

"An Introduction," *Bim*, 6 (June 1955): 66–67;

"The Negro Writer and His World," *Cross Currents*, 6 (Spring 1956): 156–162;

"Tribute to a Tragic Jamaican [Roger Mais]," *Bim*, 6 (January–June 1957): 242–244;

"Caribbean Literature: The Black Rock of Africa," *African Forum*, 1, no. 4 (1966): 32–52;

"On West Indian Writing," *Revista/Review Interamericana*, 5 (1975): 149–162;

"*In the Castle of My Skin*: Thirty Years After," *Anales del Caribe*, 3 (1983): 278–288;

"Politics and Culture," *Sargasso*, 3 (1986): 61–68.

George Lamming is one the great Caribbean writers on the subjects of decolonization and national reconstruction. He matured as a novelist of the English-speaking Caribbean at a crucial period in Caribbean history, a period of burgeoning nationalism and agitation for independence from British colonial rule. Not only are decolonization and reconstruction the main themes of his fiction, but he has also had a demonstrated commitment to use his talent as a writer, his charisma, and his skill as a public speaker for the furtherance of regional sovereignty. Lamming's importance as a writer is not simply based on his political activism, however. His work is seminal. He is foremost among those Caribbean writers who first articulated the symbolic systems that make up modern Caribbean writing. In each of his novels and in his collection of essays, *The Pleasures of Exile* (1960), Lamming conceptualizes core facets of the Caribbean experience in language and forms that continue to exercise a shaping influence over the literature of the region. From his *In the Castle of My Skin* (1953) to his *Natives of My Person* (1972), Lamming's novels engage central themes of modern Caribbean writing and the literature of decolonization everywhere: colonialism and nationalism; emigration and exile; history and myth; tradition and modernity; cultural hybridity; identity in the context of race, class, gender, and ethnicity; and the role of the writer in a time of revolutionary social change.

Lamming's fiction is characteristically political and experimental in nature. The sequence and poetic density of the novels suggest the unfolding of a great allegorical master narrative. The novels follow logically one after the other so as to suggest a single unfinished plot. The unifying theme underlying all of them is the colonial experience, broadly conceived as a continuing psychic experience after the actual colonial situation has formally ended. Lamming looks beyond the dismantling of a colonial structure of awareness to the task of revising Caribbean destiny. Chief among his concerns are the cultural orphanage engendered by slavery and colonialism and the attendant crises of alienation, exile, and reconnection; the recovery of African and Asian influences as a necessary step in the refashioning of the multicultural, multiracial, multiethnic Caribbean; the restructuring of Caribbean societies around the needs of its peasant and working-class majority; and the roles of artists and working-class men and women in any refashioning of Caribbean society.

Lamming's preoccupations as a writer mirror his experience in the Caribbean. He was born on 8 June 1927, on Hawkins Road in Carrington Village, about two or three miles from the center of Bridgetown, the capital of Barbados. A former sugar estate, Carrington Village was self-sufficient to a certain degree, with its own carpenter, shoemaker, shops, and public baths. The only child of a devoted, unmarried mother, Lamming recalls the sense of privilege she imparted to him even in the limited circumstances of a peasant and working-class environment. In a similar vein Lamming recalls the interest and attention of Papa Grandison, his mother's godfather, who gave him pocket change and always had a meal for him when he visited. (Lamming explains the importance of Papa

George Lamming (photograph copyright by the Longman Group, Ltd.)

Grandison as a formative influence in his life as a writer in the concluding chapter of *The Pleasures of Exile*.) When Lamming's mother married, that gave him yet another place to experience, St. David's Village, where his stepfather worked. But Lamming was raised primarily in Carrington Village and attended Roebuck Boys School there. From Roebuck he won a rare scholarship to attend Combermere High School, where he was befriended by Frank Collymore, a member of the faculty at Combermere and editor of *Bim*, a literary journal that published and promoted Caribbean writers. Collymore gave Lamming the freedom of his extensive personal library and encouraged him to start writing poetry. In 1946 Lamming left Barbados for Trinidad. With Collymore's help he had secured a teaching position at El Collegio de Venezuela, a school for boys in Port of Spain. In Trinidad he also acted as an agent for *Bim*, and this job brought him into contact with others like himself, young men such as Cecil Herbert and Clifford Sealy who wanted to be writers and poets. Feeling keenly their peripheral status in a colonial society with little interest in aspiring local artists, Lamming was drawn to London as the place where he might realize his ambitions. He sailed for England in 1950, by coincidence on the same ship as Trinidadian novelist Sam Selvon. As Lamming

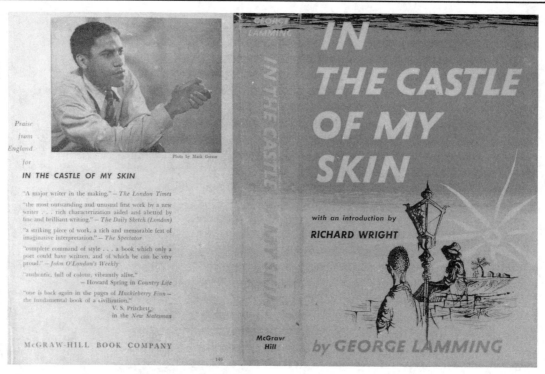

Dust jacket for Lamming's autobiographical novel, set in the Caribbean during the years of rebellion against colonialism

observes in *The Pleasures of Exile*, they were part of a larger migrating labor force that went to Britain after World War II in search of opportunities not available to them at home.

When Lamming left for England, he was primarily a poet, though he had written some short fiction. His early work was published in such journals as *Bim* and broadcast on the BBC radio program *Caribbean Voices*. Only a few of these pieces have been reprinted in anthologies. They are important for the light they throw on Lamming's early development as a writer and on his masterful first novel, *In the Castle of My Skin*. As Ian Munro points out (in "The Early Work of George Lamming," 1976), the short stories "David's Walk" (*Life and Letters*, November 1948) and "Birthday Weather" (*Bim*, December 1951) and poems such as "The Rock" (in *The Pleasures of Exile*; originally published in *Life and Letters*, November 1948) are intimately related to Lamming's first novel. In fact, "Birthday Weather" appears to be an early version of the first chapter. In *The Pleasures of Exile*, Lamming uses two of his early poems, "The Rock" and "The Boy and the Sea" (first published in *Bim*, December 1951), as the occasion for a retrospective commentary on the English audience for his early poetry and on the ideological underpinnings of his writing before his departure for London.

While in England, Lamming quickly established himself as a writer and intellectual of influence and great promise. He published four novels in quick succession: *In the Castle of My Skin*, *The Emigrants* (1954), *Of Age and Innocence* (1958), and *Season of Adventure* (1960). He also published *The Pleasures of Exile*, his pioneering collection of essays on intellectual history and cultural politics; the book was a forerunner of current postcolonial formulations around identity and cultural hybridity. During this period Lamming worked for the overseas department of the British Broadcasting Service and traveled extensively. He visited the United States in 1955 on a Guggenheim Fellowship and traveled to West Africa and the Caribbean. In 1956 he was one of the participants in the first international Congress of Black Writers and Artists in Paris; among the other participants were Jacques-Stephen Alexis, Aimé Césaire, Cheikh Anta Diop, Frantz Fanon, Jean Price-Mars, and Richard Wright.

Lamming's first novel was an immediate success, and he found himself in the vanguard of a new literary movement. It was bought by Jean-Paul Sartre for translation into French and publication in the journal *Les Temps Modernes* in 1954, and it was published in the United States with an introduction by Wright. In 1957 it received the Somerset Maugham Award for Literature. The 1983

Schocken edition includes an introduction by Lamming, offering a retrospective commentary on the nature of his art and what he hoped to accomplish in writing the novel. This introduction is also included in the University of Michigan Press reprint (1991).

In the Castle of My Skin is a Caribbean classic, an autobiographical novel of childhood and adolescence; it is also one of the great novels of decolonization. Lamming draws heavily on his childhood experiences as he describes the protagonist G.'s growth to manhood in the context of the social and political changes in the Caribbean in the 1930s and 1940s. The changes that disrupt life in the fictional Creighton's Village and displace many of its inhabitants mirror the labor unrest and consequent social upheaval that occurred throughout the Caribbean at the time. Those events made a great impression on Lamming as a boy. He was nine years old when week-long riots erupted in Barbados in 1937, following the deportation of the Trinidadian unionist Clement Payne.

The novel selectively reconstructs Lamming's boyhood and adolescence. In a fine balance of first-person and omniscient narrative Lamming describes what it meant to grow up poor and black in a British colony in the Caribbean. When the novel begins, G. is celebrating his ninth birthday rather miserably, since his birthday coincides with the floods that beset the village annually. The novel ends with the dismantling of Creighton's Village and G.'s impending departure, at age eighteen, for Trinidad. G.'s growth to manhood and his moving to another island are paralleled in the novel by the disintegration of the feudal structure of life in Creighton's Village. The first-person narrative of G.'s childhood and adolescence is interwoven with omniscient narrative that is explicitly concerned with private and public social and political issues affecting the lives of the villagers, issues that G. is either ignorant of or comprehends in a limited way. Lamming uses omniscient narrative to provide an overview of the feudal structure of village life, which is dominated by the white landlord, Mr. Creighton, who owns the land on which the village stands. Feeling threatened by the organization of labor and islandwide riots, Creighton sells his estate and the village (in secret) to island entrepreneurs who have a purely speculative interest in the resale of the village lands for a profit. The result is that many of the villagers are displaced, losing their homes, their community, and their livelihood. The tension between the first-person narrative and the omniscient narrative is at the heart of the novel,

structurally and thematically. The betrayal of the villagers by their leadership, and the dislocation that follows, gives a heightened sense of displacement and dispossession to G.'s departure at the end of the novel.

In the Castle of My Skin has assumed importance not only as a Caribbean novel but as a novel that describes, in specific yet representative terms, the revolt against colonialism in many parts of the Third World. This interpretation was put forward by Wright in his introduction to the McGraw-Hill edition. Ngugi wa Thiong'o, in his collection of essays titled *Homecoming* (1972), describes Lamming's first book as "one of the great political novels in modern 'colonial' literature." This classification is the basis of Sandra Pouchet Paquet's study of the book in *The Novels of George Lamming* (1982) and, more recently, of Wilfred Cartey's look at the novel in his *Whispers from the Caribbean* (1991). In *The Novel in the Third World* (1976) Charles Larson offers a context for the study of *In the Castle of My Skin* in relation to novels by Third World writers such as René Maran, Yambo Ouologuem, Vincent Eri, and Hyemeyohsts Storm.

A minority has resisted the elaborate architecture of Lamming's first novel: they complain of a certain heaviness and insistence in his style, and they mistrust Lamming's use of fiction to describe the structure of power in the colonial Caribbean. In a 1978 essay, "Lamming and Naipaul: Some Criteria for Evaluating the Third World Novel," Elizabeth Nunez-Harrell argues that Lamming's children are mere mouthpieces for "the inexplicable yet inevitable working-out of fate." Yet for others, such as Edward Kamau Brathwaite and the late Michael Cooke, *In the Castle of My Skin* is a transformative experience, an epiphany. In "The Strains of Apocalypse" (1990) Cooke describes it as the "consummate text of growing up male in the Caribbean," and he discusses some of the ways in which the key tropes and rhetorical strategies are repeated and revised in Erna Brodber's *Jane and Louisa Will Soon Come Home* (1980). Kenneth Ramchand also admires Lamming's use of childhood and adolescence to illuminate the troubled beginnings of a society, while Paquet's foreword to the University of Michigan reprint stresses Lamming's brilliant use of autobiography as a fictional device. Two other approaches to the book, by Patrick Taylor and Joyce Jonas, are especially illuminating. Taylor interprets the text in the light of Frantz Fanon's "narrative of liberation," and Jonas uses anthropological concepts of liminality to flesh out parallels between Lamming's use of the literal and metaphorical topography of "the plantation landscape" and Wilson Harris's approach to the same subject matter in his *Genesis of the Clowns* (1977).

Lamming's second novel, *The Emigrants*, follows thematically and logically from *In the Castle of My Skin*, in which G.'s departure for Trinidad is partly the result of his colonial education and upbringing and partly the result of poverty and limited opportunities at home. In *The Emigrants* Lamming explores emigration as a regional phenomenon that affects West Indians of all classes regardless of their island of origin. Lamming represents the massive post–World War II migration of West Indians to Great Britain not simply in terms of economic necessity but as part of the cultural legacy of colonization. The migration and the West Indians' subsequent attempts to adjust to the incomprehension and lack of welcome they encounter on arrival provide the framework for Lamming's continuing exploration of the alienation and displacement occasioned by colonialism in the Caribbean.

Lamming uses the device of the emigrant ship to assemble a representative Caribbean community that splinters and fragments on arrival in England. This fragmentation is reflected in the dispersal of the emigrants on their arrival and also in the novel's imagery and narrative strategy. As in Lamming's first novel the narration is shared by first-person and omniscient narrators. Once the emigrant ship arrives in Britain and the emigrants are scattered in different directions, the first-person narrator gives way to an omniscient narrator until the third and final section of the novel, when the reintroduction of the first-person narrator suggests the contours of a controlling sensibility. In the interim, omniscient narrative organizes time and perspective; it provides an overview of the emigrant experience and imparts a sense of simultaneity to the individual experiences of many emigrants.

The Emigrants is elaborately conceived and crowded with characters, as Lamming focuses on the emigrant journey and then the settling-in process. There are abrupt shifts of scene from one place to another and from one group of characters to another that structurally correspond to the growing disconnection and isolation of the emigrants themselves. The fragmented form mirrors the emigrants' loss of community and their ensuing disorientation in self-perception and purpose. In this novel emigration is at best a purgatorial experience. For the most part, the experience is projected in images of obscured vision, imprisonment, and death – a powerful dramatization of the alienation that afflicts a rapidly growing immigrant community settling into marginality in an increasingly hostile and unfriendly country.

Some critics have complained about the novel's fragmentary form, others about its slow pace and the psychic disintegration of its characters. However, Paquet, Gareth Griffiths, and, more recently, Cartey have high praise for the power and integrity of Lamming's fictionalization of the Caribbean emigrants' expectations and experiences. There has been a resurgence of interest in *The Emigrants* of late, partly because it has proved so prophetic about the experience of Caribbean immigrants in Britain since the 1950s and partly because of the careful and inspired interpretation of critics such as Ngugi in *Homecoming*. Lamming's second novel was certainly important to his development as a novelist and can be usefully read in conjunction with *The Pleasures of Exile* and *Water with Berries* (1971). In addition *The Emigrants* must be viewed as a seminal work in Caribbean literature; it anticipates the better-known novels of emigration and exile such as Selvon's *The Lonely Londoners* (1956), Jean Rhys's *Wide Sargasso Sea* (1966), and V. S. Naipaul's *The Mimic Men* (1967). Certainly the only prior work in West Indian fiction that comes close to it in vision and focus is Eric Walrond's *Tropic Death* (1926), a collection of short stories set in the Caribbean and Panama.

The years immediately following the publication of *The Emigrants* were important ones for Lamming. He not only visited West Africa and the United States, but he also spent several months touring the Caribbean for *Holiday* magazine. While the magazine did not publish the work he produced, its financial support allowed him to explore the Caribbean at will. He went everywhere he wanted, except to Cuba, which refused him entry. He involved himself where he could in the independence movements sweeping the Caribbean. Lamming was involved with the People's National Movement (PNM) in Trinidad and, speaking at a convention, introduced the party's candidates for their first election in 1956. He wrote for the PNM's weekly publication, the *Nation*. But most important for his third novel, *Of Age and Innocence* (1958), was his extended visit to Guyana. The politics of race had emerged as a major issue in the struggle for power between Forbes Burnham and Cheddi Jagan. The constitution was suspended in 1953, and Lamming witnessed firsthand the ruthlessness of imperialism in action under Governor Rennison, a former colonial secretary of Trinidad and Tobago, who was governor of Kenya during the Kikuyu rebellion and Jomo Kenyatta's trial. Guyana seemed a case study for ev-

GEORGE LAMMING was born of mixed African and English parentage in Barbados in 1927. After leaving school he taught French and English for four years at a boarding school in Trinidad. He came to England in 1950, and for some months worked in various factories in the London area. Early in 1951, he began to broadcast a weekly programme of reviews of books and films on the B.B.C.'s Colonial Service. His poems have been broadcast in the B.B.C. Overseas Service, and published in English and West Indian magazines. *In the Castle of My Skin* was his first prose work.

'He is a pioneer, creating a literature that is West Indian in its content and yet within the tradition of English literature. A major writer in the making' THE TIMES LITERARY SUPPLEMENT

Dust jacket for Lamming's second novel, in which he examines the plight of the many Caribbeans who immigrated to Britain after World War II

erything that could go wrong in the struggle for independence in the colonial Caribbean.

The politics of independence dominate *Of Age and Innocence*, but it is not simply about the struggle in Guyana. Lamming invents a Caribbean island called San Cristobal, the island of Columbus. It references the entire Caribbean, with place-names and distinctive features of Caribbean communities from Haiti to Trinidad and Guyana. It is a rich invention that Lamming returns to again and again in subsequent novels, which facilitates his desire to write comprehensively about the Caribbean as a post-Columbian phenomenon. The fictional location and society represent his idea of the Caribbean societies as one people. Moreover, as a microcosm of the Caribbean region, San Cristobal lends itself to Lamming's often-stated perception of the Caribbean as a kind of laboratory for exploring various interests. Because of the Caribbean's strategic importance, all the major powers have been involved there at one time or another. Additionally it is multicultural, with a history of sharp conflicts between Europeans and Amerindians, Europeans and Africans, and Africans and Indians in one area or another. All this, Lamming explains, makes the Caribbean a good place for exploring the struggle of the Third World to define its own destiny even in

the face of sharp conflicts with the interests of major world powers, whether capitalist or socialist. These issues are at the heart of the novel *Of Age and Innocence*, in which the struggle for independence fails because Britain is not ready to relinquish authority over the region and because the deep-seated mistrust Africans and Indians have toward each other outweighs their shared perception of what is in their mutual interest.

The novel is saved from the inherent pessimism of this political vision by Lamming's use of a multiracial group of children, Bob (African), Singh (Indian), Lee (Chinese), and Rowley (British). Though the racial composition of the group mirrors that of the major actors in the struggle for independence, the boys are able to set their growing sense of racial and class differences aside in their personal relationships and in their commitment to an ideal of brotherhood. Yet the hope for the future that Lamming invests in these children is tentative, as he conceptualizes it in *The Pleasures of Exile*: "Innocence and Age are two sides of the same coin."

Of Age and Innocence is also interesting because of the way Lamming returns to the emigrant experience delineated in his two previous novels, as a point of departure. In his third novel the immigrant experience in Great Britain, however traumatic, is a catalyst for social and political change in the Caribbean. Returning to the Caribbean is presented as an opportunity for redefinition of self in terms other than a colonial relationship to Europe. The opportunity for redefinition in this novel is extended to the colonizer as well as the colonized. The novel begins with a planeload of returning emigrants and British expatriates who are leaving the security of their homeland for San Cristobal. The major characters are the returning emigrants Mark Kennedy and Isaac Shephard and Britishers who plan to settle on the island: Mark's lover Marcia and their friends Penelope and Bill. The political events at the center of the novel have a dramatic impact on how these and other characters think and feel about themselves and each other. Personal relationships are extremely volatile in the jockeying for power that consumes different factions in the struggle for independence. The psychological drama of collapsing relationships and changing identities in a time of radical social change is drawn with great sensitivity to the politics of race, class, and gender in the economic and social life of the colonial Caribbean. Mark discovers that his well-established relationship with Marcia is incompatible with his longing for reconnection at home. Isaac, on the other hand, is charged with a sense of political mission fueled by the humiliations he experienced in England. San Cristobal provides all the main characters with an opportunity for life-renewing redefinitions of self in the ensuing struggle for independence from colonial rule, a fight led by the embittered Isaac, who is on a mission of personal and national reconstruction.

Of Age and Innocence has received strong praise and also some rather pointed criticism. On the one hand, Mervyn Morris describes the novel as a triumphant and masterly critique of Caribbean society. Gerald Moore concludes that as "the novel of a dying colonialism and the struggle for a new vision of life in the Caribbean, *Of Age and Innocence* stands complete." Ngugi writes appreciatively and at length about Lamming's treatment of the themes of exile and alienation. Griffiths finds the novel exceptionally successful "in creating a world which reflects the general experience of the West Indies, without losing the force of specific experience." Paquet (in *The Novels of George Lamming*) discusses the elaborate architecture of the novel, its symbolic resonance and comprehensive vision, and its rich use of the region's strong oral tradition of storytelling and mythmaking. But others have not been quite so appreciative. Brathwaite (in "The New West Indian Novelists," *Bim*, July–December 1960) complains that the novel reads like a case history

rather than a work of art, while Ramchand finds it improbable in comparison with Naipaul's *The Mimic Men.* Selwyn R. Cudjoe concludes that the novel "is inherently shallow because we are not presented with the kind of therapeutic violence necessary to insure a new relationship" between colonizer and colonized.

Lamming's fourth novel, *Season of Adventure* (1960), is also set on the fictive island of San Cristobal, now an independent republic, but in this novel the politics of race and class are perceived in terms of the conflicting claims of Europe and Africa in the postcolonial Caribbean. The political event at the center of the novel is the fall of the first postindependence republic after a popular uprising of the poor and oppressed. The president of the republic is murdered by Powell, a musician who plays the steel drums. The revolt has been inspired by the government's attempt to ban the drums in order to help preserve law and order. The uprising is led by Gort, a master steelbandsman. He is assisted by Chiki, a painter with some formal education, who remains committed to his origins among the poor and dispossessed. He is, in turn, assisted by Fola, a rebellious daughter of the ruling elite, who shifts her allegiance from the materialistic, self-serving values of her class to the needs of the poor and dispossessed. The novel ends with the emergence of a new republic under the enlightened leadership of Kofi-James-Williams Baako, a composite of political leaders from Trinidad and Ghana whom Lamming admired at the time, but the revolt itself is not led by politicians.

In *Season of Adventure* the public drama of political conflict between the ruling class and the poor revolves around Fola, a young woman of European and African parentage. The larger political drama of national reconstruction is individualized in Fola as she is transformed by a traumatic experience: she becomes an unwilling participant in a so-called Ceremony of Souls she has come to observe. Her experience inspires her to seek her father's identity. His identity remains unresolved in the novel because Fola's mother had been raped by two men in quick succession, one white and one black. But Fola's quest leads to the recovery of her peasant and African roots and the abandonment of her class, which defines itself in opposition to the peasant majority and their culture of survival. Under the guidance of Chiki, Fola commits herself politically to the rebellious poor and becomes a crucial figure in the popular uprising that topples the first republic.

The novel pulls together many of Lamming's major concerns, among them the centrality of the peasant majority in the Caribbean, the recovery of Africa as a place of cultural value and a base of power in the postcolonial Caribbean, and the roles of the artist and of women in the process of national reconstruction. The novel is among the most engaging of Lamming's works, and it appeals to a wide readership. Lamming tells a good story and makes a strong political statement at the same time. The central symbols work well. The Haitian Ceremony of Souls is represented as a remnant of African culture that exercises compelling and transforming power over a disbelieving middle class, as well as the poor and illiterate. In the novel the drums represent another direct cultural link between West Africa and the Caribbean; the drums symbolize an alternative structure of values that exists in opposition to the unjust rule of law. In San Cristobal the popular music of the steel drum is the music of African-Caribbean religious ritual. Fola's cultivated, socially acceptable taste for this music as popular entertainment leaves her vulnerable to the other values of the drums as the music of the poor and dispossessed.

Season of Adventure makes a strong statement about reconnection with Africa as the key to national reconstruction in the postcolonial Caribbean. This novel also makes a statement about the role of women in this process. The central character is a young woman and one of the most sympathetically drawn of Lamming's main characters. For the first time in Lamming's fiction a woman is cast as an active agent of national reconstruction, as the initiator of a revolutionary break rather than a repressive principle. This book is also the most optimistic of Lamming's novels. It speaks confidently of the future of the Caribbean community and of its power to renew itself in a continuing struggle for freedom and justice.

Despite an overwhelmingly favorable response to *Season of Adventure*, there is some controversy among critics and scholars about three facets of Lamming's crafting of this novel. According to Morris, Lamming is preoccupied "with themes at the expense of credible life." It is for this reason that Morris rejects the "Author's Note," which Lamming interjects as if to confirm his novel's engagement with the reader's world. Morris also argues that Lamming's "attempt to make some centrally significant myth out of the music of the steelband" does not succeed. But others judge this novel quite differently. Ramchand argues in *The West Indian Novel and Its Background* (1970) that Lamming's note "seems in theory to break the fictional illusion but in fact serves to strengthen it."

Ramchand is not only sympathetic to Lamming's symbolic use of the steel drum but also praises the novel as a major achievement. Ramchand's appreciation of the novel is shared by others, including Cartey and Paquet, who praise it for its artistic integrity and creative vision. Making use of the insights of symbolic anthropology, Jonas compares *Season of Adventure* with Harris's *The Whole Armour* (1962): both novelists "invert the extant social structures so that the center of sacredness located formerly in the Great House is now relocated among the houseless folk." In Lamming's *Season of Adventure*, she argues, the margins of the "Great House" are transformed into the threshold of a new world.

Lamming's collection of essays, *The Pleasures of Exile*, was published in the same year as *Season of Adventure*. The 1984 Allison and Busby edition of the text carries a short retrospective by Lamming (which is reproduced with a foreword by Paquet in the 1992 University of Michigan Press reprint of the novel). Written in self-imposed exile, the introduction by Lamming engages powerfully and directly with the contrary legacies affecting the social, political, and artistic dimensions of black writing. The geographical context of the issues ranges from the Caribbean to Europe, West Africa, and the United States, and they have relevance for students of Caribbean literature and black cultural studies everywhere. Lamming illuminates contemporary literary and philosophical debates around minority discourse and postcolonial writing.

The Pleasures of Exile is a seminal work of self-inquiry and cultural assessment in the context of Caribbean life. It incorporates select memoirs of Lamming's life as a writer in England and his travels in the Caribbean, West Africa, and the United States. It includes extended discussions of William Shakespeare's *The Tempest*, C. L. R. James's *The Black Jacobins* (1938), and Lamming's own fiction and poetry. Lamming's ideas anticipate many postcolonial critics' preoccupations with the politics of migration, cultural hybridity, and the prerogatives of minority discourse. He conjures up a specific subjectivity, his own, as the evidence and example of a wide range of physical, intellectual, psychological, and cultural responses to colonialism. His theme is "the migration of the writer from the Caribbean to the dubious refuge of a metropolitan culture." Lamming's perspective is that of a Caribbean writer committed to "the dismantling of a colonial structure of awareness" and the reconstruction of the colonial's psyche.

In *The Pleasures of Exile* Lamming enters into

Gambian poet Lenrie Peters and Lamming at a party (photograph by Marilyn Stafford; Transcription Centre Archive, Harry Ransom Humanities Research Center, University of Texas at Austin)

dialogue with the cultural assumptions of classic texts of imperialism and decolonization, and in the process he creates a counterdiscourse of his own, concerning his lived experience as a migrating writer in the country (England) that colonized his history. He critiques British cultural icons and institutions from Shakespeare to the Institute of Contemporary Arts, the British Broadcasting Corporation, the *Times Literary Supplement*, and the *Spectator*. He names an alternative hierarchy of values rooted in the Caribbean of the Haitian Ceremony of Souls, James's *The Black Jacobins*, his own childhood, and a community of writers from the colonial Caribbean. As intellectual history, *The Pleasures of Exile* is specific to the colonial Caribbean; it also illuminates the coercive, transgressive processes of production in colonial societies everywhere. Underlying the text is a theory of language, discourse, and representation that transforms the author as colonial subject and consumer of British intellectual and cultural history into a self-conscious producer of alternative discourses.

The Pleasures of Exile is a useful complement to Lamming's fiction. The parallels and connections between the essays in this collection and his fiction are seemingly endless, whether it be his personal view of the United States — a view that surfaces as early as *In the Castle of My Skin* and reappears throughout the body of his work — or his idea of Africa that develops from a dimly remembered dream in *In the Castle of My Skin*, or the thematically and structurally important use of African cultural remnants in *Season of Adventure*. From Lamming's use of the Haitian Ceremony of Souls in *Season of Adventure* to his use of Papa Grandison in *In the Castle of My Skin* and the voyages of Richard Hakluyt in *Natives of My Person*, these essays are endlessly informative about the nature and scope of Lamming's artistic vision.

Some critics have expressed reservations about the volume, but it endures as a major statement on Caribbean culture and society and current postcolonial debates on migration, identity, and cultural hybridity. Morris calls it "a rag-bag collection," however. Cudjoe takes issue with Lamming's ideological positioning in relation to the poetics of imperialism. But *The Pleasures of Exile* remains one of the most frequently cited works of its kind in Caribbean literary criticism and cultural theory, and it continues to offer valuable insights into Caribbean culture and society. In her 1989 essay "Rites of Resistance" Helen Tiffin stresses Lamming's self-conscious exploration of "the tyranny of the text" in his extended critique of *The Tempest*; at issue is the creation of a counterdiscourse rather than the "simple extension of a European mode." In her foreword to the 1992 reprint Paquet stresses the nature and scope of Lamming's interpretive vision in relation to the production of literature as a national enterprise and to postcolonial formations of identity, race, ethnicity, and cultural hybridity.

Though he published no new fiction in the decade following the publication of *The Pleasures of Exile*, Lamming remained active in several ways. In 1962 he received a Canada Council Fellowship. He traveled extensively in the Caribbean and North America and was actively engaged in the political debates affecting the status of black Americans and West Indians. He wrote the script for a television documentary about the so-called Freedom Rides in Alabama. He was a guest editor for the Guyana and Barbados Independence Issues of the *New World Quarterly* in 1965 and 1966–1967, respectively. He was a member of the jury for the Casa de las Américas Prize for literature when it was awarded for the first time to a writer from the English-speaking Caribbean. And in 1967 he was writer in residence at the Mona, Jamaica, campus of the University of the West Indies.

During this period Lamming published two statements on West Indian culture and society that are of particular interest to students of his work. One is his address to the Conference on West Indian Affairs held in Montreal in 1965, in which he links the Haitian Ceremony of Souls to his sense of purpose as a writer. This paper was published as "The West Indian People" in *New World Quarterly* in 1966 and collected in *Caribbean Essays* (1973). The other essay, "Caribbean Literature: The Black Rock of Africa," was published in the journal *African Forum* (1966). It is a seminal statement on the African presence in Caribbean literature and is also a restatement of Lamming's personal commitment as a writer on cultural reconstruction after colonialism. "This new independence," he told the Conference on West Indian Affairs, "is insubstantial topsoil; the real battle is below." Lamming stayed close to political developments in the Caribbean, but no new novel of his appeared until the publication of *Water with Berries* in 1971.

Water with Berries is set in postcolonial England as racial hostility toward the West Indian immigrant community is reaching critical proportions. It might be read as the preface to Lamming's own return to the Caribbean at the end of the 1970s. In *Water with Berries* Lamming returns to the themes of emigration and exile previously treated in *The Emigrants* and *The Pleasures of Exile*. His 1971 novel is about the migration of three West Indian artists to Great Britain: Derek, an actor; Roger, a musician; and Teeton, a painter. After initial success Lamming's three artists gradually reach a point of crisis in their professional and personal lives. After seven years of accommodation and gratitude, their peripheral status threatens to overwhelm them with a sense of alienation and futility; each turns violent and destructive against the society in which they sought refuge and fulfillment. In the cases of Roger and Derek, their acts of violence are self-destructive and futile. In the case of Teeton, violence occurs as a result of his failed plan to return to the Caribbean and take part in the growing rebellion there. At the end of the novel Teeton and Roger stand trial for murder and arson; the violence that consumes their lives appears unavoidable.

In *Water with Berries* Lamming returns to an earlier preoccupation with *The Tempest* as a master text of imperialist discourse. As in *The Pleasures of Exile* Lamming uses *The Tempest* as the basis for a profound examination of the colonial experience. There are explicit references to Shakespeare's play in Lamming's plot and characterization. As versions of Caliban, Prospero, Ferdinand, Miranda, and Miranda's mother, Lamming's characters, both Caribbean and British, embody significant areas of the colonial experience relative to time and place. The three artists are represented as descendants of Caliban who trade their birthright for marginality in Prospero's homeland long after Prospero has relinquished control of theirs. In *The Pleasures of Exile* Lamming refers to such misplaced trust and affection as "the gift in its most destructive form" and "the worst form of colonization: colonization through a process of affection." *Water with Berries* is a complex representation of this dilemma.

Though the novel ends in violence that is represented as the logical outcome of colonialism, a significant part is devoted to exploring the possibilities of reconciliation based on the recognition of wrongs done. Once again Lamming returns to the Haitian Ceremony of Souls as an aesthetic principle and symbol of constructive dialogue between the past and the present, the colonizer and the colonized. But in this novel all such efforts end in failure. The text suggests that constructive dialogue is unlikely and that increasing racial conflict is inevitable in the aftermath of colonialism.

In *Water with Berries* Lamming reworks the "backward-glance" theme of *Season of Adventure* and *The Pleasures of Exile*. Attempts at dialogue end in failure because important areas of personal history remain unexamined. Thus Myra, one of two versions of Miranda in the novel, though ready to talk about the abuses she has suffered at the hands of her father's servants in San Cristobal, is unable to accept the fact that her father cruelly abused his servants and that she is indirectly the victim of her father's tyranny and oppression. The truth is a liability between husbands and wives, and friends and relatives, as well as between strangers. Roger Capildeo, a composer of Indian descent, is unable to tell his white American wife of his horror of a racially mixed child, so he fabricates a lie about her infidelity. Derek, the actor, refuses to be complicitous in the lie and undertakes to tell Roger's wife the truth. With each round of betrayal the three move closer to disaster. In such a climate of deceit and conflict, attempts at dialogue are doomed to failure. The novel delivers something of an apocalyptic threat for all concerned, for returning to the Caribbean is not an option available to the immigrant artists at the end of the novel.

Structurally *Water with Berries* achieves a new compactness of form through political allegory. The novel is heavily symbolic in its rendering of character and situation. The thematic issues remain the same, however. Lamming's political vision, his preoccupation with colonialism as the key to understanding the Caribbean psyche, and his perception of the Caribbean experience as a laboratory for the study of colonialism worldwide – coupled with his elaborate narrative designs and ornate prose style – continue to divide critical response rather sharply and at times illogically. In his 1973 article "A West Indian Novelist" Cooke finds Lamming's Caliban idea "self-indulgent and senseless." He characterizes the novel as "neo-Gothic" and says it is overly contrived and tendentious. Others, such as William Curtin (*Commonweal*, 1973), find Lamming's use of *The Tempest* a powerful point of departure in the novel. Paquet and Tiffin stress the artistic power and complex vision of Lamming's sustained use of allegory to convey his perception of history as a trap from which men and women are unable to escape. Readers ought to be aware that the U.S. edition of the novel differs from the British edition published by Longman. There is a brief concluding chapter to the British edition that alters the novel

Dust jacket for the historical novel that Lamming has described as "a way of going forward by making a complete return to the beginnings" of Caribbean colonization in the sixteenth century

rather dramatically: the three artists are to be tried for murder and arson, and they become the center of a raging controversy that threatens to erupt into a continuation of the earlier violence.

Lamming's next novel, *Natives of My Person*, is about the men who made those first voyages of exploration, plunder, and conquest in the sixteenth century, who decimated the indigenous population, and who rationalized the African slave trade as a necessary component of their settlements in the New World. The novel reconstructs a voyage in the late sixteenth century from the fictive kingdom of Lime Stone to the Isles of Black Rock. The object of the voyage is to found a new settlement. The enterprise is led by the commandant of the ship the *Reconnaissance*; he is a national hero who plans a model settlement on the island of San Cristobal as a way of atoning for barbaric acts he perpetrated there earlier. The motivations of his officers and crew are mixed. Some share the commandant's vision of a model society, but others are motivated by greed, ambition, poverty, religious persecution, and criminal pasts. The enterprise itself is funded by the commandant's mistress, "the Lady of the House," a woman of wealth and influence. She has plans to join the men at their destination in what she intends as a joint enterprise in which the wives of the officers will be working partners in their new venture.

The enterprise ends in failure because of conflicts among the ship's crew and officers about the obligations of leadership and the goals of the enterprise. The officers lose interest in the enterprise when the fact and terms of the women's participation in their venture become clear. Finally the commandant himself loses interest when he learns that his mistress has been sexually promiscuous with the boatswain during one of the commandant's long absences from Lime Stone. In the mutiny that follows the collapse of leadership, he and two of his officers are killed. The ship's crew finds a new leader in the powder maker and continue on to their planned destination in San Cristobal, where the women wait in vain for the murdered commandant and his officers.

In *Natives of My Person* Lamming uses the psychosocial conflicts of a specific historical era to illuminate the bias and function of power in the postcolonial present. The narrative unfolds gradually through a mixture of omniscient narrative and the diaries of the commandant, officers, and various members of the crew, who are named according to their function: the commandant, priest, pilot, boatswain, surgeon, surgeon's wife, the Lady of the House, and others reflect a wide range of society in terms of class and geography, so that Lamming contrives a cast of characters that is explicitly representative of the age and the enterprise. He uses the *Reconnaissance* and its sister ship, the *Penalty,* to isolate and dramatize those elements in European society that shaped the spirit of territorial conquest and commercial enterprise, elements that came to distinguish the first European settlements in the Americas. The commandant's enterprise becomes an occasion for examining the inner lives of the ship's officers and crew. As they leave the Guinea coast for the Isles of Black Rock, all the major characters are tormented by past failures of one kind or another. All try to leave their past behind, their personal history of failure, to be the kind of people their ambitions or consciences require. But they are unable to sever private and public tyrannies of the past on a ship that is a microcosm of the world they leave behind.

In *Natives of My Person* issues of female difference and of discrimination are presented in the context of imperial history. The oppression of women is linked to a pervasive corruption in the society that envelops men and women in ways specific to their class and gender. Women are a distinct category; their liberation from notions of female dependency and male privilege becomes a necessary precondition to a just society. Lamming places special emphasis on the inability of the men to accept women as partners in their enterprise. The men cling to notions of peculiarly male spheres of activity and see the exclusion of women as a necessary reinforcement of difference and privilege. Lamming explores the meaning of this history of exclusion and its impact on intimate relations between men and women and on their New World settlement.

As Lamming explained it in an interview with George E. Kent, *Natives of My Person* follows up logically on his earlier novels, which deal with recent developments in the Caribbean. This continuity is "a way of going forward by making a complete return to the beginnings; it's actually the whole etiology of *In the Castle of My Skin, The Emigrants* and *Season of Adventure.*" Indeed there are many parallels and interconnections with Lamming's earlier work. Among the more obvious is the one with *The Emigrants*, which in part describes the sea journey of men and women who anticipate new lives and new beginnings. There are also parallels with *Of Age and Innocence* and *Season of Adventure* in the way the structure of power is perceived. In *Natives of My Person* Lamming returns to the familiar themes of decolonization but in the context of New World beginnings and the historic inequities in relations between men and women and between the privileged and the oppressed. The progression from *In the Castle of My Skin* to *Natives of My Person* establishes Lamming's growing interest in gender issues as a structural component of desired social and political change. *Natives of My Person* also invites a careful rereading of *The Pleasures of Exile*, for it is there that Lamming first identifies Herman Melville's *Moby-Dick* (1851), Shakespeare's *The Tempest*, and Hakluyt's *Voyages* as keys to his understanding of the social and psychological forces that shaped the course of colonialism in the New World. The commandant of the *Reconnaissance* is at once a composite of historical figures such as Francis Drake and John Hawkins and literary ones including Ahab and Prospero.

Critical issues surrounding *Natives of My Person* follow a predictable pattern, centering on Lamming's use of allegory. Some critics have a marked prejudice against allegory; others, such as Stephen Slemon, find that Lamming's use of allegory fundamentally revises the relationship of alle-

Lamming reading from his works (photograph copyright 1986 by Dr. Peter Stummer)

gory to history and tradition, and "helps produce new ways of seeing history, new ways of 'reading' the world." Cooke complains about Lamming's "idiolectal scene-setting" and a certain "malaise [of] tendentiousness" in his mediation of history, and so does Paul Theroux (*Encounter*, May 1972). Others have no such reservations. Jan Carew, writing for the *New York Times Book Review* (27 February 1972), claims that it is Lamming's finest novel, "a profoundly revolutionary and original work" that illuminates new areas of the colonial past. Michael Gilkes finds it "an exceedingly complex work, full of allegorical and historical meanings and echoes . . . an embodiment of all his themes." Tiffin reads the novel as "a quasi-allegorical exploration of that early slave and colonial history which produced the twentieth century." Susan Craig expresses some reservations about Lamming's use of allegory but praises *Natives of My Person* as a major West Indian novel. Craig and Paquet emphasize Lamming's complex and insightful representation of the sexual politics of imperialism in their readings of the novel, and Jonas clarifies and expands the discourse of imperial conquest explicit in the allegorical configurations of the novel.

In 1974 Lamming edited and published an anthology of poetry and prose titled *Cannon Shot and*

Glass Beads. As he explains in his introduction, the book is a comparative survey of the black response to the politics and culture of white racism. The central theme of the volume is the encounter between Europe and Africa. It includes twenty-eight selections by black writers from Africa, the Caribbean, and the United States. Since editing this anthology Lamming has returned to the Caribbean. He lives in Barbados, where he continues work on two novels. One is set in Martinique after the fall of France in World War II. The other is about the social upheaval in the Caribbean in the 1930s and how it connects with the Caribbean today.

Meanwhile Lamming continues organizing, lecturing, and teaching in the Caribbean and overseas. In 1974 he was invited by the Barbados Workers' Union to organize celebrations for the opening of its Labor College. Under his direction the Barbados Writers' Workshop did a reenactment of the 1937 labor riots, which was titled *Meet Me at Golden Square.* In 1975 he was writer in residence at the University of Dar-es-Salaam and the University of Nairobi. In 1976 he was awarded a British Commonwealth Foundation grant. It was a traveling fellowship that took him to major universities in India and Australia. He has also been a visiting professor at the University of Texas at Austin, the University of Connecticut, the University of Pennsylvania, Cornell University, and the University of North Carolina. Despite the traveling, Lamming remains active in regional politics and culture. In September 1981 he was elected to the twelve-member Standing Committee of Intellectuals at the First Meeting of Intellectuals for the Sovereignty of the Peoples of Our America. He has also acted as the director of the fiction workshop at the University of Miami's Summer Institute for Caribbean Creative Writing. Lamming is an active, talented, committed writer who will continue to influence readers, critics, and students for many years to come. His view of Caribbean affairs and world history is a personal one but has always had universal appeal and relevance.

Interviews:

Ian Munro and Reinhard Sander, "Interview with George Lamming," in *Kas-Kas: Interviews with Three Caribbean Writers in Texas* (Austin: University of Texas, African and Afro-American Research Institute, 1972), pp. 5–22;

George E. Kent, "A Conversation with George Lamming," *Black World*, 22 (March 1973): 4–14, 88–97;

Robert Lee, "Caribbean Politics from 1930's to Tense 70's: A *Contact* Interview with the Author of *Natives of My Person*," *Caribbean Contact*, 5 (March 1978): 10–11;

Lowell Fiet, "Intersections and Divergences: Interview [with Lamming and Gordon K. Lewis]," *Sargasso*, 3 (1986): 3–30;

Yannick Tarrieu, "Caribbean Politics and Psyche: A Conversation with George Lamming," *Commonwealth Essays and Studies*, 10 (Spring 1988): 14–25;

Frank Birbalsingh, "George Lamming in Conversation with Frank Birbalsingh," *Journal of Commonwealth Literature*, 23, no. 1 (1988): 182–188.

Bibliographies:

George Lamming: A Select Bibliography (Cave Hill, Barbados: University of the West Indies, 1980);

Arturo Maldonado-Díaz, "George Lamming: A Descriptive Bibliography of Criticism and Reviews," *Journal of Commonwealth Literature*, 16, no. 2 (1982): 165–173.

References:

F. Aiyejina, "The Backward Glance: Lamming's *Season of Adventure* and Williams' *Other Leopards*," *African Literature Today*, 14 (1984): 118–126;

Bonnie Barthold, *Black Time: Fiction of Africa, the Car-*

ibbean and the United States (New Haven: Yale University Press, 1981), pp. 85–88, 150–157;

Edward Baugh, "Cuckoo and Culture: *In the Castle of My Skin*," *Ariel*, 8 (July 1977): 23–33;

Edward Kamau Brathwaite, "Jazz and the West Indian Novel," *Bim*, 11 (January–June 1967): 275–284; 12 (July–December 1967): 39–51; (January–June 1968): 115–126;

Brathwaite, "The New West Indian Novelists," *Bim*, 8 (July–December 1960): 199–210; (January–June 1961): 271–280;

Brathwaite, "West Indian Prose Fiction in the Sixties: A Survey," *Critical Survey* (Winter 1967): 169–174;

Carolyn T. Brown, "The Myth of the Fall and the Dawning of Consciousness in George Lamming's *In the Castle of My Skin*," *World Literature Today*, 57 (Winter 1983): 38–43;

Lloyd W. Brown, "The Crisis of Black Identity in the West Indian Novel," *Critique*, 11, no. 3 (1969): 97–112;

Brown, "The Isolated Self in West Indian Literature," *Caribbean Quarterly*, 23, nos. 2–3 (1977): 54–65;

Elaine Campbell, "Two West Indian Heroines: Bita Plant and Fola Piggott," *Caribbean Quarterly*, 29 (June 1983): 23–29;

Campbell, "West Indian Sea Fiction: George Lamming's *Natives of My Person*," *Commonwealth Novel in English*, 3 (Spring–Summer 1984): 56–65;

W. I. Carr, "Reflections on the Novel in the British Caribbean," *Queen's Quarterly*, 70 (Winter 1963–1964): 585–596;

Carr, "The West Indian Novelist," in *Consequences of Class and Color: West Indian Perspectives*, edited by David Lowenthal and Lambros Comitas (New York: Anchor/Doubleday, 1973), pp. 281–301;

Wilfred Cartey, "George Lamming and the Search for Freedom," *New World Quarterly: Barbados Independence Issue* (1966–1967): 121–128;

Cartey, *Whispers from the Caribbean: I Going Away, I Going Home* (Los Angeles: Center for Afro-American Studies, University of California, 1991);

Eugenia Collier, "Dimensions of Alienation in Two Black-American and Caribbean Novels," *Phylon*, 43 (March 1982): 46–56;

Michael Cooke, "The Strains of Apocalypse: Lamming's *Castle* and Brodber's *Jane and Louisa*," *Journal of West Indian Literature*, 4 (January 1990): 23–39;

Cooke, "A West Indian Novelist," *Yale Review*, 62 (Summer 1973): 616–624;

Carolyn Cooper, "Divergent Accounts of Slavery in Two Novels of Barbados," in *West Indian Literature and Its Social Context*, edited by Mark McWatt (Cave Hill, Barbados: University of the West Indies, 1985), pp. 3–11;

George R. Coulthard, *Race and Colour in Caribbean Literature* (London: Oxford University Press, 1962), pp. 105–106, 111–114;

Coulthard, "The West Indian Novel of Immigration," *Phylon*, 20 (1959): 32–41;

Susan Craig, "Some Notes and Reflections on Reading *Natives of My Person*," *Race Today*, 7 (January 1975): 21–22;

Selwyn R. Cudjoe, *Resistance and Caribbean Literature* (Athens: University of Ohio Press, 1980), pp. 179–211;

Michael Gilkes, *The West Indian Novel* (Boston: Twayne, 1981), pp. 86–115;

Gareth Griffiths, *A Double Exile: African and West Indian Writing Between Two Cultures* (London: Boyars, 1978), pp. 80–87, 91–106, 135–144;

Helmut Gunter, "George Lamming," *Black Orpheus*, 6 (November 1959): 39–43;

Stuart M. Hall, "Lamming, Selvon and Some Trends in the West Indian Novel," *Bim*, 6 (December 1955): 172–178;

Leonie B. Harris, "Myths in West Indian Consciousness: An Examination of George Lamming's *Natives of My Person*," in *Critical Issues in West Indian Literature*, edited by Erika Sollish Smilowitz and Roberta Quarles Knowles (Parkersburg, Iowa: Caribbean, 1984), pp. 46–53;

Louis James, "The Sad Initiation of Lamming's G and Other Caribbean Green Tales," in *Commonwealth*, edited by Anna Rutherford (Aarhus, Denmark: Akademisk Boghandel, 1972), pp. 135–143;

Joyce Jonas, *Anancy in the Great House: Ways of Reading West Indian Fiction* (New York: Greenwood, 1991), pp. 12–30, 58–71, 94–113;

Jonas, "Carnival Strategies in Lamming's *In the Castle of My Skin*," *Callaloo*, 11 (Spring 1988): 346–360;

Ambroise Kom, "George Lamming et la conscience historique," *Komparatistische Hefte*, 9–10 (1984): 115–121;

Kom, *George Lamming et le destin des Caraïbes* (Quebec City: Didier, 1986);

Kom, "*In the Castle of My Skin*: George Lamming and the Colonial Caribbean," *World Literature Written in English*, 18 (November 1979): 406–420;

Kom, "Londres des nègres dans *The Emigrants* et dans *Water with Berries* de George Lamming," *Etudes anglaises*, 34 (January–March 1981): 44–60;

Neil ten Kortenaar, "George Lamming's *In the Castle of My Skin*: Finding Promise in the Land," *Ariel*, 22 (April 1991): 43–53;

Charles Larson, *The Novel in the Third World* (Washington, D.C.: Inscape, 1976);

Gloria Lyn, "Once Upon a Time: Some Principles of Storytelling: *In the Castle of My Skin*," in *Critical Issues in West Indian Literature*, pp. 112–124;

Arturo Maldonado-Díaz, "Place and Nature in George Lamming's Poetry," *Revista/Review Interamericana*, 4 (Fall 1974): 402–410;

Avis McDonald, " 'Within the Orbit of Power': Reading Allegory in George Lamming's *Natives of My Person*," *Journal of Commonwealth Literature*, 22, no. 1 (1987): 73–86;

Gerald Moore, *The Chosen Tongue* (London: Longman, 1969);

Mervyn Morris, "The Poet as Novelist," in *The Islands in Between*, edited by Louis James (London: Oxford University Press, 1968), pp. 73–85;

Ian Munro, "The Early Work of George Lamming: Poetry and Short Prose, 1946–51," in *Neo-African Literature and Culture: Essays in Memory of Janheinz Jahn*, edited by Bernth Lindfors and Ulla Schild (Wiesbaden, Germany: Heymann, 1976), pp. 327–345;

Munro, "George Lamming," in *West Indian Literature*, edited by Bruce King (London: Macmillan, 1979), pp. 126–143;

Munro, "George Lamming's *Season of Adventure*: The Failure of the Creative Imagination," *Studies in Black Literature*, 4 (Spring 1973): 6–13;

Munro, "The Theme of Exile in George Lamming's *In the Castle of My Skin*," *World Literature Written in English*, 20 (November 1971): 51–60;

Ngugi wa Thiong'o, *Homecoming: Essays on African and Caribbean Literature, Culture and Politics* (London: Heinemann, 1972), pp. 110–144;

Margaret Nightingale, "George Lamming and V. S. Naipaul: Thesis and Antithesis," *ACLALS Bulletin*, 5 (December 1980): 40–50;

Rob Nixon, "Caribbean and African Appropriations of *The Tempest*," *Critical Inquiry*, 13 (Spring 1987): 557–578;

Elizabeth Nunez-Harrell, "Caliban: A Positive Symbol for Third World Writers," *Obsidian*, 8 (Summer/Winter 1982): 42–56;

Nunez-Harrell, "Lamming and Naipaul: Some Criteria for Evaluating the Third World Novel," *Contemporary Literature*, 19 (Winter 1978): 26–47;

Sandra Pouchet Paquet, Foreword to Lamming's *In the Castle of My Skin* (Ann Arbor: University of Michigan Press, 1991), pp. ix–xxxiii;

Paquet, Foreword to Lamming's *The Pleasures of Exile* (Ann Arbor: University of Michigan Press, 1992);

Paquet, *The Novels of George Lamming* (London: Heinemann, 1982);

Paquet, "The Politics of George Lamming's *Natives of My Person*," *College Language Association Journal*, 17 (September 1973): 109–116;

Kirsten Holst Petersen, "Time, Timelessness and the Journey Metaphor in George Lamming's *In the Castle of My Skin* and *Natives of My Person*," in *Commonwealth Writers Overseas*, edited by Alastair Niven (Brussels: Didier, 1976), pp. 283–288;

Kenneth Ramchand, "The Artist in the Balm-Yard: *Season of Adventure*," *New World Quarterly*, 5, nos. 1–2 (1969): 13–21;

Ramchand, *An Introduction to the Study of West Indian Literature* (Kingston, Jamaica: Nelson Caribbean, 1976), pp. 42–57;

Ramchand, "The Theatre of Politics," *Twentieth Century Studies*, 10 (December 1973): 20–36;

Ramchand, *The West Indian Novel and Its Background* (London: Faber & Faber, 1970);

Jeff Robinson, "Mother and Child in Three Novels by George Lamming," *Release*, 6 (1979): 75–83;

Gordon F. Rohlehr, "The Folk in Caribbean Literature," in *Critics on Caribbean Literature*, edited by Edward Baugh (New York: St. Martin's Press, 1978), pp. 27–30;

Stephen Slemon, "Post-Colonial Allegory and the Transformation of History," *Journal of Commonwealth Literature*, 23, no. 1 (1988): 157–168;

K. T. Sunitha, "The Theme of Childhood in *In the Castle of My Skin* and *Swami and Friends*," *World Literature Written in English*, 27 (Autumn 1987): 291–296;

Craig Tapping, "Children and History in the Caribbean Novel: George Lamming's *In the Castle of My Skin* and Jamaica Kincaid's *Annie John*," *Kunapipi*, 11, no. 2 (1989): 51–59;

Patrick Taylor, *The Narrative of Liberation: Perspectives on Afro-Caribbean Literature, Popular Culture, and Politics* (Ithaca, N.Y.: Cornell University Press, 1989), pp. 183–227;

Helen Tiffin, "Freedom after the Fall: Renaissance and Disillusion in *Water with Berries* and *Guerrillas*," in *Individual and Community in Commonwealth Literature*, edited by Daniel Massa (Malta: University Press, 1979), pp. 90–98;

Tiffin, "The Novels of George Lamming: Finding a Language for Post-Colonial Fiction," in *Essays on Contemporary Post-Colonial Fiction*, edited by Hedwig Bock and Albert Wertheim (Munich: Max Hueber Verlag, 1986), pp. 253–274;

Tiffin, "Post-Colonialism, Post-Modernism and the Rehabilitation of Post-Colonial History," *Journal of Commonwealth Literature*, 23, no. 1 (1988): 169–181;

Tiffin, "Rites of Resistance: Counter-Discourse and West Indian Biography," *Journal of West Indian Literature*, 3 (January 1989): 28–46;

Tiffin, "The Tyranny of History: George Lamming's *Natives of My Person* and *Water with Berries*," *Ariel*, 10 (October 1979): 37–52;

David D. West, "Lamming's Poetic Language in *In the Castle of My Skin*," *Literary Half-Yearly*, 18 (July 1977): 71–83;

Susan Willis, "Caliban as Poet: Reversing the Maps of Domination," *Massachusetts Review*, 23 (Winter 1982): 615–630;

Gloria Yarde, "George Lamming: The Historical Imagination," *Literary Half-Yearly*, 11 (July 1970): 35–45.

Earl Lovelace

(13 July 1935 –   )

Chezia Thompson-Cager
Smith College

BOOKS: *While Gods Are Falling* (London: Collins, 1965; Chicago: Regnery, 1966);

The Schoolmaster (London: Collins, 1968; Chicago: Regnery, 1968);

The Dragon Can't Dance (London: Deutsch, 1979; Washington, D.C.: Three Continents, 1981);

The Wine of Astonishment (London: Deutsch, 1982; New York: Vintage, 1984);

Jestina's Calypso, and Other Plays (London: Heinemann, 1984);

A Brief Conversion and Other Stories (Oxford: Heinemann, 1988).

PLAY PRODUCTIONS: *The New Boss*, Matura, Trinidad, 1962;

My Name Is Village, Port of Spain, Queens Hall, September 1976;

Pierrot Ginnard, Port of Spain, 1977;

Jestina's Calypso, Saint Augustine, Trinidad, University of the West Indies, 17 March 1978; revised, Northampton, Mass., Mendenhall Center for the Performing Arts, 21 April 1988;

The New Hardware Store, Saint Augustine, Trinidad, University of the West Indies, 21 March 1980;

The Dragon Can't Dance, Port of Spain, Queens Hall, 30 January 1986;

The Wine of Astonishment, Port of Spain, Queens Hall, February 1987.

OTHER: "Caribbean Folk Culture within the Process of Modernisation," in *El Caribe y América Latina*, edited by Ulrich Fleischmann and Ineke Phaf (Berlin: Vervuert, 1987), pp. 153–156;

The Dragon Can't Dance, in *Black Plays 2*, edited by Yvonne Brewster (London: Methuen, 1989).

SELECTED PERIODICAL PUBLICATIONS – UNCOLLECTED: "Plain Talk," *Voices*, 1, no. 1 (1964): 3–7;

"Ingratitude?," *Voices*, 1, no. 3 (1965): 13;

Earl Lovelace

"Engaging the World," *Wasafiri*, 1 (Autumn 1984): 3–4;

"Pan in Danger," *Trinidad and Tobago Express*, February 1985;

"Praise Singer of the West Indies – C. L. R. James," *South Magazine* (London, September 1985);

"The Problem Is One of Colour Rather than Race," *Trinidad and Tobago Express*, March 1989.

Among the many letters (in the Lovelace Archives in Port of Spain) documenting Earl Lovelace's public-service record is a letter labeled

"Memorandum Presented to the Right Honorable Dr. Eric Williams, Prime Minister, on Behalf of the Rio Claro Youth Organizations." Lovelace's letter elucidates both the method of his writing and the reason why he has become a powerful voice in Caribbean literature. He makes the following statement: "In our part of the nation, there has been domination by an element with a retrogressive, narrow, colonial outlook.... We believe that progress in a community is not measured only by what Government provides but chiefly by what the community is prepared to do for itself, to solve its own problems." This basic proposition translates itself as Lovelace's responsibility as a West Indian writer, or warrior, in combat with neocolonialism in any form. The argument for the enlightenment and growth of the West Indian community is the hallmark of Lovelace's work and the popular response to it. He is perceived in Trinidad as "a man of the people." In each of his works Lovelace argues against "retrogressive, narrow, colonial" concepts, while simultaneously revealing the community's and the individual's adaptation mechanisms for the reader to critique and modify. This demystification of the forces that manipulate daily life in Trinidad provides the subtext of the cinematic descriptions of the landscape and the lilting, rhythmic voices of the people inhabiting it.

Lovelace pursues the path to selfhood through his male and female characters with the brilliance of a linguist recording with precision the speech he has heard. Unlike many of his contemporaries, he has remained in Trinidad. His presence in the community has given him access to dramatic forms through which he has ultimately reached a wide audience in Trinidad, the United Kingdom, and America. All of Lovelace's writing and work displays an uncommon love for himself as a black man, for his language, for his people, and for their potential greatness.

Earl Lovelace's personal family history is shrouded in mystery, despite the quasi-autobiographical revelations in *A Brief Conversion and Other Stories* (1988). Nevertheless it is known that he was born in Toco, Trinidad, on 13 July 1935. Shortly thereafter he moved to Tobago, where he lived with his maternal grandparents. He remembers that his grandmother Eva Watley (a Saint Vincentian of African and Amerindian descent) and his mother, Jean Watley Lovelace, had a profound impact on his development during this period. Lovelace attended Scarborough Methodist Primary School in Tobago and the Nelson Street Boys Roman Catholic School in Port of Spain. He then went to Ideal High School

from 1948 to 1953 before moving to Centeno, Trinidad, to study at the Eastern Caribbean Institute of Agriculture and Forestry from 1961 to 1962. His first job was as a professional proofreader for the *Trinidad Guardian* from 1953 to 1954. Later as a government employee in the civil service, he served first in the Department of Forestry as a field assistant and then in the Department of Agriculture as an agricultural assistant from 1956 to 1966. Characters with the same professions appear in *A Brief Conversion and Other Stories*. Both positions allowed him to study the Trinidadian landscape and its people in great detail.

Lovelace was an agricultural assistant living with his family in Tobago when he won the British Petroleum Independence Literary Award in 1964 for the manuscript of his first novel, *While Gods Are Falling* (1965). In 1966 he was awarded the Pegasus Literary Award for outstanding contributions to the arts in Trinidad and Tobago. *The Schoolmaster* (1968), his second novel, was published after a year he spent in residence at Howard University in Washington, D.C., from 1966 to 1967. Moving his family, which then included his wife, Jean, two sons, Walt and Che, and a daughter, Lulu, to Port of Spain in 1967, Lovelace divided his time between novel writing and journalism as editorial writer, columnist, and reviewer for the daily *Trinidad and Tobago Express*.

From 1971 to 1973 he was a lecturer in the English department at the University of the District of Columbia in Washington and visiting novelist in residence at Johns Hopkins University in Baltimore, where he earned a master of arts degree in English. He began teaching literature and creative writing in the English department at the University of the West Indies at Saint Augustine in 1977. The recipient of a Guggenheim Fellowship in 1980, Lovelace was also invited to participate in the International Writing Program at the University of Iowa the same year and the International Seminar Program for the Eastern Virginia International Studies Consortium in 1981. He received a National Endowment for the Humanities grant as writer in residence at Hartwick College in Oneonta, New York, in 1986. His controversial *Wine of Astonishment* (1982), written in the voice of a woman named Eva, was completed before the earlier-published novel *The Dragon Can't Dance* (1979).

Lovelace began experimenting with folk drama as a method of positive community interaction in Tobago and Matura, Trinidad, before he moved to Port of Spain. His play *The New Boss* was performed from 1962 to 1964 in Trinidad and To-

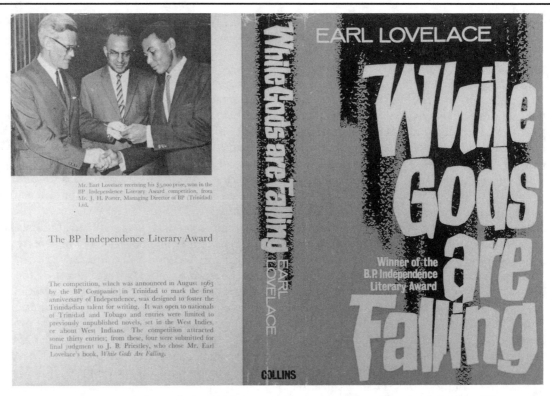

The BP Independence Literary Award

Mr. Earl Lovelace receiving his $5,000 prize, won in the BP Independence Literary Award competition, from Mr. J. H. Porter, Managing Director of BP (Trinidad) Ltd.

The competition, which was announced in August 1963 by the BP Companies in Trinidad to mark the first anniversary of Independence, was designed to foster the Trinidadian talent for writing. It was open to nationals of Trinidad and Tobago and entries were limited to previously unpublished novels, set in the West Indies, or about West Indians. The competition attracted some thirty entries; from these, four were submitted for final judgment to J. B. Priestley, who chose Mr. Earl Lovelace's book, *While Gods Are Falling*.

Dust jacket for Lovelace's first book, in which he presents the struggles of lower-class people in Port of Spain and their need to find "something to look up to"

bago. *My Name Is Village* won the Best Play Award and Best Music Award competition at its premiere performance in September 1976 at Queen's Hall, Port of Spain. It was performed by the villagers of Matura with Lovelace acting as director. The musical *Pierrot Ginnard* was produced in 1977 and followed by *Jestina's Calypso*, which blends Lovelace's talent for dialogue with a ritualistic use of space and cyclical approach to time. *Jestina's Calypso* was first performed by the University of the West Indies Players – under the direction of Gregory McGuire – on 17 March 1978 at the Saint Augustine campus. The play received mixed reviews, which lauded the issues that the play raised but criticized its interior-exterior stage structure. It had its American premiere on 21 April 1988 at the Mendenhall Center for the Performing Arts on the Smith College campus, under the direction of Chezia Thompson-Cager with a new prologue, musical score, and staging concept. *The New Hardware Store* opened as a production of the University of the West Indies Players on 21 March 1980 at Saint Augustine, under the direction of McGuire. The London performance of the play at the Camden Arts Theatre received good reviews during its week-long run in March 1985.

The Lovelace Archives collection contains manuscripts of plays that have yet to be produced, as well as scripts for dramatic readings and stage versions of some of the novels. *The Dragon Can't Dance* premiered on 1 February 1986 during the period preceding the annual carnival in Port of Spain. The play was the first venture of Dragon Productions – Lovelace's production company. A production of *The Wine of Astonishment* followed in spring 1988. A consistent blend of folk music, choreography, and ritual stylistically marks all Lovelace's plays and may account for why reviewers using a more European concept of drama often cite problems with dramatic movement and development.

A Brief Conversion and Other Stories is the first collection of many of the short stories in the Lovelace Archives. Lovelace currently teaches at the University of the West Indies in Trinidad and lectures and reads periodically at American and English universities.

Lovelace writes eloquently of a culture of resistance that has sprung up within black communities in Trinidad. However, his definition of this culture embraces all New World communities that utilize resistance as a survival strategy. The necessity for cultural, socioeconomic, and political resistance is central in the evolution of the major male character in each of his works. Lovelace's writing also incorporates a critique of societies that still regard the descendants of Africans as unequal participants in the political experiment called democracy.

The climaxes of Lovelace's novels, plays, and stories usually depend on two elements: the decision of one individual to be the person who makes the sacrifice that facilitates positive change within the community; and the emergence of a partnership or love relationship that strengthens or affirms familial and communal bonds. In addition any analysis of his work must take into account the milieu out of which he creates characters. His work avoids a stereotypical dissecting or deconstruction of reality; he reassembles the critical elements of his social environment in a format that is politically astute and culturally comprehensive.

Lovelace's *While Gods Are Falling* was written before he was married or became a permanent resident of Port of Spain, which may account for the utopian tone of the novel. The novel is narrated by alternating a chronicle of present events with the past. The structure reinforces the idealization of humankind as needing "something to look up to. Something outside of self, something bigger than self," as the narrator says. In the novel, that need has reduced Port of Spain to mass poverty, disorder, crime, fear, and a special, narrow way of thinking about life: "indeed, it is as if all Gods have fallen and there is nothing to look up to, no shrine to worship at, and man is left only bare flesh and naked passion."

The novel defines "the Gods" as the priests, police, magistrates, parents, teachers, and the values traditionally represented by words such as *family* and *community*. Like George Lamming's protagonist in *In the Castle of My Skin* (1953), Walter Castle in *While Gods Are Falling* feels imprisoned by his identity and stifled by the poverty into which his father's misfortune has cast the family. Walter's body and mind become the symbolic castle of the black Trinidadian who feels compelled to fortify himself against failure and mediocrity by cutting himself off from his community. The novel anticipates the basic themes, techniques, and characters Lovelace later isolates and develops in other novels. Readers see for the first time his use of the prologue to visualize an environment in great physical and emotional detail before the action of the story formally begins, as well as his preoccupation with the struggle of women trying to come to terms with their status in a "man's world."

In *The Schoolmaster* Lovelace turns from the brutal reality of the city to the idyllic existence of a remote Trinidadian village called Kumaca and warns against using colonial education as a fail-safe solution to the problems raised in *While Gods Are Falling*. Plantation owner Paulaine Dandrade envisions Kumaca as becoming a prosperous center of business and culture, and he foresees the need to educate all its citizens, but especially the young, including his daughter Christiana. Christiana is reminiscent of Castle's sisters, and she anticipates the more fully developed character Sylvia in *The Dragon Can't Dance*. Dandrade's vision is opposed by Constantine Patron as well as the local Catholic priest, Father Vincent. Patron concedes that change must come to Kumaca but maintains that it must be carefully orchestrated. Consequently he opposes the plan to put the education and reorientation of the village into the hands of strangers who neither know nor understand the villagers.

All the stock figures of the pastoral are represented faithfully. Dardain, the shopkeeper, brings metropolitan wily entrepreneurism and modern morals to the village. Pedro Assivero (a youthful laborer on the Dandrade estate) reiterates Lovelace's belief in the family as the fundamental unit of the society in his gentle courtship of Christiana. Both Father Vincent and the nameless schoolmaster are creatures apart. The foreshadowing of the schoolmaster's imperfections comes in a Bible verse read by the priest at a mass before the schoolmaster's arrival in Kumaca. The verse alerts the community to its responsibility to watch the schoolmaster, "lest ye enter into temptation. The spirit truly is ready, but the flesh is weak." When the mystery of who fathered Christiana's unborn child is solved at her death, questions about the place of traditional values and communal decision-making come into the discussion of progress and the choice of leadership. The schoolmaster confesses to rape but does not understand – since he tried to force her to marry him – that he is responsible for Christiana's suicide and must face the judgment of the community that loved her.

The survival strategies that Lovelace's characters employ do not always fit the pattern of logical behavior sanctioned by mainstream society. The concept of mainstreaming appears frequently in literature about urban societies of color in the United States. Lovelace's exploration of poor people's political hierarchical relationship with the power establishment in *The Dragon Can't Dance* comes painfully close to a desperate truth about both societies. Set in the troubled Port of Spain encountered in *While Gods Are Falling*, the novel reveals the impact of the characters known as the Dragon, the Badjohn, and the Calypsonian as innovators of strategies of resis-

Sheila M. Petigny as Jestina in an April 1988 production of Lovelace's play Jestina's Calypso *at the Mendenhall Center for the Performing Arts in Northampton, Massachusetts (photograph copyright 1988 by Ahzar Al-Uqdah)*

tance in a Trinidadian culture of poverty – described by Hyman Rodman in *Lower-Class Families: The Culture of Poverty in Negro Trinidad* (1971) and Michael Lieber in *Streetlife: Afro-American Culture in Urban Trinidad* (1981). Lovelace's novel challenges controversial assertions about the motives and methods that black men in the New World use to assert their personhood.

Aldrick Prospect as Dragon and Belasco John, or Fisheye, as Badjohn assume the power of men "to turn beast" and wreak havoc on their enemies. The Badjohn and the Dragon openly combat the attempts of oppressive elements of society to imprison them in what Bonnie Barthold in *Black Time* (1981) calls "the void of timeless estrangement." It is the legacy of the power of Dionysus – the lord of the carnival – to destroy as an act of re-creation and to dance as an act of power. Therefore, a dragon that cannot dance is not a dragon, not a force of power. In the novel, dancing becomes a metaphor for successful adaptation in Trinidadian society. To dance is to live, to experience the fullest realization of one's humanity and one's right to move in a world ordered by one's mortality: "Dancing is a chant that cuts off the power from the devil."

Using the ritual preparation and enactment of

the carnival to structure the plot, Lovelace introduces the major characters and their problematic intertwined lives in successive chapters. Again the ways in which characters are paired argues for the importance of family, however unorthodoxly defined, and the viability of love relationships as a political base from which to create a new social order. Aldrick as Dragon and Street Prince extraordinaire has emotionally isolated himself in a material and spiritual poverty, which Sylvia as the community Princess challenges. The Dragon is a classical carnival character in Trinidad that represents the spirit of black people to resist political and social disenfranchisement in a society favoring the white, the wealthy, and the educated. Aldrick's occupation as Street Prince means the community both loves and takes care of him in exchange for his commitment to represent them – to do battle for them in the arena of the carnival. The Princess, as an archetype of the feminine in the New World, is perceived as a virginal young woman, a beautiful and fragile example of femininity at risk in an environment "where the gods have fallen." She represents light, life, and energy in a war zone where the battle is simply to survive, eat, and sleep.

Dolly and Pariag constitute an East Indian

family living in the margin between native black and East Indian societies in Trinidad. The two characters struggle to redefine the nature of marriage in a modern New World society in which cultural norms are no longer prescribed. Cleothilda, the shopkeeper and aging mulatto leader of the Calvary Hill Steelband, confronts ingrained class and color-caste prejudices in her relationship with the black-skinned calypsonian Philo. The tradition of calypso as the origin of political rap, the living record of the history of struggle of the people, is a legacy Philo abandons to become the mouthpiece for contrived musical fantasies beginning with the sexually provocative "Axe Man" calypso. His choice of this role provides a way for him to acquire the affection and sexual favors of Cleothilda at great cost to himself and his culture.

Fisheye as Badjohn, in his relationship to Yvonne, enacts the tragedy of unsuccessful adaptation in the migration from the country to the city — from nineteenth-century machismo and chauvinism in defining gender roles to latter-twentieth-century neocolonialism, which functions on its own behalf. The novel explores the lives of the couples as they struggle to survive as individuals and families in an era when the Dragon can no longer dance a symbolic resistance. The Dragon chooses to become Aldrick and accept the real challenges, to brave real dangers in the dance of life in support of the society that loves him.

In *The Wine of Astonishment* Lovelace returns to the Trinidadian countryside to the town of Bonasse, but takes readers back in history to the time of the persecution of the Spiritual Baptists. On 28 November 1917 the colonial government approved a bill that targeted the Spiritual Baptists as religious heretics and prohibited them from practicing certain aspects of their African/New World syncretized religion. The Spiritual Baptists suffered open political and social persecution until the minister of education and social services, R. A. Joseph, proposed a bill on 30 March 1951 to "remove from the Statute Books of the Colony an Ordinance entitled the Shouters Ordinance, Chapter 4, Section 19." *The Wine of Astonishment* chronicles the survival of one Spiritual Baptist church during the period of persecution and teaches a clear lesson on the impact of the American military occupation in Trinidad during the same era.

As Marjorie Thorpe notes in the introduction to the 1983 Heinemann edition of the novel, Lovelace's use of the first-person feminine voice of Eva, the Mother of the Church, is a significant departure from Lovelace's third-person narration in

the other novels. His handling of Eva's language and character is indeed a masterful representation of "a simple country peasant" whose sense of the collective body of the church and community flows through her account of herself and her family. However, Lovelace does not always convince the reader that the perspective is feminine, especially in Eva's accounts of her interaction with her husband and sons. What readers learn about her feelings from her narration has to be read as subtext, as she focuses on describing the environment and history controlling her life.

The three plays in the collection *Jestina's Calypso* (1984) dramatize problems that Lovelace has isolated in his newspaper editorials or in his public-service work. The play *Jestina's Calypso* is about a woman named Jestina who cannot get anyone to marry her. She has been writing to an expatriate Trinidadian who decides to return to his native land and marry her. Her anxiety causes her to mislead him by sending a picture of her more-European-looking neighbor, Laura, to represent her own beauty. The denouement that takes place when Laura and Jestina go to meet him is presented as a play inside the play, acted out by other neighbors who have been mocking her all day. Black men lead the tirade of laughter against Jestina, and Lovelace suggests that black men must lead the movement to accept the diversity of black people, which includes having more than one standard of feminine beauty. Structurally problematic, with the dual-set staging and the simultaneous talking in the script, in addition to the problem of balancing the voices, the play is still one of the few that directly confront this important issue.

The New Hardware Store portrays one set of answers to Lovelace's challenge to Trinidadians to improve their lives and communities. Change has occurred in *The New Hardware Store*, but whether or not it is improvement is the focus of the play. A. A. Black has acquired the business and its employees from its previous white owner, after a political protest by black Trinidadians that Lovelace describes fully in "The Coward," a story in *A Brief Conversion and Other Stories*. The protesters demand economic parity with the white English expatriates and are given token concessions that allow designated blacks to be assimilated into the middle class. However A. A. Black's attempts at capitalism do not appear to make a significant difference in the lives of his middle-aged bookkeeper, Calliste; his advertising agent and night watchman turned calypsonian, Rooso; or his promising, young, educated assistant, Miss Prime. How they finally reach a consensus on how to work together for the shared benefit of the community makes for a humorous plot.

My Name Is Village delivers an allegorical blow to the concept of Western progress in the form of urbanization, symbolized by Mr. Towntest, the exponent of progress. Like the rural youths in *The Schoolmaster* and *The Wine of Astonishment* and many of the stories in *A Brief Conversion and Other Stories*, the youths in this play are restless to experience life outside of their country-village existence. Roy Village, like his antagonist Elena, believes that his future lies in the world of Mr. Towntest. Elena's education is designed to get her out of the village, but Roy is trapped in village life and must begin to chart a future there instead of planning to escape. When Roy manhandles Elena because she will not pay any attention to him, Cyril Village, who has recovered his dignity and authority in a stick fight, confronts him with the idea of love for his island home, doing so in beautiful lyrical language with the emotional tonality that crosses the boundaries of language and cultural difference. Roy is reconciled with Elena in a remarkable scene of masculine sensitivity. He tells her, "Look I bring these flowers for you Elena. A man is flowers too and I sorry." The musical interludes provide essential transitions between the actions of the characters in the play and (like the other plays) require a knowledge of the Trinidadian cultural music tradition to produce. Lovelace's plays are, in the best sense of the phrase, morality plays, structured around the folk-cultural, performing-arts tradition indigenous to Trinidad. Structurally they invite comparison to plays such as Wole Soyinka's *The Lion and the Jewel* (1959) and *Death and the King's Horseman* (1976), Langston Hughes's *Black Nativity* (1961), or Bob Telson and Lee Breuer's more modern *Gospel at Colonus* (1985).

A Brief Conversion and Other Stories brings together previously published stories as well as new work. The stories focus generally on the advent of modernity in Trinidad as seen through the eyes of individuals who remain in the country or move from the country to the city. The tone of the story "A Brief Conversion" is autobiographical, as Lovelace details the confrontation of an adolescent youth with conflicting definitions of manhood. The youth is only momentarily converted to an ideal that works against his personality. Nevertheless the process teaches him to appreciate his parents' struggle to love him and provide for the family. It teaches him respect for life and a willingness to fight to preserve dignity.

Lovelace is master of what Henry Louis Gates in *The Signifying Monkey* (1988) calls "the paradox of

representing, of containing somehow, the oral within the written." The stories and novels speak in distinct codes, codifying black history and tradition in Trinidad. They chronicle with great detail and emotional clarity the problem of being a threat to the ancient, fundamental prejudices of a society born out of slavery. Lovelace's literature speaks to "the folk" in any country in the twentieth century, reproducing their voices and their concerns. His work is in the best tradition of art that helps a society see and educate itself and its young.

Interviews:

Victor D. Questel, "Views of Earl Lovelace," *Caribbean Contact*, 5 (June 1977): 15–16;

Peter Fraser and E. A. Markham, "Just Talking: Interview," *Artrage*, 13 (Summer 1986): 4–5;

Maya Jaggi, "Interview: Earl Lovelace," *Wasafiri*, 12 (Autumn 1990): 25–27;

H. Nigel Thomas, "From 'Freedom' to 'Liberation': An Interview with Earl Lovelace," *World Literature Written in English*, 31 (Spring 1991): 8–20.

Bibliography:

Chezia Thompson-Cager, "Earl Lovelace: A Bibliography," *Contributions in Black Studies*, 8 (1986–1987): 101–105.

References:

Harold Barratt, "Metaphor and Symbol in *The Dragon Can't Dance*," *World Literature Written in English*, 23 (Spring 1984): 405–413;

Barratt, "Michael Anthony and Earl Lovelace: The Search for Selfhood," *ACLALS Bulletin*, 5 (December 1980): 62–73;

Edward Kamau Brathwaite, "Priest and Peasant," *Journal of Commonwealth Literature*, 7 (July 1969): 117–122;

Diana Brydon, "Trusting the Contradictions: Competing Ideologies in Earl Lovelace's *The Dragon Can't Dance*," *English Studies in Canada*, 15 (September 1989): 319–335;

Norman Reed Cary, "Salvation, Self, and Solidarity in the Work of Earl Lovelace," *World Literature Written in English*, 28 (Spring 1988): 103–114;

Carolyn Cooper, Introduction to Lovelace's *The Dragon Can't Dance* (London: Longman, 1985), pp. 9–21;

H. H. Anniah Gowda, "A Brief Note on the Dialect Novels of Sam Selvon and Earl Lovelace," *Literary Half-Yearly*, 27 (July 1986): 98–103;

Jenny Green, "Moving Spirit – *The Wine of Astonishment* by Earl Lovelace," *Race Today* (May/June 1982): 110;

Robert Hamner, "The Measure of the 'Yard Novel': From Mendes to Lovelace," *Commonwealth Essays and Studies*, 9 (Autumn 1986): 98–105;

Steve Harney, "Nation Time: Earl Lovelace and Michael Anthony Nationfy Trinidad," *Commonwealth Essays and Studies*, 13 (Spring 1991): 31–41;

Louis James, "Making the Dragon Dance," *Wasafiri*, 1 (Autumn 1984): 13–15;

Evelyn O'Callaghan, "The Modernization of the Trinidadian Landscape in the Novels of Earl Lovelace," *Ariel*, 20 (January 1989): 41–54;

Margarita Mateo Palmer, "Earl Lovelace, *The Dragon Can't Dance*," *Anales del Caribe*, 2 (1982): 308–315;

Helen Pyne-Timothy, "Earl Lovelace: His View of Trinidad Society in *While Gods Are Falling* and *The Schoolmaster*," *New World Quarterly*, 4 ("Cropover" 1968): 60–65;

Kenneth Ramchand, "Indian-African Relations in Caribbean Fiction Reflected in Earl Lovelace's *The Dragon Can't Dance*," *Wasafiri*, 1 (Spring 1985): 18–23;

Ramchand, Introduction to Lovelace's *The Schoolmaster* (London: Heinemann, 1979), pp. v–xvii;

Angelita Reyes, " 'All o' We Is One' or Carnival as Ritual of Resistance: *The Dragon Can't Dance*," in *African Literature in Its Social and Political Dimensions*, edited by Eileen Julien and others (Washington, D.C.: Three Continents, 1986), pp. 59–68;

Reyes, "Carnival: Ritual Dance of the Past and Present in Earl Lovelace's *The Dragon Can't Dance*," *World Literature Written in English*, 24 (Summer 1984): 107–120;

K. T. Sunitha, "The Discovery of Selfhood in the Fiction of Earl Lovelace," in *Subjects Worthy of Fame: Essays in Commonwealth Literature in Honor of H. H. Anniah Gowda*, edited by A. L. McLeod (New Delhi: Sterling, 1989), pp. 123–132;

H. Nigel Thomas, " 'Progress' and Community in the Novels of Earl Lovelace," *World Literature Written in English*, 31 (Spring 1991): 1–7;

Chezia Thompson-Cager, "The Dialectical Voices of Black Men: An Analysis of Giant Talk," *Fairfax Magazine*, 2 (Winter 1991): 93–100;

Thompson-Cager, "Earl Lovelace's Bad Johns, Street Princes and the Masters of Schools," in *Imagination, Emblems, and Expressions*, edited by Helen Ryan (Bowling Green, Ohio: Bowling Green State University Popular Press, 1992), pp. 213–229;

Marjorie Thorpe, "In Search of the West Indian Hero: A Study of Earl Lovelace's Fiction," in *Critical Issues in West Indian Literature*, edited by Erika Sollish Smilowitz and Roberta Quarles Knowles (Parkersburg, Iowa: Caribbean, 1984), pp. 90–100;

Thorpe, Introduction to Lovelace's *The Wine of Astonishment* (London: Heinemann, 1983), pp. vii–xiv;

Maureen Warner-Lewis, "Rebels, Tyrants and Saviours: Leadership and Power Relations in Lovelace's Fiction," *Journal of West Indian Literature*, 2 (December 1987): 76–89;

David Williams, "The Artist as Revolutionary: Political Commitment in *The Dragon Can't Dance* and *Interim*," in *West Indian Literature and Its Social Context*, edited by Mark McWatt (Cave Hill, Barbados: UWI Department of English, 1985), pp. 141–147.

Papers:
The Lovelace Archives are in Port of Spain, Trinidad.

Roger Mais
(11 August 1905 – 21 June 1955)

Kamau Brathwaite
New York University

BOOKS: *Face, and Other Stories* (Kingston, Jamaica: Universal Printery, 1942);

And Most of All Man (Kingston, Jamaica: City Printery, 1942);

The Hills Were Joyful Together (London: Cape, 1953; Kingston, Jamaica: Heinemann, 1981);

Brother Man (London: Cape, 1954; London & Kingston, Jamaica: Heinemann, 1974);

Black Lightning (London: Cape, 1955; London & Exeter, N.H.: Heinemann, 1983);

Listen, the Wind and Other Stories, edited by Kenneth Ramchand (Harlow, U.K.: Longman, 1986).

Collection: *The Three Novels of Roger Mais* (London: Cape, 1966) – comprises *The Hills Were Joyful Together, Brother Man*, and *Black Lightning.*

OTHER: *George William Gordon: A Historical Play in 14 Scenes,* in *A Time . . . and a Season: 8 Caribbean Plays*, edited by Errol Hill (Trinidad: University of the West Indies, Extramural Studies Unit, 1976), pp. 1–92.

SELECTED PERIODICAL PUBLICATIONS – UNCOLLECTED:

POETRY

"All Men Come to the Hills," *Yearbook of the Poetry League of Jamaica* (1940);

"Men of Ideas," *Focus* (1948);

"Epitaph (From 'Deirdre')," "Last Night I Was Aweary of the Wind (From 'Comedy Above the Stars')," "Last Night When It Was Very Still (from 'Deirdre')," "Static (From 'Deirdre')," and "I Shall Wait for the Moon to Rise," *Kyk-over-al*, 20 (Mid-Year 1955): 149–152.

DRAMA

The Potter's Field, Public Opinion (23 December 1950);

The First Sacrifice, Focus (1956): 186–211.

FICTION

"The White Wing," *Focus* (1943): 16–23;

Roger Mais

"The House of the Pomegranate," *Focus* (1948): 100–126;

"You Gotta Go Home," *Bim*, 3 (June 1950): 336–337;

"The Springing," *Kyk-over-al*, 20 (Mid-Year 1955): 153–157.

NONFICTION

"Now We Know," *Public Opinion* (14 July 1944);

"Why I Love and Leave Jamaica," *Public Opinion* (10 June 1966): 3.

Roger Mais was born on 11 August 1905 in

Kingston, Jamaica, into a "brown," respectable, middle-range-landowning, middle-class family and came to maturity in the 1930s, when these inherited categories were coming under pressure due to the sociopolitical changes of the time. That Mais had not only the artistic gift but made the decision to develop that gift into a life of letters was, at the time he began writing, still unusual for a West Indian, let alone a brown, middle-class man. It involved him in learning about the black underclass with the kind of innocent but informed creative attention that made it possible to report back accurately in the three novels that were published toward the sudden end of his short life (he died of cancer at age forty-nine). It also involved him in the kind of political commitment and cultural reorientation that not only inform the novels but caused him literally to change sides during the workers' antihardship and anticolonial uprisings of 1938, when, in the middle of his going to enlist as an antiriot special constable, he joined the freedom fighters instead. This commitment brought him to write the anti-British satirical tirade "Now We Know" (1944), which resulted in his suffering six months of imprisonment in the Spanish Town Penitentiary. Above all, this conversion/commitment to the black, underprivileged majority of his country hooked Mais, especially as a creative writer, into a search for a nativist aesthetic, which he pursued until the day he died.

Mais began as a journalist and contributor of short stories, plays, reviews, and "think pieces" for the left-wing political/cultural journal *Public Opinion* from 1939 to 1952, when he left Jamaica soon after he learned that *The Hills Were Joyful Together* (1953), his first published novel, had been accepted by Jonathan Cape in London. In quick succession there followed *Brother Man* (1954) and *Black Lightning* (1955), the three novels forming a kind of trilogy. They were collected in one volume in 1966.

Mais had gone to Europe – London, Paris, and the south of France – not to "find" but to fulfill himself. He hired a literary agent, assumed a nom de plume (Kingsley Croft), and presented an art exhibition in Paris under the patronage of Richard Wright and André Breton (there had been earlier exhibitions of Mais's work in Jamaica); his publishers used his illustrations in and on the covers of the first editions of his three novels.

Mais's lasting contribution to Caribbean literature lies in those novels and, from an aesthetic point of view, in some of the large quantity of unpublished material that now forms the Roger Mais Special Collection at the University of the West Indies Library at Mona, Jamaica.

Cover for the 1974 Heinemann edition of Mais's second novel. He was the first Jamaican novelist to write about the powerful influence of the Rastafarians.

The Hills Were Joyful Together is the first Jamaican "yard" novel: several families and individuals rent rooms in a collection of ramshackle houses (shacks) enclosed in a characteristic African compoundlike space, the houses forming a square with a yard in the middle, a kind of theater where the public life of the tenement takes place. The Trinidadian writers C. L. R. James and Alfred Mendes had already written about such yards a generation before but not with Mais's sense of duality and drama.

In *Brother Man* Mais makes a dramatic change from his earlier style of narrative reportage with chorus effects into a remarkably structured "jazz novel" (as Edward Kamau Brathwaite calls it in his introduction to the 1974 Heinemann edition of *Brother Man*), where words are "notes" that develop into riffs, themes, and "choruses," themselves part of a call/response design based on the aesthetic principle of solo/duo/trio improvisations, with a return, at the end of each "chorus," to the basic group/ensemble/community.

In addition Mais was the first Jamaican writer to bring into the novel the powerful subterranean influence of Rastafarianism, the Jamaican religious and cultural phenomenon that first appeared in the 1930s, part of the anticolonial push for a new Jamaica — a new African Jamaica. The Rastas claimed descent from the "Lion of Judah" and marked their "birth" as being simultaneous with Prince Ras Tafari's ascension to the Ethiopian throne, when he was renamed Emperor Haile Selassie I. Brother Man, the protagonist of the novel, is not the "dread" figure that some Rastafarians would soon become (as in Orlando Patterson's *The Children of Sisyphus*, 1964) but rather a benign Christ figure, in keeping with Mais's own aesthetic iconography — the quest for transcendent "mythopoets" in whom individualism would be eventually subsumed.

In Mais's last published novel, *Black Lightning*, the mythopoetic idea is larger than ever, represented by Jake, the blacksmith and secret sculptor, and even more so by the "Samson" he is carving out of a huge block of mahogany. But the Gnostic nature of his enterprise is signaled by the relative lack of detail about the act of carving and its inevitable collapse; he chops it up for firewood.

Most critics and commentators believe Mais was interested in symbols stemming almost exclusively from the stories about biblical characters (Samson, David and Bathsheba, Joshua, Judas, and Lazarus) and from Greek mythology (Zeus, Apollo, and Aulis). But the reinterpretation of the iconography of *Brother Man* as "jazz" and Rastafarian — involving the search for a New World aesthetic and form of expression — is fruitful. It has in turn led to a reinterpretation of *Black Lightning* as a search for ancestral (African) symbolism, which (because of his class and education) Mais might not have known much about but which (because of his nativist commitment) he felt he ought to explore. And this exploration, surely, must have been influenced by the long tradition of Jamaican black consciousness, mediated through the Bible and Greek mythology and the affinity of these with African/ancestral beliefs.

In *Black Lightning* the title term, though widely used among contemporary Rastas to mean "black transcendence," is not used by Mais in the Rastafarian sense but in the traditional African sense of the "negative — or visual imprint — of the (blinding) face of god." The god in this case is Shango, *orisha* (god) of thunder and lightning, who, in Yoruba tra-

dition, is a blacksmith and brother of Ogun (also a blacksmith and sculptor). According to legend, sometimes Shango is mistaken for Jakuta, the stone thrower.

Mais's choice of a blacksmith and carver deeply involved with thunder and lightning and called Jake thus seems meaningful. One can add to this matrix the continuing Shango legend that his wife, Oya, goddess of the Niger, was said to have had such an influence over him that he could do nothing without her — which is apparently the case with Jake's wife, Estella, or so she says. Shango was a mortal king who dared to become a god. Like Jake and the legendary Prometheus, Shango wanted the "lightning," in other words to see God's face, this desire being evidence of what Wole Soyinka has called Shango's "destructive egotism." Who in *Black Lightning* is more destructively egotistical than Jake?

The novel fails, though, because Mais, like Jake, abandoned an enterprise (Africanism) that he was not fundamentally happy with, that he did not or could not at that time properly understand. But the attempt helps readers recognize that, though it failed, it was part of a theme, judging from the Mais archives, with which he was deeply involved (the combination of biblical, Greek, Gnostic, agnostic, and African symbols in Jamaican culture).

All Mais's published novels had been written before he left Jamaica for Europe, and they represent the mature and optimistic phase of his career. He began his ancestral research with the European roots of Jamaican culture but developed an increasing awareness that Africa had to be included to make sense of his country's plural society. *Black Lightning* was the result.

As well as the ancestral, he was interested in the creole, the political reconstructionism of the 1930s, and the sociocultural problems of the "yards." There was a need for a nativist aesthetic. Many at that time were asking and writing about West Indian culture, and by 1948 there was the University of the West Indies; there was also renewed talk of self-government and the new, exciting prospect of a West Indian federation; and writers, artists, and intellectuals from the region were beginning to reflect this optimistic future and to search for forms to give it a local face. *The Hills Were Joyful Together* and *Brother Man* are Mais's contribution to this movement. *Brother Man*, certainly, is a major contribution to a nativist aesthetic.

When he left for London, Roger Mais was probably hoping to consolidate his achievements. Like the other West Indian novelists then gathering in London, he must have been hoping to extend his concerns into the cosmopolitan and the international. His untimely death from cancer (in Jamaica in 1955) ended those aspirations.

Interview:

Andrew Dakers, *John O'London Weekly* (1 May 1953).

References:

Edward Kamau Brathwaite, Introduction to Mais's *Brother Man* (London & Kingston, Jamaica: Heinemann, 1974), pp. v–xxi;

Brathwaite, "The Unborn Body of the Life of Fiction: Roger Mais' Aesthetics with Special Reference to *Black Lightning*," *Journal of West Indian Literature*, 2 (December 1987): 11–36; (October 1988): 33–35;

Bill Carr, "Roger Mais: Design from a Legend," *Caribbean Quarterly*, 13 (March 1967): 3–28;

Jean Creary, "A Prophet Armed: The Novels of Roger Mais," in *The Islands in Between*, edited by Louis James (London: Oxford University Press, 1968), pp. 50–63;

Oscar R. Dathorne, "Roger Mais: The Man on the Cross," *Studies in the Novel*, 1 (Summer 1972): 275–283;

Barrie Davies, "The Novels of Roger Mais," *International Fiction Review*, 1, no. 2 (1974): 140–43;

Jean D'Costa, Introduction to Mais's *Black Lightning* (London & Exeter, N.H.: Heinemann, 1983), pp. 7–22;

D'Costa, *Roger Mais: "The Hills Were Joyful Together" and "Brother Man"* (London: Longman, 1978);

Winnifred Grandison, "The Prose Style of Roger Mais," *Jamaica Journal*, 8 (March 1974): 48–54;

Evelyn J. Hawthorne, *The Writer in Transition: Roger Mais and the Decolonization of Caribbean Culture* (New York: Lang, 1989);

John Hearne, "The Persistence of Mais," *Jamaica Journal*, 22 (May–July 1989): 57–58;

Hearne, "Roger Mais: A Personal Memoir," *Bim*, 6 (December 1955): 146–150;

R. M. Lacovia, "Roger Mais and the Problem of Freedom," *Black Academy Review*, 1 (Fall 1970): 45–54;

George Lamming, "Tribute to a Tragic Jamaican," *Bim*, 6 (January–June 1957): 242–244;

Rupert Lewis, "Roger Mais' Work as Social Protest and Comment," *Public Opinion* (6 March 1967);

Daphne Morris, Introduction to *The Hills Were Joyful Together* (Kingston, Jamaica: Heinemann, 1981), pp. iii–xix;

Kenneth Ramchand, "The Achievement of Roger Mais," in his *The West Indian Novel and Its Background* (London: Faber & Faber, 1970), pp. 179–188;

Ramchand, "*The Hills Were Joyful Together*," in his *An Introduction to the Study of West Indian Literature* (Kingston, Jamaica: Nelson Caribbean, 1976), pp. 13–26;

Ramchand, Introduction to *Listen, the Wind and Other Stories* (Harlow, U.K.: Longman, 1986), pp. vi–xxxii;

Sydney Singh, "*The Hills Were Joyful Together*: Art and Society," *World Literature Written in English*, 29 (Spring 1989): 110–120;

Marjorie Thorpe, *Roger Mais, "Brother Man"* (Harlow, U.K.: Longman, 1979);

Karina Williamson, "Roger Mais: West Indian Novelist," *Journal of Commonwealth Literature*, 2 (December 1966): 138–147;

Fred Wilmot, "Roger Mais," *Kyk-over-al*, 33/34 (April 1986): 134–138.

Papers:

The Roger Mais Special Collection at the University of the West Indies Library, Mona, Jamaica, includes Mais's journalism, unpublished manuscripts and typescripts, exercise books, xerographic copies of his contributions to *Public Opinion*, clippings, and other miscellaneous material.

Ali A. Mazrui

(24 February 1933 –)

Omari H. Kokole
State University of New York at Binghamton

BOOKS: *The Anglo-African Commonwealth* (Oxford & New York: Pergamon, 1967);

On Heroes and Uhuru-Worship (London: Longmans, 1967);

Towards a Pax Africana (London: Weidenfeld & Nicolson, 1967; Chicago: University of Chicago Press, 1967);

Violence and Thought (London & Harlow, U.K.: Longmans, 1969; New York: Humanities, 1969);

The Trial of Christopher Okigbo (London: Heinemann, 1971; New York: Third Press, 1972);

Cultural Engineering and Nation-Building in East Africa (Evanston, Ill.: Northwestern University Press, 1972);

World Culture and the Black Experience (Seattle: University of Washington Press, 1974);

Soldiers and Kinsmen in Uganda: The Making of a Military Ethnocracy (Beverly Hills, Cal. & London: Sage, 1975);

The Political Sociology of the English Language: An African Perspective (The Hague & Paris: Mouton, 1975);

A World Federation of Cultures: An African Perspective (New York: Free Press, 1976);

Africa's International Relations: The Diplomacy of Dependency and Change (London: Heinemann / Boulder, Colo.: Westview, 1977);

Political Values and the Educated Class in Africa (London: Heinemann, 1978; Berkeley: University of California Press, 1978);

The African Condition: A Political Diagnosis (London: Heinemann, 1980; New York: Cambridge University Press, 1980);

Nationalism and New States in Africa, by Mazrui and Michael Tidy (London, Nairobi & Portsmouth, N.H.: Heinemann, 1984);

The Africans: A Triple Heritage (Boston: Little, Brown, 1986; London: BBC, 1986);

Cultural Forces in World Politics (London: Currey / Portsmouth, N.H.: Heinemann, 1990).

Ali A. Mazrui, 1986 (photograph: BBC Enterprises)

TELEVISION: *The Africans* [series], BBC, 1986.

OTHER: *Protest and Power in Black Africa*, edited by Mazrui and Robert I. Rotberg (New York: Oxford University Press, 1970);

Africa in World Affairs: The Next Thirty Years, edited by Mazrui and Hasu H. Patel (New York: Third Press, 1973); republished as *Africa: The Next Thirty Years* (Lewes, U.K.: Friedmann, 1974);

"State of the Globe Report, 1977," *Alternatives*, special issue, 3 (December 1977), edited, with contributions, by Mazrui;

The Warrior Tradition in Modern Africa, edited, with contributions, by Mazrui (Leiden, Netherlands: Brill, 1977);

The Africans: A Reader, edited by Mazrui and T. K. Levine (New York: Praeger, 1986).

SELECTED PERIODICAL PUBLICATIONS – UNCOLLECTED: "Nkrumah: The Leninist Czar," *Transition*, 4, no. 26 (1966): 9–17;

"The Poetics of a Transplanted Heart," *Transition*, 7, no. 35 (1968): 51–59;

"Miniskirts and Political Puritanism," *Africa Report*, 13 (October 1968): 9–12;

"Zionism and Apartheid: Strange Bedfellows or Natural Allies?," *Alternatives*, 9 (Summer 1983): 73–97;

"The Third World and International Terrorism: Preliminary Reflections," *Third World Quarterly*, 7 (April 1985): 348–364.

Ali A. Mazrui is one of the most prolific and most controversial African writers. He has addressed a wide spectrum of issues and ideas, and his publications reveal the fertility of his mind, his imaginative powers, and his immense capacity for intellectual work. His writings in political science can be grouped in the following broad categories: comparative politics; international relations; political theory and philosophy; sociology; and sociolinguistics and literary studies. To Mazrui's critics his high productivity is a defect rather than an asset. How can one shift from an analysis called "The Poetics of a Transplanted Heart" (an article Mazrui wrote in 1968 for *Transition*, based in Kampala) to an investigation of "Miniskirts and Political Puritanism" (*Africa Report*, October 1968)? Is Mazrui's writing speed and range intellectually dangerous? The burden of proof rests with those who would claim that writing slowly results in greater profundity and depth. Those scholars (African as well as non-African) who have been rather slow in writing have not necessarily produced more impressive contributions than Mazrui. Yet some of Mazrui's detractors ("professional Mazrui bashers," as he prefers to call them) contend that his compulsion to write and lecture relentlessly reveals a major weakness – the tendency not to engage in research and to gather data before putting his scholarly observations and thoughts into writing.

The son of Al'Amin Ali Mazrui, a judge of Islamic law, and Safia Suleiman Mazrui, Ali Al'Amin Mazrui was born in Mombasa, Kenya, on 24 February 1933. After receiving his early education in local schools, Mazrui left for England to study at Huddersfield College of Technology in Yorkshire; then he attended the University of Manchester, where he earned his B.A. in 1960. Having won a Rockefeller Foundation fellowship, he went to Columbia University in New York, receiving his M.A. in 1961. He then returned to England and began working for the BBC as an associate political analyst, a job he held on a part-time basis from 1962 to 1965, also writing and broadcasting for Radio Uganda and Radio Tanzania during 1964 and 1965. Mazrui earned his D.Phil. at Oxford University in 1966. Beginning in 1963 he had lived in Kampala, Uganda, and taught political science at Makerere University, where he became head of the department in 1965, then (after his return from Oxford) dean of the Faculty of Social Sciences in 1967. Mazrui also taught in the United States as a visiting professor at several schools, including the University of Chicago, Northwestern, UCLA, and Harvard. In 1973 he accepted a full-time professorship in political science at the University of Michigan. In 1989 he was appointed Albert Schweitzer Professor in the Humanities at the State University of New York at Binghamton, where he lives with his wife, Pauline Uti Mazrui, a teacher from Nigeria. He also directs the Institute of Global Cultural Studies.

Throughout his wide-ranging career Mazrui has consistently refused to be restricted, by others as well as by himself, to a narrow field of specialization. Some of his critics argue that, by rejecting limitations, he has sacrificed intellectual depth and genuine scholarly sophistication. Because he does not spend enough time on one theme or subfield, these critics claim that Mazrui only scratches the surface. Some of his readers wish he would return to certain issues and questions he has raised in the past, but he never seems to find time to do so. Mazrui continually tantalizes and excites the reader's mind; he also keeps moving on to new frontiers.

Mazrui maintains an enormous volume of correspondence – sufficiently large to constitute, for many people, a full-time vocation. Some of this correspondence concerns debates with intellectual interlocutors or adversaries. Some of it involves merely acknowledging greetings from his many admirers. But the scale of his personal correspondence is truly remarkable. This side of Mazrui – his immersion in a correspondence-based cultural exchange – is probably derived from his Westernization. Not many Africans or Muslims worry unduly about responding to every letter addressed to them.

Future biographers of Mazrui may want to examine this side of his literary productivity.

A typical characteristic of Mazrui is his capacity for generating debate and controversy. His provocations are usually carefully thought out, including an anticipation of likely hostile responses and preparation for rebuttal when the occasion arises. One example is Mazrui's early article "Nkrumah: The Leninist Czar," published in *Transition* in 1966. The very title of the article is unusual and was carefully calculated to stimulate critical thinking and examination of the legacy of one of Africa's postcolonial heroes. If one is a Marxist-Leninist, how can one also be a czar? This apparent contradiction betrays Mazrui's fascination with paradoxes and his inclination to illustrate how things that may, on the surface, appear vastly different from each other, even opposites of each other, are reconcilable when probed to their depths. Indeed they may be curiously similar in some fundamental respects.

In the essay on Kwame Nkrumah, Mazrui's main argument is that by leading the former British colony of the Gold Coast to independence, Nkrumah was a great Gold Coaster. Also, by being a deeply dedicated proponent of the continental unity of Africans and a great source of inspiration for and a major force behind Pan-Africanism, Nkrumah was also a great African. However, Nkrumah invested far more time, energy, and resources on the dream of continental unity than he seemed to have invested in enhancing the new nation of Ghana's socioeconomic well-being and development. Thus, as he increasingly became a tyrant who behaved more like a monarch (hence a czar), and as his ideology and political behavior moved increasingly to the left, borrowing overtly from Lenin (hence a Leninist), Nkrumah came to combine the seemingly contradictory attributes of a czar and a Lenin. To some extent, Nkrumah, Mazrui suggests, even became a fusion of the two. The controversy generated by Mazrui's brief piece on Nkrumah clearly illustrates how Mazrui excels in provoking critical thinking and spirited debates.

Mazrui's writing style — elegant, tasteful, artistic, memorable, and highly quotable — also contributes to the longevity and passion of the debates he unleashes. He breathes life and excitement into most of the things he writes about. It was not entirely in jest that one of his critics, Colin Leys, stated, "Ali A. Mazrui is incapable of writing a dull paragraph." He writes zestfully, producing racy and vigorous prose.

Adept at thinking quickly and synthesizing ideas, Mazrui is a witty, articulate, and dangerous

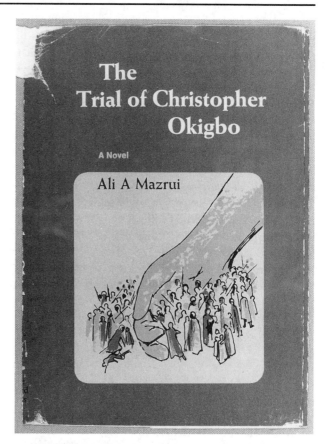

Dust jacket for Mazrui's 1971 novel, which is set in heaven, where Okigbo, a poet killed in the Nigerian civil war, engages in debates over the political role of the artist

intellectual adversary, especially in public exchanges. His most potent intellectual weapon is his capacity to see through ideas and arguments and to point out quickly any internal contradictions or irrationality. He reminds one of what German sociologist Max Weber once termed an "exposer of nonsense."

By identifying two broad and seemingly contradictory tendencies in Nkrumah, Mazrui was doing what has since become his consistent trademark — attempting to reconcile paradoxes. For example, Mazrui's BBC Reith Lectures of 1979, subsequently published in an expanded version as *The African Condition: A Political Diagnosis* (1980), focus on six major paradoxes: (1) although Africa was the first habitat of humankind, the continent has been the last to become comfortably habitable; (2) while Africans may not be the most brutalized of all peoples, they are probably the most humiliated in modern history; (3) African societies are not the closest to the West culturally, but they are experiencing the most rapid pace of Westernization in this century; (4) even though Africa is not the poorest of the regions of the world in resources, it is the least socioeconomically developed of the inhabited continents; (5) Africa is not the smallest of the continents, but it is probably the most fragmented; and (6) Africa is the most central of all continents in geographical location, but politically and to some extent militarily it may be the most marginal.

Akin to Mazrui's fascination with paradoxes is his tendency to state things in a paradoxical or dialectical way, or to invert what others may have said before. For example, as he says in his 1983 essay "Zionism and Apartheid," "Hitler was at once the greatest enemy of the Jews in history and the greatest (if unconscious) friend of the concept of 'Israel.' " In *The African Condition* he writes: "Although the Second World War was . . . politically liberating for Africans . . . that same war was an important stage in the incorporation of Africa into the world capitalist system [thereby leading to Africa's economic enslavement]." Inverting Lord Acton's well-known dictum about power, Mazrui asserts that "powerlessness corrupts – and absolute powerlessness corrupts absolutely" ("The Third World and International Terrorism," *Third World Quarterly*, April 1985).

Side by side with the exploitation of paradoxes as analytical tools is Mazrui's recurrent use of analogies as heuristic devices. His comparison of Nigeria's soldier/statesman Yakubu Gowon to Abraham Lincoln, or of Kenya's Tom Mboya to John F. Kennedy, or of Lebanon to the "first Israel" (or a "Christian Israel") are all examples of a persistent tendency to understand and to instruct by associating seemingly unrelated ideas and categories.

Mazrui's love for uniting qualities that may appear to be contradictory is evident from his early work to his latest books, including *The Africans: A Triple Heritage* (1986) and *Cultural Forces in World Politics* (1990). The Reith Lectures of 1979 probably influenced the BBC to choose Mazrui as the writer and presenter of the television series *The Africans*, telecast in 1986, a nine-part series with the book version accompanying it (both series and book are also available in the United States). Mazrui's television debut thrust him to what is probably the pinnacle of controversy and visibility in his career. His provocative views on the three legacies influencing the African experience and identity – indigenous, Islamic, and Western (especially the negative impact of the West) – irritated many conservatives in the West and even some of his fellow Africans.

The director of the U.S. National Endowment for the Humanities (NEH), Lynne Cheney, denounced Mazrui's series as an "anti-Western dia-

tribe" and as "pro-[Muammar] Qaddafy." The NEH even went to the extent of removing its name from the list of credits for the series. Mazrui must have realized and appreciated the irony that by removing its name from the list of credits and by noisily refusing to donate some sixty thousand dollars for promoting the program, the NEH had unintentionally but effectively contributed to the profitability of the series well in excess of the sum the NEH had refused to make available. As a result of the controversy generated by the NEH, far more people had their curiosity aroused, and many who otherwise would not even have noticed the series subsequently watched the nine-part program in its entirety.

In this series Mazrui ultimately places the blame for most of Africa's problems (political, economic, and social) at the doors of the three culprits: Western imperialism, Africa's environment, and poor judgment and lack of vision on the part of Africa's leaders. Many viewers of the series preferred to select arbitrarily only one of these culprits and to respond as if Mazrui had intended to hold not all three but only one of them responsible for Africa's predicament.

The dynamics of the controversy that ensued are fascinating in themselves. At one time some African-American ultranationalists charged that Mazrui's series amounted to a betrayal of the black race by one of its own. But when these same black critics discovered that Reaganite right-wingers had denounced the series, they quickly decided to reassess their position. The last thing they wanted to do, as marginalized black Americans, was to share an irritation with those they probably regarded as their worst enemies – conservative right-wingers. Perhaps Mazrui's greatest gift to Africa and its descendants is the soul searching and reexamination of ideas that his consciously provocative work has generated, not only in Africa itself but, to some extent, worldwide. His television series, the most internationalized and globally known of all his works, has to be placed at the heart of this legacy.

These two major works (Mazrui's Reith Lectures and *The Africans: A Triple Heritage*) initiated serious debates not only in the West but in Africa as well. Most of his audience either like his work deeply or dislike it intensely. In the latter case the hostility is sometimes so intense that it stretches to the point of irrational hostility. Balanced or middle-of-the-road positions are rare among responses to "Mazruiana." An even more intriguing phenomenon is that some of Mazrui's ardent critics seem to be unfamiliar with his works. This category in-

Mazrui interviewing a war widow in Zimbabwe, March 1982

cludes people who have never read his works but feel strongly about them on the basis, not of disagreement with his ideas, but rather of a stereotyped perception of Mazrui that they have somehow acquired. Perhaps no other scholar from Africa incites such passionate responses among people who have neither familiarized themselves with his writings nor met him. What these tendencies reveal is how debates and discussions initiated by Mazrui tend to take on a life of their own. In the end some of these debates retain very little of what Mazrui's ideas were. To some extent Mazrui himself invites this kind of reaction. One has to be unusually reserved or inhibited to remain silent about the many ideas Mazrui communicates either orally or in writing.

Although Mazrui has published over twenty books, he remains essentially an essayist. Indeed most of the chapters in his books were originally individual essays. Likewise it is defensible to suggest that Mazrui's innumerable public lectures are "oral essays." Mazrui is at his best as an essayist.

There is some truth in the charge that, because Mazrui does so many things at the same time,

his many writing projects often seem to need more solid supporting data than he provides. By attempting to be a jack-of-all-trades, Mazrui has, in a sense, denied scholarship as well as himself the best that his gifts might have yielded had his scholarly and intellectual activities been more focused. It is not easy to sustain theoretical coherence when one's intellectual net is cast so widely. The questions Mazrui has raised on all kinds of issues, less than the theoretical thrust of his wide-ranging contributions, will constitute the backbone of the Mazrui legacy in academia, both in Africanist circles and beyond.

There are times when Mazrui seems to engage in intellectualizing for the sake of intellectualizing. And there is also the problem of internal consistency whenever one writes as much as Mazrui does. For example, the seven strategies he recommends for combating underdevelopment in Africa (indigenization, domestication, diversification, horizontal interpenetration, vertical counterpenetration, domestic austerity in the Third World, and encouraging northern extravagance), while insightful and suggestive, do pull in contradictory directions.

Mazrui can at times be the victim of his own fecundity.

If Mazrui is the most prolific of black Africa's social scientists, he is probably also its most "cultural." While he does not entirely ignore the role of material forces in shaping Africa, he places far greater importance on the impact of culture on African realities than most of his peers do. This preoccupation is reflected by how often the terms *culture* or *cultural* appear in the titles of his books. Apart from the word *Africa* itself, no other term is more recurrent. In fact Mazrui's longest book has both terms in the title: *A World Federation of Cultures: An African Perspective* (1976). In this book Mazrui recommends a strategy for attaining world peace and social justice based on the concept of world culture rather than on the dream of world government.

Mazrui's fascination with cultural phenomena tends to encourage him to look into indigenous sources of the African condition. For example, rather than look outside Uganda in order to understand and explain the phenomenon wrought by Amin, Mazrui instead sought to examine the personality of the man and the environment that produced him. While Amin operated in an international system characterized by the competitive imperialism of the Soviet bloc versus the Western powers, there was a lot in Amin's character and behavior that was either intensely personal and idiosyncratic or partially rooted in his Kakwa-cum-Islamic heritage. To some leftist analysts the cultural aspects of sociopolitical behavior are essentially part of the superstructure, a reflection of factors far more concrete and fundamental than the aspects themselves. Culture, is, therefore, relatively unimportant to most economic determinists. By contrast, by focusing on the more elusive perceptual and cultural factors that would otherwise have been lost if the materialist approach were permitted to go too far (as so often is the tendency among the leftists in African scholarship), Mazrui's cultural approach restores some of the balance needed in understanding the African experience in all its comprehensiveness. In Mazrui's article "The Resurrection of the Warrior Tradition in African Political Culture: From Shaka the Zulu to Amin the Kakwa" (collected in *The Warrior Tradition in Modern Africa*, 1977), he attempts to examine the Zulu and the Kakwa sources of the behavior of two important figures in Africa's modern history.

The fact that Mazrui, deeply Westernized as he appears to be, should, in the majority of his works, pay careful and sustained attenion to African culture would at first appear to be puzzling. But he is not distanced from that culture and never has been. His early tendency to use non-African sources rather heavily in his writing was partly a result of working at a time when there were few fellow African scholars to consult or quote. Second, Mazrui is not always citing Western scholars because he is in agreement with all they say. On the contrary, the evidence suggests that Mazrui's evaluation of European scholars is almost evenly mixed. Third, some of the aspects of his writing, which may at first sight appear to be a reflection of how deeply Westernized he is, are, in reality, part of his African and Islamic heritages rather than purely Western in derivation. This phenomenon is perhaps most clearly reflected in his use of creative literature in his social-science works.

There are few mainstream social scientists, not just in Africa but worldwide, who draw on material from creative literature – poems, plays, and novels – more often than Mazrui does. Quotations from the works of major literary figures, both Western and African, appear repeatedly in his books and articles, reflecting to some extent his cultural Westernization. But he cites them only partly because he has absorbed them through his education and recollects them with enthusiasm. An often-overlooked factor is that as a product of the Swahili culture of coastal Kenya, Mazrui would have developed a predilection for poetry and verbal rhythm even if he had not gone to Western-type schools. The Swahili are great lovers of words and poetry, and written forms of Swahili literature were in existence several centuries prior to the European intrusion in Africa. The alphabet used in the early years was the Arabic script, and only much later was the Roman alphabet adopted. Moreover, among the Swahili people, conversation is an art, and elegance in that art is highly regarded. Therefore, it is not too farfetched to suggest that Mazrui's abundant writing is, in part, motivated by a desire to communicate, to converse with others. This attribute he owes to the Swahili culture and to his own communicative nature.

The unusual utopian novel written by Mazrui, *The Trial of Christopher Okigbo* (1971), is only partly Western. Equally crucial to the formation of this kind of futuristic fiction, set in an African afterworld, is a Swahili literary tradition in which fantasy, theology, and ethical concerns are intermingled. The tale takes the form of a debate in heaven over major moral issues. Okigbo, the Nigerian poet who died in combat in Nigeria's civil war, serves as the focal point for arguments concerning the political commitment of the artist. The content, structure, and style of narration are as much African as they are Western. Mazrui's novel is a syncretic work fusing Christian, Islamic, and indigenous cultural elements. So what may at first sight appear to be an excessive use of Western literary figures and forms is in reality a manifestation of what Mazrui would probably call "the triple heritage" at work. No genuine attempt at understanding Mazrui's work can afford to neglect such interactions.

To be eclectic, selectively to borrow aspects of one school of thought while rejecting others, to synthesize a new and distinctive position of his own — these have been the hallmarks of Mazrui's contributions to political science and literature. His life, which he once summarized as "one long debate," has been an unrelenting quest for synthesis.

References:

Kofi Awoonor, "The Writer and Politics in Africa," in *African Cultural and Intellectual Leaders and the Development of the New African Nations*, edited by Robert W. July and Peter Benson (New York & Ibadan: Rockefeller Foundation & Ibadan University Press, 1982), pp. 184–196;

Omolara Leslie, "Malignant Schizophrenia in After-Africa," *Ba Shiru*, 4, no. 2 (1973): 81–86;

Colin Leys, "Tanzaphilia and All That," *Transition*, 7 (December 1967–January 1968): 51–53;

Peter Nazareth, "The Trial of a Juggler," in his *The Third World Writer: His Social Responsibility* (Nairobi: Kenya Literature Bureau, 1978), pp. 50–61;

Charles E. Nnolim, "African Utopia and Ali Mazrui's *The Trial of Christopher Okigbo*," *New Literature Review*, 11 (n.d.): 53–62;

Sulayman S. Nyang, *Ali A. Mazrui: The Man and His Works* (Lawrenceville, Va.: Brunswick, 1981);

Kole Omotoso, "The Ideas of Ali Mazrui," *West Africa* (7 March 1983): 605–606;

Chris L. Wanjala, "The Growth of a Literary Tradition in East Africa," *Journal of East African Research and Development*, 11 (1981): 122–142.

Es'kia (Ezekiel) Mphahlele

(17 December 1919 –)

Ursula A. Barnett

BOOKS: *Man Must Live, and Other Stories* (Cape Town: African Bookman, 1946);

Down Second Avenue (London: Faber & Faber, 1959; Garden City, N.Y.: Anchor/Doubleday, 1971);

The Living and Dead, and Other Stories (Ibadan: Ministry of Education, 1961);

The African Image (London: Faber & Faber, 1962; New York: Praeger, 1962; revised, London: Faber & Faber, 1974; New York: Praeger, 1974);

A Guide to Creative Writing (Dar es Salaam: East African Literature Bureau, 1966);

In Corner B (Nairobi: East African Publishing House, 1967);

The Wanderers (New York: Macmillan, 1971; London: Macmillan, 1972; Cape Town: Africasouth, 1984);

Voices in the Whirlwind, and Other Essays (New York: Hill & Wang, 1972; London: Macmillan, 1973; Dar es Salaam: Tanzania Publishing House, 1973);

Chirundu (Johannesburg: Ravan, 1979; Walton-on-Thames, U.K.: Nelson, 1980; Westport, Conn.: Hill, 1981);

Let's Write a Novel (Cape Town: Miller, 1981);

The Unbroken Song: Selected Writings (Johannesburg: Ravan, 1981);

Afrika My Music (Johannesburg: Ravan, 1984);

Father Come Home (Johannesburg: Ravan, 1984);

Let's Talk Writing: Prose (Johannesburg: African Writers' Association & Council for Black Education and Research, 1985);

Let's Talk Writing: Poetry (Johannesburg: African Writers' Association & Council for Black Education and Research, 1986);

Poetry and Humanism (Johannesburg: Witwatersrand University Press, 1986);

Echoes of African Art (Braamfontein, South Africa: Skotaville, 1987);

Renewal Time (London & Columbia, La.: Readers International, 1988);

Es'kia (Ezekiel) Mphahlele (Transcription Centre Archive, Harry Ransom Humanities Research Center, University of Texas at Austin)

Mandela: Echoes of an Era (London & New York: Penguin, 1990).

OTHER: "Exile in Nigeria," in *Poems from Black Africa*, edited by Langston Hughes (Bloomington: Indiana University Press, 1963), pp. 116–122;

Modern African Stories, edited by Mphahlele and Ellis Ayitey Komey (London: Faber & Faber, 1964);

African Writing Today, edited by Mphahlele (Harmondsworth, U.K.: Penguin, 1967);

Bernard B. Dadié, *Climbié*, translated by Karen C.

Chapman, foreword by Mphahlele (London & Ibadan: Heinemann, 1971), pp. ix–xii;

Kofi Awoonor, *Night of My Blood*, introduction by Mphahlele (Garden City, N.Y.: Doubleday, 1971), pp. 9–20;

"Death," in *New African Literature and the Arts I*, edited by Joseph Okpaku (New York: Crowell/Third Press, 1987), pp. 144–147.

SELECTED PERIODICAL PUBLICATIONS – UNCOLLECTED: "Out of Africa," *Encounter* (April 1960): 61–63;

"Black and White," *New Statesman* (10 September 1960): 342–346;

"Travels off an Extra-Mural Donkey," *Transition*, 3 (November 1963): 46–50;

"Why I Teach My Discipline," *Denver Quarterly*, 8 (Spring 1973): 32–43;

"The Tyranny of Place," *New Letters*, 40 (Autumn 1973): 69–84;

"Portrait of a Man Who Lives in a Glass House," *Era*, 12 (Spring 1976): 4–7;

"The Voice of Prophecy in African Poetry," *English in Africa*, 6 (March 1979): 33–44;

"Oganda's Journey" [play], *Staffrider*, 2 (July-August 1979): 38–47;

"South African Literature vs. the Political Morality," *English Academy Review*, 1 (1983): 8–26;

"Women and Their Men," *Classic*, 2, no. 1 (1983): 3–5;

"Literature: A Necessity or a Public Nuisance," *Classic*, 3, no. 1 (1984): 14–16;

"Mongane Serote's Odyssey: The Path that Breaks the Heels," *English Academy Review*, 3 (1985): 65–79.

Es'kia (born Ezekiel) Mphahlele has been involved in almost every phase of black, English-language African literature, either as a participant or commentator. His importance lies in the bold and clear formulation of his ideas on African humanism, a view of life in which humankind is an expression and extension of the supreme force, in harmony with the environment. Against a dual background of Western culture and African tradition, his writing and the direction he has given his life illuminate the courage with which people survive oppression. He has a vision of a liberated land in South Africa where every human life is valued.

Mphahlele's father, Moses, who worked as a messenger, came to Pretoria from the district of Sekhukhuneland, where his forefathers of the Mphahlele clan had been chiefs and headmen. Mphahlele's origin is of concern to students of his writing in view of the contention of some of his critics that his social and educational background was a purely Western one.

Mphahlele was born in Pretoria on 17 December 1919, but from the age of five till he was thirteen, he lived in the village of Maupaneng with his paternal grandmother, Mathebe. In one of his earliest works, the story "Tomorrow You Shall Reap," in *Man Must Live* (1946), he describes nostalgically the beautiful mountains, the sparkling rivers, and the songs of the birds in his early surroundings. But as the circumstances of his life became more bitter, so the scenery of his early childhood seemed to grow darker, the mountains more ominous, and the river more chaotic. The feeling of terror remained with him until he went there in the late 1970s and allowed the nightmares to "shrink into a manageable world" in his adult mind, as he says in his autobiography *Afrika My Music* (1984).

At age thirteen Mphahlele joined his parents in Marabastad, a township in Pretoria, and they lived on Second Avenue – thus the title of his first autobiography (1959). His father habitually treated his mother badly, and, after a ghastly attack on her with a pot of boiling stew, Moses Mphahlele was arrested. The parents were divorced and the young Mphahlele never saw his father again. His mother, Eva Mogale Mphahlele, supported her children by doing domestic work. Marabastad was a typical township slum, with overcrowded homes, streets full of rubble and dirt, and nights of frightening sounds, but Mphahlele lived in a close-knit community; it was there, mainly from the strong women in his family – his mother, maternal grandmother, and his Aunt Dora – that he learned about survival. *Man Must Live* was consequently the title of his first collection of short stories.

By the time the book was published, Mphahlele was teaching high school in the township of Orlando. On her meager earnings his mother had put him through a leading high school (Saint Peter's) and a private mission institution (Adams Teachers Training College in Natal), where he gained a teaching diploma in 1940. He felt insufficiently educated to teach, though, so he first took a clerical post at an institute for the blind and continued to study. On 29 August 1945 he married Rebecca Mochadibane who was then a student teacher at a Johannesburg training college and who later became a social worker. They have five children.

From his first years on Second Avenue, Mphahlele had been an avid reader. In a small, one-room tin shack, which served as a reading room, he read anything from cookbooks and astrology to *Don*

Quixote: "I went through the whole lot like a termite," he says in *Afrika My Music*. "But Cervantes was to stand out in my mind, forever." He was also fascinated by the silent films of Charlie Chaplin. In Mphahlele's school days, however, the British classics by Sir Walter Scott, Jane Austen, John Milton, William Makepeace Thackeray, and others – with the settings so remote from an African township – had little meaning for him. It was only when he himself was teaching that he learned to appreciate Charles Dickens, the American writers William Faulkner and Ernest Hemingway, Russian writers, and ancient Greek drama, which he found close to African life. Later Rabindranath Tagore, the black American writers Richard Wright and Langston Hughes, and South African writers William Plomer, Nadine Gordimer, Alex La Guma, and others had a significant effect on him.

Mphahlele spoke Northern Sotho at home, and the language of the neighborhood was a mixture of Southern Sotho and Afrikaans. The medium of instruction at school was English, in which he soon became proficient. Then, he says, "Something strange happened to me as I studied by candle-light listening to the throb out there. I found myself writing a short story. I know I had been burning with an urge to say something in writing." The African Bookman in Cape Town, which had been publishing monographs on political and social subjects, ventured into producing *Man Must Live*, comprising five of Mphahlele's stories. All seven hundred copies of the book were soon sold.

The stories describe the experiences of characters involved in an often losing battle against circumstances, characters who come to realize that they must survive as individuals by strictly adhering to a moral code. This code is not necessarily identical with the morals accepted by the community in which they live. Courage, for example, does not have to mean facing the common enemy but rather maintaining the truth as you see it. One of the stories takes place in a period in history when black congregations were resenting white supervision of their churches. The Reverend Katsane Melato in Mphahlele's story "The Leaves Were Falling" cannot agree with the method employed by his congregation in protesting against raised fees. Like a leaf falling from a sapless twig destined to decay, Melato removes himself from the conflict.

Zungu, the hero of the title story, makes a cult of survival but misunderstands the philosophy he has chosen, in that he relies on the "machine" – the system in the form of the railway organization for which he works as a policeman – for survival at the

Dust jacket for Mphahlele's first novel (1971), a roman à def about his experiences on the staff of Drum *magazine during the mid and late 1950s and his problems in exile in the 1960s*

expense of the men and women over whose lives he holds sway. Except for "Man Must Live," which he has included in a later collection (*In Corner B*, 1967), Mphahlele has virtually disowned his first collection as escapist. Yet, although the stories do not overtly blame the social system for the dramas and tragedies of the lives they describe, most of them portray the struggles of the black man to survive in a segregated society. This is certainly how most reviewers in the white South African press saw them. The reviews were mainly favorable but expressed surprise that a black man should be able to write. On the other hand the critic for the *Guardian*, a Marxist-oriented newspaper, took Mphahlele to task for not making his characters complain about the pass laws, pickup vans, or the insolence of the white man, and accused Mphahlele of allowing the gods of his father to be exorcised by the white man. Criticism of escapism in these stories was disputed many years later by Sipho Sepamla, one of the leading African critics of the 1970s and 1980s, who had read the book in 1948 as a prescribed text at Orlando High School, where Mphahlele was teaching. In a 1976 article titled "The Black Writer in South Africa Today: Problems and Dilemmas," he says that even then the quality of self-consciousness or black consciousness was there in that Mphahlele was portraying the black experience.

In the late 1940s and early 1950s Mphahlele began concentrating on teaching, which, right from the beginning, he has always loved. Teaching gives him an opportunity to share his passion for literature with others. There has always been an intense rapport between him and his students, and former students have described him as a man dedicated to his profession. Although he disliked politics, Mphahlele was drawn into educational politics because of his ability and fearlessness in expressing his convictions. As general secretary of the Transvaal African Teacher's Association, he, with others, led the opposition against the Eiselen Commission's Report, which eventually led to the Bantu Education Act and total apartheid in education with an inferior education for the black child. Shortly after a paper voicing his opposition was published in 1952, he received a letter from the Transvaal Education Department dismissing him from the teaching profession in government schools in South Africa. Pupils decided to stay out of school in protest, and as a result he and two others were arrested on charges of inciting a boycott and public violence. They were subsequently acquitted.

There followed a period during which he taught in Lesotho (then Basutoland) and at his old school, Saint Peter's. But Saint Peter's refused to accept the new educational provisions and was compelled to close down. (Adams Teachers Training College was taken over by the government and eventually also went out of existence.)

In 1955 Mphahlele entered a brief and unhappy career as a journalist, when he accepted a position as reporter and literary editor of the journal *Drum*. He also became a leading contributor of fiction. The idea of this journal for black readers in English was conceived by Bob Crisp, a white journalist and broadcaster, who persuaded Jim Bailey, son of a gold millionaire, to finance him. It began in March 1951 as *African Drum*, a publication of what whites imagined blacks would want to read – ethnic stories and articles; installments of Alan Paton's *Cry the Beloved Country* (1948); features about religion, farming, sports, and famous men; and strip cartoons about Gulliver and Saint Paul. Under subsequent editors Anthony Sampson, Tom Hopkinson,

and Sylvester Stein, and contributors Can Themba, Todd Matshikiza, Casey Motsisi, Lewis Nkosi, and Mphahlele, *Drum* attempted to become a "people's paper." It became known for its fearless investigative journalism, and although it vied for black readership with the *Daily Mirror* in providing pinups, crime, and romance, it also represented African literature in South Africa for almost a decade.

Mphahlele hated his journalistic assignments on the magazine, yet they provided the raw material for much of his later writing. He covered most of the important events of the period: a boycott of the buses against raised fares, the 1956 march of twenty thousand women to the government buildings in Pretoria to protest against passes for women, and finally his swan song assignment for *Drum*: a late-1950s trial of 156 men and women for treason.

As literary editor Mphahlele was able to help publish works by young, talented writers, such as Nimrod Mkele, Richard Rive, Peter Clarke (writing as Peter Kumalo), and James Matthews, many of whom became well known later. Some of Mphahlele's own best early work appeared in *Drum* between 1953 and 1959. For instance, his series about the Lesanes, a fictional family in Newclare Township, was published between 1956 and 1957 (but has not been collected). Although there is rollicking fun at times in that series, it is the stark, grim realism of the life of the people, the desperate day-to-day struggle to survive, that makes up most of the action. What hope is there for the Lesane family, housed in two rooms, which Ma-Lesane desperately but unsuccessfully tries to keep clean? The father, discharged from the mines because of ill health, is afraid of his wife and takes out his frustrations on his teenage daughter, Diketso, by beating her. The young boys eat their supper secretly so that they need not feel obliged to invite their friends to share their meager meal. The daughter realizes that she is hurting her family and herself by going to live with her lover, but it is the only way she can vent her frustration at having to leave school because her parents can no longer afford to keep her there. But Diketso has not given up all hope and aspiration. There must be a future for her, she feels, and even the present has some happy moments: unexpectedly her lover gives her a gift on her birthday. Toward the end of the series, though, there seems to be less and less hope. The series was written at one of the most devastating periods of Mphahlele's life, when he first considered exiling himself from South Africa. Yet there is always a note of optimism expressed in the toughness of the people, who refuse to submit to circumstances.

In 1949 Mphahlele had earned a B.A. from the University of South Africa, and in December 1956 he presented his master's thesis, "The Non-European Character in South African English Fiction," to the university and was awarded his M.A. with distinction in a segregated ceremony. He joined the Orlando Study Circle and became interested in helping organize cultural and extramural educational activities, a pursuit to which he has devoted himself intermittently throughout his life. Among his colleagues on the staff of *Drum* and its sister publication, *Golden City Post*, who formed a close coterie in Sophiatown, he was treated with respect, although he rarely joined in their sessions of discussing culture and drinking alcoholic beverages.

At the beginning of 1957 his gradual conviction that he would have to leave South Africa came to a head. Like the character Timi in Mphahlele's autobiographical novel *The Wanderers* (1971), he had known that eventually he would "have to decide whether to stay and try to survive; or stay and pit my heroism against the machine and bear the consequences if I remained alive; or stay and shrivel up with bitterness; or face my cowardice, reason with it and leave." Just as later they would try to stop him from returning, friends attempted to dissuade him from leaving. As he writes in *Down Second Avenue*, "Stay on in the struggle," they kept saying; "I'm contributing nothing, I told them. I can't teach and I want to teach, I can't write here and I want to write." In September 1957 he exiled himself and his family, as he put it, in Lagos, Nigeria.

There he completed *Down Second Avenue*. It was accepted almost immediately and published in 1959, to be followed by a spate of autobiographies by other black South Africans. *Drum* had ceased to be an outlet for serious fiction, there was no other in South Africa, and the writers had a great deal left to say. They needed to confirm a sense of identity, and they found publishers abroad for the stories of their lives because their experiences were far more exciting than anything they could invent. Moreover the black American writers whom they admired, such as James Baldwin and Richard Wright, had all written about themselves.

Mphahlele describes himself in his 1959 book as sitting on the veranda of a shop in Marabastad: "If you were alone, you were in a position to view critically what you considered to be the whole world passing down Barber Street, half detached, half committed." From this point of view he looks at his life and that of those around him. Life is harsh on Second Avenue, and it was there that Mphahlele learned that one must live and make the most of circumstances. Readers watch Mphahlele's world deteriorate politically and socially and his own tension mount; they see him in school and college and watch him gain honor and distinction, followed by defeat and disillusionment.

In *Down Second Avenue* Mphahlele sought to give an account of himself at a time when he desperately needed to take stock. But the work also goes beyond that. The story of Mphahlele's early life is typical in many ways of that of all black South Africans, and so, perhaps unconsciously, he speaks on their behalf, too. Mphahlele found it difficult to speak of private matters, but as the self-expression of an articulate, sensitive, and perceptive black man in South Africa, the book never falters. His search for an African identity had begun.

At the beginning *Down Second Avenue* is held together not so much by the chronology of Mphahlele's life as by the control and dramatization of his feelings. He applies his skill in storytelling and in building up events and feelings. The work vibrates with the active life around him. The graphic pictures portray bitterness, for instance, as something one can almost grasp with one's hands, as when his bicycle, laden with the washing he has fetched from a white suburb, crashes into a group of white boys riding abreast. They kick and curse him as he goes down, then they ride away leaving him "with the cold, the pain, the numbness, and a puncture and bent front wheel." Above all, the aliveness of the characters and their efforts to rise above circumstances distinguish this work and set it above the autobiographies of Mphahlele's contemporaries among black South African writers.

Once the young Mphahlele leaves Second Avenue, the work becomes more conventionally autobiographical. The interest for the reader begins to lie in admiration for Mphahlele's achievements and for his political stand. There is no longer the spontaneity and aliveness of the earlier chapters, and the narrative tends to ramble.

Between the chapters there are "interludes," in which Mphahlele stops the narrative to report his thoughts. For example, he mourns the passing of Marabastad, which shared the fate of many black townships that were dissolved to make way for white, colored, or Indian communities under apartheid laws. Mphahlele saw such developments as symbolic of blacks always being on the move, and of their poverty and despair. In another interlude, toward the end of the book, he tries to describe his quest for an answer to his hopes and yearnings as he stands on top of a high mountain in Basutoland, but the writing becomes self-conscious and tends to hide rather than expose his feelings. The work regains its emotional impetus near the end when Mphahlele describes the most bitter period in his life, culminating in his voluntary exile.

In spite of some unevenness the total effect of *Down Second Avenue* is overwhelming. It is a social record and a moving human document, as relevant today as it was in 1959. Critics and the public alike approved of it. C. O. Gardner, in his laudation speech at the University of Natal at Pietermaritzburg, when presenting Mphahlele with an honorary doctorate in April 1983, said:

> Zeke Mphahlele (as he is commonly known) was born and bred in poverty and hardship. In this respect he was of course like most Africans in South Africa. One needs to begin with this point, because the earlier parts of his life – most memorably described in his autobiography *Down Second Avenue* – are both unique and typical. And the element of typicality Zeke Mphahlele would wish to insist on, since he has always wanted to be associated with his fellow black South Africans. The words "poverty and hardship" do not adequately sum up the tone of the autobiography, however. The story is a complex one, and it is told with lively vividness and with terse irony – sometimes with quiet anger, sometimes with humour, never with self-pity.

Down Second Avenue was translated into eleven languages, and innumerable extracts have appeared in anthologies. It is regarded as one of the few classics to emerge from South Africa.

Although he enjoyed freedom in Nigeria and felt that Africa had been given back to him, Mphahlele missed the sense of community living. He also felt that the "crutch" that had given one an identity at home – the anger and the bitterness – had been removed. And however much success he gained academically and with publications, what he missed everywhere was an emotional and intellectual commitment to place.

From 1957 to 1961 he served as a lecturer in the Department of Extra-Mural Studies of the University College of Ibadan, a job that entailed much traveling. In 1958 he attended the All-Africa People's Conference in Accra, Ghana, as leader of the South African delegation, having promised Nelson Mandela to represent the African National Congress (ANC). It was his one foray into active politics.

In 1961 he received news that he was one of several writers listed by the South African government under the Suppression of Communism (later Internal Security) Act. The listing meant that none of his work could be circulated or quoted by South Africans, for whom and about whom he was writing. "We would never know the reactions of those whose concerns we shared in South Africa," he writes in *Afrika My Music*. "We were indeed like disembodied voices crying out for a dimension that will give them meaning." The ban remained in force until after his return to South Africa in 1977, but several of his books remain banned individually under the Publications Act.

In the 1950s in Nigeria a literary renaissance was in full swing, and Mphahlele met many of its exponents, among them Kofi Awoonor (who became a lifelong friend), Wole Soyinka, Chinua Achebe, Christopher Okigbo, J. P. Clark, and Ama Ata Aidoo. He joined the editorial board of the journal *Black Orpheus*, became a contributor and eventually coeditor. In 1961 *Black Orpheus*, under sponsorship of the Ministry of Education, published a collection of his stories, *The Living and Dead, and Other Stories*. The stories were written in South Africa, all except one had previously been published in journals – *Drum*, *Africa South*, *Fighting Talk*, *New World Writing*, and *Black Orpheus* – and two are very similar to incidents in *Down Second Avenue*. Unlike his first collection, in the 1961 book black people are shown in relation to the white world around them and often in conflict with it.

The title story concerns a white official, Stoffel Visser, who almost comes to accept his servant Jackson as a human being. Stoffel has just completed a report to the government urging that servants not be allowed to live on the premises of the white areas in which they work. A railway sweeper comes to him with a letter that seems to indicate that a man just killed by a train is Jackson. Stoffel is full of repentance about the way he has treated his servant, such sorrow and regret being comfortable feelings when no further steps need to be taken. When it turns out that Jackson is alive, and Stoffel thus has a second chance to rectify his attitude, he relapses and decides to let Jackson continue to be "a machine to work for him."

In "We'll Have Dinner at Eight" there is a confrontation between Miss Pringle – a do-gooder who asks Mzondi, a black man, to dinner in a conscious effort to win black friends – and the crippled Mzondi, who kills her in the mistaken belief that she wants to get him drunk in order to make him reveal where he has hidden stolen money. The spinster hides her sexual longings behind a mask of good deeds, and the cripple believes anyone white represents an unjust law and therefore danger. Unfortunately there is neither tragedy nor pathos in the story, partly because of the poorly motivated murder – all Mzondi need to have done was stay away from the dinner – but more so because Mphahlele fails to raise any sympathy for or interest in either of the main characters.

In "The Master of Doornvlei" there is also a confrontation, but this time the labels are less distinct. Sarel Britz, the owner of a farm called Doornvlei, knows that it is necessary to establish a workable relationship with his laborers. Sarel is prepared to listen to them when they have complaints, but when their leader imposes an ultimatum on him to dismiss his foreman, he cannot tolerate this from a black man. He dismisses the worker and keeps the foreman. Ironically the confrontation that follows later is between Sarel and the foreman, who has taken advantage of the situation. The symbolic battle between the foreman's bull and Sarel's pedigree stallion is very effective. Although the bull gores the horse, Sarel triumphs when he gives the foreman the choice between killing his bull and leaving. But it is a Pyrrhic victory: Sarel is left in fear of his laborers.

The two stories based on incidents in *Down Second Avenue*, "The Woman" and "The Woman Walks Out," feature Ma-Lebona, called Madira in *The Living and Dead*, and are typical of the kind of writing that gives the autobiography so much of its appeal. They are compassionate and amusing sketches of a selfish and vain woman so clean that she often took meat out of boiling water to be rewashed.

"The Suitcase" is a well-constructed, ironic story about a man named Timi, unemployed and desperate, who is relying upon "sheer naked chance" to provide him with a present for his wife on New Year's Eve. He thinks he is in luck when a woman passenger on a bus apparently forgets to take her suitcase. But he plays with fate and loses. Not only is he caught in the act of stealing, but the case contains a dead baby. The theme of the story is not the vagaries of fate but the choices humankind has. Timi makes the mistake of relying on an arbitrary provision by Providence. Some years before, Mphahlele had shown some of his unpublished writings to Gordimer, and she had liked this story particularly. She told him to submit it to *New World Writing*, where it appeared in the seventh Mentor Selection in 1955, in company with works by Heinrich Bon Thomas, and others.

"He and the Cat," the last story in the 1961 collection, is very different from any other fiction by Mphahlele. The reader is not told what the burden is that will be dropped off as soon as the narrator has spoken to the lawyer for whom he is waiting

Cover for the 1979 novel based on political events Mphahlele observed while a teacher at the University of Zambia in 1968 and 1969

on a hot afternoon. The story is an impressionistic reflection of the narrator's self-centered thought processes, which lead him to the recognition that a nearby man with a fixed smile, who is interminably closing envelopes, is blind. The blind man's silent activity and his detachment, with the picture of the cat behind him, reveal to the narrator the temporal nature of day-to-day concerns.

Mphahlele enjoyed his teaching experiences in Nigeria and felt very much part of the intellectual life of the country. But he was disillusioned with the educational system. Although well-qualified for a permanent position in the English department of the University of Ibadan, as an outsider without a British postgraduate degree, such a job was denied him. He was offered a post as director of the African Program for the Congress for Cultural Freedom in Paris, which he accepted in 1961. The congress had been formed in the early 1950s with the purpose of upholding and defending intellectual freedom. Mphahlele maintained a Paris home but also toured Africa as a part of his job. Together with Africanist Ulli Beier and Nigerian writers Soyinka, Clark, and others, he formed the Mbari Writers Club in Ibadan. The name Mbari was symbolic of renewal. It was derived from an Igbo religious practice whereby a house, dedicated to Mbari, the earth goddess, is left to decay and a new house is built. The club held art exhibitions, concerts, dramatic performances, and writers' workshops, and the meeting place housed an African reference library. Mbari Publications was founded to publish African writing. Conferences on African culture and writing were held regularly, and centers were set up in other parts of Nigeria. In Paris itself Mphahlele felt isolated and unhappy, finding he could not identify with French intellectual life. He enjoyed the visits of friends and described his home as a crossroads for writers and artists from Africa.

In 1962 a collection of his essays was published – *The African Image* – in which he investigates "The African Personality," a term coined by Kwame Nkrumah at the All-African People's Conference in Accra. Mphahlele identifies it as a "beacon on the battlefield, a thrust, an assertion of the African presence . . . a coming into consciousness. . . ." *The African Image* began as an exploration of the African image in literature but went on to include the sociopolitical sphere. It includes his master's thesis and articles previously published in journals such as the *Twentieth Century*, *Transition*, *Encounter*, and the *New Statesman*. (Mphahlele revised *The African Image* for a second edition, published in 1974, and a further collection of essays was published under the title *Voices in the Whirlwind, and Other Essays* in 1972.)

In 1963 the Congress for Cultural Freedom sent Mphahlele to Kenya to establish a center like Mbari. Two months after his arrival, in October 1963, Kenya celebrated its independence. In Nairobi, Mphahlele was in charge of writing and theater at the new cultural center, called Chemchemi, Swahili for "fountain," and he also traveled to other districts to run writers' workshops and introduce his drama group.

In *Afrika My Music* he says, "my soul was in the job," but toward the end the experience began to sour. There were quarrels with members of the center's committee and a lack of support from the government. Furthermore, the Congress of Cultural Freedom had lost a great deal of its credibility when it became public knowledge that it was sponsored by the Central Intelligence Agency (CIA)

through the Farfield Foundation. He left in 1965, and as there was no one suitable to succeed him, the congress closed down the center.

These frustrations during the mid 1960s were not conducive to producing literary work, and he wrote very little; however, some stories he had finished in Paris were ready to be prepared for publication. He did finish editing two anthologies, *African Writing Today* (1967) and (in collaboration with Ellis Ayitey Komey) *Modern African Stories* (1964).

The administrators of a girls' high school near Nairobi had asked him to write a play for its yearly drama festival. He turned a short story by the Kenyan writer Grace Ogot, "The Rain Came," into a verse drama with African music. "Oganda's Journey" was subsequently also produced in Tanzania and the United States, and published in the South African journal *Staffrider* (July-August 1979). Ogot had based the story on the traditions of her Luo people. It tells how two young lovers cheat the gods who demand a human sacrifice to bring rain. Mphahlele makes some changes to the story and introduces a chorus but retains the essence of a traditional tale simply told.

Mphahlele had long loved theater, writing, producing, and acting in some sketches while still in school. Later he wrote some verse plays; one, an ambitious effort about the life of Shaka Zulu, was unfortunately lost. Apparently none of the plays has been performed or published. While teaching at Orlando High School, he attended a private class in drama with Norah Taylor, a producer and teacher. She became his mentor, benefactor, and friend, helping him with early productions and encouraging the Syndicate of African Artists, which he and musician Khabi Mngoma had founded in Soweto in 1952. It was a black community-based performing arts group at a time when most black drama was organized by whites, and it presented drama performances in the 1950s. Mphahlele dramatized Dickens's *A Tale of Two Cities* (1859), and other classics, and various folktales. The syndicate failed in its efforts, mainly due to police harassment, and was forced to disband in 1956, but Mphahlele maintained his interest in African drama and encouraged it whenever he had an opportunity.

After his experiences in Kenya, Mphahlele was anxious to return to teaching. He was able to obtain a teaching fellowship at the University of Denver and arrived there in May 1966.

Mphahlele's next collection of short stories, *In Corner B*, was published in Nairobi in 1967. Several of the stories had appeared in such journals as the *Classic* and *Drum*, others in his earlier collections. Although Mphahlele had been away from South Africa for ten years, only two of the stories are not set there.

The best-known story, of almost novella length, is "Mrs. Plum." It concerns a liberal, white widow who lives in a suburb with her daughter, her servants, and her dogs. Karabo, the female domestic worker who narrates the story, finds Mrs. Plum's liberalism puzzling but accepts it at first as one of the eccentricities of the white race: "my madam . . . loved dogs and Africans and said that everyone must follow the law even if it hurt. These were three big things in Madam's life." That is how the story opens. Relations between them deteriorate when there is trouble in the neighborhood. At first Mrs. Plum supports her servants against the police to the extent that she goes to jail. Karabo is impressed, but among her friends and at her home in Phokeng there is only poverty and tragedy; suddenly she is sickened by the smell of the cosmetics she secretly shares with Mrs. Plum, by the dogs, and by Dick, the other servant, who cleans out the dirt of Madam's body from the bathtub. Dick is suspected of poisoning dogs in the neighborhood, and Mrs. Plum dismisses him. In protest Karabo leaves her employ. The story ends when Mrs. Plum visits Karabo in her home village and asks her to return. She tells Karabo that two pet dogs have died. Did this woman, Karabo wonders, come to ask her to return because she had lost two animals she loved? "You know, I like your people, Karabo, the Africans," Mrs. Plum says. Karabo wonders if Mrs. Plum likes her as an individual.

In the course of the story readers gradually realize that while Mrs. Plum's liberalism is quite genuine, unlike that of Miss Pringle in "We'll Have Dinner at Eight," it is completely impersonal. Mphahlele dislikes this type of liberalism intensely because it lacks the one characteristic that is his own ruling passion – a feeling of compassion for one's fellow human beings. By bringing into the story a historical character, the black leader Lillian Ngoyi, as a teacher in a women's club Karabo attends, Mphahlele shows the white liberal as irrelevant to the education and maturity of a young black girl. Only by sharing a common cause with other women in her position can Karabo become conscious of her worth as a black woman.

"Grieg on a Stolen Piano" is a strong condemnation of a society in which a black man of intellect and integrity can easily founder. The main character goes through many harrowing experiences, some of them similar to Mphahlele's own. He rises to the position of school inspector. Like "Man Must Live," which precedes it in this collection, the story tells of deterioration, triggered by circumstances but intrinsically arising out of the man's character. Like Zungu, Uncle in "Grieg" never loses faith in survival as a necessity, but he is cynical in the way he applies this idea to his own life. The central plot is amusing. Uncle has a foolproof scheme for making money: he gets a pretty girl from the country and trains her for a beauty contest. The judges are bribed, but unfortunately it is decided that the winner shall be chosen by popular vote. Uncle is a likable and complicated character who faces adversity with dry humor to hide his pain. Mphahlele also introduces a new element by presenting a character embodying a synthesis of traditional and Western civilization, a blend Mphahlele has discussed throughout his nonfiction writing. Sometimes Uncle plays music by Edvard Grieg on the piano he bought, which turns out to be stolen, and sometimes he improvises on well-known African tunes. The story is also notable for its dialogue, which captures the idiom of popular speech, doing violence to standard English and thus injecting it with a new vitality.

The stories selected from Mphahlele's previously published work include some of his best, such as "He and the Cat," "Man Must Live," "Down the Quiet Street," "The Coffee-Cart Girl," and "The Suitcase." In the story "In Corner B," township people live to the fullest. For them, even death is an occasion for eating, drinking, and laughing, while keeping a watchful eye on a mourning widow, Talita. The story also tells of the earlier relationship between Talita and her husband. It is a simple love story, tender but not sentimental. Talita, a lively and overtalkative but affectionate woman, loves her gentle and shy man. They have been married for nineteen years when she finds a love letter to her husband from another woman, Marta. After the husband's death Marta comes to the funeral and flings herself on his grave. Later she sends a semiliterate letter from which Talita learns that Marta was never "sweet chokolet of your man," that "he neva love me neva neva," and that he was only "nise leel bit nise to me." Talita's love is thus restored to her, and she feels "like a foot traveller after a good refreshing bath." The description of the funeral preparations and wake is perhaps Mphahlele's most successful scene of township life, and Marta's letter and a tender moment of love between husband and wife are the most touching. By contrast, "A Point of Identity," about a man of mixed blood who betrays the black community he has joined through marriage, makes its political

Mphahlele circa 1980

point but without capturing the imagination of the reader.

"The Barber of Barigo" and "A Ballad of Oyo" are the only stories in the book that have backgrounds set outside South Africa. The former is the story of a man who refuses to become emotionally and actively involved in the rich life around him. Mphahlele has no difficulty in absorbing the atmosphere of a new milieu, but the story suffers under its theme of passivity, which is not illustrated dramatically.

Mphahlele calls his story about the Yoruba market of Oyo a ballad to emphasize the folktale element, and he uses various devices to create the illusion of a tale told by someone who has fallen under a spell. Mphahlele is obviously fascinated with the market but fails to make it an integral part of this story of a vegetable seller caught in a conflict between justice and tradition. The story foreshadows the novel *Chirundu* (1979), in which Mphahlele goes much more deeply into these concerns.

In the later stories of the 1967 collection – especially "In Corner B" and "Mrs. Plum" – Mphahlele's creative skills have matured. There is an economy of words and a conciseness of imagery

lacking before. They mark the height of his creation of short fiction.

By the time *Voices in the Whirlwind* and the revised version of *The African Image* were published, Mphahlele had become known as a major author and a controversial critic. All his essays have a unity in that they express his ideas and ideals in the search for an African identity and for an African context for humankind's place in the universe. Again and again he comes back to the subject of exile, to the "tyranny of place," the pull of the place of one's early experiences – the need for being in a community with whose cultural goals and aspirations one can identify.

As a teacher of English he discusses subjects largely through the eyes of a literary critic. His research into South African literature began with his master's thesis and still continues. Besides his essays he contributes occasional reviews to newspapers and journals, including the *Sowetan*, the *Star*, *English in Africa*, *English Academy Review*, *Tribute*, and *Staffrider*, commenting on writers he admires, such as Njabulo Ndebele and Oswald Mbuyiseni Mtshali. His love for literature comes through clearly in his critical writing. Tradition in Africa, for instance, is not an academic subject for him but a living theme in literature. His lengthy quotations often seem selected not just to prove a point but to share with his readers his intensely personal reading.

All Mphahlele's critical writing, as well as his other essays, fiction, and autobiographical writing, contributes toward formulating his philosophy of African humanism. He cherishes, he says in *Afrika My Music*, the African's belief in the supreme being as a vital force, a dynamic presence in all organic matter, in the elements, and in humankind. He has listed the ingredients of African humanism as being "the love of life for its own sake, while holding it sacred; belief in the interconnectedness of all forms of life, of all nature; our sense of community; our neighbourhood sense of collective responsibility; our desire to touch one another physically; family concern for protection of the old; our capacity to absorb influences from other cultures because of the openness of our traditional religious beliefs. . . ."

In *Afrika My Music* he says that ghetto life in South Africa was fashioned "out of our own ghetto culture, out of the bits and pieces of what was available to us in Western culture, and the stubborn sediments of the indigenous that could still be stirred up from the depths of our collective personality." Thus when Mphahlele turned away from Christianity toward African religion and values, it did not mean a total rejection of the West. His theory of synthesis has often been misunderstood and interpreted as integration and compromise. Nothing could be further from the truth. The idealism he shared in the 1950s with the ANC, an idealism that advocated a nonracial society, died for him with the arrest and trials of its leaders and with the tragic events at Sharpeville. But because African humanism is inclusive, not exclusive, blacks must leave the door open for others to come in. However, "They must earn their entry," he says. "No longer can we . . . make ourselves available on the white man's terms."

For Mphahlele, synthesis is something inherent in African thinking. He says in his 1971 introduction to Awoonor's collection of poetry *Night of My Blood* that the African has a keen sense of relationship between phenomena, of interconnection. And so Mphahlele warns against the danger of completely dismissing the Western aesthetic out of sheer crusading zeal. He feels that there is no need for conflict in the critic's mind whether to adhere to Western values or to reject them. In *Voices in the Whirlwind* he explores African and black American poetry against a background of modern European thought, as represented mainly by the critical writings of Christopher Caudwell, I. A. Richards, and Laurence Lerner. A work of art, Mphahlele insists, must express the artist's personal emotions and communicate these to the reader. At the same time, it must integrate and unify his personal experience and the sum of the experience of his fellow human beings.

Negritude, the early concept of black consciousness initiated in black French Africa and the Caribbean, Mphahlele initially rejected with vehemence because he regarded it as a pose, an artificial structure, a museum artifact. In South Africa, where black people face a fight against government efforts to legislate them back to their tribes, they dare not look back with nostalgia. In the revised edition of *The African Image* he says that negritude can have meaning only "if one regards it as a social force, never static, a tension, a continuing movement that asserts the value of African culture and its constitutions." In an open letter to Léopold Sédar Senghor – president of Senegal and a leading poet in the movement – Mphahlele revisits negritude and explains the effect Senghor's *Chants d'Ombre* (Songs of Shadow, 1945) had on him, how it entranced him, knocked him off balance, and helped to "measure the energy of Africa" in him, "the thing we had taken for granted in ghettos where you could never efface your blackness" (*The Unbroken Song*, 1981). Today Mphahlele feels comfortable with the successor to negritude, black consciousness, and with the related ideology, though not the politics, of Pan-Africanism. On his return to South Africa in 1977 he Africanized his first name to Es'kia.

In "African Writers and Commitment," one of the essays in *Voices in the Whirlwind*, Mphahlele turns to the question of a writer's commitment to a political purpose. He finds Jean-Paul Sartre's insistence on social and political programs too rigid. While Mphahlele feels that every writer "is committed to something beyond his art," to a statement of value not purely aesthetic, to a "criticism of life," he finds this functional meaning a dangerous tendency since it limits the author's vision. "Live and go out. / Define and / medicate the whirlwind," he says, quoting the 1964 poem by Gwendolyn Brooks that gives the collection its title.

By 1968 Mphahlele had felt ready to write a novel. When he wrote *Down Second Avenue* and his short stories, he was an unknown black man turning to a mainly white readership in South Africa and Britain. Later he knew that he would be measured against novelists of the stature of Achebe.

Africa and its interaction with displaced authors is the theme of Mphahlele's *The Wanderers*. He told Cosmo Pieterse in an interview for the BBC (published in 1972) that it was the first time he had tried to give a panoramic view of Africa and the torments Africa was going through. "I wanted to bring out the life of exile and put myself as the central character at different points," he told Ursula A. Barnett. If *The Wanderers* says anything at all, it should . . . be a personal record of [a] search for place." Yet he insisted that it was more fiction than autobiography since it had an imaginary plot.

The story opens with the news of the death of Felang, Timi Tabane's eldest son. Along with twenty-six other black African nationalist freedom fighters, he had been captured by a commando group of white farmers on the borders of Zimbabwe and thrown to the crocodiles. The narrative basically follows Mphahlele's experiences in South Africa, which Timi, as narrator, describes in the beginning of the book in a flashback to the time before the birth of Felang. This first of five parts is an account of Timi's life and hardships in the South African township in which he lives and of his work on the magazine *Bongo*; it closely follows Mphahlele's life during the same period, as does *Down Second Avenue*, depicting the people living there amid the misery and the violence who are trying to maintain their human dignity. Timi, like Mphahlele, frustrated in his work for the magazine, has to decide whether to leave the country. Timi's life intertwines with that of Steven Cartwright, editor of *Bongo*, who, in a country ruled by what he calls "white thugs and Nazi-headed hoodlums," battles constantly with a feeling of guilt.

In exile Timi's life continues more or less to follow the events in the life of Mphahlele. Readers learn of the problems Timi and his wife, Karabo, have with Felang, who is rebellious, will not apply himself to his schoolwork, and will not communicate with his parents – a parallel to the relationship Mphahlele and his wife had with their oldest son, Anthony.

When Timi leaves Africa, he feels he must stay out until he is needed, until the "waspish imperialism" and the "mute arrogance" of the conservative Africans has been replaced. Then Africa would come into its own, "a land of theatre, gaiety, of hot humid days and grey harmattans, of warm rain showers. Cities with vibrant night life." He might return to Africa, but not soon. He has expected a "roar of triumph, the triumph of black rule." Instead, there has been the plaintive sound of defeat.

Within the framework of his own life story and a loosely woven and rambling account of real and imaginary characters, their wanderings, and their relations with each other, Mphahlele uses this novel as a vehicle for all the themes that concerned him during his years of exile. He states his beliefs more clearly than in any of his earlier works. African humanism, in the novel, is seeking "harmony with other men, without letting anyone trample on you."

Youth is a strong theme for Mphahlele. Felang's life and his martyrdom and death are symbolic of young Africa's search for identity. Readers are given a further clue about the significance of the theme in Timi's recurring dream of terror: he is pursued, but the faces of the pursuers elude him. Only toward the end of the story does he recognize them to be young, black South Africans. Timi/Mphahlele as father, narrator, individual, and teacher, is burdened with an overwhelming sense of responsibility for future generations.

Mphahlele also shows Timi thinking deeply about the meaning of exile and trying to come to terms with bitterness. While investigating for *Bongo* the death of the husband of a young woman, Naledi, he has been rereading Wright's *Uncle Tom's Children* (1938) and wonders whether he, too, will continue to hate and curse and burn with the same anger. Timi discovers that exile is not the solution, for he has not reckoned with the all-encompassing feeling of guilt engendered by his departure from the scene of action.

The Wanderers is thus also about the tragedy and the hope of Africa. Mphahlele has tried to symbolize all this in a story about his wanderings and of the conflicts of those who will have to carry Africa's heritage. The novel fails because the tale is too diffuse, being far too long and rambling. The work is often interesting, often poignant, but there is little coherence. The theme based on the relationship between Timi and his son begins too late and lacks depth. The other themes are, however, often presented consistently. The search for a place in which a person can practice simple human ideals is expressed in the intertwining lives of Timi and Steven—black and white – and in the death of Felang. White people must break out of their cruel heritage, and black people for whom self-fulfillment lies only in exile and death must learn actively to control their own destiny. Embodying this control is Naledi, who acquires it as a result of suffering. While helping the wounded during unrest in her parents' village, she becomes the victim of an attempted rape and later sees her attacker, a policeman, receive a suspended sentence and remain on the force. As a symbol, she combines the traditional values of Africa with adaptation to what is useful in Western civilization. She marries Steven, who has moved to Britain. He then returns to Africa to work for a news magazine and later dies there. After her husband's death she remains in Britain to study nutrition and will no doubt bring her skills back to Africa.

A strong-willed, maturing girl of charm and grace, Naledi still does not match Karabo in "Mrs. Plum," Pinkie in "The Coffee-Cart Girl," and Diketso in the Lesane stories. The character of Karabo in the novel, on the other hand, comes through in successive glimpses that make up a convincing whole. She is patient and loyal in following her husband, because she never questions her function as a traditional African wife. When it comes to others, however, she is capable of spirited and determined action. She will not take nonsense from anyone. To the doorman of a nightclub who will not admit a friend of hers without a tie she says, "Why all the fuss about ties anyhow? We didn't go about dangling rags round our necks before you whites came to Africa." Mphahlele, in his autobiographical writing before his return to South Africa, did not tell much about his own wife, but it is clear that someone who had supported him in all his wanderings, who stood by his side in adversity and success, and who managed to study and graduate as a social worker, must be a woman of the same stamina, courage, and forthrightness that he successfully depicts in Karabo.

Mphahlele describes *The Wanderers* as a personal account of a search. One wonders why he chose to present it as fiction at all. Names of characters and places are sometimes changed and sometimes left intact. If one is acquainted with the life story of Mphahlele, it becomes an amusing game to find the key. Don Peck of *Bongo* is Jim Bailey, owner of *Drum*. Steven Cartwright is Sylvester Stein, the editor. Tom Hobson is Tom Hopkinson, his successor; Lazy is Casey Motsisi, one of the journalists on the magazine; Emil is Ulli Beier, and so forth. Awoonor's name is left unchanged. Felang's death and the story of Naledi seem to be almost the only additions to a nearly chronological account of Mphahlele's life. Yet he seems to have lost his skill in stirring up a lively interest in narrative episodes. The general effect is one of lack of movement. Most of the time nothing happens, and when it does, readers often know about it from hearsay. The story of the rape attempt on Naledi, for instance, reaches the reader thirdhand via her lawyer and the narrator. The story of Naledi's first husband, a prisoner who has been abducted for slave labor on a farm, lacks the power of Henry Nxumalo's exposé about the notorious Bethal potato farms in *Drum* and, indeed, of Mphahlele's own reports in that journal. The mingling of fact and fiction in *The Wanderers* neither enables readers to identify with the passion of the characters as in an imaginary story, nor to share the urgent indignation of a successful journalistic exposé. The only events that seem to happen before readers' eyes are those concerning Felang. He is seen arguing with his parents, misbehaving at school and at home, running away, and returning. Although Timi as narrator tells about the situation, the anguish of the three people concerned makes it real and immediate.

One gathers from Mphahlele's writing that his marriage to Rebecca, with him as the "thinker" and Rebecca as the "doer," has been an exceptionally happy one. Mphahlele takes parenthood very seriously but there was at one time a lack of communication with the boys in the family. The heroic death of Felang in *The Wanderers* is not symbolic infanticide but rather a transferred attempt to give Mphahlele's purposeless son direction.

The Wanderers was widely reviewed throughout the United States. Most critics were disappointed, more so because Mphahlele had become an established writer and a first novel was a literary event. Many reviewers, however, found much that was good. James Olney, in his *Tell Me Africa* (1973) says the novel is "aimless and disjointed, an account of a simple, inert, mass wandering." But later, in a letter to Mphahlele included in N. Chabani Manganyi's *Exiles and Homecomings* (1983), Olney conceded "its many virtues," among which he includes the depth and intensity of thought at the end and the success in conveying experience. James R. Frakes, writing in the *Washington Post* (11 April 1971), felt that *The Wanderers* could have been one of the masterpieces in fiction if passionate involvement — anger, firsthand experience, outrage, compassion, and topicality — were enough. But he, like several other critics, found that a firm narrative line and full development of character were missing. The most scathing comment came from Lewis Nkosi, in his *Tasks and Masks* (1981): "Mphahlele seems to have given up the cool objectivity of his short stories." Nkosi describes the novel as a turgidly voluminous prose work without a creative purpose behind it.

As a student once again, and as a teacher, writer, and critic, Mphahlele had found his two years in Denver satisfactory. In 1968 he was awarded his Ph.D., having presented *The Wanderers* in lieu of a dissertation, in the Creative Writing Program of the English department. He was also elected to Phi Beta Kappa for academic excellence.

In 1968 he accepted a post as senior lecturer in the English department of the University of Zambia. He was ready to make a permanent commitment to this country, the closest he could get to home. As usual he enjoyed teaching, both at the university and in the community, and he was happy to be among many fellow black South African exiles. But he was upset by some activities of the government, which sometimes evicted or jailed black South African and Zimbabwean refugees. Disillusioned once more, he left before his contract expired and joined the English department of the University of Denver as an associate professor in 1970.

His experiences in Zambia became the subject of *Chirundu*. This time, however, the only factual elements were the historical events, not his own personal experiences. *Chirundu* is the story of the fall from power of a cabinet minister, Chimba Chirundu, and of the dissolution of his marriage. Mphahlele explores the dynamics of power in relation to domestic life, sex, the African's attitude toward polygamy, and the modern woman's rejection of it. At the same time the novel is a study of African independence and its effects of hope and disillusionment.

Chirundu's wife Tirenje lays a charge of bigamy against him when he marries a sophisticated young woman named Monde. Chirundu contends that Bemba marriage laws, according to which he married Tirenje, look upon marriage as having ended if a wife leaves her husband and her family takes no steps to bring her back. Tirenje counters that the traditional marriage was subsequently registered under the old colonial ordinance, the divorce laws of which supersede the traditional ones. Since no divorce proceedings took place, Tirenje claims, her marriage still holds and Chirundu's marriage to Monde is bigamous. Chirundu does not expect to win the case but defends it nonetheless, so that, when marriage laws are revised, traditional marriage will be recognized as something that cannot be superseded.

When independence came to Chirundu's (unnamed) country he was at the height of his power. Two years later, however, his fortune has changed. He has been demoted from minister of the interior to minister of transport and public works because he is thought to have been too tough when handling the more responsible portfolio. There is unrest in the country, and strikes occur in which Chirundu's nephew Moyo plays a leading role. Chirundu is found guilty of bigamy and is given a jail sentence. The house he built is burned down. There is a subplot concerning the political prisoners Pitso and Chieza, who form a kind of chorus commenting on political developments. There is bitter humor in their explicit exchanges about the situation in the country. The South African Dr. Studs Letanka is a brilliant mathematician who has abandoned his post at the University of Fort Hare because it fell under the Bantu Education system and began to concentrate on African history.

One would expect a writer of the standing of Mphahlele to return to the novel form after an interval of several years only if he had something important to communicate. Yet at the beginning *Chirundu* seems almost trivial. It opens by introducing the cabinet minister Chirundu as having committed bigamy, a crime so petty that even his fellow prisoners are unimpressed. They feel, however, that there must be something more to it than just the simple crime, and obviously Mphahlele intended something deeper in the novel than displaying the chicaneries of the unprepossessing character of the title.

Chirundu is about the abuse of power. It is a dirge for Africa, in which anguished disillusionment is the keynote. Hope for "a bright new day," the phrase with which the prison warder greets his charges each morning, and which was the original, satiric title of the novel, is dim indeed. But all is not gloom: there is a glimmer on the horizon, and for the new generation, exemplified by Moyo, there might yet be a bright new day. His house has not burned down; on the contrary, it has yet to be built. And its foundations will be solid. He has not lost touch with real tradition; his faith in the power of continuity, in his ancestors, remains strong.

Mphahlele does not see the confrontation between Chirundu and Tirenje as a clash between tradition and Western values. Rather he is investigating the impact of a foreign culture on an African one and the problem of how one should deal with the resulting conflicts. All Western culture should not be discarded, he says. Synthesis is still Mphahlele's answer, and Tirenje and Moyo are its representatives. In her schooldays Tirenje had fallen under the influence of a young female teacher who told her students to wake up and fend for themselves. Tirenje is contrasted with Monde, who has gained only a veneer of Western civilization.

For the South African refugees in the novel, exile has meant disillusionment. Letanka drinks too much and dies in a car crash. Pitso decides to return to South Africa, even though it is likely he will be arrested as a terrorist. For black South Africa the message is clear: beware of the slogans and easy answers. Above all, beware of the abuse of power. As vehicles for all these themes, the events and characters are handled with skill. Tirenje is another of Mphahlele's forceful women. Moyo is a vibrant and attractive young man symbolizing young Africa, and the minor characters fulfill their functions well. But what of Chirundu himself? Are readers to admire and sympathize with this vain, power-hungry sexist character, and, if not, how can they care whether he triumphs or suffers defeat? In a 1981 seminar at Rand Afrikaans University in Johannesburg, Mphahlele, in reply to the question of whether or not he saw Chirundu as a tragic hero, said that he simply thought of the character as a product of history, as a symbol of a people rather than as a hero. Chirundu never loses faith in himself, and after his downfall he feels sure he will make a comeback. One is reminded of Zungu in "Man Must Live." Has Mphahlele then come full circle, abandoning his search, to conclude that all one can do is cling tenaciously to one's faith and destiny? This conclusion would be understandable because Mphahlele, when he wrote *Chirundu* in the early 1970s, was still in exile, displaced, with hope of a return to the country of his destiny as remote as ever, and almost devoid of hope for Africa.

Chirundu is not easy to read. The many threads give an initial impression of confusion, but this is deceptive. The novel is carefully constructed, the themes holding together the stories (told from different perspectives) to a far greater extent than in *The Wanderers*. Mphahlele, in a 25 April 1977 letter to Barnett said that his structure is an attempt "to suggest, if not to adopt wholesale, folk narrative."

Although completed in 1974, *Chirundu* remained unpublished for several years, but in 1979 it became Mphahlele's first book-length work since *Man Must Live* to be published in South Africa. The ban on him had been lifted, and Ravan Press immediately availed itself of the opportunity to add the doyen of black South African writers to their growing list. Reviews in South Africa showed a certain bewilderment about the subject matter and about the author himself. Most white South African readers simply did not know this professor of English literature, doctor of philosophy, Nobel Prize candidate, and author of many books, who had been banned from their libraries and bookshops for most of his writing life. However, among black readers his name had been kept alive.

Mphahlele taught at Denver until 1974, when he joined the University of Pennsylvania, in Phila-

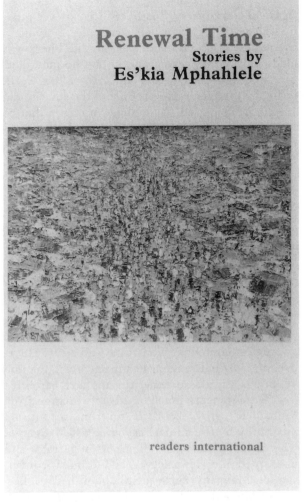

Dust jacket for Mphahlele's 1988 book, in which he collected some of his favorite previously published stories

delphia, as a full professor of English. He was happy in the United States when immersed in his teaching of a variety of courses in African, Caribbean, Afro-American, American, and British literatures. But within himself, he says, he always felt that he was an uncommitted outsider. He was not reaching the people he wanted to teach, young, black South Africans. He was writing but outside the cultural milieu in which his work was relevant and without the feedback for which he yearned.

Since 1972 he had considered returning to South Africa. All he wanted was to claim his ancestral heritage and assert his simple role as a humanist. "I want to teach in a community whose cultural goals or aspirations I comprehend, because education is for me an agent of culture even as it is culture itself," he wrote in an article titled "The Tyranny of Place" (1973). Exile had become for him "a ghetto of the mind." Once it became known that he was contemplating a return to South Africa, he became a figure of controversy. South African exiles felt that he was betraying the people's cause by applying to the regime for a visa and accepting it. There was also surprise and consternation that he should accept a post at Turfloop, the University of the North in Lebowa, which was a product of the educational system he abhorred. Mphahlele countered that he would teach African students wherever he found them. However, he never took the post. The South African government, which had granted him a visa on the condition that he confine himself to Lebowa, then proceeded to veto the unanimous decision of the university council to appoint him as head of the Department of English. He arrived in Lebowa in 1977 and stayed through 1978 as an inspector of schools, then in 1979, ironically, accepted a post at the mainly white University of the Witwatersrand in Johannesburg. For a year he was a senior research fellow in the African Studies Institute; then he became an associate professor. In 1981 he was appointed a professor of African literature and awarded a tenured position at the university. He retired in 1987 but remained connected with the university as a professor emeritus and a research fellow. Readers learn much of this information from Mphahlele's *Afrika My Music* and from the unusual biography by the clinical psychologist Manganyi, who casts Mphahlele as a first-person narrator and uses taped interviews, letters, and dramatic conversations. Manganyi subsequently published a collection of Mphahlele's letters under the title *Bury Me at the Marketplace* (1984). In *Exiles and Homecomings* Manganyi shows Mphahlele delving deeply into his soul, yet sometimes the gentle tolerance of the Mphahlele one knows from his other writing is lost in the biography and one wonders whether it is a salutary experience for a writer to find his psyche dissected through words put in his mouth by a therapist. In both the biography and the second autobiography (*Afrika My Music*) readers lose something of the spontaneity of *Down Second Avenue*.

In the published letters, readers find a rather different Mphahlele from the man who muses about life in his autobiography. As a letter writer, he always has something specific to say, and he says it clearly without embellishment. It could be a request to a friend or mentor, an admonition to one of his children, a comment on something he has read or done, a progress report on a project, or a personal note to a friend telling what a recent visit has meant. "What a spiritual uplift it was," he once wrote to his lifelong friend the musician Khabi Mngoma, "even though we had you but a day and a

half. . . In all the 18 years of exile, we hadn't experienced an occasion like our reunion and I mean it. We are grateful you came." To a friend who had sent him a monograph on William Faulkner, he wrote: "I enjoyed [it]. I find it stimulating, so balanced, so sane, so economically done, yet with so much intellectual toughness. I always wondered what to make of Faulkner's religious beliefs and moral stand. Now I think I see. Thanks for the illumination." There is less obvious endeavor to put himself and his ideas across. Rather Mphahlele seems to have the confidence of releasing his words into the care of someone who will understand. The letters were not necessarily written on the spur of the moment. Writing to his daughter, Teresa Kefilwe, to tell her how much she had recently hurt her mother's feelings, he explained that it was his habit to wait until he found the right vocabulary to phrase his indignation, that he would do so only to someone he cared about, and that if he was unable to express himself the way he wanted, he would rather keep quiet.

Manganyi has done a splendid job in collecting and selecting the letters and providing explanatory notes and arranging them so that Mphahlele's professional and intellectual life, thoughts, ideals, friendships, and interests can be followed. A fresh and uncluttered picture of the man himself emerges: compassionate, tolerant, vibrant, patient, and optimistic, willing to impart and accept favors and knowledge. Yet his unhappiness in exile is almost tangible in letters to friends, and in his letters to his daughter, the child to whom he is obviously closest, who shares his impulse to write, he pours out his hopes and fears for the family. To others he writes of his moral dilemma in accepting a post at a white university. Readers also learn a great deal about the background to his writing. His correspondence in the early years of his writing career with the drama teacher and producer Norah Taylor offers a rare testimony of friendship and a set of documents well worth preserving.

Afrika My Music takes up his life story where *Down Second Avenue* left off, and the greater part covers the years of exile. He tells of literary matters in African countries in which he played a role, all seen from the viewpoint of a newcomer to these regions. The word portraits of writers such as Camara Laye, Ngugi wa Thiong'o, Soyinka, Clark, Okigbo, Awoonor, and others are too brief to be revealing, but they give thoughtful glimpses of the people he met. The South African section takes readers only as far as his work in Lebowa. Mphahlele calls the first chapter "The Sounds Begin Again," but the sounds are not the "siren in the night," the "thunder at the door," or the "wordless endless wail / only the unfree know," to which Dennis Brutus refers in his well-known poem "Sirens, Knuckles, Boots" (from the 1963 book of that name), the first line of which Mphahlele chose as the title of this second autobiography. Neither are the sounds the earthy, vibrant ones he records in *Down Second Avenue*. They are the thinner plaintive noises of a man whose homecoming was not a triumphant return to his roots. The picture he draws of modern South Africa is an impersonal one, which is available to readers in greater detail in many social documents.

Reviews of *Afrika My Music* in the black as well as the white press in South Africa were very favorable. Sol Makgabutlane in the *Star* (8 November 1984) wrote that the book lived up to the high standards set by Mphahlele's previous books and overflowed with taut, simple language. Lewis Nkosi, however, writing in the London-based *Third World Review* in 1986 described it as a "self-indulgent apologia for returning to South Africa."

The collection *The Unbroken Song*, also published in South Africa, is a reprint of short stories and poems almost all previously published elsewhere. (Some of these same stories were reprinted in *Renewal Time*, published in 1988.) Although the contents of *The Unbroken Song* are mostly not new, Mphahlele with his preface tries to put them into a fresh perspective. South African readers had not previously had an opportunity to read the stories, well known as many of them were abroad. Although the ban had been lifted much earlier, some of the individual works were still banned, and the rest were not readily available. Mphahlele therefore felt it necessary to explain in the preface how a barrier between black and white writers arose as a result of the rejection by whites of an African humanistic worldview of an undivided society. Both those who attempt to live outside history and those who insist that literature in South Africa must be placed within the struggle are reminded that social concerns change and shift from time to time. In the unbroken music of black communal experience, revolution means renewal, and in every community "renewal has a cultural purpose, its own." All his best-known stories are included in the collection: "Mrs. Plum," "In Corner B," "Grieg on a Stolen Piano," "He and the Cat," "The Suitcase," "The Master of Doornvlei," and others.

Although Mphahlele's poems have been included in such anthologies as Langston Hughes's *Poems from Black Africa* (1963), Joseph Okpaku's *New African Literature and the Arts* (1967), Paul Breman's

You Better Believe It (1973), and Michael Chapman and Achmat Dangor's *Voices from Within* (1982), they are rarely discussed in critical works, perhaps because they lack the lyrical or revolutionary fire of works by other poets in exile – such as Brutus, Arthur Nortje, and Mazisi Kunene – and the innovative vigor of the 1970s generation of South African poets, including Mongane Serote and others, who were drawing both on their immediate experience within the country and on oral tradition. Mphahlele's concerns throughout his poems have been the same as those of his prose: exile, the pull of place, and concern for the painful events in South Africa. In a prose poem, as he calls it, "Portrait of a Man Who Lives in a Glasshouse," written in the United States and published in *Era* (Spring 1976), Mphahlele uses a metaphor for the fear of forgetting one's origins while the storm around one rages: that of living in a house in which it would be easy to renew one's lease, to shut the door, and to coast along. But he feels he can never do such a thing because deep inside he "hears the bangs and clatter of the door in the storm of memory."

In *The Unbroken Song* "Death II" is based on John Keats's sonnet "When I Have Fears that I May Cease to Be," but Mphahlele's fear is that he will die in an alien land. Returning to South Africa shortly after the infamous killings of the Soweto children, he had an impulse, like that of most black poets in South Africa, to write a tribute to the children and give vent to his anger and bitterness. The result is a dramatic poem, "Fathers and Sons," about a fifteen-year-old imprisoned boy, whose father was executed at the time of the boy's birth. In "A Prayer," written after a brief visit to South Africa in 1976, Mphahlele speaks of having been "reconnected and / becoming renewed on this killing ground." When he speaks of his sorrow and guilt for being out of the fray, and refusing to be lulled into a false peace, he is writing in the mainstream of South African poetry in exile. But the sounds do not linger in the ear as do Brutus's, and Mphahlele's isolation in exile is less evocative than that of Nortje.

The Unbroken Song has not been published abroad, and the available reviews are South African. The white press tended to be patronizing, especially about the stories that have been anthologized again and again. *Charming* is hardly a term critics acquainted with Mphahlele's ideas would use in describing them, nor would anyone but a white South African see "Mrs. Plum" as a cool but sympathetic picture of the troubles of a liberal white woman. Academics were better informed. Michael Chapman in *UNISA English Studies* (20 April 1982) found the perceptions and images of the poems acutely attuned to post-1976 South Africa.

Mphahlele's interest in traditional literature goes back to his student days when he won a prize at Adams College for the retelling of a folktale. It was in his play writing rather than in his poetry that he drew on traditional literature, but from early on he was aware of the importance of preserving every kind of traditional literature. His interest in traditional literature was never merely a search for artifacts. The first stage of a research project into African poetry resulted in a paper delivered at Rhodes University in April 1979 and published almost simultaneously as "The Voice of Prophecy in African Poetry." In it he relates the prophetic voice of oral poetry, with its resonance of organic unity in the universe, to the public voice in modern African poetry, which has to deal with new imperatives. Upon his return to South Africa, Mphahlele had almost immediately embarked on research into the oral poetry of the Venda, North Sotho, and Tsonga in the Northern Transvaal. He has plans to do English adaptations.

There is one more book-length work of fiction Mphahlele has written and published. *Father Come Home* (1984) is a historical novel for children that takes place in the early 1920s after the Native Land Act had been passed, driving Africans from large, fertile areas into small, arid reserves. As a consequence, men were forced to leave their families and work in mines. The story concerns the growth to independence of fourteen-year-old Maredi Tulamo, whose father has left the family and returns only many years later. Adventures occur when the boy goes off in search of his father, but he gets only as far as a farm where he remains to work. The white farmer is not an important character in the novel. White life has become peripheral again, as it was in Mphahlele's earliest fiction. The man is neither unkind nor cruel: "he was simply in charge of their [the laborers'] fate." It is with life in the village that Mphahlele is primarily concerned, the suffering of the wives and mothers left behind and the hardships and values of the community. The narration is filled with folklore and includes epics about warriors, sung by the stranger Mashabela, a musician, poet, and healer, who moves into the village.

Mphahlele draws on his own life as a herd boy in the northern Transvaal, where he suffered the pain of growing up without a father. There is psychological insight in the story of the boy whose life is ruled by a longing for his father, but when at last the father comes home, there is no fairy-tale ending. Maredi finds it difficult to relate to the man and has

Drawing of Mphahlele by Nils Burwitz (National English Literary Museum, Grahamstown, South Africa)

to learn to adjust. The story is told in simple language for children, but the touching plot and the vividly depicted geographical and historical background appeal equally to adults. The work fills part of a great need in South Africa for a childrens' literature that is meaningful for black children.

Mphahlele's return to South Africa, on the surface, seems to have been a failure. He came back to the only place where he could find inspiration to write, yet his literary output has been small and disappointing. His ideas have often been misunderstood both at home and abroad. Yet he is doing what he has struggled to do throughout his career, something that has given meaning to his life and his writing: establishing a central base from which to spread African cultural values among the people of the land. In Nigeria, in the Mbari centers, he gloried in success. In Kenya he failed. It remains to be seen whether he can fully succeed in the country where it matters most to him and where the difficulties are the greatest.

In a graduation address at Witwatersrand in 1980 Mphahlele criticized the university for putting off far too long any serious program for African education in the content and thrust of its disciplines. He wanted to see the university establish community colleges in or near Soweto to meet the needs of the black population. Also in 1980 Mphahlele, with a Carnegie grant, founded in Johannesburg the Council for Black Education (COBERT) and became its director. The main purpose of the council is to create a climate for the education of black people instead of merely reacting to government policy. It works toward a formulation of educational theory that will reflect black aspirations for self-determination. The council is national in scope. It conducts programs of informal education in the form of lectures on a variety of interests and for various groups: students, teachers, and other groups of adults. These lectures are published periodically as *The Capricorn Papers*. The council also has an arts program. A fine-arts study section and drama and music centers are being contemplated. For his work in the council Mphahlele was awarded the 1985 Claude Harris Leon Foundation prize for outstanding community service. He has retired from the University of the Witwatersrand but is still associated with COBERT. He lives in Lebowa and is involved in community education; he is also writing short stories for children.

In 1972, in a letter to John Wideman of the University of Pennsylvania recommending Mphahlele for a position there, Robert Richardson of the University of Denver called Mphahlele one of the half dozen distinguished African men of letters and said he regarded Mphahlele as the leading African figure then teaching in the United States. In most academic circles worldwide and in many writing, teaching, and student groups, Mphahlele is still recognized as a leader in the field of African literature, a writer and teacher who has devoted his life to the propagation of his ideals, and a man of compassion and integrity. He is much sought after as a visiting lecturer and public speaker and is an advisory editor for several publications. In 1989 he was honored with a festschrift, *Footprints Along the Way*, with contributions by leading writers from Africa and elsewhere.

Es'kia Mphahlele's vision of an African culture with a creative energy strong enough to survive and renew itself perpetually is responsible for his involvement in every phase of black life, literature, and education in South Africa. Because his vision is essentially a Pan-African one, his legacy will survive the present regime in South Africa and will benefit future generations in his own country and beyond.

Letters:

N. Chabani Manganyi, ed., *Bury Me at the Marketplace: Selected Letters of Es'kia Mphahlele 1943–1980* (Johannesburg: Skotaville, 1984).

Interviews:

Lewis Nkosi, "Conversation with Ezekiel Mphahlele," *Africa Report*, 9, no. 7 (1964): 8–9;

Ian Munro, Richard Priebe, and Reinhard Sander, "An Interview with Ezekiel Mphahlele," in *Palaver: Interviews with Five African Writers in Texas*, edited by Bernth Lindfors, Munro, Priebe, and Sander (Austin: African and Afro-American Research Institute, University of Texas at Austin, 1972), pp. 39–44;

Cosmo Pieterse and Dennis Duerden, eds., *African Writers Talking: A Collection of Radio Interviews* (London: Heinemann / New York: Africana, 1972), pp. 95–112;

Ossie Onuora Enekwe, "From an Interview with Ezekiel Mphahlele," *Greenfield Review*, 5, nos. 3–4 (1976–1977): 72–76;

Phanuel Akubueze Egejuru, *Towards African Literary Independence: A Dialogue with Contemporary African Writers* (Westport, Conn.: Greenwood, 1980), pp. 98–105, 132–141;

Noel Manganyi, "The Early Years . . . ," *Staffrider*, 3, no. 3 (1980): 45–46.

Bibliography:

Katherine Skinner and Gareth Cornwell, "Es'kia Mphahlele: A Checklist of Primary Sources," *English in Africa*, 13 (October 1986): 89–103;

Catherine Woeber and John Read, *Es'kia Mphahlele: A Bibliography* (Grahamstown, South Africa: National English Literary Museum, 1989).

Biography:

N. Chabani Manganyi, *Exiles and Homecomings: A Biography of Es'kia Mphahlele* (Johannesburg: Ravan, 1983).

References:

Samuel Omo Asein, "The Humanism of Ezekiel Mphahlele," *Journal of Commonwealth Literature*, 15, no. 1 (1980): 38–49;

Ursula A. Barnett, "Africa or the West? Cultural Synthesis in the Work of Es'kia Mphahlele," *Africa Insight*, 14, no. 1 (1984): 59–63;

Barnett, *Ezekiel Mphahlele* (Boston: G. K. Hall, 1976);

Barnett, "The Legend of Zeke Mphahlele," *Contrast*, 11, no. 2 (1977): 20–24;

Barnett, *A Vision of Order: A Study of Black South Afri-*

can Literature in English (1914–1980) (London: Sinclair Browne / Amherst: University of Massachusetts Press, 1983), pp. 25–29, 141–149, 169–181, 222–226, 254–262;

'Bayo Ogunjimi, "Mphahlele: The Aesthetics and Ideology of Alienation," *Présence Africaine*, 135 (1985): 120–128;

Gerald Chapman, "Exile in Denver," *Denver Quarterly*, 21, no. 2 (1986): 120–154;

Sarah Christie, Geoffrey Hutchings, and Don Maclennan, *Perspectives on South African Fiction* (Johannesburg: Donker, 1980);

Phanuel Akubueze Egejuru, *Black Writers, White Audience: A Critical Approach to African Literature* (Hicksville, N.Y.: Exposition, 1978);

C. O. Gardner, "The Laudation Spoken by the University Orator, Professor C. O. Gardner, in Presenting Es'kia Mphahlele to the Chancellor at the Graduation Ceremony of the University of Natal Held in Pietermaritzburg on the 16th April, 1983," *English Academy Review*, 1 (1983): 131–134;

R. Dorian Haarhoff, "The Southern African Setting of *Chirundu*," *English in Africa*, 13 (October 1986): 39–45;

Norman Hodge, "Dogs, Africans and Liberals: The World of Mphahlele's 'Mrs. Plum,' " *English in Africa*, 8 (March 1981): 33–43;

Hodge, " 'The Way I Looked at Life Then': Es'kia Mphahlele's *Man Must Live, and Other Stories*," *English in Africa*, 13 (October 1986): 47–64;

Martin Jarrett-Kerr, "Exile, Alienation and Literature: The Case of Es'kia Mphahlele," *Africa Today*, 33, no. 1 (1986): 27–35;

Joyce Johnson, "Culturally Derived Motifs and Symbols as Structural Features in Es'kia Mphahlele's *Chirundu*," *Kunapipi*, 6, no. 2 (1984): 109–120;

Vladimír Klíma, *South African Prose Writing in English* (Prague: Oriental Institute in Academia, 1971), pp. 102–119;

Leon de Kock, "Literature, Politics and Universalism: A Debate between Ezekiel Mphahlele and J. M. Coetzee," *Journal of Literary Studies*, 3, no. 4 (1987): 35–48;

Gerald Moore, *Twelve African Writers* (London: Hutchinson / Bloomington: Indiana University Press, 1980);

G. M. Nkondo, "Apartheid and Alienation: Mphahlele's *The Wanderers*," *Africa Today*, 20, no. 4 (1973): 59–70;

Lewis Nkosi, *Home and Exile* (London: Longman, 1965), pp. 125–136;

Nkosi, *Tasks and Masks: Themes and Styles of African Literature* (Harlow, U.K.: Longman, 1981), pp. 16–19, 91–99;

Okpure O. Obuke, "South African History, Politics and Literature: Mphahlele's *Down Second Avenue* and Rive's *Emergency*," *African Literature Today*, 10 (1979): 191–201;

James Olney, *Tell Me Africa: An Approach to African Literature* (Princeton, N.J.: Princeton University Press, 1973), pp. 248–282;

Adrian Roscoe, *Uhuru's Fire: African Literature East to South* (Cambridge: Cambridge University Press, 1977), pp. 228–232;

Damian Ruth, "Through the Keyhole: Masters and Servants in the Work of Es'kia Mphahlele," *English in Africa*, 13, no. 2 (1986): 65–88;

Hilary Semple, " 'Brother Mortals': Robert Burns and Es'kia Mphahlele," *Contrast*, 17, no. 4 (1989): 25–41;

Sipho Sepamla, "The Black Writer in South Africa Today: Problems and Dilemmas," *New Classic*, 3 (1976): 18–26;

Peter N. Thuynsma, ed., *Footprints Along the Way: A Tribute to Es'kia Mphahlele* (Johannesburg: Skotaville/Justified, 1989);

Brian Worsfold, "Growing Up with Apartheid: A Look at the Socio-political Background in Ezekiel Mphahlele's *Down Second Avenue* and Peter Abrahams's *Tell Freedom*," in *Autobiographical and Biographical Writing in the Commonwealth*, edited by Doireann MacDermott (Barcelona: AUSA, 1984), pp. 255–259.

Papers:

Unpublished correspondence (1959–1979) between Mphahlele and Ursula A. Barnett is in the National English Literary Museum, Grahamstown, South Africa.

Oswald Mbuyiseni Mtshali

(17 January 1940 –)

Cecily Lockett
Rand Africaans University, Johannesburg

BOOKS: *Sounds of a Cowhide Drum* (Johannesburg: Renoster, 1971; London: Oxford University Press, 1972; New York: Third Press, 1972);
Fireflames (Pietermaritzburg, South Africa: Shuter & Shooter, 1980; Westport, Conn.: Hill, 1980).

OTHER: "Mtshali on Mtshali," *Bolt*, 7 (March 1973): 2–3;
"Black Poetry in Southern Africa: What It Means," in *Aspects of South African Literature*, edited by Christopher Heywood (London: Heinemann / New York: Africana, 1976), pp. 121–127.

Oswald Mbuyiseni Mtshali's volume of poetry *Sounds of a Cowhide Drum*, published in 1971, gave the original impetus to what became known as "New Black Poetry," or Soweto poetry, during the 1970s in South Africa. It was a poetry closely aligned with the rise of the "Black Consciousness" movements in the late 1960s, and it reflected the temper of protest and resistance that was given expression in the Soweto uprising on 16 June 1976. Mtshali's work also helped engender a climate of radical revision in thought about South African literature in the local university English departments, as the forthright, sometimes crude, but always powerful nature of his poetry challenged accepted Western notions of good taste. His first collection was, in 1971, awarded the Olive Schreiner Prize for poetry by the English Academy of Southern Africa. Hailed in the South African press as the first black voice in Southern African English poetry since H. I. E. Dhlomo in the 1940s and as a Zulu "scooter messenger" who could write poetry, Mtshali gained wide recognition both at home and abroad. *Sounds of a Cowhide Drum* was later published in Great Britain and the United States and was received as the voice of a black man speaking out against his oppressors. It has sold a record number of copies for a book of poems from South Africa.

Mtshali was born of Zulu parents on 17 Janu-

Oswald Mbuyiseni Mtshali (photograph by Ad Donker)

ary 1940 in the village of Kwa-Bhanya near Vryheid in the province of Natal, South Africa. He was educated at Kwa-Bhanya Primary School and Saint Joseph's College, from which he graduated in 1958. He was refused entry to the University of the Witwatersrand on the basis of the University Education Extension Act of 1959, which made provisions for separate educational facilities for the different racial groups. Like so many talented black people in South Africa whose aspirations are thwarted by apartheid legislation, he was then forced into a series of menial occupations, as a laborer, clerk, messenger, driver, and chauffeur. In 1969 he enrolled at the Premier School of Journalism for a diploma in creative writing and journalism, which he earned in two years. By this time his poetry, highlighting the plight of black people in the township surrounding Johannesburg, was appearing in local journals as well as in international publications such as *Playboy*. In 1971 Mtshali was accepted by the University of South Africa (an "open" correspondence institution), and he commenced working toward a B.A. He completed his degree in the United States at the New School of Social Research in New York. Mtshali then earned an M.F.A. in creative writing from Columbia University and an M.Ed. from the same university in 1979. After his return to South Africa in 1980, he worked briefly as a reporter and art critic for a Johannesburg newspaper. In 1981 he was employed as deputy headmaster at Soweto Commercial College, where he later worked as the principal. He is married to a medical doctor, and they have four children.

Sounds of a Cowhide Drum was first published by a small company, Renoster Books, because no established publisher would at the time consider the writing of an unknown black poet. Renoster's founder, the writer Lionel Abrahams, operating on a shoestring budget, was prepared to give Mtshali's poetry a wider audience, and Nadine Gordimer wrote an appreciative introduction to the volume. The immediate success of *Sounds of a Cowhide Drum* among a largely white, liberal readership can be ascribed to both the lyrical intensity of the poems and to their appeal to humanist ideals of justice and dignity. Mtshali's poetic skill is evident in his powerful combination of simple yet vivid images of black, urban existence and his colloquial appeal for the recognition of individual value in a distorted society. In "Always a Suspect" Mtshali reveals the predicament of the black man living on the periphery of the "white" city of Johannesburg:

> I trudge the city pavements
> side by side with "madam"
> who shifts her handbag
> from my side to the other,
> and looks at me with eyes that say
> "Ha! Ha! I know who you are;
> beneath those fine clothes
> ticks the heart of a thief."

Labeled a criminal, the black man in Johannesburg is forced to endure such insults to his personal integrity. In "The Watchman's Blues" Mtshali describes a similar situation, that of Makhubalo Mag-

udulela, a "man amongst men" in his rural home, who in the city is merely a "boy" called Jim for the convenience of whites. "The Moulting Country Bird" also examines the transition from rural to urban life but suggests an accompanying moral and cultural breakdown: a young man's urbanization results in his rejection of tribal values and his desire to embrace Western materialism. "Pigeons at Oppenheimer Park" satirizes legislation that is degrading; the poem ironically suggests that the pigeons are defying the Separate Amenities Act by perching on "Whites Only" benches. Mtshali also notes a more fundamental aspect of apartheid: besides demeaning blacks, the laws also destroy families. In the poignant "Boy on a Swing" he conveys the bewilderment of a child whose father has been imprisoned: "Where did I come from? / When will I wear long trousers? / Why was my father jailed?"

Mtshali is sensitive to individual suffering among blacks, and he knows that the exploitation of black workers by racial capitalism in the South African marketplace results in extreme hardship and the need for resilience. In "An Old Man in Church" Mtshali's voice is ironic and bitter, as he satirizes a society that propagates Christian humility as a religious and social doctrine while ensuring that blacks remain in humble and poverty-stricken surroundings. The old man is described as "a machine working at full throttle" during the week to make a profit for his master, and he goes to church on Sundays to "recharge his spiritual batteries":

> The acolyte comes round with a brass-coated
> collection plate:
> the old man sneaks in a cent piece
> that raises a scowl on the collector's face
> whose puckered nose sneezes at such poor generosity
> instead of inhaling the aromatic incense smoke.
> Then the preacher stands up in the pulpit,
> his voice fiery with holy fervour:
> "Blessed are the meek for they shall inherit the earth."

With its ironic ending, alluding to the Sermon on the Mount and the parable of the widow's mite, the poem censures an exploitative and materialistic society that claims to be Christian.

Religious imagery is again used ironically in "An Abandoned Bundle," where Mtshali examines the distortion of the human psyche under the pressures of apartheid. The mythic image of the Virgin Mary is juxtaposed against that of a young black mother who has dumped her newborn child on a rubbish heap. Mtshali's intention is apparently to exonerate the black woman and to locate her crime in the society that has produced her:

an infant dumped on a rubbish heap –
"Oh! Baby in the Manger
sleep well
on human dung."

Its mother
had melted into the rays of the rising sun,
her face glittering with innocence
her heart as pure as untrampled dew.

Further comment on the social and psychic sickness of township life is found in poems such as "Intake Night – Baragwanath Hospital," where the casualty ward at the hospital serves to mirror a violent society: "So! It's Friday night! / Everybody's enjoying / in Soweto." Similarly "Nightfall in Soweto" portrays a society in which "Man has ceased to be man / Man has become beast / Man has become prey."

In *Sounds of a Cowhide Drum* Mtshali is also concerned with what he terms the preservation of his "shattered culture." This concern led him to produce poems such as "The Birth of Shaka," "Inside My Zulu Hut," "I Will Tell It to My Witchdoctor," as well as the title poem, where he appeals to blacks not to forsake their African heritage:

Let me tell you of your precious heritage,
of your glorious past trampled by the conqueror,
destroyed by the zeal of a missionary.
. . . .
O! Hear me, Child!
in the Zulu dance
shaking their hearts into a frenzy.
. . . .
Boom! Boom! Boom!
That is the sound of a cowhide drum –
the Voice of Mother Africa.

Mtshali's first volume of "township poetry" (as it was referred to at the time by several critics) was enthusiastically received by white readers in South Africa. Jean Marquard, for example, suggests that *Sounds of a Cowhide Drum* is one of the most worthwhile publications to have appeared in South Africa. Yet Mtshali has been severely criticized by some black commentators, disappointed at the lack of revolutionary fire in the poems. And Njabulo Ndebele points out that Mtshali seems to portray an utterly hopeless situation with no possibility of change. Ndebele accuses the poet of merely confirming oppression without offering a challenging alternative and of ignoring the black people's struggle to re-create themselves both psychologically and socially. Mtshali was sensitive to such criticism, for he later commented (in an interview with Ursula A.

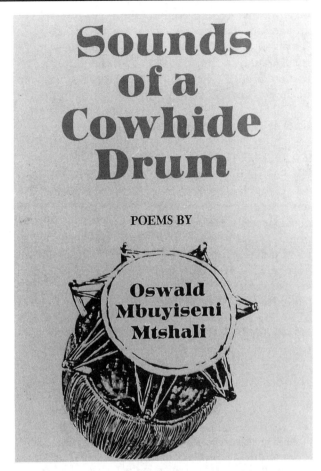

Cover for the New York edition of Mtshali's first book, which won the Olive Schreiner Prize, awarded by the English Academy of Southern Africa, in 1971

Barnett in 1973) that he ascribed the success of his book to the curiosity and skepticism of the whites who were amazed that a black "scooter messenger" could write so well. He appeared to repudiate the type of poetry he had produced in *Sounds of a Cowhide Drum* when he noted in the interview that, although he had once thought that on behalf of black dignity he could evangelize and convert whites, he realized he had been naive. His new direction lay in inspiring his fellow blacks to be proud and to strive to find their true identity in group solidarity.

This statement marked a change in the tenor of Mtshali's work. His second collection, *Fireflames* (1980), shows the influence of the radical and revolutionary climate of the 1970s in South Africa. Although it includes poems written during his stay in the United States, as well as some English translations of Zulu lyric poems, the collection is composed mainly of heroic poems of resistance to oppression, characterized by what Es'kia Mphahlele terms a "hard apocalyptic tone." The organizing metaphor is fire, representing the anger of blacks as an agent of destruction, cleansing, and renewal. In "A Big Question Sonnet" Mtshali likens the struggle for freedom to the "fireflame" on the tail of a "relentless firefly," one that acts as a "torch of freedom in the darkness," and in "I'm a Burning Chimney (A Militant's Cry)" fire defines black anger: "I grow blacker and blacker by the day / as my heart crackles with fires of fury, / stoked by the daily degradations for my blackness."

Mtshali dedicated *Fireflames* "to all our heroes, especially the brave schoolchildren of Soweto, who have died, been imprisoned and persecuted in the grim struggle for our freedom," and he included poems to the new heroes of black resistance: "Hector Peterson—the Young Martyr (Whose Death Triggered the Soweto Uprising)"; "Abram Ongkoepoetse Tiro, a Young Black Martyr"; and "The Raging Generation," in which Mtshali writes of young people whose rallying cry is "Amandla! Ngawethu!" (Power! To the People!). The struggle for freedom is portrayed in terms of traditional black life, as the freedom fighter is compared to the glorious African warrior in "Weep Not for a Warrior":

> a warrior never perishes;
> he is sustained by the glorious deeds of the departed;
> he eats the raw meat of fearlessness
> and awaits his canonisation in the realm of heroes,
> where all the freedom fighters dwell;
> their numerous names are inscribed for posterity
> in the massive girth of the baobab tree.
> . . . .
> As the clouds of war gather,
> and the southern sky frowns with rage,
> and the mountains quiver like broth,
> and the lightening swords the firmament
> . . . .
> the death knell will echo to every corner.

Whereas *Sounds of a Cowhide Drum* had depended largely on the techniques of irony and the vividly precise image, *Fireflames* turns from "protest" to "resistance" in favoring the rhetorical devices – repetition and parallelism – of traditional African oral poetry. Thus the shift of style and diction is in itself part of the political statement.

Marxist historicist thinking (which coexisted with the nationalist directions of black consciousness in the black politics of the 1970s) comes to the fore in "The Dawn of a New Era." Mtshali highlights the inevitability of social change: "History is spring cleaning," he claims, "the cobwebbed corners of the earth"; and the poem concludes with a list of countries where the colonial regimes have been eliminated in favor of a new order – Vietnam, Cambodia, Guinea-Bissau, Mozambique, and Angola. South Africa, he intimates, will soon be added to the list. Such a desire for revolutionary change in the land of his birth involves Mtshali in a rejection of First World intervention in Africa, as he explains in "Flames of Fury":

> you heard the prattle and cackle
> of the so-called Super Powers,
> and I beg you, for the cause of our liberation,
> ignore the two cackling hens of senility –
> Mr. Tear-him-apart from the West,
> Mr. Look-at-the-chin from the East –
> sitting at the conference table in the House of Monkeys,
> dishing to the Third World a porridge of lies called detente,
> cooked in a broken pot of empty promises.

"Back to the Bush" is a virulent attack on Christianity, which, according to Mtshali, has destroyed the fabric of black life and replaced it with lies, falsehoods, and double standards. He suggests that the black nation should turn its collective back on Western religion and return, metaphorically, to the bush, to its own culture and religion, as a means of reestablishing true identity and communal authenticity.

Given the revolutionary nature of *Fireflames*, with its glorification of the black struggle and its violent rejection of Western and Christian values, it is not surprising that it was banned in South Africa soon after publication and only unbanned in 1986. Critical reception of *Fireflames* was mixed. White critics who had previously championed *Sounds of a Cowhide Drum* were disappointed by what they felt to be a lack of poetic resonance and achievement in the later collection. Mphahlele, by contrast, considered that the early Mtshali had been overrated and that *Fireflames* presented a new voice, that of a spokesman for his people. In an essay titled "Black Poetry in Southern Africa: What It Means," published in 1976, Mtshali defends his work, and that of fellow black poets, when he says that black poets do not have time to embellish their urgent message with unnecessary and cumbersome ornaments such as rhyme, iambic pentameter, abstract figures of speech, and an ornate and lofty style. Such poetic devices he considers to be the luxuries of a free people, luxuries blacks can ill afford at a time when harsh realities are the tenor of their lives.

Although he has not published many poems since *Fireflames*, Oswald Mbuyiseni Mtshali has continued to be active in the field of education. In 1982 he enrolled in a doctoral program at Rhodes University in Grahamstown, and he has done a Zulu translation of William Shakespeare's *Romeo and Juliet*. He has also written a one-act play, "Black Dawn – White Twilight," which he describes as "a socio-political skit on township life."

Interview:

Ursula A. Barnett, "Interview with Oswald Mtshali," *World Literature Written in English*, 12 (April 1973): 27–35.

Bibliographies:

Gillian Goldstein, *Oswald Mbuyiseni Mtshali, South African Poet: An Annotated Bibliography* (Johannesburg: University of the Witwatersrand, Department of Bibliography, Librarianship and Typography, 1974);

S. Williams, H. Colenbrauder, and C. Owen, *A Bibliography on Oswald Mbuyiseni Mtshali (1940–   )* (Pretoria: Subject Reference Department, University of South Africa Sanlam Library, 1980).

References:

Jacques Alvarez-Peyre, "Le masque et la transparence: Introduction à une lecture d'Oswald Mtshali," *Commonwealth Essays and Studies*, 2 (1976): 9–23;

Charles R. Larson, "Books in English from the Third World," *World Literature Today*, 58 (1984): 383–384;

Jean Marquard, "Shocking Insights," *Contrast*, 27 (November 1971): 85–90;

Es'kia Mphahlele, "*Fireflames*: Mtshali's Strident Voice of Self-Assertion," *Rand Daily Mail* (Johannesburg), 19 December 1980;

Njabulo Ndebele, "Artistic and Political Mirage: Mtshali's *Sounds of a Cowhide Drum*," in *Soweto Poetry*, edited by Michael Chapman (Johannesburg: McGraw-Hill, 1982), pp. 190–193;

Makhudu Rammopo, *Mtshali's Sounds of a Cowhide Drum* (Zaria, Nigeria: Institute of Education, Ahmadu Bello University, 1981);

Cecelia Scallan Zeiss, "Landscapes of Exile in Selected Works by Samuel Beckett, Mongane Serote, and Oswald Mbuyiseni Mtshali," in *Anglo-Irish and Irish Literature: Aspects of Language and Culture*, edited by Birgit Bramsback and Martin Croghan (Uppsala, Sweden: Uppsala University, 1988), pp. 219–227.

Meja Mwangi

(December 1948 –)

Simon Gikandi
University of Michigan

BOOKS: *Kill Me Quick* (London: Heinemann, 1973);

Carcase for Hounds (London: Heinemann, 1974);

Taste of Death (Nairobi: East African Publishing House, 1975);

Going Down River Road (London: Heinemann, 1976);

The Cockroach Dance (Nairobi: Longman Kenya, 1979);

Bread of Sorrow (Nairobi: Longman Kenya, 1987);

Weapon of Hunger (Nairobi: Longman Kenya, 1989);

The Return of Shaka (Nairobi: Longman Kenya, 1989);

Striving for the Wind (Nairobi: Heinemann Kenya, 1990; London: Heinemann, 1991).

OTHER: *The Bushtrackers*, adapted by Mwangi from a screenplay by Gary Strieker (Nairobi: Longman Drumbeat, 1979).

When Meja Mwangi was awarded the Jomo Kenyatta Prize for literature in 1974 for *Kill Me Quick* (1973), he was hailed as the most significant and exciting figure to emerge on the East African literary scene since the publication of Ngugi wa Thiong'o's *Weep Not, Child* in 1964. Mwangi was received enthusiastically by the reading public and the local literary establishment. Both groups seemed eager to confirm that East Africa was no longer the literary wilderness it had been assumed to be by certain influential sectors of the Afro-Saxon literati. In the next six years, during which Mwangi published five more novels (including his adaptation *The Bushtrackers*, 1979), the reading public continued to receive him avidly, but the literary establishment was having doubts. In fact Mwangi's image has since been transformed from that of a wunderkind of East African literature to that of a persistent enigma; his career is one no critic has written about without either marked reservations or significant qualifications. He seems to stand, like many of his heroes, as a loner in the literary world.

Meja Mwangi (photograph by George Hallett; Transcription Centre Archive, Harry Ransom Humanities Research Center, University of Texas at Austin)

Indeed loneliness and ambiguity seem to mark Mwangi's life itself. Born in Nyeri, Kenya, in December 1948, he grew up under the shadow of the Mau Mau conflict in Kenya. He was brought up in Nanyuki, a military-barracks town from which the British colonial government mounted its operations

114

against the Mau Mau revolutionaries in the nearby forests. His mother worked as a maid for white families in the area, and through her Mwangi had some access to the culture of the settler establishment. By the time Mwangi went to Nanyuki Secondary School for his high-school education, Kenya was on its way to independence. He later went to Kenyatta College, then a preuniversity institution, where he majored in "A-level" science. But apart from a year he spent in the International Writing Program at the University of Iowa in 1975, Mwangi is distinguished from many of his literary contemporaries in Africa by the fact that he never studied at a university. He has the status of being a self-made man of letters, and most significantly, in the extremely limited East African literary market, he is one of the very few locally based professional writers.

Mwangi has justifiably been compared to Charles Dickens in terms of both his career and literary method. Like the great Victorian novelist, Mwangi has staked his claim as the special correspondent of the metropolis who goes out of his way to probe the arteries that define and move the city, vividly dramatizing the lives of alienated and dehumanized characters. Like that of the young Dickens, Mwangi's career has moved toward its pinnacle without the critical recognition it deserves. Indeed what F. R. Leavis said of Dickens in *The Great Tradition* (1948) is often said of Mwangi: he is a great entertainer but not a profound novelist. This attitude has bred polite neglect in critical circles, the most obvious reason being that Mwangi does not theorize about his method and ideas. His works are often praised for their sense of realism, but his novels suffer from a want of informing ideas.

However, Mwangi's rejection of ideological self-consciousness and methodological self-reflectiveness is compensated for by the experiences narrated in his novels. Again, as in the writing of Dickens, the authority of Mwangi's works is what the novelist has gone through or seen. He may not theorize on politics or history, but Mwangi's career was shaped, almost subconsciously, by the history of colonial Kenya. Indeed, as a young boy growing up in the 1950s, Mwangi was literally caught in the middle: on one side were relatives who were involved in the revolutionary movement, some of whom had been sent to detention camps and villages; on the other side were the white families from whom his mother brought him books. Thus, together with an emerging literary sensibility shaped by European children's literature, came the harsh experience of what was euphemistically referred to as "the trouble." Even as he read white people's

books, Mwangi was being made keenly aware of the nature of the larger political conflict. He could not help but become involved. He recalls being detained in a camp with his mother, and he is quick to note (as he told Bernth Lindfors) that nobody growing up in Kenya at the time could avoid awareness of what was happening: "You just couldn't help feeling the tension of the conflict between the forest fighters and the colonial government. Everyone was caught up in this movement."

These experiences gave Mwangi his first and most persistent literary subject: the Mau Mau revolution and the quest for national independence. So at the age of seventeen Mwangi embarked on his first literary project, which was to be published later as *Taste of Death* (1975). Although this work is intended for teenagers and cannot be considered as anything more than juvenilia, it points to those themes and concerns Mwangi has made his own; it is an important crystallization of the political tensions in Kenya under the state of emergency. The hero of the novel, Kariuki, has become caught up in the Mau Mau conflict even before he has developed an understanding of what the struggle is all about. He must be courageous and heroic, because the times demand it, although he is not psychologically prepared for absolutist commitments.

The chasm between conviction and courage also characterizes Mwangi's adult characters in *Taste of Death*, including Mbogo, who is tempted to desert his movement and betray his leader, and Inspector John Cowdrey, the English hunter of men, operating in a terrain that can never be home for him. Thus if *Taste of Death* is a depressing story, it is partly because, at a time when many Kenyan novelists were writing about the heroism of the past, Mwangi's novel is about trying to survive against the odds, a theme seen most vividly in the futile attempt by the freedom fighters to avoid extermination by the colonial forces. The acute sense of landscape that is a prominent feature of Mwangi's style is apparent in this early work, but *Taste of Death* is significant mostly as an act of memory: Mwangi represents facts heard and experiences seen or retold, but there is no profound understanding of the historical conflict itself.

Mwangi came into literary prominence with his second (but first published) novel, *Kill Me Quick*, whose poignancy and immediacy overshadow its limited literary achievement, for its subject had a fundamental, even utilitarian, meaning to its first readers. The tale is simple enough, but its implications remain very real. The story of two friends who go to school to uplift themselves and who perform as well as everyone else, but discover that their education is hardly the passport to a comfortable middle-class life, is one that many of Mwangi's friends were living daily. Mwangi told Lindfors that many of his friends had finished school in the early 1970s and could not find jobs: he felt "it was important to tell their story, to show their plight in the city."

The setting of *Kill Me Quick* is the neocolonial present: national independence has been won but not consummated, and the people have woken up to the reality that the dream of prosperity and opportunity promised by the native elite is never going to be fulfilled, and that hope and determination must inevitably change to despair and acceptance. The two heroes of the novel go to Nairobi, the capital city, but instead of discovering a metropolis paved with gold, they encounter a world that seems to exist solely to oppress its inhabitants. With this realization, the two boys move aimlessly from one situation to another like proverbial rogues, but their lives are not surrounded by the romance readers have come to associate with the picaro. On the contrary, every movement accentuates their oppression: they cannot find meaningful work, and when they do, their labors are fruitless; they cannot return to their rural homes because they have not acquired the benefits of their education – they have nothing to show for it.

With *Kill Me Quick* Mwangi succeeded because he said the right things at the right time, giving his audience what he aptly described to Lee Nichols as "a realization of the atmosphere." However, atmosphere in Mwangi's literary lexicon refers, first and foremost, to the sense of situation, and this sense, unfortunately, is the only memorable aspect of Mwangi's literary method in this novel. *Kill Me Quick* strikes many as a significant novel not because of its innovativeness but because of Mwangi's profound sense of situation, succored by a journalistic style; he renders scenes with the hard and sharp ear of a reporter on the beat. There is finally the authorial penchant for details, which often leads to an unintended symbolic structure centering on the consciousness of hopelessness.

This structure of despair and defeat defines Mwangi's naturalistic modernism. Usually his works emphasize a situation in which a character has lost the will to act and hence must strive aimlessly against an absurd universe. The result is a situation in which a formal and contextual naturalism is informed by a modernist vision with a sense of pessimism and angst. Readers see this combination in Mwangi's treatment of the Mau Mau theme in his

third novel, *Carcase for Hounds* (1974). A Mau Mau commander, General Haraka, is trapped in the forest waiting for supplies that never arrive; he is surrounded by British colonial forces and cannot escape. As Haraka lies wounded and dying in the arms of his faithful lieutenant, Kimamo, readers begin to realize that Haraka's physical entrapment is a metaphor for a larger state of doubt and weariness that afflicts both sides in the conflict.

Carcase for Hounds is remarkable for the sheer amount of detail that Mwangi provides about the logistics and organization of the Mau Mau movement. It is also the first novel in which he seems conscious of his style. Yet this new stylization strikes one with its inappropriateness. Mwangi has usurped the language of the American thriller, of Raymond Chandler, Mickey Spillane, and Chester Himes. His characters speak in an American idiom that is incongruous with their situation, and the authorial descriptions also seem more appropriate for the "jungles" of Harlem or the Bronx than for those of Kenya. For the first time it becomes clear that, although Mwangi has discovered appropriate contents from his own experiences, the appropriate style does not come easily to him.

However, a balance between form and content characterizes *Going Down River Road* (1976), considered by many to be Mwangi's major literary achievement. This novel is not remarkable for its themes; strictly speaking it is just a restatement of the same subjects and issues that have provided Mwangi with a recurrent and almost obsessive pattern. As in *Kill Me Quick*, readers encounter an urban jungle, this time the world of the construction laborer and the slum mechanic, characters for whom failure has become a raison d'être. The protagonist is Ben, who has been cashiered from the army for illegal arms dealing and has been reduced to being a laborer, working in a monstrous construction project that dehumanizes people, and living in a dirty slum surrounded by the putrid smell of those who have been reduced to human garbage. Ben seeks love and solace from his girlfriend Wini and her baby, but the few moments of escape they offer him from the drudgery of daily life in the city are limited. And as his sense of failure increases, as he becomes more aware of the futility of his job, the strain on Ben's relationship with Wini is too much to bear. She abandons him, and as the novel moves to its close the reader quickly realizes that for Ben, as for many of his friends in the slum, there will never be any opportunity for self-improvement.

Thus, in the gloominess of his message and the bleakness of the landscape, Mwangi has expanded and amplified the themes of his earlier novels. However, what is remarkable about *Going Down River Road* is the stark, detailed images with which Mwangi represents the vital and volatile clandestine culture of the Nairobi underworld. Nobody else has captured this subculture with as much understanding and empathy. Moreover, descriptions of the city are not marred by the haphazardness of style and structure in Mwangi's earlier novels. The cityscape is presented through a series of images and binary oppositions, combined to project Mwangi's modernist weltanschauung. Along with the lives and views of characters who have "some sort of a permanency," such images lead to a more comprehensive articulation of Mwangi's modernist vision than can be found in any of his other novels. In other words, the gap between form and ideology is not as pronounced as before.

Mwangi's literary ambition is to articulate his vision through method rather than discourse. In *The Cockroach Dance* (1979) readers find a concerted attempt at self-conscious psychological examination of a character trapped in an indifferent metropolis. The hero of the novel is Dusman Gonzanga, a meter inspector with the city water department, who is literally driven to despair and revolt by his job, which has become a symbol of a vengeful, malignant fate. Gonzanga's psychological problems are exacerbated by his identification with the poor in their struggle against the ruling elite. Although his identification is more of a knee-jerk action than the result of ideological reflection, he is able to negotiate a physical and social landscape littered by human junk and scavengers. By leading readers into the stressful lives of urbanites and by providing commentary on this scene, he becomes the articulator of a world dominated by the acquisitive desire of the African ruling class, which has turned the city into a constellation of bars and brothels.

Because of his self-consciousness Gonzanga is able to crystallize the binary oppositions that have hitherto defined Mwangi's novels: limited achievement and absolute failure; mechanical order and total chaos; and urban overcrowding and complete isolation. Thus the achievement of the novel is precisely the character's ability to link the broken-down physical landscape with the psychological displacement it triggers. It is through Gonzanga that the impact of an alienating social system, as it imprints itself on one man, is vividly rendered. And yet, as Angus Calder has argued, this novel exposes Mwangi's primary dilemma as a novelist – how to balance the imperative for entertainment with the need for social commentary. Calder sees him as

Cover for Mwangi's novel about two boys on an unsuccessful quest for employment and prosperity in postindependence Nairobi

"torn between tough-guy movie-style individualist values and the claims of social conscience." How to reconcile these claims is the challenge that continues to face Mwangi as a novelist.

At this point Mwangi's career reached an impasse or temporary hiatus. With his more recent works it is becoming clear that the balance he sought between entertainment and serious ideological narrative has not materialized in any fundamental way. A novel published in 1979, *The Bushtrackers*, compounds this problem. Adapted from the screenplay for the film of the same title, written by Gary Strieker and directed by the late Gordon Parks, Jr., this novel belongs in the world of Himes and the thriller tradition. The protagonist, Johnny Kimathi, is a former game ranger in Tsavo National Park who has retired to what he believes is a quiet life, until his wife is kidnapped. He embarks on a mission of vengeance that pits him against Al Haji, a black American with lethal Mafia connections, and this situation leads to a predictable cinematic confrontation, complete with gun battles and helicopter chases. For readers of Himes's *Cotton Comes to Harlem* (1965) and viewers of such American macho movies as *Shaft* (1971), there is a transparent commonality that provides no new thrills or frills. The only remarkable thing about this story is Mwangi's mastery of the thriller idiom.

Indeed, if there is any critical consensus about Mwangi's career, it is to be found in the admiration with which many critics write about his mastery of the thriller and the general appeal his works have for the African urban reader. Mwangi also possesses the powerful sense of situation that evokes the surfaces of the contemporary African urban scene with an acute awareness of the sights and smells of a rapidly changing community. Even when he seems to dwell on the surfaces too much, there are always hints of the deeper malaise that moves his characters, a sense of overwhelming psychological displacement in a world that promises so much and provides so little. In this sense alone Mwangi's novels are informed by a coherent vision. Far from adopting an unself-conscious technique, Mwangi's adoption of the forms of popular fiction is a manifestation of his modernist ideology – what Calder aptly calls "movie-style values."

Mwangi's ambiguous literary status, then, has to do with the disjunction between these essentially Western values and the communal demands of the situations about which he writes. Calder argues that Mwangi has to make a choice between entertainment, which on the contemporary African scene is synonymous with the celebration of "American individualism," and a deeper ideological commitment, which often works against this creed. But Mwangi may see the problem essentially as one of medium; in this case the choice is merely one of using the medium and language that put him in touch with the urban petite bourgeoisie, the so-called popular readers. In this connection his involvement in the 1985 Sydney Pollack film *Out of Africa*, in which he is listed as an assistant director, may indicate directions to be taken. He was also part of the production team that worked on the 1988 film adaptation of James Fox's *White Mischief* (1982). Film may provide Mwangi with the exact balance of form and content that his written works lack.

One can see, in retrospect, how by 1979 Mwangi was struggling to find a novelistic method that could allow him to continue writing thrillers while providing serious commentary on the African social and political landscape. By the time he came to write *Bread of Sorrow* (1987), it seems he was con-

vinced that his primary duty as a novelist was to represent the African social and political scene as he saw it, bringing his sharp sense of observation and detail to bear on the continent and the diverse social and cultural groups that occupied it. But, unlike other novelists who were turning their talents to this allegorization of Africa – one thinks of the Zimbabwean writer Dambudzo Marechera – Mwangi could not abandon his "popular" style for the "high modernist" language that appeared suited for his subject.

There were two reasons for Mwangi's decision to employ the popular style even as he tackled serious political themes: he was most at home using the kind of language he had inherited from popular culture in general and the movies in particular; and he was a professional writer who, if he had to make a viable living out of writing, needed to compete with imported pulp literature on its own terms. Mwangi seemed well suited for this kind of writing: he could import the popular idiom of the thriller and the movies to the Kenyan landscape, thus domesticating movie-style values, such as romance and individualism, and making them more palatable to his local audience; he could also use the thriller framework to introduce themes and issues from the newspaper headlines.

In *Bread of Sorrow*, for example, Mwangi turns to the most persistent of Pan-African themes – racial oppression in South Africa and the culture of apartheid – and tries to dress it up in the language and structure of popular literature. The novel, then, has all the ingredients of a major thriller: arms smuggling across the border, illicit romance, stolen diamonds, and numerous double crosses. But it also provides a serious exploration of the racist mentality, especially as readers encounter the tensions and conflicts in the Afrikaner family that provides the cultural center of the novel. Yet one is never sure whether Mwangi's main focus is intended to be this cultural center or the adventures of his main character, Peter Jones, a Welsh orphan who becomes involved with dangerous gangs in London and eventually ends up as a diamond pilot in South Africa before he betrays his employers. The seriousness of the novel is often sublimated under its action, a series of adventures that take readers across several countries in what often appears to be a gratuitous display of geographical settings. At the same time, however, one has to concede that it is precisely Mwangi's penchant for thrills that enables readers to "ride along" as they traverse various cultural spaces and witness the transformation Africa has undergone since independence.

Bread of Sorrow seems to have succeeded most in using the thriller format as a point of entry into a serious discourse on apartheid and the politics of colonialism and independence, but the same cannot be said of *Weapon of Hunger* (1989) and *The Return of Shaka* (also 1989). In these two novels Mwangi seems to have given in to movie-style values, especially the desire to entertain and thrill the audience; his unabashed celebration of Americana is often embarrassing, not only because his vision of America seems to be drawn from superficial sources but also because it always degenerates into cultural and linguistic clichés.

There is no doubt that *Weapon of Hunger* emanates from the horror stories of war and hunger that have gripped the African continent in the last twenty years. As a matter of fact, Borku, the fictional country in which the story is set, is a thinly disguised portrait of Ethiopia under the grips of revolution, civil war, and drought. Mwangi has a keen knowledge of this landscape, but what does he do with this knowledge? He gives readers the embarrassing story of an American pop singer called Jack Rivers, who has raised a lot of money to buy food for the starving people of Borku but finds it impossible to get the food to its destination because of civil war. So Rivers decides to organize a group of American volunteers to drive several trucks of food, illicitly through the Sudan, to Borku. From this point on the story degenerates into banalities of plot and language: Rivers faces treachery from the natives, is arrested several times by the warring factions, and falls in love with a beautiful guerrilla woman, much to the chagrin of his girlfriend who had earlier given up her lucrative medical practice to accompany him to Africa. By the time one finishes reading this novel, one has probably been thrilled, but this thrill offers no comfort because it is not original; on the contrary, one has likely read or seen a similar plot somewhere else – in almost any Western-made movie that is set in Africa, for example.

Reading *The Return of Shaka* is like watching an old movie, too, for while this novel follows the struggle of a South African prince to emplace himself in an alien landscape, and while it presents a taut and exciting Greyhound tour of the United States, it brings out the worst elements in Mwangi's work. Readers are not placed in a specific time and place: the United States toured with Moshesh is a place from old movies or movies about old places. There is no plausible reason for Moshesh's journey across America, only the mere hint of a mental crisis he must resolve: should he return home to help

in the liberation of his people, or should he settle in his comfortable university job? Should he marry his longtime (white) partner, Karen, or the black woman (Loretta) whom he just met on the bus? In the meantime there are echoes of Alfred Hitchcock's *North by Northwest* (1959) as the African man is chased across the country by a mob of white men who have been hired to kill him for reasons that are never made clear. This novel seems to have been written for no other reason but to sell copies of it.

In *Striving for the Wind* (1990), on the other hand, Mwangi tries to return to his roots as they were so powerfully displayed in *Kill Me Quick* and *Going Down River Road*. The fact that this novel has been published in Heinemann's canonical African Writers Series, and was even nominated for the Commonwealth Writers Prize, indicates the serious intent behind it. Mwangi's attention is focused on a world of rural poverty and greed, a world he knows firsthand, in which the future of Kenya is continuously being debated between Baba Pesa (meaning "Father of Money") and his university dropout son Juda (Judas, the betrayer). Mwangi rejects the shifting spaces of his thrillers, focusing instead on a static, weary, and worn-out landscape; he rejects the idiom of the movies, seeking instead to capture the language of rural despair and the tyranny of the nouveau riche; the alienated authorial tone of the thrillers gives way to a profound voice that sustains the pessimism and angst of the rural poor.

So in *Striving for the Wind* readers see Mwangi at his most serious. But this novel is as dull as the land and people it represents, and by the time readers finish it, and as they reflect on the labor and pain Mwangi has put into it, they begin to realize that his real talents are not in this kind of "tractor" fiction, but in the phantasmal world of the thrillers and movies he loves so much. One cannot help but wonder what Mwangi has inherited from the movies tradition. On the one hand, the movies have endowed him with the palpable wealth of Americana – in habits and idiom – that is largely responsible for his artistic fluency and his engagement with his African popular audience, which lives and thrives on such material. On the other hand, however, this appropriation of Americana has impoverished him as a novelist in the areas in which he was strongest – his sense of the African landscape and its people, the language of the urban poor, and the discourse of contemporary politics. Mwangi's real talent is manifested in the novels in which he marries the techniques of the thriller with a profound exposition of the African scene.

Interviews:

Bernth Lindfors, "Interview with Meja Mwangi," in *Mazungumzo*, edited by Lindfors (Athens: Ohio University Center for International Studies, 1980), pp. 74–79;

Lee Nichols, "Interview with Meja Mwangi," in his *Conversations with African Writers* (Washington, D.C.: Voice of America, 1981), pp. 195–204;

"Audience, Language and Form in Committed East African Writing: An Open Discussion with Meja Mwangi," *Komparatistische Hefte*, 3 (1981): 64–67.

References:

Angus Calder, "Meja Mwangi's Novels," in *The Writing of East and Central Africa*, edited by G. D. Killam (London: Heinemann, 1984), pp. 177–191;

David Dorsey, "Didactic Form of the Novel with Evidence from Meja Mwangi and Others," in *Interdisciplinary Dimensions of African Literature*, edited by Kofi Anyidoho, Abioseh M. Porter, Daniel Racine, and Janice Spleth (Washington, D.C.: Three Continents, 1985), pp. 11–25;

Simon Gikandi, "The Growth of the East African Novel," in *The Writing of East and Central Africa*, pp. 231–246;

Lars Johansson, *In the Shadow of Neocolonialism: Meja Mwangi's Novels, 1973–1990* (Umeå, Sweden: English Department, University of Umeå, 1992);

Elizabeth Knight, "Mirror of Reality: The Novels of Meja Mwangi," *African Literature Today*, 13 (1983): 146–157;

Ayo Mamudu, "Hovering Between Two Worlds: Meja Mwangi and the Urban Poor," *Association for Commonwealth Literature and Language Studies Bulletin*, 7, no. 4 (1986): 45–52;

David Maughan-Brown, "Four Sons of One Father: A Comparison of Ngugi's Earliest Novels with Works by Mwangi, Mangua, and Wachira," *Research in African Literatures*, 16 (Summer 1985): 179–209;

Peter Nazareth, "Bringing the Whole Mountain Down," *Afriscope*, 6 (April 1976): 25–28;

Eustace Palmer, "Meja Mwangi's *The Cockroach Dance*," *Fourah Bay Studies in Language and Literature*, 2 (1981): 50–68.

V. S. Naipaul

(17 August 1932 –)

John Thieme
University of Hull

See also the Naipaul entry in *DLB Yearbook: 1985*.

BOOKS: *The Mystic Masseur* (London: Deutsch, 1957; New York: Vanguard, 1959);

The Suffrage of Elvira (London: Deutsch, 1958);

Miguel Street (London: Deutsch, 1959; New York: Vanguard, 1960);

A House for Mr. Biswas (London: Deutsch, 1961; New York: McGraw-Hill, 1961); republished with a foreword by Naipaul (New York: Knopf, 1983; London: Deutsch, 1984);

The Middle Passage: Impressions of Five Societies — British, French and Dutch — in the West Indies and South America (London: Deutsch, 1962; New York: Macmillan, 1963);

Mr. Stone and the Knights Companion (London: Deutsch, 1963; New York: Macmillan, 1964);

An Area of Darkness (London: Deutsch, 1964; New York: Macmillan, 1965);

The Mimic Men (London: Deutsch, 1967; New York: Macmillan, 1967);

A Flag on the Island (London: Deutsch, 1967; New York: Macmillan, 1967);

The Loss of El Dorado: A History (London: Deutsch, 1969; New York: Knopf, 1970; revised edition, Harmondsworth, U.K.: Penguin, 1977);

In a Free State (London: Deutsch, 1971; New York: Knopf, 1971);

The Overcrowded Barracoon and Other Articles (London: Deutsch, 1972; New York: Knopf, 1973);

Guerrillas (London: Deutsch, 1975; New York: Knopf, 1975);

India: A Wounded Civilization (London: Deutsch, 1977; New York: Knopf, 1977);

The Perfect Tenants; and, The Mourners (Cambridge: Cambridge University Press, 1977);

A Bend in the River (London: Deutsch, 1979; New York: Knopf, 1979);

The Return of Eva Perón; with The Killings in Trinidad

V. S. Naipaul (photograph copyright by Jerry Bauer; courtesy of the British Council, London)

(London: Deutsch, 1980; New York: Knopf, 1980);

A Congo Diary (Los Angeles: Sylvester & Orphanos, 1980);

Among the Believers: An Islamic Journey (London: Deutsch, 1981; New York: Knopf, 1981);

Finding the Centre (London: Deutsch, 1984); republished as *Finding the Center* (New York: Knopf, 1984);

The Enigma of Arrival (Harmondsworth, U.K.: Vi-

121

king, 1987; New York: Knopf, 1987);

A Turn in the South (London: Viking, 1989; New York: Knopf, 1989);

India: A Million Mutinies Now (London: Heinemann, 1990; New York: Viking, 1991).

Collection: *Three Novels* (New York: Knopf, 1982) – comprises *The Mystic Masseur, The Suffrage of Elvira,* and *Miguel Street.*

OTHER: Seepersad Naipaul, *The Adventures of Gurudeva*, foreword by V. S. Naipaul (London: Deutsch, 1976).

SELECTED PERIODICAL PUBLICATIONS – UNCOLLECTED: "Literature in the West Indies," *Trinidad Guardian*, West Indies Federation Supplement, 20 April 1958, p. 54;

"The Documentary Heresy," *Twentieth Century*, 173 (Winter 1964): 107–108;

"What's Wrong with Being a Snob?," *Saturday Evening Post*, 239 (3 June 1967): 12, 18;

"Without a Dog's Chance," *New York Review of Books*, 18 May 1972, pp. 29–31;

"Indian Art and Its Illusions," *New York Review of Books*, 22 March 1979, pp. 6–14;

"Writing *A House for Mr. Biswas*," *New York Review of Books*, 24 November 1983, pp. 22–23;

"Heavy Manners in Grenada," *Sunday Times Magazine* (London), 12 February 1984, pp. 23–31;

"An Island Betrayed," *Harper's*, 268 (March 1984): 61–72;

"Among the Republicans," *New York Review of Books*, 25 October 1984, pp. 5–17;

"On Being a Writer," *New York Review of Books*, 23 April 1987, p. 7.

V. S. Naipaul is both one of the most highly regarded and one of the most controversial of contemporary writers. Widely admired in North America and Europe for the lucidity of his prose style, his incisive travel journalism, and his ironic accounts of colonial and postcolonial societies, Naipaul has not generally met with the same favorable reception in Africa, Asia, and the Caribbean. Comments he has made on places he has visited for his disaffected newspaper reports on the Third World have stirred up considerable animosity against him in many of the countries he has visited in Asia and Africa. His dismissal of his native Trinidad as "unimportant, uncreative, cynical" and of the West Indies as the "Third World's third world" has elicited a similar response in the Caribbean, while two of his books about his ancestral homeland of India, *An Area of Darkness* (1964) and *India: A Wounded Civilization*

(1977), which dwell on the outdoor defecation habits of Indians and the way in which the Hindu doctrine of karma has enmeshed the populace in a quietism tantamount to psychic paralysis, have brought his name into fairly general disrepute among intellectuals on the subcontinent.

However, Naipaul has never compromised his highly personal vision of experience. In the many books he has published since 1957 (roughly half of them fiction and the other half nonfiction), he has displayed a profound skepticism about social and political ideologies – whether they manifest themselves in the form of the stultifying conventions of traditional value systems or in what he sees as the fashionable shibboleths of contemporary liberal and radical perspectives – and a recurrent concern with what he appears to regard as the quintessential twentieth-century predicament, that of human displacement. Satire of the religious and social tenets of Hinduism in his early novels has been replaced by more somber accounts of the ways individuals become entrapped by systems and causes in his more recent fiction and nonfiction, and the mode of his writing has changed considerably, from broad comedy in his early work to a flatter and more neutral narrative style, but throughout there is a remarkable consistency of attitude and similarity of theme. Whether writing of people who have been denied opportunities for self-development because they have been born into colonial societies, of metropolitan misfits, or of postcolonial "casualties" of the downsizing of the British Empire; whether describing white "revolutionaries who visit centers of revolution with return air tickets" or satirizing the clichés of black radicalism; whether chronicling "the curious reliance of men on institutions they were yet working to undermine" or the attitudes of Islamic fundamentalists who deride the West for its materialism while continuing to base their very existence on its technology, Naipaul has maintained the same detached, ironic approach to human behavior in cross-cultural situations.

His most serious criticisms of the Third World, which have guaranteed that the critical response to his work has seldom been lukewarm, have mainly appeared in his nonfiction. In his novels and short stories there is a more oblique approach to the malaise that he finds endemic in colonial and postcolonial societies, and social themes are subsumed in narratives that primarily focus on the psychology of trapped and displaced individuals. In all his books personal and public themes interlink in mutually enriching ways. Nonfiction works such as *An Area of Darkness* and *India: A*

Wounded Civilization, which initially appear to be social diatribes, can be read as intensely personal documents dramatizing Naipaul's own sense of deracination. Similarly novels such as *A House for Mr.
Biswas* (1961), *Guerrillas* (1975), and *A Bend in the
River* (1979), which initially appear to be concerned
with specific interpersonal relationships, can be
read as allegories about colonial and postcolonial
experience. Part of Naipaul's achievement is that he
has managed to transform his own highly personal
sense of displacement into a fictional subject that
has touched chords in the experience of readers
from totally different backgrounds. He has brought
about such identification by resisting the temptation
to write about his Third World milieus in a manner
that would render them exotic, preferring to confine
himself to a style founded on the conventions of circumstantial realism and ironic social observation.

Naipaul's origins cast considerable light on the
theme of personal displacement in his work. Although his subsequent absorption into the English
tradition has tended to obscure his West Indian origins and East Indian heritage (he is frequently referred to as a "British writer"), his early life and the
family structure into which he was born prove to
have been crucial determinants of his personality
and writings. His grandparents migrated to Trinidad from India under the system of indentureship
that, in the latter half of the nineteenth century, replaced slavery as the main source of labor for the
West Indian sugar plantations. The Naipauls and
Capildeos (Naipaul's maternal ancestors) were,
however, untypical of the majority of Trinidad's
East Indian population in that they were Brahmans,
and both sides of the family had pundits who minis-
tered to the spiritual needs of the new agricultural
work force.

To be a high-caste Hindu in Trinidad was to
be something of a contradiction in terms, since, as
Naipaul's younger brother Shiva points out in his
African travel journal *North of South* (1978), "Our
ancestors, when they crossed the black water (the
kala pani), lost caste. Complex purification rituals
would have to be performed if they were to be
cleansed of their defilement and restored to the
fold." Naipaul frequently illustrates the problematic
situation of the high-caste East Indian/West Indian
and provides extended commentary on it in *A House
for Mr. Biswas*, in which the Tulsi family, closely
modeled on the Capildeos, are depicted as a bastion
of old India in Trinidad that is fighting a losing
rearguard action against the encroachments of the
larger creole society of the West Indian melting pot.

Yet displaced Hinduism is only one aspect of

the sense of deracination that pervades Naipaul's
early fiction. In *The Mimic Men* (1967) the narra-
tor/protagonist, Ralph Singh, says of the history of
the British Empire he once dreamed of writing, "It
was my hope to give expression to the restlessness,
the deep disorder, which the great explorations, the
overthrow in three continents of established social
organizations, the unnatural bringing together of
peoples who could achieve fulfillment only within
the security of their own societies and the landscapes hymned by their ancestors, it was my hope
to give partial expression to the restlessness which
this great upheaval has brought about." And, while
Singh's narrative persona should not simply be
identified with Naipaul, these sentiments provide a
useful summary of both this novel's larger concerns
and those of Naipaul's writing more generally. The
disharmony engendered by the sundering of organic links with ancestral landscapes lies at the
heart of his view of the colonial predicament.

On a more personal level his father, Seepersad
Naipaul, proved a crucial formative influence, as
V. S. Naipaul makes clear in his foreword to *The
Adventures of Gurudeva* (1976), the revised British edition of a volume of short stories that Seepersad
Naipaul had originally published in Trinidad in the
early 1940s. Seepersad was for many years a journalist on the *Trinidad Guardian*, the island's leading
newspaper, and both his journalism and his fiction
provided inspiration for the young Naipaul. This influence is particularly evident in *A House for Mr.
Biswas*, where, following his father's advice to take
him as a subject, Naipaul wrote a fictionalized version of his father's life story, based on aspects of the
latter's fiction and journalism and details from his
life, particularly his response to the practices of
Hinduism.

Vidiadhar Surajprasad Naipaul, the first son
and second child of Seepersad and Dropatie
Capildeo Naipaul, was born on 17 August 1932 in
Chaguanas, a small town in the central sugarcane
belt of Trinidad. His specific birthplace was the
Lion House, an imposing building with an unusual
Indian design, located on the town's main street.
The house provided the original on which Hanuman House in *A House for Mr. Biswas* was based, and
it was in the Lion House that Naipaul spent his earliest years. He attended Chaguanas Government
School for two years, until the family moved in
1938 to Port of Spain. There he went to Tranquility
Boys' School, a school famed for its success in preparing pupils for Trinidad's "exhibition examination," via which free secondary-school places could
be gained. In 1942 Naipaul, like Anand in *A House*

for Mr. Biswas, placed third on the island and won a place at Queens Royal College, Trinidad's leading secondary school and, like its equivalents in other parts of the British Empire at that time, an institution with exceptionally high academic standards. Naipaul attended Queens from 1943 to 1949, specializing in French and Spanish in the upper forms. During these years, in a manner akin to the nomadic wanderings of Mr. Biswas and his family, the Naipauls moved several times before eventually settling, in 1947, in a house in the Saint James area of Port of Spain. This house was the original for the final setting in *A House for Mr. Biswas*.

In 1949 Naipaul was awarded a Trinidad government scholarship to study abroad and, after brief periods working as a master at his old school and as a temporary clerk in the Port of Spain Registrar's Department, on 2 August 1950 he left Trinidad to attend University College, Oxford. It was a wish come true. As he once said, "When I was in the fourth form I wrote a vow on the endpaper of my *Kennedy's Revised Latin Primer* to leave within five years. I left after six; and for many years afterwards in England, falling asleep in bedsitters with the electric fire on, I had been awakened by the nightmare that I was back in tropical Trinidad." So, like the unnamed boy narrator of *Miguel Street* (1959), though in rather different circumstances (the boy secures a scholarship through bribery), Naipaul left Trinidad through the escape route offered by a metropolitan education. Yet the island society and, more specifically, his Hindu origins had left an indelible mark on him.

At Oxford, Naipaul studied English literature but was disappointed to find himself studying a syllabus "seemingly aimed at juvenile antiquarians." His tutor recalls him as "a smiling diffident little boy with a deep, grave voice" reading his first essay. It was on John Milton's *Paradise Lost* and is reported as beginning: "In [George Orwell's] *Animal Farm* [1945] some animals are created more equal than others. The same is regrettably true of Milton's angels." Although Naipaul distinguished himself at Oxford – J. R. R. Tolkien, one of his examiners, rated his Anglo-Saxon translation the best of the year – he was disenchanted with the academic curriculum and already determined to become a writer. While still at Oxford he completed a long novel, which has never been published.

After leaving Oxford in 1954, Naipaul worked briefly in the cataloguing department of the National Portrait Gallery, London. Apart from his Trinidad jobs and a period of ten weeks writing advertising copy after reading an unfavorable review

Dust jacket for the 1959 New York edition of Naipaul's first book, a picaresque novel about a masterful con man

of his first novel, *The Mystic Masseur* (1957), the cataloguing job is the only nonliterary work Naipaul has undertaken, and it is one of his proudest boasts that he has known no other profession than that of writer. His early years in London were spent in its less fashionable parts. After initially staying with relatives in Paddington, where he suffered from asthma attacks for four months, he subsequently lived in Kilburn, Muswell Hill, and Streatham. It was in Streatham that *A House for Mr. Biswas*, a novel he has referred to as "very much a South London book," was written. His experience of living there also clearly lies behind the first of his two "English" novels, *Mr. Stone and the Knights Companion* (1963). In 1955 Naipaul married Patricia Ann Hale, an Englishwoman he had met at Oxford.

From 1954 to 1956 Naipaul worked for the British Broadcasting Corporation (BBC), writing and editing for the program *Caribbean Voices*. It was broadcast weekly from London to the West Indies and had already, under the editorship of Henry

Swanzy, built up a considerable reputation as a showcase for new Caribbean writing; it had provided several of the important generation of West Indian writers who came to the fore in the 1950s with an invaluable early outlet for their work. Naipaul's job was part-time and provided him with his sole source of income at this time: "eight guineas a week, less 'deductions.' " During this period he started work on another unsuccessful, unpublished novel.

While he was working for the BBC, Naipaul began to write stories for what was eventually to take shape as *Miguel Street*. In his "Prologue to an Autobiography" (in *Finding the Centre*, 1984) he records how one afternoon in the Langham Hotel, opposite Broadcasting House, he casually typed the first sentence of "Bogart," the opening story in the volume, without having any notion where it might lead: "It was in that Victorian-Edwardian gloom, and at one of those typewriters, that late one afternoon, without having any idea of where I was going, and not perhaps intending to type to the end of the page, I wrote: Every morning when he got up Hat would sit on the banister of his back verandah and shout across, 'What happening there Bogart?' " A second sentence – "Bogart would turn in his bed and mumble softly, so that no one heard, 'What happening there, Hat?' " – followed rapidly. The two sentences had, Naipaul records, "created the world of the street" and established prose rhythms that were to inform the remainder of the narrative. The rest of the story was written quickly by a writer afraid to pause for breath, lest this sudden discovery of a subject slip away. The story was finished that same afternoon, by which time it "had developed a first-person narrator," who, unlike Naipaul himself at such a young age, was fatherless and who, Naipaul says, was "more in tune with the life of the street than I had been." While it includes no explicit commentary on the historical and social background from which it was drawn, the story is based on wartime neighbors of Naipaul's family in Port of Spain. Like the rest of the volume that was to follow, the story shows Naipaul to be reticent on the subject of race, and many readers have not unreasonably assumed that Naipaul is writing about Trinidad's urban black population. However, in his illuminating comments in "Prologue to an Autobiography," he has revealed that both Bogart and Hat were based on Indian originals. Of the latter he writes, "Hat was our neighbour on the street. He wasn't negro or mulatto. But we thought of him as half-way there. He was a Port of Spain Indian. The Port of Spain Indians – there were pockets of them

– had no country roots, were individuals, hardly a community, and were separate from us for an additional reason: many of them were Madrases, descendants of South Indians, not Hindi-speaking, and not people of caste. We didn't see in them any of our formalities or restrictions; and though we lived raggedly ourselves . . . we thought of the other Indians in the street only as street people." Thus, like Naipaul's other early fiction, where the theme is more obvious, *Miguel Street* can be read as a set of fables about the acculturation of the East Indians in Trinidad, as the young narrator encounters the creolized "individual" Indians of the city.

"Bogart" led Naipaul to write other stories in the same free-lancers' room. They continued to flow, though less rapidly and with a greater sense of self-conscious technique. "And then," Naipaul says in the "Prologue to an Autobiography," "the material, which at one time had seemed inexhaustible, dried up." The writing had taken five to six weeks, and it left him with the feeling that he had written a "real" book. Disappointment was to follow: his manuscript was rejected by publishers, and *Miguel Street* only secured publication four years after it was written, when the success of his first two novels, *The Mystic Masseur* and *The Suffrage of Elvira* (1958), had paved the way for a volume in the commercially less-viable genre of the short story.

The majority of the seventeen stories that make up *Miguel Street* are sketches centered on the fortunes of one of the street's inhabitants. However, the apparently autonomous accounts of these individuals' lives are subtly interlinked to form a developing pattern, and the seeds of the climax, which is reached in the final two stories, are already being sown in the opening pages. A recurrent pattern focuses on the attempts of the street's men to find avenues for self-expression, attempts that are usually unsuccessful.

In some cases such an endeavor takes the form of a seemingly unrealizable quest for metropolitan achievement. B. (for "Black") Wordsworth dreams of emulating the English poet whose name he has adopted. Elias sits for the Cambridge School Certificate exam on three occasions with scant success, and the narrator comments, "We felt it wasn't fair, making a boy like Elias do litritcher and poultry." Titus Hoyt, a kind of adult equivalent to Elias, is the philosopher of the street and a travesty of a European scholar, whose crowning glory is the attainment of a London external intermediate arts degree, which enables him to place the letters "I.A." after his name. The most extreme of these metropolitan fantasies is acted out by Man-man, who assumes the persona of a hellfire preacher and shows himself to have a Christ complex when he stages his own crucifixion. After being stoned by an excited crowd, he is taken away to a lunatic asylum. In each case the character who aspires to the chimera of a metropolitan goal is disappointed.

In other instances characters seek self-fulfillment through life-styles that blend elements from the local culture with influences from Hollywood cinema. Thus Bogart's modeling himself on the American film star whose name he has taken is part of the distinctively Trinidadian macho persona he has constructed for himself. He appears to be a strong, silent man who has no need of women, and so it comes as something of a surprise when he is finally revealed to be a bigamist. The story ends with Hat, who has a choric role in the work, as well as being an important character in his own right, explaining why Bogart has left his second wife and come back to the street. He has done so, Hat says, "To be a man, among we men."

The ideal of manliness is central to *Miguel Street*, recurring in one form or another in twelve of the seventeen stories. While the acting styles of certain American film stars, about whom Naipaul writes in *The Middle Passage* (1962), may be seen as important contributory influences in the shaping of this myth of manliness, its origins lie within the local society. Manliness is a major concern of calypso, the dominant narrative genre of Trinidad and a form to which Naipaul is indebted in *Miguel Street* for numerous specific allusions and much of the work's comic and episodic storytelling mode, and his treatment of the man/woman relationship involves an ironic investigation of gender mythologies prevalent in the society and celebrated in such classic calypso lines as these: "Black up their eyes and bruise up their knee / And then they love you eternally," and "Man centipede bad. / Woman centipede more than bad," which are quoted in the text.

In story after story there is an ironic exposure of the macho pose: a terror of the street is revealed to be a coward; a supposed wife beater turns out to be receiving beatings from his wife; a father of ten becomes a laughingstock when his wife, on discovering him in bed with another woman, holds him up by the waist for the people in the street to see his puny, near-naked body and taunts him about his lack of virility. In each case the assumed persona of manliness fails to conceal the underlying insecurity of those who adopt it. Like those who base their life-styles on metropolitan fantasies, they are unable to sustain the role.

The last two stories, which center on the

Dust jacket for Naipaul's first collection of short stories, most of which were written while he was a free-lance writer in the mid 1950s

youthful narrator and Hat, the most fully developed character, provide the climax. Throughout the volume Hat has demonstrated an ability to see through the masks assumed by others, and at the beginning of the story that bears his name, he is presented as uniquely self-sufficient. He appears, from the boy's account, really to be the kind of man that the other characters aspire to be. This, however, is not the case. The story reveals him to be as much a victim of the pose of manliness as any of the other men on the street. It repeats the formula of the ironic exposure of pretense that has operated throughout, only now there is an added level of poignancy, since Hat has become familiar to readers in a way that previous characters have not. The final story completes the pattern. The narrator is now eighteen and able to see the reality underlying the surface gaiety of Miguel Street, but this does not insulate him against succumbing to the street's conception of manliness himself. He turns to drink and womanizing, largely because he feels the society offers no real alternatives. Society emerges as the villain that renders the individual powerless to achieve self-fulfillment. Finally the narrator is saved by being sent abroad for his education. Escape, a recurrent Naipaulian motif that subsequently reappears at the end of several of his books, seems to offer the only possibility of success for those born in the calypso society of Trinidad. Beneath the comic surface of *Miguel Street* and its engagement with the culture at a grass-roots level, lies a pessimistic assessment of colonial Trinidad, which culminates in rejection.

A similar view pervades Naipaul's first two novels. As in *Miguel Street* he portrays a predatory society in which the trickster has usurped the role traditionally accorded to the hero in fiction. His most explicit comment on this society comes in *The Middle Passage*: "Nationalism was impossible in Trinidad. In the colonial society every man had to be for himself. . . . To understand this is to understand the squalor of the politics that came to Trinidad in 1946 when, after no popular agitation, universal adult suffrage was declared. The new politics were reserved for the enterprising, who had seen the prodigious commercial possibilities. There were no parties, only individuals. Corruption, not unexpected, aroused only amusement and even mild approval. Trinidad has always admired the 'sharp character' who, like the sixteenth-century picaroon of Spanish literature, survives and triumphs by his wits. . . ." Both *The Mystic Masseur* and *The Suffrage of Elvira* depict this kind of society, in which conventional moral codes have been replaced by picaroon cunning, and the novels show particular attention to the "new politics": the later stages of the former novel show the protagonist, Ganesh Ramsumair, campaigning in the 1946 election; and the latter novel is a wry fictional exposé of Trinidad's second general election held under universal adult suffrage.

The Mystic Masseur is a picaresque novel, both in the sense that it has an episodic structure and because it has a trickster hero. Through the eyes of a boy-narrator, whose voice is similar to that of the first-person narrator of *Miguel Street*, it traces the various stages in Ganesh's career. After a brief introductory section in which the narrator relates how he was taken to Ganesh, at that time only a struggling masseur, for a foot ailment, a problem Ganesh treated unsuccessfully, the novel provides a chronological account of Ganesh's rise from East Indian nonentity to unsuccessful masseur, successful "mystic masseur," author, radical politician, and finally colonial statesman. The epilogue shows the narrator being coldly received years afterward by Ganesh, now a bulwark of the colonial establishment, when the narrator meets him on the platform of an English railway station.

Throughout the novel Naipaul employs a deadpan ironic style, the apparent neutrality of which is the hallmark of the comic method of his early fiction. This style leaves open until almost the end the central question of whether or not Ganesh is a charlatan. An accumulation of circumstantial evidence suggests that he must be, but it is only his final political volte-face, when he changes sides overnight, that confirms beyond any shadow of a doubt that he is an opportunist. Even then condemnation is withheld. Ganesh is presented as a champion con man in a world of small-time tricksters, and the double-edged ironic approach compels one to see him as both hero and villain. The picture of the society suggests that subterfuge is necessary for survival and that for Ganesh and his fellow Trinidadians expediency has replaced the luxury of free moral choice.

Naipaul's irony is directed not only at individuals but also at social forms and customs, particularly those of Hinduism. While *The Mystic Masseur* is far more than just a satirical portrait of a putative Hindu guru, those sections that focus on Ganesh's reaction to Hinduism as a boy are the most memorable parts of the novel. Beside them other sections appear labored, and the final chapters in particular seem hurried and perfunctory. As an adolescent, Ganesh, like his creator, shows himself to be disenchanted with Hinduism, and this feeling comes out vividly in three set-piece scenes that dramatize the futility of observing Hindu rites in Trinidad: Ganesh's Brahman initiation ceremony (or *janaywa*); his father's funeral; and his wedding. In the first of these Ganesh is told to "go to Benares and study" and appears to be taking the advice literally, by beginning to walk. The passage is typical of Naipaul's neutral presentation and leaves it unclear whether Ganesh is being naive or is consciously trying to draw attention to the irrelevance of the custom in Trinidad. Either way the irony and the skepticism about the attempt to perpetuate Hindu forms in the Caribbean are inescapable, and in *An Area of Darkness* Naipaul records how he refused to go through the *janaywa* when some of his cousins donned the garb of Hindu mendicant-scholars to do so.

In view of Ganesh's obvious estrangement from Hinduism as a young man, it is extremely ironic that his subsequent rise to prominence comes about as a result of his assumption of the role of a guru and his use of the same kind of religious theater as is satirized in the set-piece accounts of Hindu rites. Ultimately, however, Hinduism for Ganesh is no more than a mask to be worn as long as it pays dividends to do so, and he richly deserves the "business man of God" label one of his enemies gives him. While his success as a popular politician is founded on a sub-Gandhian synthesis of the roles of spiritual guide and public man of affairs, he finally deserts his Hindu heritage completely and in the last sentence of the novel is seen as having anglicized his last name from Ramsumair to that of a prominent historian of the empire, Ramsay Muir.

The Suffrage of Elvira is written in a very similar satirical vein. It centers on the character Mr. Harbans, a candidate from Port of Spain who comes to the constituency of Elvira in South Trinidad to buy himself a seat in the island's Legislative Council in the 1950 election. In an early passage Naipaul anticipates his subsequent *Middle Passage* attack on Trinidad's "new politics": "Democracy had come to Elvira four years before, in 1946; but it had taken nearly everybody by surprise and it wasn't until 1950, a few months before the second general election under universal adult franchise, that people began to see the possibilities." The "possibilities" are, of course, commercial and not humanitarian and appear to indicate the extent to which the coming of full democracy has provided the trickster with a profitable hunting ground. However, the narrative is strongly influenced by Seepersad Naipaul's *Trinidad Guardian* reports on prewar electioneering in rural areas, particularly a fiercely fought contest for the Caroni seat in the 1933 legislature elections. So before V. S. Naipaul turned to an exhaustive fictionalized treatment of his father's life in *A House for Mr. Biswas*, he was already making use of his father's journalism in *The Suffrage of Elvira*.

Harbans's encounter with the people of Elvira suggests that everyone sees the "possibilities." Forced to deal with a variety of social and religious groups and frustrated at almost every juncture, he finds the price of a seat going up and up as he is forced to bribe sections of the electorate again and again. The formula of *The Mystic Masseur* has been reversed: Ganesh is a trickster; Harbans, though hardly a more exemplary character, is tricked. As polling day approaches, he begins to fear defeat, but no such peripeteia occurs. He has paid through the nose for the seat, and he wins it. Naipaul's deadpan irony seems to insist that this is the way things work in Trinidad. Everyone and everything has a price, and to be a success one must pay it. The ground rules are clear enough. The humorous irony of *The Suffrage of Elvira*, Naipaul's most richly comic novel,

emerges not (as is frequently the case in ironic fiction) from an exposure of the characters' deviations from accepted moral norms but from the omission of reference to such norms and from their silent replacement by trickery.

Hilarious though *The Mystic Masseur* and *The Suffrage of Elvira* are, their manner of presenting society raises questions. Some critics have felt that Naipaul's stance in these early novels is disdainfully aloof. George Lamming (whose novel *Of Age and Innocence* Naipaul had reviewed dismissively when it was published in 1958) attacked them in 1960, saying, "His books can't move beyond a castrated satire; and although satire may be a useful element in fiction, no important work . . . can rest safely on satire alone. When such a writer is a colonial, ashamed of his cultural background and striving like mad to prove himself through promotion to the peaks of a 'superior' culture whose values are gravely in doubt, then satire . . . is for me nothing more than a refuge." Naipaul's response to such assessments of his work has been to insist that, while he may be an ironist, he is not a satirist: "I am not a satirist. Satire comes out of a tremendous optimism. . . . Satire is a type of anger. Irony and comedy, I think, come out of a sense of acceptance." Nevertheless it is hard not to see satire in his approach to the Hindu community and to Trinidadian life in these first two novels. They are broad Dickensian comedies peopled by two-dimensional characters and full of farcical situations. As satires they lack only the ameliorative function that, in Western notions of the medium, traditionally accompanies the element of ridicule. Naipaul's subsequent fiction has, however, with the exception of an occasional shorter piece, been more restrained in its use of comedy and tends to support the statement that he is not a satirist.

By 1961 Naipaul's British reputation was already considerable. He was the author of three successful books, two of which had won prizes (the 1958 John Llewellyn Rhys Memorial Prize for *The Mystic Masseur* and the 1961 Somerset Maugham Award for *Miguel Street*), and he had been reviewing fiction for the *New Statesman* since 1957. He was, however, still struggling to make a living as a writer. He was hard at work on *A House for Mr. Biswas*, his longest novel and the work many critics came to regard as his masterpiece. The inspiration had come to him in 1958 while living in a flat in Muswell Hill in North London: "it occurred to me then that one might write a book about possessions and one might look at a room and consider everything in it and trace the history and I threw this back into a setting such as I had known in Trinidad and that was the beginning of *A House for Mr. Biswas*." Coupling this with his father's advice to use him for a subject, Naipaul set to work on the novel in the kitchen of the next London house in which he lived, on Streatham Hill. Writing it totally absorbed him for three years, and he has said of this period (in his 1963 interview with David Bates), "It was like a career – I've been feeling unemployed ever since."

A House for Mr. Biswas is both a minutely circumstantial account of an individual life and a novel that may be read as an allegory of the East Indian's situation in Trinidad or of the colonial predicament more generally. From early on in his life the protagonist, Mohun Biswas, feels a sense of displacement and resolves to own a house. The succession of houses in which he lives – mostly as a tenant – forms a structural pattern that covers many aspects of Hindu life in preindependence Trinidad.

As a small boy in his parents' home, Mr. Biswas, as he is already called, is regarded as an ill-fated child. Everything he does has unfortunate consequences, and his many "crimes" culminate in his indirectly causing his father's death. Though he is for the most part passive, he is unable to escape the role assigned to him in his horoscope as a generator of tragedy. It is a fitting beginning to a life history of dependence and dignity denied.

After his mother, Bipti, sells the house where he has been born and where his navel string and a redundant sixth finger have been buried, Biswas is dispossessed of his origins. Later he comes to see this house as the only place where he has ever truly belonged. The rest of his boyhood is spent passively being a dependent on the bounty of his well-off relatives. As an adult he is trapped into marriage with Shama, daughter of the wealthy Tulsi family, and his subsequent life involves an alternation between periods of dependence on the Tulsis, who represent the older Hindu way of life, and attempts to escape their clutches. First he lives among them at Hanuman House, which, with its uniquely Indian architecture, its backyard named "Ceylon," and its arcade where old men born on the subcontinent meet to reminisce about the mother country, is clearly a bastion of Indian culture being preserved against incursions from the larger creole world of Trinidad. Biswas's dependent situation gives rise to satire on the Hindu family style, which is compounded by the daughter-in-law nature of his role in the household: he is "like a newly-married girl," for "the Hindu custom of [wives] living with their husbands' families" has been reversed. Twice Biswas is given a longer leash and allowed to venture beyond Hanu-

man House. First the Tulsis install him in their more or less defunct shop in an area known as the Chase; later they appoint him as a suboverseer on their sugar estate at Green Vale. Both these forays into the wider world end in disaster. At Green Vale he makes the first of two abortive attempts at emancipation from the Tulsis through building his own house. The collapse of this house is paralleled by his own nervous breakdown, and since throughout the novel the houses in which Biswas lives provide an index of his state of mind, the implication seems to be that he is not yet a sufficiently integrated person to stand alone.

While the vicissitudes of Biswas's life are closely tied to his response to Hinduism, his dependent status also fits Naipaul's paradigm of the colonial psychology: "to be a colonial is, in a way, to know a total kind of security. It is to have all decisions about major issues taken out of one's hands. It is to feel that one's political status has been settled so finally that there is very little one can do in the world." On this level Biswas's odyssey within the small society can be seen not only as an attempt to escape the more stultifying aspects of his ancestral culture but also, though he is not aware of it, as an endeavor to exercise some control over his destiny, which has largely been determined by his colonial situation.

The pattern is continued in part 2 of the novel, in which Biswas and his family move to Port of Spain. There, after a brief spell of staying with his sister and brother-in-law, he experiences two further forms of dependence on the Tulsis: in Mrs. Tulsi's Port of Spain house, where the old Hindu values are shown to be fighting a losing battle against Creolization; and at Shorthills, a former French estate house, where the family's attempts to step into the shoes of the "plantocracy" only serve to demonstrate how irrevocably alienated from the land they are. While at Shorthills, Biswas builds his second house and, shortly after its completion, accidentally burns it down. Finally he is duped into paying too much for a jerry-built modern house, where he dies at the age of forty-six. The wheel has come full circle, since the novel's prologue adumbrates this conclusion. The ending is, however, after the full story has been told, fraught with ambiguity. Though Biswas has been cheated, and though the expense and worry over his final house may well have contributed to his early death, he has succeeded in attaining his ideal of having a house, in claiming his own "portion of the earth." The prologue concludes with the remark that it would have been "terrible" for Biswas to have died "unnecessary and unaccommodated," and this situation has been averted, since he is accommodated both literally and metaphorically. The acquisition of the final house may be seen as representing the partial freedom that may be attained once one has learned to accept one's limitations and live within the realms of the possible.

A House for Mr. Biswas is still a comic novel in the Dickensian mode – and it owes a particular debt to H. G. Wells's *The History of Mr. Polly* (1910) – but its tone is more complex than that of Naipaul's earlier fiction. Comedy is interlaced with more naturalistic passages, and the treatment of the "little man" protagonist that Naipaul has taken over from Wells, along with the inspiration of his own father's life and short stories, frequently evokes pathos. Although there is further satire of Hindu rites and customs, it is no longer the diminishing satire of the first two novels. *A House for Mr. Biswas* is both a satirical critique of the older Hindu way of life and an elegiac lament for the irrevocably lost "pastoral" world of the old Indian society. The novel is regarded as one of the great twentieth-century novels because of the fullness and the comic-epic quality of the world Naipaul has created and the multiplicity of responses to this world that the narrative mode invites. The sardonic quality that commentators such as Lamming have found in Naipaul's early fiction has been replaced by a more balanced comic technique, which tends to support Naipaul's own remark that he is an ironist not a satirist.

After completing *A House for Mr. Biswas*, Naipaul was awarded a three-month scholarship by the Trinidad and Tobago government, which enabled him to return to Trinidad. While he was there the prime minister, Dr. Eric Williams, the distinguished West Indian historian, suggested that Naipaul should write a book about the Caribbean, and his scholarship was extended to enable him to visit other parts of the region. Naipaul spent a total of seven months traveling in the Caribbean, visiting Dutch and French societies as well as anglophone territories. Initially he hesitated over accepting the scholarship, uncertain as to whether he would make the transition from fiction to nonfiction successfully ("The novelist works towards conclusions of which he is often unaware; and it is better that he should"). Once he agreed to write the book, he did not allow the patronage he had received to compromise him in any way. In the foreword to the book, published as *The Middle Passage*, he asserts that it is in no sense an " 'official' book," and this claim is borne out in the text itself, which is often scathingly critical of Trinidad and Caribbean society in general.

In *The Middle Passage* Naipaul records his im-

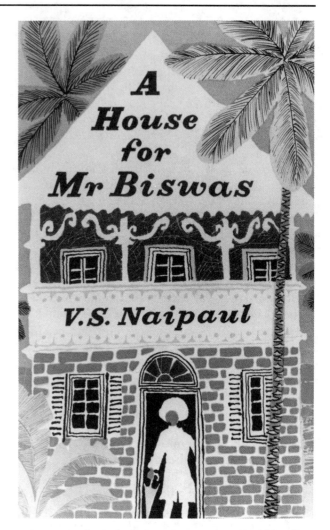

Dust jacket for the book that many critics consider Naipaul's finest novel, a fictionalized account of his father's life

pressions of five societies: Trinidad, British Guiana (now Guyana), Suriname, Martinique, and Jamaica. The book is as much a social investigation as a traveler's journal, and it demonstrates a concern with cultural identity in the Caribbean. While the section on British Guiana is the longest, the Trinidad chapter looms largest, for here Naipaul is writing as much from past experience as from his present visit, and the result is a response characterized by provocative remarks about the island's inhabitants, such as these: "Port of Spain is the noisiest city in the world. Yet it is forbidden to talk"; and "Like monkeys pleading for evolution, each claiming to be better than the other, Indians and Negroes appeal to the unacknowledged white audience to see how much they despise each other." Not surprisingly such remarks have made the book notorious in the West Indies, and attacks on it include a review by the Jamaican novelist John Hearne, who raises the charge of negrophobia. Outside the Trinidad chapter the record is more matter-of-fact, and while the remainder of the work is not without its moments of waspish satire, it lacks the vitriolic and tendentious quality of the Trinidad section.

In the early pages of *The Middle Passage* Naipaul comments on the difficulties encountered by historians trying to find an appropriate tone in which to write about the West Indies, and he appears to experience a similar problem in attempting to discover a suitable stance as a travel writer. Within the work he adopts a variety of personae, among them those of a Victorian traveler, enfeebled explorer, novelistic observer, cultural analyst, and recorder of secondhand information. His failure to assume a unitary persona has the positive effect of dramatizing the problem of choosing an appropriate tone, but it also leads to his frequently donning the role of an outsider, which seems strange for someone born within the region. Strangest of all are Naipaul's numerous self-conscious references to earlier travel books about the Caribbean, particularly those of the Victorian writers Anthony Trollope, James Anthony Froude, and Charles Kingsley. Early on Naipaul writes, "No attitude in the West Indies is new," and he comments, "This was no landscape for the camera: the tropical forest cannot be better suggested than by the steel engravings in the travel books of the last century." Such remarks present the West Indies on the eve of independence as a static, unchanging world. Despite this failure of vision, *The Middle Passage* is a work many readers find a compelling introduction to the Caribbean, and, as the first of his travel books, it is an important landmark in Naipaul's career.

In 1962 Naipaul received a Phoenix Trust Award to write a book about India (which was published two years later as *An Area of Darkness*). He has always felt it necessary to be physically absent from the places about which he writes in his fiction, and, while in India, he wrote his first novel with an English setting, *Mr. Stone and the Knights Companion*. It was written in Srinagar, Kashmir, in 1962. As with *A House for Mr. Biswas*, a significant part of the inspiration for the novel had come to Naipaul while he was living in Muswell Hill: "there was a tree at the back of the flat in Muswell Hill – the flat overlooked a bowling green. I saw the tree get bare and then in the spring I saw it putting out shoots. That was a great rebuke. It was also for me after more than seven years my first acquaintance with the seasons." This tree is clearly the real-life original of the tree at the back of Mr. Stone's house, which is an important symbol in the novel. Like Naipaul, Mr.

Stone, an elderly South London bachelor, feels a sense of rebuke when he realizes that the seasonal renewal ingrained in the natural cycle of the tree is missing from the human cycle. He seeks renewal through a late marriage and his conception of the Knights Companion scheme, a project designed to assist retired employees of the company for which he works. So, on one level, the novel is about the effects of aging.

On another level it can be read as an allegory about art, with the Knights Companion providing the outlet through which Mr. Stone attempts to express his latent artistic inclinations, and from this point of view one can see an element of self-projection on the part of Naipaul, who had doubts about his ability to write another novel after *A House for Mr. Biswas*: "I had to write another book to prove to myself that I could write, that it wasn't all over, that one had a talent. It wasn't written out of anything else but that and the subject did present itself to me." Nevertheless, although *Mr. Stone* may have been less a labor of love than *A House for Mr. Biswas* and although it is only of novella length, it is a miniature masterpiece, exhibiting the same sureness of touch as the previous novel while exploring similar themes from a very different angle of vision. These themes include the struggle of a "little man" to overcome his sense of anonymity (Mr. Stone is as much a displaced person in his English milieu as Mr. Biswas is in Trinidad), a struggle worked out particularly through his attitude toward accommodation, in both literal and metaphorical senses, and through his relationship with the landscape in which he lives. Like *A House for Mr. Biswas* and Naipaul's next novel, *The Mimic Men, Mr. Stone* explores these themes through the use of recurrent house and tree imagery; like Naipaul's earlier novels it is a fable about cultural identity, and after Mr. Stone journeys to Cornwall on his honeymoon and conceives the idea of the Knights Companion, which, with its basis in the Arthurian legend, alludes to the definitive British myth, it becomes increasingly clear that it is a "condition of England" novel.

In his 1971 interview with Adrian Rowe-Evans, Naipaul said, "In writing my first four or five books (including books which perhaps people think of as my big books) I was simply recording my reactions to the world; I hadn't come to any conclusions about it. . . . But since then, through my writing, through the effort honestly to respond, I have begun to have ideas about the world. I have begun to analyse." This statement suggests that a change occurred in his attitude toward writing and responding to experience about the time he first went to India, and the journey to the subcontinent did mark a watershed in Naipaul's development. Never having felt at home in Trinidad or England, he traveled to India in the hope that it would offer a culture wherein he would experience a sense of belonging. He came away feeling that "It was a journey that ought not to have been made; it had broken my life in two." His experiences in India are recorded in *An Area of Darkness,* but an article reprinted in *The Overcrowded Barracoon* (1972) provides the most succinct account of his reactions as a returned colonial: "A colonial in the double sense of one who had grown up in a Crown colony and one who had been cut off from the Metropolis, be it either England or India, I came to India expecting to find metropolitan attitudes. I had imagined that in some ways the largeness of the land would be reflected in the attitudes of the people. I have found . . . the psychology of the cell and the hive."

An Area of Darkness is a highly personal book, finally far more an account of personal trauma than an analysis of the social malaise Naipaul detects in India. It does, however, attack India on several levels. The hierarchical division of labor occasioned by the caste system, the Indian lack of a sense of history, and the conflicts he finds between Hindu tenets on cleanliness and the omnipresent excrement he sees are all particular objects of his irony, revealed in remarks such as these: "It is well that Indians are unable to look at their country directly, for the distress they would see would drive them mad"; and "Indians defecate everywhere. They defecate, mostly, beside the railway tracks. But they also defecate on the beaches; they defecate on the hills; they defecate on the river banks; they defecate on the streets; they never look for cover." Though Naipaul may appear to be attacking a variety of targets, virtually all the Hindu failings he documents in *An Area of Darkness* can be traced to the influence of karma, the doctrine that says that one's fate in life is determined by one's behavior in previous incarnations. Naipaul sees it as a paralyzing, defeating philosophy, which induces a quietism that precludes Western-style self-realization and progress. It is a theme he subsequently returned to more fully in his second book about the subcontinent, *India: A Wounded Civilization.*

Naipaul's voice in *An Area of Darkness* purports to be that of a detached outsider. Throughout, however, he emerges as an irritable and hypersensitive traveler, and this has the effect of undermining the credibility of his reportage. Toward the end of the book this pattern comes to a head, when he goes on a pilgrimage to see the Siva lingam in the Cave of

Dust jacket for the first of Naipaul's novels to be set in England

Amarnath. Disgusted by the unsanitary habits of his fellow pilgrims, he finally refuses to enter the cave. His Muslim companion returns to say that no lingam has formed this year, but this situation does not obviate the fact that Naipaul has declined to encounter the symbol of Hindu continuity. He remains a spectator, retaining an aura of detachment through nonparticipation. It is an attitude close to the karma-induced resignation that he deplores, and, to his credit, Naipaul subsequently admits as much in a passage that links Indian noninvolvement with his own: "It is only now, as the impatience of the observer is dissipated in the process of writing and self-inquiry, that I see how much this philosophy has also been mine." Apparently this discovery led to the more analytical stance in Naipaul's later work.

In 1966 Naipaul spent six months as writer in residence at Makerere University in Uganda. His stay there was financed by the American Farfield Foundation. His writing students, whom he usually saw at his house, were sometimes advised not to write, and Naipaul reportedly put in few appearances at the university, acquiring a reputation as a difficult and uncompromising personality. During this period he traveled in East Africa and Zaire. His stay in Africa provided the material from which the title novella of *In a Free State* (1971) grew. Toward the end of his time there Naipaul lived in a hotel in western Kenya. While in Uganda and Kenya he wrote the London sections of *The Mimic Men*; the West Indian parts were written in London.

The Mimic Men resembles *Mr. Stone* in the desertion of the comic mode of Naipaul's early fiction. It is one of his finest works and a major exploration of colonial psychology, as the protagonist, Ralph Singh, seeks, like Mr. Biswas and Mr. Stone, to impose order on his life. The novel takes the form of Singh's autobiographical memoir, and finally he concludes that the act of writing has provided the order for which he has previously searched without success. This stance, too, is a direct development of themes explored in Naipaul's previous two novels. One of the avenues through which Mr. Biswas seeks self-fulfillment is writing, and Mr. Stone's Knights Companion scheme is very much a literary project.

The Mimic Men is in three parts. Part 1 begins with Singh describing his first experience of London, when he lived amid a motley collection of people in a Kensington boardinghouse, an apt opening since, throughout, his story is one of displacement. He goes on to record his experiences while a student at a London college, his marriage to the English Sandra, and his return with her to his home island of Isabella, where the marriage breaks up. Part 2 moves back in time to describe his childhood in Isabella, where, like Naipaul, he attends the country's leading secondary school. This part of the novel mainly deals with Singh's early life until he first leaves for England, although a brief final section describes the event that precipitated his first return to Isabella, the news of his father's death. Part 3 takes up the narrative where part 1 ended. It describes Singh's subsequent career as one of a new generation of local politicians, an abortive mission to London as a representative of his country, his ensuing political disgrace on Isabella, and a final period of exile in London, where he seems more displaced than ever but sets about ordering his experience through the writing of the autobiographical memoir. Such an account of the narrative structure of *The Mimic Men* suggests a fairly straightforward linear progression with a long central flashback. The pattern is, however, more complex than this,

since Singh's mood throughout is reflective – so that the reader is constantly drawn back to the moment of writing – and Singh frequently records brief details out of sequence.

For the first time in his career Naipaul was strongly indebted to Joseph Conrad, the novelist who supplanted Naipaul's early masters, Charles Dickens and H. G. Wells, as the most significant literary influence on his work. In *The Mimic Men* the Conradian influence can be seen in incidental allusions, but more generally it is manifest in the use of a fragmentary and unchronological narrative structure, a form employed by Conrad in such novels as *Lord Jim* (1900) and *Nostromo* (1904), and in the use of a narrator through whom events are filtered. In Conrad, Naipaul found a kindred spirit. Both were non-English writers whose absorption into the English tradition did little to dispel their sense of displacement. Such displacement shows itself in their work on both formal and thematic levels. Formally the disjointed narrative method and the use of a narrator whose values may be questioned have the effect of creating a relativistic atmosphere, far removed from the certitudes of most traditional English novels. On a thematic level Naipaul attempts to dramatize the relationship between the sociopolitical and the psychological consequences of imperialism in *The Mimic Men*, and in words he was later to use in an essay on Conrad, he follows the Pole in writing, "Not as a man with a cause, but a man offering, as in *Nostromo*, a vision of the world's half-made societies, as places which continuously made and unmade themselves, where there was no goal, and where always 'something inherent in the necessities of successful action . . . carried with it the moral degradation of the idea.'"

Singh's quest for an ideal order takes many forms. He looks for it in London ("centre of the world"); the Aryan past of his ancestors; the Edenic state of pre-Columbian America; the pastoral world of Latin literature (like his creator, he particularly enjoys reading Martial); and even, when he dreams of retiring to one of the few cocoa-estate houses remaining on Isabella, in the heyday of the plantocracy. Yet from the outset the voice of Singh the narrator makes it clear that "All landscapes turn eventually to land, the gold of the imagination to the lead of reality." He fails to find the fulfillment he is seeking through any of these avenues and turns all too easily to vapid sexual encounters and a cynical political role, which involves "the moral degradation of the idea." Only writing appears to offer any release from the disorder that characterizes his life, but even in this aspect the problematic use of Singh as the narrative persona leaves open the question of whether he has truly progressed. More complex than any of Naipaul's previous novels, *The Mimic Men* ushered in a new period in his writing, in which there is a more overt concern with imperialism and its latter-day consequences.

In the same year as *The Mimic Men*, Naipaul also published *A Flag on the Island* (1967), which comprises several short stories written between 1950 and 1962, and the title novella, which had been, according to Naipaul, "specially written for an American film company." The shorter pieces include three stories with a boy-narrator similar to that of *Miguel Street*. "The Mourners" (dated 1950) is Naipaul's earliest piece of published fiction and, though little more than a sketch, demonstrates the mastery of prose style he already commanded while still in his teens; "My Aunt's Gold Teeth," originally broadcast on *Caribbean Voices* in 1954, is a study in "religious schizophrenia" brought on by Hindu acculturation in the West Indies; "The Enemy," originally written as part of *Miguel Street* but omitted from that volume, explores the narrator's relationship with his mother, the "enemy" of the title.

Other stories include two satires of English suburban life, "Greenie and Yellow" and "The Perfect Tenants." The former examines the struggle for survival of three pet budgerigars in a London home. Initially it appears to have little in common with Naipaul's other fiction, since it deserts the theme of personal displacement in colonial and postcolonial societies. However, its dramatization of the deleterious effects of the enforced bringing together of captive creatures provides a spare, elemental working out of the dominant theme of Naipaul's later fiction, the intrusion of outsiders into a restricted environment.

In the title story, "A Flag on the Island," the figure of the outsider takes the form of an American narrator who revisits the Caribbean island on which he was stationed in World War II. Naipaul's primary concern seems to be to illustrate the injurious effects of American involvement in the island's affairs, an influence exercised through Uncle Sam's military presence in the war, through imported Hollywood cinema, through tourism, and through foundation money. Frank, the narrator, is a personification of this influence, since he has had a disruptive effect on the lives of the islanders with whom he has come into contact. The novella is cinematic both in form and theme but ultimately subverts the very conventions it appears to be employing. Not surprisingly no film of it has ever been made.

Two other pieces in *A Flag on the Island*, "A Christmas Story" and "The Baker's Story," demonstrate Naipaul's ability to achieve delicate ironic effects through first-person narrative, while "The Night Watchman's Occurrence Book" is a miniature masterpiece of deadpan comedy. These three stories, all written in 1962, show the refinements in comic technique Naipaul had achieved before he virtually deserted the comic mode in the mid 1960s.

In *The Middle Passage* Naipaul had written about the difficulties encountered by historians trying to find an appropriate tone in which to write about the West Indies. With *The Loss of El Dorado* (1969), a highly personal history of Trinidad, he faced the past once again. The method he adopted was unusual. He decided to confine himself to an account of "the two moments when Trinidad was touched by 'history' ": the latter stages of the quest for El Dorado by Sir Walter Ralegh and the Spanish conquistador Antonio de Berrio; and the attempt to make Port of Spain a lucrative trading post during the period of political turmoil in the Caribbean at the end of the eighteenth century. Both stories are fully documented (Naipaul's wife, Pat, helped him with research in the British Museum) and bring to life figures who receive comparatively little attention in other historical accounts: de Berrio; Thomas Picton, the British governor of Trinidad at the end of the eighteenth century; and Luisa Calderon, a mulatto girl falsely accused by her lover of theft in the same period.

Despite the scholarship that informs *The Loss of El Dorado*, it is, as Robert Hamner remarks in his *V. S. Naipaul* (1973), "a novelist's history." Naipaul eschews both academic detachment and concerned indignation, two of the stances he has identified as typical of West Indian historiography, in favor of a meticulously detailed account, in which he endeavors to illustrate the nature of colonial society and the extent of its dependence on the metropolis. The "history" of Trinidad consists, in Naipaul's view, only of a narrative of encounters with the metropolis: "A place like Port of Spain, in the uncluttered New World has no independent life; it alters with the people who come to it." He regards Trinidad as "exempt from history" during the long interval between the two periods on which he focuses.

In short, Naipaul's one and only incursion into the realms of history writing to date is characterized by its novelistic accretion of circumstantial detail and an authorial stance that denies colonial society any autonomous life. The tone is much less dispassionate than that of most historians, and one is always aware of a voice that, without ever quite identifying itself with the colonizer, holds itself aloof from the society that is being discussed.

By this point in his career Naipaul had won all Britain's leading literary awards with the exception of the Booker Prize, and he received that for *In a Free State* in 1971. He was subsequently short-listed for the Booker Prize on a second occasion – for *A Bend in the River* in 1979 – and his name has been mentioned in connection with the Nobel Prize for Literature. Rumor has it that the Swedish academy's judges have failed, as yet, to confer this award on him because his work has not been seen to show sufficient humanitarian concern.

Like *A Flag on the Island*, *In a Free State* brings together a novella, in which two English expatriates journey through an independent East African country, and several shorter pieces: a prologue and epilogue from an otherwise unpublished Egyptian travel journal and two stories about displaced Indians. However, unlike the stories in *A Flag on the Island*, the various constituent parts of *In a Free State* form a unified whole, and Naipaul has said, "I shouldn't wish the African story to be published independently of the other parts." All the sections of *In a Free State* treat the theme of displacement in the neocolonial world. In the first story, "One out of Many," Santosh, a Bombay domestic, goes to Washington with his diplomatic-service employer and finds himself lost in the "capital of the world"; in "Tell Me Who to Kill" two Trinidadian brothers are affected in different ways by their experience of deracination in England; in the novella which gives the work its title, neither of the two protagonists belongs in England any longer. The excerpts from the travel journal first center on an elderly English tramp, a self-styled "citizen of the world" who, during a crossing from Piraiévs to Alexandria, succeeds in stirring up his cabin mates' enmity through an unspecified offense; and in the epilogue the ultimate displaced character of Naipaul's fiction is shown to be the author himself. Naipaul has confessed to being "totally involved" in all the characters of *In a Free State*, and in the final section the mask drops, at least partially, as he becomes the central persona.

In each of the sections freedom proves to be an uneasy, anguished state. The geographical freedom of the tramp in the prologue renders him an outcast, and the reader is left feeling that the tramp's unrevealed crime may well be his failure to belong. Santosh runs away from his employer, only to find he has exchanged one kind of bondage for another since he is, by himself, an illegal immigrant. In "Tell Me Who to Kill," the Trinidadian Indian

narrator, nourished on Hollywood myths, devotes himself to furthering his younger brother's education in England but comes to realize that metropolitan achievement is as far beyond his brother as himself. He is left with a desire to kill the "enemy" responsible for his sufferings. But no enemy is to be found. Once again Naipaul is dramatizing the psychology of the colonial, who has been denied freedom by forces beyond his control.

The title story corroborates the view that displacement is a general twentieth-century predicament. Naipaul's two English expatriates are as much in limbo as his Third World immigrants. During a political crisis, Bobby, a government servant, and Linda, the wife of a colleague, journey by road from the capital of the East African free state (the title has both political and psychological reverberations) to the exclusive compound in the south where they live. Bobby is a homosexual, who, after a nervous breakdown at Oxford, has found a modicum of personal salvation in Africa. Linda is equally deracinated. Only at home in the elitist situation of the compound, she is estranged from both English and East African life. When she and her husband leave the free state, they will probably "go south."

The journey proves to be an assault course for the liberal Bobby, who is genuinely committed to the society through an ideal of modest, unmeddlesome service: he is subjected both to isolated but cumulative acts of aggression against him by Africans and to verbal attacks on his liberalism by Linda. His freedom in Africa has brought him only isolation and humiliation, and he is as far from personal fulfillment as Santosh and the narrator of "Tell Me Who to Kill."

Thus far *In a Free State* follows the negative vision of Naipaul's earlier fiction, but in the epilogue he becomes involved in the action with a positive gesture of commitment. As he watches desert children being lured to approach an oasis rest house for scraps of tourists' food and then horsewhipped by the coffee waiter for coming too near, Naipaul suddenly becomes incensed, rushes into the middle of the scene in protest, and abruptly stops the flagellation. Subsequently he feels the act has been futile, but it has demonstrated the extent of Naipaul's movement away from the inertia of the karma psychology and the colonial mentality. Similarly the more-analytical mode of *In a Free State* represents a development in Naipaul's approach, and, in the year of its publication, he said in his interview with Rowe-Evans, "I've decolonized myself through the practice of writing, through what I've learned from writing, looking at the world."

After his first journey to India in 1962, Naipaul began to travel widely, often recording his impressions of the societies he visited in in-depth articles for the British and North American press. *The Overcrowded Barracoon* comprises twenty-one journalistic pieces he published between 1958 and 1972. The volume is divided into four sections: "An Unlikely Colonial," comprised of articles on Naipaul's West Indian origins; "India," the longest section in the book; "Looking Westward," which has essays on John Steinbeck, Norman Mailer, Jacques Soustelle, and a Japanese businessman, Mr. Matsuda; and "Columbus and Crusoe," a collection of more-general essays on the Caribbean and Mauritius, where there is a society that, through Naipaul's presentation, is made to look very similar to that of the Caribbean and is the "overcrowded barracoon" of the title.

In a 1965 article on "Indian Autobiographies," collected in *The Overcrowded Barracoon*, Naipaul laments the failure of Indian writers overseas – Nirad Chaudhuri apart – to provide authentic witness to what they see. In 1967, in "Columbus and Crusoe," one of the finest pieces in the volume, he levels a similar charge against Columbus. Like the Indian autobiographers, the explorer is seen as an inadequate chronicler because he was insensitive to the imaginative promise of the lands he "discovers"; his "banality of expectation matches a continuing banality of perception." This statement is not only interesting criticism; it is revealing where Naipaul's own travel writing is concerned. His ability always to offer sensitive witness makes him a good travel journalist, even when his vision is at its most sardonic. It is as if his sense of placelessness has given him a chameleonlike ability to be equally ill at ease and equally perceptive anywhere. His articles on India, Belize, Saint Kitts, Anguilla, and Mauritius bring these places alive through carefully chosen details in a way travel writing that includes more hard information frequently does not.

Paul Theroux describes Naipaul as "a writer who doesn't have what is called a journalistic style." Insofar as Naipaul operates through a mode that has much in common with his novelistic practice, there is a grain of truth in this idea, but his ability to blend firsthand observation, carefully chosen details, and impish editorial comment makes for a style that suggests that the journalistic and the novelistic are not mutually exclusive. Theroux reinforces his contention that Naipaul lacks a journalistic style by saying that "The Election in Ajmer," the longest of the pieces in *The Overcrowded Barracoon*, is a "little novel." However, the article succeeds bril-

Poster advertising Naipaul's controversial nonfiction book about the practice of Islam in Iran, Pakistan, Malaysia, and Indonesia, places he visited in 1979 and 1980

liantly as journalism, not only because it shows Naipaul as a sensitive witness and because of the adeptness with which he conveys his ironic vision in an apparently deadpan account of incestuous local politics, but also because the "story" provides a microcosm of the wider political situation in India. And this approach is typical of Naipaul's practice in *The Overcrowded Barracoon*.

During the 1970s Naipaul saw his younger brother, Shiva (born in 1945), also rise to literary prominence. Though only a dozen years younger than V. S., Shiva was, in his older brother's opinion, representative of a later generation, since the Trinidad in which V. S. grew up had changed so much in the interim. Shiva followed his older brother from Queen's Royal College to University College, Oxford, where he read classical Chinese. His novels and nonfiction books, which include *Fireflies* (1970); *North of South: An African Journey* (1978); *Black and White* (1980), a book about the Jonestown Massacre and its background; and the posthumously published *An Unfinished Journey*

(1987), treat many of the same themes as those of V. S. Naipaul and are informed by similar powers of ironic observation. Shiva died, tragically young, of a heart attack in 1985.

In 1973 Naipaul traveled to Trinidad to research material for two long *Sunday Times* articles on the so-called Abdul Malik ("Michael X") killings. (These articles were subsequently republished in his 1980 book *The Return of Eva Perón; with The Killings in Trinidad*). This material provided the germ for his next novel, *Guerrillas* (1975), where Malik's career is paralleled by that of the fictional Jimmy Ahmed. Like Malik, Jimmy is a self-styled "black" radical of mixed parentage who has risen to fame in England and has adopted a Muslim name that conceals his ethnic origins: Malik's original surname was Portuguese; Jimmy's is Chinese. Like Malik, Jimmy has been deported from England as a criminal and attempts to set up an agricultural commune on his home island. Like Malik, he has leadership fantasies that manifest themselves in clumsy attempts at fiction, and he suffers from paranoiac tendencies and a love/hate relationship with the white world – in particular white women – traits that lead to his instigating the murder of an English girl, who is unceremoniously buried in a shallow grave.

All these details serve to establish the link between these two versions of the false redeemer, but Naipaul's portrayal also suggests considerable differences. In *Guerrillas* the treatment of Jimmy Ahmed is less concerned with the damage such a figure does to a certain section of society than with his own personal tragedy. The emphasis is shifted so that it falls mainly on Jimmy as a displaced person, a typical Naipaul protagonist, trying, like Ralph Singh, to order his life through writing and also close to Mr. Biswas in his belief that "men must claim their portion of the earth."

Jimmy is, however, only one element in a larger design, one of a triptych of main characters. The others are Jane, a middle-class Englishwoman who becomes involved with Jimmy but has come to the island secure in her sense of being privileged and her knowledge that she has a return air ticket; and Roche, her lover, who, though he has the best of white liberal credentials, having been imprisoned and tortured in South Africa, is revealed as a man lacking in ideology or any form of personal belief. Both characters provide case studies in what Naipaul has referred to, in his Conrad essay, as the "corruption of causes."

As *Guerrillas* builds toward a climax, it seems possible that a social apocalypse will occur, but Naipaul frustrates the neat completion of this pattern by having Jane struck down by one of Jimmy's followers instead of having the city burned by fire, which has seemed the most likely culmination of the story because of Naipaul's recurrent use of fire imagery. Though the political dimension is emphasized, the primary concern is with individuals, and the implication, as in the title story of *A Flag on the Island*, is that the apocalyptic situation is an ongoing one for the society.

The title of *Guerrillas* may seem slightly puzzling, since guerrilla warfare is only a minor theme. The title is, however, explained in the epigraph (a quote attributed to Jimmy Ahmed): "When everybody wants to fight there's nothing to fight for. Everybody wants to fight his own little war, everybody is a guerrilla." This situation, Naipaul appears to imply, is the tragedy of all the characters in the novel. All fall short of their "hopeful and noble illusions of righteous anger, pity and revolt" and succumb to the "corruption of causes"; in a world where radical idealism has become a commonplace, the quest for identity through this avenue proves as abortive as the quests of Naipaul's earlier displaced protagonists. *Guerrillas* is a powerful and disturbing novel that did much to consolidate Naipaul's growing reputation in the United States.

Since his first journey to India in 1962, Naipaul has revisited his ancestral homeland on several occasions, and his next book, *India: A Wounded Civilization*, was based mainly on his fourth visit to the subcontinent, in 1975, during the state of emergency. Though ostensibly less personal than *An Area of Darkness*, *India*, too, is a passionate and polemical book, dedicated to developing the thesis that the real "emergency" of India is not political but psychological, since the stumbling block that prevents progress in the postindependence period is the fatalistic acceptance induced by karma, referred to by Naipaul as "the Hindu killer, the Hindu calm, which tells us that we pay in this life for what we have done in past lives: so that everything we see is just and balanced, and the distress we see is to be relished as religious theatre, a reminder of our duty to ourselves, our future lives."

Whereas in *An Area of Darkness* karma seems to underlie a great deal of Indian behavior, in *India* Naipaul detects its influence everywhere: in the complacency of a Rajasthan prince; in the perpetuation of beggary; in the Indian attitude to history and the past; and in literary works as diverse as the novels of R. K. Narayan, the plays of the Marathi dramatist Vijay Tendulkar, and U. R. Anantha Murthy's Kannada novel *Samskara*. Karma, as Naipaul sees it, arrests all growth and guarantees the ossification of the wounded civilization, which is slowly destroying itself.

India differs from *An Area of Darkness* in that the prose style is even more sparkling. Aphorisms fit together with all the satisfactoriness of a well-made jigsaw puzzle, as Naipaul develops his thesis with an appearance of essayistic detachment. However, occasionally the rhetorical smoothness is disturbed by passages such as the following, which indicate that he remains far from composed on the subject of India: "When men cannot observe, they don't have ideas; they have obsessions. When people live instinctive lives, something like a collective amnesia steadily blurs the past. The development . . . hadn't yet begun to show . . . children were stunted, their minds deformed, serf material already, beyond the reach of education where that was available." *India* may seem to be a more balanced work than *An Area of Darkness*, since by 1975 Naipaul had sufficiently digested the shock of his first visit to the extent of being able to generalize more successfully and even to offer a hint of a positive approach through "social inquiry," which slightly mitigates his otherwise remorselessly negative vision. But, like the earlier work, the book is ultimately very personal and says more about the psychology of the deracinated Indian and Naipaul's own particularly ambiguous love/hate relationship with Mother India than about the actual India he visits.

In *An Area of Darkness* Naipaul makes the comment that nineteenth-century English travel writers frequently reported "not on themselves but on their Englishness." The implication is that he expects such writers to be reporting on themselves rather than the places they visit. Apparently this approach is for Naipaul a normal facet of travel writing. What is distinctive about the nineteenth-century English exponents of the genre to whom he refers (Charles Darwin, Anthony Trollope, Charles Kingsley, and James Anthony Froude) is their participation in and perpetuation of "the English national myth." Naipaul is himself influenced by these writers. However, his background prevents him from following his mentors in reporting on his "Englishness"; his travel writing is characterized instead by the insights it offers into the colonial psychology and, more specifically, into his own paradoxical East Indian/West Indian origins. Nowhere is this more prominent than in his Indian travel books.

A 1975 return visit to Zaire provided Naipaul with material for another in-depth journalistic essay, "A New King for the Congo" (included in *The Return of Eva Perón*), and his next novel, *A Bend in the River*. The relationship between fictional and nonfictional accounts is similar to that between "The Killings in Trinidad" and *Guerrillas*. Some refinement naturally took place between the writing of the essay, which is characterized by Naipaul's familiar dismissive approach to the Third World, and the novel, which is more concerned with the plight of individuals. In both works the present predicament of Africa is encapsulated in a powerful image of a world gradually becoming more and more clogged up and moving toward stasis, represented by the water hyacinths on the Zaire River, which in the last generation have increasingly disrupted navigation. However, whereas in "A New King for the Congo" these are seen as threatening to "imprison the river people in the immemorial ways of the bush," in *A Bend in the River* they become a more multivalent image, relating to personal as well as social paralysis. Both books show postindependence Africa as reverting back to the bush, after what the novel calls "the miraculous peace of the colonial time," but in *A Bend in the River*, while the personal and the public cannot finally be separated from one another, this situation is more the backdrop for another Naipaul study of individual displacement than the epicenter of the narrative.

The narrator/protagonist Salim begins his story with the words "The World is what it is; men who are nothing, who allow themselves to become nothing, have no place in it," and survival is at the heart of the novel from this moment until the end, which sees Salim taking flight from the town at the bend in the river (primarily based on Kisangani), where, after previously fleeing the East African coast, he has built up a business as a shopkeeper. Salim, like so many of the characters of Naipaul's later novels, emerges as a "casualty" of imperialism and finds himself running out of places that offer him a secure existence. Where he differs from many of these characters, however, is in his capacity for pragmatic action to ensure his own survival. Naipaul has said that he chose the title of the novel for the "uplift" in it, and while at first sight this remark may puzzle many readers, Salim's capacity to adapt and take a new direction, when his world falls apart at the end, does offer a more positive vision than that in *Guerrillas*.

Though set in Zaire, *A Bend in the River* is primarily concerned with expatriates of one kind or another, and even the two main African characters – Metty, Salim's servant from the coast, and Ferdinand, a "new man of Africa" from the south of the country – who are characterized quite fully, have mixed backgrounds (Metty has "the blood of

Gujarat in his veins," and Ferdinand is "of mixed tribal heritage"); thus they are also outsiders in their present environment. As so often in Naipaul's fiction, this setting is a world in which no one belongs. The various other Asian characters in the novel all seek to find a safe haven, whether it be in nostalgia for the ancestral past, in flight to the metropolis, or in attaching themselves to the international organizations that are seeking to create a new modern Africa. The Europeans – Raymond, a historian who has previously been high in the country's president's esteem, and Yvette, his young wife with whom Salim has an affair – also emerge as characters who are among Naipaul's lost people. Raymond finds himself suffering from the president's studied neglect, and Yvette's relationship with Salim, which seems to depend as much on Raymond's health and well-being as their own, comes to an end in circumstances that, while they suggest mutual betrayal, are more injurious to her than to Salim.

The Zaire setting has inevitably led to comparisons with Conrad's Congo, and Salim emerges as the Marlow-like figure whose pragmatism ensures his survival where others are destroyed by their encounter with the darkness of the African interior. *A Bend in the River* can be read as a postindependence *Heart of Darkness* (1899) in which many of the earlier patterns have been reversed, with Africans now occupying roles previously reserved for Europeans and the president offering the closest model for a latter-day Kurtz, but ultimately Naipaul shows far greater concern with how individuals cope with social, political, and psychological crisis, and this approach makes it possible to view *A Bend in the River* as essentially similar to *Heart of Darkness* rather than as a text that simply inverts the major patterns of Conrad's novella.

During the 1970s Naipaul wrote several in-depth journalistic pieces for the British and American press, and his next book, *The Return of Eva Perón; with The Killings in Trinidad*, brought some of these together as four long essays: the pieces on Michael X and Zaire; the long title essay on Argentina; and a shorter piece on Conrad. While initially this volume may appear, like *The Overcrowded Barracoon*, simply to be a collection of Naipaul's journalism, in fact there are clear thematic parallels between the various component parts, and this structure, in addition to providing a compendium of the issues that had most absorbed Naipaul during the 1970s, makes for a sense of overall unity.

The accounts of Malik, Eva Perón, Mobutu (the Congo's "new king"), and their societies all show how charismatic leadership can minister to the fantasies of those who find their lives deficient but can ultimately fail to offer anything other than a leadership cult, which can destroy leaders and followers alike while contributing nothing to the improvement of society. In "The Killings in Trinidad" Naipaul is once again treating one of his earliest subjects, the confidence man/trickster who is as much a victim of his deception as those he exploits: like Man-man in *Miguel Street*, Malik is a fantasist who effectively destroys himself. In "The Return of Eva Perón" Argentina is "an artificial, fragmented colonial society, made deficient and bogus by its myths," and Perón is seen as central to its contemporary mythology: twenty years after her death she has the cult following of a saint, but such social reforms as those for which she stood have been forgotten or obscured, and the country's problems continue to multiply. In "A New King for the Congo" Mobutu, like the president in *A Bend in the River*, is viewed as a latter-day Kurtz, a leader whose fanaticism is derived from a direct reversal of the circumstances that produced Conrad's megalomaniac: Naipaul describes Mobutu as having been "maddened not by contact with wilderness and primitivism, but with . . . civilization." The essay on Conrad puts Naipaul's other essays in the volume into context by focusing on Conrad's absorption with the forerunners of today's Third World societies, the juxtaposition of cultures, and the "corruption of causes." In each of the previous pieces there is at least one reference to Conrad's work, and in retrospect his influence appears to have been underlying the whole book.

During the latter part of 1979 and early 1980 Naipaul spent seven months traveling in Muslim societies in the Middle and Far East, and this experience provided the subject of *Among the Believers: An Islamic Journey* (1981). He visited four non-Arab Muslim nations – Iran, Pakistan, Malaysia, and Indonesia – and his account is a personal attempt to explain the "Islamic revival." The "believers" of the title are for the most part the young Muslims who have been in the forefront of the revival, and, as is often the case in Naipaul's travel writing, social analysis mainly takes the form of a narrative of encounters with individuals. Sometimes these individuals are public figures, such as the Ayatollah Khalkalli, the Ayatollah Khomeini's "hanging judge," but more frequently they are ordinary people caught between the resurgence of the old faith and the acculturation engendered by the spread of a global consumer culture.

The picture of contemporary Islam that

emerges is for the most part a negative one characterized by confusion and contradiction, and the believers' passionate conviction is seen as a force that is impotent to bring about greatly needed social change. As in *The Mimic Men* Naipaul suggests it is paradoxical that Third World societies that reject the West nevertheless depend on it for technology and material goods. Thus the section on Iran ends with his comment that Khomeini expresses the "confusion" of his people: "the confusion of a people of high medieval culture awakening to oil and money, a sense of power and violation, and acknowledgment of a great new encircling civilization. That civilization couldn't be mastered. It was to be rejected; at the same time it was to be depended on." Of the four countries he visited, Naipaul sees Pakistan, the pioneer of the revival after its founding as a Muslim state in 1947, as the place where Islam "as a people-building force, has worked at its best." But even in Pakistan the sense of cultural definition and "personal salvation" is seen to go hand in glove with a political regime that justifies its despotism, public whippings, and curtailment of the freedom of the press as "the true Islamic way."

In Malaysia the contradictions between a return to the old Islam and reliance on the appurtenances of modern consumer culture are presented as particularly acute. The believers there are the educated young, for whom the religious revival has provided a "weapon," a "way of getting even with the world. It serves their grief, their feeling of inadequacy, their social rage and racial hatred." With its high standard of living, Malaysia is seen as the Asian society most distant from traditional Islam. In Indonesia the situation is different again. There Naipaul finds a sense of uniqueness among the populace, which he attributes to their reverence for the "great civilization" of the past, but it is a hybrid past, since the culture has only been Muslim since the fifteenth century and before that had been predominantly Buddhist and Hindu for more than a millennium.

Among the Believers has been criticized by Muslim intellectuals, who have found it superficial, biased toward Western rationalism, and finally unrepresentative because of its exclusion of Arab and African Islamic societies. Despite the considerable amount of penetrating firsthand observation and analysis offered in the text, its point of view remains blinkered and guaranteed to reinforce Western prejudices. The disenchanted polemical stance is comparable with *An Area of Darkness* and *India: A Wounded Civilization*. All three works offer an account of how Islam and Hinduism are stultifying in-

Dust jacket for Naipaul's book about his travels in the southeastern United States

dividual development in Asia. But whereas the Indian books are written out of a passionate love/hate relationship with Hinduism and considerable knowledge of the culture, *Among the Believers* finally comes across as more of a tourist's-eye view, redeemed only by sensitivity and a sense of authorial integrity.

Naipaul's next book, *Finding the Centre*, ostensibly brings together two very different pieces of narrative: "Prologue to an Autobiography," described by Naipaul as "not an autobiography, a story of life or deeds done," but "an account of something less easily seized: my literary beginnings and the imaginative promptings of my many-sided background"; and "The Crocodiles of Yamoussoukro," a travel essay about a journey to the Ivory Coast. In fact the two pieces have much in common, for both – like much of Naipaul's work – deal with a quest for signification. The search for a center comes to stand for both the attempt by marginalized countries and peoples to find order and the writer's search for kernels of narrative that can express this predicament. In his foreword Naipaul says that "both pieces are about the process of writing" and "seek in different ways to admit the reader to that process."

"Prologue to an Autobiography" takes the reader into the origins of *Miguel Street* and is interesting not only for the light it sheds on the beginnings of Naipaul's writing career in the free-lancers' room of the Langham Hotel but also for the insights it offers into the ethnic backdrop to that book. The revelation that characters such as Hat and Bogart are based on Indian originals shows that, early on, the theme of East Indian acculturation in the Caribbean was in Naipaul's work, even if it is far from immediately apparent to most readers. Subsequent sections of the essay provide further details about Seepersad Naipaul and the importance his influence had on his son, particularly in the writing of *A House for Mr. Biswas*, and Seepersad's life and career are related to his Hindu background.

At one point Naipaul writes of having grown up with "two ideas of history, almost two ideas of time": the former — "history with dates" — encompassed the knowledge of ancient Rome and nineteenth-century England, as well as the growth of the nationalist movement in India; the latter was concerned with the world beyond dates of his local Hindu origins in rural Trinidad. The recent past of the Trinidad East Indian community is viewed as "a time beyond recall," a world Naipaul had seen as almost as mythical as the India of the *Ramayana*. "Prologue to an Autobiography" succeeds in bringing together personal and public history and in rendering this mythical world "real" for the reader.

In "The Crocodiles of Yamoussoukro" Naipaul focuses on people he has met in the Ivory Coast, provides insight into the society, and comes to the conclusion that they are like himself in that they, too, are "trying to find order in their world." In one sense this situation is hardly surprising, since several of them are expatriate Caribbean women and so have a relationship to Africa similar to his own, but the search for a center affects the local populace as well.

Naipaul's approach to the Ivory Coast seems to be more sympathetic than his attitude toward Africa in his other writing about the continent. The country is presented as one of the success stories of black Africa, and he sees the president as a man who has used French technical expertise to bring about significant material advances. However, Naipaul still manages to find in the Ivory Coast the Africa of *In a Free State* and *A Bend in the River*, for, along with the world of modern hotels, golf clubs, and highways, he discovers an antique bush culture that comes into its own at night, a culture based on superstition and ritual. The coexistence of these two

worlds is seen at Yamoussoukro, a modern city of fine avenues in the middle of the bush, where, at a lake beside the president's palace, tourists come to see a regular daily ritual in which crocodiles devour a live sacrifice, a chicken. As Naipaul presents it, this ritual symbolizes the modern French-educated president's reliance on a display of potency and cruelty that has its roots in the old tribal Africa, the intrusion of the Africa of the night into the Africa of the day. So, while the tone is less negative than in Naipaul's earlier writing about Africa, the fundamental vision remains unchanged.

Between 1963 and 1979 Naipaul published novels at regular four-year intervals. But after the appearance of *A Bend in the River* no new novel of his appeared until *The Enigma of Arrival* (1987). During the intervening years he suffered from a serious illness and was deeply moved by the deaths of his younger sister and his brother, Shiva. *The Enigma of Arrival*, which is Naipaul's most autobiographical piece of fiction to date, is pervaded by a sense of personal loss and fragility. It is also an elegy for a vanishing English landscape. The narrator writes about his experience living as a tenant on a manorial estate in Wiltshire, and, like *Mr. Stone and the Knights Companion*, the book can be read as a "condition of England" novel. The narrator's surroundings are presented as an ancient, multilayered landscape, containing numerous "sacred sites," among them Stonehenge, Winchester — a candidate for Arthur's Camelot — and Victorian churches expressive of the certitudes of the "Indian Summer of Empire." Initially he sees this landscape as "natural" and immutable, but he comes to realize the extent to which it is a "constructed" landscape, liable to change and decay, forces that begin to loom particularly large in the latter stages of the book.

His particular situation, on the gradually decaying Victorian/Edwardian estate, provides a central image. The manor is presided over by a reclusive landlord who has been suffering from "accidia" since his early manhood and, though actually in residence, is effectively almost as much an absentee as many of the owners of Caribbean sugar plantations were in the heyday of the British Empire. The writer (not named as Naipaul, but so similar to him that the distance between autobiographical fiction and fact has to all intents and purposes been collapsed) never meets him, but there is a clear suggestion that their relationship represents a final chapter in the history of imperialism, when the writer points out that his own presence on the estate, far from being accidental, is a product of the migrations caused by imperialism. Characteristically for

Naipaul, the narrator identifies with his landlord's sense of inertia, which is symbolized by his allowing ivy to proliferate and gradually strangle the trees on his grounds. The colonial man has found a haven in a landscape that seems "benign" to him, but the manor is a semiruin, without the traditional appendages of farms and lands, and the remains of the older management that it represents crumble during the course of the narrative.

Loss is central to *The Enigma of Arrival* in other ways. The title derives from a surrealist painting by Giorgio De Chirico, which the writer had thought might provide him with the inspiration for a story. He envisaged that the narrative would tell of a traveler's arrival in a classical city, his involvement in a mysterious religious ritual, his gradual realization that he is its intended victim, his narrow escape back to the wharf of his arrival, and his discovery that his ship has gone and that his life is over. Ostensibly this story – perhaps not surprisingly, since it is more Borgesian than Naipaulian – has never been completed. But the writer comes to see that it has permeated an African story he did complete (obviously "In a Free State") and that it is the story of his own life and present work.

The idea of enigmatic arrival informs all the book's major concerns: the writer's journey to the metropolis, which fails to match his youthful fantasies about it; his relationship to his Hindu past; his success as an author exploring the predicament of colonial fragmentation he has tried to escape; his disappointment when the history of Trinidad he wrote in the late 1960s (exactly similar to *The Loss of El Dorado*) was rejected by the publisher who had commissioned it and failed to afford him the sense of fulfillment he had anticipated; and his discovery that his Wiltshire surroundings are largely a product of human artifice and not organically whole.

Like the traveler in the planned story, he is left contemplating the prospect of his own mortality. Death is prominent throughout this elegiac, autumnal work, and in the final section, titled "The Ceremony of Farewell," the writer is taken back to Trinidad by his sister Sati's death. The remnants of Hinduism – even more vestigial than in Naipaul's early novels – suggest that the valediction of the title of this section makes it as much a requiem for his ancestral culture as for his sister. But the novel is full of intimations of mortality, and ultimately it is as much a generalized lament for human transience and an expression of the writer's all-pervasive sense of vulnerability as an elegy for any particular person or community.

The Enigma of Arrival provides a fitting conclu-

sion to Naipaul's career as novelist so far, not only because it is so strongly autobiographical and because it brings together so many strands of his previous writing in one volume, but also because, in its vision of a world running down and of human vulnerability, it seems to be the culmination of much of what he has been writing about over the years. But, although there is a uniformity of theme in Naipaul's work, the diversity of modes in which this unity has expressed itself and the multiple changes of direction it has so far taken warn one against seeing anything he writes as final.

Naipaul's two most recent travel books, *A Turn in the South* (1989) and *India: A Million Mutinies Now* (1990), make extensive use of a method employed more sparingly in his earlier nonfiction: large sections of both works take the form of quasi-verbatim transcriptions of the remarks of people he has interviewed. Devoting so much space to such reportage has the corollary function that the persona of Naipaul is less prominent than in works such as *The Middle Passage* and *An Area of Darkness*. Nevertheless both the recent books propound strong central theses, and the 1990 book on India is as passionate and polemical as anything Naipaul has written.

A Turn in the South describes his travels in "the old slave states of the American southeast." Having written about the former slave colonies of the Caribbean in his first travel book, he saw it as "fitting" that what he (wrongly) assumed would be his last such book should explore similar terrain. Consequently "the race issue" is high on his agenda at the outset, but it is increasingly less so as the work proceeds. Although Naipaul occasionally finds similarities between the American South and his own early experiences in Trinidad and the Caribbean, gradually he moves away from interviewing southern blacks and becomes more and more absorbed in anatomizing the culture of rural white southerners.

More than halfway through *A Turn in the South* Naipaul admits that an element of arbitrariness determined the structure of the book. Comparing his approach to that of film directors who like to work in natural light, he says, "travel of the sort I was doing, travel on a theme, depends on accidents." Ironically at this point the book begins to take on more of a definite shape. Naipaul tells of his encounter with a man named Campbell who seems to be a graphic, lyrical redneck. This happy accidental meeting provides the spine around which the remainder of the text, and in retrospect the earlier sections, can be seen to coil. Naipaul opens a vivid window on the world of redneck culture, tracing its links with the Old South and its contemporary manifestations in country-and-western music, fundamentalist religious sects, and the cult of Elvis Presley. Episodes that find Naipaul at Graceland and among the country-music publishers of Nashville may initially sound unlikely (he confesses to having little interest in such music before), and yet, curiously, he manages to fit in.

The book ends with his identifying with the North Carolina poet James Applewhite – both with Applewhite's expressed sense of separation from the community in which he grew up (an alienation presented as typifying the artistic psychology) and more generally with Applewhite's sense of history as a wound. The extent to which people's lives are affected by what Naipaul refers to as a "desperate kind of New World history" has been a subtext of the entire book, and as the conclusion shows his comments on the psychic accommodations individuals are obliged to make because of their society's past, this characteristically Naipaulian idea is explicitly identified as a central theme.

This travel book about a society far removed from Naipaul's habitual Third World terrain ends with reflections that project a psychic geography similar to all his other travel writing. If this conclusion suggests a capacity for discursively reconstituting any social world according to his own predilections, *India: A Million Mutinies Now* surprises readers by moving in the opposite direction. Naipaul's two earlier books about India, with their thesis that the country is enmeshed in a quietism engendered by adherence to the Hindu doctrine of karma, promote a monolithic view of Indian cultural identity; they offer an essentialist construction of India that leaves Naipaul open to the charge that he engages in the kind of Western appropriation that Edward Said attacks in *Orientalism* (1978). Naipaul's view in these two earlier works is, after all, little more than a highly subjective version of what one aspect of India (Brahmanic Hinduism) means to him, and the real dynamic of the books is less concerned with India as an observed reality than with the author's attempt to achieve self-definition (as a "wounded man," because he is the displaced product of a "wounded civilization").

In his 1990 book he narrates travels to various parts of India, encountering "twenty kinds of group excess" – Sikh, Muslim, Dalit, and Shiv Sena among them – which are seen as expressions of the million mutinies in contemporary India. The overall effect is a book that offers a powerful argument for diversity, not only through Naipaul's contention

Naipaul circa 1988 (photograph by Thomas Victor)

that the range and number of such "mutinies" are evidence of the "truest kind of liberation" but also through its method – even more heavily reliant on the words of interlocutors than is *A Turn in the South* – a method that allows a multiplicity of Indians and Indias to speak for themselves.

Both Naipaul and his subjects have come a long way from the passive victims of the colonial psychology about which he writes in his early works. And while he seems to have lost the talent for comedy that played such a large role in his early fiction, he remains at the height of his creative and perceptive powers. He received the T. S. Eliot Award in 1986 and was knighted in 1990, his name appearing on the British New Year's Honours List.

Interviews:

David Bates, "Portrait Gallery," *Sunday Times Magazine,* 26 May 1963, pp. 12–13;

Derek Walcott, "Interview with V. S. Naipaul," *Trinidad Guardian,* 7 March 1965, pp. 5–7;

Ian Hamilton, "Without a Place," *Times Literary Supplement,* 30 July 1971, pp. 897–898;

Adrian Rowe-Evans, "The Writer as Colonial," *Transition,* 40 (1971): 56–62;

Ronald Bryden, "V. S. Naipaul," *Listener,* 89 (22 March 1973): 367–370;

Raoul Pantin, "Portrait of an Artist: What Makes Naipaul Run," *Caribbean Contact,* 1 (May 1973): 16–19;

Charles Wheeler, "It's Every Man for Himself – V. S. Naipaul on India," *Listener,* 98 (27 October 1977): 535–537;

Elizabeth Hardwick, "Meeting V. S. Naipaul," *New York Times Book Review,* 13 May 1979, pp. 1, 36;

Linda Blandford, "Man in a Glass Box," *Sunday Telegraph Magazine,* 23 September 1979, pp. 77–90;

Bharati Mukherjee and Robert Boyers, "A Conversation with V. S. Naipaul," *Salmagundi,* 54 (Fall 1981): 4–22;

Charles Michener, "The Dark Visions of V. S. Naipaul," *Newsweek,* 98 (16 November 1981): 104–117;

John Cunningham, "Floating up to a Point," *Guardian,* 30 April 1984, p. 9;

Mel Gussow, "V. S. Naipaul: It Is out of This Violence I've Always Written," *New York Times Book Review,* 16 September 1984, pp. 45–46;

Constantin von Barloewen, "Naipaul's World," *World Press Review,* 32 (April 1985): 32–33;

"V. S. Naipaul Answers Questions from a Trinidad Audience," in *Passion and Exile,* by Frank Birbalsingh (London: Hansib, 1988), pp. 162–165;

"Andrew Robinson Meets V. S. Naipaul," *Literary Review* (October 1990): 21–24.

Bibliographies:

Robert Hamner, "V. S. Naipaul: A Selected Bibliography," *Journal of Commonwealth Literature,* 10 (August 1975): 36–44;

Hamner, "Annotated Bibliography," in *Critical Perspectives on V. S. Naipaul,* edited by Hamner (Washington, D.C.: Three Continents, 1977; London: Heinemann, 1979), pp. 263–298;

Harveen Sachdeva Mann, "Primary Works of and Critical Writings on V. S. Naipaul: A Selected Checklist," *Modern Fiction Studies,* 30 (Autumn 1984): 581–591;

Kelvin Jarvis, *V. S. Naipaul: A Selective Bibliography with Annotations, 1957–1987* (Metuchen, N.J. & London: Scarecrow, 1989).

References:

Anthony Boxill, *V. S. Naipaul's Fiction: In Quest of the Enemy* (Fredericton, N.B.: York, 1983);

Commonwealth, special issue on Naipaul, 6 (Autumn 1983);

Selwyn R. Cudjoe, *V. S. Naipaul: A Materialist Read-*

ing (Amherst: University of Massachusetts Press, 1988);

Robert Hamner, *V. S. Naipaul* (New York: Twayne, 1973);

Hamner, ed., *Critical Perspectives on V. S. Naipaul* (Washington, D.C.: Three Continents, 1977; London: Heinemann, 1979);

Dolly Zulakha Hassan, *V. S. Naipaul and the West Indies* (New York: Lang, 1989);

Peter Hughes, *V. S. Naipaul* (London & New York: Routledge, 1988);

Journal of Commonwealth Literature, symposium on Naipaul's *Guerrillas,* 14 (August 1979);

Shashi Kamra, *The Novels of V. S. Naipaul: A Study in Theme and Form* (New Delhi: Prestige, 1990);

Richard Kelly, *V. S. Naipaul* (New York: Continuum, 1989);

Modern Fiction Studies, special issue on Naipaul, 30 (Autumn 1984);

Robert K. Morris, *Paradoxes of Order: Some Perspectives on the Fiction of V. S. Naipaul* (Columbia: University of Missouri Press, 1975);

Peggy Nightingale, *Journey Through Darkness: The Writing of V. S. Naipaul* (Saint Lucia, Australia & New York: University of Queensland Press, 1987);

Rob Nixon, *London Calling: V. S. Naipaul, Postcolonial Mandarin* (New York & Oxford: Oxford University Press, 1992);

Paul Theroux, *V. S. Naipaul: An Introduction to His Work* (London: Deutsch, 1972);

John Thieme, *V. S. Naipaul: The Mimic Men* (London: Collins Nexus/British Council, 1985);

Thieme, *The Web of Tradition: Uses of Allusion in V. S. Naipaul's Fiction* (Aarhus, Denmark: Dangaroo, 1988);

Michael Thorpe, *V. S. Naipaul* (London: Longman/British Council, 1975);

Thorpe, *V. S. Naipaul: A House for Mr. Biswas* (London: Collins Nexus/British Council, 1985);

William Walsh, *V. S. Naipaul* (Edinburgh: Oliver & Boyd, 1973);

Timothy F. Weiss, *On the Margins: The Art of Exile in V. S. Naipaul* (Amherst: University of Massachusetts Press, 1992);

Landeg White, *V. S. Naipaul: A Critical Introduction* (London: Macmillan, 1975).

Ngugi wa Thiong'o
(James Ngugi)
(5 January 1938 –   )

David Maughan-Brown
University of Natal, Pietermaritzburg

BOOKS: *Weep Not, Child* (London & Ibadan: Heinemann, 1964; Evanston, Ill.: Northwestern University Press, 1967);

The River Between (London: Heinemann, 1965; Evanston, Ill.: Northwestern University Press, 1967); translated into Swahili as *Njia Panda* (Nairobi: East African Publishing House, 1974);

A Grain of Wheat (London: Heinemann, 1967; New York: Humanities, 1968; Harare: Zimbabwe Publishing House, 1984);

The Black Hermit (Nairobi, London & Ibadan: Heinemann, 1968; New York: Humanities, 1969);

This Time Tomorrow: Three Plays (Nairobi: East African Literature Bureau, 1970);

Homecoming: Essays on African and Caribbean Literature, Culture and Politics (London: Heinemann, 1972; New York: Hill, 1973);

Secret Lives, and Other Stories (London: Heinemann, 1975; New York: Hill, 1975);

The Trial of Dedan Kimathi, by Ngugi and Micere Githae-Mugo (Nairobi: Heinemann, 1976; London: Heinemann, 1977);

Petals of Blood (London: Heinemann, 1977; New York: Dutton, 1978; Cape Town: Philip, 1982);

Caitaani Mutharaba-ini (Nairobi: Heinemann, 1980); translated as *Devil on the Cross* (London: Heinemann, 1982; Harare: Zimbabwe Publishing House, 1983);

Ngaahika Ndeenda: Ithaako ria Ngerekano, by Ngugi and Ngugi wa Mirii (Nairobi: Heinemann, 1980); translated as *I Will Marry When I Want* (London & Exeter, N.H.: Heinemann, 1982);

Detained: A Writer's Prison Diary (London & Nairobi: Heinemann, 1981);

Writers in Politics (London & Exeter, N.H.: Heinemann, 1981);

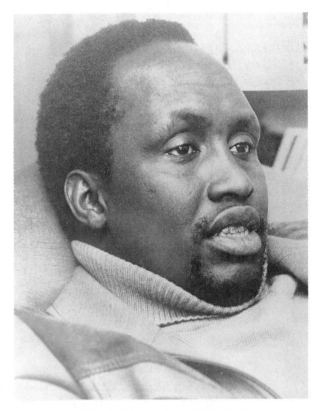

Ngugi wa Thiong'o (photograph copyright by the Guardian, *Lagos, Nigeria)*

Education for a National Culture (Harare: Zimbabwe Publishing House, 1981);

Njamba Nene na Mbaathi i Mathagu (Nairobi: Heinemann, 1982); translated as *Njamba Nene and the Flying Bus* (Nairobi: Heinemann, 1986);

Barrel of a Pen: Resistance to Repression in Neo-Colonial Kenya (London: New Beacon, 1983; Trenton, N.J.: Africa World, 1983);

Bathitoora ya Njamba Nene (Nairobi: Heinemann, 1984); translated as *Njamba Nene's Pistol* (Nairobi: Heinemann, 1986);

Decolonising the Mind: The Politics of Language in African Literature (London: Currey / Portsmouth, N.H.: Heinemann, 1986);

Matigari ma Njiruungi (Nairobi: Heinemann, 1986); translated as *Matigari* (Oxford: Heinemann, 1989);

Writing Against Neocolonialism (London: Vita, 1986);

Njamba Nene na Chibu King'ang'i (Nairobi: Heinemann, 1986);

The First Walter Rodney Memorial Lecture, 1985 (London: Friends of Bogle, 1987);

Moving the Centre: The Struggle for Cultural Freedoms (London: Currey / Portsmouth, N.H.: Heinemann / Nairobi: East African Educational Publishers, 1993).

PLAY PRODUCTIONS: *The Black Hermit*, Uganda National Theatre, November 1962;

The Trial of Dedan Kimathi, Nairobi, 1974;

Ngaahika Ndeenda, Kamiriithu, Kenya, Kamiriithu Community Education and Cultural Centre, October 1977.

RADIO: *This Time Tomorrow*, BBC Africa Service, 1967.

OTHER: Okot p'Bitek, *Africa's Cultural Revolution*, introduction by Ngugi (Nairobi: Macmillan, 1973).

SELECTED PERIODICAL PUBLICATIONS – UNCOLLECTED: "The Tension between National and Imperialist Culture," *World Literature Written in English*, 24 (Summer 1984): 3–9;

"On Writing in Gikuyu," *Research in African Literatures*, 16 (Summer 1985): 151–156.

When he was incarcerated as a political detainee in Kamiti Maximum Security Prison near Nairobi in 1978 for his part in the production of his Gikuyu-language play *Ngaahika Ndeenda* (performed, 1977; published, 1980; translated as *I Will Marry When I Want*, 1982), Ngugi wa Thiong'o caused consternation among the warders by refusing to submit to the ritual of being chained before being transported out of the prison for medical treatment or family visits. It was made clear that refusing to be chained meant he would receive no visits from his family and no treatment for his abscessed tooth, but for Ngugi, always alert to the symbolism of colonial and neocolonial oppression, being chained was too high a price to pay for the privileges.

Ngugi's refusal to submit to shackles in Kamiti can be seen as an appropriate symbolic culmination of nearly twenty years of writing and lecturing in which he released himself, link by link, from the mental shackles of his colonial education, with all the attendant assumptions about race, class, and language. Throwing off those shackles has brought Ngugi persecution and an enforced exile, but it has also led to the production of a body of fiction, drama, and essays so original, technically assured, politically committed, informative, and influential that many of Ngugi's admirers regard him as the most important African writer.

Ngugi was born on 5 January 1938 as James Ngugi, son of a Kenyan peasant farmer who, having no access to land of his own, was forced to live as an *ahoi*, a squatter or "tenant-at-will" on the land of "one of the very few African landlords in pre-independence Limuru," as Ngugi says in *Detained* (1981). Ngugi was one of about twenty-eight children in a polygamous household in which his father had four wives: Ngugi was the fifth child of the third wife. Describing his childhood, Ngugi says in "The Writer in a Changing Society," an essay in *Homecoming* (1972): "Harvests were often poor. Sweetened tea with milk at any time of day was a luxury. We had one meal a day – late in the evening. Every day the women would go to their scruffy little strips of shamba [garden]. But they had faith and they waited."

Ngugi received his first schooling in 1946 at Kamaandura, a missionary-run primary school about two miles from his home. In 1948 he was taken out of the mission school and sent to Maanguuu, a school run by Gikuyu nationalists. The changing of schools had clear political overtones. Ngugi told Amooti wa Irumba in a 1980 interview that, while he cannot remember precisely what occasioned the change, "It was thought that in missionary schools some things were deliberately held back from students, and that in Gikuyu *Karinga* [independent] schools nothing would be hidden from the students to keep them ignorant." With the declaration of the "State of Emergency" in Kenya in 1952, all the independent schools were either closed down or taken over by district education boards; English became the medium of instruction, and so Ngugi learned English.

In 1955, largely on the strength of a credit in English, Ngugi won a place at the prestigious Alliance High School at Kikuyu, "one of the most elitist institutions for Africans in colonial Kenya," as Ngugi describes it in *Decolonising the Mind* (1986). He was "the only student from virtually the whole of Limuru" to be there. Ngugi's subsequent comments

Ngugi in a Nairobi bookstore in 1964 signing copies of Weep Not, Child, *his first published novel (photograph: East African Standard)*

on the prevailing ethos of the school have been scathing, as is this one in the Irumba interview: "I think the education offered to us at Alliance was intended to produce Africans who would later become efficient administrators of a colonial system. . . . We were being trained to become obedient servants of Her Majesty the Queen of England, to serve her and the British Empire, and never to question the legitimacy or correctness of that Empire."

What Alliance High School did for Ngugi in a positive sense was to sustain his interest in reading and arouse a speculative desire to write, though this direction was achieved perhaps more through random novel reading in the comparatively well-stocked library than through the formal curriculum. Ngugi read widely, works by Charles Dickens, Sir Walter Scott, Rider Haggard, John Buchan, Alan Paton, and W. E. Johns being explored by him. But it was of Robert Louis Stevenson that Ngugi was

later to say (in his 1964 interview with Dennis Duerden): "He is the one who really set my imagination flying, and I thought that one day I would like to write stories like those which he himself had written." However, in 1967, when interviewed by Alan Marcuson and others at Leeds University in England, Ngugi said, "I wrote, I suppose, because I had been moved by the bloodshed and violence during the Mau Mau uprising [in Kenya from 1952 to 1956]."

Although Ngugi's formal education was not seriously interrupted by the state of emergency, he could not be left unaffected by the turmoil in central Kenya resulting from the armed revolt of the Land and Freedom Army (called the "Mau Mau" by the settlers) against the inequities – particularly the unequal distribution of land – of the colonial system. Ngugi's elder brother, Wallace Mwangi, joined the guerrillas in the forests between 1954 and 1956, as a consequence of which Ngugi's mother was detained for three months and tortured at the home-guard post at Kamiriithu, where the family then lived. In an interview with Reinhard Sander and Ian Munro, Ngugi addressed the question of the extent of his awareness of the emergency: "As a child growing up during this period, it would be silly and not true to say one was aware of all implications of even the struggle itself. But one did get the impressions. You are so young. You see your uncles being killed. . . . You see some of your friends being taken from their homes. These things stay with you. You see an old man you respected being emasculated as a condition of war. These things leave you with an impression. . . ."

On his return to Kamiriithu after his first term at Alliance, Ngugi found that, as part of the colonial forces' anti-insurgency "protected" village strategy (designed, in fact, to cut the forest fighters off from their food supplies), his home had simply disappeared. As he says in *Detained*, "My home was now only a pile of dry mud-stones, bits of grass, charcoal and ashes. . . . Not only my home, but the old village with its culture, its memories and its warmth had been razed to the ground." The trauma of this experience led to the attempted return home being a recurrent motif in Ngugi's fiction, and his writing is often at its most powerful when re-creating the anguish and heroism of the Mau Mau revolt.

From Alliance High School, Ngugi, like many of his classmates, went on to Makerere University College, Kampala, where in 1959 he embarked on a four-year honors degree in English. In retrospect Ngugi regards the real importance of his time at Makerere as being his exposure to African and West Indian writers for the first time, though they had no place on the syllabus. Ngugi singles out three works as having impressed and influenced him in particular: Chinua Achebe's *Things Fall Apart* (1958), George Lamming's *In the Castle of My Skin* (1953), and Peter Abrahams's *Tell Freedom* (1954).

At Makerere, Ngugi joined the University Drama Club and Play Reading Circle, and in 1960 he wrote a short story, "The Fig Tree," as a result of telling a member of the editorial committee of *Penpoint*, the English-department literary journal, that he had already written one. This story was the start of an intensely creative three-year period during which Ngugi wrote six other stories later collected in *Secret Lives* (1975), three one-act plays (in *This Time Tomorrow*, 1970), a full-length play (*The Black Hermit*, performed, 1962; published, 1968), and two novels: "The Black Messiah" (published as *The River Between*, 1965) and *Weep Not, Child* (1964).

In 1962 Ngugi participated at Makerere in the historic Conference of African Writers of English Expression, which was attended by most of the better-known anglophone African writers, including Achebe, Wole Soyinka, Christopher Okigbo, and Es'kia Mphahlele. Writing in prison in 1978, Ngugi commented: "What I remember most about the conference was the energy and the hope and the dreams and the confidence: after all, we were part of a continent emerging from a colonial era into . . . what? We never answered the question, but the hopes and the dreams and the confidence remained. Now we have no doubt, two decades later, about the answer" (*Detained*).

In addition to his burst of creative writing, Ngugi was also, by the end of his four-year degree, editing *Penpoint*, which had become a vehicle for writers from all over east and central Africa, and writing a regular column for the *Sunday Nation* in Nairobi. He still found time to obtain a good upper-second-class honors degree, writing his major essay on Joseph Conrad.

The first novel Ngugi wrote (but the second one he published) started life as "The Black Messiah" and was begun in March 1961 in response to a challenge posed by an East African Literature Bureau novel-writing competition whose deadline was in December that year. Ngugi won the competition.

The action of the novel takes place among the ridges in the heartland of Gikuyu territory in the late 1920s, at the time of the conflict between the Church of Scotland missions and Gikuyu traditionalists over female circumcision – described by Ngugi in a 1962 *Sunday Nation* article as a "brutal" custom (as quoted by Bernth Lindfors). Ngugi makes use of a symbolic topographical setting: two ridges, Kameno and Makuyu, the homes of Gikuyu traditionalists and Christian converts respectively, confront each other across the river noted in the published title. This setting provides him with a simple but effective schematic base from which to explore the relationships between Christianity and Gikuyu tradition (including the similarities between the mythologies underlying each), between private and public responsibilities, and between education and political activism.

Waiyaki, the "Black Messiah" of the original title, is last in a line of descent from the Gikuyu seer Mugo wa Kibiro, and is looked to by his father, Chege, an elder from Kameno, to fulfill Mugo's prophecy: "Salvation shall come from the hills. From the blood that flows in me . . . a son shall rise. And his duty shall be to lead and save the people." To this end, Waiyaki is sent by his father to a

church mission to learn the wisdom and secrets of
the white man – but he is enjoined to be true to the
Gikuyu people and their ancient rites. The inherent
contradiction proves insurmountable.

When circumcised Gikuyu children are excluded from Siriana, the mission school, Waiyaki
returns to the ridges and establishes the first Gikuyu independent schools. He fires the people of
the ridges with his enthusiasm for education – seen
by him as the solution to the encroaching domination of the colonial power – and comes to be seen as
a savior. But Waiyaki is so single-mindedly intent
on his schools that he fails to give due recognition
to the political significance of the Kiama, a Kameno-
based, proto-"Mau Mau" organization led by Kabonyi, a lapsed Christian who is intensely jealous of
Waiyaki. The Kiama is dedicated to the "purity of
the tribe" and prepared to use more direct forms of
political activism than Western education to oust
Christianity and colonialism.

Like Romeo with Juliet, Waiyaki falls in love
with Nyambura, the daughter of Joshua, the fanatical leader of the Christian converts of Makuyu,
who is the archenemy of the Kiama. Kabonyi manages to engineer a public trial of Waiyaki for betraying the tribe by associating with the Christians,
Waiyaki refuses to renounce his love for Nyambura, and the pair are handed over to the Kiama for
judgment and, presumably, execution.

Asked about his writing by an interviewer at
Leeds in 1967, Ngugi's comment on *The River Between* was, "I had come from a missionary school
and I was deeply Christian. . . . In school I was concerned with trying to remove the central Christian
doctrine from the dress of Western culture, and seeing how this might be grafted onto the central beliefs of our people. *The River Between* was concerned
with this process."

That the novel is, to some extent, a project in
contextualizing theology is borne out by its extensive use of biblical language and imagery, by the
way it sets the Gikuyu creation myth beside the
Christian one, and by such recognitions as the one
arrived at by Waiyaki toward the end: "Even his
[the white man's] religion was not essentially
bad. . . . But the religion, the faith, needed washing,
cleaning away all the dirt, leaving only the eternal.
And that eternal that was the truth had to be reconciled to the traditions of the people."

But this project, which suggests that Ngugi's
sympathies lay on the Makuyu side of the river,
does not come across as the dominant concern of
the novel to most readers. Christianity in the novel
is represented by the somewhat caricatured Joshua

*Cover for the 1986 Heinemann African Writers Series edition
of Ngugi's most autobiographical novel, set during the state
of emergency in Kenya during the 1950s*

("he would never refrain from punishing a sin, even
if this meant beating his wife"), and while much of
the novel is concerned with the foundation of the
Gikuyu independent schools movement, there is no
mention of the historically parallel independent
church movement. The focus on Christianity is similar to that in Achebe's *Things Fall Apart*: it is a divisive influence that produces a violent reaction on
the part of traditionalists and provides the obvious
focus for an exploration of the impact of colonial
penetration on traditional ways of life. Not that the
Kiama finds much favor either; it is characterized
by "extravagant enthusiasm," led by a jealous fa-
natic, and its members are symbolically depicted as
"figures lurking in the edges of darkness."

The two themes most critics have seen as dominant in the novel are the relationship between education and political activism, and the relationship

between private commitment and public responsibility. Waiyaki's preoccupation with education leads him to lose contact with the people he wants to serve, or perhaps more accurately – considering his messianic sense of his own destiny – to lead and save. Only at the end of the novel does he come to recognize that "The Kiama was right. People wanted action now," and he decides that, if he had the opportunity, he would preach "education for unity. Unity for political freedom." He is repeatedly described as "confused" and is often unaware of the implications, and sometimes even the origins, of his actions.

Ngugi is clearly inviting readers to be critical of Waiyaki's simplistic positing of Western education as the cure-all for political ills, and his divorcing of education from political action. Waiyaki has no reply to Kabonyi's crucial question: "do you think the education of our tribe, the education and wisdom which you all received, is in any way below that of the white man?" Waiyaki does not, however, appear to come in for authorial criticism in his quest for the reconciliation of the ultimately irreconcilable opposites represented by Kameno and Makuyu.

The focus on Waiyaki's public role as founder of the independent schools is to some extent eclipsed in the second half of the novel by the attention given to his love for Nyambura. It is this shift in emphasis that has led some critics to regard the theme of private conscience and commitment set against public responsibility as carrying the main weight of the novel's message. G. D. Killam, for example, says the theme that most interests Ngugi in this novel is "the place of love as a means of achieving personal redemption and by extension as an agent for redemption in the community" (*An Introduction to the Writings of Ngugi*, 1980).

The novel is characterized by simplicity of language and the schematic opposition of contending values and their champions, which have much in common with the myths on which the novel draws so heavily. The complexity of the themes could well have borne the fuller and more complex treatment given to themes in Ngugi's later novels, but the critical tendency to sum up the novel in the manner of Killam's opinion—"it is a modest beginning in a small novel" – does perhaps not do justice to what was a remarkable achievement for a university student producing the first novel in English by a Kenyan writer.

If, as David Cook and Michael Okenimkpe claim, Ngugi now finds *The River Between* embarrassing, that is because he has traveled a long way, ideologically, in the interim. He would no longer endorse either the Christianity, underpinning the novel, or the subordination of the education/political-activism debate to the slightly cliché love story at the end. But Ngugi has no need to feel that *The River Between* is an embarrassingly weak first novel.

In January 1962 Ngugi started on his second novel, *Weep Not, Child*. Set twenty years later than *The River Between*, at the time of the state of emergency in Kenya in the 1950s, when many of the latent tensions and antagonisms explored in the earlier novel boiled over in armed conflict, *Weep Not, Child* is generally held to be the most autobiographical of Ngugi's fictional works.

The protagonist is a young boy, Njoroge, through whose often naive perceptions most of the action of the novel is filtered. The youngest boy in a polygamous family renowned for its domestic harmony, Njoroge, like Ngugi himself, plays no active role in the armed rebellion in which his family becomes caught, but he carries on with his schooling, placing his faith, like Waiyaki, in education: "He always thought that schooling was the very best that a boy could have. It was the end of all living."

The novel traces Njoroge's career as a scholar, which takes him to Siriana (a fictional version of Alliance High School) as "the only boy in all that area" to get there – again like Ngugi himself. At the same time, the story charts the progressive disintegration of the ideally harmonious home and family. When the novel opens, Ngotho, Njoroge's father, is a landless peasant living as an *ahoi* (tenant farmer) on the land of Jacobo, a rich African farmer, and tending the tea plantation being grown on his own ancestral land, now "alienated" and given to a Mr. Howlands under the post–World War I soldier-settler scheme. Ngotho loses his job as a result of taking part in a strike and leading an attack on Jacobo, who, true to his collaborationist role, is trying to persuade the strikers to return to work. This wholly uncharacteristic action on the part of Ngotho is embarked on in an attempt, in part, to appease his son, Boro, who is an embittered former serviceman who despises his father and his father's generation for their passive submission to colonial rule.

These four characters exemplify, emblematically and with great economy, the forces unleashed in central Kenya with the declaration of the state of emergency in October 1952. Howlands becomes a fanatical district officer who plays a brutal role in the repression of the revolt; Jacobo becomes a "loyalist" home-guard leader who viciously exploits his position to settle the score with Ngotho; Boro takes to the forest as a guerrilla leader and is responsible for killing both Jacobo and Howlands, but Boro is captured in the process; and Ngotho is the hapless victim, the peasant caught in the cross fire, who confesses falsely to the killing of Jacobo and is tortured and castrated before dying. Njoroge's part is to be a passive spectator until arrested at school on suspicion of complicity in Jacobo's killing, whereupon he too is tortured – both physically and, more particularly, by the denial of further schooling.

Ngugi's attitude toward his protagonist is difficult to discern. Njoroge's response to the gathering conflict, described sparingly but with considerable historical authenticity, is to retire behind fantasies of his destiny: "he was lost in speculations about his vital role in the country. He remembered David rescuing a whole country from the curse of Goliath." In comparison with Waiyaki, Njoroge has no basis for his fantasies in achieved action or in heredity and prophecy, and it is clear that the reader is not intended to take them very seriously. But Ngugi's characterization of Njoroge seems almost wholly without irony, and the reader is not invited to take up the same position of detachment in relation to Njoroge's other main line of escape – another Romeo-and-Juliet love relationship, with Mwihaki, the daughter of Jacobo.

Even the ending of the novel is somewhat ambivalent. With his father dead, his brothers all in prison or detention, and Boro to be hanged, Njoroge tries to commit suicide when Mwihaki refuses to elope to Uganda with him. His courage fails him, however, when his two mothers (from his polygamous family), Nyokabi and Njeri, true to the life-giving and supporting role they play throughout the novel, come to find him in the darkness. The act of attempting suicide is presented as a cowardly escape, yet Njoroge appears to escape censure. He is allowed to run ahead as the three return home and symbolically to "open the door" of the future for his mothers.

Ngugi's apparent ambivalence toward Njoroge extends to his attitude toward the Mau Mau movement itself, whose effects on the Gikuyu villagers form the central concern of the novel. As Ngugi put it in his interview with Dennis Duerden: "Actually in the novel I have tried to show the effect of the Mau Mau war on the ordinary man and woman who were left in the villages. I think the terrible thing about the Mau Mau war was the destruction of family life, the destruction of personal relationships." Many critics incorrectly interpret this novel, presumably on the basis of their readings of later ones, as sympathetic toward the guerrillas.

The novel is successful in both the depiction of the bitter disillusionment of former servicemen who returned from fighting for freedom to discover that freedom was not about to be extended to them, which was one of the main catalysts of the revolt, and in the depiction of the plight of the landless Gikuyu peasantry, the main spur to the revolt. Indeed Ngugi's description of Ngotho lovingly watching over his land by working on it as a "shamba-boy" for the colonial-settler usurper, Howlands, is likely to bring home to the reader the anguish of the dispossessed with a far more memorable poignancy than any statistics about the square miles of land "alienated." Ngugi is also unflinching in his portrayal of the ruthlessness and brutality of the colonial response to the Mau Mau. But the movement itself, as represented in the person of Boro, is kept at a firm distance from the reader's sympathies and is depicted as motivated by revenge and as fighting for nothing more principled than "To kill. Unless you kill, you'll be killed. So you go on killing and destroying. It's a law of nature."

Three major themes can be identified in the novel: education and messianism, which are carried over from *The River Between*; and the suffering of the ordinary villagers because of the revolt. This last was intended by Ngugi to have a representative dimension: "in my approach to the novel you use even a small village as a symbol of a larger concern. . . . I use a small village as a guide for the whole African struggle for identity."

In comparison with the treatment of education in *The River Between*, Njoroge's notion of education is abstract and theoretical, and the novel does not explore the tension between education and political activism at all, although in many ways it is better set up to do so. Although it could be argued that Ngotho's recounting of the Gikuyu creation myth is designed to show that education is not, in fact, the exclusive preserve of schools, the novel as a whole seems to endorse a generally uncritical acceptance of Western education, along the lines of Ngugi's comment in his interview at Leeds: "The gospel of the peasant has always been: 'Get ye first education, and all other things will be added unto you.'"

Even if we are not expected to take Njoroge's messianic urgings seriously, no skepticism is shown in Ngugi's identification of Kenyan leader Jomo Kenyatta variously with Moses and with Christ. As a student at Makerere, Ngugi clearly shared the popular conception of the still-detained Kenyatta as a savior; as Ngotho sees it, "To him Jomo stood for custom and tradition purified by grace of learning and much travel." Kenyatta's condemnation of the Mau Mau and the resort to political violence, both before and during his detention, must have had considerable influence on the distance the novel puts between itself and the movement.

Where the sufferings of the ordinary villagers under the state of emergency are concerned, Ngugi uses Njoroge's family as a microcosm of the Gikuyu peasantry, ninety percent of whom, though one would certainly not guess it from the novel, are estimated to have taken the movement's oath of loyalty. The breakup of the home is intended to exemplify the breakup of the larger Gikuyu society, and the tragic dimension of this disintegration is personified in Ngotho and dramatized in his decline in public esteem and self-respect as a result of his conflict with Boro. One of the problematic aspects of Ngugi's fictionalization of the state of emergency is that it appears to invite its readers to see the Mau Mau, rather than the repressive colonial dispensation against which the movement was revolting, as being responsible for the disintegration of Ngotho's family and the wider society it represents.

Generally evaluated by critics as a work of apprenticeship, paving the way for *A Grain of Wheat* (1967), *Weep Not, Child* manages, nonetheless, to evoke the conditions of the state of emergency in Kenya with considerable power and poignancy. Ngugi's style is sparser and less biblical than in his earlier novel, in keeping with a project in fictional realism that is more firmly based in history and has less of the air of mythmaking about it. Where the novel has weaknesses – for example in the imprecision of the treatment of the central question of education, and the partial nature of the analysis of the revolt – they can be attributed not simply to the technical consequences of the choice of Njoroge's consciousness as a vehicle but also to the closeness of the subject matter to Ngugi's own experience and the interpretations a privileged university student, a product of the colonial educational system, would inevitably place upon that experience.

The Black Hermit, a play, was written as the Makerere Students Dramatic Society contribution to Uganda's Uhuru celebrations and was first produced in the Uganda National Theatre in November 1962; it was published in 1968. In the play Remi, the only son of his people to have achieved a university education, is confronted with the choice of remaining as a "black hermit" in the city or returning home to provide political leadership for his people, which would bring material benefits all around but would take him back to Thoni, his brother's widow, whom custom decrees that he should marry. He returns, but the failure of each to communicate his or her love for the other leads Thoni to commit suicide. The first act, with stylized

Dust jacket for the first novel written by Ngugi. Originally titled "The Black Messiah," it was published following the success of Weep Not, Child

and generally formal language, focuses on the traditional world of the village; the second act, in which the language is colloquial and informal, deals with the city; the third act deals with the fatal intersection of the two. In the preface for the publication of the play, Ngugi distances himself from its main concern: "I thought then that tribalism was the biggest problem besetting the new East African countries. . . [that] all we had to do was to expose and root out the cantankerous effects of tribalism, racialism and religious factions."

The Black Hermit, like Ngugi's other early plays, has tended to receive short shrift from literary critics, who have lambasted it for didacticism, cumbersome themes, and characters who are not developed and are used as mere "mouthpieces for views on political education," as Clifford B. Robson says. It is by no means certain, however, that those who watched the plays in performance shared these views.

Ngugi filled the interval between graduating from Makerere and going to Leeds in September

1964 with work as a junior reporter on the *Daily Nation* in Nairobi. His regular column during this period, called "As I See It," ranged widely, from William Shakespeare to African socialism, and provides useful insights into Ngugi's liberal ideological position at this time.

At Leeds, once again it was on the fringe of the formal curriculum that the development of Ngugi's thinking and writing received its major boost. Formally Ngugi spent most of his time at Leeds engaged in research for a two-year M.A. in Caribbean literature. Informally Ngugi's political thinking was revolutionized by his first exposure to works by Karl Marx and Frantz Fanon; by his interaction with other students including Grant Kamenju, Peter Nazareth, Ime Ikiddeh, and Alan Hunt; and, perhaps more particularly, by socialist academics such as Arnold Kettle. Apart from the West Indian writers on whom Ngugi's research focused, the specifically literary influences to which he was first exposed at Leeds were Bertolt Brecht's plays and Robert Tressell's *The Ragged Trousered Philanthropists* (1914), described by Ikiddeh as a "major influence" on Ngugi.

Ngugi took the opportunity while in Great Britain to travel extensively. He not only toured England and Scotland and visited the continent but also attended the 1966 Afro-Asian Writers Conference in Beirut, from where he went on to visit Palestinian refugee camps in Lebanon and to travel to Damascus with a group from the conference. He also visited the United States as a guest of honor at the international P.E.N. conference. His first impressions of the United States were mixed, as he told a Leeds interviewer: "I was impressed by the actual material progress. But in the streets of New York, one of the richest cities in the world, I found beggars crawling in the streets and people who had nowhere to sleep. I couldn't believe it."

Ngugi's main preoccupation while he was at Leeds, however, the writing of *A Grain of Wheat*, which was completed in November 1966. The action of the novel covers a time span of four days leading up to Kenyan Independence Day, 12 December 1963, and involves four main characters, who are all from the Gikuyu village of Thabai: Mugo, Gikonyo, Mumbi, and Karanja. Within the four-day fictional present, Ngugi manages, principally by means of a series of interlocking flashbacks, to convey not only the personal histories of the important characters, focusing in particular on their experiences under the state of emergency, but also an outline of the history of Kenyan resistance to colonial rule.

The most significant structural break with the pattern of the earlier novels is his abandonment of the single central protagonist, who is replaced by a group of protagonists. The intention, derived from Ngugi's exposure to socialist thinking at Leeds, and to that of Fanon in particular, is clearly to employ a fictional form better suited to the rendering of collective consciousness. This plan does, however, run into problems. The first one is apparent from the title, whose meaning is made explicit in the epigraph to the last section: "Except a corn of wheat fall into the ground and die, it abideth alone: but if it die, it bringeth forth much fruit." The novel makes extensive use of biblical imagery and also takes as its "metadiscourse" the Christian model of individual guilt, expiation, and redemption.

Second, the plot parallels that of Joseph Conrad's *Under Western Eyes* (1911) very closely; Conrad's influence is clearly discernible elsewhere in the novel and can be seen to have provided Ngugi with a model of a secular pattern of betrayal, remorse, and redemption. The result is an internal tension between a fictional structure designed as a historical project, which explores Kenya's past and present from the collective vantage point of the Kenyan peasantry, and a fictional rendering – at times almost obsessive in its minuteness – of the states of mind and the spiritual redemption of a group of essentially isolated individuals. Gikonyo's perception, "To live and die alone was the ultimate truth," seems definitive.

The opening of the novel focuses on Mugo, whose solitariness and air of self-sufficiency, combined with his reputation as a hero of the struggle, have led the villagers to see him as their choice to be the main speaker at the independence celebrations. One of the purposes of the celebrations is to honor those who died in the struggle, most notably Kihika, a Mau Mau leader from the village who was betrayed and hanged.

Mumbi, Kihika's sister, fulfills a key role as the catalyst for the development away from the pervasive atmosphere of guilt, self-doubt, and betrayal that characterizes the villagers' preparations for the *Uhuru* (independence) for which they endured so much. Gikonyo and Karanja are long-standing rivals for Mumbi's affections. Gikonyo, the village carpenter, marries Mumbi, is sent to a detention camp, and betrays the movement in order to return to Mumbi. On his return he finds Mumbi suckling a child she has had by Karanja, who, in spite of having lost her to Gikonyo, has also betrayed his people and joined the "loyalist" home guard in order to avoid detention and remain near Mumbi. Having held out against his advances for six years – during which Karanja becomes a sadistic and much-hated home-guard chief – Mumbi yields to him in her ecstasy at hearing of Gikonyo's impending release. The existence of the child acts as a total block on communication between Mumbi and Gikonyo.

As the action unfolds, it becomes apparent that the apolitical Mugo, who, resentful like Conrad's Razumov at having the even tenor of his solitary existence intruded upon, had betrayed Kihika when the latter came to him for shelter after assassinating a notoriously brutal district officer. Mugo initially refuses to speak at the celebrations, which are to be used by Kihika's former comrades as an opportunity to denounce and execute Karanja as Kihika's betrayer. But as a direct result of Mumbi's confiding her marital problems to Mugo and his own private confession of the betrayal of Kihika to her, Mugo makes a public confession at the meeting in order to save Karanja and is himself duly executed.

Mugo's courage in publicly confessing and expiating his act of betrayal provides the inspiration for Gikonyo to reconsider his harsh rejection of Mumbi and her child. Their reconciliation – which, through the closeness of their names to those of Gikuyu and Mumbi, the mythical founders of the Gikuyu nation, implicitly symbolizes the regeneration of the Gikuyu people and postindependence Kenya as a whole – is emblematized at the end of the novel in Gikonyo's plans for the carving of a traditional stool as a gift for Mumbi. The stool will not only incorporate a figure of a woman pregnant with a child as a symbol of hope for the future, but Gikonyo contemplates working into beads on the seat an image of "a field needing clearance and cultivating." The struggle is not over with the celebration of independence: much clearing still needs to be done if the ground for genuine freedom is to be successfully cultivated.

The focus of *A Grain of Wheat* is predominantly on the past. The criticism of the post-independence political dispensation in Kenya is low-key and almost incidental, in spite of Ngugi's author's note: "But the situation and the problems are real – sometimes too painfully real for the peasants who fought the British yet who now see all that they fought for being put on one side." The closest Ngugi gets to a critique of the direction of Kenya's independence is in the pillorying of the member of Parliament for Thabai. Gikonyo, anxious to buy a farm for a cooperative farming venture, goes to the M.P. to ask him to organize a loan. The latter, who is clearly intended as a representative of post-

independence corruption, buys the farm in question for himself.

Where *A Grain of Wheat* breaks most significantly with the earlier novels is in the abandonment of education as containing the key to Kenya's problems and in the acceptance, at least in the abstract, of the necessity for armed struggle. Kariuki, Mumbi's younger brother, who, like Njoroge and Ngugi himself, "was the only boy in these ridges to get a place in Siriana secondary school," is a wholly insignificant character who plays no part in the action. His acceptance at the school, as the brother of a Mau Mau leader, is not, as with Njoroge, treated as a potential political reconciliation deriving from universal aspirations for education but is more realistically made politically contentious: "why . . . should a boy whose brother was in the Forest, be allowed to go to a government school, while the sons of loyalists could not?" The main characters are not singled out by their education: they are all uneducated peasants, and Kihika is shown to have run away from the brutality and blinkered vision of formal education.

The endorsement of the Mau Mau remains at an abstract level. Kihika is the only major character in the novel who is not guilty of betraying some person or ideal, and is explicitly likened to Christ at certain points, but he is characterized as insensitive to the needs of his girlfriend Wambuku; as contemptuous of what he sees to be the weakness of his father's generation; and, essentially, as the Conradian man "haunted by a fixed idea." The living Mau Mau representatives in the novel are portrayed as obsessed by guilt over their past acts of individual violence, a pervasive guilt that implicitly expunges any political legitimacy the novel might elsewhere be seeming to try to establish for the movement's resort to violence. Despite Ngugi's reading of Fanon, this novel is clearly not informed by the surprisingly Fanonist view expressed in Ngugi's 1963 review of Fred Majdalany's *A State of Emergency* (1962): "Violence in order to change an intolerable, unjust social order is not savagery: it purifies man."

Although *A Grain of Wheat* does provide some evidence of an ideological shift, Ngugi's exposure to socialism at Leeds was too recent to have been fully assimilated, and this novel, like the previous ones, can be seen to be predominantly informed by liberalism. Aesthetically this slant is perhaps most evident in the impulse toward balance in structure and characterization. So Ngugi is at pains to explore the consciousness of, and invite sympathy for, politically antipathetic characters such as Karanja and John Thompson, a once-idealistic colonial administrator who ends up being responsible, in the novel's fictional version, for the Hola detention camp massacre.

The major development demonstrated by this novel is in the area of fictional technique. Apart from his assured handling of the fractured time scheme, Ngugi makes effective use of some intricate patterns of symbolism and develops a flexible prose style far better adapted to the complexity of many of the issues raised by the novel than the brevity and simplicity of the two earlier novels. Songs become part of the texture of the narrative, the narrative voice assumes an identity as one of the Thabai villagers in the second half of the novel, and, in general, Ngugi can be seen to be making a concerted attempt to adapt the novel form to make it an appropriate vehicle for the consciousness of a group of Gikuyu peasants with little formal Western education. The attempt is somewhat undermined by Ngugi's residual liberalism, leading to the contradictory focus on individual consciousness, usually of guilt, but this does not prevent *A Grain of Wheat* from being one of the major accomplishments of African literature; nor has it hindered most critics from recognizing it as such.

A Grain of Wheat was the major outcome of Ngugi's stay at Leeds. He did not complete his M.A. thesis, clearly regarding the production of his novel as more important and possibly becoming skeptical about the value of postgraduate degrees. His decision not to complete the M.A. may also have been connected to a more radical and far-reaching questioning, which first found expression in the interview he gave to fellow students at Leeds before returning to Kenya. When asked whether he had plans for any other books, Ngugi replied, "No plans at present. You see I have reached a point of crisis. I don't know whether it is worth any longer writing in English. . . . I am very suspicious about writing about universal values. If there are universal values, they are always contained in the framework of social realities. And one important social reality in Africa is that 90 percent of the people cannot read or speak English. . . . The problem is this – I know whom I write about, but whom do I write for?"

In less formal terms what Leeds did for Ngugi is perhaps best summed up in a comment he made to Micere Githae-Mugo: "I think I was confused at Makerere. I had more questions than answers and by the time I left I was disillusioned about many things. Leeds systematized my thinking."

In 1967 Ngugi returned to Kenya as a special lecturer in English at University College, Nairobi, having earlier in the year attended the African Scan-

Ngugi in the 1970s (photograph: the Nation, *Nairobi, Kenya)*

dinavian Writers' Conference. He had apparently overcome his doubts about writing in English sufficiently to sign a contract with Heinemann to write a book, to be titled "A Colonial Affair," about the social life of European settlers in Kenya. Significantly, however, although he embarked on serious research for the project, he found himself unable to write the book. As he puts it in *Detained,* "An account of their social life would have to include a section on culture, and I was by then convinced that a Draculan idle class could never produce a culture."

Ngugi's stay at University College was brief but productive. During this time he edited *Zuka,* the English department literary journal, and he was one of the driving forces behind the move to abolish the department and replace it with a Department of African Literature and Languages. In "On the Abolition of the English Department," in *Homecoming,* he argues that "The primary duty of any literature department is to illuminate the spirit animating a people, to show how it meets new challenges, and to investigate possible areas of development and involvement," and is predicated on a central question: "If there is need for a 'study of the historic continuity of a single culture,' why can't this be African?" The outcome of the debate was the establishment of two departments: Languages and Literature.

Early in 1969 Oginga Odinga was invited to speak on campus but was prevented from doing so by the government; the students boycotted lectures in protest; the police intervened with considerable violence; and the college suspended five students. As he told Peter Darling, Ngugi resigned his post in protest "against the mishandling of the crisis by the College administration, and . . . the failure of a large body of members of staff to come out clearly and publicly with their views or attitude towards issues underlying the crisis."

Ngugi was immediately offered a year's fellowship in creative writing in the Department of Literature at Makerere University, during the course of which his 1970 collection of short plays, *This Time Tomorrow*, was published, his last work to appear under the name James Ngugi. In March 1970, since he was not a Christian, Ngugi decided he would begin using the name Ngugi wa Thiong'o rather than his Christian name, James Ngugi. *This Time Tomorrow* consists of three one-act plays: "The Rebels" and "The Wound in the Heart," which were written at Makerere; and the title play, which was written as a radio play for the BBC Africa Service and first broadcast in 1967.

"The Rebels" deals with the return of the university-educated favorite son of a village, who is unexpectedly accompanied by his foreign (but African) girlfriend, to be confronted by the parental demand that he marry a less-than-enthusiastic village woman chosen for him by his father. "The Wound in the Heart," rejected for the 1962 Uganda Drama Festival by censors, reads like a preliminary sketch for Gikonyo's return from detention in *A Grain of Wheat*, the major difference being that the patiently waiting wife has eventually remarried as a result of having been misled into believing that her husband has been killed. In both plays the solution to the dilemma is found in the somewhat improbable death or suicide of the woman the protagonist loves. "This Time Tomorrow" is an account of the destruction of a Nairobi shantytown. In highlighting the poverty of the majority of Nairobi's inhabitants and their disillusionment with independence, it presages Ngugi's later works.

On completing his fellowship at Makerere, Ngugi accepted a year's visiting professorship in African literature at Northwestern University in Evanston, Illinois – where the long process of writing *Petals of Blood* (1977) was begun – before returning to Nairobi in August 1971 to take a lectureship in University College's Department of Literature. He was rapidly promoted to senior lecturer and before long was acting chairman and then chairman of the department.

In 1972 Ngugi published his first collection of critical prose, *Homecoming*, which brings together essays, speeches, and reviews written from 1962 to 1970 and thereby provides documentation, invaluable to the interpretation of the fiction, on the shift in Ngugi's thinking over this crucial period in both Kenya's and his own political development. Ngugi argues in the author's note that *Homecoming* "is an integral part of the fictional world" of the early novels: "Literature does not grow or develop in a vacuum; it is given impetus, shape, direction and even area of concern by social, political and economic forces in a particular society."

The collection is divided into three sections. The essays in the first, "On Culture," lead from an early critique of racism and tribalism, through a scathing indictment of the role of Christianity in serving colonial expansion, most obviously through the destruction of traditional culture, to the advocacy of a national culture that will depend on "a completely socialized economy, collectively owned and controlled by the people," and on the prior "complete and total liberation of the people through the elimination of all exploitative forces."

The second section, "Writers in Africa," includes essays on Chinua Achebe, Wole Soyinka, T. M. Aluko, Okot p'Bitek, and East African writing. The literary criticism is always related to the overall polemical thrust of Ngugi's lucid and impassioned attack on monopolistic capitalism, and he comes to the conclusion that "It is not enough for the African artist, standing aloof, to view society and highlight its weaknesses. He must try to go beyond this, to seek out the sources, the causes and the trends of a revolutionary struggle which has already destroyed the traditional power-map drawn up by the colonialist nations."

The third section, "Writers from the Caribbean," the fruits of Ngugi's research at Leeds, consists of two essays on George Lamming and two broad surveys of Caribbean fiction. The volume concludes with an appendix containing the memorandum "On the Abolition of the English Department," prepared as part of the Nairobi debate, which has been the single most influential document in the revision of university-level English-department curricula in anglophone Africa.

In 1974 a joint project by Ngugi and Micere Githae-Mugo, which had been conceived in 1971, finally found fruition in the play *The Trial of Dedan Kimathi* (published in 1976). The final spur to completion was the 1974 publication of Kenneth Watene's play *Dedan Kimathi*, which, following the pattern of colonial writings about the Mau Mau, depicts the leader Kimathi as a crazed and brutal paranoiac. Ngugi and Githae-Mugo, by contrast, in what they call in the preface "an imaginative re-creation and interpretation of the collective will of the Kenyan peasants and workers in their refusal to break under sixty years of colonial torture and ruthless oppression by the British ruling classes," were determined to re-create Kimathi as the "great man of courage, of commitment to the people" of popular memory. The content of the play derives from the actual trial of Kimathi after his betrayal and capture in 1956, but the polemical thrust is aimed at highlighting another, contemporary, kind of trial: "We believe that Kenyan Literature – indeed all African Literature, and its writers is on trial. We cannot stand on the fence. We are either on the side of the people or on the side of imperialism."

The play makes no attempt at a naturalistic re-creation of the trial and makes extensive use of mime, dance, and song, with the songs frequently in Gikuyu. It is episodic, with the action in the courtroom being interrupted by scenes depicting other, related, action. In a scene early in the play, the actors enact black history – from the time of the slave traders to the continuing struggle against imperialism – as an overarching historical context for the action of the play. There is a series of scenes in which a symbolically unnamed Kenyan woman, representative of the Kenyan people, recruits a boy and a girl as her helpers in an attempt to assist Kimathi to escape.

Toward the end of the play there is a long flashback to Kimathi's time in the forests: he is seen putting on trial a group of guerrillas, including his brother, who have betrayed him. In the depiction of Kimathi's ultimate betrayal as resulting from his having "so hated the sight of Africans killing one another that he sometimes became a little soft with our enemies," Ngugi and Githae-Mugo directly repudiate Watene's interpretation.

There is also a series of scenes in the middle of the play in which Kimathi is subjected to private trials in his cell. These scenes depict the colonial magistrate's promises to spare Kimathi's life in return for his acknowledging the jurisdiction of the court; the blandishments of black businessmen and the exhortations of the clergy; and, finally, his tor-

Dust jacket for the 1975 New York edition of the collection that Ngugi calls a "creative autobiography" covering the years 1962 through 1974

ture. While these trial-cum-temptation scenes are reminiscent of T. S. Eliot's *Murder in the Cathedral* (1935), the play as a whole is far closer in genre to Brecht's epic theater – if one is looking for Western antecedents to set beside its obvious debt to the Gikuyu oral tradition.

"We believe," say Ngugi and Githae-Mugo in their preface, "that good theatre is that which is on the side of the people, that which, without masking mistakes and weaknesses, gives people courage and urges them to higher resolves in their struggle for total liberation." That this idea of what constitutes "good" theater was shared by many among the enthusiastic audiences who attended its first (1974) run in Nairobi was attested to by a first-night review in the *Sunday Nation*: "a degree of audience participation and appreciation which one seldom sees in Nairobi – culminat[ed] in many of the audience joining in the final triumphant dance down the central aisle and spilling out into the street." This kind of audience response, rather than official approval of the content of the play, led to its being sent to Lagos as one of Kenya's official entries for the 1977 Festival of Arts and Culture.

In 1975 Ngugi published *Secret Lives*, a collection of thirteen short stories, which he describes in the preface as his "creative autobiography over the last twelve years." Many of the stories were published (usually in *Penpoint*) while Ngugi was at Makerere, and many of them feature characters, themes, or situations that recur in the novels. Thus, for example, "The Return" is another variation on a theme that has its fullest exploration in Gikonyo's return from detention in *A Grain of Wheat*; "Goodbye Africa" deals with a situation and relationship similar to that of John Thompson and his wife in the same novel; and the ghoulish political competition to see who can provide the most extravagant coffin for the character Wahinya in "A Mercedes Funeral" presages the competition of thieves and robbers in *Caitaani Mutharaba-ini* (1980; translated as *Devil on the Cross*, 1982).

The collection is divided into three sections. The first, "Of Mothers and Children," includes three of Ngugi's earliest stories and conveys a profound concern for the hardships endured by women in traditional Gikuyu society, particularly the plight of barren women, thereby presaging the dominant role played by women in much of Ngugi's fiction. The stories in the second section, "Fighters and Martyrs," either explore the confusion and indecision that result from the conflict between Gikuyu tradition and Christianity, perceived in terms very similar to those of *The River Between*, or deal with the state of emergency and its aftermath.

The last section, "Secret Lives," is notable for three much longer stories, written after Ngugi's return to Kenya from Evanston in 1971. "Minutes of Glory," "A Mercedes Funeral," and "Wedding at the Cross" focus on the victims of postindependence Kenya's much-bruited economic "success": those left behind or trampled underfoot in the scramble for wealth and status. These are highly accomplished stories, scathingly satirical, and similar in mood to much of *Petals of Blood*; they conclusively give the lie to Ngugi's 1973 comment to Sander and Munro: "I don't think I'm particularly good at them [short stories] myself."

Ngugi spent September 1975 as a guest of the Soviet Writers Union at Yalta, where he completed *Petals of Blood*. "It was not," said Ngugi in a 1978 *Weekly Review* interview, "a very easy novel to write. It kept changing all the time. I grew with it all the time. And that is why it took so long to write."

Change is a word that recurs repeatedly in Ngugi's answers to questions about how *Petals of Blood* relates to his other works: "I feel that I have changed, in terms of outlook," he told Anita Shreve in 1977.

The fiction Ngugi produced in the 1970s does not simply embody more explicit statements of positions already held when writing the earlier works, as one might infer from many of Ngugi's critics. Killam, for example, in discussing *Secret Lives* in his *Introduction to the Writings of Ngugi*, says: "Ngugi's position in the stories as in *A Grain of Wheat* and *Petals of Blood* is that of a humane socialist. . . . " In fact *Petals of Blood* reveals a marked break from the liberal humanism of his early works, mediated aesthetically through Christian and Gikuyu mythology, and a shift to a militant socialism informed by Marx, Fanon, and Amilcar Cabral.

Ngugi has been quite explicit about the ideological thrust of his 1977 novel compared to the previous ones. Referring to the characters, he said in his 1978 *Weekly Review* interview: "I am more interested in their development from the stage of black cultural nationalism to the stage of class consciousness. From a stage when he [a character] sees oppression in terms of culture alone, to the stage when he can see oppression and exploitation as being total, that is, as being economic, political and cultural." Ngugi sees this novel, as he told Jürgen Martini in 1981, as representing "a shift . . . from a concentration on the vacillating psychology of the petite bourgeoisie to the position of the worker and the peasant." However, none of the four main characters is, strictly speaking, a representative worker or peasant.

The central focus of the novel is on the fictional village of Ilmorog, which changes, in the twelve years the action of the novel takes, from a drought-stricken dereliction in the middle of nowhere to a commercial boomtown astride the Transafrica Highway. Ilmorog's "progress," representative of that of postindependence Kenya as a whole, is the vehicle for the most comprehensive critique in African literature of the corruption and indifference of the neocolonial elite. The practical consequences of the village's economic and cultural dependency are seen most starkly in the poverty and dispossession of the peasantry. Ilmorog's condition at the beginning of the novel is described as being that of "an island of underdevelopment which after being sucked thin and dry was itself left standing, static, a grotesque distorted image of what peasant life was and could be."

In order to place Ilmorog's fate in its proper historical context, Ngugi reconstructs Kenya's history from precolonial times. As the character Karega puts it: "To understand the present . . . you must understand the past. To know where you are, you must know where you came from. . . ." Knowing where one came from, in this novel, involves, in marked contrast to Ngugi's early novels, understanding the relationship between education and the ideology it serves.

The structure of the novel is borrowed from the detective story. Three prominent company directors in New Ilmorog have been murdered by arson; the four main characters in the novel, Munira, Wanja, Karega, and Abdulla, have been arrested as suspects; and the present time of the novel is taken up with Inspector Godfrey's investigation of the murder, conducted mainly by the extraction of a lengthy written statement from Munira, the headmaster of the village school, in which he recounts events in Ilmorog since he arrived there twelve years earlier. Much of the narrative thus takes the form of extended flashbacks that, in turn, allow scope for the reminiscences of the other three main characters. The four individual histories are gradually laid bare, as are the many coincidental points at which those histories intersect with each other and with those of the three murdered men. The history of the community in the days before Munira's first arrival is reconstructed through the reminiscences of Nyakinyua, Wanja's grandmother, an archetypal village elder who is the guardian of Gikuyu myth, legend, and lore.

Of the four central characters Wanja is the dominant personality. Her promising school career is terminated by her seduction, impregnation, and abandonment by Kimeria, who becomes one of the murdered men, and she earns a precarious and sordid living as a barmaid before arriving in Ilmorog. Once there, her dynamism leads to her becoming a successful businesswoman, initially via the brewing of Theng'eta, a traditional herbal spirit made from flowers with the "petals of blood" of the title. She becomes involved in relationships with Munira, Karega, and Abdulla in turn, but, bitterly disillusioned by the loss of her brewing business (as a result of the greed of capitalist investors in New Ilmorog) and by her abandonment by Karega, she uses her remaining money to set herself up as the madam of the brothel in which the three company directors are incinerated. The philosophy by which Wanja then regulates her life is: "This world . . . this Kenya . . . this Africa knows only one law. You eat somebody or you are eaten. You sit on somebody or somebody sits on you."

Munira is a portrait of inadequacy – the epit-

ome in fact of the "vacillating psychology of the petite bourgeoisie." Expelled from Siriana for his part in a pupils' strike, he becomes a schoolteacher and accepts a post in Ilmorog as a refuge from his rigid, Christian wife and father and from his sense of failure in the face of the worldly success of his siblings. Munira's father, Waweru, is a wealthy landowner who acquired his wealth through collaboration with the colonial government and carries much of the weight of Ngugi's criticism of institutionalized Christianity. Inadequate as a teacher, anxious to avoid having to make choices and become involved in other people's lives, and unable to have a fulfilling relationship with Wanja, Munira eventually consigns himself to a fanatical revivalist Christianity.

Karega, as part of a pattern of repetition to be found throughout the novel, was also expelled from Siriana for his involvement in a pupils' strike in protest against an inflexibly Eurocentric education. Karega becomes Munira's assistant and conceives of the villagers' epic journey to Nairobi – consciously reminiscent of the march of the women in Ousmane Sembène's *God's Bits of Wood* (1960) – to seek drought aid from Ilmorog's absentee member of Parliament. The journey rekindles the collective spirit in the community, but its end result, the development of New Ilmorog, brings, by a bitter irony, the final destruction of that community. Dismissed because of Munira's jealousy, Karega leaves Ilmorog but returns to become the trade-union organizer at the Ilmorog brewery. Of all the characters, Karega learns most during the course of the action, and through his perceptions much of the novel's criticism of the neocolonial dispensation in Kenya is voiced.

Abdulla is the novel's representative former Mau Mau guerrilla, whose unqualified heroism, depicted in Fanonist terms, is a marked change from the equivocation surrounding the treatment of the Mau Mau in Ngugi's earlier novels. Maimed in the forest and unrewarded for his sacrifice after independence, he returns as a petty trader and storekeeper to Ilmorog. Infused with the spirit of the warrior heroes of Kenya's first resistance to colonialism, he comes into his own as the community's chief storyteller and inspiration on the journey to Nairobi.

Abdulla, dispossessed and impoverished in New Ilmorog, fathers the child Wanja conceives, after so many years of waiting, at the end of the novel. This child serves the same symbolic function as the pregnant woman Gikonyo plans to incorporate in his carved stool. The baby signifies, as Ngugi

Cover for Ngugi's 1977 novel, which he completed while a guest of the Soviet Writers Union in Yalta. The book shows his change of attitude from humanism to militant socialism.

told Shreve, that "There are always possibilities of renewal and growth . . . possibilities of creating a new world through a united people's determined resistance against imperialism, against foreign domination, against all other social forces that diminish men and women."

In keeping with the movement away from the liberal individualism of his earlier fiction and the focus on the history of Ilmorog as a community, Ngugi makes extensive use of community-oriented fictional techniques. The Ilmorog community as a whole is the narrator of the first part of the novel; there is frequent recourse to untranslated passages of Gikuyu and Kiswahili; many more songs are incorporated into the text than was the case in his earlier novels; the names of the characters have suggestive meanings in the vernacular; and the recounting of myth, legend, and history, as well as the frequent reminiscences of the main characters, fits into the pattern of traditional storytelling.

Ngugi no longer feels the aesthetic need to construct a fictional balance by interiorizing villains such as Kimeria. This new approach led to adverse critical response, such as that by Gerald Moore, who castigates the "melodramatic encounters with

figures of corruption and evil . . . cardboard 'baddies' who are never anything but bad. . . ." Taxed about such reactions, Ngugi explained to Shreve: "In this novel there are individual characters that are not fully explored. They are supposed to stand as class types, as typical of a class that has come to be completely indifferent to the cry of the people."

The critical reception of *Petals of Blood* has tended to be rather less enthusiastic than that accorded to *A Grain of Wheat*, generally as a result of uneasiness about Ngugi's conflation of the categories of literature and politics. Robson, for example, says, "in *Petals of Blood* Ngugi goes beyond what is acceptable in fiction; he is giving us polemic." Cook and Okenimkpe assert that "the intellectual skeleton grins through the vital literary flesh in a number of places in *Petals of Blood*," but they conclude, "*A Grain of Wheat* is the more perfect novel, but *Petals of Blood* is arguably the greater." Eustace Palmer almost certainly speaks for the majority of Ngugi's readers in Africa when he concludes, "It is enough that he [Ngugi] has presented the problems of his society as powerfully as anyone can." Taking *A Grain of Wheat* and *Petals of Blood* together, Moore would find a good deal of critical support for his assertion that these two novels "form the most impressive and original achievement yet in African fiction."

In 1976, responding to a request from a woman from Kamiriithu village – "Why don't you and others of your kind give some [of your] education to the village?" – Ngugi became involved as chairman of the cultural committee of the Kamiriithu Community Education and Cultural Centre, which was being transformed from a disused youth center into a cooperative labor project focusing on adult education, cultural development, craft production, and health awareness.

After a successful initial literacy project the next step was a venture into cultural activities, and in December 1976 Ngugi and Ngugi wa Mirii, chairman of the center's education committee, were commissioned to produce the working script for a play. By the time the play, *Ngaahika Ndeenda*, opened in October 1977, the script had been transformed by additions made by the local peasants; an open-air theater with raised stage, roofed dressing rooms, and a two-thousand-seat auditorium had been built; and a cast and orchestra consisting entirely of local talent had come together in a production that drew enthusiastic audiences of thousands.

The symbolic focus of the play is the framed deed, to one and a half acres of land, that hangs in the house of a farm laborer, Kiguunda wa Gathoni, and his wife, Wangeci. The plot shows how Kiguunda's employer, Kioi, a wealthy Christian businessman, gains possession of the land (so that a foreign-owned insecticide factory can be built on it) by persuading Kiguunda to join the church and to mortgage the land so that he can pay for a Christian wedding service in order to "cleanse" his "sinful," traditional marriage. Kiguunda succumbs because he and Wangeci are led to believe that this service is to enable their daughter Gathoni to marry Kioi's son John. But John seduces her and abandons her to the life of a barmaid when she becomes pregnant. When Kigunda fails to repay the loan, the bank, of which Kioi is a director, forecloses; the land is auctioned; and Kioi buys it. In broad terms the play, as Ngugi puts it in *Decolonising the Mind*, "depicts the proletarisation of the peasantry in a neocolonial society." This play is relentless in its attack on imported religions, particularly Christianity: "Religion is the alcohol of the soul! Religion is the poison of the mind!" It concludes, strikingly, "The voice of the people is the voice of God."

Formally the most important elements of the drama are mime and, particularly, song and dance, which are integral parts of the action. As Ngugi says

(in *Decolonising the Mind*), "The song arises from what has gone before and it leads to what follows. The song and the dance become a continuation of the conversation and of the action."

The success of a venture in community theater such as *Ngaahika Ndeenda* will ultimately be measured in social and political, rather than purely literary, terms, but the verdict of Magayu K. Magayu in the *Weekly Review* (25 April 1980) seems apt when he describes the play as "a revolutionary classic of our time."

A self-help cultural center that gave peasants and workers a collective confidence in their abilities and a collective cultural focus was seen by Kenyan authorities as posing a political threat – far more of a threat than that posed by the chairman of a university literature department occupying his time with the writing of novels and plays in English, however critical those might be of the government. On 16 December 1977 the district commissioner of Kiambu withdrew the license for any further performances of the play, and on 31 December Ngugi was taken to Kamiti Maximum Security Prison as a political detainee.

Detained: A Writer's Prison Diary, published in 1981, provides a vivid account of Ngugi's experience during his year in detention. But *Detained* is more than just an account of the day-to-day life of a political prisoner; it also presents Ngugi's impassioned reflections on Kenya's colonial and post-independence history and on the transformation of Kenyatta from the anticolonial nationalist of the 1930s to the self-serving president of the 1980s; and it provides an invaluable account of the gestation of Ngugi's prison novel, *Caitaani Mutharaba-ini* (*Devil on the Cross*).

The writing of a novel in Gikuyu while in detention was conceived of by Ngugi as not only "an insurrection of a detained intellect" but also "one way of keeping my mind and heart together." The first draft of *Caitaani* took Ngugi ten months to write and was virtually complete when he was released on 12 December 1978. It was originally written on toilet paper, discovered, confiscated, and then returned to Ngugi by the senior superintendent with a critical comment destined for immortality: "I see nothing wrong with it." *Caitaani* is the classic prison novel.

Like *Petals of Blood*, *Caitaani* has four main protagonists. Of these the most important is Wariinga, a young secretary whose promising academic career has been ruined as a result of her seduction and impregnation by a rich old man. When the novel opens, she has been sacked for refusing her boss's advances, but by the end she has become an emancipated and self-confident motor mechanic, a "heroine of toil." Ngugi describes her genesis in *Detained*: "Because the women are the most exploited and oppressed section of the entire working class, I would create a picture of a strong determined woman with a will to resist and to struggle against the conditions of her present being."

The other three characters are Gatuiria, a radical music student attempting to compose an oratorio that will convey the whole of Kenya's history; Wangari, a heroine of the liberation struggle, a dispossessed peasant whose attempts to find employment in Nairobi have led to her arrest for vagrancy; and Muturi, who is an enigmatic leader of an undefined workers' revolutionary movement.

The four meet for the first time in a *matatu* (a transport for hire – usually a minibus), on their way to a cave near Ilmorog to attend, as spectators, a "Competition in Modern Theft and Robbery." The journey provides the framework for the recounting of their individual histories. They attend the competition and are duly appalled by the barefaced cynicism with which the competitors, all members of the bourgeoisie, boast of their various methods of exploiting the Kenyan masses.

Wangari reports the presence of these robbers and thieves to the local police (her promise to do so having been the condition of her release) and is arrested for her pains. Muturi leads a procession of peasants and workers in a march on the cave, where they disrupt the competition but are violently dispersed by the police, and Muturi is also arrested. Wariinga is profoundly affected by the experience and devotes herself to the workers' cause, while Gatuiria, with whom she falls in love, gets on with his composition. The novel ends when, prior to their marriage, Gatuiria takes Wariinga to meet his parents. His father turns out to be the rich old man, who tries to seduce Wariinga again, so she shoots him.

Roughly half the novel is taken up with the description of the competition in the cave, a tour de force of satire and burlesque, combining an irrepressible imaginative inventiveness with a relentless exposure of political corruption and economic chicanery. The competitors, who have to announce their credentials in terms of the cars and women they possess, recount their methods of achieving wealth – which range from land speculation to employing aged or crippled white women as headmistresses and motorized white mannequins as dummy pupils in order to attract the children of the black elite to "international" schools – and con-

Caricature of Ngugi by Terry Hirst (from Joe Magazine, *August 1977)*

clude with their blueprints for novel ways of exploiting the masses in the future.

Ngugi's satire is at its most devastating. The mildest suggestion is that the air should be canned for sale to the peasants and that they should be sold earth by the potful for cultivation. One competitor envisages a factory for making human parts: "This would mean that a really rich man would never die. . . . We could purchase immortality with our money and leave death as the prerogative of the poor." But the climax comes when Kimeenderi wa Kanyuanjii plans to pen his workers on his farm with barbed wire and fix machines to their bodies for milking their sweat, their blood, and their brains, which can then be piped away for export.

In *Caitaani* the unequivocal political stance of Ngugi's fiction is assured – drawing ultimately perhaps on Wariinga's recognition that "There is no love that is not linked with hate. How can you tell what you love unless you know what you hate?" The novel's ending countenances no doubt as to the moral and political correctness of Wariinga's resorting to the gun as a necessary instrument of class struggle in her execution of the symbolic representative of Kenya's neocolonial bourgeoisie, "parasites that live on the trees of other people's lives!" Before she pulls the trigger, Wariinga speaks "like a people's judge about to deliver his judgement."

Ngugi's control of fictional form is masterly, particularly in the adroitness with which he manages to dovetail the widely divergent modes of fictional realism – employed in the framing narrative and the flashbacks conveying the life stories of the main characters – and burlesque satire, which informs the cave scene. The finished product fully justifies Ngugi's resolve, described in *Detained*, to "use any and everything I had ever learnt about the craft of fiction – allegory, parable, satire, narrative, description, reminiscence, flash-back, interior monologue, stream of consciousness, dialogue, drama – provided it came naturally in the development of character, theme and story." Cook and Okenimkpe rightly assert that "Ngugi's determination to communicate more generally has led him not towards technical crudity but to a new and more appropriate kind of technical brilliance."

In formal terms the writing of this novel in Gikuyu has resulted in a far heavier reliance even than that in *Petals of Blood* on devices drawn from, and deliberately signaling the novel's relationship with, an oral tradition. The narrator refers to himself as "Prophet of Justice" and is addressed as Gicaandi Player on the opening page; extensive use is made of proverbs and riddles in dialogue; figurative language almost always has a local reference; and songs, particularly Mau Mau liberation songs, are integrated into the narrative. As in his previous novel the plot relies on coincidence and the chance intersections of the lives of the main characters in the past.

In keeping with his unequivocal political position and the challenge he poses to half-committed intellectuals (not, however, his main target group), there is a strong element of the medieval morality play about *Caitaani*. As Muturi puts it, "Our lives are a battlefield on which is fought a continuous war between the forces that are pledged to confirm our humanity and those determined to dismantle it. . . ." Satan himself is one of the dramatis personae, in the form of "The Voice," which speaks to Wariinga in a vision. He is allowed some of the most penetrating criticisms of neocolonial Kenya in the novel (giving rise to the most complex ambiguity from an interpretive point of view), but he is unsuccessful in tempting her toward a self-seeking individualism.

The title's reference to the devil – crucified (historically perhaps at "Independence") but rescued from the cross and nursed back to health by his worshipers, the postindependence bourgeoisie – is only the most obvious of many ironic references made to Christianity, whose mythology remains, in Ngugi's view, more widely accessible than any other to an audience consisting of all the peoples of Kenya. Ngugi's irony at the expense of institutionalized religions also extends to Islam.

Ngugi's project in *Caitaani* can best be summed up by reference to part of the testimony of Kihaahu wa Gatheeca, one of the competitors in the cave, who says: "I'm very grateful to the masses of the Kenyan people. For their blindness, their ignorance, their inability to demand their rights are what enable us, the clan of man-eaters, to feed on their sweat without their asking us too many awkward questions." The novel is addressed primarily to the peasants and workers of Kenya and is designed to encourage the asking of awkward questions and the demanding of rights.

On its publication in Gikuyu in Nairobi, the novel was an instant success, going almost immediately into second and third printings. It reached a wide audience of nonliterate Gikuyu via, among other means, public readings in *matatus* and by professional readers who sprang up in bars, timing the emptying of their glasses to coincide with climaxes in the plot. Ngugi's assertion of the political role of fiction makes it difficult to assess the novel's success in any terms other than his own: how many more people are asking awkward questions?

Ngugi was eventually released from detention in 1978 as part of a general amnesty following Kenyatta's death earlier in the year. Ngugi was never given any reasons for his detention. If the expectation was to intimidate him, or, as he speculated, that his "brain would turn into a mess of rot," the exercise was obviously a signal failure. In terms of the production of fiction, Ngugi's spell as prisoner K6.77 in Kamiti was his most intensely productive period since his days at Makerere. Writing in prison, Ngugi said, "I am where I am because I have written about and believed in a Kenya for Kenyans, because I have attempted to hold up a mirror through which Kenyans can look at themselves in their past, their present and perhaps in their future." Ngugi continued to hold up that mirror, his determination to do so merely strengthened by his imprisonment.

Ngugi was never reinstated in his post at the university or given any explanation as to why he was not. Instead he was consigned to what Victoria Brittain describes in her preface to *Barrel of a Pen* (1983) as "the limbo Kenya reserves for its most articulate government critics. They become unemployable and isolated – a form of subtle torture which has broken less resilient people." Apart from trips abroad, such as his visit to Denmark in response to an invitation to take part in the 75th anniversary celebrations of the Danish Library Association in December 1980, and his visit to Zimbabwe in 1981, Ngugi was occupied for the next two years with the English translation of *Caitaani* (*Devil on the Cross*) and the publication of *Detained* and his second collection of essays, *Writers in Politics* (1981).

The collection comprises thirteen essays, written between 1970 and 1980, the main concern of which is summed up by Ngugi in the preface: "what's the relevance of literature to life?" Ngugi explains that he has titled the book *Writers in Politics* "because literature cannot escape from the class power structures that shape our everyday life. Here a writer has no choice. . . . Every writer is a writer in politics. The only question is what and whose politics?"

As *Homecoming* is integral to the world of his early novels, so these essays are the obvious secondary source to turn to for an elaboration of the ideas embodied in Ngugi's fiction and drama in the 1970s. The attack on imperialism, monopoly capitalism, and cultural dependency is unremitting and more forthright than in *Homecoming*. The topics range from the teaching of literature in schools, to the appropriate language for African literature (during which discussion Ngugi coins the term "Afro-Saxon" literature for African literature written in English), to tributes to the assassinated J. M. Kariûki. Ngugi's concern for the plight of the oppressed reaches out from Kenya to America and Asia, and he focuses, in particular, on South Korea.

During the early 1980s Ngugi also maintained his involvement with the Kamiriithu Community Education and Cultural Centre, though there were no plays for three years after the closing of *Ngaahika Ndeenda*. In 1981 he wrote the working script for a musical "Maitu Njuriga" (Mother Sing For Me), which the group hoped to perform at the Kenyan National Theatre in February 1982. Unlike that of *Ngaahika Ndeenda*, the setting for this play is not contemporary; it deals with the colonial system in the 1930s and, as Ngugi says in *Decolonising the Mind*, "depict[s] the heroic struggle of Kenyan workers against the early phase of imperialist capitalist 'primitive' accumulation with confiscation of the land, forced labour on the same stolen land and heavy taxation to finance its development into settler run plantations."

The play's focus on the colonial rather than neocolonial system in Kenya was not enough, however, to deflect the unwelcome attentions of the state. The play was not granted the necessary li-

Cover for the 1989 English translation of Ngugi's Matigari ma Njiruungi *(1986), originally published in Gikuyu, his native language*

cense to open at the National Theatre. The university authorities were instructed to keep the performers out of the university theater when the group tried the expedient of continuing "open" rehearsals there – but not before some ten thousand people had attended such "rehearsals." On 10 March 1982 Ngugi published a hard-hitting statement, which is reprinted in *Barrel of a Pen*, condemning the government's suppression of the play. On 11 March the government revoked the license for Kamiriithu Community Education and Cultural Centre. On 12 March three truckloads of armed policemen arrived and razed the Kamiriithu people's open-air theater.

Three months later, in early June 1982, in an atmosphere of mounting tension as the government once again set about detaining progressive politicians, lawyers, and academics, Ngugi left Nairobi to attend the launching of *Devil on the Cross* in London. An attempted coup in August took place in his absence, the climate of repression has intensified ever since, and Ngugi has been unable to return to Kenya.

Since mid 1982 Ngugi has been based mainly in London but has traveled extensively: to Sweden and West Germany in 1982; to Zimbabwe; to West Germany again, where he was a guest professor at Bayreuth University for two months; to Fiji; and to New Zealand, where he gave the Robb lectures at Auckland University, subsequently published as *Decolonising the Mind*; and to the United States in 1985 and intermittently between 1989 and 1992, when he taught at Yale University. He is currently teaching at New York University.

Although it contains little new material, *Decolonising the Mind* is a valuable addition to Ngugi's publications in that it neatly condenses many of his earlier arguments on language, literature, and society into four, often informatively autobiographical, essays: "The Language of African Literature"; "The Language of African Theatre"; "The Language of African Fiction"; and "The Quest for Relevance."

Ngugi spent the first half of 1986 taking a film course in Sweden, and he completed a twenty-minute feature film, "Blood-grapes and Black Diamonds," which examines the South African sanctions issue and draws attention, in particular, to the economic self-interest underlying Western opposition to sanctions. Besides publishing *Barrel of a Pen*, a collection of essays in the same vein as those in *Writers in Politics*, and *Decolonising the Mind*, Ngugi has also published three children's books in Gikuyu and a booklet, *Writing Against Neocolonialism* (1986), as well as a second novel in Gikuyu, *Matigari ma Njiruungi* (1986; translated as *Matigari*, 1989).

As an adaptation of the novel form to the purpose of raising the revolutionary consciousness of Gikuyu peasants and workers through the incorporation of elements of an oral tradition, *Matigari* takes up where *Caitaani* left off, though the greater use of repetition, the stronger adventure-story plot, and the tendency toward a less baroque mode of satire all suggest that the novel is aimed at an even wider popular audience of Gikuyu-speakers, including children (judging by the prominent role given to the young boy Muriuki).

The unspecified setting of the allegorical story is evidently Kenya. The story tells of the emergence from the forests of Matigari ma Njiruungi (whose Gikuyu name means "the patriots who survived the bullets"), who has finally managed, after many years of hunting and being hunted, to kill Settler Williams and his faithful retainer, John Boy. Matigari symbolically buries his weapons, girds

himself with a belt of peace, and sets out to find his "people" ("my parents, my wives, my children") so that together they can reclaim Williams's house, which Matigari built and which he has since fought for and won. When he tries to claim the house, he finds it has been sold by Williams's son to John Boy's son, John Boy Junior, the continuity of the name, with its weight of colonial insult, connoting a role for the postindependence elite indistinguishable from the servile collaboration of their parents.

Matigari is arrested and thrown into jail but mysteriously escapes. This experience, together with his earlier bravery in confronting the police, the way he appears at times to be miraculously protected from bullets and stones, and the way his appearance changes from youthfulness to age depending on his mood, lends him mythical status. He travels the country with dreamlike rapidity, asking everyone he meets where he can find truth and justice, and eventually he confronts the Minister of Truth and Justice himself with the same question. Matigari is sent to a mental hospital but escapes, and finally recognizing that "justice for the oppressed springs from the organised and armed power of the people," he takes off his belt of peace and determines to dig up his weapons and kill John Boy Junior to reclaim the house. Savaged by police dogs, Matigari is finally carried away by a swollen river to an indeterminate end, after having burned down the disputed house – an ironic outcome of his original intention: "We shall all gather, go home together, light the fire together and build our home together."

Again there are four main characters, though Matigari is dominant. The heroine, Guthera, is (like Wanja) a prostitute. By a bitter irony, this profession is the direct result of her religious devotion, which made her refuse to sacrifice her virginity to a policeman and thereby save her father's life after he had been arrested for carrying bullets to the forest fighters. With no father to support her she took to the streets, refusing, however, to sleep with policemen. After meeting Matigari, she abandons this principle in order to ensure his release from jail, and under his inspiration she dedicates herself to doing "something to change whatever it is that makes people live like animals, especially us women." Less idealized than Wariinga, Guthera shares her perspicuity, and her reward for her transformation is to share Matigari's fate at the end of the novel.

Another important character is Ngaruro wa Kiriro, a representative worker at the Anglo-American Leather and Plastic Works, who is inspired by an encounter with Matigari to become a leader of a strike at the factory and publicly to defy a presiden-

63

also equally extremist actors in the resistance. So at the end of the film, in a sense, we are shown that a

colonial state is really a liberal state ~~,~~ *It liberal* is a referee in a system of civil war. ~~Furthermore~~ *In th* film the

African people involved in resistance have been denied a voice. They do not even have a language, for the

language which they speak -- even when they are peasants and workers -- is good King's or Queen's

English. It is as if the Mau Mau resistance forces did not really have a language of their own.

Now this denial of the voice ~~of language~~ to those who resist is ~~in a sense~~ fairly central to the

literary consciousness in the West which on the whole has been in harmony with the forces of imperialist

domination of other countries. I want to illustrate this gradual denial of the voice to those who resist by

mentioning just a couple of texts which you will all recognize. And these texts cover the whole period of *historica*

this ~~historic~~al domination of the rest of the world by a handful of European nations.

The first text is Shakespeare's <u>The Tempest</u>. And you remember there that Caliban, whose island

has been taken over by Prospero, is represented as having no language although we presume that before

Prospero came to the island Caliban had been speaking to his mother in a certain language. But in the

play he has no language *of his own. However,* It is very interesting that Shakespeare, ~~even~~ after he has given him the English

language, at least makes Caliban have a voice even though this voice is in the English language.

We come to another text, ~~and from Caliban through transformation to Friday in~~ Defoe's <u>Robinson</u>

<u>Crusoe</u>. And you remember the contact between Friday and Crusoe: Crusoe here meets Friday and

begins to teach him a language. Again we perceive that Friday is presumed to have no language ~~and~~ He is *given*

being ~~taught~~ a language. And the first thing he is told is, "Your name is Friday." Then he is told to say,

"Master, Master," and then he is told, "that is my name." "Your name is Friday; my name is Master." It is *again* *on*

~~quite~~ interesting that ~~even then~~, Defoe was quite satiric about this whole encounter. ~~Still~~ Friday has some

kind of voice for he does, or he is made to, doubt Crusoe's conception of the origins of the world in the

divine order. *But still, Friday has much less of a voice than Caliban*

We come to the twentieth century, to Joseph Conrad's <u>Heart of Darkness</u>, a text which is in so *It* *negative*

many ways consistently anti-colonial adventurism, ~~which~~ paints colonial adventurism in very strong colors.

Nevertheless, the African people there have absolutely no voice. This time they don't ~~even~~ have a

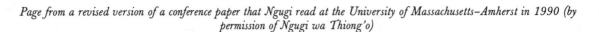

Page from a revised version of a conference paper that Ngugi read at the University of Massachusetts–Amherst in 1990 (by permission of Ngugi wa Thiong'o)

tial decree against inciting people to strike. He, too, is committed to the mental hospital and escapes, but he is shot down by the police and dies. The last of the four main characters is the young Muriuki, who ekes out an existence by scavenging off the garbage dump and living in an abandoned car. At the end of the novel Muriuki is left to continue the resistance against oppression, as he unearths and girds on Matigari's AK-47 rifle, pistol, and sword with the voices of workers, peasants, students, and "other patriots" ringing in his ears: "Victory shall be ours!"

Structurally *Matigari* is divided into three sections, whose titles reveal the symbolic significance of the names given to the main characters: "Wiping Your Tears Away" (*Ngaruro wa Kiriro*); "Seeker of Truth and Justice"; and "The Pure and the Resurrected" (*Guthera na Muriuki*). The novel has a relatively long central chapter, describing a political meeting addressed by the Minister for Truth and Justice – reminiscent of the cave scene in *Caitaani* in which Ngugi allows free rein to his delight in burlesque. Thus, for example, a member of Parliament argues that only the wealthy should be allowed to have children, and the caricatured political speeches are punctuated by a trio consisting of the editor of the *Daily Parrotry*, a "Permanent Professor in the History of Parrotology," and a lecturer in the "Philosophy of Parratology" leaping to their feet and singing songs from the governing party's hymnal, *Songs of a Parrot*.

There are two main respects in which *Matigari* differs from *Caitaani*. First, in terms of genre, it is a far less complex collage. Storytelling is the dominant mode and carries much more of the political thrust of the novel than previously, as seen, for example, in the frequent repetition of Matigari's personal history (insofar as a character who, in his author's words, "symbolizes a collective worker" can have a "personal" history), which is always dovetailed with parables of "the tiller dying of starvation, the builder sleeping on the verandah; the tailor walking about without clothes and the driver having to go for miles on foot." Generically the main variant on storytelling is parody, which takes the form of frequent news bulletins from the Orwellian "Voice of Truth" national broadcasting service being interjected into the narrative and suggests that Ngugi sees an urgent need to counteract the hegemonic persuasiveness of government-propaganda media.

Second, *Matigari* suggests a far more complex attitude on Ngugi's part toward Christianity than that to be found in the biting satire of *Caitaani*.

Much of Matigari's mystique results from the possibility raised in the popular imagination that his advent is the Second Coming, a possibility that remains open at the end of the novel. He is prone to utterances such as "Let the children come to me" and "You will see me again after only three days," and he has a miraculous ability to transcend time and space. Ngugi is not simply utilizing the imagery of Christianity as a useful point of reference; Matigari's status as hero depends on his Christ-like stature and involves an acceptance of Christian mythology. And this Christ figure is in no way undercut in the way Kihika is in *A Grain of Wheat*. This motif does not, of course, preclude a scathingly satirical depiction of the self-serving priest who represents the established church.

Matigari is a carefully crafted work that further develops the novel's potential as a cultural weapon in the fight against oppression. It is a powerful literary response to the recognition that comes to Matigari: "It dawned on him that one could not defeat the enemy with arms alone, but one could also not defeat the enemy with words alone. One had to have the right words; but these words had to be strengthened by the force of arms. In the pursuit of truth and justice one had to be armed with armed words."

The publication of *Matigari* in Kenya fired the imagination of peasants and workers in a way that closely paralleled the hero's effect on their fictional counterparts. This much is clear from the novel's postpublication history in Kenya, which also reveals just how much the Kenyan government apparently sees itself as having to fear Ngugi's "armed words." Ngugi describes how, soon after the novel's publication, Kenyan peasants started talking about a man called Matigari who was going around the country asking questions about justice. These reports were conveyed to the president, who ordered Matigari's arrest. When the police reported back to the president that Matigari was only a character in a book, the outcome was, in Ngugi's words, that "the book itself was arrested in 1987 from all bookshops – an operation involving the whole country." The "arrest" of his book effectively consigns Ngugi to a double exile: with Ngugi physically cut off from the peasants and workers in Kenya, who are the source of his inspiration, the banning of his book means that he cannot, through his fiction, communicate with those for whom he writes.

In "A Statement" at the beginning of *Decolonising the Mind* Ngugi announces that the book "is my farewell to English as a vehicle for any of my writings. From now on it is Gikuyu and Kiswahili all the way." Twenty years ago, in his interview with Leeds students, Ngugi followed up his statement that he had reached a point of crisis and did not know whether it was worth it any longer to write in English, by replying to the question of whether he intended returning to Africa: "I sincerely believe that everybody's struggle, except in very special circumstances, lies in his own country where that struggle is taking place. I don't believe in exile, although there are situations where this is unavoidable."

Ngugi still does not believe in exile, though in his situation it is clearly unavoidable until such time as the political changes that his writings are designed to hasten finally come about. A measure of Ngugi's intellectual consistency and commitment is that, although the arguments in favor of writing in Gikuyu have for him become almost moot, he still follows his original logic in the most difficult possible circumstances, thousands of miles from the peasants and workers for whom he writes. That courage and commitment, combined with a technical mastery of fictional forms and a total command of both English and Gikuyu, make Ngugi wa Thiong'o preeminent among African writers.

Interviews:

Alan Marcuson and others, "James Ngugi Interviewed by Fellow Students at Leeds University," *Cultural Events in Africa*, 31 (June 1967): i–v;

Peter Darling, "My Protest Was Against the Hypocrisy in the College," *Sunday Nation* (Nairobi), 16 March 1969, pp. 15–16;

Dennis Duerden, Interview with Ngugi, in *African Writers Talking: A Collection of Radio Interviews*, edited by Dennis Duerden and Cosmo Pieterse (London: Heinemann, 1972), pp. 121–124;

Aminu Abdullahi, Interview with Ngugi, in *African Writers Talking: A Collection of Radio Interviews*, pp. 124–131;

Anita Shreve, "*Petals of Blood*," *Viva*, 3 (1977): 35–36;

"An Interview with Ngugi," *Weekly Review* (9 January 1978): 9–11;

Margaretta wa Gacheru, "Ngugi wa Thiong'o Still Bitter over His Detention," *Weekly Review* (5 January 1979): 30–32;

Amooti wa Irumba, "The Making of a Rebel," *Index on Censorship*, 3 (1980): 20–24;

Jürgen Martini and others, "Ngugi wa Thiong'o: Interview," *Kunapipi*, 3, no. 1 (1981): 110–116; no. 2 (1981): 135–140;

Raoul Granqvist, "Ngugi wa Thiong'o: Interview," *Kunapipi*, 5 (1983): 44–48;

Reinhard Sander and Ian Munro, "Tolstoy in Africa", in *Critical Perspectives on Ngugi wa Thiong'o*, edited by G. D. Killam (Washington, D.C.: Three Continents, 1984), pp. 46–57;

Bettye J. Parker, Interview with Ngugi, in *Critical Perspectives on Ngugi wa Thiong'o*, pp. 58–66.

Bibliography:

Carol Sicherman, *Ngugi wa Thiong'o: A Bibliography* (London, Munich & New York: Zell, 1991).

References:

Jacqueline Bardolph, *Ngugi wa Thiong'o* (Paris: Présence Africaine, 1991);

Roger Berger, "Ngugi's Comic Vision," *Research in African Literatures*, 20 (Spring 1989): 1–25;

Ingrid Bjorkman, *"Mother, Sing For Me": People's Theatre in Kenya* (London & Atlantic Highlands, N.J.: Zed, 1989);

Victoria Brittain, Preface to Ngugi's *Barrel of a Pen* (London: New Beacon, 1983), pp. iii–ix;

David Cook and Michael Okenimkpe, *Ngugi wa Thiong'o: An Exploration of his Writings* (London: Heinemann, 1983);

Echos du Commonwealth, special issue on *Petals of Blood*, 6 (1980/1981);

English in Africa, special issue on Ngugi wa Thiong'o, 8 (September 1981);

Shatto A. Gakwandi, "Ngugi's *A Grain of Wheat* and Ousmane Sembène's *God's Bits of Wood*," in his *The Novel and Contemporary Experience in Africa* (London: Heinemann, 1977), pp. 108–125;

Micere Githae-Mugo, *Visions of Africa* (Nairobi: Kenya Literature Bureau, 1978);

Andrew Gurr, *Writers in Exile: The Identity of Home in Modern Literature* (Brighton, U.K.: Harvester, 1981), pp. 92–121;

W. J. Howard, "Themes and Development in the Novels of Ngugi," in *The Critical Evaluation of African Literature*, edited by Edgar Wright (London: Heinemann, 1973), pp. 95–119;

Ime Ikiddeh, "James Ngugi as Novelist," *African Literature Today*, 2 (1969): 3–10;

Ikiddeh, "Ngugi wa Thiong'o: The Novelist as Historian," in *A Celebration of Black and African Writing*, edited by Bruce King and Kolawole Ogungbesan (Zaria, Nigeria: Ahmadu Bello University Press/Oxford University Press, 1975), pp. 204–216;

Abdul R. JanMohamed, *Manichean Aesthetics: The Politics of Literature in Colonial Africa* (Amherst: University of Massachusetts Press, 1983);

G. D. Killam, *An Introduction to the Writings of Ngugi* (London: Heinemann, 1980);

Killam, ed., *Critical Perspectives on Ngugi wa Thiong'o* (Washington, D.C.: Three Continents, 1984);

Bernth Lindfors, "Ngugi wa Thiong'o's Early Journalism," *World Literature Written in English*, 20 (Spring 1981): 23–41;

David Maughan-Brown, "Not Yet the Freedom," in his *Land, Freedom and Fiction: History and Ideology in Kenya* (London: Zed, 1985), pp. 230–258;

L. A. Mbughuni, "Old and New Drama from East Africa," *African Literature Today*, 8 (1976): 85–98;

Leslie Monkman, "Kenya and the New Jerusalem in *A Grain of Wheat*," *African Literature Today*, 7 (1975): 111–116;

Gerald Moore, "Towards Uhuru," in his *Twelve African Writers* (London: Hutchinson, 1980), pp. 263–288;

Peter Nazareth, "Is *A Grain of Wheat* a Socialist Novel?" in his *An African View of Literature* (Evanston: Northwestern University Press, 1974), pp. 128–154;

Ebele Obumselu, "*A Grain of Wheat*: Ngugi's Debt to Conrad," *Benin Review*, 1 (June 1974): 80–91;

Eustace Palmer, *The Growth of the African Novel* (London: Heinemann, 1979);

John Reed, "James Ngugi and the African Novel," *Journal of Commonwealth Literature*, 1 (September 1965): 117–121;

Research in African Literatures, special issue on Ngugi wa Thiong'o, 16 (Summer 1985);

Clifford B. Robson, *Ngugi wa Thiong'o* (London: Macmillan, 1979);

Ato Sekyi-Otu, "The Refusal of Agency: The Founding Narrative and Waiyaki's Tragedy in *The River Between*," *Research in African Literatures*, 16 (Summer 1985): 157–178;

Govind Narain Sharma, "Ngugi's Apocalypse: Marxism, Christianity and African Utopianism in *Petals of Blood*," *World Literature Written in English*, 18 (1979): 302–314;

Sharma, "Ngugi's Christian Vision: Theme and Pattern in *A Grain of Wheat*," *African Literature Today*, 10 (November 1979): 167–176;

Carol M. Sicherman, "Ngugi wa Thiong'o and the Writing of Kenyan History," *Research in African Literatures*, 20 (1989): 347–370;

Sicherman, ed., *Ngugi wa Thiong'o: The Making of a Rebel: A Source Book in Kenyan Literature and Resistance* (London, Munich & New York: Zell, 1990);

Michael Vaughan, "African Fiction and Popular Struggle: The Case of *A Grain of Wheat*," *English in Africa*, 8 (September 1981): 23–52.

Arthur Nortje

(16 December 1942 – 10? December 1970)

David Bunn
University of the Western Cape

BOOK: *Dead Roots* (London: Heinemann, 1973).

OTHER: "Hollows for Travelling Music," in *Seven South African Poets*, edited by Cosmo Pieterse (London: Heinemann, 1971);
"Lonely Against the Light," edited by G. Butler and R. Harnett, *New Coin Poetry*, special issue, 9 (September 1973);
Arthur Nortje and Other Poets, includes poems by Nortje (Athlone, South Africa: COSAW, 1988).

Until recently Arthur Nortje was often referred to rather sentimentally as South Africa's "forgotten poet." Nevertheless most students of South African culture have never lost sight of Nortje's importance as a poet and as a symbol of resistance to apartheid. Ever since Nortje's apparent suicide in December 1970, a few days before his twenty-eighth birthday, writers and critics alike have been struggling to come to terms with the haunting poetry he left behind. In his career, his poems, and the manner of his death, one sees exemplified the problem of reconciling aesthetics and political commitment, for the essence of Nortje's life and work is struggle – struggle to forge a personal and poetic identity in the face of dehumanizing political forces that eventually drove him into exile. Most important of all, perhaps, Nortje represents a part of South African history that was conveniently effaced and which is only now being painfully recovered. In recent years academic interest in Nortje has been fueled by the discovery of numerous unpublished manuscripts, which hint at his unfulfilled potential.

To understand Nortje, one must understand the political forces that bore down upon him from a very early age. He was the second illegitimate son of Cecilia Potgieter, was classified as "coloured" (the racist appellation applied to individuals of mixed descent in South Africa), and had been born on 16 December 1942 into a community that was to suffer increasing alienation with the imposition of

Arthur Nortje (photograph by Hedy I. Davis)

apartheid legislation in the 1940s and 1950s. Raised initially in an Afrikaans-speaking family, then nurtured in an English-speaking environment in Port Elizabeth, he had a multilingual background that made even his earliest poems unusual.

In those early works (written between 1960 and 1964) Nortje assumes the posture of the poet manqué, a "dogsbody halfbreed" (as he once referred to himself), standing in romantic antithesis to the discriminatory conditions brought about by apartheid. This attitude is but the first of a series of poetic masks that Nortje donned throughout his career, and it is a mask that disguises a deep unease.

Underlying even his first published works readers find aesthetic, political, and personal contradictions that would have scuttled the career of many a writer, but these provide the motive force behind his verse. His is always an aesthetic forged out of crisis and a sense of injustice. Later in his career Nortje overcame some of these earlier contradictions: when one takes into account the evidence of his unpublished letters and journals, a strong sense of purpose and corpus emerges. In the late 1960s, after his exile in England and his teaching in British Columbia and Toronto, he had come to understand his life as an odysseylike progression with allegorical overtones. In the last years of his short career this idea produced some of his greatest work: poems such as "Seen One, Take One," "Native's Letter," and "All Hungers Pass Away," which are collected in *Dead Roots* (1973.) His final poems enact a rediscovery of political meaning in personal trauma; they also embody a reformulation of his own identity, the African oral tradition, and the denied history of his ancestors. This widening mythopoeic and political vision, juxtaposed against occasional poems that call from the pit of despair, has made it difficult for some critics to assess his final phase.

At the time of his death Nortje left behind a considerable collection of his poems in manuscript, many of which were published in two separate volumes: *Dead Roots* and "Lonely Against the Light" (a special issue of *New Coin Poetry*, September 1973). To this must be added the anthologies that feature his work (some of it previously unpublished), and two lengthy manuscripts consisting of journal entries, transcribed letters, and drafts of published and unpublished poems (at the National English Literary Museum, Grahamstown, South Africa).

Even in his earliest published work his technical expertise is apparent. In "Thumbing a Lift" (in *Dead Roots*) he has a highly self-conscious voice and refers to himself as a "wheedling tramp." This early persona was heavily determined by the influence of poet Dennis Brutus, now exiled, who taught English to Nortje at Paterson High School in the 1950s. Brutus, an articulate activist, was constantly challenging the younger poet to commit himself on the side of established antiapartheid organizations. Poems by Nortje such as "Preventive Detention" (in *Dead Roots*) reveal that Brutus had an almost iconographic significance for him.

"Preventive Detention," written in 1963, includes an odd allusion to Brutus's imprisonment in South Africa: "a spindly scholar's imprisoned because / winter is in the brilliant grass." Lines such

as these are characteristic of the way Nortje blends references to the seasons and images of political causation in his early work. He was interested in patterning the lyric landscape of Romantic verse against the stark South African reality. Had Nortje lived, he would probably have pared away the Romantic influence, because this paring tendency is evident in his poems written in Canada. However, the Romantics, and the cadences of Gerard Manley Hopkins, are evident in many of his South African poems. Some lines are direct imitations of Hopkins, as in the following rather overblown image from "Slip of a Girl" (in *Dead Roots*): "beautiful phantom by failed love fostered / elfin in willow woods."

The tension between romanticism and realism is not, of course, peculiar to Nortje; it is an antinomy apparent in much South African poetry written in English. Yet for Nortje, the "coloured" writer in South Africa, political realism was inescapable. His early career coincides with one of the most repressive eras in the history of apartheid, a period that included the dictatorship of Hendrik Verwoerd (the "architect" of apartheid) and a series of draconian legislative measures designed to entrench segregation.

In the early 1950s the meager privileges enjoyed by "coloureds" had been quickly eroded. Prohibitions were placed on mixed marriages, racial classification was enforced with the Population Registration Act, and the Separate Registration of Voters Bill denied parliamentary representation to all but whites. In 1959 the Extension of University Education Bill enforced apartheid at universities and schools. Nortje, a promising high-school student, was forced to attend the segregated Belleville College of the Western Cape, where he was awarded a B.A. in 1963. His dissatisfaction is evident in certain anonymous articles that criticize apartheid education. Significantly, through fear or sheer hesitancy, he refrained from claiming affiliation with any political group.

Nortje's university training was important, for it fed his academic interest in aesthetic theory and introduced him to a range of established poets. His poetic output increased during this period, and he received his first serious recognition in the form of the Mbari Poetry Prize for 1962 from Ibadan University. His expanding circle of friends included influential South African writers such as Richard Rive and Athol Fugard.

Two more somber trends began to emerge in his poetry written during his first years at Belleville. First, the theme of self-exploration started to be

AWAY SO FAR INDEED

Away so far indeed my love may never
grow actual in your home despite that need:
the waiting numbs the heart with winter wishes,
the sea between could render me its eunuch.

Tenderness keeps, & now that knowledge deepens,
through absence you are grown so dear & real.
The dross of thought sheds snow leaves from dim regions,
like presences in air, it's what you breathe.

When is your arrival? You arrange your hair
in distant places, silent to surprise me,
while I climb island paths to clearer prospects:
without your nearness worlds withold their treasures.

Keen edge of winter cleans the flesh like truth,
air with cold purity becomes your agent.
My hands bleed for your limbs, land of my own,
& fingers keen for warmth along your cheek.

With dusk descends the wilderness of dreams
in your quite usual beauty finding rare virtues.
Your moon's gift is to show my destiny,
So I shall hold you safe to man's dumb purpose.
for to some purpose will we seed the dark.

K. Oxford 1966

THIRD PERSON

He asks what tree this is what tree
So trim & slender with its various golds,
its amber fading from the eyes but then
a thrush is delivered out of the leaves.

The mint of autumn prints the changing tones
on silver ash & birch, the crisp notes spin
in showering moments when the wind
is air which melancholy stirs to motion.

No grey abstraction the the sky which keeps
the laws of the mute transfiguring waters.
Under the shifting mists he links
his words like pearls about your features.

Drafts for two of the poems Nortje wrote while a student at Oxford (Melville J. Herskovits Library of African Studies,
Northwestern University Library)

muted by images of alcoholic depression, as in "Hangover" (in *Dead Roots*):

In case of foul play, imprisonment, death
by drinking (identity is
268430: KLEURLING
Pretoria register, male 1960)
inform Mrs Halford, Kromboom Road, Crawford[.]

In a manner reminiscent of the later Soweto poets, Nortje experienced the tyranny of apartheid legislation as a form of identity crisis; he was reduced to the ciphers and categories imposed by a racist bureaucracy and stamped a *kleurling* (Afrikaans for "coloured"). Second, his independent spirit came into conflict, perhaps for the first time, with those who wished him to apply his talents directly to the overthrow of apartheid. As one anonymous critic remarked, "If only his enormous talent could have been harnessed to a cutting edge of political understanding, what a weapon he might have wielded!" (*Educational Journal*, June 1974).

Perhaps the most haunting and pervasive theme in Nortje's poetry from 1963 to 1965, when he left South Africa, is that of silence. "The long silence," he says in a poem of the same name (in *Dead Roots*), "speaks / of death and removals. . . . / I have seen men with haunting voices / turned into ghosts by a piece of white paper / as if their eloquence had been black magic." Thronging through this poetry, including the verse written soon after his arrival in London, are characters who are refugees, exiles, and detainees, men like Brutus and Nelson Mandela, whom Nortje later referred to as "the dark princes." More and more of South Africa's most talented artists and political leaders were disappearing into the void of prison and exile.

Nortje himself left South Africa for England in late 1965, after teaching for two years at South End High School in Port Elizabeth. He enrolled to study for a B.A. at Oxford on a scholarship arranged by the National Union of South African Students and the undergraduates of Jesus College, Oxford. His decision to leave South Africa was a direct response to repressive conditions that stunted his artistic and political development. Yet, even at the moment of leaving, he showed a sense of tremendous poignancy in his verse; in "Song for a Passport" (in *Dead Roots*), for instance, he comments on his difficulty in acquiring travel documents: "Who loves me so much not to let me go. . . ?" In "Transition" (also in *Dead Roots*) there is the following wistful remark: "For your success, black residue, / I bear desire still, night thing!" This last image is a characteristic one, for many of the voices of black opposition

seem distanced and diminished in his early verse. Under a system of racial capitalism, where economic inequality is the norm, those who suffer often seem reduced to a lower but resilient form of life, and this concept is a recurrent theme in his poetry between 1964 and 1966. Yet in references to blacks as "bacteria," "residue," and "autotoxins," Nortje makes it clear that, though life for the poor has sunk to its lowest ebb, the potential for subversive action still remains.

When Nortje left for England, he became part of a community of exiled writers that included legendary figures such as Brutus, Bloke Modisane, Es'kia Mphahlele, Alex La Guma, Can Themba, and Lewis Nkosi. As many critics have remarked, their leaving brought to an end a short-lived literary renaissance, which flowered in South Africa in the 1950s and 1960s. Harsh legislative measures had also brought this blossoming of talent to an abrupt end. The Sharpeville massacre and subsequent bannings of the Pan Africanist Congress and African National Congress changed the face of black protest in South Africa, sending it underground until the fiery years of 1976 and 1977. The lot of the writer was a particularly unhappy one, for the Publications and Entertainment Act of 1963 instituted the official government censorship policy, and some estimates suggest that by March 1971 over fifteen thousand books had been banned.

For writers such as Nortje the decision to leave was by no means easily made. But the choice was governed by the hope that being overseas would bring new insights and a critical, objective perspective on the troubled country of one's birth. Once in London, Nortje, a colonial immigrant, reveled in the English way of life that he had known vicariously through literature and postcards: red double-decker buses, for example, are described by him in a poem as "gentle monsters." The vastly different environment seemed to offer new possibilities for verse, and he rejoiced in the paradox that here, on an island, one seemed to have more freedom than in the open reaches of South Africa, as he indicates in "Cosmos in London" (in *Dead Roots*):

It seems at times as if I am
this island's lover, and can sing her soul,
away from the stuporing wilderness where
I wanted the wind to terrify the leaves.

In the first year of his exile Nortje felt that he had achieved a more objective perspective on South Africa. Most dominant in his clearing vision of the past is the use of the color gold and the image of the sun whenever he refers to the South African context. He had turned his back on the "opulent squalor of too much sunshine," a world where "the laager / masters recline in a gold inertia" ("Autopsy," in *Dead Roots*). Looking back on South Africa was for him like looking back through time, to a point where actions were performed with absurd slowness. In his poetry the sun's heat becomes a metaphor for the inability of the individual to act, and the "gold" or "blonde" masters of apartheid seem satiated with greed. Exile, in other words, enables one to have a critical distance. In his later writing, however, as Nortje increasingly felt the alienating effects of exile, the South African sun becomes an agent of macabre change. In "Waiting" (in *Dead Roots*) South African poets are described as speaking "through the strangled throat of multi-humanity, / bruised like a python in the maggot fattening sun."

Though Nortje felt, in 1966, that he had managed to put a critical distance between himself and South Africa, he soon began to see that writing in a foreign country is never merely an extension (though in a freer context) of writing at home. For this reason, perhaps, he used his time at Oxford to develop an individual theory of art's "objectivity." Much of what Nortje wrote on the theme of objectivity was influenced by his reading of modernists such as Ezra Pound and T. S. Eliot and was exaggerated by the New Criticism he absorbed at Belleville College. Moreover he soon became interested in the 1960s counterculture and its heroes, and popular versions of Zen Buddhism no doubt added to his sense that art must be distanced. He was also particularly taken by the standards of detachment and the bias against figurative language to be found in Alain Robbe-Grillet's *Pour un nouveau roman* (1963; translated as *For a New Novel*, 1966).

Nortje's statements about objectivity were, of course, also influenced by his need to distance himself from South Africa. His comments on aesthetic theory show certain contradictions: how can one espouse an objective theory of art without diminishing the ability of the artist to act as the subject of his own work? In short, it seems absurd to withdraw from a context where one's writing seems to be curtailed, only to erect a theory that deliberately restricts the freedom of the poet to appear as a shaping force in his work. During late 1966 all of his thoughts on the role of art were subject to the same tensions that can be found in his view of exile.

In 1966 and 1967 Nortje explored with growing urgency the relationship between exile and literary production. There is an increasing sense, in his poetry and journal writings, that exile may sever

the poet's ties with the country that first inspired him. Furthermore he discovered that it was difficult to communicate the subtle horror of apartheid to an audience that had no firsthand experience of it. Living in exile means that one has to balance one's present circumstances against insistent memories of the past. In some of his poems this balance produces a strained metaphoric relationship between foreign and familiar settings, as in the poem "In Exile," from "Lonely Against the Light":

Leaves and transient
streetscape conjure up that southern

blue sky and wind-beautiful
day, creating paradise.
Otherwise:
the soul decays in exile.

Without the direct inspiration of the southern arena, with only memory guiding it, the "soul" of poetry seems to wither and die. Winter in Oxford caused him to be "forced upon austerities," and "the soul / glimmers feebly in its bed of pork."

In his two years at Oxford, Nortje had gathered around him a small group of friends and admirers, perhaps the one effective buffer against his feeling of alienation from South Africa. However, the political and aesthetic contradictions of exile were matched, in spirit, by extreme psychological torment. In late 1966 Nortje weathered a time of suicidal bleakness while on the brink of a nervous breakdown. The period is best summed up by the following stanza from "The Near-mad" (in *Dead Roots*):

Midnight over the phosphorescent sea.
Back at the hotel hard bodies bob on the dance floor.
You lie like an assassin in wait for the moon:
but your jugular swells, your wrist can stain razors.

There is no question that this poem reflects a terrifying period of Nortje's life, but it is also an elaboration of the Baudelairean posture – the flaneur in the city – of which Nortje was so fond.

The poems written shortly before Nortje's departure for Canada in 1967 are among the most interesting of his career. In works such as "To John, Paul, George and Ringo" and "Discopoem" (both in *Dead Roots*) it is possible to see the depth of his identification with the youth culture of the 1960s. "Message from an LSD Eater" (also in *Dead Roots*), though an extremely uneven work, records his increasingly frequent experimentation with hallucinogenic drugs, and his journal for this period makes sporadic reference to Aldous Huxley, William Blake, and other heroes of the counterculture. Always, though, there is the crushing return to self that follows his alcohol- or drug-induced experience: "I am unsettled by a ghostly snore / being buried in mud, life-locked."

There is, however, a countervailing tendency in the last poems he wrote before his British Columbia experiences. In "Night Ferry" (in *Dead Roots*) a theme appears that was to become greatly significant in his last poems:

> Origins – they are dim in time, colossally
> locked in the terrible mountain, buried in seaslime,
> or vapourized, being volatile. What purpose
> has the traveller now, whose connection is cut
> with the whale, the wolf or the albatross?

It is no longer the poet's individual identity that is held up for scrutiny or demolition; rather, it is the individual in relation to a mythic past, a political unconscious. The same theme is sounded in "Waiting" but is linked to a forgotten age of South African poetry, including "all the dead poets who sang of spring's / miraculous recrudescence in the sandscapes of Karoo."

Despite periods of trial and suffering, Nortje enjoyed a growing reputation as a poet while in England. His sense of audience had matured, and he was able to elicit the help of able and sensitive friends to act as editors. When he left for British Columbia to take a teaching position in the town of Hope, he left behind a community that was extremely important for the development of his artistic and political vision. The move to Canada produced some of his most epic and haunting verse, with a breadth of vision and political understanding that had been lacking before. But silence, too, seemed to surround him once again, as seen in "Waiting":

> It is not cosmic immensity or catastrophe
> that terrifies me:
> it is solitude that mutilates,
> the night bulb that reveals ash on my sleeve.

Nortje had spoken of moving to Canada even before leaving South Africa in 1965. James Davidson, a former headmaster of his, eventually sponsored his immigration, and Nortje found a teaching position at Hope, near Vancouver. The two years in British Columbia were characterized by periods of severe depression, exacerbated by recurrent drinking bouts and frequent recourse to barbiturates and amphetamines in a desperate effort to control his

Dust jacket for the first collection of Nortje's poetry, posthumously published in 1973

wildly oscillating emotions. The lifeline of memory, too, seemed less and less secure. From the evidence of his poems alone, it would be possible to chart a cycle of disillusionment during this period. Taking all of the evidence of his letters and journals into account, however, one sees that living in North America at least enabled Nortje to broaden considerably his understanding of oppression in South Africa, linking it to his understanding of capitalism and commodity fetishism. Throughout the journal of his period in British Columbia are references to consumer insanity: "Wheels of profit revolve – turn, turn, turn, – get back. Spinning satanically in Blake fashion. The dollar axis." There is also a constant, reiterative cry of outrage at American involvement in Vietnam and Cambodia, culminating in an imaginary monologue of a war correspondent.

In Canada, Nortje began to talk and write self-consciously of a mass of people there who were divided along the lines of class. A sprawling middle class, espousing "puritan virtues that never mature," seemed hostile to his art and blind to the startling beauty of their own natural landscape: "poetry bleeds where summer / shoots sapphire through the trunks of noon." Nevertheless, though his time in Canada was lonely and difficult, Nortje managed to achieve a savage kind of resolution in his poems written in 1969. During the last two years of his life the old wish for critical objectivity was replaced by an urge to universalize his situation through metaphor and reappraise the past in mythic terms.

Throughout his life Nortje displayed an ambivalence toward the "coloured" identity that had been foisted on him in racist South Africa. For most of his life it was his habit to sign his poems with the initials "KAN" (he was baptized Kenneth Arthur Nortje), but this signature is also a revealing joke, for the word *kan* in Afrikaans means "can," as in "I can." But his humor and optimism came to an end in Canada. Nortje also returned to the question of his mixed origins. He traced in himself a mixture of Khoikhoi and Jewish blood, and then, instead of using the images of self-loathing as in some of his earlier verse, he wrote in the persona of a modern Odysseus, a cast-out wanderer. The persona in his later Canada poems is also, for the first time, a representative black artist, constantly harking back to an original colonial invasion, as in these lines:

> What do you know
> of my exodus from Kalahari, drinking from a gourd
> eating thin lizards, with the riverbed dry
> . . . .
> & the blond invaders coming on horseback[?]

The developing sense of historical continuity that is present in Nortje's later poetry is in part due to the influence of "Black Consciousness" theory and a feeling of shared suffering with black American writers. It is a perception of communal exile similar to the one Nkosi records in *The Transplanted Heart* (1975). In a sense Nortje and other exiles were ahead of their time in taking inspiration from such a theory. Even though an interest in negritude, as well as in African nationalism, was present in South Africa from an early period, it was only in the mid 1970s that black-consciousness movements came into their own in South Africa.

After two dismal years in British Columbia, Nortje took a teaching position in Toronto. In January 1970 he was forced to take sick leave; in retrospect, it is clear that he was once again on the brink of a nervous breakdown, and his alcohol and drug abuse had increased alarmingly. He was nursed back to relative health by a friend, Mrs. Olga Reed, a Toronto schoolteacher, and he recovered enough to go on a short holiday to England. (The visit is re-

corded in "Return to the City of the Heart," in *Dead Roots*.) After returning to Toronto, once again to the care of Reed, he entered one of the most productive periods of his life, writing poems such as "Nightfall," "Poem in Toronto," "Notes from the Middle of the Night," "Poem: South African," and "Native's Letter" (all in *Dead Roots*). The last is one of Nortje's greatest accomplishments, and it subjects the question of exile to intense scrutiny. The persona is a poet in exile, the bearer of "memories apocryphal / of Tshaka, Hendrik, Witbooi, Adam Kok," the unsung heroes of South Africa's repressed history. In other words, Nortje identifies strongly with the oral tradition in South African poetry, a tradition in sharp opposition to official history, and the poem concludes with a call to future generations:

> let no amnesia
> attack at fire hour:
> for some of us must storm the castles
> some define the happening.

For these comments, more than any others, Nortje has been attacked. To some, these concluding lines epitomize Nortje's lack of political commitment and his intellectual remove.

In July 1970 Nortje returned to England to earn a B.Phil. degree at Oxford. A series of dark sonnets record this period, and in poems such as "Nasser Is Dead" (in *Dead Roots*) Nortje continues his generalizing tendency, seeing world history as the history of exile and oppression. Until recently it was widely assumed that Nortje's return to London began a cycle of despair, culminating in his death in late 1970. Hedy Davis and others have argued against this interpretation, however. Perhaps Nortje's best-known poem, "All Hungers Pass Away," can be seen as closely allied to the tense but balanced examination of exile in his later Canada poems. Yet the sense of his recovery "from the wasted years" is still undermined by the final image:

> Face-down
> I lie, thin arms folded, half-aware
> of skin that tightens over pelvis.
> Pathetic, this, the dark posture.

The "dark posture" is as much a pun on the condition of black exiles as it is a reference to the final posture of death. Although the poem expresses a mature vision, many of the tensions that characterize Nortje's early work are still apparent.

Despite claims to the contrary, "All Hungers

Pass Away" is not the last poem Nortje wrote; at least three later pieces exist in manuscript form. But the work does seem to prepare readers for the events that were to follow. Nortje was under some pressure from antiapartheid organizations to read at Human Rights Day meetings in December 1970, but there is little evidence to suggest that Nortje felt harassed by their insistent requests. He was last seen alive on 8 December, and a friend, Donald Arthur, found Nortje dead in his rooms three days later. An autopsy revealed the presence of twenty-five barbiturate tablets in his stomach, yet at the inquest the coroner returned an open verdict.

The shock of Nortje's death still lingers among some critics and admirers. However, there is a new sense of urgency governing academic research into his work, and considerable energy has been expended on gathering manuscripts and dating his published work. Though the reason for his death remains a mystery, a rumor that he was about to be deported back to South Africa seems to have been dispelled.

Only by seeing Nortje as a poet deeply concerned with the question of exile itself can one gain valuable insights into the forces that shaped his life and work. Some critics still criticize Nortje for his lack of commitment, but though his political vision is unquestionably naive at times, he moved toward a comprehensive understanding of oppression and racism. The liberatory wave of protest that arose in South Africa in 1976 would have had much to offer Arthur Nortje. Since then "coloured" communities that had experienced nagging sectarian doubts during Nortje's day were bound closer together in their opposition to apartheid, and a new generation of highly politicized writers arose, including young poets such as Hein Willemse, Chris van Wyk, Donald Parenzee, and Jeremy Cronin. The tragedy is that Nortje did not live to see any of this, nor did he outgrow his reputation as a South African Charles Baudelaire.

Bibliographies:

H. Wooley and S. Williams, *A Bibliography of Kenneth Arthur Nortje, 1942-1970* (Pretoria: UNISA Sanlam Library, 1979);

Williams, H. Colenbrander, and C. Owen, *A Bibliography on Kenneth Arthur Nortje (1942-1970)* (Pretoria: Subject Reference Department, University of South Africa Sanlam Library, 1980).

References:

Jacques Alvarez-Péreyre, *Les Guetteurs de l'aube: poesie et apartheid* (Grenoble, France: Presses Universitaires, 1979), pp. 313-331; translated as *The Poetry of Commitment in South Africa* (London: Heinemann, 1984);

Jacques Berthoud, "Poetry and Exile: The Case of Arthur Nortje," *English in Africa*, 11 (May 1984): 1-14;

Dennis Brutus, "Protest Against Apartheid," in *Protest and Conflict in African Literature*, edited by Cosmo Pieterse and Donald Munro (London: Heinemann, 1969), pp. 99-100;

Michael Chapman, "Arthur Nortje: Poet of Exile," *English in Africa*, 6 (March 1979): 60-71;

Charles Dameron, "Arthur Nortje: Craftsman for His Muse," in *Aspects of South African Literature*, edited by Christopher Heywood (London: Heinemann, 1976), pp. 155-162;

Hedy Davis, "Arthur Nortje: The Wayward Ego," *Bloody Horse*, 3 (January/February 1981): 14-24;

André Lefevere, "Arthur Nortje's Poetry of Exile," *Restant*, 8, no. 2 (1980): 39-45;

Raymond Leitch, "Nortje: Poet at Work," *African Literature Today*, 10 (1979): 224-230;

Gessler Moses Nkondo, "Arthur Nortje's Double Self," *Africana Journal*, 12, no. 2 (1981): 105-121;

Nkondo, "Arthur Nortje's Microscopic Eye and Literal Imagination," *ACLALS Bulletin*, 6 (November 1982): 89-99;

Cosmo Pieterse and Dennis Duerden, eds., "Dennis Brutus," in *African Writers Talking* (New York: Africana, 1972), pp. 60-61.

Papers:

No single collection of Nortje's manuscripts exists, and controversy surrounds the private ownership of his papers. By far the most significant collection of his journals, letters, and personal documents is at the National English Literary Museum in Grahamstown, South Africa. (Authorized photocopies of much of this material are available in the Africana Library at Northwestern University, Evanston, Illinois.)

Flora Nwapa

(13 January 1931 –)

Gay Wilentz
East Carolina University

BOOKS: *Efuru* (London & Ibadan: Heinemann, 1966);

Idu (London: Heinemann, 1970);

This Is Lagos, and Other Stories (Enugu, Nigeria: Nwankwo-Ifejika, 1971);

Emeka – Driver's Guard (London: University of London Press, 1972);

Never Again (Enugu, Nigeria: Nwamife, 1975; Trenton, N.J.: Africa World, 1992);

Mammy Water (Enugu, Nigeria: Nwapa, 1979);

Wives at War, and Other Stories (Ogui & Enugu, Nigeria: Tana, 1980; Trenton, N.J.: Africa World, 1992);

The Adventures of Deke (Enugu, Nigeria: Tana, 1980);

Journey to Space (Enugu, Nigeria: Nwapa, 1980);

The Miracle Kittens (Enugu, Nigeria: Tana, 1980);

One Is Enough (Enugu, Nigeria: Tana, 1981; Trenton, N.J.: Africa World, 1992);

Women Are Different (Enugu, Nigeria: Tana, 1986; Trenton, N.J.: Africa World, 1992);

Cassava Song and Rice Song (Enugu, Nigeria: Tana, 1986).

Flora Nwapa

Flora Nwapa, a novelist, publisher, short-story writer, and author of children's books, is best known as the first female novelist in Nigeria and the first African woman to write and publish a novel in English (*Efuru*, 1966). Although early critics of African literature did not recognize the significance of her work, Nwapa is now widely praised for her ability to adapt the English language to capture the flavor of the Igbo idiom. Nwapa offers to readers a fresh perspective on traditional West African culture and modern Nigeria by exploring a woman's point of view; furthermore, her use of the oral tradition and the folk language of village women reflects a commitment to create literature from those sources.

Nwapa, the eldest of six children, was born in Oguta, in eastern Nigeria, the area in which most of her fiction is set. As a child she was surrounded by women who told tales and sang songs, and she freely admits that these women, including her mother, have informed her art. This influence is evident in all of Nwapa's work, which has been summarized by critic Prema Nandakumar as "an expansion of an African tale." Nwapa left Oguta to finish her schooling, first in the coastal town of Port Harcourt and later in Lagos. In 1957, after receiving her B.A. from the University of Ibadan, she went to Edinburgh University in Scotland for her diploma in education, which she earned in 1958. After her return to Nigeria she served as an education officer in

178

Calabar and began teaching English and geography in eastern Nigeria. She is married to Gogo Nwakuche, an industrialist.

All Nwapa's fiction for adults centers on the role of women in Nigerian society, whether urban or rural. Her earliest works are based in the rural village of her childhood, but later works have branched out into the hectic world of Lagos. Nwapa's concern for a woman's rights and position in Nigerian society is apparent in her comments on her reasons for writing (in an interview with Gay Wilentz): "Flora Nwapa writes stories about women because these stories are familiar to her. . . . If I'm trying to prove something, it is that women are first and foremost human beings!" Nwapa views women dialectically in both traditional and modern society. On the one hand they are powerful figures in traditional culture, economically secure and socially vibrant; yet on the other they are bound to a system of male dominance that limits their choices. In facing this dilemma, Nwapa's women confront both pre- and postcolonial Nigeria in their search for self-determination within the confines of their culture.

Nwapa's attention to women's lives, particularly in the villages, gives her writing an oral quality in which the voices of women define the pattern and structure of her novels and short stories. Nwapa, like many of her male counterparts, relies heavily on African oral tradition in the form of proverbs, parables, songs, and tales, thus creating a distinctly African quality to her written work in English; moreover her writing reflects the oral tradition in another way. Nwapa's style is rarely descriptive; information is passed on by dialogue. As in an oral culture the characters in her novels and short stories find out important news through contacts at the marketplace, at the farm, in town, or around the family compound. The presence of confiding conversations, sexual banter, child socialization, value judgments, and community palaver marks Nwapa's literature as both "Afrocentric" and women centered.

Efuru, Nwapa's first novel, is set in the village community of Oguta, where Nwapa was raised. Efuru, the protagonist, is a remarkable woman: beautiful, intelligent, and successful as a trader. Yet she has one severe flaw – she cannot have a child. Although she respects her village traditions, she does not always follow them. She chooses both her husbands without familial approval, and both marriages end disastrously. Yet, even though she cannot, as wife and mother, meet the conventional requirements of the society, Efuru is given another option in which to serve her community – as the

worshiper of the lake deity, Uhamiri. As a child Nwapa was fascinated with the stories of Uhamiri, and through this powerful female god Efuru takes her place as a full citizen of her society. Throughout the novel Efuru wrestles with her situation and, by the end, finds a path different from the conventional one for women; yet her choice is within the framework of the community structure. The problem *Efuru* poses is that this option is not open to all women who, for biological or other reasons, do not fit into traditional West African society. Moreover, even though the ending seems a positive one for Efuru, readers are left with a question: "Efuru slept soundly that night. She dreamt of the woman of the lake, her beauty, her long hair and her riches. . . . She gave women beauty and wealth but she had no child. She had never experienced the joy of motherhood. Why then did the women worship her?"

The themes present in *Efuru* surface in the majority of Nwapa's works, as she examines the relationship of the individual – in particular the individual woman – to the community, an important motif in contemporary African literature. Furthermore, she explores the theme of women's central roles in the society, as mothers and educators of children, as well as the painful theme of childlessness. As critic Juliet Okonkwo comments in her 1971 essay "Adam and Eve," "Since the primary purpose in the Igbo marriage is to raise a family," the childless Efuru can neither be what society expects of her nor can she fulfill herself within that context. Even though she is wealthy, beautiful, generous, and kind, the childless Efuru is seen as deficient within her cultural milieu. While there is another option for Efuru, the questions that this issue raises are left open, and Nwapa returns to this theme in her next novel, *Idu* (1970). At the time *Efuru* was published, critical response tended to be negative or indifferent at best. Nwapa was seen as a mediocre copy of Chinua Achebe, or as a writer overly concerned with unimportant things, such as women's lives. Ironically, one of her harshest critics, Eustace Palmer (*African Literature Today*, 1968), addressed in his review one of her greatest strengths as an African writer, although he saw it as a fault: "It is as if Flora Nwapa has set herself the task of writing an East Nigerian epic and wants to ensure, whatever the subject matter, her novel should embody the culture and spirit of her tribe." What Palmer failed to realize, although it has been acknowledged by recent critics of Nwapa, is that her subject matter – the place of women in a communal village society – is inextricable from her representation of her culture and its oral traditions. Today *Efuru* is seen as

Dust jacket for Nwapa's 1966 book, the first novel published in English by an African woman

an early classic of African literature, since it explores a world close to its precolonial roots and women's important roles in that world. In 1983 Adewale Maja-Pearce (writing for the journal *Okike*) called *Efuru* an "indisputable masterpiece . . . which will, I'm sure, come to be recognized as one of the greatest novels of the twentieth century."

As evinced in *Idu*, Nwapa had not in *Efuru* fully addressed all the issues that concerned her. Even with the contradictions implied in *Efuru*, it is not a gravely serious novel; *Idu*, on the other hand, is somber in tone and subject matter. Like the character Efuru, Idu is a successful trader, well thought of in her community, and known for her good deeds, but the protagonists differ in one respect: Idu is happily married to Adiewere. Idu's conflict comes because she, too, is apparently unable to have a child, and her husband refuses to marry a second wife. This conflict between the needs of the individual and the demands of the community is more intense than it is in Nwapa's earlier novel. The somber tone of the novel comes from the personal disasters that take place in an environment of natural calamities and disturbances. These incidents foreshadow the tragic deaths of Idu and Adiewere at the

end of the novel. Idu, who has finally conceived and given birth to a boy, is again pregnant when Adiewere, who has suffered from an unnamed illness throughout the novel, dies. In an ending that has disturbed both readers and critics, Idu wills herself to die, thus ending her own life and that of her unborn child. Idu states: "I am going with my husband. Both of us will go to the land of the dead. It will be even better there." For Idu, death is not the worst alternative; she sees no alternatives in life. Idu's choice is tragic, not only because of the useless death of her unborn child but because she could see no life-giving options. Although *Efuru* has a more positive approach in dealing with the conflicts of women in a male-dominated society, Idu's choice has also been a historical option for women unable to fit into society.

Critical attitudes at the time *Idu* was published appear to have been based on moral outrage: critics did not find the ending acceptable. African critic Adeola James commented in *African Literature Today* (1971) that, although the theme — which questions the dominant attitudes of Africans toward children as the sole basis of marriage — is important, Nwapa leaves the deep moral questions surrounding Idu's actions unanswered. In response to James and others who called the ending of *Idu* fantastic and morally unacceptable, Ernest Emenyonu has stated that their judgments were indicative of a larger problem: how to judge African literature without being limited by Eurocentric prejudices. He calls *Idu* a successful novel in terms of "validity of content as well as appropriateness of form." Nwapa, responding to the critics who questioned the validity of the novel, told Wilentz that the story is "authentic," one Nwapa heard from her mother. Nwapa returns to this issue of childlessness and the demand for children in her third full-length novel, *One Is Enough* (1981).

Both *Efuru* and *Idu* were published in Heinemann's African Writers Series; Nwapa's next book, a collection of short stories, *This Is Lagos* (1971), not only changed the direction of her approach and her material – moving for the most part from the rural village to the urban capital – but it was published by a Nigerian company. Although this situation helped bolster Nigerian readership and the Nigerian publishing industry, it did cut back on critical response to the book. Unfortunately the majority of critical writing on African literature still tends to focus on materials published in the United States or Great Britain. *This Is Lagos* centers primarily on young people from the villages in Nwapa's Igboland who move to Lagos; the last two stories focus on the time just before the Biafran war. The title story is about the breakdown of traditional culture and family values in Lagos. Soha, a quiet girl from a village in eastern Nigeria, goes to live in Lagos with her aunt. Her mother warns her that "Lagos men do not just chase women, they snatch them." Soha, swayed by the materialism of the big city, falls for a young man with a big car and is soon out of her aunt's control, living the high life in Lagos. Other stories revolve around female narrators and are concerned with, for example, an adolescent on "we we" (marijuana), a Lagos man trying unsuccessfully to seduce a woman in the provincial capital (Enugu), and a young woman with two small children who loses her husband and then is accused by his family of stealing his money. The last two stories recount the days after the 1966 military coup, which eventually plunged Nigeria into a devastating civil war.

Like Achebe and other Nigerian writers, Nwapa turned away from writing novels at this time, since the upheaval in their country did not offer the leisure to write at length – only snatches of time for short stories and poetry. The aftermath of this turbulence may also account for the brevity of

her next two adult-oriented works after *This Is Lagos*. The first is a novella about the civil war, *Never Again* (1975), and the second is another collection of short stories, *Wives at War* (1980). Like other Igbos during the war, Nwapa (who was then assistant registrar at the University of Lagos), her husband, and their family were forced to leave Lagos and return to Igboland, in their case Oguta. Reflections on this disruption as well as on the disaster that followed are dispassionately detailed in *Never Again*. Nwapa was well suited to write this novella on the Nigerian civil war, not only because of her past career as a writer and her personal experience during the fighting but also because she was involved in the administration of the former Biafra after the war as a member of the East Central State Executive Council. Her experiences before, throughout, and after the war inform *Never Again*, which is probably more important for its documentation than its literary merit. The novella is a mixture of personal vindication and social commentary, and it clearly reflects Nwapa's antiwar sentiments.

After the release of *Never Again*, Nwapa made a big change in her writing career: she became a publisher. Early in 1975 she had left her position as government commissioner and planned to devote her time to writing, but she was unable to write in the isolation of her house; she needed interaction with others outside the home environment. Moreover she saw her publishing role as enhancing her position as a writer, not limiting it: "I have to be very busy to be able to write," she told Wilentz. "You have greater freedom as writer and publisher in terms of what shape your book will have; you are in control of these things." Still, the relative freedom of publishing her own work (with the Tana Press) as well as others' has posed some problems for Nwapa. First, import-duty and currency changes have often left her newly published books stranded at the docks. Second, a small editorial staff has not had the resources with which to produce error-free publications. Thus the books have typographical mistakes and suffer from the want of careful editing. Finally, because of the lack of communication between Nigeria and other African countries and the West, there has not been much distribution or critical response to her later publications. However, three of her recent works for adults – *Never Again*, *Wives at War*, and *One Is Enough* – and her children's book *Mammy Water* (1979) are now being distributed by Africa World Press in Trenton, New Jersey, which may help to remedy the lack of response.

Wives at War is much more somber and angry than *This Is Lagos*, perhaps because of her experiences during the civil war. Most of the stories in the collection concern war, the aftermath of war, and the social disintegration of the society. Nwapa's emphasis – which differs from that of many male Nigerian writers – is on the role of women during the war, illustrated in the title story, "Wives at War." Moreover Nwapa explores the devastating effect of the war on women's lives. Three other stories deal with women's roles in a changing Nigeria; one, "Man Palaver," foreshadows Nwapa's novel *One Is Enough.*

In *One Is Enough* Nwapa returns to the plight of the childless woman; yet this novel exposes a more radical feminist stance than her earlier ones. The protagonist, Amaku, wants nothing more than to have a home and family, yet she cannot have a child. Ridiculed by her mother-in-law and humiliated by her husband, Obiora, she chooses to leave her matrimonial home to strike out on her own in Lagos. In the capital she quickly becomes rich working as a "cash madam" (a woman who sells building contracts) and becomes sexually involved with a priest. Eventually she becomes pregnant by this priest and gives birth to twins. The priest decides to give up his vocation to marry her, but she refuses him even in opposition to her mother, making it clear that, indeed, one husband is enough: "As a wife, I am never free. I am a shadow of myself. When I rid myself of Obiora, things started working for me. I don't want to go back to my 'wifely' days. No, I am through with husbands."

Unfortunately there has been little critical response to this novel, though it poses some interesting questions about the Nigerian woman and Nigerian society in general. Amaku appears as the independent modern woman who denies community rules and familial advice to choose her own path in life. Yet, as a heroine, Amaku is a strange choice because she is obviously a powerful woman in an illegal trade that is clearly injurious to the economic health of her country. When questioned on this issue, Nwapa told Wilentz that "it is Amaku's story and it is her *own* story. There are many people who do this in our society. If the evils are relevant to the stories I am telling, I will include them; it does not mean that I approve of it." Amaku is attractive to readers because she takes positive steps to liberate herself from the unjust restrictions placed on childless women by this West African society; yet the way she succeeds is based in a system that eventually bankrupted Nigeria. Since she tends to record rather than reform, Nwapa does not make a moral judgment on her character's actions; therefore, the reader may feel uncomfortable with Amaku's tri-

Caricature of Nwapa by Obe Ess

umph. Still, in light of Amaku's position, there are few other options open to her to support herself and preserve her dignity.

Nwapa's reflections on the role of women in both precolonial and modern Nigerian society place women at "the heart of the turmoil of their continent," as Maryse Condé notes. From rural women such as Efuru and Idu to the new urbanites Soha and Amaku, these women make choices about their lives, taking what they can from both the traditional and modern cultures to try to forge a life for themselves and their communities.

Of the early writers in anglophone African literature, Flora Nwapa has been perhaps the least acknowledged; probably this lack of attention has a simple explanation: Nwapa is a woman writing about the lives of women, a situation that makes her even further removed from the attention of the literary mainstream than the already-marginalized male African writers. With new approaches to African literature and with more women critics, Nwapa's works – particularly her first two novels, *Efuru* and *Idu* – are receiving more of the recognition they deserve. She is continuing to work with her publishing house, Tana Press/Flora Nwapa and Company, and her novel *Women Are Different*, which further explores the place of women in Nigerian society, was published in 1986. She has also published *Cassava Song and Rice Song* (1986) and is working on a collection of short stories. For most contemporary critics of African literature, Nwapa's position as a foremother of modern African women's writings is secure, for through the voices of her classic novel *Efuru* and her other works the previously undocumented women storytellers in African villages are heard.

Interviews:

John Agetua, "Flora Nwakuche," *Sunday Observer*, 18 August 1975, p. 6;

Austa Uwechue, "Flora Nwakuche, née Nwapa, a Former Cabinet Minister and One of Africa's Leading Women Writers, Talks to Austa Uwechue," *African Woman*, 10 (1977): 8–10;

Allison Perry, "Meeting Flora Nwapa," *West Africa* (18 June 1984): 1262;

Gay Wilentz, "Interview with Flora Nwapa," *Okike* (forthcoming).

References:

Brenda Berrian, "African Women as Seen in the Works of Flora Nwapa and Ama Ata Aidoo," *CLA Journal*, 25 (March 1982): 331–339;

Maryse Condé, "Three Female Writers in Modern Africa: Flora Nwapa, Ama Ata Aidoo and Grace Ogot," *Présence Africaine*, 82 (1972): 132–143;

Ernest Emenyonu, "Who Does Flora Nwapa Write For?," *African Literature Today*, 7 (1975): 28–33;

Chidi Ikonné, "The Society and Women's Quest for Selfhood in Flora Nwapa's Early Novels," *Kunapipi*, 6, no. 1 (1984): 68–78;

Kenneth Little, *The Sociology of the Urban Woman's Image in African Literature* (London: Macmillan, 1980), pp. 58, 134–135;

Adewale Maja-Pearce, "Flora Nwapa's *Efuru*: A Study in Misplaced Hostility," *World Literature Written in English*, 25 (Spring 1985): 10–15;

Prema Nandakumar, "An Image of African Womanhood: A Study of Flora Nwapa's *Efuru*," *Africa Quarterly*, 11 (1967): 136–146;

Femi Ojo-Ade, "Female Writers, Male Critics," *African Literature Today*, 13 (1983): 158–179;

Ojo-Ade, "Women and the Nigerian Civil War: Buchi Emecheta and Flora Nwapa," *Etudes Germano-Africaines*, 6 (1988): 75–86;

Juliet Okonkwo, "Adam and Eve: Igbo Marriage in the Nigerian Novel," *Conch*, 3 (September 1971): 137–151;

Okonkwo, "The Talented Woman in African Literature," *African Quarterly*, 15 (1975): 35–47;

Harold Scheub, "Two African Women," *Revue des Langues Vivantes*, 37, no. 5 (1971): 545–558;

Mineke Schipper, "Women and Literature in Africa," in *Unheard Words*, edited by Schipper (London: Allison & Busby, 1984), pp. 22–58;

Nancy J. Schmidt, "Children's Books by Well-Known African Authors," *World Literature Written in English*, 18 (April 1979): 114–123;

Gay Wilentz, *Binding Cultures: Black Women Writers in Africa and the Diaspora* (Bloomington & Indianapolis: Indiana University Press, 1992);

Wilentz, "The Individual Voice in the Communal Chorus: The Possibility of Choice in Flora Nwapa's *Efuru*," *ACLALS Bulletin*, 7, no. 4 (1986): 30–36.

Grace Ogot

(15 May 1930 –)

Brenda F. Berrian
University of Pittsburgh

BOOKS: *The Promised Land* (Nairobi: East African Publishing House, 1966);
Land Without Thunder (Nairobi: East African Publishing House, 1968);
The Other Woman: Selected Short Stories (Nairobi: Transafrica, 1976);
The Island of Tears (Nairobi: Uzima, 1980);
The Graduate (Nairobi: Uzima, 1980);
Miaha (Nairobi: Heinemann, 1983); translated as *The Strange Bride* (Nairobi: Heinemann Kenya, 1989).

PLAY PRODUCTIONS: *Simbi Nyaima*, adapted by Asenath B. Odaga, Kisumu, Kenya, Reunion Cultural Group Theatre, 28 December 1982;
In the Beginning, adapted by Michael Ogot, Nairobi, 23 March 1983.

SELECTED PERIODICAL PUBLICATIONS – UNCOLLECTED: "Ward Nine," *Transition*, 3 (March/April 1964): 41–44;
"The African Writer," *East Africa Journal*, 5 (November 1968): 35–37.

Grace Ogot (photograph: The Standard Ltd., Nairobi, Kenya)

Grace Ogot is one of the few well-known Kenyan women writers. She is also the first Kenyan woman to have her fiction published by the East African Publishing House, her first book being the novel *The Promised Land* (1966). Her major contribution to literature has been in the short-story genre; so far she has published three collections: *Land Without Thunder* (1968), *The Other Woman* (1976), and *The Island of Tears* (1980). Speaking of her preference for the short story, Ogot once said (to interviewer Shailaja Ganguly), "A novel keeps you in its grip for a longer time. But remember, while the short story is shorter . . . it is also harder to write."

Ogot is devoted to relating native Luo folktales to the younger generation of Kenyans. Many of her writings are also based on the day-to-day life of people she has known or read about. As a nurse she has been intrigued by the continuing use of tra-

ditional medical cures in Kenya. As Ogot explained to Bernth Lindfors, "Stories of African traditional medicine and of the medicine man against the background of modern science and medicine fascinated me." This fascination led to the writing of *The Promised Land*; the short stories "The Old White Witch," "The Hero," and "Night Sister," in *Land Without*

184

Thunder; and "The Family Doctor" and "The Professor" in *The Other Woman*.

The debate between a medicine man and a Western-trained doctor does not delineate the only theme in *The Promised Land*. The novel is also an exploration of marriage and a woman's duties to her husband. The characters Nyapol and Ochola are based on people known by Ogot in Seme in the Maseno division of Kenya. The plot centers on this poverty-stricken Luo couple, who migrate as farmers from Kenya to Tanzania. Their eventual success provokes the jealousy of the local Tanzanians, and one of the neighbors, a witch doctor, casts a spell on Ochola, resulting in a disfiguring skin disease. Yet Ochola is cured once he agrees to return to Kenya and to abandon the flourishing farm.

Nyapol's conduct as the dutiful wife, who follows and protects her husband, provides the role model for the majority of Ogot's women characters. Nyapol sets the trend for the naive, virginal Elizabeth of "Elizabeth"; the trustful Jedidah of "The Other Woman"; the dying Awino, who cries out for her philandering husband in "Pay Day"; and the mother Oganda, who abandons her daughter to save her marriage in "The Bamboo Hut" (all these stories being in *The Other Woman*). These women sacrifice themselves to maintain family harmony; they rarely oppose their men. Preservation of the family is more important to them, even though it can sometimes involve the subordination of a more intelligent woman to a shallow or tyrannical man. However, the wronged woman always has Ogot's sympathy. Ogot has stated (to Donald Burness) that she "sets out to write as a universal writer for both sexes. But of course one must see one's society as it is."

Grace Emily Akinyi (later Ogot) was born on 15 May 1930 at Butere, near Kisumu, in Central Nyanza, Kenya. Her primary and secondary education was acquired at Maseno Junior School, Ng'iya Girls School, and Butere Girls' High School. As a little girl Ogot's interest in writing took root when she listened enthusiastically to the folktales recited by her paternal grandmother to put her to sleep. A second influence was her father's readings from the Bible and storybooks with translations in Luo. As soon as Ogot mastered the English language, she was inspired by her father, a teacher of religion, to read the Old Testament several times. In her interview with Lindfors she recalled, "With that background, I extremely enjoyed the storytelling lessons at school, which were compulsory. I read any little booklets I could lay a hand on and discovered that some of my own stories compared favorably with those written in the booklets. But although the desire to write was stimulated in me, I never thought of writing my own stories down."

Ogot's active writing career did not begin until she corresponded with her future husband, the well-known historian Bethwell Allan Ogot, while she was training in England to be a nursing sister. Her fiancé (whom she married in 1959) encouraged her to publish some of her writings because her letters addressed to him were so poetic. Ogot first wrote short stories in her maternal language (Luo) and later in the two Kenyan national languages (Kiswahili and English). In 1962, before working as a nursing sister in charge of the Student Health Services at Makerere University College in Uganda (1963–1964), she attended a conference for African writers, held on campus. This literary meeting affected Ogot and resulted in a period of heart searching and self-examination because no book exhibits from East Africa were on display. She, Ngugi wa Thiong'o, and other East Africans took the challenge to be more productive.

During the conference Ogot gave an oral reading of the short story "A Year of Sacrifice," which became her first publication, in 1963 in the journal *Black Orpheus*, and was republished as "The Rain Came" in *Land Without Thunder*. Encouraged by the publication of this story, Ogot decided to show it, along with others, to the European manager of the East African Literature Bureau, who said he "really could not understand how a Christian woman could write such stories, involved with sacrifices, traditional medicines and all, instead of writing about Salvation and Christianity." Not easily deterred, Ogot continued to write, drawing on her training at the Nursing Training Hospital at Mengo, near Kampala, Uganda (1949–1953), and Saint Thomas's Hospital and the British Hospital for Mothers and Babies in London (1955–1958).

Not all of Ogot's fiction takes place in Kenya and is concerned with medical and women's issues. In 1975 she was one of the Kenyan delegates to the United Nations General Assembly. A three-and-a-half-month stay provided material for her story "New York," in *The Island of Tears*. Ancestral linkage between Kenyans and African-Americans is the main theme, with the action centering on a Kenyan ambassador who is directed to the subway station by an African-American. Unfortunately the ambassador is robbed and almost killed by this African-American. However, an unexpected twist occurs when the thief's parents visit the ambassador in the hospital and an offer of a job is extended to their repentant son.

As she writes, Ogot has no consistent predetermined ideology. Asked about her choice of subject material for her stories, she told Lee Nichols, "I just collect them, write them, because they stick in my mind like when you listen to the news." Ogot simply listens, observes, and records. For instance, her past work as a community development officer in Kisumu was utilized in her novella *The Graduate* (1980). The primary theme is that the former European colonial powers are still controlling independent Kenya, particularly because of its out-of-date bureaucratic system, which still employs condescending European staff members. Ogot's premise is that independence neither brings a sudden change of attitudes nor the adoption of Kenyanization.

Ogot is well aware of the social, political, and economic changes taking place around her and continues to retain a respect and a close understanding of the traditional thought of her people. An understanding and appreciation of Luo traditional ways, customs, superstitions, and history are the strengths of Ogot's writing. Her close attention to an accurate recalling of details was exhibited when she changed the title of her story "Ayiembo's Ghost" to "The Ivory Trinket" (in *The Island of Tears*) as soon as she learned that ghosts are not dead in Luo traditions. Another example is the recitation of the Nyamgondho legend in "The Fisherman" (also in *The Island of Tears*).

As for historical facts, Ogot gives thanks to her husband. Marriage to a historian has had its advantages, Ogot admits. As she told Burness, "I would have been a fool if I did not seize the opportunity to use the vast knowledge he has of the background of my people and the way he has assembled everything that has ever been written about them." Her accumulation of historical facts has resulted in the completion of a book of over four hundred pages titled "In the Beginning," based on Luo history from A.D. 97, and the manuscript "Simbi Nyaima," based on the village history of her people. The former work was adapted by Ogot's son, Michael, in 1983 as a play; the latter was also adapted as a play and was translated from Luo into English by Asenath B. Odaga, a Kenyan woman who specializes in writing children's stories. The play *Simbi Nyaima* was produced in 1982.

Miaha (1983; translated as *The Strange Bride*, 1989) is Ogot's interpretation and retelling of a popular Luo myth. Various troubles befall a village after the leader's youngest son marries a beautiful, mysterious woman.

The tragic aspects of history and life fascinate Ogot: six stories in *Land Without Thunder*, three sto-

Cover for Ogot's 1976 collection of short stories, some of which focus on wives who sacrifice autonomy and personal happiness for the sake of family harmony

ries in *The Other Woman*, and two stories in *The Island of Tears* have an element of sadness in them. Ogot's belief is that "There are more tragic incidents in life than there are comic ones" (quoted by Helen Mwanzi). To support her statement, Ogot has written about Tom Mboya's funeral in "The Island of Tears"; the death of Dr. Sserwadda from poliomyelitis in "The Hero"; the mother's desperate attempt to find a doctor to save her child's life in "The Family Doctor"; and the sacrifice of the life of Oganda, a king's daughter, for the survival of the village in "The Rain Came." In short, tragedy cuts across class lines and touches a cross section of Kenyan rural and urban society.

This preoccupation with a sacrificial act that can bring forth tragedy for some people (the king) and happiness for others (the villagers) in "The Rain Came" has been further explored in "The Professor," in *The Other Woman*. By far the most ambitious of Ogot's fiction, "The Professor" shows the negative and positive aspects of the first successful heart transplant in Kenya. From a scientist's perspective, Professor Miyare, the protagonist, needs to be commended for his skills as a surgeon. From a traditional Luo perspective, Miyare has performed an act that borders on witchcraft: he has removed the heart and soul from a deceased person and placed them in a living one. Miyare has also sacrificed precious time he could have spent with his family, parents, and clan in order to do the research necessary to conduct the transplant operation. The ironic twist is that, while Miyare is praised by the president of Kenya, he is labeled as a failure by his own father. According to his father, Miyare has not fulfilled the traditional expectation of constructing a house in the village. Unable to resist his father's and his wife's pleas, Miyare builds a village home against his will. This situation leads to his personal unhappiness. An insecure politician, fearful that Miyare might replace him, arranges an administrative position for him. The once-lively professor, who was content in his laboratory and with his patients, becomes a weary person with bowed shoulders. The burdens of society have overwhelmed another unwilling victim, who, at the end of the story, writes "AFRICA IS DEAD" on his notepad. The professor's ambition to become a doctor abroad has to take second place to the demands of his societal group.

Ogot says she got the idea for this story through contact with devoted scientists and doctors whom society will not leave alone to do their work. Furthermore, as she told Lindfors: "There are often a lot of social demands made on them, and some of these men may wonder whether you can combine being a scientist and being an African, particularly if you want to be a good African."

Earning a living solely from creative writing is unknown for most African writers. There is not a large enough literate audience to sustain them. This fact explains why Ogot has held positions as a broadcaster, scriptwriter, and editor for the BBC Africa Service in London (1959–1961); a broadcaster of a weekly radio magazine in Luo and Kiswahili for the Voice of Kenya in Nairobi; a public-relations officer for the Air India Corporation of East Africa; and the founding chairperson of the Writers' Association of Kenya. Time for writing has been allocated to the evenings, when she returns home from work.

Since 1983 Grace Ogot's attempts to write creatively have been curtailed. President Daniel arap

Moi appointed her a member of parliament (M.P.) in October 1983. In July 1985 Ogot made history when she resigned as a nominated M.P. to contest successfully the Gem constituency by-election. In Kenya this was the first time that a nominated M.P. resigned from parliament to seek an electoral mandate.

When one looks at Grace Ogot's versatile career, one must admire her energy, persistence, and pioneering spirit. She has made her distinctive mark on Kenyan literature and politics. As a writer she probably will be remembered best for her meticulous documentation in fiction of Luo customs, legends, and history.

Interviews:

Bernth Lindfors, "Interview with Grace Ogot," *World Literature Written in English,* 18, no. 1 (1979): 56–58; republished as "Grace Ogot," in his *Mazungumzo: Interviews with East African Writers, Publishers, Editors, and Scholars* (Athens: Ohio University Monographs in International Studies, Africa Series, 1981), pp. 123–133;

Shailaja Ganguly, "An Afternoon with Grace Ogot," *Femina* (8–22 September 1979): 39;

Lee Nichols, "Grace Ogot," in his *Conversations with African Writers* (Washington, D.C.: Voice of America, 1981), pp. 207–216; revised in his *African Writers at the Microphone* (Washington, D.C.: Three Continents, 1984);

Donald Burness, "Grace Ogot," in *Wanasema: Conversations with African Writers* (Athens: Ohio University Monographs in International Studies, Africa Series, 1985), pp. 59–66.

References:

Jacques L. J.-B. Bede, "La femme et le pays natal dans *The Promised Land* de Grace Ogot," in *Mélanges africains,* edited by Thomas Melone (Yaoundé, Cameroon: Editions Pédagogiques Afrique-Contact, n.d.), pp. 209–240;

Maryse Condé, "Three Female Writers in Modern Africa: Flora Nwapa, Ama Ata Aidoo and Grace Ogot," *Présence Africaine,* 82 (1972): 132–143;

Helen Mwanzi, *Notes on Grace Ogot's Land Without Thunder* (Nairobi: Heinemann, 1982);

Oladele Taiwo, *Female Novelists of Modern Africa* (New York: St. Martin's Press, 1985), pp. 128–162.

Gabriel Okara

(24 April 1921 –   )

Bruce King
University of Guelph

BOOKS: *The Voice* (London: Deutsch, 1964; New
York: Africana, 1970);
The Fisherman's Invocation (London: Heinemann,
1978; Benin City, Nigeria: Ethiope, 1979).

OTHER: "African Speech . . . English Words,"
in *African Writers on African Writing*, edited
by G. D. Killam (Evanston, Ill.: Northwestern
University Press, 1973).

SELECTED PERIODICAL PUBLICATIONS –
UNCOLLECTED: "Ogboinba: The Ijaw Creation
Myth," *Black Orpheus*, 2 (January 1958): 9–17;
"The Crooks," *Black Orpheus*, 8 (1960): 6–8;
"Tobi," *Flamingo*, 4, no. 1 (1964): 29–31;
"Poetry and Oral English," *Journal of the Nigerian En-
glish Studies Association*, 8 (May 1976): 41–49.

Gabriel Okara is the first significant English-
language black African poet, the first African poet
to write in a modern style, and the first Nigerian
writer to publish in and join the editorial staff of the
influential literary journal *Black Orpheus* (started in
1957). A Nigerian "Negritudist," he is a link between colonial poetry and the vigorous modernist
writing that began to appear in Nigeria around the
time of national independence in 1960. One of the
founders of modern Nigerian and African literature,
he has also published some short stories, a translation from Ijaw, and *The Voice* (1964), an experimental novel that was one of the more interesting works
to be published during the unusually creative period of the 1960s, when Nigerian literature was
coming into its own, providing creative leadership
for other black African and Third World literatures. If Okara has not published widely, it is partly
because many of his manuscripts were destroyed
during the Nigerian civil war and partly because he
belongs to an earlier generation than such university-educated Nigerian writers as Wole Soyinka and
J. P. Clark, who had the advantages of university
teaching careers and university support for their

*Gabriel Okara (photograph by Afolab Adesanya; Newswatch,
Lagos, Nigeria)*

creative writing. Because of his comparatively small
literary production Okara had not received as much
attention as some of his more well-known compatriots until the publication of his first collection of
verse, *The Fisherman's Invocation* (1978); since then he

has been seen as having a major place among the poets of the African continent.

Born 24 April 1921 in Bumoundi, in southeastern Nigeria, to Prince Sampson G. Okara, a Christian businessman, and Martha Olodiama Okara, Gabriel Imomotimi Gbaingbain Okara first attended local schools and then, from 1935 to 1940, Government College in Umuahia. Because of World War II he transferred to Yaba Higher College, where he passed the Senior Cambridge Examination, specializing in art, which he had studied with the well-known Nigerian sculptor Ben Enwonwu. After being a schoolteacher at the Ladilac Institute in Yaba, Okara tried to join the Royal Air Force, but, unable to become a pilot, he instead joined the British Overseas Airway Corporation auxiliary, traveled to Gambia, was briefly a businessman, and in 1945 became a bookbinder for the Government Press, for which he worked until 1954. He was sent from Lagos to start a branch of the press at Enugu in 1950. During this time he began translating Ijaw poetry and writing talks and plays for broadcasting. In 1953 his poem "Call of the River Nun" won an award at the Nigerian Festival of the Arts. In 1957 some poems of his were published in the first issue of *Black Orpheus*, in which he continued to publish. He was assistant publicity officer in the Ministry of Information from 1955 to 1959, after which he attended Northwestern University, where he studied journalism from 1959 to 1960. Returning to Nigeria, he worked as publicity officer (1960–1962), principal information officer of the Eastern Region Government Information Office in Enugu (1964–1967), and director of the Cultural Affairs Division of the Ministry of Information for Biafra (1967–1969), traveling to the United States in 1969 to speak for the Biafran cause. From 1971 to 1975 he was the general manager of the Rivers State Newspaper and Television Corporation (which he started), and he founded the newspaper *Nigerian Tide* as well as being commissioner for information and broadcasting for the Rivers State. He has also been a writer in residence of the Rivers State Council on Arts and Culture.

Okara's literary work is distinctive in its highly poetic style and his blending of private, public, and religious themes. He is concerned with the relationship of the past to the present and of tradition to modernization. His themes include biculturalism, the alienation of the intellectual from the masses and politicians, political corruption and the effect of materialism on African society, and the problems of an African writer using English. His works are marked by a consciousness of Ijaw traditions, Christianity, and a visionary mysticism close to nineteenth-century romantic pantheism. His verse and prose are symbolic, private, and "Ijawized" in language, Ijaw at times being transliterated by him into English. In his later poetry, written during and after the Nigerian civil war, Okara changes from an allegorical symbolism and an artificially African English style to a more direct, open, and natural manner.

His theory about the nature of African literature is controversial, relevant to his own writing, and apparently has not changed over the years. He came to intellectual maturity during a time when a major problem facing African intellectuals was the cultural schizophrenia of affirming their Africanism through the languages, literary forms, politics, and concepts of European culture; writers were especially concerned with the question of language and literary types, as their works of protest, cultural affirmation, or self-questioning were more likely to be read by foreigners than by their own people, for whom any literature in European languages belonged to an alien culture. Okara believes that a literature must reflect the culture and the way of thought of a country; an African writing in a European language must use it in such as way as to express African ideas, folklore, and philosophy. Okara attempts to get around the alien language in which cultural experience is being communicated by forcing himself to think of his sentences in Ijaw and then to translate them literally into English so that they remain Ijaw in symbolism, syntactical structure, idiom, and reference. In his 1973 essay "African Speech . . . English Words" he says, "I had to study each Ijaw expression I used and to discover the probable situation in which it was used in order to bring out the nearest meaning in English." The results are poetic, densely textured, serious, and sometimes obscure, like many of the symbolist and modernist works of the first half of the twentieth century. The Africanization is paradoxically part of the modernism of his work. Okara is the first Nigerian, and perhaps the first English-language, black African, modernist writer. He early rejected the outdated Victorian styles of the colonial poets and instead brought to Nigerian poetry an infusion of the styles of T. S. Eliot, Dylan Thomas, and Gerard Manley Hopkins. Okara used free verse, abandoned fixed rhyme schemes, and allowed the flow of his thought to determine the shape of the poem.

"The Call of the River Nun" is Okara's earliest surviving poem and, like most of his poetry, is collected in *The Fisherman's Invocation*. The poem was written in Enugu, where he was living in 1950. Surrounded by the local hills, the speaker is nostalgic for the Nun River he knew in his childhood; the river is also a symbol for his personal destiny and his journey through life toward death and God. In this poem Okara has already found one of his major patterns of symbols. Flowing rivers with such accompanying imagery as canoes and sea birds can be found throughout his work, the river representing the continuity of past, present, future, destiny, and the individual's pilgrimage through life.

The religious tone of the poem's conclusion is noticeable in such other early verse by Okara as "Were I to Choose" (written in 1953) and "Spirit of the Word." The former is influenced by Thomas, whose use of symbolic allegories Okara continues to develop in his own manner, while the latter poem brings to mind the seventeenth-century meditative poetry of Henry Vaughan in that the natural world is seen as being more in tune with the divine than humankind is. The conclusion of "Spirit of the Word," however, is reminiscent of some of the black-American-influenced pioneer West African poets who asked whether they could find religious salvation despite having "Singed Hair and Dark Skin." Okara's manner, symbols, and themes were established early. His poem "Once Upon a Time" could be background material for *The Voice*; it is a dramatic monologue in which a father compares the happiness and contentment of the past to the hypocrisy of the modern world; he asks his son to regain such innocence. Okara experiments with language ("officeface, streetface, hostface") and emblematic symbols ("While their ice-block-cold eyes / search behind my shadow"). The early poems show the influence of the Romantic ode in the way they begin with meditation on some object or event, the meditation then leading by a process of association to reveries, philosophical insights, or visionary experiences, which apparently cannot be sustained in this life, as the poems end in uncertainty, often about the speaker's own destiny. Such a structure is infused with late-Victorian solemnity, religiosity, seriousness, and depression in "New Year's Eve Midnight," where instead of renewal "it's shrouded things I see / dimly stride / On heart-canopied paths / to a riverside." Although the many seasonal images in Okara's poems imply life is a cyclical process of birth, growth, harvest, and renewal, the hope is weighed down by a consciousness that an individual journeys toward death. In these poems the future is gloomy, especially in comparison to reveries of childhood.

While his education and career had taken Okara from home and parents into a world of change, desire, deception, and hypocrisy, the individual's journey in his poems is also associated with modernization and Westernization. In "Piano and Drums" native ways are represented by "jungle drums," which are "urgent, raw / like bleeding flesh, speaking of / primal youth and the beginning," whereas the alien piano symbolizes "complex ways / in tear-furrowed concerto; / of far-away lands." The drums bring thoughts not only of exaggerated, romantic, primitive, communal scenes but also of childhood: "at once I'm / in my mother's lap a suckling; / at once I'm walking single paths."

As younger Ibadan writers such as Soyinka, Clark, and Christopher Okigbo rejected the francophonic-negritudist idealization of a supposed innocent, uncorrupted, primitive precolonial Africa, it is sometimes assumed that English-speaking West Africa was untouched by such views; but educated Nigerians were aware of negritude during the 1950s. *Black Orpheus* was at first, with its original German coeditors, an extension of the Paris-based *Présence Africaine* and was aimed at English-speaking West Africa. Just as the negritudists symbolized their longing for tradition and unity of self as a nostalgia for the comforting Mother Africa of their childhood, so Okara's personal unease at separation from his past and family is merged with the disturbing effects of social, cultural, and technological change as a result of education, modernization, and his own experience of the world. Significantly a "wailing piano solo" speaks of complexity, which ends "in the middle of a phrase at daggerpoint."

The way the early 1950s themes of loneliness, nostalgia for home, and a depressed fatalism have evolved into an affirmative negritude can be seen in Okara's poem "You Laughed and Laughed and Laughed." The "You" in the title is the white European who laughs at African culture as primitive and who is identified with ice blocks, motor cars, and frozen emotions, whereas the African, in the tradition of negritudist primitivism, is identified with nature. The surrealism of the penultimate stanza could be that of Léopold Sédar Senghor or Aimé Césaire, as is the claim that Africa will rehumanize the West out of the rigid, mechanical way of life:

> My laughter is the fire
> of the eye of the sky, the fire
> of the earth, the fire of the air,
> the fire of the seas and the
> rivers fishes animals trees
> and it thawed your inside,
> thawed your voice, thawed your
> ears, thawed your eyes and
> thawed your tongue.

"The Mystic Drum," which appears to be concerned with sexual desire as well as evoking the natural world, is both a celebration and rejection of the surrealist mode: "I packed my mystic drum / and turned away; never to beat so loud any more." "The Mystic Drum" is related to two other poems concerning desire for a woman, "Adhiambo" and "To Paveba." In the latter, after "young fingers stir /the fire smoldering in my inside," the poem moves into the surreal ("the eye / of the sky on the back of a fish"), until the speaker remembers "my vow not to let / my fire flame any more," and his fires dwindle to smoldering "beneath the ashes." Probably the outbursts of desire and their repression are related to Okara's personal life, which has included three marriages and divorces. (He has fathered two children.) The mystical streak in Okara's poetry is taken up again in "One Night at Victoria Beach," which also concludes with defeat before the unknown: "I felt my knees touch living sands − / but the rushing wind killed the budding words." "The Snowflakes Sail Gently Down" was written in the United States in 1959, when Okara was studying journalism at Northwestern University and doing field research in the Public Information Department of the Atomic Research Station near Chicago, where he saw snow for the first time. In the poem the speaker falls asleep in a heated room on a snowy day and dreams of tropic Africa. He dreams that colonialism and foreign exploitation will be defeated. The striking but obscure ending may imply the possibility of renewal for the West through accepting African values.

The five-part "Fisherman's Invocation," written in connection with the coming of Nigerian independence, is, as K. E. Senanu and Theophilus Vincent comment, modeled on a traditional ballad performance celebrating an important event, in this case the birth of the nation. Using the situation of two men fishing in a canoe on a river, the poem concerns the relationship of the past to the present and future: "The Front grows from the Back / like buds from a tree stump." One fisherman complains that he no longer can remember his "Back," and he is told to rediscover his origins: "let your eyes be the eyes / of a leopard and stalk the Back," in order to move into the future. Otherwise independence will be stillborn. The negritude and cultural-affirmation themes are put forward in the Ijawized imagery ("teaching hands," "sweet inside") that Okara uses in *The Voice*, which he started writing at about the same time the poem was written, in 1959. "The Fisherman's Invocation" appeared at the end of the negritude movement, which had been marked by

Okara in the 1960s (Transcription Centre Archive, Harry Ransom Humanities Research Center, University of Texas at Austin)

the self-conscious use of surrealist fantasy techniques of romantic, primitive Africa and the claims of African moral superiority over the Westernized world. The creation of independent black African nations ended the phase when the assertion of a cultural past was an analogy to political assertion of the right to self-government. "The Fisherman's Invocation," questioning the nature of the future if unimpregnated with tradition, is a sign that independence and its possible disillusionments would soon be a main theme of African literature.

Although Okara wrote many short stories, including "The Iconoclast," which won first prize in a British Council short-story contest (1954), he has only published two; the others apparently are lost. "The Crooks" (*Black Orpheus*, 1960) might be described as an updated version of a trickster folktale in which cunning is valued more than ethics and in which the deeper cunning of the peasant, or the seemingly innocent man, outwits the self-assured, sophisticated urban confidence man. In the story two dusty, dirty, barefoot travelers, who apparently have arrived from the provinces for the first time in Lagos, the Nigerian capital, are stopped by a well-dressed man who warns them against strangers and invites them to his house. He loses money to them at cards with the intent of robbing them in the morning of their bag, which he believes to contain their savings. But by morning they have disappeared and are on a train back to Enugu laughing at having tricked the trickster out of a night's food, lodgings, and the money won at cards. The bag that supposedly held their savings was filled with stones and old rags to deceive such men, as it had before in other cities: " 'They'll never learn,' said Okonkwo as he wiped his face. 'They are green as green peas, the whole batch of them. See how they left the door only bolted.' " While "The Crooks" is simple, obvious, and crudely structured, it is surprisingly effective, possibly because of its pidgin English and Okara's ability to convey a sense of location and imply the ways of a society.

"Tobi" (*Flamingo*, 1964), Okara's other published story, is a curious and less successful trickster tale about a guest who steals from his hosts, who in turn ignore his misdeeds: "He's a relative; the only son left of your great-grandfather's slaves and you mustn't do anything to make him feel we know. Only be very careful with your things, that's all." According to the curious psychology of the story, Tobi is an unwelcome guest but is needed to celebrate the harvest season.

The Voice, Okara's only published novel, was begun shortly before Nigerian independence and was seen by him as a struggle between good and evil, as represented by a young intellectual versus the Nigerian politicians who were looking forward to the expected spoils of national independence. The elders in the novel look forward to "the coming thing," over which they slap "their thighs in joy." An early version of the opening chapter was first published in *Black Orpheus* in 1961, and the style, with verbs regularly following the object, is even more based on Ijaw than in the novel, which, despite the controversy over its style, is mostly written in standard English. Okara used as a model the way Amos Tutuola translates directly from Yoruba into English, but in practice Okara found it necessary to be less rigid. As he says in "African Speech . . . English Words," "Some words and expressions are still relevant to the present-day life of the world, while others are rooted in the legends and tales of a far-gone day. Take the expression 'he is timid' for example. The equivalent in Ijaw is 'he has no chest,' or 'he has no shadow.' Now a person without a chest in the physical sense can only mean a human

that does not exist. The idea becomes clearer in the second translation. A person who does not cast a shadow of course does not exist. All this means is that a timid person is not fit to live. Here, perhaps, we are hearing the echoes of the battles in those days when the strong and the brave lived. But is this not true of the world today? . . . What emerges from the examples I have given is that a writer can use the idioms of his own language in a way that is understandable in English. If he uses their English equivalents, he would not be expressing African ideas and thoughts, but English ones."

Around the idea of the alienated, young, educated intellectual opposing the materialism of the elders and the politicians – a theme common in the 1960s in West Africa, as can be seen in Soyinka's *The Interpreters* (1965) and Chinua Achebe's *No Longer at Ease* (1960) and *A Man of the People*, (1966) – other central themes are developed by Okara, including a quest for "it," or the meaning of life; a parallel between the protagonist, Okolo, and Christ; the relationship of the African past to the future; and the individual's conscience versus conformity to the community. Many of the features of *The Voice* are characteristic of the style of early Nigerian literature, including a Nigerianized English and the use of a quest to structure the story.

While the plot has the economy and clear shape of a parable, the rich but open symbolism of *The Voice* shows its links both to Okara's reading of Christian literature and to modernist high culture. Okolo returns to his town after his schooling and finds himself out of step with almost everyone because he is searching for "it," which no longer has "roots." This situation makes him an outsider and disturbs the community. His spiritual concerns challenge the tribal elders' glee at the expected wealth and material goods they will inherit with national independence. In taking over from the white rulers, the politicians have forgotten the teachings of their fathers; by contrast Okolo is, like Christian of John Bunyan's *Pilgrim's Progress* (two volumes, 1678, 1684), someone who has learned from a book that he must give up all and search to be saved. The story is written in such a manner that Okolo, whose name means "the voice" in Ijaw, takes on the symbolic roles of conscience, Messiah, reformer, sacrificial outcast, and quester. When he is first threatened by his townspeople, "Hands clawed at him, a thousand hands, the hands of the world." Although Okolo is portrayed from the first as alone, he acquires a few disciples, including one, at the book's end, who will tell his story and care for his words. The town is Christian ("We are all church people.

We all know God"), but it suffers from old superstitions, from lack of conscience, and from a desire for worldly things.

Although the "it" Okolo seeks is purposely left vague, it seems to cover such significant things as conscience; a personal meaning in life; and perhaps the old Christian sense of vocation, truth, and the gospel: "I am the voice from the locked up insides which the Elders, not wanting the people to hear, want to stop. . . ." In this novel of few actions each confrontation between individuals or between Okolo and a group of people becomes a significant event. Okolo's secondary-school education (which even in the early 1950s would still have been uncommon in Nigeria) is contrasted to the education of Abadi, another young man who has been to foreign countries and holds a Ph.D. Abadi praises the leadership of Chief Izongo and reminds the elders that many of them were "mere fishermen and palm-cutters . . . in the days of the imperialists"; he asks them to "toe the party line" and "support our most honourable leader." When Okolo replies that the politicians and their followers are fighting no one but merely clamoring "to share in the spoils" of independence, it is worth recalling that Okara's father was a prince. As in the writings of Cyprian Ekwensi, Soyinka, and Achebe, there is a distrust of the politicians who gain their support from distributing the spoils of office rather than from the traditional customs of clan and tribe.

Okolo is made to leave the town because he will not do as others do and betray his conscience. He insists on following what he believes to be the timeless, straight ways of the past, whereas "Everybody's inside is now filled with money, cars and concrete houses and money." Just as Okara notes the creation of a new political class coming into being before national independence, so he records, as do the novels of Achebe and Soyinka, the increasing materialism and obsession with Western comforts that result in spiritual corruption and a disregard for the past.

Okolo's trip to Sologa corresponds to the period of exile before return in messianic literature. In Sologa, Okolo finds people who brag of such things as being "a whiteman's cook." The white man's money economy has corrupted people, and money is the only social value. The city of Sologa is not a community but a conglomeration of various tribes and languages: "cars honking, people shouting, people dying, women delivering, beggars begging for alms, people feasting, people crying, people laughing, politicians with grins that do not reach their insides begging for votes, priests building houses, peo-

ple doubting, people marrying, people divorcing, priests turning away worshippers, people hoping, hopes breaking platelike on cement floors." Justice is corrupt, there is tribal favoritism, and the powerful are beyond the law. In contrast to the people of the city who have no sense of purpose and "think nothing," there is the carver, an artist who believes "everything . . . the whiteman's God, the blackman's God. . . . The carver believes and puts even his shadow into creating faces out of wood and his inside is sweeter than sweetness." In Sologa, Okolo also learns that the white men have become corrupted; they tell him that truth and honesty do not exist for the person who wants to get ahead. Okolo, still searching for a purpose, a faith, a belief, realizes that he must return home in search of "it."

Meanwhile in his town some people have been influenced by Okolo's words. They start changing their ways, which threatens Chief Izongo. Part of Okolo's message is to return to the "earth's knowledge which has come down from our ancestors. . . . They are the words of your father's father's father." Eventually Okolo understands that his purpose in life is to plant "it in people's insides by asking if they've got it." In what appears to be a comment on Okara's treatment of "it" in the novel, Okolo says that there is no single meaning to life; each person has his or her own purpose: "Names bring division and divisions, strife. So let it be without a name." The syncretism is African and an adaptation of African beliefs to those of Christianity and Islam; there is an implication (as in Soyinka's works) that life is cyclical and that people will be reborn in different forms. As a cult of Okolo's followers forms, Chief Izongo decides that Okolo must be destroyed and has him tied and set adrift in a canoe floating down a river toward a whirlpool.

The novel shows Okolo's discovery of a need to have a purpose in his life, the beginning of his teaching to others, his expulsion from the village, his trial in the outside world, his discovery of his message, his return, the formation of the cult of his word, and his death. Because of the language and themes, the novel appears to blend Christianity with a negritudist concern to preserve or adapt African traditions in the new materialist society created by European influence on Africa. People and events seem emblematic, symbols of ideas, and much of the book gives the impression of occurring in a dark, shadowy, dimly lit place. As in many epics, the hero begins as an isolated individual but eventually learns that lives interact and that he is a part of society. His "spoken words" enter other people, "remain there and grow."

The language of *The Voice* is the most controversial aspect of the novel. As the Nigerian poet Clark, also an Ijaw, complains in *The Example of Shakespeare* (1970), "With commands and requests like 'Your nonsense words stop,' Mr. Okara is no doubt trying to recreate the original sentence structure of object-verb, but he has no justification for converting the normal . . . order of straight statements." Clark writes that Okara "has no cause to resort to the biblical verb ending -*eth*, very rare as plural even in Elizabethan usage, and the odd use of both the negative and verb *to be*. The result is not the reproduction of Ijaw rhythms in English, but an artificial stilted tongue, more German than Ijaw. It is a creation completely devoid of the positive attractions of a living language like pidgin English." While objecting to the method, Clark explains some of the words and idiomatic expressions Okara transliterated: "the *it* of the story . . . is the Ijaw *iye*, meaning from the most to the least tangible of things"; "the term *inside* . . . is *biri*, the belly as the seat of human passion and will. . . . Okara's use of the expression 'Your head is not correct' also derives directly from Ijaw idiom and usage." The poetic quality resulting from Okara's use of unusual word order (especially of verbs), repetition of words (especially verbs, adverbs, and adjectives), parallel constructions, recurring symbols, and similes and metaphors based on nature (such as fish, water, river, and fire) has been discussed by J. Shiarella, while Donald Burness also notes syntactic inversions, uses of nouns as modifiers, simultaneous usage of an adjective and a noun that are the same word, and use of a standard adjective as a qualifying adverb (as in "black black" or "cold cold"). Other language features include unusual comparative forms, many proverbs, and the rephrasing of English sayings so that they appear Ijaw – instead of "out of sight, out of mind," Okara writes, "When I do not see you, you will not be in my inside." In general, critics assume that Ijaw ways of thinking are accurately reflected in Okara's text. Burness feels that, whereas English speakers choose from a rich store of adverbs, in Ijaw emphasis is achieved by such simple repetitions as "black black" or "slowly, slowly." Adrian A. Roscoe claims Okara's style reflects characteristics of Ijaw thinking with a limited number of antonymic pairings: " 'Straight' and 'crooked' dispose of every variety of truth and untruth," while " 'sweet' and 'sour' represent all shades of happiness or misery."

After being principal information officer of the Eastern Region Government Information Office in Enugu during the mid 1960s, Okara worked during the civil war as director of the Cultural Affairs Division of the Ministry of Information for Biafra. In contrast to the introvertedness of his earlier poetry, the poems in *The Fisherman's Invocation* written during and after the Nigerian civil war have a new urgency and directness of experience. In the twelve lines of "Moon in the Bucket," the word *look* occurs five times; the innocence and peace of the moon are contrasted to those people in the Nigerian Federal Republic "who shout across the wall / with a million hates." In "Suddenly the Air Cracks" the repeated use of *suddenly* and *cracks,* and such similar-sounding words as *striking* and *cracking,* suggests the unexpectedness, drama, and danger of an air raid by the Nigerians on a Biafran village, as the airplanes dive, fire at the people, drop bombs, and are driven out by antiaircraft fire. Afterward children running with their arms stretched out play at being diving jets, while bodies are stacked in the morgue.

While poems treating the contrasts of war and the drama of a bombing raid have a new concreteness, in many of Okara's poems of the Biafran period there is too much sentiment, thought, and rhetoric. "Cross on the Moon" begins with the complex imagery he often uses in which one association leads to another: the dew on the leaves of trees reflects the moonlight on hedges from which one can hear crickets and see fireflies, while overhead an airplane waits its turn to bring in relief supplies to "whimpering children / on the backs of fearless mothers." The airplanes are "A testimony of Man's humanity." While such sentiments are to be expected in the situation, they do not necessarily make for good poetry. Some poems, such as "Expendable Name," appear to be written directly as appeals to Roman Catholics abroad for aid to Biafra. At his best in the early poems Okara is a symbolist, most effective when treating a theme by metaphor; in the war poems imagistic descriptions too often become prose statements. In "Cancerous Growth," "Today's wanton massacre / burns up tender winds / and from the ashes / hate is growing." These poems do show Okara's control of rhetorical forms. Kenneth L. Goodwin calls "Expendable Name" "a powerful but unbitter reproach to the comfortable warmongers" and finds "Rain Lullaby" "an unsentimental poem" that condemns the war fought by day in contrast to the nighttime mercy flights to Biafra.

Many of the wartime and more-recent poems use traditional Christian imagery and associations. "Come, Come and Listen" loosely imitates Christ's Good Friday reproaches on the Cross to those who pass and is perhaps related to George Herbert's

Cyprian Ekwensi, Okara, and John Updike at the University of Lagos on 26 January 1973 for a symposium, "The Novel and Reality in Africa and America" (photograph by Bernth Lindfors)

well-known "The Sacrifice." Besides pleading with Nigerians to think of the mothers and children they are killing, the speaker in the final stanza of "Come, Come and Listen" appears to ask why the God brought by the Christians has deserted him. In "Christmas 1971," "love and peace" are sacrificial Christlike figures "caricatured, maligned / taunted and rejected." In many of the late war poems there is a feeling of betrayal because of the bombings and deaths of civilians, the wall created between the Federal Republic and Biafra, the unwillingness of the leaders to compromise and seek peace, and the attitudes of those who profit from the war. Christian images are used in these disillusioned, often satiric poems, forming a pattern of irony. "The Revolt of the Gods," a long poem from 1969, begins with a debate between the gods during which readers learn that humans make and kill gods by their need, love, and hatred. The scene next shifts to earth, where two men mock the idea of divine

power, while another seemingly believes in the Judaic god, and a fourth is a Christian doomsayer prophesying the end of the earth and the coming last days. The poem concludes with the old gods dying with the apparent triumph of the scientific and skeptical, although they will eventually return for another cycle of belief and disbelief.

The problem of faith haunts Okara's later poems. In "The Glowering Rat," written in Port Harcourt in 1970, shortly after the war, the spiritual life – its comforts and sense of being at ease – is dispossessed by a symbolic rat "whetted on yesteryears." As Susan Beckmann says, the poem is a "mindscape" of someone returning to a war-scarred city and stumbling physically over shell craters, while his spirit, attempting to return to its home in faith, stumbles mentally over the emptiness left within by the war experience.

Although Okara in his later poems does not experiment with language and symbol, he uses syntax in a new way, often delaying or not using punctuation, with the result that stanzas, as in "Suddenly the Air Cracks," or entire poems, such as "Cancerous Growth," "Freedom Day," "Rain Lullaby," and "The Dead a Spirit Demands," flow on continuously and gain greater force for the momentary suspensions caused by line endings, dashes, or a few capital letters at the start of a line. In place of the earlier concentration on image and song, the later poems are whiplike, depending on energy, repetitions, and ideas for their force. Often they project the state of the poet's psyche on the external world, as in "Flying Over the Sahara," where "Here all is dead." The expected picture of a lost man's dying search for water is transferred to the water itself, "sucked away by craving sands," like the mind eternally searching for "fulfillment." The speaker sees smoke from "oil in flames," an example of the human mind creating "to build / and destroy, to nurture life and kill." The Nigerian civil war was fought partly because of rights to the oil in Okara's native delta area.

After the defeat of Biafra, Okara founded and wrote for a newspaper, the *Nigerian Tide*, and started the Rivers State Newspaper and Television Corporation, of which he was general manager until 1975. His manuscripts containing all his unpublished poems were destroyed during the chaos of war, and *The Fisherman's Invocation* includes mostly previously published poems. In his interview with Bernth Lindfors, Okara said that since the end of the Nigerian civil war he no longer could write, but *The Fisherman's Invocation* has a few poems from 1976, including "To a Star" and "Celestial Song," which refer to a renewal of poetic, and perhaps amorous, energies. In these poems Okara alludes to the symbolism of both his earlier and his wartime poems, with the result that his work takes on self-referential, autobiographical, and myth-making qualities, with each poem being part of a continuing story. Unfortunately the diction is sometimes Victorian or late Romantic: "O let not this be as those / which lie scotched like rose / trampled by passing years." While it is generally felt that Okara's best verse was written during the late 1950s, when he was both a modernist and negritudist poet, some poems of the Biafran period seem more powerful now than when they first were published.

Okara's reputation has been influenced by the small quantity of his publications and by changing fashions in the criticism of African literature. As one of the first modern Nigerian poets, he has poems in all the influential anthologies of African and Commonwealth verse published during the 1960s; there was, however, little criticism of African poetry written at that time, and much of the criticism was introductory or polemical. Critics have remarked on Okara's inwardness and mysticism. As Clark says, "This concern with the self, the soul, runs through all his work." In regard to Okara's primitivism and romantic images of jungle drums, innocent virgins, mystic rhythms, and dark flesh, Clark feels that Okara showed characteristics of the early West African poets, and Clark places Okara's verse midway between the large public statements and public oratory of the pioneer poets and the more concise, imagistic, purer poetry of Okigbo and Soyinka.

Others felt that, despite the mysticism and experimentalism, Okara aimed to be a poet of the African continent. Noting his intensity of mood, richness of soul, and sense of an inner life, Roscoe claims Okara's *I* signifies the communal *we*: "He is Nigeria's best example of the poet singing in solitude yet singing for his fellow men." A similar line is taken by P. N. Njoroge, who calls Okara one of Africa's greatest poets and the embodiment of the continent's experiences; the poet in expressing his soul expresses the soul of society.

Although hailed as more successful as a poet than a novelist, Okara received little sustained critical attention as a poet until the appearance of *The Fisherman's Invocation*, which shared the Commonwealth Poetry Prize with *Ladders of Rain* (1978) by the New Zealander Brian Turner. A revival of interest in Okara's poetry immediately followed, with reviews and articles appearing in literary journals as distant from Nigeria as Canada, Denmark, and India. Bruce King describes Okara as one of the first and best of the African poets, who after being lost is being rediscovered. Beckmann notes that while Okara's work is indispensable to any general anthology of African poetry, the award of the Commonwealth Poetry Prize was an indication that he was at last gaining the wider recognition he deserved. Beckmann and King, like most reviewers, feel that his best poetry preceded the Nigerian civil war. Kirsten Holst Petersen claims that Okara debated the relationship between the past and the present in traditional African imagery rooted in oral literature: "Through this use of imagery . . . he moves effortlessly between private, public and cosmic levels."

Others have commented that Okara's poems share negritudist themes and concerns, including identification with Africa symbolized by the natural world. Noting that Okara's style changed at the time of the civil war from lyric and celebratory to satiric, bitter, and lamenting, S. A. Gingell comments that, while the Christian vision appears to suffer, a belief in the creative spirit remains. The difference between Okara's early and later verse, according to Goodwin, is representative of a shift in African poetry from early-twentieth-century modernist models to a freer, more oratorical American manner. This change in direction reflected a new interest by radicalized poets in using verse as a means of communicating with an African readership about social and political matters. Okara has emancipated himself from European influences and writes like an African for Africans; he is "one of the first truly African poets in English," according to Goodwin. Samuel O. Asein says that Okara's early poetry failed to gain attention among critics because in the 1960s he was absorbed in "an individualized quest . . . to find meaning in human existence" rather than public issues. In the later poems Asein sees signs of someone shocked by the effects of the civil war; instead of imagination, vigor, verbal energy, and fluid oratory, there are pathos, sentimentality, banality, and labored rhetoric. Asein feels that Okara's value as a poet lies in his experiments with language and his cultural nationalism, which made an important contribution to the development of modern African literature.

Critics of *The Voice* were at first concerned with its poetic style, then with interpreting its symbolism; recently there has been a feeling that the novel is most significant for its criticism of African society and politics and its prophetic truth. Early commentators on *The Voice* were puzzled by its unusual English and by the alienation of the main character from his society. The novel was unlike the previous West African literature of anticolonialism and cultural assertion. Sunday Anozie compares the novel to *Hamlet*, seeing Okara's book as the portrait of an African intellectual caught up in a double alienation from himself and from his society. Anozie finds Okolo's search for "it" pretentious, the disillusionment unmotivated, and the novel too static. That it resembles the novels of Ekwensi and Achebe in being concerned with the disrupting and corrupting effects of modernization and social change was overlooked, as were similarities to the work of Soyinka — such similarities including an unillusioned view of national independence and the feeling that the hero is a representative of a group of young, self-destructive, truth-seeking intellectuals. No one at the time noticed that Okolo could just as well be a character in Soyinka's novel *The Interpreters*.

While a characteristic of early Nigerian litera-

Gabriel Okara

ture is experimentation with language to create an African style, as shown by Tutuola's successful use of transliteration from Yoruba and Achebe's more sophisticated "Igboization" of English, critics have long discussed whether or not Okara's experiment in using Ijaw language is successful. In *The Example of Shakespeare* Clark claims that *The Voice* offers conclusive proof that such devices as special syntax and sentence structures based on the vernacular are likely to lead the African writer to disaster; in contrast to such external forms, Clark argues for reliance on images.

After the initial negative evaluation of *The Voice*, opinion began to shift as interpretation became more subtle. The Canadian novelist Margaret Laurence claims that *The Voice* is one of the most memorable novels to have come out of Nigeria, and she comments on its power and poetic imagery. She finds the use of imagery and Ijaw speech patterns fresh, says that the rhythms are those of prose poetry, and notes the use of Ijaw proverbs and parables, including imagery from Ijaw mask drama. Although set within Ijaw tribal society, *The Voice* is universal in its picture of a man who questions pretense, rigidity, and the establishment. For Shiarella, Okolo is a Messiah figure, and Tuere, the outcast woman who befriends him, is a type of Mary Magdalene, while the cripple is the apostle who will carry the message to others. Okolo seeks the inner peace of "it" in contrast to the new ways that have replaced African tradition. Shiarella notes that many of the poetic devices, such as rhyme, alliteration, inverted word order, and repetition result from transliteration; the style and technique make *The Voice* a new form of experimental, poetic novel. Okara's attempt to bridge the distance between European literary models and an African point of view and style, as represented by Tutuola's fictions, is noted by Roscoe, who claims that *The Voice* blends the realism of Western fiction with the fantasy in traditional African tales. While its origins are in contemporary life, the novel is an allegory of the struggle between good and evil in a symbolic, dark, and hazy landscape. Okolo is a modern character, a man of inner tensions and depressions; but the "it" he seeks is too vague, according to Roscoe.

Later criticism praises Okara's achievement in *The Voice* as a successful attempt at creating in English the manner of African oral literature. Whereas older critics complain about Okolo's alienation, recent emphasis is on the political relevance of the satiric elements. More attention has also been given to the details of the symbolism. Lindfors sees a poet's concern with form, symbol, and language in the novel; it represents for him the most eloquent African vernacular style in English. It is a brilliant achievement, a moral allegory about the search for truth and purpose in a corrupt world, and it is concerned about the moral consequences of rapid Westernization. Eustace Palmer also sees its imagery, style, and quest plot as being influenced by the oral tradition of the storyteller. Noting similarities to Eliot's *The Wasteland* (1922), Palmer finds *The Voice* religious, moral, and extremely pessimistic, although one of the most significant African novels.

The tight, closely drawn structure, symbolism, and solemn, moralizing tone create a nightmare world dominated by tyranny and materialism, says Emmanuel N. Obiechina, who also comments on the novel as parable and the analogy between Okolo's life and the Passion story. Burness claims identity is a main concern of any African novelist who is working within a European literary genre; no other African novelist has reconstructed a Western language so drastically to fit the rhythms of a tribal language. Okolo is a symbol of the pilgrim frustrated by the moral laxity of his society and its leaders, a situation that can occur in any society or culture; the political leaders are mediocre, not evil. Reinhard Sander, however, sees the situation depicted in the novel as typical of postcolonial Africa, where a white ruling class was exchanged for a similar black ruling class, resulting in disillusionment and cynicism. The rebel is at a loss for progressive allies as the establishment crushes opposition. Hugh Webb sees Okara as having transferred to the novel the characteristic features of the African oral tale, such as moralizing parables to form group conscience. Okara's narrative is stripped of all detail not essential to parable, making the characters figures in an allegory. Although alienated, Okolo is a crusader, and his search threatens the conservatives' retention of power.

Noting a similarity of techniques and themes between *The Voice* and works of the early 1960s by Soyinka, Albert Olu Ashaolu sees the novel as concerned with the corrupting effects of Western materialism on traditional Nigerian society at the time of national independence. Okolo is one of the intellectuals who preach reform. *The Voice* is "one of the finest African novels of social analysis," according to Solomon Iyasere; no other novel has so successfully captured the social injustice, corruption, and spiritual emptiness of contemporary Nigeria.

Okara appears to have evolved from a late-Romantic religious poet to a negritudist, then in *The Voice* to a critic of the materialism of Nigerian politics. Afterward he became a Biafran poet recording the pains of the secession movement, while beginning to question his religious faith. His style changed from the romanticism of his first poems to the modernist and surrealist tendencies of his negritude phase. With the Biafran poems his style became more open and his subject matter more clearly in view. He has written little since the end of the Nigerian civil war, but his reputation as an important writer is secure.

Interview:

Bernth Lindfors, "Interview with Gabriel Okara," *World Literature Written in English*, 12 (November 1973): 133–141; reprinted in *Dem-Say: Interviews with Eight Nigerian Writers*, edited by Lindfors (Austin: African and Afro-American Studies and Research Center, University of Texas, 1974), pp. 41–47.

References:

Sam A. Adewoye, "The Effects of the Hand of the Past on the Protagonist in Gabriel Okara's *The*

Voice," *Journal of African Studies*, 12 (1985): 77–81;

Sunday Anozie, "The Theme of Alienation and Commitment in Okara's *The Voice*," *Bulletin of the Association for African Literature in English*, 3 (1965): 54–67;

Samuel O. Asein, "The Significance of Gabriel Okara as Poet," *New Literature Review*, 11 (November 1982): 63–74;

Albert Olu Ashaolu, "A Voice in the Wilderness: The Predicament of the Social Reformer in Okara's *The Voice*," *International Fiction Review*, 6 (July 1979): 111–117;

Susan Beckmann, "Gabriel Okara, *The Fisherman's Invocation*," *World Literature Written in English*, 20 (Autumn 1981): 230–235;

Donald Burness, "Stylistic Innovations and the Rhythm of African Life in Okara's *The Voice*," *Journal of the New African Literature and the Arts*, 13/14 (1972/1973): 13–20;

J. P. Clark, *The Example of Shakespeare* (Evanston, Ill.: Northwestern University Press, 1970);

R. N. Egudu, "A Study of Five of Gabriel Okara's Poems," *Okike*, 13 (1979): 93–110;

S. A. Gingell, "His River's Complex Course: Reflections on Past, Present and Future in the Poetry of Gabriel Okara," *World Literature Written in English*, 23 (Spring 1984): 284–297;

Kenneth L. Goodwin, "Gabriel Okara," in his *Understanding African Poetry: A Study of Ten Poets* (London: Heinemann, 1982), pp. 142–153;

Solomon Iyasere, "Narrative Techniques in Okara's *The Voice*," *African Literature Today*, 12 (1982): 5–21;

Bruce King, "The Poetry of Gabriel Okara," *Chandrabhaga*, 2 (1979): 60–65;

Margaret Laurence, *Long Drums and Cannons* (New York: Praeger, 1969), pp. 193–198;

Bernth Lindfors, "Gabriel Okara: The Poet as Novelist," *Pan-African Journal*, 4 (Fall 1971): 420–425;

Obi Maduakor, "Gabriel Okara: Poet of the Mystic Inside," *World Literature Today*, 61 (Winter 1987): 41–45;

Ayo Mamudu, "Okara's Poetic Landscape," *Commonwealth Essays and Studies*, 10 (Autumn 1987): 111–118;

Emmanuel Ngara, *Stylistic Criticism and the African Novel: A Study of the Language, Art and Content of African Fiction* (London: Heinemann, 1982), pp. 39–57;

Alastair Niven, "Gabriel Okara's *The Voice* and

What It Utters," *Commonwealth Novel in English*, 1, no. 2 (1982): 121–126;

P. N. Njoroge, "Gabriel Okara: The Feeler of the Pulse of Africa's Soul," *Busara*, 5, no. 1 (1973): 48–56;

Emmanuel N. Obiechina, "Art and Artifice in Okara's *The Voice*," *Okike*, 1 (September 1972): 23–33;

Emeka Okeke-Ezigbo, "The 'Sharp and Sided Hail': Hopkins and His Nigerian Imitators and Detractors," in *Hopkins among the Poets: Studies in Modern Responses to Gerard Manley Hopkins*, edited by Richard F. Giles (Hamilton, Ont.: International Hopkins Association, 1985), pp. 114–123;

Eustace Palmer, *An Introduction to the African Novel: A Critical Study of Twelve Books by Chinua Achebe, James Ngugi, Camara Laye, Elechi Amadi, Ayi Kwei Armah, Mongo Beti and Gabriel Okara* (London: Heinemann, 1972), pp. 155–167;

Kirsten Holst Petersen, "Heterogeneous Worlds Yoked Violently Together," *Kunapipi*, 1, no. 2 (1979): 155–158;

Adrian A. Roscoe, *Mother Is Gold* (Cambridge: Cambridge University Press, 1971), pp. 27–35, 44–48, 80–81, 113–121;

Reinhard Sander, "A Political Interpretation of Gabriel Okara's *The Voice*," *Omaba*, 10 (1974): 4–15;

Patrick Scott, "The Older Generation: T. M. Aluko and Gabriel Okara," in *European-Language Writing in Sub-Saharan Africa*, edited by Albert Gérard (Budapest: Akadémiai Kiadó, 1986), II: 689–697;

K. E. Senanu and Theophilus Vincent, eds., *A Selection of African Poetry* (Harlow, U.K.: Longman, 1976);

J. Shiarella, "Gabriel Okara's *The Voice*: A Study in the Poetic Novel," *Black Orpheus*, 2, nos. 5–6 (1971): 45–49;

Vincent, ed., *The Novel and Reality in Africa and America* (Lagos: U.S. Information Service and University of Lagos, 1974), pp. 11–13, 34–35;

Hugh Webb, "Allegory: Okara's *The Voice*," *English in Africa*, 5 (September 1978): 66–73;

Noel Woodroffe, "The Necessity for Cultural Redefinition in Gabriel Okara's *The Voice*," *World Literature Written in English*, 25 (Spring 1985): 42–50;

Derek Wright, "Ritual and Reality in the Novels of Wole Soyinka, Gabriel Okara and Kofi Awoonor," *Kunapipi*, 9, no. 1 (1987): 65–74.

Christopher Okigbo

(16 August 1930 – August 1967)

Donatus Ibe Nwoga
University of Nigeria, Nsukka

BOOKS: *Heavensgate* (Ibadan: Mbari, 1962);
Limits (Ibadan: Mbari, 1964);
Labyrinths; with Path of Thunder (London: Heinemann, 1971; New York: Africana, 1971);
Collected Poems (London: Heinemann, 1986).

OTHER: "Lament of the Mask," in *W. B. Yeats 1865–1965: Centenary Essays*, edited by D. E. S. Maxwell and B. S. Bushrui (Ibadan: Ibadan University Press, 1965), pp. xiii–xv;
"Dance of the Painted Maidens," in *Verse & Voice: A Festival of Commonwealth Poetry*, edited by Douglas Cleverdon (London: Poetry Book Society, 1965);
"Lament of the Deer," in *How the Leopard Got His Claws*, by Chinua Achebe and John Iroaganachi (Enugu, Nigeria: Nwamife, 1972; New York: Third Press, 1973).

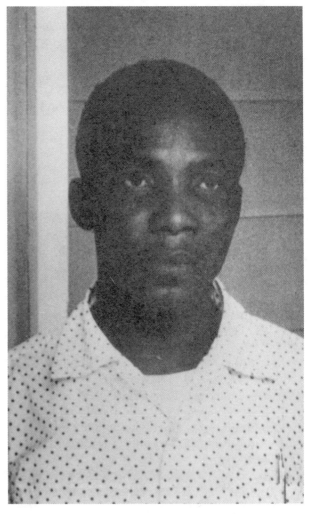

Christopher Okigbo, 1963 (photograph by Bernth Lindfors)

The centrality of Christopher Okigbo in the development of modern poetry in Africa is an acknowledged reality. Perhaps the greatest tribute to him has been that by his friend and contemporary Wole Soyinka, who won the Nobel Prize for Literature in 1986 and associated Okigbo with this great honor by setting up an African poetry prize in his name. The irony of this recognition would not be missed by Okigbo himself, who, when asked by interviewer Marjory Whitelaw whether he thought of himself as an African poet, answered, "I think I am just a poet. A poet writes poetry and once the work is published it becomes public property. It's left to whoever reads it to decide whether it's African poetry or English." But beyond the irony is the reality of the acclaim with which Okigbo's poetry continues to be received. He achieved a legendary status in African literature within a short lifetime, with publications that would all fit into a slim volume. When he died in August 1967 during the Nigerian civil war, there were extensive and intense reactions to the news of his death both inside and outside Africa. Within Biafra the legendary Okigbo was mourned not only by intellectual and artistic colleagues who wrote memorial poems and biographical works in Igbo and English but by the common people and soldiers who immortalized his name in a chant about lamented Biafran heroes. Indeed there were many who shed tears for him who were never to cry again over the death of a colleague; the shock was that traumatic. In Nigeria, Okigbo was considered important enough for his death to be announced on the national radio network. J. P. Clark revived the journal *Black Orpheus*, on which they had worked together at Ibadan, and published a full-page obituary followed by the last poems of Okigbo.

Christopher Okigbo was a controversial poet and has been generally recognized as one of the most innovative to have written in English in the middle of the twentieth century. In the discussion of African poetry his work is a significant basis of several debates: on the nature and conception of poetry (poetry as ritual; as a religious, prophetic, mystic activity; as a communal exposition; and as personal expression of the realistic and the mythopoeic); about poetry and meaning (should a poet aim at a paraphrasable meaning or express his deeper impulses and leave the issue of meaning to the reactions of the recipients? what level and complexity of language should the poet use?); about the role of the poet (the question of persona; the audience of the poet; the poet as poet and the poet as citizen; poetry as a revolutionary tool or agent of self-release for the poet); and about the tradition of poetry (the place of traditional African, foreign, European, and other elements; the sources of image and metaphor and myth; and the influences on poetry in terms of concept, nature, and language). In the discussions and debates on these issues Okigbo's ideas and poems have featured prominently.

Christopher Ifekandu Okigbo was born on 16 August 1930. (Perhaps the 1932 date used by some biographers was introduced during Okigbo's university days, when peer competition made some people reduce their ages to indicate how young they were for their achievements.) The importance he was to attribute to his role in traditional religion makes it necessary to go into some detail about his origins. Ojoto, Okigbo's hometown, is about ten miles southeast of Onitsha, on the eastern bank of the river Niger in eastern Nigeria. Ojoto is a rural community with the river Idoto running through it, and it is the home of certain high priests and the location of the shrines of two major deities: Idoto and Ukpaka Oto. James Okoye Okigbo, Christopher's father, and Anna Onugwalobi Okigbo, his mother, were both raised in Ojoto. The Nweze family, from which she came, held the priesthood of Idoto, and Christopher was thought to be a reincarnation from his mother's line of a former chief priest, his maternal grandfather. Indeed it was his maternal uncle Ikejiofor Nweze who held the priesthood as Christopher's surrogate. James Okigbo was a traveling teacher and headmaster in the service of the local Roman Catholic mission. His travels provided the background experiences of Christopher's childhood, which feature prominently in his early verse. Christopher's father lived in mission-school stations extending through most of Igboland. In August 1930 he was living and teaching in Onitsha, and Anna Okigbo had to go home to the village to deliver their child Christopher. The boy spent his first six years living alternately in Onitsha and Ojoto because most teachers spent their Christmas holidays in their villages, and teachers' wives who were industrious took their young children with them during planting and harvesting seasons in their villages while the teachers stayed at the mission.

When Christopher Okigbo was six, his mother died. His eldest brother, Lawrence, remembers him calling to their mother as she lay in the coffin, and he suggests that this is the basis of the address to "Anna of the panel oblong" in some of Okigbo's poems. From then on he and the others were looked after by Eunice, a relation of their mother who served as their father's housekeeper. Eunice is reputed to have had a lovely voice and to have been an expert in telling folktales and singing the accompanying songs. James Okigbo moved with Eunice and the children to Ekwulobia in 1936. This location was important for Christopher Okigbo's later poetry, for it was the place in which the madman Jadum lived, making his witty claims to all wisdom and all women. It was also where Christopher started primary school and encountered the comic teacher that became Kepkanly in his poems. In 1939 or 1940 the Okigbo household moved to Asaba, on the western side of the river Niger across from Onitsha, and it was there that Christopher completed his primary-school studies. He later passed the entrance examination and went to Umuahia Government College.

The implications for his poetry of the life of Okigbo as the son of a traveling teacher are many. One of these relates to the general style of life of a teacher's child in those days; another is particular to the character and temperament of Okigbo himself. At the general level those who were the offspring of such headmasters in the late 1930s and early 1940s were the children of two homes, one the variable home dependent on the regular postings and transfers of their fathers, the other the village home to which they had to return with their mothers during school term, if they were young enough, or during school holidays, or generally at Christmas with the mass return to the villages of all those who lived in towns. Whether at the mission station or in the village, there was always an element of differ-

Okigbo (seated, far right) on the soccer team at Umuahia Government College, circa 1949

ence and separateness between teachers' children and other children. Such an atmosphere could engender a feeling of isolation, but the life-style also had its rewards. The multifarious experiences of the teachers' children would encompass the religious and educational activities of the mission station, as well as the village activities – work, leisure, festivals, and song and dance, watched from a distance or perhaps engaged in.

Umuahia Government College, in 1945 when Okigbo began his studies there, was an elitist institution to which a few of the best students from the eastern region of Nigeria were admitted via a competitive entrance examination. In the tradition of the colonialists, only a few were supposed to go to secondary school or university, and those were supposed to be trained to be English-type gentlemen, eventually to be admitted into the colonial civil service. Eastern Nigeria was provided for educationally by the religious groups who had set up some high-quality secondary schools and teacher-training institutions. Government College gave excellent academic and sports education and produced some of the best writers in English from Igboland. The principals were English gentlemen and clerics, the games of England – including cricket, hockey, football, tennis, and boxing – were played, and the

piano and other forms of artistic activity were introduced.

Okigbo learned and became proficient in several games – soccer, cricket, hockey, track events, boxing, and chess. As Bernth Lindfors has further established through a study of the *Umuahia Government College Magazine* of 1949–1950 and other sources, Okigbo was "quite active in extra-curricular activities, serving as a member of the Arts Society and the Chess Club, editing a house magazine with Vincent C. Ike, and playing the role of Defending Counsel in a dramatic production of 'The Trial of Hitler.' He was also entrusted with certain responsibilities: it is recorded that when a new wireless set was installed in the assembly hall on September 22, 1949, Okigbo was put in charge." Lindfors also gives specific information on the games in which Okigbo excelled, the prizes he won, and his style of play.

From Umuahia, Okigbo succeeded in gaining admission to University College, Ibadan. This was an important academic achievement, considering that Ibadan was then an elite colonial institution designed to train the few graduates that the British believed were all they needed for the colonial educational and administrative services. Though Okigbo was admitted to study medicine, he transferred to classics after his intermediate examinations. In this change he was following in the footsteps of another, older writer who was then also a University College student, Chinua Achebe.

Okigbo's academic performance was not outstanding and was complicated by personal habits that were not best suited for scholarly achievement. Though he had won a Latin prize in secondary school, classical studies involved Greek, which he had never studied before. But Okigbo could have achieved better than his third-class honors degree at the end of his classics studies if he had put his full energies to the assignment. He did not. Athletic and sporting activities featured prominently in Okigbo's student career in Ibadan. In the 1950–1951 session he was the best batsman on the cricket team. He also devoted vigorous energies to trying to help build a strong soccer team.

Okigbo also broadened his artistic and social horizons. He read vast amounts of all kinds of literature, engaged in musical activities, and enjoyed female company. With regard to music, Okigbo said he composed seriously up to the end of his undergraduate days. The intensity of his interest in music was to show itself later when he described its influences on his imagination at the time he wrote his poem sequence *Heavensgate* (1962). In addition Okigbo tried to run a student newspaper, the *University Weekly*, but gave up when he realized he did not have enough money to continue publishing it.

When he graduated with his B.A. in 1956 Okigbo went to Lagos, where he ran through a gamut of different jobs. He worked with private business companies, such as the Nigeria Tobacco Company and the United Africa Company, before he was reclaimed by the federal government, with whose scholarship he had studied. In the federal service he was engaged as a private secretary to the federal minister of research and information until, in 1958, he was sent to Fiditi, near Ibadan, to teach at Fiditi Grammar School. He taught there from 1958 to 1960.

This period is marked by four important aspects: his literary and other leadership activities in the school, his interaction with the University of Ibadan, his involvement in other Ibadan cultural activities, and the blossoming of his poetic talents. Lindfors's explorations of Okigbo's activities as a teacher, derived from reports in the school's annual, *The Fiditian*, show that Okigbo contributed much more than the teaching of Latin to the school. He gave much encouragement and skilled coaching to the soccer team and provided them with modern equipment. He became the patron of the boxing so-

ciety and gave them hope. Table tennis improved in the school because of his guidance and example. Beyond sports he also became the patron of the Senior Literary and Debating Society. The secretary of the society reported that Okigbo was an "energetic and virtuous leader," and the secretary praised Okigbo's initiative in "influencing other educational giants to give lectures to boys." The list of these lecturers included Dr. Pius Okigbo, the brother of the poet, and important names from the University of Ibadan. The topics, in addition to more general ones, included classical and poetic subjects. Christopher Okigbo proposed a series of six lectures as an "Introduction to Poetry" and delivered at least one of them himself. Before the end of his teaching career at Fiditi Grammar School, Okigbo had also participated in founding a Prose and Poetry Society, which, according to the annual, was "inaugurated on amount [sic] of the burning enthusiasm of boys to study prose and poetry."

Okigbo was a young man dedicated to sports, to the uplifting of youth, and to wide intellectual and literary pursuits. Being in Fiditi, which was only a few miles away from the University of Ibadan, made it possible for him to pursue these enthusiasms further in contact with people who had similar interests. Some of the lecturers Okigbo attracted to his school – including Professor John Ferguson, who gave a series of lectures, the last one of which was "The Love of Aeneas and Dido" – showed that he was taken seriously by the academics at the university.

In addition to this level of contact, it was during this period that Okigbo started his interaction with the younger generation of students who were going to be important figures along with him in the development of modern African literature. He met Clark, who was then a student in the English department at the university. Okigbo's eldest brother, Pius, and Clark's eldest brother were friends and prepared their brothers for the meeting. Clark spoke of Okigbo as not being associated with the *Horn*, the university literary magazine, "except while he was at Fiditi and shunting to Ibadan to and from me in 1959–60. I introduced him to the paper as he spouted the Old Classics to me and I the New Greats to him. That's how he met [Ezra] Pound, [T. S.] Eliot, and [W. B.] Yeats. . . ." It might be more valid to say that Clark intensified Okigbo's awareness of and interest in the poetry of the moderns since Okigbo had an earlier interaction with modern poetry of various types introduced to him by Pius.

One of the consequences of Okigbo's involve-

Okigbo, Chinua Achebe, and Alex Ajayi while they were students at University College, Ibadan (photograph by Modern, Enugu, Nigeria)

ment with this literary environment and his interaction with the students was the first publications of his poetry, in the *Horn* in 1959 and 1960. "Debtor's Lane," the first Okigbo poem to be published, was later to be republished with "Song of the Forest," the oldest of his poems, dated 1957; "Lament of the Flutes" (1960); and "Lament of the Lavender Mist" (1961) in the journal *Black Orpheus* (1962). "On the New Year" was published in the *Horn* in 1960. Also "Love Apart," which was to become the fourth movement of "Lament of the Lavender Mist," and "Moonglow" were written in Ibadan in 1960, and "Moonglow" was published in the student magazine *Fresh Buds* that same year. (All these works are in *Collected Poems*, 1986.) These poems constitute the early poetry of Okigbo and mark his entry into the career that would make him one of the great African poets of his time.

A perception of the themes of Okigbo's poetry depends on whether one is considering individual poems, poem sequences, or the total framework of Okigbo's work. For example, one of the earliest debates on his work was the series of analyses and counteranalyses of "Love Apart" after it was published individually, and yet it was to turn out that the piece was one movement in a poem of four movements. Various critics have studied individual poem sequences, and, in line with Okigbo's own in-

troduction to *Labyrinths* (1971), others have taken an overall look at the progression of the sequences in the Okigbo canon. From the combination of these, a preliminary summary may be made of his topics and themes.

The bulk of the poetry of Okigbo is aimed inward, at the exploration of the nature of experience. On the public level, the poems incorporate references to and inspiration from the events of African and Nigerian history: the processes and implications of colonization and cultural and religious conversion; the political tragedies of the murder of Patrice Lumumba of the Congo and the imprisonment of Obafemi Awolowo of Nigeria; and ultimately the mad rush of events that led to the 1966 military takeover of the government in Nigeria, the subsequent pogrom against eastern Nigerians, and the civil war that took Okigbo's life. However, he subsumes most of these events into a series of poems that form what he describes as a "fable of man's perennial quest for fulfillment." Okigbo's mythopoeic imagination led him to transcend each given event or memory, surround it with myths and symbols from various cultural and literary traditions, and derive from it a poetic statement that is not merely a comment on or a description of the event or memory but a distillation of what he considered to be the eternal essence of that experience.

The nature of this quest and how each poem sequence contributes to the total exploration, and Okigbo's development as a poet and how influences of various traditions contributed to the content and manner of each presentation continue to interest readers and critics of his work.

"Song of the Forest," though it was not to be published until 1962 as one of the "Four Canzones" (in *Black Orpheus*), was written even before Okigbo came to teach at Fiditi Grammar School. It is dated "Lagos 1957" and is thus known as Okigbo's oldest extant poem. "Song of the Forest" was a direct outcome of Okigbo's Latin studies. It is a translation and adaptation of the first verse of Virgil's first eclogue, *Tityrus*. The model suited him because he was then living in Lagos and could, from there, reflect on his home village and see and project the life of ease in the open air of his youth:

> You loaf, child of the forest,
> beneath a village umbrella,
> plucking from tender string, a
>   Song of the Forest.

Contrasting his own life to that of the village youth, he calls himself a "runaway," a term that, in the form of "prodigal," was to feature centrally in his poetry. But here he emphasizes the element of compulsion — "[we] must leave the borders of our / land, fruitful fields, / must leave our homeland." This nostalgic preference for the village environment could have been an unconscious influence from negritude, but it was already there in the Virgil model. What Okigbo did to the pastoral form he borrowed was to transform it from a vehicle for urban discussion among the urban elite about the pastoral shepherds into a modern subjective tool for reflecting on the position and feelings of the poet himself.

Though "Song of the Forest" was written in Lagos, the Fiditi environment produced the first published poems of Okigbo, "Debtor's Lane" and "On the New Year." "Debtor's Lane," written in 1959, was republished in *Black Orpheus* as the second poem of the "Four Canzones." "On the New Year," written earlier, in 1958, was not republished until it was included in Okigbo's *Collected Poems*. Robert Fraser, in his *West African Poetry* (1986), after explaining how "the experimental poetry of the Modernist source had a deleterious effect upon early West African poetry in English," makes one exception: Okigbo. He attributes Okigbo's success in this mode to the fact that "the allusions and echoes Okigbo found in those [modernist] poets were to literatures which he had encountered in their own language. He was thus not dependent on the kind of second-hand acquaintance with the international classics to which lesser talents fell foul." Fraser illustrates the "unforced cosmopolitanism" of Okigbo's early poetry by referring to "On the New Year."

The poem is not as tight and firm as Okigbo's later poetry, but it is important in two ways. It carries a theme central to Okigbo's poetry, and it is an early manifestation of his approach to poetic style, both in terms of picking up echoes from other poets and juxtaposing them to make his points, and in the use of private and public symbols and images whose meanings are ultimately cumulative. "On the New Year" presents a reflection, provoked by the transition from the old year to the new, on the cyclic pattern of human hope and frustration. At this stage of Okigbo's writing, the concept is manifested as romantic despair, shown by events, situations, fragments of memories, and half-forgotten statements. The active elements are "the midnight funeral," a warder, a wagtail singing over lost souls, a church bell, a pilgrimage, a cross, and, above all, time — in its hourly, seasonal, and eternal cycle:

> We have to think of ourselves as forever
> Soaring and sinking like dead leaves blown by a gust
> Floating choicelessly to the place where
> Old desires and new born hopes like bubbles burst
> Into nothing. . . .

With hindsight the critic today can appreciate that one of the difficulties of Okigbo's poetry arose from the fact that the elements of his mythic structures came to him almost fully formed at the start of his career, before his readers knew that such structures were there, within which to seek meaning in Okigbo's poetry. While readers were looking for the usual type of meaning in individual poems to emerge from the simple collection of words and lines that form the poems, Okigbo was working with a set of words, images, and concepts whose full meanings would emerge with the fullness of their exploration in the full corpus of his poetry.

"Debtor's Lane," the first Okigbo poem to be published, was next in the line of Okigbo's production. Some structural peculiarities of the poem may be noted immediately as characteristic of Okigbo's writing. One is the instruction after the title that the poem is to be performed with the accompaniment of "drums and ogene" (an *ogene* being a type of gong). The instruction with "Song of the Forest" was that it should be accompanied with an *ubo*, a local "hand piano." This idea helped create for the reader a picture of the "child of the forest," in his hands the *ubo*, with which he is "plucking" a song of the forest under a village umbrella tree. Later Okigbo poems not only request accompaniment with musical instruments but some of them are named after musical instruments: "Lament of the Flutes," "Lament of the Drums," "Elegy for Alto," and so on.

Though "Debtor's Lane" was written in Fiditi in 1959, its theme is provoked less by that environment than by literary sources. The element of Fiditi being a hideout is there in the statement of the speaker, who contrasts a putative past of hectic social activity with the present:

> No heavenly transports now
> of youthful passion
> and the endless succession
> of tempers and moods
> in high societies... [.]

But "Debtor's Lane" is heavily dependent for its sounds and images on Eliot's "The Hollow Men" (1925).

"Love Apart," written in 1960, is a translation and reworking of an extract from the Spanish poet Miguel Hernández's "El amor ascendia entre nosotros" (Love Has Risen Between Us). "Love Apart" became the final coda of the long sequence "Lament of the Lavender Mist," the fourth of the "Four Canzones." "Moonglow," also written in Ibadan, is a reworking of the Igbo children's story that the dark image in the full moon is that of a man who went to work on Sunday and so was given the punishment of forever hewing wood:

> And there engraved on the dead world,
> Moonman,
> bowed in shame over the beam
> I see you,
> hear ever your penance as you measure
>   cup after cup your strength,
> and Time
>   day after day its length.

"Lament of the Flutes" was written in Ojoto in 1960 and represents a homecoming both at the physical and the emotional levels, what Sunday O. Anozie calls "a feeling of *reconciliation* in the poet" (*Christopher Okigbo: Creative Rhetoric*, 1972). It recalls, with some imagistic adaptation, memories of childhood activities and environments:

> Day breathes,
> panting like torn horse –
> We follow the wind to the fields
> Bruising grass leafblade and corn
> . . . .
> Night falls

> smearing sore bruises . . .
> boring new holes in old sheets . . . [.]

The central questions concern what future to pursue – the religious service of Idoto or the sacrifice to Idoto through poetic activity:

> Shall I offer to *Idoto*
> my sandhouse and bones
> then write no more on snow-patch?

The flavor of imagery from old English is there in the kenning "sandhouse and bones" for the human body. To "write no more on snow-patch" carries the connotation of ephemerality, as whatever is written in a patch of snow quickly dissolves in the melting of the snow. But "snow-patch" is also a likely play on words and concepts by Okigbo suggesting the empty sheet of paper on which one writes. He suggests one answer to his question about the avenue of service, not directly but through the combination of the old and the new in the poetic personality and style he was to evolve: "Sing to the rustic flute. / Sing a new note." Okigbo once described to Lewis Nkosi his style of work: "As much as possible, I keep practising – I mean I try to keep informed. If I have nothing to say, I translate from Latin verse into English verse or from Greek verse into English verse and vice versa. I mean if I have nothing to say, I just keep translating – keep playing with work because I have seen that a poet, apart from being a writer, is also a technician." Clearly most of the early published poems of Okigbo are reworkings of poems – some translated, some reconstructed, from other poets – that he has given a local setting and flavor.

Okigbo joined the staff of the new University of Nigeria, Nsukka, in October 1960 as the officer in charge of the library. He was not professionally qualified and had never worked in a library before then. Achebe has told the story of Okigbo's quest for this job: "he relished challenges and the more unusual or difficult the better it made him feel." Okigbo bought a book on librarianship, read it on the journey from Fiditi to Nsukka, attended the interview, and won the job.

Okigbo's sojourn in the Nsukka environment was brief but centrally significant to his growth and achievement, and his death in Biafra. He told Ike that it was a compulsive urge to keep the federal troops off "the sacred grove of academe" that made him take up arms.

The library to which Okigbo came in 1960 was two rooms in the Faculty of Education building. He was responsible for organizing the collection of books and other documents and the management of the staff. Perhaps the largest single collection was the twelve thousand books, journals, and pamphlets donated by the founder of the university, the Right Honorable Dr. Nnamdi Azikiwe. In October 1961 Okigbo was posted to the Enugu campus of the university, where, again, he had to take charge of the campus library, acquired as part of the merger process that made the Nigeria College of Arts, Science and Technology at Enugu part of the University of Nigeria. By the middle of 1962 Okigbo had resigned his library job at the university and taken on the challenge of representing Cambridge University Press in West Africa.

During his time with the university, Okigbo had continued his interest in sports. He coached and captained the Nsukka community soccer team, which was successful in some of the intercity competitions in eastern Nigeria. Chess was another game that held much interest for him, and he was an aggressive, enthusiastic player who spent long hours at the game. Clearly games played a large part in his life, and he showed proficiency and dedication to playing and coaching several of them. The strategies he adopted in his gamesmanship are evident, too, in his poetry. As Lindfors notes, "He excelled in offensive rather than defensive positions – inside forward in soccer, batsman in cricket, aggressive puncher in boxing and ping-pong. He was the kind of player accustomed to making moves to which others had to respond. . . . He was, in other, words, a quick and elusive trickster-athlete bent on avoiding capture and scoring goals."

Okigbo's involvement in games effectively drew to a close, though, at Nsukka. The main opportunity his position in Nsukka offered him was in the area of vigorous literary communion. The University of Nigeria opened with a higher percentage than it would ever achieve again of undergraduates studying English language and literature. Some of these students were very bright and enthusiastic. Among their lecturers were some enterprising staff members from England and America, particularly Peter Thomas, who was to offer the opportunity for intense communication among Okigbo, himself, and his students.

Thomas has described how one evening, soon after he started his seminars in his house for his Honours English students in October 1960, "somewhere about dusk, a slim, trim, round-face young Ibo, with close-cropped hair, and a quizzical, slightly brooding look, appeared" and asked for permission to sit in on the seminar. This man was Okigbo, who was then, as Thomas noted, "a very

Cover for the sequence of poems that Okigbo once described as "a ceremony of innocence"

efficient" librarian. The relationship blossomed into an association of minds that Thomas has written about in memorials and which Okigbo recognized in his poem "For Peter Thomas," published in *Heavensgate*. The poem concludes with an affirmation of intimacy and acknowledgment of inspiration.

I am mad with the same madness as the
    moon and my neighbour
I am kindled from the moon and the
    hearth of my neighbour.

Thomas has a copy of "Lament of the Flutes" in which Okigbo inscribed "I could never have written this if I did not meet you." Thomas's summary of these meetings in Nsukka and later in other places is that "always there was in our meetings a sharing of views, of music, or of silences, and an exchange reading of our poems – though he preferred to have me read his for him, because he said I made them sound better."

One of the students at the seminars taught by Thomas was Anozie, now a critic and publisher. Anozie has given a description of the impression Okigbo made on the students, especially himself, and how Okigbo was regarded on campus. In *Christopher Okigbo: Creative Rhetoric* Anozie reports that Okigbo struck him as "very individualistic, impressive and learned," a first impression that was to be "borne out by later experiences." This relationship also grew. Okigbo was inclined toward bright younger people whom he would encourage to develop the best potential in themselves and to whom he would give his company, advice, books, and friendship.

Most noticeable were Okigbo's informality and unconventionality, which appeared especially in his mode of dress. In a university campus that was formal enough to demand that the staff give lectures in academic gowns and that students not be admitted into the august presence of the vice-chancellor unless also clad in such an outfit, it was exciting and liberating for the young students to see their librarian moving about "in a pair of Khaki shorts and an open-breasted short-sleeved shirt with the bottom all loose, and roughly shod in an old pair of sandals." His style of dress attracted a lot of the students to him, and he gave much hospitality and encouragement to those he found mentally exciting. His conversations were vigorous and literary. Michael J. C. Echeruo, then a young colleague, says, "He had a passionate involvement in poetry and an eccentric manner which made that involvement all the more exciting; it was fun talking poetry with him."

Part of Okigbo's style in life and letters may have been deliberately designed to shock neighbors and friends with unconventionality and mischievousness. For example, when he lived in Nsukka, one of his neighbors was the expatriate British head of the English department, whose wife was very inquisitive about the comings and goings in Okigbo's house and would constantly peep out through her curtains. Okigbo decided to shock her. One afternoon he brought out his straw mat to the veranda of his house and, having ensured that the woman was peeping out, began vigorously to divest himself of all his clothes. The woman was so shocked she nearly fell out through the window. Such a provocation accords with Okigbo's personality. He had a tendency to create an atmosphere, to generate vigorous scenes.

To complete the picture of Okigbo's life in Nsukka and its impact on his poetic development, one must refer to his contact with the noncampus life of the Nsukka environment. He developed an interest in village people and activities and, given his talent for absorbing creative inflences, derived new inspiration from village rituals, festivals, masquerade performances, and poetry.

While he was in Nsukka and later Enugu, he completed "Lament of the Lavender Mist," published the "Four Canzones," and wrote the final drafts for *Heavensgate* and *Limits* (1964). "Lament of the Lavender Mist" is a love poem, and there is an addressee. In its style and phraseology it comes close to the *Heavensgate* poems. The opening stanza of the first of the four movements of the poem appears to present two pictures with no apparent link:

> Black dolls
> Returning from the foam:
> Two faces of a coin
> That meet afar off...[.]

This passage is characteristic of early Okigbo poetry: a staccato juxtaposition of logically unrelated phrases, images, and concepts. These certainly alert the reader to an approach to meaning that is not based on the logical or even visually or imaginatively coherent elements. One is alerted to a variety of incoherent and even discordant bits of experience. The meaning one obtains may or may not be definable in an encapsulated summary but is vigorous and occasionally illuminating.

In prosaic terms, one is tempted to identify "Black dolls / Returning from the foam" with village belles returning from the ocean. The juxtaposed image of the coin, again in prosaic terms, suggests some comment on the communality of the nature of women, whether black or white, rural or urban. But there is too much other material in the poem to allow one to settle for these prosaic equivalences.

The next stanza personifies the sea and draws a visually vivid and sensitive picture of it, of the foam where it hits the shore, and of the serenity beyond the foamy contact line:

> Sea smiles at a distance
>   with lips of foam
> Sea walks like a rainbow
>   beyond them[.]

The next stanza takes readers away from the black dolls and the sea into the psyche and memory where the dolls are redefined and qualified:

DOLLS . . .
Forms
Of memory,
To be worshipped
Adored
 By innocence:

Creatures of the mind's eye
Barren—
Of memory—
Remembrance of things past.

That last line again presents the compositional strategy of using phrases from just about anywhere in contexts not related to their original use. *Remembrance of Things Past* is, of course, the English title of a series of novels by Marcel Proust. Thematically one is tempted to adopt this unit of lines as a statement on the nature of the man-woman relationship, but readers are swept onto another plane when violent images of external and internal reality are juxtaposed intrusively:

Eagles in space and earth and sky
Shadows of sin in grove of orange
Of altar-penitence . . .

Echoes in the prison of the mind
Shadows of song of love's stillness . . .[.]

The section ends with a surprisingly vivid, humanized image of dead leaves in a garden, seen as "wounded by the wind."

The second movement of the poem takes readers further away from a realistic interpretation. The Lady of the Lavender Mist is seen as a powerful, threatening, and fruitless force:

scattering
Lightning shafts without rain,
came forging
Thunder with no smell of water . . .[.]

The third and fourth movements present the processes and phases of contact between the persona of the poem and the Lady of the Lavender Mist. She is further identified with the "spirit of the wind and the waves." The interaction is staccato and violent, partly insulting and frustrating, and finally unfulfilled.

The fourth movement ends with the often anthologized and debated "Love Apart." In its full context it clearly reflects a physically unconsummated love. The earlier lines show the disheartening progression from the insulting offer of "love in a / Feeding bottle" to the statement that "the outstretched love / Dried as it reached me...." Those earlier lines also contain an example of Okigbo's use of what are supposed by some to be private symbols but are actually images taken from Igbo tradition. "Kernels of the water of the sky" is a direct translation of "*aki mmili igwe*," which was what Igbo children called the hailstones that came with the stormy rains. And the children used to run around in the rain and pick these hailstones, but they quickly melted and hardly got into their mouths — an apt image for the frustrating love relationship being described in this movement.

"Lament of the Lavender Mist," which may be taken to conclude Okigbo's juvenilia, is not a meaningless poem. Yet it presents, in characteristic Okigbo fashion, a challenging code that points to a meaning outside the logic of presentation. Indeed it carries much of interest — thematically, symbolically, and stylistically — that prepares one for his major works. As Omolara Leslie wrote, "the theme of memory as an important experiential dimension to our poet's imaginative vision . . . is now [in "Lament of the Lavender Mist"] more symbolically expressed than previously. In style, the canzone is more broken in rhythm than the earlier pieces. It is evocative of meaning cumulatively through phrase juxtapositions; repetitions and rephrasings; freely collocating images from Christianity and African religion."

Heavensgate and *Limits* were written and refined at Nsukka between 1960 and 1962. Anozie has described in his 1972 book how he met Okigbo in his house while he worked on the poems: "I arrived promptly at 5 o'clock and saw him lying down in short pants on his raffia carpet, with papers and books scattered all over the table and the floor; there was also a small typewriter in a leather case. These papers, I later found out, were the original manuscripts of *Heavensgate* and *Limits*, nearly all completed but being retyped and, as was Okigbo's wont, retouched." *Heavensgate* was Okigbo's first major publication. It was one of the publications produced by the Mbari Writers and Artists' Club at Ibadan in 1962, and it was instantly recognized as an important new development in African poetry.

The poem sequence *Heavensgate* was republished in *Labyrinths* and is more widely available in that 1971 publication. As usual, before the republication, Okigbo reworked sections of the poem, combined some units, and dropped some others. D. S. Izevbaye has presented these revisions in his 1973 essay "Okigbo's Portrait of the Artist as a Sunbird: A Reading of *Heavensgate*." But basically the poem retains the same structure and meaning. In *Labyrinths* Okigbo added an introduction, which gives

Okigbo as a young man (photograph by Donatus Ibe Nwoga)

his perception of the poems, and some notes to the most-often-mistaken elements of private symbolism. In that introduction Okigbo gives this information on *Heavensgate*: "*Heavensgate* was originally conceived as an Easter sequence. It later grew into a ceremony of innocence, something like a mass, an offering to Idoto . . . ; the celebrant, a personage like Orpheus, is about to begin a journey. Cleansing. . . . The various sections of the poem, therefore, present this celebrant at various stations of his cross."

This is far from being an easy statement on the meaning of a difficult work. But some key factors toward the comprehension of as much of the poem sequence as possible are to be extracted from this presentation: Easter, innocence, offering, cleansing, and celebration. The striking juxtaposition of Christianity and Idoto worship with the Orpheus myth also alerts one to strands of religious and mythical traditions that informed the imagination of Okigbo.

Heavensgate, in Okigbo's chosen final version, consists of five sections: "The Passage," "Initiations," "Watermaid," "Lustra," and "Newcomer." Early reviewers of the publication spoke of the "rit-

ualistic feeling of the whole poem," the "organic fusion of Christian and pagan imagery," the "atmosphere of myth and legend," and of Okigbo as "a poet for the ear and not for the eye." They spoke of "measure, control, craft, and a refinement of utterance that at time verges on the precious" and of "honesty and rigor." But there was hesitation in attempting to interpret the poem until Anozie suggested "the totality of this poem as richly exploratory of the creative process in poetry and of what has earlier been referred to as the poet's own personal myth or predicament."

As more of Okigbo's poems were published and the organic link between them was seen as intrinsic, later critics began to articulate the position of *Heavensgate* as the first stage in a journey that was Okigbo's poetic life and myth. Izevbaye claims that "*Heavensgate* is an account of its own uncompleted quest only," but Nyong J. Udoeyop contends that "*Heavensgate* is the beginning of Okigbo's journey into consciousness."

Heavensgate is Okigbo's presentation of the growth of his mind/personality/psyche up to and during the time of its writing. This growth is figured in both religious and artistic terms in poetry of great musical effects and humorous play with the sound and meaning and even appearance of words. The element of humor is most often neglected, and this neglect has led to the search for deep meaning where the play on words should be enjoyed for its own value. Indeed, friends coaxed Okigbo into revising the poem and removing some of the wittiest punning and nonsense word collocations possible in the English-language usage prevalent in Africa.

"The Passage" starts with a poem about obeisance to Idoto, the female deity of the River Idoto, an obeisance that involves humility, contemplation, and expectation, and the section also identifies the protagonist as one who is crying "out of the depths." The opening poem is not an invocation in the sense of inviting the presence of the deity. It is more a prayer of acknowledgment and supplication. With this prayer, readers are introduced to the village deity of the poet's birthplace and to the totems and legends of her worship. The two other poems that make up "The Passage" call up the experiences of childhood – not only Okigbo's childhood but the childhood of the world, the "Dark waters of the beginnings"; and the childhood of a day: "Rays, violet and short, piercing the gloom / Foreshadow the fire that is dreamed of." But this sunrise presages the end of the world, because the Bible says that, since the first destruction of the world was by water, the next and final one will be by fire. The protagonist emerges as a sad, lonely person, a mournful prophet with a mother to lament. Readers also experience an environment, recalled by phrases, references, and echoes – the active childhood environment of Okigbo in Catholic mission compounds: "orangery," with "silent faces at crossroads," "festivity in black," and "loft pipe organs."

"Initiations" re-creates the various learning experiences through which he grew. The first poem of the sequence concerns the religious and educational elements of modernity, especially the mystery of initiation into the Christian religion. An attitude of rejection of that initiation emerges, but there is the characteristic Okigbo humor in this poem. Kepkanly, mentioned three times in the poem, is described in Okigbo's footnote as "A half-serious, half-comical primary school teacher of the late thirties." The hidden linguistic joke is that the teacher's name was derived from the fact that he used to command the marching schoolboys by shouting, "*Aka ekpe, aka nli*" (left, right), which, pronounced fast, yields Kepkanly. Indeed the end of that poem is nostalgic: "but the solitude within me remembers Kepkanly. . . ."

The other two poems of "Initiations" draw on village aspects of the learning process and on encounters with spectacular wits. Jadum was a madman who got his name from his prefix to riddling statements: "Jam Jam Dum Dum . . . / Say if thou knowest." Upandru, the other wit, is described in the footnotes as "a village explainer." What emerges from these two poems is a conception of poetry as "logistics," a manner of statement that is affective but not necessarily logical and which is open to "the errors of the rendering. . . ."

"Watermaid" shows a solitary child mourning his dead mother; he has matured through a learning experience to the stage of expecting and encountering briefly the ultimate object of human desire. The poems in the "Watermaid" sequence constitute the sensitive highlights of *Heavensgate*. The four poems of the sequence re-create anticipation, brief encounter, the sense of loss, and concluding despair. These poems have been the least revised of Okigbo's poetry, and this fact indicates how nearly perfect they were when they came to him from the beginning. The object of desire, the "Watermaid," could quite easily be whatever girl Okigbo was interested in at this phase of his growth, but, within the mythic framework of his poetry, the figure has grown into the figure of the "mammywater" of local legend and may also be interpreted as another shape taken by the goddess/muse of the poet's quest. Thematically, therefore, "Watermaid" reflects another facet of the frustrating development of the solitary protagonist – the urge to write with the goddess/love/muse and the disappointment and despair that arises from her brief but unfulfilling appearance.

"Lustra" portrays the attitude and process of cleansing. Okigbo did say that the process was a ritual necessitated by his almost constant moving from place to place. But it fits into the *Heavensgate* sequence in terms of the protagonist's having to resort to the act of penitence to improve his readiness for a successful encounter with his goddess after the aborted encounter in "Watermaid." The ritual is set in a clearing among the hills, and the offerings are traditional gifts. The tendency has been to see this poem in terms of Okigbo's return to traditional, Igbo religion. But he refused to be tied to any religion, for the second poem of the sequence takes its image from the Christian liturgical system.

"Newcomer" has been seen as Okigbo's vision of his readiness, after the cleansing, for a new life of communion with his muse/goddess. However, this unit is also a mixed bag of poems written for occasions such as the birth of Okigbo's niece, and, in the original version, for his friend Peter Thomas. The first poem, known as the Angelus poem, shows a violent reaction to the Angelus bells, the phrase "the bells of exile" indicating a withdrawal from the demands of Catholic devout practice of saying the Angelus prayers at the six hourly intervals. But Okigbo is careful to indicate also that the mask over his face is "my own mask – not ancestral" and that the mask is generated out of two traditions, one derived from calvary (Christianity) and the other from the "age of innocence" (traditional religion). The violence directed against Christianity is because it is the most serious prison out of which he is breaking.

At the time *Heavensgate* was published in 1962, it was not clear to anybody that it was the first sequence in a set of poems that would be organically linked to explore experiences of the type Okigbo's poetry was to illuminate. What was strikingly evident was that there was a new, strong voice in modern African poetry. As Anozie correctly writes, "*Heavensgate* is indeed a serious slap in the face of our Nigerian poetry readers who have not yet grown out of the 'patriotic' nausea, the 'palmtree' and 'River Niger' sentimentalism of Chief Osadebay's 'Africa Sings' and its coterie." Okigbo indeed was a vibrant music maker with words, whose poems could be heard more than seen; a sensitive and controlled craftsman who was jolting the sensibility of the complacent modern audience with the introduction of ritual paraphernalia from traditional religion and confronting the taken-for-granted Christian orthodoxy; and a cultural revivalist who, calling himself a prodigal, returns in his poems to pay obeisance to his traditional deity Idoto.

The overall meaning of *Heavensgate* emerged when the set of poems to which it belonged was complete and the mythic pattern of Okigbo's development became manifest. What was clear from the beginning was the set of concerns that was featured in the sequence: religion, both Christian and traditional; education and childhood experiences; love and desire; frustration; and, above all, the mentality of a suffering and confused protagonist confronted with these experiences – "the Orpheus figure at the beginning of his quest."

Another aspect of interest immediately generated by Okigbo's poetry was the matter of the influence that liberated his imagination into the creation of this vibrant, new poetry in Africa. Okigbo himself was to assert in reply to a *Transition* questionnaire, and in his interview with Nkosi, that he wrote under the spell of the impressionist composers. As he said to Nkosi, "when I was working on 'Heavensgate,' I was working under the spell of the impressionist composers Debussy, César Franck, Ravel, and I think that, as in the music of these composers who write of a watery, shadowy, nebulous world, with the semitones of dream and the nuances of the rainbow, there isn't any clearly defined outline in my work." He also acknowledged the influences of Raja Ratnam, Malcolm Cowley, Stéphane Mallarmé, and Rabindranath Tagore. But it has been established that he was also intensely influenced by Ezra Pound, whom he probably deliberately neglected to mention. Clark has noted, concerning the "Watermaid" sequence, "The bright aura and dazzle, the armpit, the lioness, the white light, the waves as escort, the crown and moonlight, the transience of the maid like 'matchflare in the wind's breath,' the mirror and gold crop, all constitute an apparatus completely taken from Pound's Cantos 6 and 104. . . ." Romanus N. Egudu has established (in 1971) that even beyond these phrases and images, Okigbo was heavily influenced by the technical aspects of Pound's work, especially the techniques of *phanopoeia, melopoeia,* and *logopoeia* – "throwing the object (fixed or moving) onto the visual imagination"; "inducing emotional correlation by the sound and rhythm of the speech"; and "inducing both of the effects by stimulating the associations (intellectual and emotional) that have remained in the receiver's consciousness in relation to the actual words or word groups employed."

In *Heavensgate*, then, Okigbo establishes his protagonist as a prodigal – a consciousness aware of the need for a new journey of self-discovery, which has to start with a cleansing – a traveler who has to restore himself to a unified personality and psychic stability.

The other major work completed at Nsukka was *Limits*. Okigbo described it, even before it was published, in his interview with Nkosi: "My *LIMITS* was influenced by everything and everybody. But this is not surprising, because the *LIMITS* were the limits of a dream. It is surprising how many lines of the *LIMITS* I am not sure are mine and yet do not know whose lines they were originally. But does it matter?" He also described its parts and the stages of the writing.

Limits is in two sections, first published separately in two 1962 issues of *Transition*. These two parts are named "Siren Limits" (parts 1–4) and "Fragments out of the Deluge" (parts 5–10). In the Nkosi interview, Okigbo spoke of "Siren Limits" as the prelude and said that he wrote it early in August 1961, that there was a gap of three months before he wrote the other parts, and that the whole work

Cover for the last book by Okigbo to be published in his lifetime

was not revised and ready until May 1962. Okigbo also spoke of the sections of *Limits* in classical-music terms, showing how much his imagination was suffused with the strategies of the musical composers: "The limit is, I will say, the limit of a dream and the prelude is about one-quarter of it divided into four parts, the first one which is the prelude to the preludes, and the second one which is a response by a chorus, the third one is the first development, and the fourth one is a divagation. Then we go into the heart of the work itself; there are six parts to the main work itself and the last one is almost an epilogue."

These statements by Okigbo introduce one to an appreciation of his mode of thought in connection with the poem. But in terms of the usual approach of extracting meaning out of a poem, they are not very helpful. The central concerns of *Limits* have been seen as divided into two spheres: the private/personal and the public/national/cultural.

"Siren Limits," the first four poems of the book, operate mainly at the private level. The first poem reintroduces the *Heavensgate* protagonist at an act of sacrifice. Okigbo sets the scene in a time-space environment that is mysterious – a "palm grove ... between sleep and waking" – and speaks of the Idoto/watermaid figure of devotion, now addressed as "Queen of the damp half light." The claim at the end of the poem, that the protagonist has had his cleansing, links *Limits* with the preoccupation in *Heavensgate*. The quest for self-fulfillment, which is the speaker's predilection, is seen in terms of a desired union with the "Queen," and this union requires an act of subjection and self-purification by him.

The second poem of the sequence gives a sedate picture of achievement, sustained through a single, consistent, growing-plant image, but the third poem strains to convey the picture of a frustrating and frustrated pilgrimage. These two poems have formed the basis of several interpretations of "Siren Limits" – as a statement on national cultural suppression or on artistic achievement and frustration.

The third poem is also an illustration of how an incident can be changed, in the imagination and poetry of Okigbo, into a much larger phenomenon and be so treated as to assume the dimensions of a universal myth. Okigbo's statement to Nkosi that "*Limits* was written at the end of a journey of several centuries from Nsukka and Yola in pursuit of what turned out to be an illusion" contains a mythic time factor ("a journey of several centuries"). But the poem in which this journey is re-created is much broader in its use of the pilgrimage motif set in a large, nebulous world and ending in a mysterious awakening to failure. Izevbaye attributes this technique to "the basic symbolist preoccupation to distill the poet's personal experiences into an aesthetic experience not necessarily related to the original experience."

The fourth poem reintroduces readers to the predominant female again, the subject of dedication and devotion by the poet, but this time made ugly, dangerous, and distracting:

> Oblong-headed lioness—
> No shield is proof against her—
> Wound me, O sea-weed
> Face, blinded like strong-room.

At the end of "Siren Limits," readers again encounter the perennial quest motif, after a presumed (momentary) fulfillment of the persona/poet and an apparent disastrous failure of action, a continuation of the theme and quest is promised in the concluding lines:

> When you have finished
> & done up my stitches,
> Wake me near the altar,
> *& this poem will be finished.* . . .

"Fragments out of the Deluge," the second part of *Limits*, re-creates a more external environment of cultural and national conflict. Okigbo himself described it as rendering "in retrospect certain details of the protagonist and of his milieu – the collective rape of innocence and profanation of the mysteries, in atonement for which he has had to suffer immolation." This section takes its images and allusions from various historical and literary sources, going back to the beginning of literature in the Sumerian epic of Gilgamesh, but the references also come as close and personal as Flannagan ("a well-known Irish priest of the 1940s") and Eunice ("my childhood nurse known for her lyricism"). Reference is also made to Pablo Picasso and his painting *Guernica* (1939).

The "Fragments" sequence is not purely external. At various points readers are again presented with images of a suffering, rejected protagonist. But the main parts of the section reflect vigorously on the destruction of the innocence and traditions of the protagonist's environment. Parts 8 and 10 are the most dramatic in presenting political activities as "a fleet of eagles" swooping "out of the solitude" over "the forest of oil bean." The destructive action is described in terms of authorities entering the grove of mystery and despoiling the twin

gods of the forest. The rout, which Okigbo attributes to external forces as part of his strategy for symbolically referring to the impact of the colonial political and religious activities on African culture, was historically committed by the people of Ojoto in 1929 against their gods, who had turned vicious toward them. It is part of Igbo tradition for people to destroy and remove their deity if the deity fails in the duties for which it was recognized or breaks the "contractual" relationship with the people by inflicting unexplained violence on them. But Okigbo uses even that successfully in this poem to revive in dramatic imagery the history of colonial cultural contact and exploitation.

What links together the whole book is the figure of the colorful, singing bird. At the beginning of "Siren Limits" readers are introduced to the noisy weaverbird. In part 8 they meet the sunbird, which warns of the impending attack and doom. Nobody listens, and a holocaust ensues. But at the end, "The sunbird sings again / From the LIMITS of the dream. . . ." An underlying theme is the validity and undying nature of the creative ideal and the fate of the community that rejects it. *Limits* therefore includes Okigbo's statement on the growth and nature of the poet and on his position in the community.

Though his first two major books were finished by the time Okigbo left the University of Nigeria, their publication belongs to a slightly later phase of his life, during which he married a teacher, Sefi, daughter of the Atta of Igbira, in 1963. Not much is said about this aspect of Okigbo's life, but it was important to him. Thomas has mentioned how much Okigbo was in love with Sefi. Living near him as a close friend, Thomas was able to separate Okigbo's internal moods from his outside behavior. In his 1968 memorial to Okigbo, he declared, "In private, the mask of mischief and bonhomie would sometimes be discarded – though seldom for very long – and I could see why it was that most of the poems made such profoundly sad, often nostalgic, music. For one thing, there was his wife, bonded to a school in the North, up near Lake Chad. 'Every time I meet her,' he told me once, 'I fall in love all over again.' And I remember his radiant face and contagious joy when he announced the birth of the daughter." The couple's daughter, Ibrahimat, was born in Ibadan in 1964. But Okigbo's separation from Sefi had lasted through most of his time at the University of Nigeria.

It is not clear, however, that Okigbo wanted to live permanently on a full-time basis with her. Anozie has said that Okigbo could not live happily under the same roof for a long time with a woman. How much of this reputation was bravado and how much represented Okigbo's true sentiments? Since he said that "*Limits* was written at the end of a journey of several centuries from Nsukka to Yola in pursuit of what turned out to be an illusion," one is tempted to speculate that this journey may have been a frustrating visit to the location where Sefi was engaged in teaching at the time.

By the time *Heavensgate* was published in 1962, Okigbo was living in Ibadan as the West African representative of Cambridge University Press. As the Nsukka phase had given him an opportunity to read more books, to listen to more music, and to make more contact with traditional realities, this Ibadan phase was to expose Okigbo to more public events, more contact with other writers, and more international travel.

At the Kampala Conference of African Writers of English Expression in June 1962, Okigbo initiated a discussion on the thorny question of what constitutes African literature. He was later to refuse to tie any tag of "African" or "Negro" to his own writing. But during this conference he posed searching speculations as to the definition of African literature – whether it was literature written by Africans, or by anybody on African subjects, or possessed of special characteristics that are African. The tendency of the conference was not to be too emphatic on circumscribing and localizing literature.

He was an eccentric, highly respected member of the conference, and practical discussions led to his being appointed the West African editor for *Transition*, the intellectual journal then being edited in Kampala by Rajat Neogy. Okigbo's poems soon started to appear in *Transition*.

Okigbo set up house in Ibadan in a rather grand fashion. Marjory Whitelaw took note of his home when she interviewed him in 1965: "His house was large and well-furnished, with possibly an Italian air about it." The poet and critic Paul Theroux, also in 1965, described its "white rugs and fake fur walls and white cushions everywhere. Americans told me they hated the decor – 'It's not African,' they said. 'It looked Italian, like something out of Fellini.' It was clean and very comfortable and it was obvious that Okigbo was very happy in the house." His house and furniture reflected his attitude of eclecticism, his willingness to use whatever resources were available to him from anywhere in the world to fashion his life, facilities, and poetry – the more striking the factors the better.

Okigbo's life-style in Ibadan did not include a family. Though he married Sefi there, he did not bring his wife to live in Ibadan with him. This may have been because she was still teaching in northern Nigeria. But she had enough social connections to be released from her government-scholarship bond and transferred to Ibadan if Okigbo had so insisted. Most likely he could not have shared the same house with a wife. He said as much to his friends, and Kole Omotoso has reported the influence this statement made on him: "Okigbo said he could not imagine a situation whereby he would live in the same house with a woman as his wife. I knew he was married. . . . At that time I had read the biography of writers, poets, artists and it seemed that there was one constant problem: they never seemed capable of sustaining a marriage relationship. Being in close contact with one poet who expressed the same sentiment must have predisposed me to the feeling I carried about with me for many years that one could not be a writer or an artist or a poet at the same time as a husband and a father." However, Okigbo maintained good contact with his wife. When their child was to be born, he insisted that Sefi come to Ibadan to give birth to the baby at the University Teaching Hospital. Yet, when the period of serious labor started, he ran away from the hospital. He did not show up at home until his elder brother Lawrence had paid the bills and brought the wife and child from the hospital.

Okigbo was devoted to his daughter, and he acquired a reputation as a lover of children. The memories held by Achebe of the pranks played between Okigbo and Achebe's son of three illustrate how playful Okigbo could be. Indeed he had inspired so much affection in the boy that when Achebe brought the news of Okigbo's death, the boy was provoked to a sensitive cry of "Daddy, don't let him die," which provided the title for Achebe's anthology of memorial poems in honor of Okigbo.

Okigbo did not, obviously, have much of a chance to play with his daughter, but there must have been some regular contact. When he came back from the Commonwealth Arts Festival in Edinburgh and a business trip to London in July 1965, he wrote to his father indicating that he would be visiting home with his wife and daughter. And when, in 1965, he completed work on the final edition of his poem sequences for *Labyrinths*, his dedication of the book was to "Sefi and Ibrahimat: Mother and Child."

Ibadan was the center of a very vibrant literary and artistic culture, and Okigbo participated fully. O. R. Dathorne has written of the almost interminable discussions that used to continue from house to house: "When everybody did meet in Clark's flat just under mine, J. P. talked J. P.; Okigbo talked Okigbo; Soyinka refrained, saying that it was a mutual admiration society. But everybody wrote. Okigbo always introduced himself by proclaiming 'I am Okigbo' and his volatile temperament seemed curiously crystallized in those words." Wole Soyinka, Clark, and Okigbo were then all living in Ibadan along with a large group of expatriate art-and-literature scholars, such as Ulli Beier, Gerald Moore, and Denis Williams. There was also a growing body of young Nigerian artists and scholars, including Demas Nwoko, who did the illustrations for *Heavensgate*; Abiola Irele; Omolara Leslie; Femi Osofisan; and Omotoso. The Mbari Centre in Ibadan provided a focus for these literary and cultural activities, and Okigbo's regular presence there was an inspiration to many young artists and budding creative writers.

The tribute by Omotoso in his essay "Christopher Okigbo: A Personal Portrait" gives a vivid picture of a man who was a "vibrant personality," who took an interest in young talents, and who was ready to spend a great amount of time with them, encourage them with his conversation, lend them books that he thought would sharpen their imaginations, and be generally available. These attributes remind one of the descriptions by Anozie of his own contacts earlier with Okigbo at Nsukka. The last telephone conversation between Omotoso and Okigbo, after the mass exodus of eastern Nigerians from other parts of Nigeria, epitomized the physical, emotional, and psychological break in communication that was the prelude to the Nigerian civil war.

Okigbo's work with Cambridge University Press also put him in contact with many writers and made international travel routine for him. His job also gave him access to cultural activities at the international level, and some of his later poems were first read in such contexts.

During the period from 1962 to 1965 Okigbo was interviewed both in Ibadan and London. These interviews offer insights into his ideas on life, art, and criticism. He spoke to Nkosi of the kind of audience he wished for his poetry. Okigbo was aware that not many Nigerians read poetry, and even among these there were few who would be naturally attracted to the kind of poetry he wrote, which they would consider difficult. For his audience, therefore, he wanted kindred spirits, "other poets all over the world to read and see whether they can share in my experience." Applause was not what he

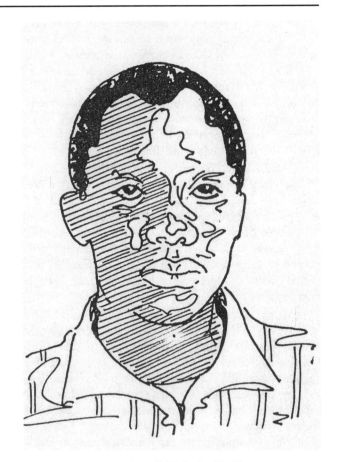

Caricature of Okigbo by Obe Ess

wanted, since quite often the applause would be for the wrong reasons: "I don't think I have any ambition to become a very popular poet. I think I am just satisfied if a good deal of friends come by my work and get something out of it." About the need for craft he said, "A poem can come by accident and a lot of it does come by accident, but it has to be moulded into the form in which you want it preserved and this means a lot of — this embraces the question of craftmanship. I believe that there is craft apart from the art — if there is craft alone, then you can easily see through the thing and see that there isn't any feeling but art isn't enough, there must be craft also." He insisted on his preference for sensitive poetry as against "academic versifying," he rejected the concept of the "black mystique" inherent in the negritude movement, and he found disfavor with the tendency of Beier to give prominence, and indeed pride of place, to experimental work which did not show enough evidence of originality.

Two issues discussed by Okigbo in interviews are important for the consideration of his life and poetry: the issue of poets and commitment, and that of meaning in poetry. He rejected the overt commitment that seemed to be demanded as a program for the creative writer. In his interview with Whitelaw he was very explicit on the question. He did not see that self-exploration was an irrelevance in the crisis of change taking place in Africa: "Because the writer isn't *living* in isolation. He is interacting with different groups of people at different times. And any inward exploration involves the interaction of the subject with other people, and I believe that a writer who sets out to discover himself, by so doing will also discover his society. I don't think that I like writing that is 'committed.' I think it is very cheap. I think it is the easy way of doing it."

As a corollary to this position, he gave no special place to the creative writer in terms of national political or social roles. Poems were expressions of states of mind, and they could affect readers in different ways; it was up to readers to do what they preferred with the poetic product. He did not think that "it is necessary for the writer to assume a particular function as The Messiah or anything like that." Okigbo made a distinction between the person as a citizen and the person as a writer, and he thought that though the individual may assume any role he chose, "I don't think that the fact that he's a writer should entitle him to assume a particular role." The example Okigbo chose to illustrate his point was that of the role of teacher, which put him at the opposite end of the argument from Achebe, who had spoken in 1964 of the role of the novelist as teacher. For Okigbo, "If he [the writer] wants to educate people he should write textbooks. If he wants to preach a gospel he should write religious tracts. If he wants to propound a certain ideology he should write political tracts." This attitude toward the role of the writer/citizen was ominous and indeed prepares one to understand why, when the Nigerian crisis came to the point of war, Okigbo did not retire to the role of poet of the revolution but took up arms physically as a Biafran citizen.

The second issue is related to the first and concerns the intention of the poet in terms of meaning. Okigbo's "Lament of the Drums" was featured at the 1965 Commonwealth Arts Festival, and Robert Serumaga asked him how the poem came about. Okigbo's response attributed the poem to the drums. He created the drums all right, but what they said in the poem was their own: "the drums spoke what they spoke." To Serumaga's further comment on the immense difficulty of intellectually comprehending the poem, Okigbo made this often-quoted statement which explains his attitude toward meaning in poetry:

> Well, because what we call understanding – talking generally of the relationship between the poetry-reader and

the poem itself – passes through a process of analysis . . . there is an intellectual effort which one makes before one arrives at what one calls the meaning. Now I think it is possible to arrive at a response without passing through that process of intellectual analysis, and I think that if a poem can elicit a response, either in physical or emotional terms from an audience, the poem has succeeded. Personally I don't think that I have ever set out to communicate a meaning. It is enough that I try to communicate experience which I consider significant.

This statement is very important for the formulation of strategies for participating in the experience embedded in the Okigbo oeuvre.

Okigbo's poetic creativity flourished and came to a conclusion in Ibadan. In 1962 he completed "Lament of the Silent Sisters," which was immediately published in *Transition* (1963). In 1964 he completed two poems: "Lament of the Drums" and "Distances." "Lament of the Drums" was the second part of the "Silences" sequence, and "Distances" concluded Okigbo's quest poetry. These represent major poem sequences. When *Transition* published "Distances" in 1964, the editors promised that "with the publication of 'Lament of the Drums' in *Transition* 18 next year, Okigbo will have created a body of poetry that will rank him the major poet in English-speaking Africa."

Though "Lament of the Silent Sisters" was written in 1962 and was closer in time to *Limits*, it was "Distances," written and published in 1964, that Okigbo saw as the complement to *Limits*. In the introduction to *Labyrinths*, he wrote of them as follows: "*Limits* and *Distances* are man's outer and inner worlds projected – the phenomenal and the imaginative, not in terms of their separateness but of their relationship." He went further to say of "Distances" that it is "a poem of homecoming, but of homecoming in its spiritual and psychic aspect."

There have been several studies of "Distances," and these all confirm it as the poem that shows the fulfillment of the quest at the center of Okigbo's poetry. In many ways it is a terrifying poem, and Okigbo takes full advantage of a dreamy, euphoric state. He also said in the *Labyrinths* introduction that " 'Distances' was written after my first experience of surgery under general anesthesia."

The homecoming, as he writes in the poem, was "from flesh into phantom on the horizontal stone," the horizontal stone being both the operating table and the altar of a deity. "Distances" has been illuminatingly studied from the "speech-act-theory" perspective by John Haynes (in 1986) to show how an awareness of the stances taken by the poet further reveals the characters at work in the poem. The study helps to expose each character's field of discourse and allusion and therefore the meaning of the poem. This poem declares three times, "I was the sole witness to my homecoming," and readers may ask where he has arrived, where he was coming from, and the context and meaning of *homecoming*.

Some critics have been tempted to declare that this homecoming was the final arrival at the worship of, and reunion with, Idoto, and a final rejection of Christ and Christianity. Others have seen it in terms of the achievement of a stage of aesthetic grace after a cycle of spiritual and historical exploration. Still others have used the Jungian proposal of the anima and animus to posit the theme of self-fulfilling reunion of the two parts of the poet's self.

What is clear is the pattern set up by the poem. Starting from the euphoric but obviously religious state of awakening, Okigbo moves on to a pilgrimage motif, the journey being endangered by the environment in poem 2: "Death lay in ambush that evening in that island, / voice sought its echo that evening in the island." Indeed this poem contains what may be called the most realized visual image in Okigbo's oeuvre, a terrifying transfiguration of the White Goddess Idoto, the Lioness, into the uncaring figure of Death – reminding one of Okigbo's reference to the object of his devotion as "the supreme spirit that is both destructive and creative":

> and behind them all,
> in smock of white cotton,
> Death herself,
> the chief celebrant,
> in a cloud of incense
> paring her fingernails. . . .
>
> At her feet rolled their heads like cut fruits;
> about her fell
> their severed members, numerous as locusts.
>
> Like split wood left to dry, the dismembered
> joints of the ministrants piled high.
>
> She bathed her knees in the blood of attendants. . . .

The third, fourth, and fifth poems of "Distances" explore the motif of pilgrimage in heavily Christian and biblical imagery, creating environments that identify and criticize various participants and actors in the journey of life – prophets, martyrs, lunatics, dilettantes, vendors, politicians, and so on.

Ultimately the confusion clears, the unity of experience is appreciated, and what Fraser calls "a spiritual apotheosis" is reached. In the end the mysterious marriage of the mortal to the immortal oc-

curs, the questing poet/protagonist makes his junction with the goddess, and this union ends in glorious terms the anguished quest of life.

"Distances" completed Okigbo's private quest for self-realization, but "Silences," in its two parts, marked his involvement with the society in which he lived. Though he had declared that one need not set out to express meaning and that the poet's exploration of his own experiences would inevitably lead to his statement on his society, he did actually react to events of his time.

"Lament of the Silent Sisters," written in 1962, was provoked by the western Nigeria crisis of that year; "Lament of the Drums" by the imprisonment of Awolowo and the tragic death of Awolowo's eldest son. "Lament of the Silent Sisters" heralds Okigbo's maturing into the poet of destiny. The agony of apprehension that had provided the internal dynamics of his internal quest yielded here a transformation of a political event into the human condition and the declaration of an attitude to that condition. As Okigbo was to say, the search in the poem was for the framework of words that could declare a rejection of the human condition: "The problem 'How does one say NO in thunder' is then finally resolved in silence. For the ultimate answer is to be sought only in terms of each poet's response to the medium."

"Lament of the Silent Sisters" also marked the peak of one style and a turning point in Okigbo's management of his words, images, and sentences. Moving from the imitativeness dominated by the concept of objective and symbolist poetry, Okigbo achieves his own voice in this poem so that any identifiably foreign elements only add external supportive imagery to his own thought and statement. He shares the concerns of his people and becomes their mouthpiece. The persistent images are of drowning, violence, the trivialization of a disastrous tragedy, and the anguish and "cadenced cry" of the perceiving consciousness.

"Lament of the Drums," on the other hand, is the attempt by Okigbo to create a dramatic self-exclusion and give the comments on the political situation to the funerary drums. To Serumaga he said that all he did "was to create the drums and the drums said what they liked. Personally I don't believe that I am capable of saying what the drums have said in that first part."

"Lament of the Drums" was a much-revised poem. The first publication in *Transition* (1965) was quite different, especially in the first movement, from subsequent publications in *Black Orpheus* (later in 1965) and in *Labyrinths*. Okigbo wrote the third

About Dakar. I did not go. Did you? I found
the whole idea of a negro arts festival based on
colour quite absurd. I did not enter any work either
for the competition, and was most surprised when I
heard a prize had been awarded to LIMITS. I have
written to reject it.

What else have you been working on besides
Creative Rhetoric? I am at the moment writing the
closing chapters of my large prose work entitled
Pointed Arches. Pointed Arches is neither fiction
nor criticism nor autobiography. It is an attempt
to describe the growth of the creative impulse in me,
an account of certain significant facts in my
experience of life and letters that conspired to shapen
my imagination. It throws some light on certain
apparently irreconcilable features of my work and life,
and places them in a new perspective. I am hoping for
publication by 1970.

With my very best wishes.

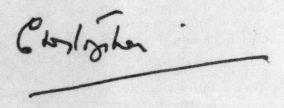

Page from Okigbo's 5 May 1966 letter to Sunday O. Anozie, author of Christopher Okigbo: Creative Rhetoric *(1972). "Pointed Arches" has not been published (Collection of Sunday O. Anozie).*

part, the section on Palinurus, some months before the other parts. The poem is a good example of how, in Okigbo's hands, an event, already perceived in an image/symbol, grows until it far outstrips its original provocation and, by drawing together relevant parallel myths from all over the world, becomes a new universal symbol. The imprisonment of Awolowo and his tragedy, first seen in the Palinurus image, goes on to memorialize Christ's martyrdom and betrayal by Judas, and ends up in the annual death ritual and renewal of the native deity Tammuz. The poem then ends with a re-creation of Ishtar's lament for Tammuz. As Fraser has noted (in "Christopher Okigbo and the Flutes of Tammuz," 1984), this use of the Tammuz death-and-resurrection myth recalls "that mysterious metamorphosis by which the authentic tragic spirit is enabled to convert devastation into matter for affirmative rejoicing."

By 1965 Okigbo was summarizing his poetry. "Distances" had concluded a phase of external and internal quest. He became lax both in his creativity and his publishing work. It was as if the spirit had left him after the disastrous movements in the politics of the Western Region of Nigeria, where he was based. The months between early 1964 and late 1965 were not very productive poetically for Okigbo. They were also months of not-very-efficient contribution by him to the publishing business of Cambridge University Press. Visitors to Okigbo over this period report much talking far into the night, much thinking of other possible directions for exhilarating activities, and a lack of interest in the mail – either his own or that of Cambridge University Press. His brother Lawrence mentions seeing a check for a fair sum of money on Okigbo's table and taking a look at it to find that it had expired after a year of not being cashed. Theroux, who visited and stayed with him for some weeks in 1965, has written of Okigbo's boredom with his job at this time. Theroux reports that, by the time he met him, Okigbo "was so bored by the job he had stopped opening his mail. It simply accumulated, like fallen leaves. A man came with mail-bags full of proof copies and catalogues, and Okigbo dumped these on the table without glancing at them."

Two poems did emerge from this period, both published in 1965: "Lament of the Masks" and "Dance of the Painted Maidens," the latter of which was Okigbo's contribution to the Edinburgh Festival of that year.

"Lament of the Masks" draws practically all its imagery from the Yoruba *oriki* (celebration) in praise of the Timi of Ede. This lament contains many images referring to violence, and even if the basis was the struggle W. B. Yeats had to wage against British supercilious disdain to establish a dignity for the Irish and their literature, there is no doubt that the violence in Nigeria also fired Okigbo's imagination, which

Charges to the assault;
. . . .
For we answer the cannon
From far off –

And from throats of iron
In bird-masks
Unlike accusing tones that issue forth javelins . . . [.]

"Dance of the Painted Maidens" is almost

pure sound. The repetitions of phrases and the choice of vowels and consonants make the poem ring with melody: "After she had set sail after she had set sail / After the mother-of-the-earth had set sail / After the earth-mother on her homeward journey. . . ." The poem sets up a pattern, like most Okigbo poems, contrasting the absence of the Earth-Mother with what one obtains when she is present.

Okigbo expressed indebtedness to Ben Obumselu of the University of Ibadan English department for criticisms that affected "the phrase and structure" of the poems he wrote at Ibadan. Obumselu has claimed that many of the poems taken with so much seriousness were jokes being played by Okigbo. Specifically he said that the "Hurry on down" sequence in *Limits*, culminating in these lines: "To pull by the rope / the big white elephant . . . ," referred to Okigbo's high expectation and his failure to perform sexually on a given occasion. One is tempted to read "Dance of the Painted Maidens" in this light. "Earth-mother" is the earth deity, but she is also the masquerade "Mother-of-the-Earth" (*Nne Uwa*). The expression can be used to describe a woman of some weight and prominence. This perspective would make sequence 3 of this poem have vivid sexual overtones. The masquerade aspect is recalled again in part 4, where the words are those with which one answers a masquerade:

We did not know you
Who were whom we hold
For to know you was
To know the infinite[.]

But no poem of Okigbo's stops with one level of interpretation of experience. The pattern set up could recapture the external reality of cultural/political alienation from colonialism and the renewal and reintegration that was being achieved. The deity Earth-Mother, different from, but serving the same function as, the river goddess Idoto, becomes the desired object for the achievement of reunion to bring protection and salvation:

Today on your homecoming
Patient mother
With you in our palm
The life horn is our cup.

The catastrophic national events toward the end of 1965 and into early 1966 inspired Okigbo to his best and most admired set of poems, "Path of Thunder: Poems Prophesying War." These poems were available to be published posthumously in

Black Orpheus (1968), and then with *Labyrinths*, only because some friend had retained a copy in Ibadan. The irrationality in Nigeria's political and economic activities led to a military coup in 1966, followed by the massacre of Igbos and other eastern Nigerians in many parts of Nigeria, especially in northern Nigeria, and the consequent exodus of eastern Nigerians from other parts of Nigeria into the Eastern Region. "Path of Thunder" reflects these events. It describes what was happening and warns against what could happen. Every critic has found these poems, except for their lack of Okigbo's characteristic revisions in some units, to be the peak of his achievement. "Path of Thunder" reconciled many otherwise disgruntled readers to the poetry of Okigbo. For some it signaled a change in Okigbo from the esoteric to the indigenous. For others it is the culmination of his chosen poetic style, the use of his trained voice, which had gathered its timbre from many sources, to speak like the prophets of old on a most crucial phase of his nation's existence. The military had taken over power in Nigeria, and Okigbo proclaimed: "Fanfare of drum, wooden bells: iron chapter; / And the dividing airs are gathered home...." The divisive politics of ethnicity and religious bigotry had led to a cataclysm, and Okigbo could see the disastrous conclusion. "Path of Thunder" is Okigbo's last communication with Nigeria and the world through poetry.

Okigbo came to Enugu with the other Igbos chased out of the rest of Nigeria. He and Achebe set up a publishing company there, aimed mainly at producing books for young readers, but it never succeeded. The political and military disagreement in Nigeria soon degenerated into a civil war. Once it was reported that a plane carrying arms to the secessionists, which crashed in the Cameroons, contained a briefcase of Okigbo's. The story was promptly denied. But when the actual fighting started, he soon joined the Biafran Army and was commissioned as a major. Two months into the war, in August 1967, he was killed at the Nsukka front.

Much is reported of Okigbo's activities within those two months that is revelatory of his character. It appears that as he lived, so he died. During the rallies of mobilization, various kinds of performers contributed their talents. Echeruo has told a story that shows how Okigbo used to react to his perception of creativity in others. Echeruo, Okigbo, and others were in the Enugu stadium during one of the solidarity rallies and suddenly Okigbo struck his hands together and asked Echeruo to drive him fast to the hotel where they were staying. One of the

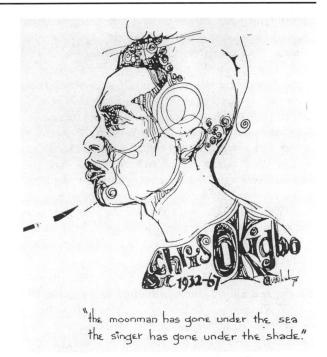

"the moonman has gone under the sea
the singer has gone under the shade."

Sketch of Okigbo by Obiora Udechukwu. The quotation is from one of Okigbo's poems (from Homage to Christopher Okigbo: Catalogue, *1975).*

marching songs had given him the inspiration and idea for a national anthem for Biafra. However, nothing apparently came of that idea.

Achebe also has a story of how, when they were staying at the Catering Rest House in Enugu, there was a performance by a local minstrel called "Area Scatter." Okigbo was so thrilled that he shouted across to Achebe, "Come and see a real poet! We are wasting our time. This is a real poet!"

Some of the generals of Biafra who have written their memoirs have imparted to Okigbo an image of bravery and courage during the war. To this picture must be added the image of the romantic. Ike followed Okigbo's war career and tells the story of how Okigbo used to go to battle sitting on the hood of a jeep. His romantic fantasy was of charging into battle bestriding his horse. He told stories of how he and others had disturbed the eating time of the Nigerian soldiers, who had no right to eat in peace in Biafra after harassing people out of their homes.

Chukwuma Azuonye and a young colleague, Columbus Ihekaibeya, rode in a car to the Nsukka front as war reporters. Okigbo commandeered their car. They complained that he could not do it because they were war columnists. At that point he turned on them and said, "if you are war reporters then you must watch a battle." So he took them toward the scene of battle. There was a heavy enemy attack taking place at the time. They had just heard that a Major Okafor had been killed. So many other names were being mentioned of people who had just been killed. The reporters were praying intensely, all their previous contact with war having been gained through their ears and through reading about Charlemagne. Still Okigbo took them forward and said they must move toward the source of the artillery fire that was being aimed at them but whose shells were falling behind them. Azuonye and his colleague escaped as Okigbo walked forward toward the source of the artillery fire. They nearly killed themselves for, while escaping, they were really running into the range of the explosions. What saved them was the cessation of the shelling.

Some days later Okigbo met Azuonye in Enugu and asked him how he had enjoyed the battle. He also showed Azuonye all the things the reporter had let fall while he ran from the front, but he said that Azuonye had to come to the field camp to claim them. The day that Azuonye went there Okigbo was already dead.

Okigbo's last moments were reported by his friend and fellow poet Gaius Anoka. Okigbo was keeping watch at Opi junction and said that the Nigerian soldiers would pass that point over his dead body. They did. Pius Okigbo has said that the bullet that killed Christopher hit him on the neck in the same spot as the bullet that killed the maternal grandfather whose reincarnation he was.

In death as in life Christopher Okigbo has been controversial. Some of the controversy has been about whether he should even have ventured into military combat, but he saw that as his fate and destiny, and he confronted it.

His reputation as an African poet writing in English has been the highest. In 1985 Fred Akporobaro observed that "With the intense personal experience of the early poems – *Heavensgate, Limits, Silences* and *Distances* – and the relevance and directness of the socio-historical experience of *Path of Thunder*, he achieves the distinction of being the most inspired, profound, stimulating and intellectually challenging of the modern African Poets." In 1986 Fraser, writing on "The Achievement of Christopher Okigbo," claimed that his slim volume of poetry (*Labyrinths*) "arguably represents the most revered trophy in the gallery of English-language verse in Africa, and Okigbo himself the most talented of modern African poets."

Polemic continues to flourish with regard to his so-called obscurity. The issue will never be exhausted, but evidence grows that his poetic strate-

gies will be further and further clarified and, at last, his poetry will be seen for its strong exploratory inspiration and for its thematic contribution to the experiencing of the nature and impact of modernity in human lives and imagination.

The context of Okigbo's major poetry was one of literary and cultural effervescence in which the creative spirit accepted no limitation as to the audience to be addressed, the sources of influence, the languages and literatures, or even the forms of art from which one could draw inspiration. The limits of one's horizon extended beyond continents and present times. The writer wrote for the world, for anybody anywhere who could respond to the literature. The world contributed to sharpening the poetic voice of Christopher Okigbo. In return he added new flavor to the world. He played poetic pranks with humor, not with viciousness, and those who wish to enjoy his early poetry must share his games. With age and with the darkening events surrounding him, he spoke with the voice of wisdom in the language and images of his people. Young poets complain of his difficulty, but the sensitive ones end up borrowing several elements from his style. His greatest tribute will be in his poetic offspring.

Interviews:

Marjory Whitelaw, "Interview with Christopher Okigbo, 1965," *Journal of Commonwealth Literature*, 9 (1970): 28–37;

Dennis Duerden and Cosmo Pieterse, eds., *African Writers Talking: A Collection of Radio Interviews* (London: Heinemann / New York: Africana, 1972), pp. 133–147;

Lewis Nkosi, Interview, in *Critical Perspectives on Christopher Okigbo*, edited by Donatus Ibe Nwoga (Washington, D.C.: Three Continents, 1984).

Bibliographies:

Joseph C. Anafulu, "Christopher Okigbo, 1932–1967: A Bio-Bibliography," *Research in African Literatures*, 9 (1978): 65–78; reprinted in *Critical Perspectives on Christopher Okigbo*, edited by Donatus Ibe Nwoga (Washington, D.C.: Three Continents, 1984), pp. 349–361;

Bernth Lindfors, "Addenda to Okigbo Bibliography," in *Critical Perspectives on Christopher Okigbo*, pp. 362–364.

References:

Chinua Achebe, Preface to *Don't Let Him Die: An Anthology of Memorial Poems for Christopher Okigbo (1932–1967)* (Enugu, Nigeria: Fourth Dimension, 1978);

J. A. Adedeji, "A Dramatic Approach to Okigbo's *Limits*," *Conch*, 3, no. 1 (1971): 45–59;

Fred Akporobaro, "Christopher Okigbo: Emotional Tension, Recurrent Motifs and Architectonic Sense in *Labyrinths*," *Nigeria Magazine*, 53, no. 2 (1985): 6–13;

Sunday O. Anozie, "Christopher Okigbo: A Creative Itinerary, 1957–1967," *Présence Africaine*, 64 (1967): 158–168;

Anozie, *Christopher Okigbo: Creative Rhetoric* (London: Evans / New York: Africana, 1972);

Anozie, "Okigbo's *Heavensgate*: A Study of Art as Ritual," *Ibadan*, 15 (1963): 11–13;

Chukwuma Azuonye, "Christopher Okigbo and the Psychological Theories of Carl Gustav Jung," *Journal of African and Comparative Literature*, 1 (1981): 30–51;

Michael G. Cooke, "Christopher Okigbo and Robert Hayden: From Mould to Stars," *World Literature Written in English*, 30 (Autumn 1990): 131–144;

O. R. Dathorne, "African Literature IV: Ritual and Ceremony in Okigbo's Poetry," *Journal of Commonwealth Literature*, 5 (July 1968): 79–91;

Dathorne, "Okigbo Understood: A Study of 'Two Poems,' " *African Literature Today*, 1, no. 1 (1968): 19–23;

Michael J. C. Echeruo, "Traditional and Borrowed Elements in Nigerian Poetry," *Nigeria Magazine*, 89 (June 1966): 142–155;

Romanus N. Egudu, "Anglophone African Poetry and Vernacular Rhetoric: The Example of Okigbo," *Lagos Review of English Studies*, 1, no. 1 (1979): 104–113;

Egudu, "Defence of Culture in the Poetry of Christopher Okigbo," *African Literature Today*, 6 (1973): 14–25;

Egudu, "Ezra Pound in African Poetry: Christopher Okigbo," *Comparative Literature Studies*, 8 (June 1971): 143–154;

Egudu, *Four Modern West African Poets* (New York: Nok, 1977);

Egudu, *Modern African Poetry and the African Predicament* (London & Basingstoke, U.K.: Macmillan, 1978; New York: Barnes & Noble, 1978);

Elaine Savory Fido, "Okigbo's *Labyrinths* and the Context of Igbo Attitudes to the Female Principle," in *Ngambika: Studies of Women in African Literature*, edited by Carole Boyce Davies and Anne Adams Graves (Trenton, N.J.: Africa World, 1986), pp. 223–239;

Robert Fraser, "Christopher Okigbo and the Flutes of Tammuz," in *A Sense of Place: Essays in Post-Colonial Literatures*, edited by Britta Olinder (Gothenburg, Sweden: English Department, Gothenburg University, 1984), pp. 190–195;

Fraser, *West African Poetry: A Critical History* (Cambridge: Cambridge University Press, 1986), pp. 104–137;

Ken Goodwin, *Understanding African Poetry: A Study of Ten Poets* (London: Heinemann, 1982);

John Haynes, "Okigbo's Technique in 'Distances I,' " *Research in African Literatures*, 17 (Spring 1986): 73–84;

Annemarie Heywood, "The Ritual and the Plot: The Critic and Okigbo's *Labyrinths*," *Research in African Literatures*, 9 (Spring 1978): 46–64;

Ime Ikiddeh, "Iron, Thunder and Elephants: A Study of Okigbo's *Path of Thunder*," *New Horn*, 1, no. 2 (1974): 46–67;

D. S. Izevbaye, "Death and the Artist: An Appreciation of Okigbo's Poetry," *Research in African Literatures*, 13 (Spring 1982): 44–52;

Izevbaye, "From Reality to Dream: The Poetry of Christopher Okigbo," in *The Critical Evaluation of African Literature*, edited by Edgar Wright (London: Heinemann, 1973), pp. 120–148;

Izevbaye, "Okigbo's Portrait of the Artist as a Sunbird: A Reading of *Heavensgate*," *African Literature Today*, 6 (1973): 1–13;

Omolara Leslie, "Christopher Okigbo: The Development of a Poet," *New Horn*, 1, no. 2 (1974): 17–32;

Leslie, "The Poetry of Christopher Okigbo: Its Evolution and Significance," *Ufahamu*, 4, no. 1 (1973): 47–54;

Bernth Lindfors, "Okigbo as Jock," *English in Africa*, 6 (March 1979): 52–59;

Ali A. Mazrui, "Meaning versus Imagery in African Poetry," *Présence Africaine*, 66 (1968): 49–59;

Gerald Moore, *The Chosen Tongue* (London: Longman, 1969);

Jonathan Ngaté, "Senghor and Okigbo: The Way Out of Exile," in *Explorations: Essays in Comparative Literature*, edited by Matoto Ueda (Lanham, Md.: University Presses of America, 1986), pp. 253–277;

Donatus Ibe Nwoga, "Okigbo's *Limits*: An Approach to Meaning," *Journal of Commonwealth Literature*, 7 (June 1972): 92–101;

Nwoga, "Plagiarism and Authentic Creativity in West Africa," *Research in African Literatures*, 6 (Spring 1975): 32–39;

Nwoga, ed., *Critical Perspectives on Christopher Okigbo* (Washington, D.C.: Three Continents, 1984);

Wole Ogundele, "From the Labyrinth to the Temple: The Structure of Okigbo's Religious Experience," *Okike*, 24 (June 1983): 57–69;

Dubem Okafor, *Nationalism in Okigbo's Poetry* (Enugu, Nigeria: Fourth Dimension, 1980);

Kole Omotoso, "Christopher Okigbo: A Personal Portrait, 1932-1967," *New Horn*, 1, no. 2 (1974): 4–15;

John Povey, "Epitaph to Christopher Okigbo," *Africa Today*, 14, no. 6 (1967): 22–23;

Annie Provinciael, "An Introduction to Okigbo's *Labyrinths*," *Restant*, 8 (Spring 1980): 57–67;

Adrian Roscoe, *Mother Is Gold: A Study in West African Literature* (Cambridge: Cambridge University Press, 1971);

Paul Theroux, "Christopher Okigbo," *Transition*, 5, no. 22 (1965): 18–20;

Theroux, "Voices out of the Skull: A Study of Six African Poets," *Black Orpheus*, 20 (August 1966): 41–58;

Peter Thomas, "The Hidden Dancer, Together with 'A Personal Note on Christopher Okigbo,'" *Compass*, 5/6 (1973–1974): 24–25;

Thomas, "An Image Insists," *Greenfield Review*, 8, nos. 1-2 (1980): 122–126;

Thomas, "Ride Me Memories: A Memorial Tribute to Christopher Okigbo," *African Arts*, 1 (Summer 1968): 68–70;

Thomas, "The Water Maid and the Dancer: Figures of the Nigerian Muse," *Literature East and West*, 12 (March 1968): 85–93;

Edwin Thumboo, "Dathorne's Okigbo: A Dissenting View," *African Literature Today*, 3 (1969): 44–49;

Nyong J. Udoeyop, *Three Nigerian Poets* (Ibadan: Ibadan University Press, 1973);

James Wieland, "Beginning: Christopher Okigbo's 'Four Canzones,'" *World Literature Written in English*, 23 (Spring 1984): 315–342;

Wieland, "From Orpheus to Town-Crier: *Path of Thunder* and the Canon," *World Literature Written in English*, 25 (Spring 1985): 31–42;

Noel Woodroffe, "Songs of Thunder: The Biafran War in the Poetry of Chinua Achebe and Christopher Okigbo," *Commonwealth Essays and Studies*, 10 (Spring 1988): 80–87.

Okot p'Bitek

(1931 – 20 July 1982)

Bernth Lindfors
University of Texas at Austin

BOOKS: *Lak Tar Miyo Kinyero Wi Lobo* (Kampala, Nairobi & Dar es Salaam: Eagle, 1953); translated as *White Teeth* (Nairobi: Heinemann Kenya, 1989);

Song of Lawino: A Lament (Nairobi: East African Publishing House, 1966; New York: Meridian, 1969); published in the original Acoli as *Wer pa Lawino* (Nairobi: East African Publishing House, 1969);

Song of Ocol (Nairobi: East African Publishing House, 1970);

Two Songs: Song of Prisoner; Song of Malaya (Nairobi: East African Publishing House, 1971); "Song of Prisoner" published separately as *Song of a Prisoner* (New York: Third Press, 1971);

Religion of the Central Luo (Nairobi, Kampala & Dar es Salaam: East African Literature Bureau, 1971);

African Religions in Western Scholarship (Kampala, Nairobi & Dar es Salaam: East African Literature Bureau, 1971; Totowa, N.J.: Rowman & Littlefield, 1972);

Africa's Cultural Revolution (Nairobi: Macmillan, 1973);

Artist, the Ruler: Essays on Art, Culture and Values (Nairobi: Heinemann Kenya, 1986).

Collection: *Song of Lawino & Song of Ocol* (Nairobi: East African Publishing House, 1972; London: Heinemann, 1984).

RECORDING: *Okot p'Bitek of Uganda*, Washington, D.C., Voice of America, 1978.

OTHER: *The Horn of My Love*, compiled and translated (from Acoli) by Okot (London: Heinemann, 1974; New York: Humanities, 1974);

Hare and Hornbill, compiled and translated (from Acoli) by Okot (London: Heinemann, 1978);

Acoli Proverbs, compiled and translated by Okot (Nairobi: Heinemann Kenya, 1985).

Okot p'Bitek (Transcription Centre Archive, Harry Ransom Humanities Research Center, University of Texas at Austin)

When Okot p'Bitek surprised the world with *Song of Lawino* in 1966, he was recognized immediately as a major African poet. No other African writer – except possibly Christopher Okigbo of Nigeria – had made such an indelible impact with his first volume of verse, creating at one stroke a new poetic idiom so entirely his own. Most African poets writing in English and French were cultural mulattoes seeking self-consciously to fuse the two disparate traditions of verbal creativity on which they had been nurtured. Léopold Sédar Senghor, for instance, certainly owed as much to French surrealism as he did to the songs of the Serer people; Okigbo was literarily descended from Ezra Pound, T. S. Eliot, and Peter Thomas, as well as from anonymous Igbo bards; and J. P. Clark had deliberately imitated the techniques of Gerard Manley Hopkins, Dylan Thomas, Japanese haiku, and Ijaw oral art while forging his early apprentice verse. But Okot was refreshingly different. No European echoes could be heard in the background. His *Song of Lawino* was the first long poem in English to achieve a totally African identity.

This was no accident, considering Okot's education, cultural interests, and literary inclinations. He was born in 1931 in Gulu, Uganda, to a schoolteacher and his wife. After attending schools in Uganda, earning a Certificate of Education at Bristol University in England, and studying law at the University of Wales in Aberystwyth, Okot went on to Oxford, where he studied for his B.Litt. at the Institute of Social Anthropology. It was here that he wrote a thesis on Acoli and Lango traditional songs, a formal academic study that must have forced him to take a closer look at the structure, content, and style of songs he had heard and sung as a young man growing up in Uganda. This project, completed three years before the publication of *Song of Lawino*, may have suggested to him a new way of singing in English.

Okot appears to have developed an interest in music, song, literature, and traditional culture while very young and to have sustained this interest throughout his life. As a schoolboy at King's College in Budo, Uganda, he composed and produced an opera, and in 1953, when only twenty-two years old, he published his first literary work, *Lak Tar Miyo Kinyero Wi Lobo* (Are Your Teeth White? Then Laugh), a novel in Acoli that was translated as *White Teeth* in 1989. After completing his undergraduate education in Britain, he returned to Uganda and joined the staff of the Extra-Mural Department at Makerere University College in Kampala; his job enabled him to carry out further research on the oral literature of the peoples of northern Uganda and to found and organize the annual Gulu Festival of the Arts. In 1966 he was appointed director of the Uganda National Theatre and Cultural Centre in Kampala, where he did much to promote local

cultural activities. At the end of 1967 he joined the Western Kenya section of Nairobi University College's Extra-Mural Department and immediately became the moving force behind the first Kisumu Arts Festival, held in December 1968. Then, in the academic year 1969–1970, he accepted a one-year appointment as fellow in the International Writing Program at the University of Iowa, a position that enabled him to write full-time. A year later he became associated with the University of Nairobi as a research fellow at the Institute of African Studies and a part-time lecturer in sociology and literature. He remained at the University of Nairobi until 1978, a year during which he held visiting appointments at both the University of Texas at Austin and the University of Ife in Nigeria. In 1979, after Idi Amin Dada was overthrown, Okot returned once more to Makerere University. In February 1982 he was appointed the first professor of creative writing in the Department of Literature, and he died at his home in Kampala only five months later, at the age of fifty-one.

Throughout his busy academic and professional career, Okot p'Bitek never stopped writing. His enormously successful *Song of Lawino* was soon followed by three other long poems of the same genre: *Song of Ocol* (1970), "Song of Prisoner," and "Song of Malaya" – the latter two being published together as *Two Songs* in 1971. That same year, he also published two scholarly works, *African Religions in Western Scholarship* (1971) and *Religion of the Central Luo* (1971). His interest in oral forms of literature was reflected in his publication of *The Horn of My Love* (1974), a collection of Acoli songs; *Hare and Hornbill* (1978), a collection of folktales; and *Acholi Proverbs* (1985). (*Acholi* is a variant spelling of *Acoli*.)

Another book, *Africa's Cultural Revolution* (1973), a collection of some of the essays he wrote for East African periodicals, magazines, and newspapers between 1964 and 1971, includes several of Okot's most candid statements on African culture, so it serves as an excellent introduction to some of the ideas in his poetry. In the preface to *Africa's Cultural Revolution* Okot says that his essays are part of the revolutionary struggle in Africa that is "dedicated to the total demolition of foreign cultural domination and the restoration and promotion of Africa's proud culture to its rightful place." In order to achieve these worthwhile nationalistic goals,

Africa must examine herself critically. She must discover her true self, and rid herself of all "apemanship." For only then can she begin to develop a culture of her own. Africa must redefine all cultural terms according to her own interests. As she has broken the political bondage of colonialism, she must continue the economic and cultural revolution until she refuses to be led by the nose by foreigners. We must also reject the erroneous attempts of foreign students to interpret and present her. We must interpret and present Africa in our own way, in our own interests.

Okot's aim as a writer was to assist in this vital task of cultural redefinition.

His essays range widely over such varied topics as literature, philosophy, religion, politics, history, education, sex, and pop music. But underlying them all is an insistence on the validity and dignity of indigenous African culture. Okot wants Africans – especially educated Africans – to accept their Africanness and stop mimicking non-African customs, traditions, fashions, and styles, which are entirely inappropriate and even a bit ridiculous in an African setting. Only by affirming the integrity of their own cultural identity will Africans find happiness and genuine fulfillment. As Ngugi wa Thiong'o puts it, Okot "is simply and rightly saying that we cannot ape and hope to create." Okot desires to release the creative potential of Africa by making Africans conscious and proud of their own rich cultural heritage.

In his essays on literature Okot begins the process of cultural redefinition by questioning the Western conception of literature itself. He points out that "in Western scholarship, literature means the writings of a particular time or country, especially those valued for excellence of form or expression. This definition, with its emphasis on 'writing,' implies that literature is the exclusive preserve of human societies which have invented the art of writing." In place of this "narrow and discriminatory definition" Okot advocates adopting a more "dynamic and democratic" notion of literature as an art embracing "all the creative works of man expressed in words," which would take in oral as well as written performances, because "words can be spoken, sung or written. The voice of the singer or the speaker and the pen and paper are mere midwives of a pregnant mind. A song is a song whether it is sung, spoken or written down." By redefining literature in this way, Okot is able to demonstrate that Africa possesses one of the richest literary cultures in the world.

He also emphasizes that literature in Africa is a living social art. It is not a collection of old classics that one reads alone or studies diligently at school in order to pass examinations and win certificates. It is an intensely expressive activity aimed at publicly communicating deeply felt emotions. Sometimes it may be designed to amuse, sometimes to instruct, but the best literature never fails to make a profound impact on the whole community. It is a totally democratic art, which attempts to reach everyone within earshot. There must always be direct communication between the artist and his audience and full participation by all present, which means that the African literary artist cannot afford to indulge in deliberate obscurity. He produces his art not for art's sake but for society's sake.

Song of Lawino was created in this spirit. It is a thoroughly indigenous poem in form, content, style, message, and aesthetic philosophy. Okot took the songs he knew best – Acoli and Lango traditional songs of praise and abuse, joy and sorrow, and sympathy and satire – and made use of their poetic resources in composing an original anthem in honor of Africa. The result is something both old and new because, while Okot exploited many of the conventions of oral art, he also invented a literary genre never before seen in African writing. He did this first in his own mother tongue and then in English, claiming to have "clipped a bit of the eagle's wings and rendered the sharp edges of the warrior's sword rusty and blunt, and also murdered rhythm and rhyme" in the process of translation. Like a traditional poet he was trying to reach the widest possible audience because he felt he had an important idea to impart. And like a literary artist he was still experimenting with his verbal medium in an effort to find a uniquely appropriate idiom to carry his message. *Song of Lawino* is thus a hybrid achievement, a successful sustained blending of oral and literary art in a long poem remarkably innovative in conception and design, yet immanently African in orientation.

Much of the Africanness of the poem shows in its imagery, ideology, and rhetorical structure. It is an oral song sung by an illiterate Ugandan housewife, who complains bitterly about the insults and ill treatment she receives from her university-trained husband. Being an unschooled village girl, Lawino speaks in the earthy idiom of the rural peasantry and sees everything from the perspective of a country cousin. She cannot understand why her husband, Ocol, follows Western ways or why he rejects her because she is clinging to the traditions of her people. She knows nothing about ballroom dancing, cooking on a modern stove, or reading clocks, books, or thermometers, and she sees no reason why she should learn such strange skills when she can get along perfectly well without them. She has been exposed to a few Christian beliefs and teachings, but these she found either incomprehensible or profoundly perplexing. Why must Ocol

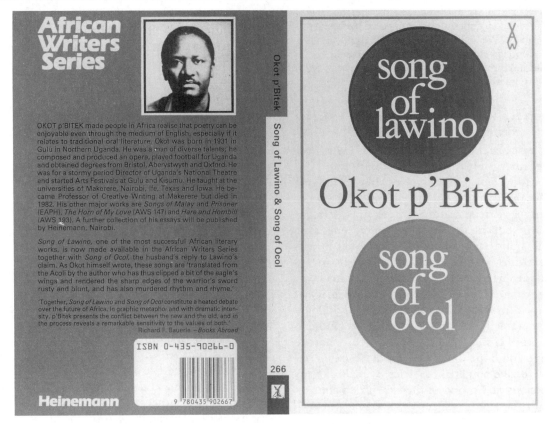

Cover for the 1984 Heinemann volume that collects Okot's first two books of poetry, the first presenting the complaints of an African wife and the second offering her husband's responses

abuse and punish her for being African? These are the questions Lawino asks repeatedly as she recounts her husband's brutality and cruel words. Recalling the time Ocol branded her and her kinfolk as ignorant, superstitious fools, she laments:

> My husband's tongue
> Is bitter like the roots of the *lyonno* lily,
> It is hot like the penis of the bee,
> Like the sting of the *kalang*!
> Ocol's tongue is fierce like the arrow of the scorpion,
> Deadly like the spear of the buffalo-hornet.
> It is ferocious
> Like the poison of a barren woman
> And corrosive like the juice of the gourd.

Everything Lawino says is rooted in the reality she has mastered, the world she knows. She speaks in a language that reveals an intimate knowledge and experience of rural African life. Obviously such a perceptive observer is neither ignorant nor foolishly superstitious. Lawino's imagery alone refutes Ocol's accusation.

Okot's strategy throughout the poem is to contrast the natural grace and dignity of traditional African ways with the grotesque artificiality of the modern habits and practices that educated Africans have copied from Europe. The primary target is Ocol's "apemanship," but Okot gradually widens the focus of Lawino's complaints to embrace larger social, political, and religious issues arising from rabid, unthinking Westernization. In his 1977 interview with Bernth Lindfors, Okot described *Song of Lawino* as "a big laugh by this village girl called Lawino, laughing at modern man and modern woman in Uganda. She thinks that the educated folk are spoiled, in the sense that they don't belong, they don't enjoy fully the culture of the people of Uganda, and she thinks that if only these educated people could stop a little bit and look back into the village they would find a much richer life altogether." Lawino provides a window on both African worlds because she is the product of one and a prisoner in the other. Like Alice in Wonderland, like Gulliver, like Medza in Mongo Beti's *Mission to Kala* (1958), she discovers herself in a strange new universe and reacts strongly to anything that deviates from her own cultural expectations and prejudices. But a major difference in her case is that most of her audience – Western as well as African – does not share her cultural perspective but rather that of

Ocol, the modern man at whom she is laughing. She forces such readers to see themselves from an entirely different point of view and to join in the laughter. By viewing modern manners through her own distorted ethnocentric lens, Lawino serves as a catalyst for satire.

But she also becomes a victim of satire, because occasionally there are significant discrepancies between her words and deeds. For instance, after beginning a devastating verbal assault on the physical appearance of Ocol's modern girlfriend Clementine (Tina), she pauses briefly to assure her audience that her motives are pure:

> Do not think I am insulting
> The woman with whom I share my husband!
> Do not think my tongue
> Is being sharpened by jealousy.
> It is the sight of Tina
> That provokes sympathy from my heart.
>
> I do not deny
> I am a little jealous.
> It is no good lying,
> We all suffer from a little jealousy.
> It catches you unawares
> Like the ghosts that bring fevers;
> It surprises people
> Like earth tremors:
> But when you see the beautiful woman
> With whom I share my husband
> You feel a little pity for her!

She then resumes her attack with gusto, ridiculing Tina's dried-up breasts and padded brassiere, insinuating that Tina has aborted or killed many children in her long lifetime, and scoffing at her slim, "meatless" figure. Obviously Lawino is more than a little jealous of the woman she claims to pity.

Okot carefully counterpoints Lawino's lapses into pure invective with her gentle, nostalgic reflections on traditional African life. These frequent changes in mood and tempo reveal the softer side of her personality while reinforcing her emphasis on differences between the old and the new. Lawino's sympathies always lie with tradition, and, through graphic images and telling details, she is able to communicate her enthusiasm for the customs and practices of her people. She describes a civilization that is wholesome, coherent, deeply satisfying to those born into it, and therefore naturally resistant to fundamental change. Her angry tirade against Tina is followed by a rosy account of how rivals for a man's love behave in Acoli society, and then by a level-headed appeal to Ocol, politely asking him to stop rejecting his own heritage:

> Listen Ocol, my old friend,
> The ways of your ancestors
> Are good,
> Their customs are solid
> And not hollow
> They are not thin, not easily breakable
> They cannot be blown away
> By the winds
> Because their roots reach deep into the soil.

This statement summarizes the theme of Lawino's entire song.

But because she tends to sing it too stridently, because she refuses to make the slightest effort to adjust to modern ways, because she remains so intractably old-fashioned, Lawino eventually shows herself to be a tribal chauvinist who is as limited in vision as her husband. Sometimes she is conscious of her inflexibility, as when she admits she cannot "cook like a white woman" or "dance the white man's dances" because she has never cared to learn such revolting skills. On other occasions she appears to be totally unaware of the strength of her own cultural prejudices, and this naiveté sets her criticism of others in an ironic light. For example, she showers insults on Tina's lipstick, powder, perfume, wig, and artificially dyed and straightened hair, yet in the very next breath goes on to extol Acoli customs of tattooing, body painting, body scenting, and hairdressing. Her aim may be to condemn Tina's "apewomanship" and to ridicule Ocol's perverse preference for Western odors and adornments, but she does not seem to realize that she is simultaneously betraying the absurdity of her own dogmatic "Acolitude." Her unconscious undercutting of her own argument is a classic example of reflexive satire: the use of satire to satirize the satirist.

This is not to say that her attacks on the follies of Westernized Africans are invalid or unjustified. Lawino has a keen eye for human stupidity, and her common sense does not allow her to be easily taken in by pretense and affectation. She views Ocol and Tina not as her superiors but as ordinary human beings who are struggling desperately to prove themselves superior by adopting Western ways. Since Lawino does not understand such ways, she raises fundamental questions about their logic and propriety, which Westerners and Westernized Africans never bother to ask. For instance, she points out:

> At the height of the hot season
> The progressive and civilised ones
> Put on blanket suits
> And woollen socks from Europe,
> Long under-pants

And woollen vests,
White shirts;
They wear dark glasses
And neck-ties from Europe.

She also cannot imagine what pleasure these people take in smoking, drinking, kissing, and other unclean, unnatural acts. Lawino regards such habits as foolish and unhealthy. Those who indulge in them ought to be avoided, not admired or emulated.

Even more difficult for Lawino to fathom are Western habits of mind. Why should Ocol reckon time by consulting a clock when there are much more natural signs by which to measure the passing of a day? Why should he want to give his children Christian names when Acoli names are more meaningful? Why should he place so much faith in Western medicine and prayer, and scorn the remedies offered by herbalists and diviners? Why should politicians who are working toward the same goals oppose one another? By asking these questions Lawino focuses attention on some of the arbitrary and seemingly irrational aspects of Western behavior, which would very likely baffle any non-Westerner encountering them for the first time. She forces readers to recognize the illogic of Western ways. Her incomprehension is both a warning and a protest against cultural arrogance.

What makes Lawino a more sensible person than Ocol is her acceptance of the validity of other cultures, despite her personal aversion to them. She does not insist, as Ocol does, that everyone conform to her own cultural pattern. She realizes that Westerners will behave as Westerners, and though she would clearly prefer Africans to behave as Africans, she is content to let Ocol eat Western foods and adopt Western eccentricities so long as he reciprocates with equal tolerance for her traditional preferences. She would like to see her husband return to the Acoli life-style he had once enjoyed, but if that is impossible (as it appears to be), then he should at least respect her right to remain loyal to the ways of her ancestors. At one point she sums it all up by saying,

I do not understand
The ways of foreigners
But I do not despise their customs.
Why should you despise yours? . . .
The pumpkin in the old homestead
Must not be uprooted!

Lawino's "lament" is a plea for tolerance, understanding, and respect for African culture.

The success of *Song of Lawino* rests primarily on Okot's creation of a convincing persona to artic-

ulate his ideas. Lawino's vibrant personality animates the entire poem, giving it the energy and earthiness appropriate to an iconoclastic assault on postcolonial "high" culture. Only a woman of her peasant origins could reject Westernization so totally. Only a scorned wife of her particular matrimonial temper could denounce her husband so passionately yet yearn to win back his love. There may be inconsistencies in her conduct and huge self-contradictions in her argument, but these simply make her a more believable human being. She wins one over by the honest eloquence of her emotion, the primitive force of her tongue.

Yet one must never forget that she is a persona and that Okot may not share all her views. *Song of Lawino* is a long dramatic monologue deliberately placed in the mouth of an invented character, and to understand its full meaning one must carefully appraise the singer as well as the song. Lawino presents a persuasive case for African tradition because she is able to perceive salient absurdities of modern African life through eyes unclouded by formal education or acculturation to Western ways. But though she sees clearly, her vision is limited to a single, circumscribed point of view by her own narrow cultural prejudices, and she has real difficulty seeing beyond her Acoli nose. This fact makes a good deal of her testimony suspect, for it is impossible to trust impassioned polemics brimming with so much overstatement and exaggeration. Lawino's argument, though tempered with unconscious irony, is too one-sided.

This situation may have been why Okot decided to write *Song of Ocol* as a reply to Lawino. By giving Ocol a chance to state his own case, Okot could examine the same social, political, and cultural issues from a different point of view. And, in the process of ostensibly redressing the balance of a biased conjugal debate, he could make clever use of satire to reassert basically the same position he had advocated in *Song of Lawino*.

In singing his song, Ocol reveals himself as exactly the type of person Lawino had described – an angry, insensitive, impatient opportunist intent on destroying African traditions and institutions in the name of progress. He hates everything black because he associates blackness with backwardness and primitivism:

What is Africa
To me?

Blackness,
Deep, deep fathomless
Darkness;

Africa,
Idle giant
Basking in the sun,
Sleeping, snoring,
Twitching in dreams;

Diseased with a chronic illness,
Choking with black ignorance,
Chained to the rock
Of poverty. . . .

Mother, mother,
Why,
Why was I born
Black?

In order to overcome his feelings of self-hatred and inferiority, Ocol is ready to uproot Lawino's pumpkins, burn mud huts, imprison witches and village poets, hang professors of African studies, and obliterate indigenous cultural treasures. His aim is to

Smash all these mirrors
That I may not see
The blackness of the past
From which I came
Reflected in them.

Much of Ocol's song is an inventory of what he intends to destroy. He speaks as a member of the ruling class that came to power after independence with the ambition of transforming a former colony into a modern nation-state. In order to bring "civilization" to their part of the world, these Westernized African leaders are planning to demolish the "Old Homestead" and build a "New City" complete with statues of European explorers, missionaries, and kings. Their notion of national progress is further imitation of Europe.

Nothing Ocol says wins the sympathy of readers. He seems so intent on ravaging the countryside and throwing harmless people into prison in order to achieve a worthless goal that it is impossible to view him in a friendly light. He is obviously a blackguard obsessed with a desire to prove himself white. He displays no love or tenderness toward his fellowman and possesses no traits worthy of admiration. Indeed, one wonders why Lawino wants him back.

As Ocol speaks, his own words condemn him, making him the butt of ridicule. For example, after outlining a strategy for wiping out African culture and traditions and replacing them with Western ways, he asks an African ambassador at the United Nations to

Tell the world
In English or in French,
Talk about
The African foundation
On which we are
Building the new nations
Of Africa.

Ocol also claims to hate poverty but does nothing to help the poor, even though he has grown wealthy as a politician. His major concern as a public servant is not with the public welfare but with keeping thieves and trespassers off his vast country estate. He is a rich landed aristocrat in a poor underdeveloped country, a contrast that points up the disparity between his nationalistic ideals and parasitic practices. Virtually every line he speaks betrays him as an arch hypocrite.

By the time readers finish *Song of Ocol*, they are aware that Lawino was right: Ocol's "apemanship" has turned him into a monster. If he had managed to retain a healthy respect for African traditions, he might have been a better person and a far more constructive influence on his society. His fanatical Westernization and rejection of himself have prevented him from developing into a creative human being. He has lost not just his ethnic identity but his humanity.

Thus *Song of Lawino* and *Song of Ocol*, though structured as a debate, actually present two sides of the same coin; they may face in opposite directions, but they have precisely the same ring. Ocol's argument is undercut so completely by irony that it reinforces Lawino's position. And Okot, by ostensibly removing himself from the quarrel between his personae, is able to establish an independent stance some distance from the ground Lawino defends. He advocates neither an atavistic return to Acoli customs and traditions nor a total abandonment of Western ways. His aim appears to be to help educated Africans to appreciate their rich cultural heritage so they can create a new culture equally meaningful and relevant to Africa.

Okot's next song is much more ambiguous. Instead of carrying the cultural debate further, he turned to an explosive new political subject and treated it in a deliberately equivocal fashion. He used the same basic poetic form — an emotionally charged dramatic monologue — but invested it with such complex irony that its moral center was difficult to discern. The poem has aroused considerable controversy in East Africa and is likely to go on provoking lively discussion for some time to come. Brief and puzzling, it has all the fascination of a conundrum.

Dust jacket for the New York edition (1971) of one of Okot's long poems, the speaker of which has been incarcerated for assassinating a head of state

"Song of Prisoner" begins as the anguished soliloquy of a man who appears to have been brutally beaten and thrown into prison for the most trivial of offenses: vagrancy and loitering in the city park. As he sits counting his wounds and cursing his captors, he seems a victim of injustice and oppression. He broods on thoughts of his starving children, complains of his own hunger and thirst, and frequently lashes out at those he imagines to be responsible for his misfortunes. He even goes so far as to blame his dead father for not having married a woman from the right clan, thereby foisting bad genes on all his descendants, then accuses his mother of the same catastrophic matrimonial misjudgment. He also imagines his wife to be sleeping with a "Big chief" who drives a Mercedes-Benz, and this vision gives him a macabre urge to "drink human blood" and "eat human liver." Imprisonment obviously is driving him insane.

Not until the middle of the poem do readers learn the real reason he has been locked up: he is a hired assassin who has killed the head of state. Though he claims to have done so out of love for his country, his charge that the leader was "a trai-tor, a dictator, a murderer, a racist, a tribalist, a clannist, a brotherist . . . a reactionary, a revisionist, a fat black capitalist, an extortioner, an exploiter" sounds suspiciously like programmatic revolutionary rhetoric. Perhaps the prisoner is the heroic liberator he claims to be; perhaps he is the dupe of sinister forces in his society. In evaluating his conduct, readers have only his own half-demented words to go by.

He shouts that he had been a minister in the government, in fact had been the one responsible for "Law and Order. . . . Peace and Goodwill in the Land." He asks for his gold pen so he can write his children and parents and send them fat checks. At this point he appears to have changed character completely, picking up a new set of parents along the way and leapfrogging from the depths of proletarian squalor to the heights of bourgeois luxury. Indeed he has been transmuted into another Ocol. Could this be the same prisoner seen and heard earlier? If so, has he gone irretrievably mad? What accounts for his sudden, magical transformation?

Okot does not stop to answer these questions before moving into the final section of the poem, which contains a morbid appeal for oblivion as a distraction from despair. The prisoner says he wants to be free so he can sing, drink, dance, and fornicate until he forgets the anguish of his insignificance. He knows he has no future and that his children will never go to school or have a chance to escape wretched poverty. His only hope for release from these depressing thoughts lies in total debauchery:

> I want to drink
> And get drunk,
> I do not want to know
> That I am powerless
> and helpless,
> I do not want to remember anything.
>
> I want to forget
> That I am a lightless star,
> A proud Eagle
> Shot down
> By the arrow
> Of Uhuru!

The poem's internal contradictions generate a confused response. Should one feel sympathy for this prisoner, or disgust? Is he worthy of pity, approbation, or condemnation? Was his crime noble or base? Okot leads readers first toward one conclusion, then toward another, until readers are trapped in the labyrinth of the prisoner's complex personality. By encouraging them to make judgments that they later feel compelled to reverse, Okot makes readers realize how difficult it is to distinguish between good and bad in contemporary Africa. Readers may applaud the guerrilla "freedom fighters" who boldly take the law into their own hands, yet readers are likely appalled by the hard-fisted tactics of military regimes founded with the same disregard for individual liberties. The political assassin is seen as a national hero by some and as a self-seeking rogue by others. Many who feel oppressed may themselves be ruthless oppressors. Okot seems to be saying that, in the confusion of post-Uhuru Africa, justice, honor, loyalty, and morality – all the social and political virtues – may be subject to reinterpretation according to the exigencies of the moment and the bias of the interpreter. There are no longer any fixed truths, only competing ideologies. This conclusion may be cynical and perhaps even a gross misreading of Okot's intention, but when confronted with such rich ambiguity in a literary work, it is easy for a reader to go astray. The fact that the poem has already stirred so much controversy suggests that it invites many different interpretations.

Although most critics have assumed that "Song of Prisoner" is the song of a single prisoner, there is some evidence suggesting that it may have been conceived as a medley of various voices. Okot is reported to have said that the "Soft Grass" episode involving the minister and the gold pen is an interpolation by "a man in the next cell, whom the Prisoner overhears." If so, what is to prevent one from identifying other lyrics that seem out of character as songs sung by other prisoners? Perhaps "Song of Prisoner" actually represents the communal wailings of an entire cell block. This view would make the poem less complex psychologically but certainly no less damning as an indictment of contemporary African experience. Despite flashes of gallows humor, it remains a very gloomy song.

"Song of Malaya," paired with "Song of Prisoner" in *Two Songs*, provides boisterous comic relief. The prostitute who sings it is good-natured, proud of her profession, and tolerant of all humankind. She invites men of every description to enter and make use of her facilities. No one is barred or refused service. She is the great social equalizer, humanity's most effective democratizer because she mixes with high and low societies indiscriminately. Thus she is in a good position to expose cant and hypocrisy. Her song is a series of rebukes to her critics – to the chief who accuses her of giving him venereal disease, to the wife who is unhappy about sharing her husband with a whore, to the priest who preaches that monogamy is morality, to the schoolmaster who calls the prostitute's children bastards, to the brother who despises her yet buys the services of other prostitutes, and to the policeman who arrests her even though he was her customer the night before. Malaya answers their charges with common sense and good humor, pointing out their failings and moral weaknesses in the process. Each of her replies ends with words of encouragement to her fellow professionals and lay workers: "Sister *Malayas* / Wherever you are, / Wealth and health / To us all."

As in *Song of Lawino* Okot's strategy is to juxtapose two different worldviews, one a commonly accepted perspective and the other a somewhat unorthodox outlook, and to slant the argument in such a fashion as to demonstrate the moral superiority of the latter. In "Song of Malaya" prostitution seems a wholesome profession when compared with marriage, priesthood, teaching, law enforcement, and other occupations that are no better ethically and spiritually than the imperfect human beings who practice them. The prostitute is at least self-reliant, open, and unpretentious – much healthier psychologically than those who condemn her. She em-

Okot p'Bitek in Nairobi, August 1976 (photograph by Bernth Lindfors)

braces all who come to her, never attempting to deny pleasure to those who are willing to pay the price. Her message, like Lawino's, is one of tolerance for human diversity. She accepts whatever seems natural and genuine, rejecting only the patently artificial and perverted. Malaya is clearly more moral than her society.

In *Artist, the Ruler* (1986), a collection of Okot's essays and unfinished works, one finds some of the same arguments about culture, art, and values that he had espoused earlier. He persisted in raising big questions and seeking to answer them in a way that affirmed the validity of indigenous social and cultural institutions. He also put forward the view that the artist had a key role to play in guiding society toward humane goals. In the title essay he asserts, "If there are two types of rulers in every society, that is, those who use physical force to subdue men, and those that employ beautiful things, sweet songs and funny stories, rhythm, shape and colour, to keep individuals and society sane and flourishing, then in my view, it is the artist who is the greater ruler." The artist is not just an entertainer but a gentle leader and legislator of social norms. And who qualifies for this special role in society? In Okot's

view, "every human being is an artist." Some may be greater than others, but all respond to beauty, all participate in creating art and investing it with social relevance.

This stance was not just empty theorizing on Okot's part, for he lived his life according to this credo. As an artist, as an educator, and as an agitator, his role was basically the same. He was quite conscious of the consistency of his position. In his interview with Lindfors he said, "I want to suggest that all my writings, whether they are anthropological monographs, studies of religion, essays, songs, poems, or even traditional stories and proverbs such as I am collecting now, all of them are ammunition for one big battle: the battle to decide where we here in Africa are going and what kind of society we are building. I think you will find great similarities in all the different things I have been producing because they all have basically the same aim." Clearly Okot was quite serious about what he was doing as a writer.

Some of the criticism directed at Okot as a commentator on East African society has asserted that his analysis of contemporary social problems is shallow, for he was more an entertainer than an incisive social scientist or political reformer. Taban lo Liyong has charged him with playfulness and insincerity: "I see more of the frivolous and more of the jester in these [sociological and anthropological] works. Only rarely do I see an Okot with tight lips and protracted visage. . . . Okot with a political temper is better than Okot the sceptic posing as a champion for dying and dead customs he doesn't believe in. These are useful only as means for giving play to sarcasm, and making fun of other people's ways in mock-revenge for their destruction of the ways of his own people, again in which he does not seriously believe." Ngugi wa Thiong'o has expressed the view that Okot is a bit shortsighted, for he fails to look at the root causes of East Africa's social problems: "While I agree with p'Bitek's call for a cultural revolution, I sometimes feel that he is in danger of emphasizing culture as if it could be divorced from its political and economic basis. . . . Can we be ourselves while our economic life is regulated by forces outside Africa?" Andrew Gurr, echoing Ngugi and quoting Frantz Fanon, has complained that Okot's diagnosis of social ills "does not go below the surface of the problem. . . . [He] is fussing over the outworn garments of the past, not the teeming present." These critics wish Okot had probed more deeply into the body politic and exposed the sources of its sickness instead of merely mocking the bizarre convulsions of a delirious, moribund society. They would like him to have behaved as a physician rather than a clown.

Yet Okot's strident style of satirical singing has won him a wider audience than any prescriptive political propaganda would have been likely to, and he achieved this immense popularity without pulling any of his punches. Indeed his four outspoken songs compel readers to listen to voices they would not ordinarily heed. Original in form, technique, and idea, these vivid lyrical soliloquys captivate the imagination and provoke the intellect while advancing half-ironic arguments that radically challenge some basic cultural assumptions. One's immediate reaction to such audacity may be to laugh in astonishment, but Okot had a talent for forcing one to think as one laughs. He never let readers rest comfortably in mindless complacency. This made him an unsettling writer, indeed a revolutionary artist, for his constant questioning teaches readers entirely new ways of seeing themselves and others. By singing comically and occasionally off-key, he drew attention to serious social disharmonies that require adjustment and correction. He was writing not merely to amuse but to instruct and guide his people. He once said that a truly African literature must have "deep human roots" and deal "honestly and truthfully with the problems of the human situation." Okot p'Bitek, who spent his life striving to produce this kind of literature, deserves recognition as one of Africa's major creative talents. Though he remained a blithe spirit throughout his career, he articulated important ideas about culture and identity that still have relevance. Okot may have been a clown, but he was a serious clown, the kind whose antics provoke wholesome, regenerative laughter.

Bibliography:

Ogo A. Ofuani, "Okot p'Bitek: A Checklist of Works and Criticism," *Research in African Literatures*, 16 (1985): 370–383.

Interviews:

Robert Serumaga, Interview with Okot p'Bitek, in *African Writers Talking: A Collection of Radio Interviews*, edited by Dennis Duerden and Cosmo Pieterse (London: Heinemann, 1972; New York: Africana, 1972), pp. 149–155;

Tony Hall, "Great Dancers, Great Poets Are Left Out," in Okot's *Africa's Cultural Revolution* (Nairobi: Macmillan, 1973);

Peter Darling, "Relevance: A Must for Our Culture," in Okot's *Africa's Cultural Revolution*;

Arne Zettersten, "Okot p'Bitek and the East African Literary Situation," *Commonwealth Newsletter*, 10 (1976): 27–32;

J. Lahui, "Okot p'Bitek . . . to Sing 'Song of Lawino,' " *Papua New Guinea Writing*, 23 (1976): 12–13;

Bernth Lindfors, "Interview with Okot p'Bitek," *World Literature Written in English*, 16 (November 1977): 281–299;

John Esibi, "Africa Is Full of Bogus Types Who Are Fools," *Sunday Nation* (Nairobi), 18 December 1977, pp. 8, 19;

Kirsten Petersen and others, "Okot p'Bitek," *Kunapipi*, 1, no. 1 (1979): 89–93;

Lee Nichols, ed., *Conversations with African Writers: Interviews with Twenty-Six African Authors* (Washington, D.C.: Voice of America, 1981), pp. 242–252;

David Rubadiri, "David Rubadiri Interviews Okot p'Bitek," *Ife Studies in African Literature and the Arts*, 1 (1982): 18–36;

Audu Ogbeh, "Thirty-Six Hours with Okot p'Bitek," *Pan African Book World*, 2, no. 2 (1982): 3–4, 6–9;

Emman Omari, "Foreign Ideologies Have Failed in Africa," *Sunday Standard* (Nairobi), 1 August 1982, pp. 11, 13.

References:

H. O. Anyumba, "*Song of Lawino*: A Creative Audacity – An Appreciation," *East African Journal*, 4, no. 6 (1967): 31–36;

Samuel Omo Asein, "Okot p'Bitek: Literature and the Cultural Revolution in East Africa," *World Literature Written in English*, 16 (April 1977): 7–24;

E. S. Atieno-Odhiambo, "The Dead End of Uhuru Worship," *Busara*, 3, no. 4 (1971): 51–65;

Françoise Balogun, "*La Chanson de Lawino*: Un plaidoyer pour l'authenticité," *Présence Africaine*, 135 (1985): 102–112;

Chinweizu, Onwuchekwa Jemie, and Ihechukwu Madubuike, *Toward the Decolonization of African Literature* (Enugu: Fourth Dimension, 1980; Washington, D.C.: Howard University Press, 1983; London: Routledge & Kegan Paul, 1985);

Romanus N. Egudu, "East African Poetry: The Surprise of Its Calm," *Nigeria Magazine*, 110–112 (1974): 105–109;

Maina Gathungu, "Okot p'Bitek: Writer, Singer or Culturizer?," in *Standpoints on African Literature: A Critical Anthology*, edited by Chris Wanjala (Nairobi: East African Literature Bureau, 1973), pp. 52–61;

Ken Goodwin, *Understanding African Poetry: A Study of Ten Poets* (London: Heinemann, 1982);

Andrew Gurr, *Writers in Exile: The Creative Use of Home in Modern Literature* (Brighton, U.K.: Harvester / Atlantic Highlands, N.J.: Humanities, 1981);

John Haynes, "Simplicity, Accessibility and Discourse in African Poetry," *Saiwa*, 3 (1985): 59–70;

George A. Heron, "The Influence of the Rhetoric of Acoli Oral Songs on the Poems of Okot p'Bitek," *Occasional Papers* (Kano), 1, no. 1 (1975): 22–53;

Heron, "Okot p'Bitek and the Elite in African Writing," *Literary Half-Yearly*, 19 (January 1978): 66–93;

Heron, *The Poetry of Okot p'Bitek* (London: Heinemann, 1976; New York: Africana, 1976);

Annemarie Heywood, "Modes of Freedom: The Songs of Okot p'Bitek," *Présence Africaine*, 113 (1980): 235–257;

Lutfurahman Jonaid-Sharif, "Okot p'Bitek's *Song of Lawino*: The Dynamics of a Voice," *Griot* (Winter 1984): 17–26;

Giovanna La Magna, "Okot p'Bitek and the Search for Self–Identity," *Quaderni di Lingue e Letterature*, 6 (1981): 67–82;

Bernth Lindfors, "The Songs of Okot p'Bitek," in *The Writing of East and Central Africa*, edited by G. D. Killam (London: Heinemann, 1984), pp. 144–158;

Ismael Mbise, "Modes of Saying, Modes of Being: The Poetry of p'Bitek, Buruga and Oculi," in *Literature, Language and the Nation*, edited by Emmanuel Ngara and Andrew Morrison (Harare, Zimbabwe: Atoll & Baobab, 1989), pp. 83–97;

Gerald Moore, *Twelve African Writers* (London: Hutchinson, 1980; Bloomington: Indiana University Press, 1980);

Keguro Muhindi, "In Memoriam: Okot p'Bitek," *Présence Africaine*, 125 (1983): 379–381;

Dominic Mwasaru, "Okot p'Bitek and Religion," *Afer*, 17 (1975): 280–289;

Ngugi wa Thiong'o, "Okot p'Bitek and Writing in East Africa," in his *Homecoming: Essays on African and Caribbean Literature, Culture and Politics* (London: Heinemann, 1972; New York & Westport, Conn.: Hill, 1973), pp. 67–77;

Lee Nichols, *African Writers at the Microphone* (Washington, D.C.: Three Continents Press, 1984);

Alastair Niven, Francis Kidubuka, and Margaret Macpherson, "A Song for Okot," *Africa Now* (October 1982): 100–102;

J. O. J. Nwachukwu-Agbada, "Okot p'Bitek and the Story of a Paradox," *Commonwealth Essays and Studies*, 12 (Autumn 1989): 95–107;

Ogo A. Ofuani, "Digression as Discourse Strategy in Okot p'Bitek's Dramatic Monologue Texts," *Research in African Literatures*, 19 (Fall 1988): 312–340;

Ofuani, "The Form and Function of Repetition in Okot p'Bitek's Poetry," *Meta*, 31 (1986): 300–313;

Ofuani, "The Image of the Prostitute: A Reconsideration of Okot p'Bitek's Malaya," *Kunapipi*, 8, no. 3 (1986): 100–114;

Ofuani, "Poetics and Syntax in Okot p'Bitek's Songs," *Jolan: Journal of the Linguistics Association of Nigeria*, 2 (1983–1984): 133–141;

Ofuani, "The Traditional and Modern Influences in Okot p'Bitek's Poetry," *African Studies Review*, 28, no. 4 (1985): 87–99;

C. O. Ogunyemi, "In Praise of Things Black: Langston Hughes and Okot p'Bitek," *Contemporary Poetry*, 4, no. 1 (1981): 19–39;

Tanure Ojaide, "Poetic Viewpoint: Okot p'Bitek and His Personae," *Callaloo*, 9 (Spring 1986): 371–383;

Ndubuisi C. Osuagwu, "A Traditional Poet in Modern Garb: Okot p'Bitek," *Literary Criterion*, 23, nos. 1–2 (1988): 13–29;

Adrian Roscoe, *Uhuru's Fire: African Literature East to South* (Cambridge: Cambridge University Press, 1977), pp. 32–66;

Taban lo Liyong, "Lawino Is Unedu," in his *The Last Word: Cultural Synthesism* (Nairobi: East African Publishing House, 1969), pp. 135–156;

Laura Tanna, "Notes Towards a Reading of Okot p'Bitek's *Song of Lawino*," *African Studies Association of the West Indies Bulletin*, 8 (1977): 18–31;

Monica Nalyaka Wanambisi, *Thought and Technique in the Poetry of Okot p'Bitek* (New York: Vantage, 1984);

Chris Wanjala, *For Home and Freedom* (Nairobi: Kenya Literature Bureau, 1980);

Wanjala, "Imaginative Writing Since Independence: The East African Experience," in *The East African Experience: Essays on English and Swahili Literature/2nd Janheinz Jahn Symposium*, edited by Ulla Schild (Berlin: Reimer, 1980), pp. 9–24;

Wanjala, *The Season of Harvest: Some Notes on East African Literature* (Nairobi: Kenya Literature Bureau, 1978);

Michael R. Ward, "Okot p'Bitek and the Rise of East African Writing," in *A Celebration of Black and African Writing*, edited by Bruce King and Kolawole Ogungbesan (Zaria, Nigeria & Ibadan: Ahmadu Bello University Press & Oxford University Press, 1975), pp. 217–231;

Mark Weinstein, "The Song of Solomon and *Song of Lawino*," *World Literature Written in English*, 26 (Autumn 1986): 243–244.

Kole Omotoso

(21 April 1943 –)

F. Odun Balogun
Delaware State College

BOOKS *Notes, Q & A on Peter* [Paul] *Edwards' West African Narrative* (Ibadan: Onibonoje, 1968);
The Edifice (London: Heinemann, 1971);
The Combat (London: Heinemann, 1972);
Miracles and Other Stories (Ibadan: Onibonoje, 1973; revised, 1978);
Fella's Choice (Benin City, Nigeria: Ethiope, 1974);
Sacrifice (Ibadan: Onibonoje, 1974; revised, 1978);
The Curse (Ibadan: New Horn, 1976);
The Scales (Ibadan: Onibonoje, 1976);
Shadows in the Horizon (Ibadan: Omotoso/Sketch, 1977);
To Borrow a Wandering Leaf (Akure, Nigeria: Olaiya Fagbamigbe, 1978);
The Form of the African Novel (Akure, Nigeria: Olaiya Fagbamigbe, 1979; revised edition, Lagos: McQuick, 1986);
Memories of Our Recent Boom (Harlow, U.K.: Longman, 1982);
The Theatrical into Theatre: A Study of the Drama and Theatre of the English-Speaking Caribbean (London: New Beacon, 1982);
A Feast in the Time of Plague (Ife, Nigeria: Dramatic Arts/Unife, 1983);
This Girl Sunshine (Ife, Nigeria: Dramatic Arts/Unife, 1983);
All This Must Be Seen (Moscow: Progress, 1986);
Just Before Dawn (Ibadan: Spectrum, 1988).

PLAY PRODUCTIONS: *Pitched Against the Gods*, Ikare, Nigeria, Deen Playhouse, March 1969;
The Last Competition, Lagos, National Theatre, 25 November 1983.

RECORDING: *Kole Omotoso of Nigeria*, Washington, D.C., Voice of America, 1978.

OTHER: "The Indigenous Publisher and the Future of Culture in Nigeria," in *The Indigenous for National Development*, edited by Omotoso, G. O. Onibonoje, and O. A. Lawal (Ibadan: Onibonoje, 1976).

Kole Omotoso (photograph by Jide Adeniyi-Jones; Guardian Newspapers, Lagos, Nigeria)

SELECTED PERIODICAL PUBLICATIONS –
UNCOLLECTED: "The Child Next-door," *Sunday Times* (Lagos), 14 April 1974;
"The End of Johnbool," *Top Life* (May 1979): 28–29, 50–51;
"The Woman and the Goat," *Sunday Concord* (Lagos), 9 March 1980;
"With Comic Commencement," *Okike*, 17 (1980): 46–49;
"Secret Histories," by Omotoso and Adewale Maja-Pearce, *Index on Censorship*, 18 (February 1989): 14–15.

Kole Omotoso belongs to, and indeed personifies, the second generation of Nigerian writers.

From the outset he began to address a local audience, often using local publishers and employing an artistic style that is accessible to common people. He is a fearless social critic whose creative writing and frequent presentations in the news media reveal the tragic situation of the common man and criticize the Nigerian intellectual, political, and business elite who are given to materialism and the perpetuation of neocolonialism. In spite of an asthmatic condition, Omotoso is energetic, tirelessly attending to many commitments, one of which involves promoting the interests of the Association of Nigerian Authors (ANA). He was national secretary for this association from its inception in 1981 until 1984 and served as its national president from 1986 to 1987.

Omotoso was born on 21 April 1943 in Akure and obtained his early education in local schools and at King's College, Lagos. His academic degrees were earned at the University of Ibadan (a B.A. in French and Arabic in 1968) and the University of Edinburgh (a Ph.D. in modern Arabic literature in 1972). He lectured briefly (1972–1976) at Ibadan before being hired by the University of Ife. He is married to a Barbadian, and they have a daughter and two sons.

Omotoso started writing while in primary school. The inspiration to write came both from listening in the evenings to the telling of tales during traditional family folktale sessions and from observing his uncle Olaiya Fagbamigbe, who wrote and published in Yoruba. Omotoso began by transcribing for the pleasure of fellow pupils the tales he had heard. This writing was done in Yoruba, his native tongue, but by the 1960s, when he was a secondary-school pupil and his stories started appearing in *Radio Times, Flamingo*, and other media, he, like most Nigerian writers of his generation, had abandoned the mother tongue for English. Omotoso, whose father died while he was in primary school, has always been adventurous, which is evident in his selection of Arabic as a major in college, even though he had no previous knowledge of the language. His adventurousness is also manifest in his attempts at various times to do creative writing in French and Arabic. Omotoso's initial plan had been to enter the foreign service, but circumstances compelled him to abandon this ambition.

His first novel, *The Edifice* (1971), was started in 1969, barely three months after Omotoso enrolled for graduate studies at Edinburgh. Writing the novel, Omotoso disclosed to Peter Nazareth, was a therapeutic exercise in coping with the hostile aspects of his new environment. The project and its success enabled him to reject the idea of giving up

his studies to return to Nigeria. The novel shows a young black man's strained relationship with his white wife, Daisy, especially on his return from Britain to Nigeria. His hypocritical radicalism is also exposed. Omotoso makes good use of irony in his characterization of this protagonist.

Omotoso's second novel, *The Combat* (1972), written in Nigeria, records his reaction to the Nigerian civil war (1967–1970). The issues raised in the novel had been touched upon in two earlier short stories: "The Nightmares of an Arch Rebel" and "Isaac" (later included in the collection *Miracles and Other Stories*, 1973). In *The Combat* Omotoso departs from the realistic method of *The Edifice* and employs allegory to expose the absurdity of the Nigerian civil war. He depicts two close friends, Chuku and Ojo, who symbolize the two sides in the war. The two men compound the stupidity of a frivolous personal quarrel by escalating it into an international military conflict. While ridiculing the major participants in the combat, Omotoso shows deep concern for the common man, represented by an orphan named Isaac, who becomes the victim of the absurd political game. Even though, in his 1973 interview with Bernth Lindfors, Omotoso faults himself with "a complete failure of tone" in the novel, there is no doubt that the plot works as an allegory. The gripping, suspenseful story is brief and universally valid. Furthermore he maintains a careful balance between comedy and tragedy, and the racy prose amuses while subtly underscoring the tragedy of the subject matter.

Omotoso's next publication, *Miracles and Other Stories*, comprises six stories that focus on children and are written in language accessible to children, but they are not really meant for children. Omotoso uses the stories to prick the consciences of his Nigerian adult readers who are responsible for the neglect and tragic circumstances of poor children. The stories also address vital national issues of primary concern to adults. The title story suggests synthesizing usable elements from both the African past and modern contact with the West to achieve self-reliance, thereby solving the problem of underdevelopment. All the stories except "The Happy Boy," an allegorically composed modern folktale, are realistic. All are brief, dramatic, and absorbing.

Fella's Choice (1974) is Omotoso's attempt at starting an African tradition in the genre of the detective novel. The book is fashioned after the James Bond series, and Omotoso's objective was to win Nigerian youths away from Western detective fiction and the ideology it propagates. In *Fella's Choice* Omotoso tempers the heroic individualism characteristic of the Western detective novel with an emphasis on communal ethics. Even though Fella remains the prime mover, the success of his actions at critical moments always depends on the cooperative effort of his gang as a united body. The novel's theme, which concerns neutralizing the anti-African designs of the secret agents of apartheid South Africa, has political importance.

The relationship between Africa's past and its future – a recurrent theme in Omotoso's works – is the major focus in his next novel, *Sacrifice* (1974). In this narrative, set in Akure, Omotoso's hometown, Dr. Siwaju is faced with the moral predicament of being a medical doctor in the same town as his mother, who has refused to abandon the profession of prostitution from which she had earned the money to give him an education. The allegorical nature of the narrative is made obvious in the dialogue and correspondence between Dr. Siwaju and Flor, his wife. Africa, the novel suggests, has first to understand and come to terms with its past, however sordid, before it can move forward. The story, rendered in naturalistic detail and making use of first person narration, is concerned with Dr. Siwaju's search for identity.

Omotoso's next published book, the one-act play *The Curse* (1976), is in the parabolic style. A misused servant overthrows his rich, vulgar, and sadistic master but immediately begins to behave worse than the old master had. The play is pessimistic and ambiguous. If it refers to history and power aggrandizement on the part of successive ruling social classes, Omotoso has unfortunately ignored the qualitative differences between these classes. But his real concern seems to be with the situation in which some of those who fought together with others in a revolution sometimes turn to usurping power and perverting the revolution to serve personal goals. There is limited stylization in characterization and some exaggeration in the use of details.

The Scales (1976) is another attempt at the genre of the detective novel. As in his first one, Omotoso jettisons individualism and underscores communalism as the basis of heroism. The novel is also Omotoso's most socialist work up to that time. The hero, Barri, who at various stages in his ideological development recalls Ofeyi and Demakin of Wole Soyinka's *Season of Anomy* (1973), organizes a commune of fighters in the fashion of Ayi Kwei Armah's protagonist in *Two Thousand Seasons* (1973) and defeats Chief Daniran, an obvious symbolic representation of the callous, rich exploiters of the poor in the society. While echoing the Soyinka and Armah novels, *The Scales* never achieves their artis-

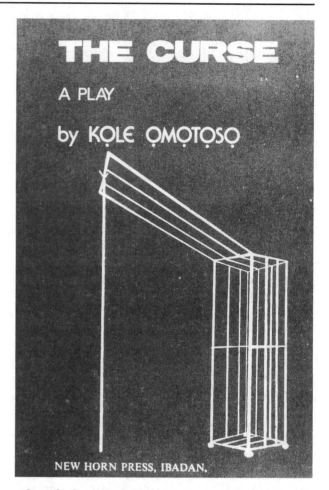

NEW HORN PRESS, IBADAN.

Cover for Omotoso's 1976 one-act play in which revolutionary goals are perverted by personal greed

tic grandeur, belonging, as intended, to the level of popular fiction. At that level, however, it is sufficiently entertaining.

The late 1970s seemed to mark the most intense period of Omotoso's interest in revolutionary, socialist ideas, for *The Scales* was immediately followed by *Shadows in the Horizon* (1977), clearly the most revolutionary of his works. It is a four-act play that Omotoso had to publish on his own as no publisher would touch it. Ironically it was the first of his major works to be translated into a foreign language (Russian). The play is an optimistic, socialist revision of the pessimistic treatment of the theme of revolution presented in *The Curse*. Dedicated to "the day when those who have not shall not be satisfied with their nothing," *Shadows* centers on how the workers of a particular country quickly regroup, recapture a revolution that had earlier been taken away from them, and establish a workers' dictatorship. The overthrown exploitative class is represented by a businessman, a former soldier, and a university professor. The play is more stylized than *The Curse*, and an audience might not immediately recognize the symbolic implications of the beginning action.

Omotoso's next work, the novel *To Borrow a Wandering Leaf* (1978), presents a group of administrative and intellectual elitists undertaking a trip to the interior of Nigeria. The trip reveals why Nigeria has continued to "wander" rather than develop. Misdirected economic planning stresses dependence on foreign aid rather than self-reliance; and the relationship between the city and the village, as well as between the elite and the common people, is exploitative rather than collaborative. Even the best among the elite, such as the character Kobina, find their efforts to set things right frustrated by the system. Through a Ghanaian character, significantly named Kwame, a radical socialist alternative is suggested as a solution. Though the narrative beauty of individual passages is captivating, the novel as a whole can leave the reader dissatisfied. The complex multiple plot produces diffuse action and a confused chronology.

The Form of the African Novel (1979) is a long essay in which Omotoso examines a selection of novels with the purpose of identifying the direction in which novelistic style is developing in Africa. He sees a shift from the critical realism of the 1950s and 1960s to the "marvelous realism" of the 1970s. The latter involves the use of varying levels of folkloric fantasy in an essentially realistic narrative. He argues against identifying the trend as modernist. He also observes that, among leading African novelists, there is a growing radicalization in the treatment of themes. Although the topic of the essay is highly relevant, its treatment is too thin and hasty to be impressive.

In his novel *Memories of Our Recent Boom* (1982) Omotoso returns once more to the theme of the wrongful application of educational training, which he treated earlier in *The Edifice* and *To Borrow a Wandering Leaf*. Thanks to the industry of protagonist Seven Alaka's mother, his own intellectual endowments, and the good fortune of an overseas scholarship, Seven escapes abject village poverty to become a rich contractor in the Nigeria of the oil-boom era. Rather than use his enormous wealth and influence to bridge the village-city, poor-rich gaps, the self-advertising Seven pursues all types of bourgeois comfort and self-glorification. He ends up dying in a car accident on the day that should have been his day of glory. This character, who bears a name with mythical, numerical significance, is the ultimate realization of earlier characters, such as Dele, the pro-

tagonist of *The Edifice*, and Professor Akowe and Kehinde George of *To Borrow a Wandering Leaf*. *Memories*, an antimaterialist narrative, is lucid and poetic, especially in the early chapters.

Omotoso's second critical book, *The Theatrical into Theatre* (1982), is a more impressive piece of scholarship than the first and is a fairly comprehensive survey of the development of Caribbean drama and drama criticism. Omotoso examines how the theatrical elements of earlier periods are being utilized with varying degrees of success to create drama. He discusses performances, language, and themes of this new drama. Omotoso sees the future of Caribbean drama in the fostering of a "community of sensibilities" rather than a "community of faiths," because the former unites while the latter fragments. Furthermore the drama must go back to its roots to exploit, without color prejudice, the theatrical resources, oral and written, of all the people of any Caribbean state. Not surprisingly Omotoso sees the greatest achievement of Caribbean drama in the works of Derek Walcott, a social critic who "has repeatedly expressed the view that the political necessity of the West Indies is socialism, very close to marxism. Such a system he feels would serve to alleviate the poverty of the masses."

All This Must Be Seen (1986), his next major publication, is an account of Omotoso's extensive journey through the Soviet Union in August and September 1983. The greater part of the book gives details of visits to administrative, educational, cultural, and economic establishments, and duplicates general information contained in tourist guidebooks; therefore, it tends to be boring. Fortunately, these materials are interspersed with more-interesting introspective chapters in which Omotoso records his intellectual and emotional responses to Soviet people, history, politics, technology, and cultural policy and practices. His responses are highly positive, even enthusiastic. The book is useful as a record of the history of Omotoso's ideological interest in the Soviet Union since 1961. It also provides a wealth of information on matters such as his unpublished early works, his reason for abandoning the detective genre, the sources of his inspiration for writing certain works, and the nature of Russian literary influence on him. The book is in a sense a restatement of Omotoso's political and literary manifesto, and thus it is a summation of views he has expressed in various media over the years.

Just Before Dawn (1988) is the most ambitious and impressive novel Omotoso has written. It employs the innovative narrative method of a new genre, "faction," which conflates historical facts and fiction. The book provides the essential details of a century of Nigeria's history from the 1880s, in the colonial times, to the collapse of the Second Republic in 1983. The root of Nigeria's postcolonial instability, characterized mainly by ethnic rivalry, is traced to the divide-and-rule policy of the British colonial administration. The British maintained power during colonialism by pitting the less-developed, but favored, North against the more-advanced South, but they also sought to assure continued control by establishing at independence a constitutional arrangement that would perpetuate ethnic divisiveness. The equally bitter personal rivalries among Nigerian civilian and military politicians and the elite, who are all depicted as corrupt, selfish, and unmindful of the common people, further aggravated the already tragic situation.

As fiction, *Just Before Dawn* rejects the strict, linear chronology of history and adopts a near-circular plot structure that traces the political intrigues of Nigerian historical characters. The story is captivating throughout, and its hold on the reader owes much to Omotoso's judicious disposition of his massive materials and the selection and arrangement of characters and incidents. Swiftly changing scenes produce cinematographic close-ups with vivid descriptions of public and private figures, historical and domestic events, private thoughts and political actions, and acts of courage and cowardice. Individual histories are dexterously woven into, and reflect, national history at every stage. *Just Before Dawn* is an interpretation of Nigeria's history by a nationalist, populist, southern Nigerian intellectual; as an interpretation, it is bound to be controversial in spite of the evident attempt at narrative objectivity.

Weighing his publications as a whole, one can say that Omotoso is primarily a novelist, even though he has written plays and has a teaching career in the field of drama. The direction in his writing has clearly been toward a gradual radicalization, as well as toward expression of a systematically firmer belief in socialism. Although the quality of his writing has not been altogether even, although there is evidence of haste in the proofreading of many works, and although the dexterity one expects from him in the handling of the technicalities of fiction is still a little deficient, there is absolutely no doubt that Omotoso, already an important writer, has steadily been acquiring what it takes to become a great African writer. His handling of language, which has consistently been the source of aesthetic satisfaction in his works, has improved; his tone is no longer shaky and juvenile but is firm and philosophical; and there is a noticeable tendency, beginning with *Memories of Our Recent Boom*, to abandon the slimness of the early books for more-ambitious, voluminous novels. All Omotoso needs to overcome his shortcomings is a little more care, a greater attention to details.

Interviews:

Bernth Lindfors, "Kole Omotoso Interviewed," *Cultural Events in Africa*, 103 (1973): 2–12;

John Agetua, *Interviews with Six Nigerian Writers* (Benin City: Bendel Newspapers Corporation, 1974), pp. 9–16;

Tola Adeniyi, "Writers' Search for Audience in Africa," *Daily Times* (Lagos), 12 March 1974, p. 12;

Hans Zell, "Interview: Kole Omotoso," *African Book Publishing Record*, 2 (1976): 12–14;

Lee Nichols, *Conversations with African Writers* (Washington D.C.: Voice of America, 1981), pp. 218–229;

Dili Ezughah, "Omotoso Banished into Creative Bliss," *Guardian* (Lagos), 9 June 1986, p. 10;

Jean Pascal Daloz, "Cette nuit: Le Nigéria: Entretien avec Kole Omotoso," *Notre Librairie*, 98 (July–September 1989): 68–70.

References:

F. Odun Balogun, "Populist Fiction: Omotoso's Novels," *African Literature Today*, 13 (1983): 98–121;

Cheryl M. L. Dash, "An Introduction to the Prose Fiction of Kole Omotoso," *World Literature Written in English*, 16 (April 1977): 39–53;

Mpalive-Hangson Msiska, "Cultural Dislocation and Gender Ideology in Kole Omotoso's *The Edifice*," *Journal of Commonwealth Literature*, 25, no. 1 (1990): 98–108;

Peter Nazareth, "The Tortoise Is an Animal, but He Is Also a Wise Creature," in his *The Third World Writer: His Social Responsibility* (Nairobi: Kenya Literature Bureau, 1978), pp. 71–86;

Olu Obafemi, "Political Perspectives and Popular Theatre in Nigeria," *Theatre Research International*, 7 (Autumn 1982): 235–244;

Eliane Utudjian Saint-André, "Political Commitment in Nigerian Drama," *Commonwealth Essays and Studies*, 7 (Autumn 1984): 36–50.

Femi Osofisan

(16 June 1946 –)

Sandra L. Richards
Northwestern University

BOOKS: *Kolera Kolej* (Ibadan: New Horn, 1975);
A Restless Run of Locusts (Ibadan: Onibonoje, 1975);
The Chattering and the Song (Ibadan: Ibadan University Press, 1977);
Who's Afraid of Solarin? (Ibadan: Scholars, 1978);
Once upon Four Robbers (Ibadan: BIO Educational Services, 1980);
Morountodun and Other Plays (Ikeja: Longman Nigeria, 1982) – comprises *Morountodun*, *No More the Wasted Breed*, and *Red Is the Freedom Road*;
Farewell to a Cannibal Rage (Ibadan: Evans, 1986);
Midnight Hotel (Ibadan: Evans, 1986);
Two One-Act Plays (Ibadan: New Horn, 1986) – comprises *The Oriki of a Grasshopper* and *Altine's Wrath*;
Beyond Translation: A Comparatist Look at Tragic Paradigms and the Dramaturgy of Ola Rotimi and Wole Soyinka (Ife, Nigeria: University of Ife, 1986);
Wonderland and Orality of Prose: A Comparative Study of Rabelais, Joyce and Tutuola (Ife, Nigeria: University of Ife, 1986);
Minted Coins, as Okinba Launko (Ibadan: Heinemann, 1987);
Another Raft (Lagos: Malthouse, 1988);
Cordelia, as Launko (Lagos: Malthouse, 1989);
"Birthdays Are Not for Dying" and Other Plays (Lagos: Malthouse, 1990) – comprises *Birthdays Are Not for Dying*, *Fires Burn and Die Hard*, and *The Inspector and the Hero*;
Esu and the Vagabond Minstrels (Ibadan: New Horn, 1991);
Aringindin and the Night Watchmen (Ibadan: Heinemann, 1991).

PLAY PRODUCTIONS: *Oduduwa, Don't Go!*, Ibadan, 1967;
You Have Lost Your Fine Face, Ibadan, University of Ibadan Theatre, 1969;
A Restless Run of Locusts, Akure, Nigeria, 1969;
The Chattering and the Song, Ibadan, University of Ibadan Theatre, 1976;
Who's Afraid of Solarin?, Ibadan, University of

Femi Osofisan

Ibadan Theatre, 1977; translated (into Yoruba) as *Yeepa Solarin Nbo*, Ibadan, University of Ibadan Theatre, 1988;
Once upon Four Robbers, Ibadan, University of Ibadan Theatre, 1978;
Farewell to a Cannibal Rage, Ibadan, University of Ibadan Theatre, 1978; revised version, Benin City, Nigeria, University of Benin Theatre, 1984;
Morountodun, Ibadan, University of Ibadan Theatre, 1979; revised version, Ibadan, Kakaun Sela Kompany [*sic*], 1980;

Birthdays Are Not for Dying, Ibadan, University of Ibadan Theatre, 1980;

The Oriki of a Grasshopper, Ibadan, University of Ibadan Theatre, 1981; revised version, Benin City, Nigeria, University of Benin Theatre, 1985;

Midnight Hotel, Ibadan, Kakaun Sela Kompany, 1982;

Altine's Wrath, Benin City, Nigeria, University of Benin Theatre, 1984;

Esu and the Vagabond Minstrels, Benin City, Nigeria, University of Benin Theatre, 1984; revised version, Ife, Nigeria, University of Ife Theatre, 1986;

Another Raft, Ibadan, University of Ibadan Theatre, 1987;

Aringindin and the Night Watchmen, Ibadan, University of Ibadan Theatre, 1988;

Yungba-Yungba and the Dance Concert, Ibadan, University Theatre, 1990;

The Engagement, St. Louis, African Studies Association, 24 November 1991.

TELEVISION: *The Visitors* [series], BCOS-TV, Ibadan, 1982;

No More the Wasted Breed, BCOS-TV, Ibadan, 1982.

OTHER: "The Origins of Drama in West Africa," Ph.D. Dissertation, University of Ibadan, 1974;

"Like a Dead Clock Now" [poem], in *Don't Let Him Die*, edited by Chinua Achebe and Dubem Okafor (Enugu: Fourth Dimension, 1978), p. 28;

"Tiger on Stage: Wole Soyinka and the Nigerian Theatre," in *Theatre in Africa*, edited by Oyin Ogunba and Abiola Irele (Ibadan: University Press, 1978), pp. 151–175;

"Anubis Resurgent: Chaos and Political Vision in Recent Literature," in *West African Studies in Modern Language Teaching and Research*, edited by Ayo Banjo, Conrad-Benedict Brann, and Henri Evans (Lagos: National Language Centre, 1981), pp. 185–198;

"Festac and the Heritage of Ambiguity," in *Survey of Nigerian Affairs, 1976 & 1977*, edited by Oyeleye Oyediran (Ibadan & London: Longman, 1981), pp. 32–46;

"The Alternative Tradition: A Survey of Nigerian Literature After the War," in *European Language Writing in Sub-Saharan Africa*, edited by Albert S. Gérard (Budapest: Akadémiai Kiadó, 1986), II: 781–798;

"And After the Wasted Breed? Responses to His-

tory and Wole Soyinka's Dramaturgy," in *On Stage*, edited by Ulla Schild (Göttingen, Germany: Mainzer Institut, 1992), pp. 59–74.

SELECTED PERIODICAL PUBLICATIONS – UNCOLLECTED: "The Quality of Hurt, (1): A Survey of Recent Nigerian Poetry," *Afriscope*, 4 (April 1974): 45–48, 51–53;

"The Quality of Hurt, (2): The New Voices," *Afriscope*, 4 (April 1974): 46–55;

"The Environment as Hero: A Note on *The Interpreters*," *Ibadan Literary Review*, 1, no. 1 (1975);

"From *Opon Ifa* . . . Prose Poems," *Opon Ifa*, 1 (March 1976): 1; (May 1976): 35; 2 (October 1976): 1–2; special issue (February 1977); new series 1, no. 1 (1982): 1–2; special issue, no. 2 (1982);

"War's Aftermath" [poem], *Opon Ifa*, 1 (March 1976): 13;

"Two Variations, a Theme" [poem], *Opon Ifa*, 1 (May 1976): 13;

"Literacy as Suicide: Artist and Audience in Contemporary Nigerian Society," *Afriscope*, 7 (February 1977): 21–23;

"Criticism and the Sixteen Palmnuts: The Role of Critics in an Age of Illiteracy," *Ch'indaba*, 3 (October 1977);

"Domestication of an Opiate: Western Paraesthetics and the Growth of the Ekwensi Tradition," *Positive Review*, 4 (January–February 1981): 1–12;

"I Remember Okigbo" [poem], *Opon Ifa*, new series 1, no. 1 (1982): 14–16;

"Enter the Carthaginian Critic?," *Okike*, 21 (July 1982): 38–44;

"Ritual and the Revolutionary Ethos: The Humanist Dilemma in Contemporary Nigerian Theatre," *Okike*, 22 (September 1982): 72–81;

"Drama and the New Exotic: The Paradox of Form in Contemporary Theatre," *African Theatre Review*, 1 (April 1983): 76–85;

"Discours (peu) académique," *Politique Africaine*, 4 (March 1984): 65–78;

"The Author as Sociologist," *West Africa* (27 August 1984): 1731–1732.

Femi Osofisan is a playwright, poet, theater director, university professor, literary theorist, and newspaper critic, and he is part of a generation of Nigerians who feel they have experienced Nigerian independence as an empty slogan. Thus he fashions a committed literature designed to shatter the enduring shackles of religion, custom, and colonialism and to stimulate a confident, imaginatively self-critical sensibility capable of charting a course toward a more humane, egalitarian society. Writing in English, he aims his dramas at those whose education enables them to manage the nation's destiny, but his manipulation of the theater's rich nonverbal resources, coupled with an exploitation of indigenous, African performance aesthetics, means that his work has the potential to reach a wider audience. Within Nigeria he is often viewed as a radical intent upon completely destroying the past, but his radicalism actually builds on the best of tradition while seeking to encourage pervasive change.

Born Babafemi Adeyemi Osofisan on 16 June 1946 in Erunwon, a Yoruba farming village located in what was then known as the Western Region, the playwright was three months old when his father died. Early experiences of poverty affected him profoundly, causing him to lack a sense of stability and to be dependent on a variety of relatives who could house him and later assist in paying his school fees at Government College, Ibadan. As a consequence, he later disavowed the privileged position of the educated elite in favor of an ideological identification with the impoverished Nigerian masses.

While at Government College he wrote short stories and poems and edited the school journal. Graduating in 1965, Osofisan won a scholarship to the University of Ibadan, where he wrote scripts for various student events and eventually became president of the Dramatic Society. As part of the requirements for the bachelor of arts in French, he spent 1967 and 1968 at the Université de Dakar in Senegal, where he trained with the Daniel Sorano Theatre Company while earning a diplôme d'etudes supérieures. Over the next two years the fledgling playwright gained additional experience in acting and directing for both theater and television through his affiliation with the Orisun Theatre, a professional company established at the University of Ibadan by drama pioneer Wole Soyinka and managed by Dapo Adelugba during Soyinka's incarceration.

A Restless Run of Locusts (performed, 1969; published, 1975), Osofisan's earliest published play, was written in 1969 while he was a senior at the University of Ibadan. Nigeria was engulfed in a civil war, which had erupted less than a decade after independence from Britain. Like several other African nations, the country had already experienced military coups. To young university men such as Osofisan, it seemed apparent that the generation who had negotiated freedom was bankrupt, and the stirring rhetoric of the negritude movement of the 1930s and 1940s had no counterpart in the sociopo-litical realm. To the young generation, so it seemed, would fall the task of building a nation and forging an art directly confronting the crises challenging the African continent. They rejected the style and vision of the earlier generation of poets and playwrights – including Christopher Okigbo, Wole Soyinka, and J. P. Clark – in favor of an art largely devoid of a metaphysical orientation and reflective of a contemporary, urban idiom.

Thus in *A Restless Run of Locusts* the protest against the devastating effects of political greed, as evidenced in the Western Region elections of 1965 and 1966, was strident, and the manipulation of plot was transparent. In the play Chief Michael Kuti, a representative of an old guard intent on consolidating privileges inherited from the British, and Sanda Adeniyi, the young reformer eager to avenge the political thuggery suffered by his brother, both resort to campaign violence. Left to mourn their deaths are their women, who recognize their failings, love them nonetheless, but can fashion no effective action against the men's excesses.

A similarly desolate situation, in which the oppressed assume the violent characteristics of their oppressors and leave the women to mourn their deaths, is found in Osofisan's *You Have Lost Your Fine Face*, originally produced in 1969 at the University of Ibadan and later retitled and published as *Red Is the Freedom Road* (in *Morountodun and Other Plays*, 1982). A disguised commentary on the regime of Lt. Col. Yakubu Gowon, who had come to power in Nigeria in 1966, the play is set within the context of nineteenth-century, intra-Yoruba warfare. It traces the meteoric rise of a warrior, Akanji, who must brutally renounce all allegiance to his own people as part of a strategy to regain their freedom. Though he mounts a successful counterattack, he also unleashes a new round of violence in which promises of liberation and dignity soon degenerate into looting and death.

Graduating from the University of Ibadan in 1969, Osofisan initially rejected a scholarship for postgraduate work, preferring instead to teach in a secondary school and launch a writing career from there. Within three months he was back on a college campus, after being disillusioned by what he describes as the other teachers' intellectual mediocrity and preoccupation with superficial values. Graduate work in drama took him to the Université de Paris III, where a quarrel with a faculty supervisor who refused to acknowledge the legitimacy of African drama led to Osofisan's withdrawal in 1973 and his return to the University of Ibadan, from which he obtained his Ph.D. the following year.

While in Paris, however, Osofisan completed his only novel to date, *Kolera Kolej* (1975). A surrealistic treatment of current events, the novel concerns a college granted its independence from the state after an outbreak of cholera quarantines faculty, students, and staff. Among predictably corrupt faculty members and female students wanders a mysterious poet with his dog; an equally elusive Muse figure seduces and yet accuses him of being a "dead conscience," unwilling to translate his beautiful words into some tangible reality. Inspired by this woman, the poet attempts to warn his society about the new messiah, whom it so eagerly embraces, but the poet is killed in a coup. At the conclusion an illusionary hope is rekindled, and the people can "begin to die again with renewed fervor."

In 1975, when New Horn Press was about to publish the book, Osofisan decided to add a postscript, largely in response to audience reactions to the dramatization of this novel as well as to productions of Kole Omotoso's *The Curse* (published in 1976) and Dejo Okediji's *Rere Run*. Because all three works concluded pessimistically with the rebel destroyed by reactionary forces, spectators seemed to interpret these plots as demonstrating the futility of struggling for positive, social change. Thus Osofisan appended a second ending, in which a scheme to silence all members of the opposition by selling them off as cheap labor to "the mother country" is defeated, and the Muse's voice is heard welcoming the imprisoned back to freedom.

Between 1970 and 1973 Osofisan wrote *Farewell to a Cannibal Rage* (performed, 1978; published, 1986) and *The Chattering and the Song* (performed, 1976; published, 1977). With these plays he began to abandon realism with its tidy categorizations, wherein minor themes or voices are subordinated to major ones, conflict is resolved, and – given the Nigerian sociopolitical reality mirrored in the plays – the general populace's powerlessness is reinforced. In its place he offered what may be described as a contemporary African total theater. The traditional, philosophical understanding of experience as a dynamic interlock of potentially competing energies is preserved through such devices as the articulation of multiple, conflicting narratives of equal value; the exploitation of music, dance, and spectacle to create moments of potentially shared transcendence; the conflation into one experiential reality of ontological and cognitive distinctions between human and supernatural, past and present; and the passage of artistic hegemony from author to audience through the conscious solicitation of in-

volvement in the production of meaning. What marks this stylistic approach is Osofisan's sustained interrogation of history: the connection between received wisdom and the material forces shaping its articulation is insisted on, and the audience is offered images of and challenges to the reformulation of that tradition in a manner that affirms its empowerment.

Thus in *Farewell to a Cannibal Rage* Osofisan relies heavily on the structural strategies of storytelling to project a tale about the triumph of young lovers over social divisions maintained by their elders. A narrator announces at the outset that he will tell a story of reconciliation, and he drafts his fellow actors into various roles. Since there are more performers than there are character parts, some people must be cajoled into playing hills, door frames, and other scenic elements. As the drama progresses, these elements are dismantled and reconstituted in accordance with the demands of the plot; Yoruba songs – adapted for the most part from popular rhythms and proverbs – and dance provide the mechanisms by which these changes are accomplished. Predictably some actors tire of playing verandas or watching from the sidelines; they seize parts from their colleagues and replay segments to accustom the audience to changes. Having stated at the beginning the outcome of the story, Osofisan continually focuses attention on the means by which illusion is created, and he thwarts tendencies toward emotional involvement with the young lovers' dilemma.

Dedicated to the survivors of the Biafran war, the play nonetheless ends on an ambiguous note, in which a vision of unity is affirmed while the difficulties of burying historic, ethnic animosities are acknowledged. Interestingly Osofisan reports that one of the play's chief stylistic features occurred almost by accident, for in selecting the script as an examination piece for Ibadan students, he found it necessary to institute frequent role changes as a means of assessing their acting skills. This anecdote highlights an important element of his creative process, for he always directs the first productions of his plays, closely scrutinizing acting problems and audience responses, a task he regards as a necessary extension of the act of writing.

The Chattering and the Song likewise utilizes a traditional performance mode, that of a riddling competition related to success in love. It also marks his interest in the Agbekoya Farmers' Rebellion of 1968–1969 as a moment in Nigerian history when a genuinely populist uprising seemed possible. In the play middle-class supporters of the Farmers' Movement gather to celebrate an impending wedding. They drink, exchange riddles, and finally enact a historical play as a way of cementing their sometimes tense relationships. But the jubilant atmosphere is disrupted when a jilted lover reveals his identity as a secret-service agent and arrests the wedding couple for their political activities; the remaining friends must decide how to translate their own rhetoric of vague opposition to the government into some concrete plan of action.

The play-within-the-play is an example of Osofisan's interrogation of history. Whereas the eighteenth-century leader Alafin Abiodun, whose story is reenacted, is usually regarded as a hero who restored peace to his kingdom, Osofisan chose to depict him as a previously benign ruler who invokes the sanctions of custom and religion to perpetuate political exploitation. The change allowed Osofisan to question the relationship between tradition and hierarchy and to dramatize the fact that individuals can disrupt a preestablished order; by inviting the audience, at the play's end, to join the actors in singing the farmers' anthem, he challenges them to decide their position vis-à-vis the struggle for social justice.

In 1977 Osofisan used the Russian writer Nikolay Gogol's 1836 comedy *The Inspector General* as the basis for *Who's Afraid of Solarin?* (performed, 1977; published, 1978). It closely follows the Russian drama of an unemployed former civil servant who manages to fleece a group of rural government officials who are fearful of having their corruption uncovered. Its title refers to the Nigerian Dr. Tai Solarin, a tireless social critic who served as a public-complaints commissioner for several western states during the Olusegun Obasanjo military regime of the mid 1970s.

Osofisan soon turned his attention to another controversial issue confronting the nation. *Once upon Four Robbers* (performed, 1978; published, 1980) questions the morality of public executions. Stylistically inspired by Efua Sutherland's ingenious use of traditional Ghanaian folklore in her writing, the play concerns a band of thieves given a trick formula by which they can successfully rob people — provided they kill no one, steal from the rich, and commit their crimes in public places. Each member is given a portion of a song, unknown to his colleagues; when they work together, their victims are entranced and leave their property untended. Bickering among the group enables government soldiers to capture them and start their public executions, but, at the last moment, the old man who has narrated the entire drama freezes the action and de-

FEMI OSOFISAN

THE ORIKI OF A GRASSHOPPER
and
THE ENGAGEMENT

November 24, 1991
8:00p.m.
African Studies Association Conference
St. Louis

Poster advertising a performance of two Osofisan plays, the second of which was a premiere presentation

mands that spectators decide the fate of these petty criminals. Stage directions indicate that should the audience choose death, the executions are to be mimed in such a way that each one becomes progressively more intolerable to watch; should it choose freedom, the actors are to proceed to rob the audience. Osofisan reports that at most performances spectators agree to spare the criminals' lives. More important, perhaps, than the specific consensus the audience finally reaches is the process of debate, for it approximates a level of responsibility the public must assume in charting a course of national development.

In 1979 Osofisan returned to the subject of the Agbekoya Farmers' Movement with his production of *Morountodun* (published in 1982), mounted first at the theater on the Ibadan campus and then toured off-campus by his theater group, the Kakaun Sela Kompany [*sic*]. The subsequent publication of the play garnered for Osofisan the first Association of

Nigerian Authors (ANA) prize for literature. Produced at a time of transition from military to civilian rule, the drama is based on archives housed in London and on local newspaper accounts concerning the government's use of a female agent to infiltrate the agrarian movement of some ten years earlier. This historical detail allows Osofisan to draw parallels with a much earlier history (or myth) of the Yoruba queen Moremi, who also infiltrated enemy ranks to save her city from destruction. Whereas the actual Agbekoya operative was successful in fundamentally compromising the protesters, in Osofisan's account the agent Titubi eventually reexamines the Moremi story and opts against the status quo and for the farmers instead.

But the actors abandon their roles before the narrative of the farmers' protest is concluded. The audience must decide which is more important: the factual detail of the farmers' eventual defeat, offhandedly mentioned as a concession to the spectators' desire to know "what happens next"; or the images of a people collectively moving to assert their interests. In making that decision, members of the audience, of course, ultimately determine the meaning of the artistic enterprise; they begin the process of their own empowerment.

Parallels between Samuel Beckett's tramps in *Waiting for Godot* (1952) and a marginalized, Third World intelligentsia led Osofisan to write *The Oriki of a Grasshopper* (performed, 1981; published in *Two One-Act Plays*, 1986). First produced for the annual African-literature conference sponsored by the Ibadan English department, the play focuses on a radical professor, Imaro, who continues to rehearse the Beckett play while waiting for secret-service agents to arrest him for allegedly fomenting campus unrest. Alienated from the university, business, and working-class communities, who find his ivory-tower protests against injustice unprofitable and therefore incomprehensible, Imaro loses even his leftist friends when it is revealed that one of his actors, who is also a wealthy businessman, has intervened with the police on his behalf. Though Imaro argues for principled, ideological flexibility, his chief collaborator sees only duplicity. Neither the Pozzo of the state nor the Godot of socialism will ever arrive for Imaro. Like Beckett's tramps, he is left alone, psychologically immobilized and chanting "Let freedom come."

In 1982 Osofisan wrote and directed thirteen episodes for the television series *The Visitors*. A murder-mystery series, it allowed the playwright to combine popular forms with social commentary. Several of those episodes have been transferred to the stage and subsequently published. During that same year, his Kakaun Sela Kompany premiered *Midnight Hotel* (published in 1986), the text of which freely acknowledges Osofisan's debt to both Ernest-Aimé Feydeau and Bertolt Brecht. A hilarious farce concerning rampant materialism, the play is set in a seedy Lagos hotel where politicians, businessmen, and various women meet to transact commerce and sex. Interviews with Osofisan reveal again the crucial connection for him between writing and rehearsal: a casual decision to include one song led to the conscious crafting of several songs, designed to contradict the slapstick quality of the spoken text, and the creation of a Brecht-like "Songmaster," who periodically brings out an oversized songbook from which cast members sing lyrics.

In more serious tones Osofisan wrote *No More the Wasted Breed*, which was filmed for television and shown in 1982 with a cast composed of members of the Unibadan Performing Company. A refutation of Wole Soyinka's *The Strong Breed* (performed, 1966; published, 1969), it renders in dramatic form Osofisan's long-standing objections to metaphysical solutions, an objection expressed in various essays of his, such as "Ritual and the Revolutionary Ethos," "Literacy as Suicide," and "The Alternative Tradition." In Osofisan's play a fisherman, Biokun, desperate to cure his dying son, is preparing to renounce his materialist views and honor the gods. Two gods, disguised as an old couple, arrive to determine whether the local inhabitants, who have for a long time ignored their divinity, should be spared ultimate destruction. A debate ensues concerning the principles of obedience and self-sacrifice demanded of the poor by a priesthood indebted to the rich. Won over by Biokun's arguments, the old man/god banishes his wife, and the religious observance surrounding her, to death. Ushered in is a new age when people will learn to master their own destinies. Thus, in place of Soyinka's allegedly elliptical style and ahistorical metaphysical vision, Osofisan posits a more pedestrian poetics and a secular humanism.

In 1982 Osofisan took a sabbatical from university teaching to serve as a founding member of the editorial board of the *Guardian* newspaper (Lagos), which had been formed during the second Shehu Shagari presidential election campaign to function as an independent voice. The position not only afforded Osofisan a forum from which to comment on important issues before a more diverse audience than might ordinarily view his plays but also provided a mechanism by which to feel the national pulse. The next year, having helped to establish the paper on a firm footing, he resumed teaching, this time as chairman of the Department of Theatre Arts at the University of Benin. Throughout his moves to Benin City, the University of Ife, and back to Ibadan, the peripatetic Osofisan maintained connections with the *Guardian*. Not only did he continue a regular column of cultural and sociopolitical commentary but from about 1987 to 1990 he also authored, under the pen name Okinba Launko, a column titled "Tales the Country Told Me." Many of them were later published as the 1989 novella *Cordelia*, and a subsequent collection of his journalistic fiction, "Ma'ami," awaits publication.

Using the Launko name again, Osofisan published *Minted Coins*, which was awarded the ANA poetry prize in 1987. Osofisan is the first author to have won this prestigious award in two different categories. As a subsequent president of ANA (1989–1990), Osofisan resumed the practice, which he and others had begun in the poetry journal *Opon Ifa*, of encouraging younger writers. This time he focused on playwrights, persuading the British Council to publish the 1989 ANA drama prizewinners' plays in a collection entitled *Five Plays*.

Esu and the Vagabond Minstrels, first produced in 1984 at the University of Benin and published in 1991, is another example of contemporary African total theater. Posing as a priest, the god Esu promises wealth to a group of starving musicians if they each bestow a gift on a truly needy recipient. Predictably all but one of the musicians choose those who can clearly reward them handsomely, while the loner selects a poor, pregnant woman and a leprous couple from whom he contracts the disease. The priest/god returns to evaluate the artists' choices, claims an inability to decide the leprous musician's case, and demands that the audience make known its opinions. Though some may argue that in a context of pervasive greed, selfishness is appropriate, spectators can be expected to vote that the generous musician be restored to health and the greedy ones punished. But the fairy-tale ending, in which the kindest man is hailed as "humanity's last remaining hero," is punctured by scripted objections from actors sitting incognito in the auditorium. They question Osofisan's alleged radicalism and argue that songs and magic have no relevance to the severe crises plaguing the nation. Again the audience must voice an opinion. The play's production history at the University of Ife, where it had an extensive run (as revised) in 1986, attests to various reactions: some religious conservatives objected to the god's desacralization; some experts in Yoruba culture deplored the Christianizing influences evident in the portrayal of the god and chief protagonist; some

leftists denounced the piece as a shift to the same mystification Osofisan found offensive in Soyinka's work; and some sympathizers applauded Osofisan's attempts to render traditional cosmology applicable to contemporary realities.

With *Aringindin and the Night Watchmen* (performed, 1988; published, 1991) Osofisan returned to the subject of armed robbery, examining what he calls in the preface "the processes by which fascism is allowed to breed. . . . " The plot involves townspeople who, out of fear and frustration, hire a retired veteran and his subordinates to defend their businesses. Though calm returns to a grateful citizenry, and the veteran, Aringindin, receives governmental honors, in time he proves to be collaborating with armed robbers and elected officials to foster social chaos that will justify his absolute rule. All the townspeople, except one young woman, seem cowed into submission, and at the end of the play she kills herself rather than submit to military detention. Though much of the drama is entertaining – given its considerable use of Yoruba songs and dance contests among female and male townspeople – its perspective is more bleak than most of Osofisan's other work. As in plays such as *Altine's Wrath*, where he wrote an ending calculated to elicit spirited objections from viewers, Osofisan concedes in his preface that he has deliberately magnified current sociopolitical conditions in Nigeria in order to challenge audiences to reconsider their responsibilities in crafting their future.

Femi Osofisan is an artist who generates controversy. Thoroughly grounded in a Nigerian social and cosmological reality, his plays also speak to those outsiders who cherish the potential of men and women to both dream and struggle. He will likely continue to exploit popular forms and traditional thought in order to create a provocative style of theater that challenges audiences to rethink basic values and reclaim the power to alter their worlds.

Interviews:

Ossie Enekwe, "Interview with Femi Osofisan," *Greenfield Review*, 8 (Spring 1979): 76–80;

Jean-Pascal Daloz, "Briser les barrières: Entretien avec Femi Osofisan," *Notre Librairie*, 98 (July–September 1989): 94–97.

References:

Muyiwa Awodiya, "Femi Osofisan's Theatre," in *Perspectives on Nigerian Literature, 1700 to the Present*, edited by Yemi Ogunbiyi (Lagos: Guardian, 1988), pp. 223–227;

F. Odun Balogun, "*Kolera Kolej*: A Surrealistic Political Satire," *Africana Journal*, 12 (October–December 1981): 323–332;

Lanrele Bamidele, "The Poet of the Theatre: Osofisan's Experiment with Form and Technique," *New Literature Review*, 4 (January 1986): 82–90;

Aderemi Bamikunle, "Nigerian Playwrights and Nigerian Myths: A Look at Soyinka, Osofisan, and Sowande's Plays," in *Critical Theory and African Literature*, edited by R. Vanamali, Emelia Oko, and Azubike Iloeje (Ibadan: Heinemann, 1987), pp. 121–131;

Bamikunle, "Nigerian Political Culture in Osofisan's *Minted Coins*," *Commonwealth Essays and Studies*, 12 (Autumn 1989): 108–116;

Chris Egharevba, "The Carrier Ritual as Medium of Vision in Nigerian Drama: The Examples of Soyinka and Osofisan," in *Critical Theory and African Literature*, pp. 25–36;

Edde Iji, "The Mythic Imagination and Heroic Archetypes: From Moremi Myth to Osofisan's *Morountodun*," in *Critical Theory and African Literature*, pp. 81–98;

Biodun Jeyifo, "Femi Osofisan as Literary Critic and Theorist," in *Perspectives on Nigerian Literature, 1700 to the Present*, pp. 228–232;

Jeyifo, "Theatrical Analogues of the Second Republic: Osofisan's *Midnight Hotel*," *West Africa*, no. 3398 (20 September 1982): 2406–2410;

Jeyifo, *The Truthful Lie: Essays in a Sociology of African Drama* (London: New Beacon, 1985), pp. 51–54, 82–87;

Rotimi Johnson, "Revolutionary Consciousness and Commitment in Osofisan's *Minted Coins*," *Neohelicon*, 17, no. 2 (1990): 157–168;

Gerald Moore, "Against the Titans in Nigerian Literature," *Afriscope*, 7 (July 1979): 19, 21–22, 25;

Moore, "L'Image de la revolution dans le théâtre africain," *Le Monde Diplomatique*, 12 September 1982, p. 23;

Olu Obafemi, "Political Perspectives and Popular Theatre in Nigeria," *Theatre Research International*, 7 (Autumn 1982): 235–244;

Obafemi, "Revolutionary Aesthetics in Nigerian Theatre," *African Literature Today*, 12 (1982): 118–136;

Odia Ofeimun, "Criticism as Homicide: A Reply to Femi Osofisan's 'Literacy as Suicide,' " *Afriscope*, 7 (July 1977): 31–32;

Yemi Ogunbiyi, "Nigerian Theatre and Drama: A Critical Profile," in his *Drama and Theatre in Nigeria: A Critical Source Book* (Lagos: Nigeria Magazine, 1981), pp. 3–53;

Chinyere Okafor, "Creating New Awareness Through Shock Drama," *Nigerian Theatre Journal*, 1, no. 1 (1984): 9–15;

Modupe O. Olaogun, "Parables in the Theatre: A Brief Study of Femi Osofisan's Plays," *Okike*, 27–28 (March 1988): 43–55;

Tess Akaeke Onwueme, "Osofisan's New Hero: Women as Agents of Social Reconstruction," *Sage: A Scholarly Journal on Black Women*, 5 (Summer 1988): 25–28;

Onwueme, "Visions of Myth in Nigerian Drama: Femi Osofisan versus Wole Soyinka," *Canadian Journal of African Studies*, 25, no. 1 (1991): 58–69;

Niyi Osundare, "Social Message of a Nigerian Dramatist," *West Africa* (28 January 1980): 147–150;

Sandra L. Richards, "Nigerian Independence Onstage: Responses from 'Second Generation' Playwrights," *Theatre Journal*, 39 (May 1987): 215–227;

Richards, "Towards a Populist Nigerian Theatre: The Plays of Femi Osofisan," *New Theatre Quarterly*, 3 (August 1987): 280–288;

Richards, "Wasn't Brecht an African Writer? Parallels with Contemporary Nigerian Drama," *Brecht Yearbook* (1989): 168–183.

Sol T. Plaatje

(9 October 1876 – 19 June 1932)

Brian P. Willan

BOOKS: *Native Life in South Africa* (London: King, 1916; Kimberley, South Africa: Tsala Ea Batho / New York: Crisis, 1921);

A Sechuana Reader, in International Phonetic Orthography, by Plaatje and Daniel Jones (London: University of London Press, 1916);

Mhudi: An Epic of Native Life a Hundred Years Ago (Lovedale, South Africa: Lovedale, 1930; New York: Negro Universities Press, 1970; Johannesburg & London: Quagga/Collings, 1975);

The Boer War Diary of Sol T. Plaatje, edited by John L. Comaroff (London & Johannesburg: Macmillan, 1973); revised and edited by Comaroff, Andrew Reed, and Brian P. Willan as *Mafeking Diary* (Johannesburg: Southern Books / London: Currey / Athens: Ohio University Press, 1990).

TRANSLATIONS: *Sechuana Proverbs, with Literal Translations and Their European Equivalents* (London: Kegan Paul, Trench, Trubner, 1916);

William Shakespeare, *Diphosho-phosho* [*A Comedy of Errors*] (Morija, Lesotho: Morija, 1930);

Shakespeare, *Dintshontsho tsa bo-Juliuse Kesara* [*Julius Caesar*] (Johannesburg: Witwatersrand University Press, 1937).

Sol T. Plaatje occupies a central position in South Africa's political and literary history. One of the most widely talented and versatile men of his generation, he was a prolific journalist and newspaper editor, one of the founders of the African National Congress, and a leader in the public affairs of the African people for much of his life. His most significant writings are *Native Life in South Africa* (1916), a powerful defense of African rights, published as a response to the Natives' Land Act of 1913; *Mhudi* (1930), the first novel in English to have been written by a black South African; and a handful of books written in Setswana (also called Sechuana),

his native tongue, which did much to preserve the language's literary form and established Plaatje as one of its leading writers and translators.

Solomon Tshekisho Plaatje was born near Boshof, South Africa, on 9 October 1876, into a Setswana-speaking family of Barolong origin, whose ancestors were among the earliest African converts to Christianity in the interior of southern Africa. His parents were Johannes and Martha Plaatje. One of a large family, Sol went to school at the Lutheran Berlin Missionary Society's mission station at Pniel, not far from the then-new diamond town of Kimberley. Much of his education he owed to the Reverend Ernst Westphal and his wife, Elizabeth, who took a close interest in his progress. From an early age he showed an unusual learning ability, in particular a remarkable facility with the various languages – African and European – spoken on the mission grounds. Plaatje's formal education, however, ended when he was seventeen: he left Pniel early in 1894 to take up employment as a messenger with the post office in Kimberley.

Over the next four years Plaatje emerged as one of the most active figures in the communal life of the polyglot African community in Kimberley and applied himself – both at work and in his spare time – to the task of acquiring a full command of the English language, one of the two official languages (along with Dutch) of the Cape Colony. On 25 January 1898 Plaatje married Elizabeth (Lilith) M'belle, sister of the well-known court interpreter Isaiah Bud-M'belle, his close friend, and later the same year the couple moved to Mafeking, where Plaatje himself had accepted a job as court interpreter, employed by the Cape civil service. The subsequent siege of Mafeking (October 1899 – May 1900), one of the best-known episodes in the Anglo-Boer War, inspired Plaatje to his first extended literary venture: his private diary, covering the period of October 1899 to March 1900. Written in English,

*Sol T. Plaatje (Department of Historical Papers, University of the
Witwatersrand Library, Johannesburg)*

it provides a lively, detailed, and personal day-to-day account of the siege, demonstrating Plaatje's already remarkable facility with the English language, a fascination with the idioms of both African and European languages, and a finely developed sense of humor and irony. Plaatje's narration of the siege also casts new light on the highly significant African contribution to the defense of Mafeking, an aspect very much underplayed in other accounts.

Although many diaries kept by whites during the siege of Mafeking were published over the next few years, Plaatje's was not, and he seems to have made no effort to have it published. It was only published in 1973, following the retrieval of Plaatje's manuscript by John Comaroff, an anthropologist doing research in the Mafeking district.

Frustrated at the lack of opportunities for advancement when the siege was over, Plaatje resigned from the civil service in 1902 in order to assume the editorship of a new Tswana-English newspaper, *Koranta ea Becoana* (The Tswana Gazette), financed by a local chief, Silas Molema. Over the next decade Plaatje emerged not only as one of the leading African newspaper editors of his day but

also as one of the most eloquent spokesmen for his people. He argued that Africans should be properly represented and protected in the new political and constitutional structures being created in the aftermath of British victory in the Anglo-Boer War.

With the creation of the Union of South Africa in 1910, Plaatje moved to Kimberley to become editor of the newspaper *Tsala ea Becoana* (Friend of the Tswana), and then *Tsala ea Batho* (Friend of the People), which achieved a circulation of several thousand for each weekly issue. Increasingly involved in national politics, Plaatje was one of the founders of the African National Congress in 1912. He became its first general secretary and in 1914 traveled to the United Kingdom as a member of a deputation to appeal to the British imperial government to repeal the Natives' Land Act of 1913, one of the most significant pieces of segregationist legislation, which severely restricted native African rights to land.

When the other members of the deputation returned to South Africa at the outbreak of World War I, Plaatje stayed on for a further two and a half years, during which time he worked on three books.

Dust jacket for the 1975 South African edition of the first novel in English by a black South African. Plaatje wrote Mhudi *in England during 1919 and 1920, but the novel was not published until 1930.*

The first was *Native Life in South Africa*, published in May 1916. In essence a fierce attack on the Natives' Land Act and written as an appeal to the British public, *Native Life* was also a wide-ranging defense of African political rights and an often-emotive account of the steps taken over the years by South Africa's rulers to exclude Africans from political power. The book is notable for its moving description of the devastating effects the Land Act had on African peasant farmers in the Orange Free State and for a personal, often nostalgic tone, which bears comparison with William Cobbett's *Rural Rides* (1830), published nearly a hundred years earlier as a response to the enclosure movement in the English countryside.

Native Life was widely reviewed in both Great Britain and South Africa. For the most part reviewers concentrated on the political stance of Plaatje and on the fact that *Native Life* was actually the first book-length exposition of African claims to have been written by a black South African. In 1917 both the book and Plaatje himself were the subject of considerable debate in the South African House of Assembly.

The other two books Plaatje worked on during his sojourn in England – his *Sechuana Proverbs*

and *Sechuana Reader* (both published in 1916) – were of a different kind: both were the product of his intense concern to preserve his native language, which he felt to be threatened by the effects of socio-economic changes and by the predominance of other, more widely spoken African and European languages. The *Sechuana Reader*, written in conjunction with Professor Daniel Jones, one of the foremost linguistic scholars of his day, was an attempt to preserve the precise sounds of the language by applying to it the phonetic alphabet – the first time this sort of project had been done with an African language. Also significant is the fact that the book includes Tswana folktales that Plaatje had collected and recorded firsthand.

Sechuana Proverbs is a comprehensive compilation of 732 Tswana proverbs, which Plaatje recorded and put alongside his own literal English translations, together with their English or European equivalents where he could identify them. Both books were welcomed by the few scholars in the field, and they remain to this day among the most important books to have been written in Setswana. However, they never achieved a wide circulation or readership.

Plaatje returned to South Africa in 1917, but

two years later he traveled to Britain as the leader of a second African National Congress deputation, again seeking the intervention of the British government in South Africa's affairs. This deputation met with no more success than its predecessor did in 1914. Plaatje then apparently completed the manuscript of a successor volume to *Native Life* (covering political affairs in South Africa between 1916 and 1920), but it was never published, and the manuscript has not survived.

In 1920 Plaatje traveled on to the United States and Canada, seeking to publicize the plight of black South Africans, and he made contact with some well-known black American leaders, such as Marcus Garvey and W. E. B. DuBois (who published the American edition of *Native Life*). Finally, in 1923, to rejoin his wife and family Plaatje returned to South Africa, having achieved scant success in his travels overseas and reconciled to his failure to secure any outside intervention in South Africa's political affairs.

During the remaining years of his life, in Kimberley, Plaatje continued to devote himself to both political and literary concerns. Although he failed to resuscitate his newspaper as he hoped, he wrote extensively for both black and white newspapers, but in the changed circumstances of South Africa in the 1920s he no longer enjoyed the influence he once had. Increasingly he devoted himself to the task of recording and preserving Tswana language and literature. He compiled an English-Setswana dictionary, designed to replace the existing published dictionary, originally compiled by J. T. Brown in the 1870s, which he felt to be wholly inadequate and inaccurate; he compiled a substantial collection of Tswana folktales and praise poems; and he prepared a second, enlarged edition of his earlier *Sechuana Proverbs*. None of these books was ever published, and only the manuscript of the revised *Sechuana Proverbs* has survived.

Plaatje's other major project in the field of Tswana literature was the translation of several of William Shakespeare's plays, reflecting — as well as his concern to create a body of written literature in Setswana — an interest and fascination with Shakespeare that dated from the 1890s. Plaatje probably completed translations of six of Shakespeare's plays, but only two were published: *Diphosho-phosho* (literally, "Mistake upon Mistake"), his translation of *A Comedy of Errors*, published by the Morija Press in 1930; and *Dintshontsho tsa bo-Juliuse Kesara (Julius Caesar)*, published posthumously in 1937.

The few people in a position to judge Plaatje's success in these translations were full of praise for the quality of his work, and the books attracted considerable interest by virtue of being the first published translations of plays by Shakespeare into any African language. Subsequent editions of both books achieved substantial sales to schools in Setswana-speaking parts of Botswana and the Republic of South Africa.

Plaatje's literary endeavors were not confined to the Setswana language. The year 1930 also saw the publication of *Mhudi: An Epic of Native Life a Hundred Years Ago*, the first novel in English to have been written by a black South African. Plaatje actually wrote *Mhudi* while in England in 1919 and 1920, and he had tried in vain to find a publisher for it during his subsequent travels.

Set in South Africa in the 1830s, *Mhudi* follows the fortunes of the two principal characters, Ra-Thaga and Mhudi (the heroine), as Barolong, Boer, and Ndebele peoples clash in the wake of the *mfecane*, a series of forced migrations set in motion by the rise of the Zulu kingdom. In this setting Plaatje combines a fast-moving plot in the style of the Western novel with a deliberate use of African oral tradition and idiom. The result is an unusual synthesis, reflecting Plaatje's enthusiasm for both African and English literary traditions, and his view that it was not only perfectly legitimate to mix the two but that much creative potential lay in doing so.

At the same time, Plaatje used *Mhudi* as a vehicle for the expression of many of his own beliefs and ideals. In the character of Mhudi is embodied the notion that women had a special contribution to make to the achievement of racial harmony in South Africa; in the individual friendship of a Boer and a Barolong is a model for the breaking down of personal prejudice, which Plaatje believed to be a precondition for the emergence of a just social order; and in his many prophetic utterances about the consequences of continued injustice and oppression, Plaatje had in mind the South Africa of his own day, not just the period in which the action of *Mhudi* occurs.

At the time of its publication and shortly afterward *Mhudi* was noted more for the fact that it was the first novel in English to have been written by a black South African than for any real appreciation of its qualities, although the reviewer for the *Times Literary Supplement* did conclude that the book was "definitely memorable — a torch for some others to carry on." Few people were aware of what Plaatje was seeking to do in *Mhudi*: the book seemed to fall between two traditions, African and European, and to be part of neither. Only in the 1970s and 1980s — particularly with its publication in the Heinemann

African Writers Series (1978) – did *Mhudi* achieve a wider readership, and recognition of its place in the development of both African and South African literature is now assured.

Shortly before his death Plaatje was working on another book in English, based on the nineteenth-century history of the Baca people of the eastern Cape. Only part of an early draft of this manuscript survives, and no conclusive assessment of it is possible. Enough of it survives, though, to suggest that Plaatje's future literary plans may well have involved exploring in greater depth the historical traditions not only of the Tswana people but of other South African peoples as well. As in *Mhudi*, one of his concerns was to preserve and uphold African historical traditions to counter the misrepresentations by white historians, writers, and officials.

Sixty years after his death Plaatje's pioneering role in both political and literary spheres is achieving a growing recognition within South Africa. The enormous range of his activities and interests, his determination to explore both African and English literary traditions, a vision that looked forward to a South Africa free from oppression and racial discrimination – all these things made Plaatje a man who in many ways rose above the constraints of the divided, polarized society of South Africa.

Biography:

Brian P. Willan, *Sol Plaatje: South African Nationalist 1876–1932* (Berkeley: University of California Press, 1984; London: Heinemann, 1984).

References:

T. J. Couzens, "Sol Plaatje's *Mhudi*," *Journal of Commonwealth Literature*, 8 (June 1973): 1–19;

Couzens, "Sol T. Plaatje and the First South African Epic," *English in Africa*, 14 (May 1987): 41–65;

Stephen Gray, "Plaatje's Shakespeare," *English in Africa*, 4 (March 1977): 1–6;

Gray, "Sol T. Plaatje's Use of John Bunyan in *Mhudi*," *Communiqué*, 9, no. 1 (1984), 3–13.

Papers:

There are three major archival collections of Plaatje papers: at the University of the Witwatersrand, Johannesburg; the University of South Africa, Pretoria; and the School of Oriental and African Studies, London. An earlier manuscript of *Mhudi* is in the Rhodes University Library, Grahamstown, South Africa. For holdings at the University of the Witwatersrand, see Marcelle Jacobson, *The Silas T. Molema and Solomon T. Plaatje Papers*, Historical and Literary Papers: Inventories of Collections, 7 (Johannesburg: University of the Witwatersrand Library, 1978).

V. S. (Vic) Reid

(1 May 1913 – 25 August 1987)

Michael G. Cooke
Yale University

BOOKS: *New Day* (New York: Knopf, 1949; London: Heinemann, 1950);
The Leopard (New York: Viking, 1958; London: Heinemann, 1958);
Sixty-Five (London: Longmans, Green, 1960; Trinidad & London: Longman, 1980);
The Young Warriors (London: Longmans, 1967; Port of Spain: Longman Caribbean / London: Longman, 1979);
Buildings in Jamaica (Kingston, Jamaica: Information Service, 1970);
Peter of Mount Ephraim: The Daddy Sharpe Rebellion (Kingston: Jamaica Publishing House, 1971);
The Jamaicans (Kingston: Institute of Jamaica, 1976);
Nanny-Town (Kingston: Jamaica Publishing House, 1983);
The Horses of the Morning: About the Rt. Excellent N. W. Manley, Q.C., M.M., National Hero of Jamaica; An Understanding (Kingston: Caribbean Authors, 1985).

PLAY PRODUCTION: *Waterford Bar*, Kingston, Jamaica, 1959.

OTHER: *Fourteen Jamaican Short Stories*, includes stories by Reid (Kingston, Jamaica: Pioneer, 1950).

SELECTED PERIODICAL PUBLICATIONS –
UNCOLLECTED: "Kingston Chronicles," *Jamaica Journal*, 19 (February–April 1986): 32–38; *Sunday Gleaner*, 30 March 1986;
"The Writer and His Work: V. S. Reid," *Journal of West Indian Literature*, 2 (December 1987): 4–10.

V. S. (Vic) Reid

Victor Stafford Reid was born in Kingston, Jamaica, on 1 May 1913 and called himself a "city-bred person." The son of Alexander Reid (in the shipping business) and Margaret Reid, he traveled a good deal in young adulthood and sought his livelihood in advertising, journalism, farming, and the book trade before he came into the limelight as a fiction writer. With prosperity he lived in a handsome apartment in upper Kingston with his wife, Monica (whom he married in 1935), and their four children. But Reid identified himself with the "country parts" of his homeland, where he set most of his fiction and to which he returned frequently, for reinvigoration and inspiration. He especially loved the mountains.

Reid made Jamaica – its history, people, needs, hopes, and powers – the focus of his work. Though he did receive the Silver and Gold Musgrave Medals (1955, 1978) from the Institute of Jamaica, and then the Order of Jamaica (1980) and the Norman Manley Award for Excellence in Literature (1981), he felt that full appreciation and impact were still to come: "My work is necessarily for the next generation," he once said. He wanted more than to be read; he wanted to effect a new consciousness, even a new temper, with his work, and he knew that would take time.

In the year preceding his death Reid published a couple of sections of "Kingston Chronicles," which he described as a "bio-poem" and which he projected to run to three volumes. He explicitly decided against any autobiographical novel. He was reluctant to discuss questions of theme or tone or design, as he was with his other unfinished works. Poetry and forthright autobiography both represented new departures for Reid, who was then in his seventies, but poetry is often an explicit concern in his fiction.

Four decades earlier Reid had adopted a grandfatherly personal voice, a voice of appealing instruction, in his first novel, *New Day* (1949). Protagonist John Campbell, a near nonagenarian, recounts his ideas about Jamaica from the Morant Bay Rebellion in 1865, when Campbell was eight, to the New Constitution in 1944. The novel is the story of the Jamaicans' first spasmodic outburst against the casually and provocatively cruel English overlordship that kept a social yoke in place three decades after the political yoke of slavery was lifted, and of the slow development of a social philosophy, a social structure, and a social and political authority that obliged the English to forego the tradition of force and negotiate in good faith Jamaica's new self-image and self-resolution.

With this novel, critic Wycliffe Bennett says, Reid brought Jamaican language forcefully to the attention of the international literati, but to some ears Campbell's idiom sounds far less deep and true than, say, Sam Selvon's speakers or Erna Brodber's characters. Selvon, Brodber, and Reid necessarily compromise or dilute the frankest demotic tongue in the interest of range and readability, but Reid slips in occasional implausibilities ("came a-ride," "began a-gather") and strains the use of inversions ("smart is my father") and elisions, such as *o'*, *no'*, or *ha'* (for *of*, *not*, and *have*). He held that "English must grow," and he was passionately interested in the Jamaican dialect as a "source of [that] growth." His love of music was also strong, and he may have had no greater interest in sounding Jamaican than in maintaining a "stately but natural rhythm in writing."

What gives focus and tension to *New Day* is Campbell's eager involvement as a patriot in the fate of the nation and his attachment to a family that has been rising to greater and greater prominence with each generation. His grandnephew, Garth Creary, as a wealthy lawyer/businessman sits on the platform with the notables and dignitaries for the New Constitution ceremonies and also stands up for the downtrodden and the exploited. (Reid may have divined the master maneuver of the Jamaican politician: to have the vote of the masses along with the ear of the few.)

Reid stresses how eager Creary is to learn about – and presumably from – the past. But the success drive of the Campbell/Creary family suggests otherwise. Creary's grandfather Davie Campbell quickly outgrows his mercurial revolutionary impulses and shows a conservative desire for dominance in his Cays community. Creary's father, James, flourishing in the Jamaican business world, cares little for the past or for the people (his wife is "of the English"). Both forebears serve to give Creary a powerful advantage in society and politics; the novel hardly substantiates the claim that Creary, rather than profiting from political gains, "is leading his people to the promised land. . . ."

John Campbell, the champion of the past in *New Day*, stands in a somewhat ironic relationship to the central action. His flashes of conceit may be understandable, but they seem distracting. In the 1865 riot he is too small to play a meaningful role; in the riot against the corporation at the novel's end he is too old to be of much account. Indeed he and his lifelong friend Timothy seem nothing but odd to the "young ones passing on the streets," and – though the story is framed as Campbell's account to readers who are beyond the action – within the action he appears a bit out of place, as the "young ones . . . wonder what [he and Timothy] must talk of all the time." The poignancy is more than that of an old man out of touch. It is the poignancy of accumulated knowledge and judgment without a ready medium of communication, or a proper audience. *New Day* has the willfulness of an important recounting, rather than the fluency and force of a story borne and shared by a cohesive cultural group.

Reid in a sense set out to generate such a cultural group with his novels for schoolchildren. As its title suggests, *Sixty-Five* (1960) focuses on the Morant Bay Rebellion of 1865; *The Young Warriors* (1967) deals with the Maroons, the runaway slaves who set up an impregnable stronghold in the "cockpit" country of Jamaica; and *Peter of Mount Ephraim* (1971) goes back to the period just prior to the abolition of slavery to treat the Samuel Sharpe slave uprising of 1831.

Reid's determination to drive home Jamaica's

Dust jacket for Reid's first novel, which is narrated by a Jamaican man in his eighties

story and make a place for John Campbell's "old things" persists in *The Jamaicans* (1976), set in the mid seventeenth century, when the English and the Spanish were vying for supremacy in Jamaica. Reid's avowed purpose is to rehabilitate the memory of Juan de Bolas, leader of a pre-Maroon band in the mountain wilds above Guanaboa Vale.

Two features stand out in *The Jamaicans*. First, Reid has his typical grandfather/bystander figure, Old Miguel, spell out the purpose of memory, which is to inspire the minds and hearts of the young in the fight against the age-old (European) enemy: the "Remembrancer" must "tell and retell the story of our past, until all our young men know it as they knew their mother's teats. . . ." The emphasis on knowledge rather than nurture may be somewhat questionable, and some may wonder whether Reid is not touting old weapons for new wars, out of nostalgia for a simpler confrontation, a surer heroism than the late twentieth century allows. Certainly it is such a confrontation, such a heroism that he pursues in his only non-Jamaican novel, *The Leopard* (1958). His muse led him more strongly toward the past than the present, and his work as chairman of the Jamaican National Trust Commission and a trustee of the Historic Foundation Research Centre in Kingston reflected that.

The second outstanding feature of *The Jamaicans* is its mystical sense of fusion with nature. De Bolas's guerrilla group enjoys almost an alliance with the forest in their struggle against superior English arms (the Spaniards having agreed to leave the guerrilla retreat alone, in a bargain that stipulated that the guerrillas would leave the Spanish haciendas alone). The trees "shared [their] secret with [the guerrillas]," Reid writes, "because [they] had become one" with the "leaves and the trees immediately around" them. It is not clear whether Reid is prompting the contemporary Jamaican to a similar relationship and state, but part of his case against the Europeans, whom he treats as avaricious poltroons, is their disharmony with nature as much as their fellowman.

The oneness with nature takes a dark and chilling turn at the end of *The Jamaicans*, when de Bolas and his closest friend and ally, Pablo, splitting over the question of whether to side with the English or the Spanish, fight and die at each other's hands. The choric voice of Old Miguel intones that they are now "of the Jamaican earth." Possibly Reid means this statement in a solemn, celebratory way, but it seems more like another dead-end conclusion in practical terms. By the same token, the fact that de Bolas's woman Kedala is with child offers no more than a vague promise, implicitly vitiated by the loss of the two principal champions of the Jamaican earth.

The national piety of Reid showed in the grim or fierce actualities of his work. Certainly fierceness is what readers encounter in two works that display his versatility as a writer. One is *The Horses of the Morning* (1985), a biography of the Jamaican national hero Norman Washington Manley, a key figure in the credibility and viability of the "New Day" that Reid so steadily espouses. He calls this work "an understanding" rather than a biography. The title harks back to *New Day* just as Garth Creary represents Reid's view of Manley. But as Reid himself put it, the spirit of "gentleness" and "prophecy" at work in *New Day* is no longer apropos. In *Horses* the situation calls for "redemption": forty years have past, and "you are trying to say to people: 'Look, you have done damn wrong, bang! bang! Therefore, now, let's change our ways.' Of course it [*Horses*] is more cross, more punishing! I see no reason at my age now not to say exactly what I've seen." The book is as much a bitter "understanding" of the middle class as a celebratory understanding of its focal figure. A more hard-hitting, acidulous Reid is heard in his description of Jamaica as "a land of shrewd, hard, fearless men in two-toned shoes and their semi-literate meddling wives."

The Leopard, Reid's second novel, is another work in a distinctive key and with a distinctive setting, the Kenya of Mau Mau times. Reid's avowed desire to counteract the negative portrayal of the Mau Mau in the British press serves almost as a red herring. Kenya's drive for political independence is far more oblique than Jamaica's is in *New Day*. More basically the novel is replete with Reid's key motifs: the harmony between nature and the black man; the inflated self-opinion of young boys; the sense of white (or "pink") smugness and ineptitude; the imagery of teats associated with learning and knowledge rather than instinct and nurture; animal imagery and hunting (Reid expressed special admiration for Ernest Hemingway); and above all the fascination with the *mano-a-mano* confrontation between males. ("I believe," Reid once averred, "in that one-on-one. It is the concept of the old-time champions doing battle.") In Reid's work the past exerts a hindering influence on Nebu, the protagonist of *The Leopard*, rather than securing his steps. The novel is Reid's most gripping and most complex. It is bold in its presentation of the sexual encounter between the nature-ecstatic protagonist, Nebu, and his nature-tormented white mistress, and in the systematic vindictiveness of her husband, Bwana Gibson, when

she bears a "gray" and lame child; the novel is stark in its portrayal of the husband hunting the despised black and finding the tables turned; and it is subtle in its play of substitutions and identifications, as Nebu and the husband switch places. Nebu's unexpected son takes up Gibson's animosity toward Nebu; then the leopard becomes the hunter in place of both Nebu and Gibson. The final scene of death, when the English lieutenant substitutes for various figures, including the leopard itself, is dramatic as well as poignant and, ultimately, peaceful.

Nanny-Town (1983), Reid's last published novel, celebrates the priestess warrior, Jamaica's aboriginal Queen Mother, who marshaled the Blue Mountain Maroons and led them to political and material independence from the English. If this work breaks new ground, it is in the depiction of a woman as hero. (Reid's admiring portrait of Edna Manley in *Horses* is notable as well.) Reid grew up in a household where the mother's influence was paramount. Being involved in the shipping business, his father spent much time away from home, and Reid's mother was the provider for body and spirit. She was a consummate storyteller and had a treasure trove of old Jamaican stories. But often women are incidental or ancillary in Reid's works. Kedala, the fighting partner/mate of de Bolas in *The Jamaicans*, dwindles into a home-standing helpmate, important for the man she maintains and the child she is to bear. And even the Queen Mother takes on more and more of a ritual quality, understandable in light of Reid's calling the novel "almost a tone-poem." Reid spoke of growing up in an aura of machismo and with the false ideal of female beauty as "blue-eyed and blond," and he avowed a strong purpose to do justice to the black woman in Jamaica, for whom he said he felt "great respect, and respectful fear."

Kedala has to struggle with two ways of relating to her man and her group. In *Nanny-Town* there is a marked tension between the conviction that youth must learn to pull together as a group and that they should have the imagination and vigor to go their own ways, for the sake of progress. Even generically a conflict appears in Reid's work, since he writes historicized rather than historical fiction and writes fiction about a past time not for its own character or even for its analogues with the present but essentially for its argumentative, directive, developmental bearing on the future.

The teaching relationship that is pervasive in Reid's work expresses that aim, but it also clashes with his sense of the cyclic character of human time, embodied in his preoccupation with morning and evening. He was taken, he said, with "the commitment of the morning, and then the thinking-back of the evening," and his love of the countryside stemmed in part from his steady, palpable experience of the natural cycle. He felt that he enjoyed morning and evening, in the spirit of that cycle, "far more than most," and appropriately he expected to die "in the evening rather than morning." Yet he saw, throughout his work, how many things failed to square with one another. The untidy dynamism of events coming into conflict with the considered and desired ritual order of interpretation poured out of Reid's own perceptions and washed through the work he wrote about, and for, his country. Perhaps it is that split vision and split sympathy, caught in a nutshell in Nebu's existence as "half Kikuyu, half Masai," as well as half penitent and half avenger, that gives Reid's work its greatest interest and impact.

Interview:

Edward Baugh, "Vic Reid in His Own Words: An Interview," *Jamaica Journal*, 20 (November 1987–January 1988): 2–9.

References:

Edward Baugh, "Tribute to Vic Reid," *Journal of West Indian Literature*, 2 (December 1987): 1–3;

Wycliffe Bennett, "Literature's Role in Developing Jamaican Society," *Daily Gleaner* (Kingston), 18 December 1987, pp. F1, F3;

Frank Birbalsingh, "Vic Reid's *The Leopard*: A West Indian View of African History," in his *Passion and Exile: Essays in Caribbean Literature* (London: Hansib, 1988), pp. 166–175;

Barrie Davies, "Neglected West Indian Writers: No. 2. Vic Reid: *The Leopard*," *World Literature Written in English*, 11 (November 1972): 83–85;

H. P. Jacobs, "The Historic Foundation of *New Day*," *West Indian Review* (Kingston), 1 (14 May 1949): 21–22; (21 May 1949): 10–11, 25; (28 May 1949): 18–19;

Louis James, "Of Redcoats and Leopards: Two Novels by V. S. Reid," in *The Islands in Between*, edited by James (London: Oxford University Press, 1968), pp. 64–72;

Mark Kinkead-Weekes, "'Africa' – Two Caribbean Fictions," *Twentieth Century Studies*, 10 (December 1973): 37–59;

Mervyn Morris, Introduction to Reid's *The Leopard* (London: Heinemann, 1980);

Morris, Introduction to Reid's *New Day* (London: Heinemann, 1973);

Kenneth Ramchand, "History and the Novel: A Literary Critic's Approach," *Savacou*, 5 (June 1971): 103–113;

Ramchand, *The West Indian Novel and Its Background* (London: Faber & Faber, 1970), pp. 154–159;

Gregory Rigsby, Introduction to Reid's *The Leopard* (New York: Collier, 1971);

Amon S. Saakana, "Vic Reid and the Self-Government Movement," in his *The Colonial Legacy in Caribbean Literature* (Trenton, N.J.: Africa World, 1987), pp. 75–82;

Sylvia Wynter, "Novel and History, Plot and Plantation," *Savacou*, 5 (June 1971): 95–102.

Richard Rive

(1 March 1931 – 4 June 1989)

Martin Trump
University of South Africa

BOOKS: *African Songs* (Berlin: Seven Seas, 1963);
Emergency (London: Faber & Faber, 1964; New York: Collier, 1970);
Selected Writings (Johannesburg: Donker, 1977);
Writing Black (Cape Town: Philip, 1981);
Advance, Retreat (Cape Town: Philip, 1983);
"Buckingham Palace," District Six (Cape Town: Philip, 1986; London: Heinemann, 1986; New York: Ballantine, 1987);
Emergency Continued (Claremont, South Africa: Philip, 1990; London: Readers International, 1990).

PLAY PRODUCTION: *"Buckingham Palace," District Six,* Cape Town, 1989.

OTHER: *Quartet,* edited, with contributions, by Rive (London: Oxford University Press, 1963; New York: Crown, 1963);
Modern African Prose, edited, with contributions, by Rive (London: Heinemann, 1964; revised, 1967).

Richard Rive, a well-known South African fiction writer, was born in Cape Town on 1 March 1931. His father was an African-American, and his mother a South African "coloured." He attended schools in the city and graduated in 1962 with a B.A. in English at the University of Cape Town. He had also trained as a teacher at Hewat Training College, Cape Town, and, in subsequent years, he earned degrees in literature from Columbia (M.A., 1966) and Oxford (Ph.D., 1974). His Oxford doctoral thesis was on the works of Olive Schreiner.

Rive spent most of his life in South Africa, a point worth noting, as virtually all black South African writers of his generation left the country as exiles during the 1950s or 1960s. Rive was a teacher or an instructor of teachers for most of his working life. He became head of the Department of English at Hewat College of Education (formerly Hewat

Richard Rive (photograph by Douglas Reid Skinner)

Training College) in 1988. On 4 June 1989 he was murdered in his home in Cape Town.

Rive grew up in a poor area of Cape Town called District Six. The district is the setting for much of his fiction. Despite its poverty and the violence that haunted its streets, District Six is recalled by Rive fondly, but with little sentimentality, as a community in which people from different backgrounds and with different creeds lived together in a harmony that is virtually unknown in the broader South African society. In 1966 the authorities declared District Six an area set aside for the exclusive occupation of white people. Over the next few years much of the district was bulldozed, and its residents were forced to seek new homes. At one and the same time, District Six symbolizes both the destructiveness of apartheid and a kind of community that gave the lie to the system of racial segregation. This dual symbolic significance is at the heart of Rive's fictional treatments of this area.

Rive's first collection of stories, *African Songs,* was published in East Germany in 1963. Rive believed that, as most of its stories were intensely critical of the forms of oppression practiced in South Africa, he was best advised to seek a publisher beyond the borders of his country. The authorities in South Africa paid ironic tribute to the force of the collection by banning it soon after it appeared. Rive's stories offer views of people battling with the particular difficulties that the system of discrimination in South Africa forces upon them. But his book is not a bleak, humorless collection. On the contrary, there is a great deal of humor in many of the stories. Indeed the humorous sense of irony here and throughout Rive's writing is possibly its most distinctive feature.

Five of the twelve stories in the collection describe the arrest of people who have defied the apartheid laws. Shame forms no part of the characters' responses to detention; their arrest simply adds to their dignity. There is pride in having defied the unjust regulations of the country. For instance, in "The Bench" the narrator comments about Karlie, one such character: "He had challenged and he felt he had won. Who cared at the result."

This spirit of courage and almost reckless defiance of authority forms an important dimension of Rive's next work, the novel *Emergency* (1964). Set against the background of the civil unrest in South Africa that followed the Sharpeville massacre of March 1960, the novel describes the difficult challenges that face a small group of characters, mainly schoolteachers and students who are hounded by the security police. Some of them flee the country, while others remain to continue the struggle against oppression. This book was banned in South Africa shortly after its publication in England.

By this time Rive had also edited and contributed to two important collections of African fiction: *Quartet* (1963) and *Modern African Prose* (1964). Writers at early stages in their careers, such as Alex La Guma, James Matthews, Chinua Achebe, and Ngugi wa Thiongo, were given a voice in these volumes.

During the 1960s and 1970s Rive traveled widely, spending a couple of years (1965 and 1966) in the United States while studying for an M.A. at Columbia. Later, from 1971 to 1974, he lived in England, where he completed his doctorate at Oxford. His output of writing was not large during these years. His keynote address at the African Literature Association conference in Bloomington, Indiana, in March 1979 formed the kernel for his autobiography, *Writing Black* (1981).

The book offers, apart from its chronicle of the life and adventures of Rive, an informal guide to the growth of African literature and its teaching since the early 1960s. Written as a kind of traveler's diary, *Writing Black* presents sketches of African and African-American writers and critics. Rive touches on some of the debates within the development of African literature. The autobiography makes it clear that Rive is little persuaded by the calls for an African or black aesthetic. For him African literature takes its place among other world literatures and must be assessed along with them and by means of the same standards and critical techniques.

In 1983 Rive's book of selected stories titled *Advance, Retreat* was published. Among the older pieces, there are some new works, such as the title story. It is among his best. "Advance, Retreat" offers a humorous account of the events surrounding the production of *Macbeth* by a "coloured" secondary school in the Cape. Rive wittily calls the characters by their stage names and plays on the incongruities that arise between the behavior of the contemporary characters and their stage personalities. Here is how Lady Macbeth is introduced:

> There was a loud bang at his door. He looked up, straining through the dull ache, to see Lady Macbeth framed in the entrance, swinging a tennis racquet in her hand. His headache cleared slightly at the sight of her. She was the very ample gym mistress who insisted on wearing very tight tights especially when she knew that he would be around. He didn't mind that. At rehearsals they had their private little game. He would slap her backside and say, "This castle hath a pleasant seat." She loved it.

Rive also gives an amusing account of the political tensions that surround the production. Many of the students and staff are troubled over the racial problems that arise in the project: "There was a spirit of rebellion especially among the more radical pupils who were strongly influenced by Macduff, who taught them history. They put up notices about a darkie Shakespeare and a coon Macbeth." Throughout this story, Rive satirizes the ways in which racial categories have come to possess the thinking of his characters to such an extent that, paradoxically, they often become the dupes of the system they are resisting.

Dissent reaches the boiling point in the story when the school learns that the principal, Macbeth, intends staging the production in a so-called white area. In an amusing denouement the chastened principal recants when it comes to taking the play out of the township, and he begs his cast to remain faithful to the production: " 'Forgive me when I break down like this. It is only because I feel so strongly for you, my people. To those who accuse Retreat Senior Secondary of racialism, I say, this is not a coloured *Macbeth,* nor a white *Macbeth,*' he stared pointedly at Macduff, 'Nor a black *Macbeth,* but a non-racial *Macbeth,* a non-ethnic *Macbeth.* And a pox on him who says otherwise!' " Like fellow South African satirical writers Herman Charles Bosman and Christopher Hope, Rive sees and exploits the absurdity and humor that often lie behind the racial obsessions of many of his countrymen.

The novel *"Buckingham Palace," District Six* (1986) travels back into the past in order to recall the defeats and the triumphs of a community that was broken up by the forces of apartheid in Cape Town. It is arguably Rive's best individual work. In it he manages, by means of chapters that focus closely on individual characters or small groups, to utilize one of his greatest talents: his ability as a short-story writer. The unity of the novel is achieved by means of the common destiny that faces all of his District Six characters. Rive later adapted the novel into a play, which was performed in Cape Town shortly after his death.

There is a great deal of potency in dealing with the destruction of a community such as District Six in the way that Rive does. He celebrates qualities in the district that are being ravaged by the policies of apartheid, such as trust between people of different backgrounds and the spirit of cooperation that exists among residents of a close-knit community. But there is no doubt whatsoever that the forces of violence ultimately have their way. District Six is finally destroyed by the authorities, and its residents are scattered. Yet out of this defeat a spirit of resistance has arisen, clearly illustrated in *"Buckingham Palace," District Six,* which brings to fruition many of his earlier treatments of this subject.

Toward the end of the novel, for example, one of the characters states what is a kind of programmatic note about the work:

> The children must be reminded of the evils that greed and arrogance can cause. We must tell about the District and the thousands of other districts that they have bro-

ken up because they wanted even more than they already had. We knew that District Six was dirty and rotten. Their newspapers told us so often enough. But what they didn't say was that it was also warm and friendly.... That it was never a place—that it was a people. We must tell how they split us apart and scattered us in many directions.... They are trying to destroy our present but they will have to deal with our future. We must never forget.

The act of recalling the past, in Rive's manner, becomes an act of resistance and affirmation in itself.

Rive is not the only author to have dealt with the destruction of a vibrant South African community. Fellow writers of his from the Cape, such as Matthews and La Guma, have also paid homage to the community that was District Six. Further afield, Can Themba, Bloke Modisane, and Miriam Tlali have written about the similar destruction of Sophiatown in Johannesburg. Rive's stories and novels about District Six share much with the work of these authors. In this respect his works form part of a central stream of South African writing that deals with communal responses to the institutionalized violence of the state. Rive, like many of his fellow writers, finds an answer to this violence in the communal strength of the people in places such as District Six.

Rive's works of the 1980s indicate that there was little falling off in his powers as a writer. Indeed, after the long gap since his first works of fiction in the 1950s and early 1960s, there had been a renewal of creative energy in his more recent work. His death deprives South Africa of one of its most urbane writers. Richard Rive was murdered in his home early on Sunday morning, 4 June 1989. A fortnight before his death Rive had completed a novel, *Emergency Continued* (1990). This work, a sequel to his earlier *Emergency,* describes conditions under the renewed South African state of emergency of the 1980s. Andrew Dreyer and other key characters from his earlier novel reappear in the later work. Rive's untimely death occurred when he was at the peak of his literary powers.

Interviews:

Robert Serumaga, "Richard Rive, South African Writer, Interviewed by Robert Serumaga in London," *Cultural Events in Africa,* 18 (1966): i–iii;

Bernth Lindfors, "Interview with Richard Rive," *Genève-Afrique,* 18, no. 2 (1980): 45–66;

"An Interview with Richard Rive," *Current Writing,* 1, no. 1 (1989): 45–55;

Frank Birbalsingh, "An Interview with the Late

Richard Rive," *ALA Bulletin,* 15, no. 4 (1989): 8–14.

Bibliography:

Jayarani Raju and Catherine Dubbeld, "Richard Rive: A Select Bibliography," *Current Writing,* 1, no. 1 (1989): 56–65.

References:

Ursula A. Barnett, *A Vision of Order: A Study of Black South African Literature in English (1914–1980)* (London: Sinclair Brown / Amherst: University of Massachusetts Press, 1983);

Grant Farred, "The Color of Writing Black," *ALA Bulletin,* 15, no. 4 (1989): 24–26;

V. A. February, *Mind Your Colour: The 'Coloured' Stereotype in South African Literature* (London & Boston: Kegan Paul, 1981);

Vladimír Klíma, *South African Prose Writing in English* (Prague: Oriental Institute, Czechoslovak Academy of Sciences, 1971);

Bernth Lindfors, "Form and Technique in the Novels of Richard Rive and Alex La Guma," *Journal of the New African Literature and the Arts,* 2 (1966): 10–15;

Ezekiel Mphahlele, *The African Image* (London: Faber & Faber, 1962);

Mbulelo V. Mzamane, "Sharpeville and Its Aftermath: The Novels of Richard Rive, Peter Abrahams, Alex La Guma, and Lauretta Ngcobo," *Ariel,* 16, no. 2 (1985): 31–44;

William H. New, *Among Worlds: An Introduction to Modern Commonwealth and South African Fiction* (Erin, Ontario: Press Porcepic, 1975);

Okpure O. Obuke, "South African History, Politics and Literature: Mphahlele's *Down Second Avenue* and Rive's *Emergency,*" *African Literature Today,* 10 (1979): 191–201;

Jean Sévry, "Un Itineraire difficile: Richard Rive, ou l'histoire d'un homme qui ne voulait pas se retrouver enfermé dans un camp," *ALA Bulletin,* 15, no. 4 (1989): 15–22.

Ola Rotimi

(13 April 1938 –)

Joel Adedeji

BOOKS: *The Gods Are Not to Blame* (London: Oxford University Press, 1971);

Kurunmi: An Historical Tragedy (London & Ibadan: Oxford University Press, 1971);

Ovonramwen Nogbaisi: An Historical Tragedy in English (Benin City, Nigeria: Ethiope / Oxford & Ibadan: Oxford University Press, 1974);

Our Husband Has Gone Mad Again: A Comedy (Oxford & Ibadan: Oxford University Press, 1977);

Holding Talks (Ibadan: University Press / Oxford: Oxford University Press, 1979);

If (Ibadan: Heinemann Nigeria, 1983);

Statements Towards August '83 (Lagos: Kurunmi Adventures, 1983);

Hopes of the Living Dead (Ibadan: Spectrum, 1988);

African Dramatic Literature: To Be or To Become? (Port Harcourt, Nigeria: University of Port Harcourt, 1991).

PLAY PRODUCTIONS: *Our Husband Has Gone Mad Again*, New Haven, Yale Theatre, 1966;

The Gods Are Not to Blame, Ife, Nigeria, Ori Olokun Theatre, 1968;

Kurunmi, Ife, Nigeria, Ori Olokun Theatre, 1969;

Holding Talks, Ife, Nigeria, University of Ife Theatre, 1970;

Ovonramwen Nogbaisi, Ife, Nigeria, University of Ife Theatre, 1971;

If, Port Harcourt, Nigeria, University of Port Harcourt Theatre, 1979;

Hopes of the Living Dead, Port Harcourt, Nigeria, University of Port Harcourt Theatre, 1985.

RECORDING: *Ola Rotimi of Nigeria*, Washington, D.C., Voice of America, 1978.

OTHER: "Traditional Nigerian Drama," in *Introduction to Nigerian Literature*, edited by Bruce King (Lagos: Evans / New York: Africana, 1971), pp. 36–49;

"Drama," in *The Living Culture of Nigeria*, edited by Saburi O. Biobaku (Lagos: Nelson, 1976), pp. 33–37.

Ola Rotimi (photograph: the Nigerian Tribune, *Ibadan, Nigeria)*

SELECTED PERIODICAL PUBLICATIONS –
UNCOLLECTED: "The Man and the Black Mosquito," *Interlink*, 4, no. 2 (1968): 29;

"The Drama in African Ritual Display," *Nigeria Magazine*, 99 (1968): 329–330.

Emmanuel Gladstone Olawale Rotimi, popularly known as Ola Rotimi, is a playwright, director, producer, actor, critic, scholar, and teacher. In 1959, as one of the first three Nigerians (the others being Joel Adedeji and Yemi Lijadu) to receive a Nigerian Government Scholarship to study drama, he attended Boston University, earning his B.F.A. in 1963; then he specialized in playwriting and directing at the Yale School of Drama and developed skills that have made him one of Africa's most popular dramatists and theater directors. His popularity derives from his use of a language capable of reaching a large audience of theatergoers and his ability to sustain dramatic interest through sheer mastery of stagecraft.

Born to parents who did not speak the same language (a Yoruba father, Samuel Enitan Rotimi, and an Ijaw mother, Dorcas Oruene Addo Rotimi), Ola Rotimi grew up in circumstances that made the problem of language and communication a real issue in interpersonal relationships. His early interest in theater and particularly in play directing was stimulated by his father who, although a steam-launch engineer by profession, directed and produced amateur theatricals. Beginning in 1963, while on a Rockefeller Foundation Scholarship, Ola Rotimi received professional training as a dramatist at Yale under John Gassner, one of America's distinguished dramatic critics, and Jack Landau, a professional New York director; Rotimi earned his M.F.A. in 1966. *Our Husband Has Gone Mad Again* premiered at Yale that year, was published in 1977, and gives greater evidence of Yale's influence on Rotimi than do his later plays, beginning with *The Gods Are Not to Blame* (performed, 1968; published, 1971), which is a reworking, in terms of Yoruba culture, of Sophocles' *Oedipus Rex.*

The Gods Are Not to Blame established Rotimi as a significant African playwright and director. The play reflects the extent of his commitment to oral tradition and to the deployment of an appropriate theatrical language to render an interpretation of Nigerian history and relate that history to recent events. This avowed double purpose propels his plays. His efforts to domesticate the English language, by striving to temper its phraseology to the ear of both the dominant, semiliterate masses and the literate classes so that the dialogue in his plays reaches out to both groups, initially claimed most of his attention. But in confronting the language question, Rotimi came to realize that his real concern as an artist was to transcend aesthetics and communicate a relevant message, one that explored the past in order to comment on the present.

Rotimi appreciates the value of history for an understanding of present sociopolitical problems. He feels that "every writer – whether a dramatist, novelist or poet – should have some commitment to his society. It's not enough to entertain; the writer must try to excite people into thinking or reacting to the situations he is striving to hold up to them in his drama or narrative." This search for social rele-

vance is a major concern in his recent plays, *If* (performed, 1979; published, 1983) and *Hopes of the Living Dead* (performed, 1985; published, 1988).

Rotimi's *Our Husband Has Gone Mad Again* paints a picture of Nigeria as a country ready for political exploitation. It is a hilarious politico-domestic comedy in which the typical Nigerian politician is portrayed as a charlatan rather than a patriot. The published play appears to have been extensively revised, for it reflects more of the Nigeria of the "oil boom" period than it does of the country during the period of Rotimi's studies in the United States (1959–1966). The aftermath of the Nigerian civil war (1967–1970) and the military government's promise of a return to civilian political rule loom large in the play, which satirizes the protagonist's acquisition of excessive influence and wealth.

Our Husband Has Gone Mad Again focuses on a former military major who leaves a lucrative cocoa business for party politics. Maj. Rahman Taslim Lejoka-Brown has seen military service in the Congo, and during his absence his father has married him to Mama Rashida, his deceased elder brother's oldest wife, without his consent. While in the Congo, Lejoka-Brown married Liza, a Catholic Kenyan nurse whom he encouraged to go to the United States to study medicine. Lejoka-Brown returns home to enter big-time politics and gets married to a third wife, Sikira, the daughter of the president of the Nigerian Union of Market Women. Lejoka-Brown then works out a plan that ensures his political future after the election, a future into which each of the three wives will fit. The situational comedy turns on his cunning manipulation of domestic circumstances to achieve political goals. The three wives represent three kinds of women: Mama Rashida is an illiterate traditionalist who accepts the situation with calm and mature decorum. Sikira is a radical young woman whose background and disposition tend toward aggression and overconfidence. Liza is an educated, Westernized, sophisticated young woman whose Catholic upbringing and acquired cultural habits are opposed to polygamy and chicanery. The high-water mark of the comedy is reached in the explosive interplay of the three women within the network of deceit set up by the exuberant Lejoka-Brown, who is always facetiously noting the common ground between tactics in military warfare and those in politics, especially the "surprise-and-attack" strategy.

The sociopolitical commentary in the play is submerged beneath forced comic situations and farfetched knockabouts, but these extraordinary events are the primary source of humor and reveal

Rotimi's robust approach to comedy. He is more interested in exploiting language to sustain the light mood than in attempting to treat the problems that have erupted in Nigeria in the wake of party and tribal politics and the interventions of the military. The skillful combination of a variety of languages, from pidgin to a broken English that incorporates words from familiar local dialects, contributes a great deal to the comic energy and enables Rotimi to achieve his ambition to reach a large and varied audience.

When Rotimi returned to Nigeria in 1966, he had been married for a year to the former Hazel Mae Gaudreau (with whom he later had four children). He soon became a research fellow in drama at the Institute of African Studies at the University of Ife, where from 1975 to 1977 he headed the Department of Dramatic Arts. Research matters very much to Rotimi, informing his concept of play writing and directing. He once stated that "historical resources offer possibilities for matching the human concerns of the past with issues that preoccupy us today." Rotimi uses his plays to draw such parallels and to show his audience that previous generations, despite their "obvious debilitating handicaps," were able to "grapple with certain sociopolitical problems that threatened their survival." This fact may help inspire present generations to deal with contemporary political problems.

The Gods Are Not to Blame is not a historical play that re-creates Nigeria's distant past. It is concerned with more-recent events. Rotimi, inspired by the Oedipus myth, wanted to criticize ethnic strife and affirm models of heroism and patriotism, so he transferred the Greek story to Nigeria, adapting it to conform to local culture. The gods are not mystic deities of an African pantheon but rather political powers outside the African continent. These "gods are *not* to blame" for the fall of any man who brings disaster upon himself through his own machinations. The tragedy of Rotimi's hero is self-inflicted, as was the tragedy of Nigeria's civil war, an ethnic conflict Nigerians can only blame on themselves. The modified Oedipus myth thus illuminates contemporary Nigerian political history.

In the play King Odewale, a stranger, becomes the ruler of Kutuje. He prepares for a peaceful and prosperous tenure. In spite of his birth into a world of predetermined conditions beyond his control, King Odewale convinces his people of his strong determination to seek and maintain their welfare. He is by nature an extremist who is also given to inquisitiveness, rash decisions, and errors in judgment. These affect his appraisal of the situation in

Cover for Rotimi's 1970 absurdist comedy satirizing African and international politics

his society and imperil his reign. He gouges out his own eyes when he discovers that he is the cause of the disaster that has engulfed his people and endangered the society. He takes his children away and abandons the society for an unknown destination. King Odewale's leadership and style of governance, however, point to the social relevance of collective leadership as an assurance for societal stability.

Kurunmi, Rotimi's next play (performed, 1969; published, 1971), concentrates on a hero who tries to uphold the dignity of tradition in the face of threats to the continued existence of his society. There is a general atmosphere of unrest and war threatening the Oyo Yoruba kingdom. Any more abuse of the age-old customs of the people will provoke the gods. The sanctity of honored traditions makes a people honorable. Must a leader therefore bow to the forces of change even when such change is harmful and ill motivated? Kurunmi, the *Are-Ona-Kakanfo* (leader of the empire), believes he must defy the pressures that undermine tradition. What is the relevance of tradition when the society demands change and the collective will of the people becomes the enabling force? Rotimi's play exposes his sympathy for inevitable change. Kurunmi plunges the state into war and ultimately becomes a victim of his own free will and action. With Kurunmi's loss and death, the forces of change win, but in the end the society suffers. The search for a patriotic leader and true nationalism continues.

Holding Talks (performed, 1970; published, 1979) has been described as an absurdist allegory. It depicts how people at critical points can dissipate their energies in interminable discussions instead of taking immediate action that results in straightforward solutions to pressing human problems. A man dies, and those investigating the cause focus not on vital issues but turn their attention to different organs of the corpse. In this way Rotimi exposes to ridicule the ineffectiveness of certain social institutions, such as the church, the school, the press, and the diplomatic service. Although *Holding Talks* does not entirely succeed as a political statement, it does succeed as an entertaining comedy. It pokes fun at the inept behavior of some African political leaders and heads of government and also satirizes international politics.

Ovonramwen Nogbaisi (performed, 1971; published, 1974) continues Rotimi's exploration of the theme of leadership and responsibility in a period of crisis. Oba Ovonramwen of the Benin Empire is under pressure. His authority is threatened both internally and externally. Ovonramwen attempts to reassert the authority of Benin over the subject areas in rebellion, but he is confronted by a devastating attack by British imperialistic forces. Rotimi sees the British punitive expedition of 1897 as unwarranted aggression by a group intent on subjugating the might of Benin with a view to exercising British jurisdiction over the people's wealth and resources. Ovonramwen takes steps that show he lacks the quality of willpower necessary to reassert his diminishing authority and influence over his chiefs. The odds against him are overwhelming, and after he has been mischievously abandoned by his warlords, the British move in. Ovonramwen's strength of character in his final hour of surrender reveals that he is a heroic leader.

If clearly expresses the wish for strong leadership, one with a rugged sense of responsibility and a commitment to "tearing everything apart and starting the entire nation-building process all over again, this time with no tolerance whatsoever for the selfish, nor for the expedient of double standards." The play captures the mood of the nation after the de-

mise of Nigeria's Second Republic. Capitalism has been enthroned with its brutal machinery for exploiting the masses. A chance for change exists "if the masses will use their votes as tools for their own freedom," but the entrenched capitalist system has cruelly dehumanized the oppressed and ultimately crushes their idealistic, enlightened leaders who have advocated solidarity with the masses.

In his latest play, *Hopes of the Living Dead*, Rotimi returns again to his preoccupation with the concept of leadership and responsibility. This time, however, he seems to realize that history is more than a record of past events. The "Lepers' Rebellion" in Nigeria from 1928 to 1932 provided the background for the play, but Rotimi weaves a parable on the theme of "collective struggle" forged through group solidarity and communicated through waves of petitions, delegations, and protests by the lepers (the living dead) to the government in an effort to assert their legitimate right to exist.

The hero is a character based on Ikoli Harcourt Whyte, one of forty lepers at Port Harcourt General Hospital who in 1924 underwent an experimental treatment for leprosy devised by a Scottish medical practitioner. In the play Harcourt Whyte organizes the leprosy patients to resist evacuation to their different villages after the abandonment of the experiment by the colonial administration. When offered special inducements to break with his fellows, Harcourt Whyte refuses the temptation and purposely binds his ethnically diverse group into an effective political force. In the end the lepers prevail and march forward to a new settlement offered them by an image-conscious government. The "living-dead" thus compel the "dead-awaken" to recognize the humanity of the sick and downtrodden.

Rotimi's genius and significance as a dramatist lie in his successful modification of traditional dramatic form and content and his creation of a language appropriate to the mass audience he wishes to address. For him, theater is a celebrative event, allegorical in essence, and capable of capturing the spirit of communal participation. His importance will emerge with time, for he will continue to develop new ways of articulating political ideas through the medium of popular theater. From 1977 to 1992 he headed the Department of Creative Arts at the University of Port Harcourt.

Interviews:

Margaret Folarin, "Ola Rotimi Interviewed," *New Theatre Magazine*, 12, no. 2 (1972): 5–7;

Bernth Lindfors, ed., *Dem-Say: Interviews with Eight Nigerian Writers* (Austin: African and Afro-American Studies and Research Center, University of Texas, 1974), pp. 57–68;

John Agetua, ed., *Interviews with Six Nigerian Writers* (Benin City, Nigeria: Bendel Newspapers, 1976), pp. 28–33;

Dapo Adelugba, *An Interview with Ola Rotimi, Senior Research Fellow, Institute of African Studies, University of Ife* (Ibadan: Department of Theatre Arts, University of Ibadan, 1984);

Understanding The Gods Are Not to Blame: *A Detailed Interview with Ola Rotimi on His Award-Winning Tragedy* (Lagos: Kurunmi Adventures, 1984);

Onuora Ossie Enekwe, "Interview with Ola Rotimi," *Okike*, 25/26 (February 1984): 36–42;

Don Burness and Mary-Lou Burness, eds., *Wanasema: Conversations with African Writers* (Athens: Ohio University Center for International Studies, African Studies Program, 1985).

Bibliography:

O. O. Lalude, *Theatre Arts: Ola Rotimi and His Works: An Annotated Bibliography* (Port Harcourt, Nigeria: University of Port Harcourt Library, 1984).

References:

Z. A. Adejumo, "Transmuting History into Drama: A Study of Ola Rotimi's *Kurunmi* and Wole Soyinka's *Death and the King's Horseman*," *Lagos Review of English Studies*, 8 (1986): 186–200;

Dapo Adelugba, "Wale Ogunyemi, 'Zulu Sofola and Ola Rotimi: Three Dramatists in Search of a Language," in *Theatre in Africa*, edited by Oyin Ogunba and Abiola Irele (Ibadan: Ibadan University Press, 1978), pp. 201–220;

Samuel O. Asein, "The Tragic Grandeur of *Ovonramwen Nogbaisi*," *Nigeria Magazine*, 110–112 (1974): 40–49;

Martin Banham, "Ola Rotimi: 'Humanity as My Tribesmen,' " *Modern Drama*, 33 (March 1990): 67–81;

Brian Crow, "Melodrama and the 'Political Unconscious' in Two African Plays," *Ariel*, 14 (July 1983): 15–31;

T. A. Ezeigbo, "Ola Rotimi and the Oedipus Legacy," *Lagos Review of English Studies*, 6–7 (1984–1985): 175–185;

Alex C. Johnson, "Ola Rotimi: How Significant?," *African Literature Today*, 12 (1982): 137–153;

Johnson, "Two Historical Plays from West Africa," *Komparatistische Hefte*, 8 (1983): 39–54;

Akanji Nasiru, "Ola Rotimi's Search for a Technique," in *New West African Literature*, edited by Kolawole Ogungbesan (London: Heinemann, 1979), pp. 21–30;

Lee Nichols, *African Writers at the Microphone* (Washington, D.C.: Three Continents, 1984);

Teresa U. Njoku, "Influence of Sophocles' *Oedipus Rex* on Rotimi's *The Gods Are Not to Blame*," *Nigeria Magazine*, 151 (1984): 88–92;

Chinyere G. Okafor, "Ola Rotimi: The Man, the Playwright, and the Producer on the Nigerian Theater Scene," *World Literature Today*, 64 (Winter 1990): 24–29;

Kalu Okpi, "Ola Rotimi: A Popular Nigerian Dramatist and Man of the Theatre," *Literary Criterion*, 23, nos. 1–2 (1988): 106–117;

V. U. Ola, "The Concept of Tragedy in Ola Rotimi's *The Gods Are Not to Blame*," *Okike*, 22 (September 1982): 23–31;

Femi Osofisan, *Beyond Translation (A Comparatist Look at Tragic Paradigms and the Dramaturgy of Wole Soyinka and Ola Rotimi)* (Ife, Nigeria: University of Ife, 1985);

Martin Owusu, *Drama of the Gods: A Study of Seven African Plays* (Roxbury, Mass.: Omenana, 1983);

Robert M. Wren, "Ola Rotimi: A Major New Talent," *Africa Report*, 18, no. 5 (1973): 29–31.

Andrew Salkey

(30 January 1928 –   )

Anthony Boxill
University of New Brunswick

BOOKS: *A Quality of Violence* (London: Hutchinson, 1959);

Escape to an Autumn Pavement (London: Hutchinson, 1960);

Hurricane (London: Oxford University Press, 1964; New York: Penguin, 1977);

Earthquake (London: Oxford University Press, 1965; New York: Roy, 1969);

Drought (London: Oxford University Press, 1966);

The Shark Hunters (London: Nelson, 1966);

Riot (London: Oxford University Press, 1967);

The Late Emancipation of Jerry Stover (London: Hutchinson, 1968);

The Adventures of Catullus Kelly (London: Hutchinson, 1969);

Jonah Simpson (London: Oxford University Press, 1969; New York: Roy, 1970);

Havana Journal (Harmondsworth, U.K.: Penguin, 1971);

Georgetown Journal: A Caribbean Writer's Journey from London via Port of Spain to Georgetown, Guyana, 1970 (London: New Beacon, 1972);

Jamaica (London: Hutchinson, 1973);

Anancy's Score (London: Bogle-L'Ouverture, 1973);

Joey Tyson (London: Bogle-L'Ouverture, 1974);

Come Home, Malcolm Heartland (London: Hutchinson, 1976);

In the Hills Where Her Dreams Live: Poems for Chile, 1973–1978 (Havana: Casa de las Américas, 1979); enlarged as *In the Hills Where Her Dreams Live: Poems for Chile, 1973–1980* (Sausalito, Cal.: Black Scholar, 1981);

The River That Disappeared (London: Bogle-L'Ouverture, 1980);

Away (London & New York: Allison & Busby, 1980);

Danny Jones (London: Bogle-L'Ouverture, 1980);

The One: The Story of How the People of Guyana Avenge the Murder of Their Pasero with Help from Brother Anancy and Sister Buxton (London: Bogle-L'Ouverture, 1985);

Andrew Salkey, circa 1969

Anancy, Traveller (London: Bogle-L'Ouverture, 1988).

OTHER: *West Indian Stories*, edited by Salkey (London: Faber & Faber, 1960);

Stories from the Caribbean, edited by Salkey (London: Elek, 1965; New York: Dufour, 1968);

Caribbean Prose: An Anthology for Secondary Schools, edited by Salkey (London: Evans, 1967);

Island Voices: Stories from the West Indies, edited by Salkey (New York: Liveright, 1970);

Breaklight: An Anthology of Caribbean Poetry, edited by Salkey (London: Hamilton, 1971); republished as *Breaklight: The Poetry of the Caribbean* (Garden City, N.Y.: Doubleday, 1972);

Caribbean Essays: An Anthology, edited by Salkey (London: Evans, 1973);

Linton Kwesi Johnson, *Dread Beat and Blood*, introduction by Salkey (London: Bogle-L'Ouverture, 1975), pp. 7–9;

Writing in Cuba Since the Revolution: An Anthology of Poems, Short Stories and Essays, edited by Salkey (London: Bogle-L'Ouverture, 1977);

Caribbean Folk Tales and Legends, edited by Salkey (London: Bogle-L'Ouverture, 1980);

Walter Rodney: Poetic Tributes, introduction by Salkey (London: Bogle-L'Ouverture, 1985).

Andrew Salkey is one of the most prolific and versatile of West Indian writers. He has written over twenty books, including novels for adults, novels for children, collections of short stories, books of poems, and travel-cum-political journals. Furthermore, as an editor he has done much to promote and make available West Indian writing both to adults and young people in no fewer than eight anthologies of Caribbean stories, poems, essays, and folktales. He was also a founding editor of the lively, if sporadic, Caribbean journal *Savacou*.

Felix Andrew Alexander Salkey was born on 30 January 1928 in Colón, Panama, to Jamaican parents, Andrew Alexander Salkey, a businessman, and Linda Marshall Salkey. At the age of two Salkey was sent to Jamaica, where he was raised by his grandmother and his mother. His father continued to work in Panama, and the two never met until Salkey was a grown man. Salkey attended two of the finest schools in Jamaica: Saint George's College, a Catholic secondary school for boys, run by Jesuits in Kingston; and Munro College, a boarding school in the rural parish of Saint Elizabeth. In 1952 Salkey left for Britain to study at the University of London. He received his B.A. (Honors) and M.A. degrees for work in English literature. Instead of returning to Jamaica, he remained in London, where there lived a small group of expatriate West Indian novelists, including George Lamming, Sam Selvon, John Hearne, and V. S. Naipaul. Salkey taught English language and literature at a comprehensive school in London from 1957 until 1959. Back in 1952 he had begun an association with the British Broadcasting Corporation that was to last until he left England in 1976. He was a free-lance writer, interviewer, scriptwriter, and reviewer for the BBC's External Services (Radio). He also served from 1955 to 1956 as an editor of a literary program broadcast to the Caribbean. In his position as editor and reviewer Salkey was able to assist and encourage many aspiring West Indian writers. Naipaul, for example, in *Finding the Centre* (1984), indicates that it was Salkey who advised him about his first story and who took his first book to a publisher. In the mid 1950s Salkey was himself trying to get started as a writer. Although his first book, the novel *A Quality of Violence*, was not published until 1959, and although Salkey's reputation depended for a long time on his fiction, his first literary success came in 1955, when he received the Thomas Helmore Poetry Prize for "Jamaica Symphony" (published as *Jamaica* in 1973). On 22 February 1957 Salkey married Patricia Verden; they have two sons, Eliot Andrew and Jason Alexander, to whom many of his books are dedicated.

Salkey's career as a novelist falls into a pattern common to many West Indian writers, such as Lamming, Selvon, and Naipaul. His first novel is set in the West Indies, and many of his later novels deal with the fate of West Indians in exile in London and with their desire, often frustrated, to return home. Also, in Salkey's first book the characters are peasants; in his later novels they are more middle-class and urban. These patterns were almost inevitable because of the powerful effect of London and exile on the imaginations of the young writers. Their physical displacement also made it possible for these writers to explore a theme central to all West Indian writing: the quest for selfhood with its concomitant theme of departure and return.

A Quality of Violence is set in the rural parish of Saint Thomas in Jamaica during a period of severe and prolonged drought, which challenges the commitment of the peasants to the land and their belief in themselves and in each other. The spiritual doubt provoked by the drought and the means the peasants use to try to remedy the related ills are the central issues of the novel. Thinking that their Christian faith is inadequate to cope with their problems, the people turn to Pocomania, a cult combining Christian and African rituals. The collision of these two sources of faith divides the people, and it results ultimately in violence and death. Eventually, when the drought does not end, many of the people leave.

A Quality of Violence is highly symbolic: the uneasy relationship of the people with the land on which they live is suggestive of the plight of West Indians in general. The journey into exile with which the novel ends is the first of the journeys of West Indians in search of a true home, as traced by

Salkey in his later novels. His first novel is considered by many critics to be his best because of its suggestiveness and the austerity of its language, which embodies the aridity of the people and the landscape. On the merits of this novel Salkey was awarded a Guggenheim Fellowship in 1960 to undertake a folklore project. He then returned to Jamaica and got acquainted with his father.

Escape to an Autumn Pavement (1960), Salkey's next novel, deals with the attempts of a young middle-class Jamaican, Johnnie Sobert, to find himself in London, to which he has fled from the social injustices of his native island. Johnnie was unsure of where he belonged in Jamaica because he was illegitimate and of mixed racial background. He grew up with knowledge of a father whose only proof of existence was an occasional airmail letter, and Johnnie was brought up in a house of women, dominated by his grandmother. He finds, however, that he does not shed his colonial sense of alienation as soon as he arrives in London. Instead his problems are compounded when he begins to have doubts about his sexuality as he feels drawn to both a man and a woman. Johnnie's journey eventually leads nowhere since he is more intent on escaping one world than on arriving in another. Salkey manages to suggest that Johnnie's apathy is the result of the style of colonial upbringing that has robbed West Indian manhood of its initiative. *Escape to an Autumn Pavement*, whose themes are more explicitly handled than those of *A Quality of Violence*, is not as successful a piece of fiction. It is nevertheless a provocative and honest exploration of a West Indian dilemma. Perhaps because the story of Johnnie is much closer to Salkey's own experience than are the peasants' lives in his first novel, it may have been more difficult for him to distance himself from his character. Many of the facets of Johnnie's life are borrowed from Salkey's: the absent father, the matriarchal household, and the job in a London nightclub.

For the next seven years Salkey devoted his energy to writing novels for children. He produced a quartet of books about Jamaica – *Hurricane* (1964), *Earthquake* (1965), *Drought* (1966), and *Riot* (1967). In 1966 he published *The Shark Hunters*, a reader for schools. The years after 1960 also saw the development of Salkey's work as an anthologist. *West Indian Stories* (1960), *Stories from the Caribbean* (1965), and *Caribbean Prose: An Anthology for Secondary Schools* (1967), all edited by Salkey, bring together the works of a variety of West Indian writers. The anthologies are aimed at schoolchildren and no doubt were inspired by intentions similar to those

Probable price: £1.50
Probable publication date: July 1982

Cover for an advance copy of the 1982 Longman edition of Salkey's tragic novel focusing on a group of restless, dissatisfied young men in Kingston, Jamaica, during the 1960s

that provoked his fiction for children: to provide West Indian youths with the opportunity to read about themselves, their landscape, and their societies so that they could develop a strong sense of who they were and so that they would not grow up to be like the lost heroes of Salkey's adult novels.

Hurricane, *Earthquake*, *Drought*, and *Riot*, all set in Jamaica, deal with children who have come to terms with disasters, both natural and man-made, which affect their societies. The incidents of the stories are from Jamaican history, and their settings are all specifically Jamaican. The language of the characters, however, does not always sound authen-

European: too generalized. Specify by nation. French, German, Dutch landowners   6

putation as a defender of the exploited canecutters, in the Bay area, had spread everywhere in the agricultural regions of the island. Even some of the more liberal-minded English, *and European* employ-ers thought of his negotiating representations, with respect and admiration; and, indeed, his approaches were ~~firm and~~ de-manding but ~~also~~ even-tempered ~~and well-mannered~~. His charac-teristic gesture, during most of his dealings with the workers, ~~when they sought his help,~~ and with management, too, was an amiable shrug and diffident smile, which soon became an emblem of his poised determination as a negotiator. *{ More on this last, pointing up B's coolth under pressure. Maybe, two sentences, only.*

↕

Bogle called the strike on his old employer's planta-tion, on the first Monday of October in 1865. That evening, he and Sarah went to see *George William* Gordon at Gordon's mother's house, a safe hideaway in a country village outside Port Morant. [Even though Gordon was a Kingston businessman and a leading member of the Urban Party of Merchants and Free Persons of Colour, he sided with the cause of the strike and with Bogle and his workers' committee plans for a possible rebellion against the Custos of the Parish and the executive council of landowners. *{Amplify.]*

A touch overly ornate. Edited closely; later on.

Prancing, looping pepperlights of moonie-kitty fireflies circled the front garden, and the veranda was dappled with lacy sprays of moonlight and spiky shadows. The setting reminded Gor-don of most evenings at his hillside home in St. Andrew, where peeny-wally *flying* beetles and their subtle filigrees of light and dark, graduated overlappings of <u>yes</u> and <u>no</u>, played around his spacious garden and hugged his old two-storey log cabin. <u>Yes</u>, there will be short bursts of clarity in black times, the evening in Port Morant seemed to be saying to Gordon; there will always be the two facing each other, even colliding side by side and fusing, but the <u>no</u> of darkness will also have its small spaces of bril-liant visions.

The <u>yes</u> and <u>no</u> metaphorical strophes might not work in the present context. Revision ahead.

Page-end in original ms (longhand).

tic. The children who are the central characters are lively and inquisitive but remarkably mature and understanding. They are helped at times of crisis in their lives by strong, loving relatives. Although some critics have accused these novels of being too nostalgic and sentimental, and although the books were not considered suitable for Jamaican children by the Jamaican Ministry of Education, Salkey's reputation as a children's novelist was established by this quartet. *Hurricane* received the Deutscher Kinderbuchpreis from Germany in 1967.

Jamaica is the setting of Salkey's next novel for adults, *The Late Emancipation of Jerry Stover* (1968). This time, however, the main characters are middle-class inhabitants of Kingston. Stover, a young civil servant, is a member of a group known as the Termites because of its disaffection with the government. Although they have a desire for change, these young people lack the maturity to take action, expressing their frustration instead in extended drinking bouts and in sexual debauchery. After they finally discover a good cause – to try to educate oppressed Rastafarians – most of them are killed in a landslide.

The central character of Salkey's next novel, *The Adventures of Catullus Kelly* (1969), is also lost and unemancipated. Kelly arrives in London and, as Salkey himself had done, gets a job as a teacher. After that he works in a coffee bar not unlike the nightclub in which Salkey had worked. During his adventures in England, Kelly's blackness causes him to be both patronized and exploited. Attempting to assert his identity and his manhood, he dabbles in the philosophy of negritude and seduces Englishwomen. His sexual exploits are so frequent and so spectacular that the reader is often incredulous. Salkey seems to be parodying the myth of the black man as superstud, but in doing so he makes Kelly less real. Kelly himself, by choosing sex as his means of self-assertion, merely conforms to the status of sexual object imposed on him and others of his race. In these two novels Salkey's ideas about race, colonialism, and politics become more obtrusive, and his fiction is more committed to protest.

In 1969 Salkey published another novel for young people, *Jonah Simpson*. It is an attempt to familiarize the young Jamaican with the exotic past of the country while suggesting that the violent history of the town of Port Royal still has an effect on the present.

With *Havana Journal* (1971) and *Georgetown Journal* (1972) Salkey took a short leave from writing fiction. These two books, as their titles suggest, are diaries he kept when he went to Cuba in 1968

for an international congress and to Guyana in 1970 for the Caribbean Writers and Artists Conference, which coincided with the founding of the Co-operative Republic of Guyana. Because of the political reasons for the trips there is more political commentary in these books than description of travel. Although there is much astute and perceptive observation in Salkey's accounts, one often feels that because of Salkey's own political convictions he gives more prominence to incidents that support his position.

In 1973 Salkey's first book of poetry was published. *Jamaica*, an epic poem, tells the history of the island from a Jamaican perspective and using Jamaican language. The poem also suggests something of the atmosphere of the society and of the character of the people. Sometimes strident in outrage over the atrocities of Jamaican history, the poem does not always live up to expectations. Too often it appears imitative of Edward Brathwaite's well-known trilogy, *The Arrivants* (1973).

A similar preoccupation with Jamaican language and folklore is evident in *Anancy's Score* (1973), a collection of stories. Anancy, the "Spiderman" and hero of many folktales, is made relevant to modern society by being shown as involved in a series of present-day adventures. These are lively stories and contain some of Salkey's best use of Jamaican patois.

Joey Tyson (1974), the most explicitly political of Salkey's novels for children, deals with the turmoil caused in Jamaica by the government's decision to revoke the work permit of Walter Rodney, a lecturer at the University of the West Indies, because the government disapproved of his involvement with the poor. A boy, Joey Tyson, has his eyes opened to the reality of Jamaican politics.

With *Come Home, Malcolm Heartland* (1976) Salkey returned to the adult novel. The central character decides to leave his career as a lawyer in London to return to his home in Jamaica, where he wishes to make a contribution, but he is murdered because he disagrees with the attitudes of the black revolutionaries with whom he is associating. This novel, like those before it, expresses Salkey's growing disillusionment with the typical West Indian's ability to find himself.

Since 1976 Salkey has been a professor of writing at Hampshire College in Amherst, Massachusetts. He has written no new adult novels; however, his two 1980 novels for children, *The River That Disappeared* and *Danny Jones*, seem to be aimed at a more mature audience. The first introduces the problem of ganja (marijuana) in Jamaica, while the second – Salkey's first children's novel set outside of Jamaica – deals with the problems of the offspring of West Indian immigrants in London.

Much of Salkey's attention since moving to America has been focused on his poetry. He won Cuba's Casa de las Américas Prize for Poetry for *In the Hills Where Her Dreams Live: Poems for Chile, 1973–1978*, published in 1979. His continued interest in the politics of the Caribbean and Latin America is evident in these poems, which protest the oppression associated with imperialism. Salkey's last book of poems, *Away* (1980), deals with exile and concludes with his assertion that "there's nothing, here, now; / nothing, back there, either!"

During the 1970s Salkey continued his work as an editor and anthologist and published five more collections of Caribbean literature, many of which, such as *Breaklight: An Anthology of Caribbean Poetry* (1971) and *Writing in Cuba Since the Revolution* (1977), demonstrate his growing preoccupation with protest in literature. In keeping with his political attitudes Salkey has published many of his books with so-called alternative presses, such as Bogle-L'Ouverture in London and Black Scholar in California.

In his 1968 essay "A Complex Fate" Bill Carr speculates that Salkey's future writing might be in the form of middle-class satire or the novel of manners. At this stage of his career, however, it seems that Salkey will devote less time to fiction than to poetry, as there he can express more directly his ideas and feelings about the political predicament of the Caribbean to which he is so committed.

References:

Anthony Boxill, "The Emasculated Colonial," *Présence Africaine*, 75 (Fall 1970): 146–149;

Bill Carr, "A Complex Fate: The Novels of Andrew Salkey," in *The Islands in Between: Essays on West Indian Literature*, edited by Louis James (London: Oxford University Press, 1968), pp. 100–108;

Barrie Davies, "The Sense of Abroad: Aspects of the West Indian Novel in England," *World Literature Written in English*, 11 (November 1972): 67–80;

C. R. Gray, "Mr. Salkey's Truth and Illusion," *Jamaica Journal*, 2 (June 1968): 46–54;

Mervyn Morris, "Anancy and Andrew Salkey," *Jamaica Journal*, 19 (November 1986–January 1987): 39–43;

Peter Nazareth, "The Fiction of Andrew Salkey," *Jamaica Journal*, 19 (November 1986–January 1987): 45–55;

Nazareth, "Sexual Fantasies and Neo–Colonial Repression in Andrew Salkey's *The Adventures of Catullus Kelly*," *World Literature Written in English*, 28 (Autumn 1988): 341–356.

Dennis Scott

(16 December 1939 – 21 February 1991)

Al Creighton
University of Guyana

BOOKS: *Terminus: A Play in One Act* (Port of Spain: University of the West Indies Extra-Mural Department, 1966);
Uncle Time (Pittsburgh: University of Pittsburgh Press, 1973);
The Fantasy of Sir Gawain & the Green Knight (New Orleans: Anchorage, 1978);
Dreadwalk (London: New Beacon, 1982);
Strategies (Kingston, Jamaica: Sandberry, 1989).

PLAY PRODUCTIONS: *An Echo in the Bone*, Kingston, Jamaica, Creative Arts Centre, 1 May 1974;
Dog, Kingston, Jamaica, Creative Arts Centre, 1978.

OTHER: "Another Country," "Journey," "Cotyledon," "Freefall," "The Dumb-School Teacher," and "Open," in *Seven Jamaican Poets: An Anthology of Recent Poetry*, edited by Mervyn Morris (Kingston, Jamaica: Bolivar, 1971), pp. 39–46;
Anthony McNeill, *Reel from "The Life-Movie,"* introduction by Scott (Kingston, Jamaica: Savacou, 1975), pp. 1–5;
An Echo in the Bone, in *Plays for Today*, edited by Errol Hill (Harlow, U.K.: Longman, 1985), pp. 73–137;
The Crime of Anabel Campbell, in *Caribbean Plays for Playing*, edited by Keith Noel (London: Heinemann, 1985), pp. 23–42.

SELECTED PERIODICAL PUBLICATIONS – UNCOLLECTED: "Walcott on Walcott" and "Bennett on Bennett," *Caribbean Quarterly*, 14 (March–June 1968): 77–82; 97–101.

Dennis Scott in 1988 (photograph copyright by A. Vincent Scarano)

The full impact of the work of Dennis Scott, its value and influence, and the totality of Scott's contribution to Caribbean literature are still, to some extent, unknown to an international audience. Much of his work is unpublished, in some cases unpublishable, and at this time unrecordable because of the variety of artistic disciplines within which he worked and the sensitive, unassuming nature of the man himself, who effectively and consistently suppressed self-promotion.

Dennis C. Scott was born on 16 December 1939 to a middle-class family in Kingston, Jamaica. He was encouraged to read and often spoke of his happy childhood. Though he found the boarding school he attended, Jamaica College, to be cold and impersonal, he nevertheless rose to the position of

276

head boy while there. After graduating, and then studying for a while at the University of the West Indies (UWI) at Mona, he left to teach English and Spanish at Presentation College in Trinidad, then later came back to Jamaica and taught at Kingston College and Jamaica College. Eventually Scott returned to UWI and completed his B.A., then moved on to graduate studies in the United States and England. After finishing his education, he again taught at Jamaica College, then became the director of the Jamaica School of Drama at the Cultural Training Centre in Kingston.

Scott was intensely aware of his role as an artist. He insisted that the work should speak for itself, and he left it to others to expound on and interpret its meaning. Yet his poetry demonstrates the maturity of Jamaican and Caribbean verse, and it charts important stylistic developments in the genre. Scott's poetry has been widely anthologized, but he was equally important as a dramatist and as a practitioner in the theater. The Nigerian writer Kole Omotoso has characterized Scott's achievement as a playwright:

> Dennis Scott's plays, especially [An] Echo in the Bone [performed, 1974; published, 1985] and Dog [performed, 1978; unpublished], constitute major contributions to the process of creating a serious-minded Caribbean theatre tradition. His poetic insight, his multiple levels of exploring the being of the Caribbean man and woman, past and present, rival the four major plays of Derek Walcott. Dennis Scott's use of unchronological timelessness as well as his use of interchangeable roles and characters make him the most important and most conscientious writer/director for the theatre in the Caribbean.

Scott's contributions as a dancer and choreographer are perhaps of lesser significance. In addition, like many of his theatrical creations, his dances were not usually recorded on film or videotape. Although his theater and his poetry overshadow his work in dance (mainly with the National Dance Theatre Company of Jamaica), they nevertheless show a choreographic ordering and sensitivity.

Edward Baugh, in his West Indian Poetry 1900–1970 (1971), has suggested that the place of Scott's poetry in regional literature has much to do with "the emergence [in the 1960s] of a new generation of poets" developing at a time when "the West Indian poet [had] at last found an audience, his own audience, to which he [could] speak without distracting anxieties and uncertainties about the relationship between that audience and himself." Scott, Mervyn Morris, Anthony McNeill, and Wayne Brown represented this "new generation." They

worked closely together, mainly on the Mona, Jamaica, campus of UWI, from which Scott graduated in 1970 with first-class honors in English, and where Morris was lecturing at that time. According to Baugh, "Each pursue[d] his individuality while benefitting from the friendly competitive spirit that exist[ed] among them." The poetry that emerged had a strong Caribbean identity, but they were not afraid to appropriate other influences. Scott went on to produce important work in Jamaican creole and to experiment with "dub" and "dread" dialect poems, which have influenced recent developments in the region's verse.

Scott won several important awards for poetry, including Jamaica's Silver Musgrave Medal for Achievement in Poetry (1976) and two international awards – the International Poetry Forum Award (1973) and the Commonwealth Poetry Prize (1974), both for Uncle Time (1973). The title poem of the volume is one of the most important single poems in the region. In it Scott takes the universal theme of time and creolizes/localizes it with a remarkable thoroughness. The archetypal Old Father Time becomes a more familiar figure, Uncle Time. Through an elusive shiftiness characteristic of the deceptive swiftness of time itself, however, he also becomes simultaneously a close relative, a village character, a destructive force, the ancient hills, a sly mongoose, the trickster/spider Anansi, a seducer and reducer of women, a separator of families, and (the agent of) death. The use of creole language engenders a deceptive informality and simplicity that enhances the poem's purpose. The Jamaican creole speaker gives the verse a sense of place as he describes his uncle, a familiar figure but one who cannot be pinned down. The poem's power and importance come from the profundity of the creolization and the thorough treatment given to the universal theme of time and its effects.

"Uncle Time" is a mature poem that anticipates later developments in Scott's poetic voice and foreshadows ways in which orality and nonstandard language are featured in later Caribbean poetry. The volume Uncle Time explores a range of themes and illustrates the ascetic honing and sensitivity to craft that is typical of Morris and of McNeill as well.

The period between Scott's two major books of poetry (1973–1982) was a politically turbulent one in Jamaica with a sharpened class struggle, fierce ideological battles, many violent crimes, an experiment in socialist government (with many members of the middle class emigrating to escape it), and the increasing significance of Rastafarianism and "Dread Talk." During that time Scott was a senior teacher at Jamaica College (1971–1976) and director of the Jamaica School of Drama (1977–1983). He could easily have become a part of academic life at UWI but apparently chose instead a closeness to student activities and community work, coming into contact with radical and Rasta elements. Unlike many middle-class West Indian intellectuals who dabbled in fashionable radicalism during this period, Scott chose such alliances because of tendencies he already had. His characteristic abandonment of the convention of wearing shoes may have been relevant to that choice, to his humility, and to his working-class sympathies, which appear as strong currents in his play *Dog* and in several poems written during this time that are collected in *Dreadwalk* (1982).

The shooting of a naked "madman" by a policeman on a Kingston street (an actual incident) is subtly protested in Scott's poem "The Infection." In "Apocalypse Dub" the Four Horsemen of the Apocalypse, in a poem reminiscent of "Uncle Time," are recast in the Kingston ghettos, performing their "danse macabre" to "dub" music, which serves as an escape and a disguise. The poem "Dreadwalk" presents Rasta "dread talk" and consciousness, with the emphasis on "I" as first, second, and third person pronoun, subject, and object. Scott's poem titled "Mouth" paints a picture of sufferers struggling to find food, in contrast to the indifferent, affluent middle class against whom they seem about to rise in violent revolt. Many poems in the volume had been circulated among members of the poetic avant-garde of the 1970s. Some were published in *Arts Review*, founded by Morris in 1975 largely as an outlet for students' work on the Mona campus of UWI (but also including many new poems by established artists).

In other publications the proletarian sensitivity/empathy of Scott and his determination to speak in an ordinary language become associated with characteristic idiosyncrasies other than his familiar barefootedness. He prefaces his introduction to *Reel from "The Life-Movie"* (1975) – the first book of poems by his friend McNeill – with these words: "To be read, if at all, after the poems have spoken for themselves." He then allows McNeill's comments, extracted from letters, to lead the discourse rather than foregrounding his own ideas. Asked to give a lecture to a group of (mainly student) dramatists at the university's Creative Arts Centre, he elected to have them speak for themselves by giving them play excerpts to act out, basing his brief comments on their efforts. But sarcasm, wit, and a

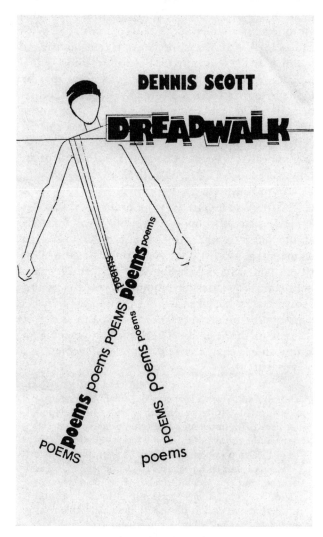

Cover for Scott's 1982 collection of poems, written in the years 1970 through 1978

sometimes sardonic, usually cutting humor were very much a part of Scott's style. He once remarked, after a poetry reading that some felt went on too long, that since it had taken him several months of hard work to produce the poems, the audience should not grumble if they had to sit and listen for a mere hour or two.

Many of Scott's plays are unpublished. However, his first effort, *Terminus*, was published in 1966. *Terminus* presents a purgatorial trial of corrupt, middle-class antagonists, condemned for their crimes, and it demonstrates Scott's social conscience even at that early stage. Scott taught at Presentation College in Trinidad between September 1961 and July 1963 and had a brief letter exchange in the *Trinidad Guardian* with Derek Walcott, who severely criticized a production Scott had directed. After his return to Jamaica, during a period of unemployment, he won a Gold Medal in playwriting in the 1966 Jamaica Festival literary competition.

During these years Scott reached, and passed, the height of his dancing career; married Joy Thompson on 4 October 1969; fathered a son, John-David, and a daughter, Danielle Justine; and edited *Caribbean Quarterly* at UWI between 1968 and 1970. He also reached some of his milestones as a director, including his production at the Barn Theatre in Kingston of *Smile Orange*, Trevor Rhone's satire on the tourist industry, which broke attendance records in 1971, becoming the first play to run for over a year in that city. In 1970 Scott won a Schubert Playwriting Fellowship, which allowed him to travel to the University of Georgia, and in 1972 the Jamaica Festival Best Director Award. A Commonwealth Fellowship enabled him to gain a diploma in drama in education from the University of Newcastle-upon-Tyne in 1973.

An Echo in the Bone is Scott's first play of major importance. Its first performance on 1 May 1974 by the students' Drama Society, as part of the University of the West Indies' twenty-fifth-anniversary celebrations, further demonstrates his close associations with the students and the Creative Arts Centre staff. In this play Crew, a Jamaican peasant and farmer, kills Mr. Charles, a white estate owner, and then disappears, by all indications electing to kill himself rather than face arrest. His family holds a traditional "Nine Night" rite to appease and rest his spirit. During the ritual Crew's story is revealed when his spirit returns and possesses one of his sons.

The ceremony, of which possession is a central component, serves Scott well as a medium through which the historical past of slavery, the "middle passage," dispossession, and injustice are invoked in several flashback scenes. The play establishes organic links between the present and the past, using the callousness and dehumanizing crimes of past and present plantocracies to explain why Crew, who has suffered "for four hundred years," killed Mr. Charles, who was oppressive and had to pay for the sins of his prototypes.

Scott's second major play, *Dog*, which was first produced within a year of his assuming the directorship of the Jamaica School of Drama, was, like *An Echo in the Bone*, performed by students at the Creative Arts Centre. In 1981 it was also performed at Carifesta in Barbados, under the direction of Rawle Gibbons. In *Dog* the characters Mommy and Daddy live barricaded and sheltered in their middle-class home while Daddy (with sadistic pleasure and bourgeois contempt) goes out nightly hunting and killing

dogs that seem to have gone on a threatening rampage around the city. Mainly through the sensitive intervention of Finger, the yard boy, the family adopts a young dog (named Dog) whose mother has been killed. But Finger wields an almost subversive influence over Dog as well as over Mommy and Daddy, who, having grown tired of hunting dogs (and perhaps subconsciously insecure), plans to fly to Canada with Mommy, leaving Dog and Finger behind. Scott deliberately draws a vague line between the dogs and people. The threat and unrecognized fear that the middle class feels in confronting the dogs is indivisible from an identical situation in the human society, and Scott's dogs may be considered representatives of the increasingly restless and volatile class of sufferers.

Even though *Dog* remains unpublished and *An Echo in the Bone* was not published until 1985, they have been among the most influential plays in the Caribbean since they were first performed. In *An Echo* Scott employed a traditional, ritual enactment as form, a convertible set and costuming, and considerable role and character changing by the actors. *Dog* has a versatile, multifunctional narrator, in addition to the role switching and a light, flexible set. Scott has generally not received very much published critical attention, but reviewers were impressed by these plays. The avant-garde art, rather than popular, theater that they promoted made an impact on dramatists throughout the region. After Scott left the Jamaica School of Drama in 1983 to become a visiting professor at the Yale School of Drama, where he became cochair of its directing department, his work continued to move in the same direction.

In 1989 Scott's third poetry collection, *Strategies*, was published. It includes excerpts from the impressive cycle of "letter" poems in which he explores his relationship with his son. Also evident is a preoccupation with birds as symbols, already recurrent images in the poetry of *Uncle Time* and *Dreadwalk*. As Scott once explained, "Birds appear to function for me as icons of freedom, imagination, the creative impulse, the subconscious, the part of us that denies mortality and its grossness."

Dennis Scott died on 21 February 1991, after a prolonged illness. In the years preceding his death, he was working on a play called "Four Birds Crossing a Field of Bright Desire," which he described as "totally apolitical." It is an unlikely description that suggests a departure from his other major works. Scott intended the play to be a four-character piece but to be played by two actors, and this concept places it in line with current directions in Caribbean theater, where dramas for two actors, role-shifting techniques, and sparseness of set and narrative style have received new attention. Many of these features are characteristic of the developing brand of director's theater with which Scott experimented widely at home and at national playwrights' conferences at the Eugene O'Neill Memorial Theater Center in Waterford, Connecticut.

Scott will certainly be remembered for the economical, multidimensioned, and modernist theater for which he was well known in both the Caribbean and the United States. His influence remains in the work of some of the leading directors, some of whom were either students or tutors at the Jamaica School of Drama. Some of what he bequeathed to Caribbean poetry in the uses of language, rhythms, and subculture may be seen in the 1989 anthology *Voiceprint*, which captures the mood of contemporary Caribbean poetry by other writers.

Interview:

"Interview: Dennis Scott Talking to Mervyn Morris," *Caribbean Quarterly*, 30 (March 1984): 48–50.

References:

Lloyd W. Brown, *West Indian Poetry* (Boston: Twayne, 1978), pp. 168–171;

Stewart Brown, "New Poetry from Jamaica," *New Voices*, 3, no. 5 (1975): 48–50;

Errol Hill, Introduction to *Plays for Today*, edited by Hill (Harlow, U.K.: Longman, 1985), pp. 1–14;

Joyce Jonas, "The Carnivalesque World of Dennis Scott's *Strategies*," *Kyk-over-al*, 42 (July 1991): 69–70;

Renu Juneja, "Recalling the Dead in Dennis Scott's *An Echo in the Bone*," *Ariel*, 23 (January 1992): 97–114;

Anthony McNeill, "Dennis Scott, Maker: Part 1, 'Journeys,'" *Jamaica Journal*, 5 (December 1971): 49–52;

Mervyn Morris, "Dennis Scott (1939–1991)," *Journal of West Indian Literature*, 4 (November 1990): 164–165;

Morris, Introduction to Scott's *Uncle Time* (Pittsburgh: University of Pittsburgh Press, 1973), pp. xvii–xxiii;

Kole Omotoso, *The Theatrical Into Theatre: A Study of the Drama and Theatre of the English-Speaking Caribbean* (London: New Beacon, 1982), pp. 94–95;

Ian D. Smith, "The Poetics of Self: Dennis Scott's Dangerous Style," *Caribbean Quarterly*, 30 (March 1984): 23–32.

Sam Selvon

(20 May 1923 –)

Harold Barratt
University College of Cape Breton

BOOKS: *A Brighter Sun* (London: Wingate, 1952; New York: Viking Press, 1953; Trinidad & Jamaica: Longman Caribbean, 1971);

An Island Is a World (London: Wingate, 1955);

The Lonely Londoners (London: Wingate, 1956; New York: St. Martin's Press, 1956; Port of Spain: Longman Caribbean, 1972); also published as *The Lonely Ones* (London: Brown, Watson, 1959);

Ways of Sunlight (London: MacGibbon & Kee, 1957; New York: St. Martin's Press, 1957; Saint Andrews, Jamaica: Longman Caribbean, 1973);

Turn Again Tiger (London: MacGibbon & Kee, 1958; New York: St. Martin's Press, 1959);

I Hear Thunder (London: MacGibbon & Kee, 1963; New York: St. Martin's Press, 1963);

Carnival in Trinidad (Wellington, New Zealand: Department of Education, 1964);

The Housing Lark (London: MacGibbon & Kee, 1965; Washington, D.C.: Three Continents, 1990);

A Cruise in the Caribbean (Wellington, New Zealand: Department of Education, 1966);

A Drink of Water (London: Nelson, 1968);

The Plains of Caroni (London: MacGibbon & Kee, 1970);

Those Who Eat the Cascadura (London: Davis-Poynter, 1972);

Moses Ascending (London: Davis-Poynter, 1975);

Moses Migrating (Harlow, U.K.: Longman, 1983; Washington, D.C.: Three Continents, 1991);

El Dorado West One (Leeds, U.K.: Peepal Tree, 1988);

Foreday Morning: Selected Prose 1946–1986, edited by Kenneth Ramchand and Susheila Nasta (London: Longman, 1989);

Highway in the Sun and Other Plays (Leeds, U.K.: Peepal Tree, 1991).

PLAY PRODUCTION: *Switch*, London, Royal Court Theatre, 1977.

Sam Selvon

MOTION PICTURES: *The Lonely Londoners*, screenplay by Selvon, London, BBC Films, 1958;

Pressure, screenplay by Selvon and Horace Ové, London, British Film Institute, 1978.

TELEVISION: *Anansi the Spider Man*, BBC, 1974; *Home, Sweet India*, BBC, 1976.

RADIO: "Village in the Bambbees," *Tea-Time Talk*, BBC, 19 June 1952;

"English Goes Abroad: English as Spoken in the West Indies," *The English Tongue*, BBC, 30 August 1955;

"A Multi-Racial Society," *The Changing Caribbean*, BBC, 12 October 1960;

Lost Property, BBC, 1965;

Perchance of Dream, BBC, 1966;

Rain Stop Play, BBC, 1967;

Highway in the Sun, BBC, 1967;

You Right in the Smoke, BBC, 1968;

El Dorado, West One, BBC, 1969;

Bringing in the Sheaves, BBC, 1969;

Turn Again Tiger, BBC, 1970;

Voyage to Trinidad, BBC, 1971;

Those Who Eat the Cascadura, BBC, 1971;

Mary, Mary Shut Your Gate, BBC, 1971;

Cry Baby Brackley, BBC, 1972;

Water for Veronica, BBC, 1972;

The Harvest in the Wilderness, BBC, 1972;

Milk in the Coffee, BBC, 1975;

Zeppi's Machine, BBC, 1977.

OTHER: "A Note on Dialect," in *Commonwealth*, edited by Anna Rutherford (Aarhus, Denmark: Aarhus University Press, 1971), p. 124.

SELECTED PERIODICAL PUBLICATIONS – UNCOLLECTED: "The Leaf in the Wind," *Bim*, 4, no. 16 (1952): 286–287;

"Little Drops of Water," *Bim*, 11, no. 44 (1967): 245–252;

"Three into One Can't Go – East Indian, Trinidadian or West Indian?," *Wasafiri*, 5 (Autumn 1986): 8–11;

"Finding a West Indian Identity in London," *Kunapipi*, 9, no. 3 (1987): 34–38.

Sam Selvon is one of the important writers who contributed to the remarkable development of West Indian fiction in the 1950s and 1960s. Within recent years his work has been critically examined by scholars from several countries. To date he has published ten novels and written two screenplays, numerous short stories, several books of fiction for children, and many plays for radio and television. But even if he had written nothing else, *A Brighter Sun* (1952) and *The Lonely Londoners* (1956) assure him a permanent place in the history of West Indian literature.

Born in South Trinidad on 20 May 1923, Samuel Dickson Selvon, the son of an Indian father and a half-Indian, half-Scottish mother, graduated from San Fernando's Naparima College in 1938. Selvon grew up in Trinidad's multiracial society and regards himself as a creolized West Indian, as he has suggested in more than one interview. But he has a strong sense of displacement, and this feeling some-

times emerges as a subtle theme in his fiction. He began to write fiction and poetry while he worked as a wireless operator for the Royal Navy Reserve during World War II. When the war ended, he turned to journalism and served as the fiction editor of the literary magazine of the *Trinidad Guardian* newspaper until 1950, when he left for England in search of other employment. In London his short stories began to be published in journals and newspapers, and in 1954, before the publication of his second novel, he was awarded his first Guggenheim Fellowship. Six additional fellowships and assorted scholarships, including a second Guggenheim (1968), followed, and in 1969 the Trinidad and Tobago government awarded him the Humming Bird Medal for literature. Selvon married Draupadi Persaud in 1947, was later divorced, and married Althea Nesta Daroux in 1963. He has one child from his first marriage and three from his second.

A Brighter Sun, Selvon's first novel, is a pivotal work in the development of West Indian fiction because the central character's compelling quest for self-awareness and wholeness in colonial and pluralistic Trinidadian society is a particularly significant theme. Selvon's central concern in *A Brighter Sun* is the growth of Tiger, the young hero, from childish dependence upon his parents to adult responsibility. The story is an examination of the developing sensibilities of a youngster who, soon after his arranged marriage, is suddenly uprooted from the Chaguanas cane fields and the security of parents and must fend for two people in Barataria, a considerably more complex and cosmopolitan part of the island. At the beginning of the novel Tiger is an innocent boy, ignorant and rather stupid about everything. His conception of manhood is adolescent: "men smoked: he would smoke." Selvon also draws one's attention to Tiger's childlike desire, even after his marriage to Urmilla, to return to the protection of the womb. But early in the story one can see in Tiger signs of a growing self-assertiveness and the beginnings of a political and social sensitivity, all of which underlie his restless urge to enlarge the horizons of his limited mind. As Tiger and Urmilla establish themselves in racially mixed Barataria, his growing awareness and commitment to personal development is increasingly internalized. When he is negotiating for land, for instance, Tiger "wished his father or one of his uncles was there with him." But the thought "made him ashamed," Selvon writes; Tiger "was married . . . he might as well learn to do things without the assistance of other people."

Although his East Indian parents disapprove

of his relationships with Trinidadian blacks, Tiger wisely rejects such advice, cultivating friendships with neighbors. Tiger's relationship with Joe and Rita is particularly important. Selvon carefully draws one's attention to Joe's smug satisfaction with physical, ephemeral pleasures and then sets it against Tiger's hunger for knowledge. "I used to think," Tiger tells Joe, "as long as you have wife and child, you is a man. So long as you drink rum and smoke, you is a man." In time, however, Tiger discovers that manhood means achieving self-awareness or, more pertinently, awareness of one's individual identity: "ain't a man is a man, don't mind if he skin not white, or if he hair curl?" Tiger, furthermore, discovers that maturity is accepting the consequences of one's actions and decisions. The discovery marks the end of his boyhood.

There are other signs of Tiger's growing maturity. Of these, two are crucial. The first is his anxiety about national independence. Tiger may not know how Trinidad can achieve independence; he does know, however, that the island, like himself, must take charge of its own destiny. This desire for national independence matches Tiger's drive for personal integrity, and Selvon subtly conveys this relationship in strategic places in the novel. The second sign is Tiger's acceptance of sober reality. To the irresponsible and cavalier Boysie, Tiger says: "it different with me. It ain't always a man does be able to do the things he wants to do." There are, moreover, Tiger's pithy words to Urmilla at the end of the novel: "You don't start over things in life. . . . You just have to go on from where you stop. It not as if you born all over again. Is the same life."

While Tiger tries to find a place in his complex and racially divided society, while he is preoccupied with "the great distance which separated him from all that was happening," he loses many of his already tenuous links with his Indian heritage. The loss facilitates his growing creolization. Total assimilation, however, does not follow. One thinks here of Pariag, the Indian outcast in Earl Lovelace's *The Dragon Can't Dance* (1979). Like Tiger, Pariag comes to the urban center in search of an awareness beyond that of Indian and black, and he is anxious to be integrated into and accepted by the black, hostile community of Calvary Hill. But he, too, discovers that "all o' we" is not one. Pariag and Tiger also share something else: Pariag's rejection and symbolic crucifixion are transformed into a regeneration when he becomes "a person" to his neighbors, which is "a sacred moment," Lovelace writes, "for it joined people together to a sense of their humanness and beauty." This sense of a primal, inviolable humanness is also implicit in Tiger's hunger for

an individuality that transcends racial divisions. Tiger's sensibility also resembles Selvon's own conception of a united Caribbean free of racial and religious divisiveness.

Tiger's relationship to the land is also important to his developing consciousness. His bond with the land is considerably more than an economic necessity. He does give up farming in order to earn better wages working for the Americans who are building a road through the village; however, his attachment to the land is intimate and permanent. References to this strong bond are written deep into the idiom of several scenes. Consider, for example, this passage, strategically placed at an early period in Tiger's life, a time of confusion and bewilderment about the war raging in Europe, a time of doubt about his worth and capacity for growth and understanding:

> Sometimes in the morning when he got up early and dew was still heavy on the grass, he used to watch at what he could see of the world – the sky light blue with promise of a sunlit day, the low hills that break away from the Northern range and run hunchbacked for some miles, and the trees on the hills, dark green before the sun rose and made them lighter. With all this he felt a certain satisfaction, as if he were living in accordance with the way things should live. These sensations happened too when he was working in the fields. Sometimes the sun burned into him so he raised his back and tried to look at it, knowing there was power and bigness there.

The passage shows Tiger's abiding love and respect for a power he cannot comprehend but of which he is nonetheless totally cognizant. One may see parallels with Samuel Taylor Coleridge's sense of an "eternal language" as well as William Wordsworth's "sense sublime." The feeling of oneness with the land, sky, and sun gives Tiger the solace he needs. And the land does more: it gives Tiger the strength to persevere. "Whenever big things happen," he says, "I does go out and look all about, at the hills, and the trees, and the sky, and them. And I does get a funny feeling, as if strength coming inside me. That must be God."

There are two crucial periods in Tiger's life when his bond with the land is given special emphasis. The building of the road will provide Tiger and other villagers with jobs; nevertheless the road is disruptive and brings uneasiness. Instinctively Tiger counteracts his anxieties through a simple communion with the land:

> The gardeners did odd jobs about their huts. Only Tiger went to the fields every morning. He wanted to

Dust jacket for the 1958 sequel to Selvon's first novel, A Brighter Sun. *The novels follow the growth of Tiger, a Trinidadian, from youth and innocence to maturity and wisdom.*

impress the landscape on his mind, how the trees grew, how the drains near the ricefields ran. . . . Because he knew it would all change, and he wanted to be able to remember how it was at first, before the road was built.

At the end of the novel Tiger's house has been built, and a brighter sun is in the offing. At once he thinks of returning to the Chaguanas cane fields, but this urge "made him laugh." Ostensibly Tiger has rejected the land and the past when he toiled in the hot sun. But Tiger feels the land in his blood: "now is a good time to plant corn," he says, "gazing up at the sky." These are the novel's final words, and they are instructive. They tell us that even though he is committed to economic improvement, Tiger is strongly drawn to the land as the source of an undefined, but nonetheless certain, strength. Selvon, moreover, skillfully parallels Tiger's bond with the land and his growing awareness that a man must educate himself. Tiger refuses to accept Joe's complacent attitude: "dey have plenty people who can't write and dey living happy." Instead Selvon's youngster is "conscious only of the great distance which separated him from all that was happening."

Tiger's quest for maturity continues in *Turn Again Tiger* (1958), which has several important links with *Those Who Eat the Cascadura* (1972). Both

novels examine the individual's search for integrity in a society psychologically crippled by years of moribund colonialism. Five Rivers, where Tiger and Urmilla sojourn, is a somnolent backwater, and Sans Souci is the equally isolated setting of *Those Who Eat the Cascadura*. Sans Souci is also politically isolated and is a microcosm of preindependent colonial Trinidad, complete with the three-tiered racial hierarchy and its resultant antagonisms and divisiveness.

Tiger's integrity is a central issue in *Turn Again Tiger*. The internalizing of his identity, which began in *A Brighter Sun*, is consolidated in this later novel. Five Rivers is more cohesive than Sans Souci, and racial tensions are muted and subordinated to Tiger's goal: "when I come a man in truth, I want to possess myself." Tiger's desire for self-possession can be seen in his bouts of introspection and assertion of his own dignity in the presence of the white Robinson. His father's attitude toward Robinson, on the other hand, foreshadows Prekash's obsequiousness in *Those Who Eat the Cascadura*. Nowhere is Tiger's desire for self-possession more effectively conveyed than in his violent sexual encounter with Doreen, Robinson's wife. Tiger's attitude toward Doreen is ambivalent and disingenuous. When, panic-stricken, he flees at the sight of

Doreen bathing naked in the river, he has an ostensibly honest explanation for his shameful action: "it had nothing to do with colour or the generation of servility which was behind him. He had fled because she was a woman, a naked woman, and because he was a man." But the references to color and servility, which Tiger dismisses with revealing glibness, are crucial. He cannot come to terms with the luscious, forbidden, white female, and his fear reduces him to a terrified, cringing boy. When Tiger does make love to Doreen, his motives are mixed. The frisson of interracial sex is obvious, and so, too, is the revenge motive, a feature of the black male/white female syndrome often explored in West Indian fiction; but there is an even-more-basic motive: "I wonder," Tiger says with blunt directness, "if under all the old-talk, all I wanted to do was screw a white woman?"

However important these motives are, they lack the compelling urgency of Tiger's need to restore his shattered self-esteem, to free himself of the degrading fear of the untouchable, but eminently desirable, white woman. Tiger's calculatedly cold and brutal union with Doreen should be set alongside the shopkeeper Otto's thrashing of Singh, an Indian laborer, who has cuckolded him. Like Otto, who must thrash Singh in order to exorcise self-destructive jealousy and the wound his ego has sustained, Tiger must possess Doreen in order to exorcise his own devils. For both men the acts bring relief and victory over their fears and torments. Tiger, with Monday-morning hindsight, comes to his own sense of the matter: "There was no pleasure in the memory for him . . . no satisfaction, no extension of desire to make him want to do it again. Just relief, as if he had walked through fire and come out burnt a little, but still very much alive." The act, furthermore, is immediately followed by Tiger's symbolic purification in the river. Tiger's life changes noticeably after his encounter with Doreen: he discards the crutch of heavy rum-drinking and sullen withdrawal, and he returns to the right path after walking off the trail.

Tiger's communion with the land is no less intimate than in the earlier novel. The older, wiser Tiger still turns to the land for comfort and understanding, and it continues to play a part in his growing maturity. "If ever he was going to make up his mind, it would be out here in his garden," Selvon writes; "burn, sun, burn, he thought, and blow wind blow, as if in these abstract, irrelevant thoughts there was a wisdom to help." Unlike Sarojini in *Those Who Eat the Cascadura*, who will never set herself free of the white man Johnson –

she is carrying his child – Tiger can look forward to continued growth. "It just like we," he says of the land; "we finish one job, and we got to get ready to start another."

Roger Franklin, the Englishman who owns Sans Souci in Selvon's 1972 novel, is an emotionally alienated expatriate who is concealing a dark secret. Prekash is Sans Souci's overseer and has a gnawing jealousy and obsession with the beautiful Indian woman Sarojini. Prekash's sullen pettiness and obsequiousness are emphasized to the point of caricature, and he is depicted as insecure and contemptuous of blacks. While she rejects Prekash's amorous advances, Sarojini shares his defiant sense of Indianness as well as his strong contempt for blacks. Sans Souci, for all its superficial unity, is a divided community; however, the Indians and blacks do share a common trait: they are without the sort of palpable identity that separates and distinguishes them as assertively strong individuals. For instance, Manko, the obeah man who does not hesitate to exploit gullible people, finds a fragile identity in the vestiges of African religion; and Kamalla, the lusty sensualist, subordinates her identity as a person to the service of Franklin's aberrant sexual tastes. Eloisa, Franklin's black cook, is also his surrogate wife and mother, but she lives with him in what might perhaps be described as a state of bovine bliss.

The theme of individual integrity is emphasized in Johnson's relationship with Sarojini, who is a motherless beauty of low self-esteem frustrated by an ineffectual, drunken father. Her self-image is important: for a backward village girl, union with the Englishman Johnson is the zenith of achievement. Meanwhile Johnson's perception of Sarojini is noticeably ambiguous. He protests love for Sarojini, but he is not at all confident of his motives. Sarojini, one feels, is a sort of West Indian dryad with whom Johnson can couple in the bush, at the same time freeing himself of all the responsibilities such a relationship would normally entail. Sarojini's symbolic raping of Johnson – a loveless act of Bacchic frenzy – is a gratuitous reversal of sex roles; but this vicious sexual union brings her neither insight nor any sort of self-awareness. Nor, significantly enough, does it change her dependence on the white male. At the end of the novel Selvon shows Sarojini as pathetic, living in hope of Johnson's unlikely return from England. This ending is appropriate: her integrity has always given way to her fantasy of permanent union with a white male.

Critics have tended to neglect Selvon's *An Island Is a World* (1955) and *I Hear Thunder* (1963) in favor of his less ponderous, more satirical and humorous fiction. This situation is unfortunate because these two early novels show his meditative and philosophical side. Although he has expressed a desire to rewrite *An Island Is a World* – its structure being somewhat experimental – Selvon has described it as a very personal work and indeed his favorite of his novels. There is some fine writing in both novels, although at times the dialogue, especially the philosophically reflective exchanges between characters in *An Island Is a World*, seems contrived and starchy; nevertheless, both novels offer a sharp, finely focused and particularly accurate picture of Trinidadian society in the 1940s and 1950s: a society of petty racism and of men and women lost in the void of colonial neglect; a society with which Selvon is familiar and from which he sought escape.

Many of the characters, Adrian and Mark of *I Hear Thunder* and Foster and Rufus of *An Island Is a World*, for example, are carefully developed, and some of Selvon's best female portraits can be found in these novels. Women such as Rena, Jennifer, Polly, and Marleen do not resemble the caricatured playthings of Selvon's London fiction. They are self-possessed and, with the possible exception of Marleen, they are unwilling to accept total dependence on the male. Rena and Polly are strongly assertive and are not willing to be treated with short shrift.

Other characters, such as Randolph, the indefatigable womanizer of *I Hear Thunder*, are less fully drawn but are nevertheless interesting. It can be argued that Randolph is a caricature; he is, however, drawn from reality. In an insignificant crown colony in which feelings of racial inferiority or insignificance are tenaciously embedded, Randolph's white skin gives him carte blanche. But even while he is using this power to exploit others, the shallow Randolph is hounded by the fear of waning youth and the inevitable ebbing of passion; so he flees his small island in search of an illusive perpetual youth.

Some of Selvon's central themes, such as the West Indian's search for identity and the stasis of a neglected colonial society, appear in both novels. The individual's sense of entrapment and rootlessness is an equally strong and important theme in *An Island Is a World*. Many of the characters are given to brooding; ready to philosophize at the slightest encouragement; introspective; and, at times, melancholy. Foster, the "lost soul groping in the dark," is confined by the smallness of his world, and his mind and vision are said to be "cramped and limited." Desperate, he flees the narrowness and claus-

Cover for the 1972 publication of the first volume in Selvon's London trilogy, which presents the experiences and attitudes of West Indian immigrants

trophobia of Trinidad in search of fulfillment in London, where he agonizes over his amorphous identity as a Trinidadian and has bouts of melancholy reflections. He discovers, like so many other West Indians of the 1940s and 1950s, that the mother country is not, and probably never will be, his home. Foster merely becomes part of the alienation and general hopelessness he notices in other West Indians who have come to "the old Brit'n" in search of some kind of fulfillment. Rufus, his less introspective, less neurotic brother, also flees Trinidad and a loveless marriage for the greener pastures of America in search of a profession. But America is not the promised land, and it tends to exacerbate Rufus's own angst: "tangled in the net, he was crazily tempted to ensnare himself still further," which he achieves when he commits bigamy. At the end of the novel Rufus is denied permission to return to America, and Selvon seems to have deliberately consigned him to the void.

Other characters, the fugitive Father Hope of *An Island Is a World*, for example, are driven by their secret devils. Having killed a man several years ago in London – while defending a woman being attacked – Father Hope flees England but is pursued by paralyzing guilt. In Trinidad he sets himself up as a minister in Veronica, an isolated, bucolic, and hauntingly beautiful hamlet, where he administers to the simple villagers and expects to find spiritual peace. But peace is as elusive as his determination to found a new, less restrictive, more liberal religion. His mysterious death at the end of the novel (suicide or an accident) matches the sort of nebulous resolution with which Rufus's search ends. Johnny, the Indian jeweler whose daughters Rufus and Foster marry, is an equally well-drawn character. Although he has lived, raised a family, and prospered in Trinidad for several years, Johnny regards India as his home, and as he becomes increasingly alienated from all but one member of his family – the sensitive Jennifer, who understands his loneliness – he is drawn into the islandwide scheme of returning to India with other disaffected Trinidad Indians. As his alienation and frustrations grow, Johnny sublimates his failures by excessive drinking. Prime Minister Jawaharlal Nehru, to whom the disaffected have written for comfort and support, has responded with no encouragement, and indeed he sees no place for Johnny and his exiles in turbulent, postcolonial India.

The characters of *An Island Is a World* and *I Hear Thunder* are palpably West Indian in that they struggle to come to terms with a society they regard as unimportant. Foster is "a member of a cosmopolitan community who recognized no creed or race, a creature born of all the people of the world, in a small island that no one knew anything about," Selvon writes; "of what material loss would it be to the world if the island suddenly sank under the sea?" These characters are also uniquely West Indian to the extent that they seek fulfillment somewhere else; however, their relentless search for self-awareness and strong roots also makes them universal men.

In his London fiction Selvon explores the plight of largely unskilled West Indians struggling to survive in a decidedly hostile society. Much of the critical response to these novels focuses on this particular aspect of Selvon's immigrants. There are, however, other, perhaps more subtle, issues in the London novels. Of these the attitude of Selvon's immigrants toward women and marriage is worth exploring. In London "the boys" rigidly maintain a cohesive male community closed to women. Women

and family are peripheral, marriage is undesirable, and those who do marry are either ridiculed or they come to grief. Moses, the charismatic persona of Selvon's trilogy – *The Lonely Londoners, Moses Ascending* (1975), and *Moses Migrating* (1983) – argues that the "lonely miserable" city of London is not conducive to family life, but this idea is somewhat disingenuous. Moses and his companions consistently regard the female as a nuisance, however necessary she may be as a plaything. Women are merely "things" or "children" or "pieces" to be enjoyed and discarded at the males' discretion. Accordingly women such as Teena of *The Housing Lark* (1965), who will not be treated as pieces of skin to be sloughed off at the males' discretion, are disconcerting to Selvon's West Indians. For example, in the same novel, Battersby's attempt to engineer a Trinidad-style *boballe* (con game) is stymied by the intervention of the abrasive Teena, who demands a strict accounting of all monies collected; and Moses' descent into the claustrophobia of basement living in *Moses Ascending* is precipitated by the arrival of Jeannie and his liaison with her. Moses attributes his fall to his lust for women, but he immediately qualifies his own responsibility: "it is a pity that Adam had that spare rib what God make Eve with, for from the moment woman come into this world it was as if a Pandora Box open and let loose evils in Paradise."

Some of Selvon's immigrants reveal a subconscious fear of women, a fear mixed with anger and hate. These responses are noticeable, for example, in the story of Small Change, the bus driver in *Ways of Sunlight* (1957), whose rising fortunes with London Transport are ruined by an aggressive woman. One also thinks here of Galahad's first date in London, which he describes as a "battle royal" (*The Lonely Londoners*). His choice of words is revealing: for a man infected with colonial self-contempt, to say nothing of an indoctrinated belief in the superiority of whiteness, the bedding of the white Daisy is a considerable victory. An examination of the immigrants' self-image helps to explain their attitude toward women. In a predominantly white, antagonistic, and "superior" society, Selvon's West Indians are frequently objects of ridicule, laughter, and contempt; and, more important, they often reveal self-contempt. "You see how it is," Moses remarks in *The Lonely Londoners*, "one worthless fellar go around making bad and give the wrong impression for all the rest." Again and again there are candid comments about the alleged inability of blacks to thrive. Moses, long since wrung through the London mill, says to Galahad in *Moses Ascending*: "I will tell you one thing I have learnt in this life. It is that

287

Samuel Selvon (photograph copyright 1989 by Dr. Peter Stummer)

the black man cannot unite. I have seen various causes taken up and dropped like hot coals." Nor is Moses the only West Indian who mulls over the alleged deficiencies of blacks.

Unquestionably the discrimination and bigotry the West Indian immigrant encounters in London exacerbate his less-than-mediocre self-image and inferiority complex. Racism depersonalizes its victim, and it reduces him to the status of an object, as episodes in Moses' stream-of-consciousness reflections demonstrate. This stunting of the personality sometimes forces the victim to treat others as objects. More pertinently, some of Selvon's West Indians depersonalize women as they themselves have been depersonalized. The female, furthermore, is both lifeline and whipping boy. This antithesis is evident in Syl's frantic attempts to bed Pat, the "Irish thing" of *The Housing Lark*. When she refuses, Syl's behavior becomes desperate and bizarre, and his deeply embedded insecurities surface: he threatens to beat up Pat, and his fantasies of sexual union with her are violent.

The stasis one notices in Selvon's immigrants is also worth examining. Many of them are trapped in a pleasure-seeking syndrome against which more than one woman vociferously rebels. Teena is char-

acteristically blunt: her fellow West Indians have come to London to "full [their] belly with rum and food . . . belch and fart around . . . catch women, stand up by the market place talking a set of shit day in and day out." The immigrants' tendency to fantasize also contributes to the stasis. The con-artist Battersby fantasizes about a compliant genie who will produce a variety of women playmates on demand. On three occasions the narrative voice interrupts the action of *The Housing Lark* to make comments such as this one: "Look at all these dreamers, and imagine that characters like these could get serious."

Racism and rejection, however, only partly explain the stagnation and feelings of hopelessness so noticeable in Selvon's immigrants. Galahad's attitude ("we only want to get by, we don't even want to get on") and Moses' remark "I does always think poor" are self-defeating and merely serve to perpetuate the immigrant's second-class status in London. After some ten years in London, Moses concludes that his chief ways to spend time are to sleep and to feed and hustle women. Moses sees "a great aimlessness, a great restless, swaying movement . . . leaving you standing in the same spot."

Alienation and discrimination force Selvon's

West Indians into a cohesive group; but these two important factors only partly explain this close bonding. Moses, although he acts as father, mother, and mentor to "the boys," also requires the emotional security of the group for survival. Even the older Moses, for all his posturing and alleged abhorrence of "the old brigade," grudgingly recognizes that his connection with the group cannot be severed.

Selvon's West Indians have moved from what may be regarded as an open to a closed society, and their cohesiveness can be explained as a defense mechanism against what appears to be a permanently closed society. None of Selvon's immigrants has a sense of belonging in British society. But there is more to this cohesiveness: one of the pernicious consequences of a totally dependent colonial society – the sort of society from which Selvon's immigrants come – is that it ill prepared native residents for independent and effective existence in a society perceived of as superior. Selvon's West Indians have a psychological need to form a colony with a governor/leader if they are to survive in the "superior" metropolitan society. The formation of a colony satisfies this need and ensures survival; however, it retards the individual's development.

Selvon's career has been shaped in the first instance by his nurture in West Indian society. His West Indian roots are deep. But he also lived in England for some twenty-eight years, and that has influenced his sensibilities as well. He has lived in Canada since 1978. To date, however, no substantial work has come from this third area of experience.

Interviews:

"British Caribbean Writers" [Selvon interviewed by Stuart Hall], BBC Radio, 21 April 1958;

Rosemary Stone, Interview with Selvon, *Express*, 2 March 1972, p. 13;

"Samuel Selvon Talks to Gerald Moore," BBC Radio, 1 January 1974;

"Samuel Selvon Talks to Norman Jeffares," in *Commonwealth Writers Series* (London: British Council Literature Department, 1975);

Peter Nazareth, Interview with Selvon, *World Literature Written in English*, 18 (November 1979): 420–437;

J. Ursulet, Interview with Selvon, *Afram Newsletter*, 13 (1981): 14–16;

Clement Wyke, "Interview with Samuel Selvon," *Chimo*, 3 (Spring 1981): 30–38;

"Sam Selvon Talking: A Conversation with Ken-

neth Ramchand," *Canadian Literature*, 95 (Winter 1982): 56–64;

"The Moses Trilogy: Sam Selvon Discusses His London Novels with Susheila Nasta," *Wasafiri*, 1 (Spring 1985): 5–9;

Jean-Pierre Durix, "Talking of *Moses Ascending* with Samuel Selvon," *Commonwealth Essays and Studies*, 10 (Spring 1988): 11–13;

Frank Birbalsingh, "An Interview with Sam Selvon," in his *Passion and Exile: Essays in Caribbean Literature* (London: Hansib, 1988), pp. 147–161;

Michel Fabre, "Samuel Selvon: Interviews and Conversations," in *Critical Perspectives on Sam Selvon*, edited by Susheila Nasta (Washington, D.C.: Three Continents, 1988), pp. 64–76;

John Thieme and Alessandra Dotti, " 'Oldtalk': Two Interviews with Sam Selvon," *Caribana*, 1 (1990): 71–84.

Bibliography:

"Bibliography," in *Critical Perspectives on Sam Selvon*, edited by Susheila Nasta (Washington, D.C.: Three Continents, 1988), pp. 267–282.

References:

Harold Barratt, "Dialect, Maturity, and the Land in Sam Selvon's *A Brighter Sun*: A Reply," *English Studies in Canada*, 7 (Fall 1981): 329–337;

Barratt, "From Colony to Colony: Selvon's Expatriate West Indians," in *Critical Perspectives on Sam Selvon*, edited by Susheila Nasta (Washington, D.C.: Three Continents, 1988), pp. 250–259;

Barratt, "Individual Integrity in Selvon's *Turn Again Tiger* and *Those Who Eat the Cascadura*," *Toronto South Asian Review*, 5 (Summer 1986): 153–159;

Edward Baugh, "Exiles, Guerillas and Visions of Eden," *Queen's Quarterly*, 84 (Summer 1977): 273–286;

Baugh, "Friday in Crusoe's City: The Question of Language in Two West Indian Novels of Exile," *ACLALS Bulletin*, 5 (December 1980): 1–12;

Stephen Bernhardt, "Dialect and Style Shifting in the Fiction of Samuel Selvon," in *Studies in Caribbean Language*, edited by Lawrence Carrington (Saint Augustine, Trinidad: Society for Caribbean Linguists, 1983), pp. 266–276;

Frank Birbalsingh, "Samuel Selvon and the West Indian Literary Renaissance," *Ariel*, 8 (July 1977): 5–22;

Edward Kamau Brathwaite, "Jazz and the West Indian Novel," *Bim*, 11 (January–June 1967):

275–284; 12 (July–December 1967): 39–51; (January–June 1968): 115–126;

Brathwaite, "The New West Indian Novelists: Part One," *Bim*, 8 (July–December 1960): 199–210;

Brathwaite, "Roots," *Bim*, 10 (July–December 1963): 10–21;

Brathwaite, "Sir Galahad and the Islands," *Bim*, 7 (July–December 1957): 8–16;

Barrie Davies, "The Sense of Abroad: Aspects of the West Indian Novel in England," *World Literature Written in English*, 11 (November 1972): 67–80;

Michel Fabre, "From Trinidad to London: Tone and Language in Samuel Selvon's Novels," *Literary Half-Yearly*, 20 (January 1979): 71–80;

Fabre, "Moses and the Queen's English: Dialect and Narrative Voice in Samuel Selvon's London Novels," *World Literature Written in English*, 21 (Summer 1982): 385–392;

Fabre, "The Queen's Calypso: Linguistic and Narrative Strategies in the Fiction of Samuel Selvon," *Commonwealth Essays and Studies*, 3 (1977–1978): 69–76;

Fabre, "Samuel Selvon," in *West Indian Literature*, edited by Bruce King (London: Macmillan, 1979), pp. 111–125;

H. H. Anniah Gowda, "A Brief Note on the Dialect Novels of Sam Selvon and Earl Lovelace," *Literary Half-Yearly*, 27 (July 1986): 98–103;

Jane W. Grant, *Samuel Selvon: Ways of Sunlight* (London: Longman, 1979);

Stuart M. Hall, "Lamming, Selvon and Some Trends in the West Indian Novel," *Bim*, 6 (December 1955): 172–178;

Katie Jones, "Dialect, Idiolect, Sociolect: Transformations of English in the Work of Raja Rao, Samuel Selvon and Alice Walker," *Chimo*, 11 (1985): 4–13;

Bruce MacDonald, "Language and Consciousness in Samuel Selvon's *A Brighter Sun*," *English Studies in Canada*, 5 (Summer 1979): 202–215;

Christian Mair, "Naipaul's *Miguel Street* and Selvon's *Lonely Londoners* – Two Approaches to the Use of Caribbean Creole in Fiction," *Journal of Commonwealth Literature*, 24, no. 1 (1989): 138–154;

Mervyn Morris, Introduction to Selvon's *Moses As-*

cending (London: Heinemann, 1984), pp. vii–xviii;

Susheila Nasta, ed., *Critical Perspectives on Sam Selvon* (Washington, D.C.: Three Continents, 1988);

Peter Nazareth, "The Clown in the Slave Ship," *Caribbean Quarterly*, 23 (June–September 1977): 24–30;

Sandra Pouchet Paquet, Introduction to Selvon's *Turn Again Tiger* (London: Heinemann, 1979), pp. vii–xxiv;

Kenneth Ramchand, "*A Brighter Sun*," in his *An Introduction to the Study of West Indian Literature* (London: Nelson, 1976), pp. 58–72;

Ramchand, "The Fate of Writing in the West Indies: Reflections on Oral and Written Literature," *Caribbean Review*, 11, no. 4 (1982): 16–17, 40–41;

Ramchand, "Song of Innocence, Song of Experience: Samuel Selvon's *The Lonely Londoners* as a Literary Work," *World Literature Written in English*, 21 (Autumn 1982): 644–654;

Victor J. Ramraj, "The Philosophy of Neutrality: The Treatment of Political Militancy in Samuel Selvon's *Moses Ascending* and *Moses Migrating*," in *Literature and Commitment: A Commonwealth Perspective*, edited by Govind Narain Sharma (Toronto: Tsar, 1988), pp. 109–115;

Gordon Rohlehr, "Samuel Selvon and the Language of the People," in *Critics on Caribbean Literature*, edited by Baugh (London: Allen & Unwin, 1978), pp. 153–161;

Rohlehr, "Selvon on Stage," *Moko*, 10 (March 1969): 3;

R. Sutherland, "Sam Selvon – The Caribbean Connection," *Toronto South Asian Review*, 2, no. 1 (1983): 44–46;

John Thieme, " 'The World Turn Upside Down': Carnival Patterns in *The Lonely Londoners*," *Toronto South Asian Review*, 5 (Summer 1986): 191–204;

Maureen Warner-Lewis, "Samuel Selvon's Linguistic Extravaganza: *Moses Ascending*," *Caribbean Quarterly*, 28 (December 1982): 60–69;

Clement H. Wyke, "Language and Sense of Place in Naipaul and Selvon," *Toronto South Asian Review*, 16, no. 2 (1987): 36–56;

Wyke, *Sam Selvon's Dialectal Style and Fictional Strategy* (Vancouver: University of British Columbia Press, 1991).

Mongane Wally Serote

(8 May 1944 -)

David Attwell
University of Natal, Pietermaritzburg

BOOKS: *Yakhal'inkomo* (Johannesburg: Renoster, 1972);

Tsetlo (Johannesburg: Donker, 1974);

No Baby Must Weep (Johannesburg: Donker, 1975);

Behold Mama, Flowers (Johannesburg: Donker, 1978);

To Every Birth Its Blood (Johannesburg: Ravan, 1981; London: Heinemann, 1983);

Selected Poems, edited by Mbulelo Vizikhungo Mzamane (Johannesburg: Donker, 1982);

The Night Keeps Winking (Gaborone, Botswana: Medu Art Ensemble, 1982);

A Tough Tale (London: Kliptown, 1987);

On the Horizon (Johannesburg: Congress of South African Writers, 1990);

Third World Express (Cape Town: Philip, 1992).

OTHER: "Power to the People: A Glory to Creativity," in *Criticism and Ideology*, edited by Kirsten Holst Petersen (Uppsala, Sweden: Scandinavian Institute of African Studies, 1988), pp. 193–197.

SELECTED PERIODICAL PUBLICATIONS –
UNCOLLECTED: "When Rebecca Fell," "Fogitall," and "Let's Wander Together," *Classic*, 3, no. 4 (1971): 5–7; 8–10; 11–14;

"A Look at the Line," *Bolt*, 9 (1973): 4–8;

"The Nakasa World," *Contrast*, 31 (1973): 16–21;

"Feeling the Waters," *First World*, 1 (March–April 1977): 22–25.

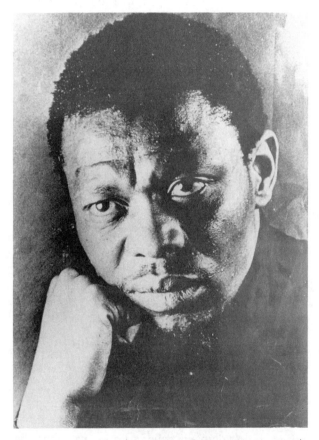

Mongane Wally Serote (photograph: Africamera, Johannesburg)

From the early poems of *Yakhal'inkomo* (1972), where the anguish of black life in South Africa becomes compressed into a personal lyricism of unusual intensity, to the epic expansiveness of *A Tough Tale* (1987), with its directly referential and secular celebration of a revolutionary movement, the career of Mongane Wally Serote spans an important period in the history of resistance and its cultural expression in South Africa over the past two decades.

Serote is widely recognized in South Africa and beyond as a leading figure in the generation of writers who emerged in the 1970s (known as the era of "Soweto Poetry"), including Oswald Mbuyiseni Mtshali, Sipho Sepamla, and Mafika Gwala. This group's work – which includes the collective output of those publishing in *Staffrider* magazine – inaugurated a resurgence of black literary activity in the country after the chilly silence produced by the banning and exile of the writers of the late 1950s and early 1960s, the generation associated with *Drum* magazine.

Serote was born in Sophiatown on 8 May 1944, but he grew up and went to primary school in Alexandra, a township in Johannesburg, which "was not meant for people to live in," as he told Mbulelo Vizikhungo Mzamane in an interview. The child of parents who were, as he puts it, neither very rich nor very poor, Serote was able to feel part of a community whose common experience was impoverishment and also to reflect on and articulate that experience. As he explained to interviewer Michael Chapman, "that position makes you keenly aware of other people being extremely poor, and that in fact you are closely related to poverty. Poverty is a constant threat. You become aware that it is a miracle that you have meals daily, that you have a chance to go to school. Living a miracle is like hanging from a very high, high building, held there only by a strand of hair. That is Alexandra; that is South Africa." From the time he wrote his early poem titled "Alexandra," Serote's hometown has remained a distinctive signature for him, a specific urban geography transformed by experience into an ambivalent symbol of both mothering and oppression.

Serote left Morris Isaacson High School in Soweto before matriculating at a college, having been among the earliest victims of the segregationist Bantu Education Act. In 1969 he was detained for nine months under the Terrorism Act; no charges were brought against him. Before leaving South Africa in 1974, Serote worked in advertising and as a free-lance journalist for the *Post* in Johannesburg, and he collaborated with several cultural groups, such as the Mihloti Black Theatre, MDALI (Music, Drama, Art, Literature Institute), and SABTU (South African Black Theatre Union). From 1975 to 1979 he studied fine arts and creative writing at Columbia University in New York, where he received an M.A. On his return to southern Africa in 1979, Serote chose voluntary exile in Botswana, where he cofounded the Medu Art Ensemble. He has published poetry in *Ophir*, *New Coin*, *Classic*, *Contrast*, *Staffrider*, *Purple Renoster*, and *Playboy*. Having worked in London for several years in the Department of Arts and Culture of the African National Congress (ANC), he returned to South Africa in February 1990.

Serote's first two collections, *Yakhal'inkomo* (the title of which means the cry of cattle going to slaughter) and the 1974 book *Tsetlo* (whose title is the name of a bird with a mysterious, luring whistle that can lead the listener to either pleasure or danger – perhaps a symbol of the poet), consist mainly of lyric poems and dramatic monologues, the formal antecedents of which can be found, by and large, in the Anglo-American tradition; in later work Serote begins to explore the resources of a more indigenous form, the epic. The early poems, written in free verse, present a reflective persona who witnesses and evaluates his world in a language that is sharply metaphoric and whose tones are sometimes bitter, sometimes ironic, but invariably passionate and authoritative. Serote's predominant themes focus on the waste and suffering that are encountered in the midst of ordinary, daily experience under apartheid. While this experience is filtered through anguish, the feeling seldom lapses into sentimentality or an acceptance of easy solutions; Serote's control is a function of a defiant spirit, and his imagery can sharply articulate social commentary, as in "Burning Cigarette" (from his first book):

> This little black boy
> Is drawn like a cigarette from its box,
> Lit.
> He looks at his smoke hopes
> That twirl, spiral, curl
> To nothing.
> He grows like cigarette ashes
> As docile, as harmless;
> Is smothered.

The final poem in *Yakhal'inkomo*, however, called "Black Bells," reveals an explicit frustration with both the language and the formal limitations of the dominant pattern, and it points the way to Serote's experiments with longer structures (a process that also led eventually to Serote's one and only novel, *To Every Birth Its Blood*, 1981). The protagonist in "Black Bells" complains of being "trapped twice," both by the apartheid society and by the language of "whitey." The poem ends in a scramble to get out: "You've trapped me whitey! Meem wanna ge aot Fuc / Pschwee e ep booboodubooboodu blllll / Black books, / Flesh blood words shitrr Haai, / Amen."

Serote's exasperation with the social, linguistic, and formal constraints of his situation, together with a brief, longing glance at the possibility of an alternative, black, cultural authority – the "Black books" containing "Flesh blood words" – are seldom completely suppressed below the unstable surface of most of the early poems. The struggle with language and form, however, is part of the struggle to come to terms with and articulate the black experience. "Where's the world?" asks the speaker in "The Face of a Happening" in the same book, "How do you look at it? / It's like you are trying to put the wind into bed." In the early poems Serote does turn in a few instances to indigenous resources for appropriate formal models, and the results are such poems as "City Johannesburg" and "Alexandra" in *Yakhal'inkomo*, and "Introit" in *Tsetlo*, which have links with the traditional *izibongo* and *lithoko*, especially the device of "making by naming." Some of the poems – for example, "Hell, Well, Heaven" in *Yakhal'inkomo* and "Mother Dada and Company" in *Tsetlo* – make use of an African-American vocabulary and idiom, notably in their jazzlike parallelisms and refrains. But it is in the longer poems of *No Baby Must Weep* (1975) and *Behold Mama, Flowers* (1978) that Serote attempts a more complete integration of his formal versatility and a historic vision of the black struggle, although the personal or existential emphasis remains strong in the longer poems as well.

No Baby Must Weep is a single poem of fifty-three pages, which attempts to chart the course of the "blackmanchild" in its journey of self-discovery and self-emergence. The poem establishes many of the formal and symbolic patterns that Serote was to use in later work. The journey begins with a return to childhood, to the familial relations and peer-group associations that develop within the scarred urban landscape of the township; the consistent thread through this experience is the bond with the mother, who is the addressee of the poem. The growth to adult consciousness involves a sense of internal loss, an existential pain – the recurrent metaphor for which is a bleeding wound – generated by questions about selfhood and identity ("mama / you grew a hollow and named it me"); but the pain is also secular, and more than individual, in that it involves an internalization of the wider social malady. Serote's imagery of the body in various forms – youthful, aged, in childbirth, wounded – serves as a register of immediate pressures in the experiences of individuals in a brutal environment. Toward the end of the poem the self's transcendence is sought through the deployment of organic metaphors: the sea, sky, landscape, and trees; but, finally and most powerfully, the river. The river gives coherence and historical depth to the black experience, thereby assuaging it symbolically:

> this river is dark
> this river is deep
> this river coils its depths and hides its flow
> the river is dark
> the deaths that emerged from a creation into a hole
> fell and formed little ripples on the surface of the river
> the deaths that came rushing like a mad train
> crushed
> smashed
> and there were no screams

> there were no tears
> nobody mourned
> the corpses still stride the streets like scarecrows[.]

No Baby Must Weep ends with an affirmation of the self, through its transcendence and integration with the collective history imagined in the river, but there is also an affirmation of the value of the poetic language that gives expression to this process: "i have gone beyond the flood now / i left the word on the flood / it echoes in the depth the width / i am beyond the flood."

The relationship between "the word" and "the flood," between the resources of language and the black historical experience, provides the titular motif for Serote's next long poem, *Behold Mama, Flowers*. From the artist Skunder Boghossian, Serote learned the story of a man who chopped a body into pieces, and when he threw them into a river, a child looking on said, "Mama, look at the flowers." The river in this poem – whose waters are "no longer clean" – runs not only through the black diaspora but also through the entire colonized world: it is the Limpopo, the Zambezi, the Nile, the Mississippi, the Amazon, and the Ganges. This larger perspective is probably attributable to the poem's having been written outside South Africa, in 1975, during Serote's period in the United States as a student at Columbia. This sojourn was clearly not a happy one for Serote: some of the anguish of what was surely Serote's own sense of isolation comes through in the portrayal of Yao in *To Every Birth Its Blood*; Serote is also on record as having said to Chapman, perhaps impulsively, that "going to America was a waste of time." But the experience did provide him an expanded sense of historical horizons. In addition to South Africans such as Albert Luthuli and Robert Sobukwe, who are given a united "voice" in the poem, there are, for example, scattered references to such figures as Angela Davis, Malcolm X, and George Jackson, and to the leaders of anticolonial struggles in Mozambique and Guinea-Bissau – Eduardo Mondlane and Amilcar Cabral. As in *No Baby Must Weep*, the poem develops from an existential center involving a journey of self-discovery. This point of departure is located in the only repeated refrain, "where is it that i am not there / what is it that i do not know." The search for identity that the poem records, however, is constructed from the capacity of the speaking subject to witness pain and give it a historical dimension by recalling it in memory and by summoning the collective will to endure and transcend it. (The appeal to a historical memory, followed by a call for mobiliza-

MONGANE SEROTE

the night keeps winking

Mongane Serote was born in 1944 in Sophiatown, South Africa. He has published four previous volumes of poetry:
Yakhal'inkomo (1972); Tsetlo (1974); No Baby Must Weep (1975); and Behold Mama, Flowers (1978). He published
his first novel, To Every Birth its Blood, in 1981. Serote presently lives in exile in Botswana, and is an active member
of Medu Art Ensemble.

Cover and Illustrations by Thamsanqa Mnyele.   published by Medu Art Ensemble

*Cover for a collection of poems in which Serote calls for revolution in South Africa. The book was written and published in
Botswana, where Serote went into voluntary exile in 1979.*

tion, is a pattern that Serote repeats in later, more explicitly revolutionary poems.)

The first of what Serote called "the storms of the future" was closer than he might have anticipated in 1975, when *No Baby Must Weep* was published, for in June of the following year the Soweto revolt erupted. *To Every Birth Its Blood* incorporates the "days of Power," as they became known in subsequent literature. The novel does not narrate the course of the revolt, nor does it directly tell the story of the students who were involved in it, but it does explore the experience of a range of people whose lives are thrown into crisis by the revolt and its consequences. The novel falls into two parts. Part 1, presented in the first person, deals with the personal history and early, unfulfilled working life of protagonist Tsi Molope. (Much of the anguished subjectivity of Serote's poems is filtered through the character of Tsi, for whom the drinks and jazz of the townships provide supports against the alienating and brutalizing effects of black life.) Part 2 is in the third person and deals more fully with Tsi's family and associates. The deepening historical crisis is shown to affect the characters in different ways, but most notably readers see the emergence to mature political leadership of Michael Ramono; the absorption into activism of his daughter, Dikeledi, through the agency of Oupa, Tsi's illegitimate and disregarded nephew; and the growth of guerrilla activity linking the remaining individuals into the loosely defined political association termed the Movement. At times the Movement is indicative

of the popular swing to the ANC, which followed on the revolt, at other times it operates as an organic metaphor (like the river of Serote's longer poems) linking disparate elements into an affirmation of collective resistance. The treatment of the Movement as both secular and organic remains a consistent feature of Serote's poems, and it appears in *A Tough Tale*.

Criticism of *To Every Birth Its Blood* is divided over the question of whether the work is structurally coherent. Dorian Barboure argues that it is formally and thematically unified by a shift from an individual to a collective focus, and from alienation to commitment. Nick Visser, who values formal unity less highly than the relationships between fiction and history, contends that the novel comprises two distinct fictional projects, that the existential bildungsroman involving the life of Tsi is overtaken, but not completely erased, by the larger, more radical narrative of social conflict and resistance. The latter reading relies on calculated guesses about the revolt being incorporated into the novel as it happened.

To Every Birth Its Blood and, by implication, the events at Soweto in 1976 are clearly pivotal in Serote's development. In fact one might argue that the changes that began to occur in Serote's work at this time reflect wider shifts of allegiance within black political life and that Serote was close to the pulse of these developments. In the poems up to and including *Behold Mama, Flowers*, Serote's work has close affinities with "Black Consciousness," the philosophy of black self-reliance pioneered by the South African Students Organization (SASO) and given its most articulate expression in the work of Steve Biko. It was the most significant ideological rallying point of the 1970s up to and including the revolt. In keeping with this consensus, Serote's earliest categories of social analysis are racial ones, and he unmistakably deploys formal and ideological strategies that show a conscious identification with the black world and its traditions. Mzamane, in his introduction to Serote's *Selected Poems* (1982), argues explicitly that Serote is "the poet of Black Consciousness." Serote also worked with CULCOM, the cultural committee within SASO, and was an associate of Biko. (Interestingly, it was Biko who persuaded Serote to continue a working relationship with the white poet Lionel Abrahams, who had been instrumental in publishing Serote's first collections but whose editorial suggestions Serote found difficult to accept.) The involvement with Black Consciousness also extended to Serote's work with theater groups. Serote himself, on the other hand, is cautious about the label and says laconically that it was given to him partly by unsympathetic readers. What emerges in *To Every Birth Its Blood*, however, is an uneven process in which the struggle is seen to be most usefully advanced by a secular ideology – rather than the racial or cultural ideology characteristic of Black Consciousness – and a form of collectivization that is most obviously represented by the ANC. The character Ramono, whose activism stretches back to the nonracialism of the 1950s (which distinguishes him from the Soweto generation) and whose political wisdom carries the most weight in the novel, tells Dikeledi in what is undoubtedly the clearest ideological statement of the novel, "I want you to understand that colour must not be the issue. Once we get to understand that, then we can talk on, but I am afraid that you have put too much emphasis on the colour question."

Serote's ideological emphases are not sectarian, however; it is indeed a question of emphasis, as Ramono puts it. In Serote's next work, *The Night Keeps Winking* (1982), written wholly under conditions of committed exile in Botswana and given over unambiguously to the ideal of "national revolution," there is an opening tribute to Biko. The poem is the most directly revolutionary of Serote's works until this point, ending with a celebration of the spectacular effects of ANC sabotage attacks, notably one on a prestigious oil refinery in which "red, blue, green and yellow flames scream into the sky."

The book falls into three sections. The first,

"Time Has Run Out," deals once again with memory and establishes the record of resistance in the popular consciousness. Throughout this section the night is seen as the suprahistorical witness to the decades of black suffering; the night is a knowing consciousness that enables Serote to posit the historical continuity demanded by the resistance movement. In the second section, "The Sun Was Falling," there are two poems: "Exile," which deals with the silence surrounding the exile in his adopted home; and "Notes," which traces the growth of a "secret" into a "song," in this context a revolutionary commitment to armed struggle that brings assurances of a transformed future. The names of ANC fallen, notably Solomon Mahlangu, are given as rallying calls. The final section, "Listen, the Baby Cries and Cries and Cries," similarly consists of two poems: "Once More, the Distances," a lyrical poem that anticipates the birth of a love child (presumably also a representative of the new society); and "The Long Road," which celebrates the successes of ANC attacks while asking repeatedly, "how is a long road measured?"

A Tough Tale, Serote's long poem published in 1987, continues the revolutionary dedication of *The Night Keeps Winking*, but there is a deepened sense of the costs of the struggle; Serote intimates that its human and historical dimensions are, in the final analysis, beyond the capacity of language or narrative to grasp, for in the poem he asks, "how can this tale be told?" It would be useful to recall the period prior to the poem's publication, 1985–1987, which involved three successive states of emergency declared by the government. There were well over ten thousand detentions of suspects, there were complete news blackouts, and more deaths were recorded than in any of the other major conflicts with which South Africa's recent history is littered, including the Soweto revolt. Implicitly Serote's poem asks what support literature can provide in such a context. No narrative seems to be adequate to such a moment, other than as a reminder of the power of people to endure: "my people / I cannot be rash with this tale / you taught me to wait and be patient / so you – / through your wealth of life / you tell this tale as your life unfolds." Serote also speaks soberly about this tale being "a song whose strength like strong wind / can blow and reveal our weaknesses." The difference between *The Night Keeps Winking* and *A Tough Tale* is the latter's sharper sense of historical limitations. *A Tough Tale* is not lacking in commitment; on the contrary, the poem ends by drawing strength from the continued existence and resilience of what for Serote are the key resistance organizations, the ANC and its allies, the South African Congress of Trade Unions (SACTU), and the South African Communist Party (SACP). But Serote's tale, in the final account, is the one these organizations tell of themselves.

On the Horizon, published in 1990, is a collection of talks and interviews given by Serote between 1986 and 1989 in his capacity as cultural attaché of the ANC in London. If, in his creative work, Serote gradually allows his personal voice to merge with that of the ANC and its allies, the process is fulfilled in this collection, where he spells out his movement's position explicitly on such questions as the meaning of Black Consciousness in the 1970s, the function of cultural activism, the cultural boycott, censorship, and so forth. It is a valuable collection for anyone interested in the maturation of Serote's views and in the position of the ANC on important issues during a crucial period of its struggle. However, the collection offers more than the party line; Serote's vision of the end of apartheid is an expression of his faith in ideas of modernity and freedom for humanity as a whole: "The struggle for the destruction of apartheid and for the abolition of the exploitation of the majority by the minority in South Africa is, on the one hand, a re-entering of history by over twenty million people who are black; and on the other hand, their entering the civilised world which, for many years, has been expressing a select culture which consciously excludes the majority of the world, and this will contribute to the totality and dynamism of human civilisation."

Serote's most recent poem, *Third World Express* (1992), develops this intrinsic optimism. Similar in scope to *A Tough Tale*, the later poem reflects on new conditions in South Africa. The present is seen as dangerous and confusing, a far cry from the vision of freedom that stirred the imaginations of the Soweto youth sixteen years previously. However, the poem also recalls "simple things which are forgotten" – the loyalty, camaraderie and humanity of friends – and says, "Let the men and women of this earth / . . . claim the past for the future." Characteristically Serote is sensitive to the moment and deals with the situation in terms of a dialectic of frustration and hope. But Serote's poem also embodies a larger, utopian vision that extends beyond the present to a time when peace and democracy will be shared by all.

Interviews:

Jaki Seroke, "Poet in Exile: An Interview with Mongane Serote," *Staffrider*, 4, no. 1 (1981): 30–32;

Michael Chapman, "Interview with Mongane Serote," in *Soweto Poetry*, edited by Chapman (Johannesburg: Donker, 1982);

Liz McGregor, "A Far-Away View of Home," *Rand Daily Mail*, 29 July 1982;

Mbulelo Vizikhungo Mzamane, "Literary Responses to Apartheid (1): Interview with Mongane Wally Serote," *Saiwa, A Journal of Communication*, 2 (February 1984): 56–62.

Bibliography:

S. Williams, H. Colenbrander, and C. Owen, comps., *A Bibliography on Mongane Wally Serote (1944–)* (Pretoria: Subject Reference Department, University of South Africa Sanlam Library, 1980).

References:

Cecil Abrahams, "The South African Writer in a Changing Society," *Matatu*, 2, nos. 3–4 (1988): 32–43;

Lionel Abrahams, "Black Experience into English Verse: A Survey of Local African Poetry," *New Nation*, 3, no. 7 (1970): 10–11, 13, 20–21;

Jacques Alvarez-Péreyre, *The Poetry of Commitment in South Africa*, translated by Clive Wake (London: Heinemann, 1984);

Dorian Barboure, "Mongane Serote, Humanist and Revolutionary," in *Momentum: On Recent South African Writing*, edited by M. J. Daymond, J. U. Jacobs, and M. Lenta (Pietermaritzburg: University of Natal Press, 1984), pp. 171–181;

Ursula Barnett, *A Vision of Order: A Study of Black South African Literature in English (1914–1980)* (London: Sinclair Brown / Amherst: University of Massachusetts Press / Cape Town: Maskew Miller Longman, 1983);

Guy Butler, "The Language of the Conqueror on the Lips of the Conquered Is the Language of Slaves," *Theoria*, 45 (1975): 1–11;

Michael Chapman, *South African English Poetry: A Modern Perspective* (Johannesburg: Donker, 1984);

Chapman, ed., *Soweto Poetry* (Johannesburg: McGraw-Hill, 1982);

Jeremy Cronin, " 'The Law that Says / Constricts the Breath-Line,': South African English Language Poetry Written by Africans in the 1970's," *English Academy Review*, 3 (1985): 25–49;

Leigh Dale, "Changing Places: The Problem of Identity in the Poetry of Lionel Fogarty and Mongane Serote," *Span*, 24 (1987): 81–95;

Tony Emmett, "Oral, Political and Communal Aspects of Township Poetry in the Mid-Seventies," *English in Africa*, 6, no. 1 (1979): 72–81;

Stephen M. Finn, "Poets of Suffering and Revolt: Tschernichowsky and Serote," *UNISA English Studies*, 26, no. 1 (1988): 26–32;

Colin Gardner, "Irony and Militancy in Recent Black Poetry," *English Academy Review*, 3 (1985): 81–88;

Gardner, " 'Jo'burg City': Questions in the Smoke – Approaches to a Poem," *Bloody Horse*, 5 (1981): 38–45;

Gardner, "Poetry and/or Politics: Recent South African Black Verse," *English in Africa*, 9, no. 1 (1982): 45–54;

Nadine Gordimer, *The Black Interpreters* (Johannesburg: Spro-Cas/Ravan, 1973);

Gordimer, "In a World They Never Made: Five Black South African Poets Write About Life in the White-Makes-Right Land of Apartheid," *Playboy* (May 1972): 166–169;

Geoffrey Haresnape, " 'A Question of Black or White?': The Contemporary Situation in South African English Poetry," in *Poetry South Africa*, edited by P. Wilhelm and J. Polley (Johannesburg: Donker, 1976), pp. 35–46;

Peter Horn, "When It Rains, It Rains: U.S. Black Consciousness and Lyric Poetry in South Africa," *Speak*, 1, no. 5 (1978): 7–11; republished in *Soweto Poetry*;

Douglas Livingstone, "The Poetry of Mtshali, Serote, Sepamla and Others in English: Notes Towards a Critical Evaluation," *New Classic*, 3 (1976): 48–63;

Es'kia Mphahlele, "Mongane Serote's Odyssey: The Path that Breaks the Heels," *English Academy Review*, 3 (1985): 65–79;

Mbulelo Vizikhungo Mzamane, Introduction to Serote's *Selected Poems*, edited by Mzamane (Johannesburg: Donker, 1982);

Arthur Ravenscroft, "Contemporary Poetry from Black South Africa," *Literary Criterion*, 12, no. 4 (1977): 33–52;

Richard Rive, "Black Poets of the Seventies," *English in Africa*, 4, no. 1 (1977): 47–54;

Sheila Roberts, "The Black South African Township Poets of the Seventies," *Genève-Afrique*, 18 (1980): 79–93;

Robert Royston, "A Tiny, Unheard Voice: The Writer in South Africa," *Index on Censorship*, 2, no. 4 (1973): 85–88;

Kelwyn Sole, "The Days of Power: Depictions of Politics and Community in Four Recent South African Novels," *Research in African Literatures*, 19 (1988): 65–88;

A. G. Ullyatt, "Dilemmas in Black Poetry," *Contrast*, 11, no. 4 (1977): 51–62;

Attie van Niekirk, "Wit op Swart: Gedigte van die Sewentigerjare," *Bloody Horse*, 4 (1981): 73–79;

A. S. van Niekirk, *Dominee, Are You Listening to the Drums?* (Cape Town: Tafelberg, 1982);

Nick Visser, "Fictional Projects and the Irruptions of History: Mongane Serote's *To Every Birth Its Blood*," *English Academy Review*, 4 (January 1987): 67–76;

Clive Wake, "Practical Criticism or Literary Commentary," *Research in African Literatures*, 16 (1985): 5–19;

Cecelia Scallan Zeiss, "Landscapes of Exile in Selected Works by Samuel Beckett, Mongane Serote, and Mbuyiseni Oswald Mtshali," in *Anglo-Irish and Irish Literature: Aspects of Language and Culture*, edited by Birgit Bramsback and Martin Croghan (Uppsala, Sweden: Uppsala University, 1988): 219–227.

Wole Soyinka

(13 July 1934 –)

James Gibbs

See also the Soyinka entry in *DLB Yearbook: 1986.*

BOOKS: *A Dance of the Forests* (London & Ibadan: Oxford University Press, 1963);

The Lion and the Jewel (London & Ibadan: Oxford University Press, 1963);

Three Plays (Ibadan: Mbari, 1963); republished as *Three Short Plays* (London: Oxford University Press, 1969);

Five Plays (London & Ibadan: Oxford University Press, 1964);

The Interpreters (London: Deutsch, 1965; New York: Collier, 1970);

The Road (London & Ibadan: Oxford University Press, 1965);

Idanre & Other Poems (London: Methuen, 1967; New York: Hill & Wang, 1968);

Kongi's Harvest (London, Ibadan & Nairobi: Oxford University Press, 1967);

Poems from Prison (London: Collings, 1969);

The Trials of Brother Jero, and The Strong Breed: Two Plays (New York: Dramatists Play Service, 1969)

Madmen and Specialists (London: Methuen, 1971; New York: Hill & Wang, 1972);

A Shuttle in the Crypt (London: Collings/Eyre Methuen, 1972; New York: Hill & Wang, 1972);

The Man Died: Prison Notes of Wole Soyinka (London: Collings, 1972; New York: Harper & Row, 1972; Lagos: University of Lagos Press, 1972);

Before the Blackout (Ibadan: Orisun Acting Editions, 1972?);

Camwood on the Leaves (London: Eyre Methuen, 1973);

Collected Plays, 2 volumes (London & New York: Oxford University Press, 1973, 1974);

The Jero Plays (London: Eyre Methuen, 1973);

Season of Anomy (London: Collings, 1973; New York: Third Press/Okpaku, 1974);

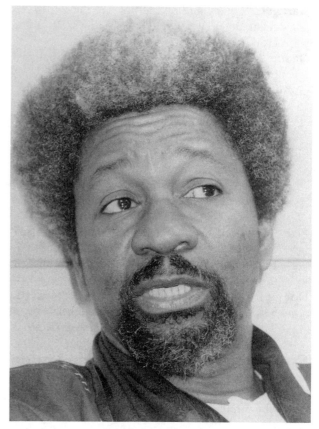

Wole Soyinka, 1986 (photograph by Lasse Hedberg; Pressens Bild AB, Stockholm)

Death and the King's Horseman (London: Eyre Methuen, 1975; New York: Norton, 1975);

Myth, Literature and the African World (Cambridge & New York: Cambridge University Press, 1976);

Ogun Abibimañ (London: Collings, 1976);

Aké: The Years of Childhood (London: Collings, 1981; New York: Random House, 1981);

Opera Wonyosi (London: Collings, 1981; Bloomington: Indiana University Press, 1981);

The Critic and Society (Ife, Nigeria: University of Ife Press, 1982);

A Play of Giants (London & New York: Methuen, 1984);

Six Plays (London: Methuen, 1984);

Requiem for a Futurologist (London: Collings, 1985);

Art, Dialogue and Outrage: Essays on Literature and Culture (Ibadan: New Horn / Oxford: Zell, 1988);

Mandela's Earth and Other Poems (New York: Random House, 1988; London: Methuen, 1989; Ibadan: Fountain, 1989);

This Past Must Address Its Present (New York: Anson Phelps Stokes Institute, 1988);

Isara, a Voyage around Essay (Ibadan: Fountain, 1989; New York: Random House, 1989; London: Methuen, 1990);

The Credo of Being and Nothingness (Ibadan: Spectrum, 1991);

From Zia, with Love, and A Scourge of Hyacinths (London: Methuen, 1992); *From Zia, with Love,* published separately (Ibadan: Fountain, 1992).

PLAY PRODUCTIONS: *The Swamp Dwellers*, London, National Union of Students' Drama Festival, 31 December 1958;

The Lion and the Jewel, Ibadan, University College Arts Theatre, February 1959; London, Royal Court Theatre, December 1966;

The Invention, London, Royal Court Theatre, 1 November 1959;

The Trials of Brother Jero, Ibadan, Mellanby Hall, April 1960;

A Dance of the Forests, Lagos, Yaba Technical College, October 1960;

The Republican, Ibadan, University College Arts Theatre, November 1963;

The (New) Republican, Ibadan, University College Arts Theatre, March 1964;

Before the Blackout, Ibadan, University College Arts Theatre, 11 March 1965;

Kongi's Harvest, Lagos, Independence Hall, 12 August 1965;

The Road, London, Theatre Royal Stratford East, September 1965;

The Strong Breed, Ibadan, Secondary Schools, 1966;

Madmen and Specialists, Watertown, Conn., Eugene O'Neill Memorial Theatre Center, 2 August 1970;

The Bacchae of Euripides, adapted by Soyinka, London, Old Vic, August 1973;

Jero's Metamorphosis, Bristol, U.K., Van Dyke Theatre, February 1974;

Death and the King's Horseman, Ife, Nigeria, University of Ife, Oduduwa Hall, December 1976;

Opera Wonyosi, Ife, Nigeria, University of Ife, Oduduwa Hall, December 1977;

Before the Blow-Out, Ife, Nigeria, 1978;

Rice or Rice Scene, Lagos, Museum Kitchen, 1981;

Camwood on the Leaves, Lagos, National Theatre, March 1982;

Priority Projects, Ife, Nigeria, December 1982;

Requiem for a Futurologist, Ife, Nigeria, University of Ife, Oduduwa Hall, January 1983;

A Play of Giants, New Haven, Conn., Yale Repertory Theater, 27 November 1984;

Before the Deluge, Lagos, 18 October 1991;

From Zia, with Love, Siena, Italy, June 1992.

MOTION PICTURES: *Culture in Transition*, commentary by Soyinka, Esso World Theater, 1964 (includes an abbreviated version of *The Strong Breed*);

The Swamp Dwellers, screenplay by Soyinka, London, Transcription Centre, 1967;

Kongi's Harvest, screenplay by Soyinka, Lagos, Calpenny-Nigeria Films, 1970;

Blues for a Prodigal, scenario by Soyinka, Ife, Nigeria, Ewuro, 1985.

TELEVISION: *My Father's Burden*, Western Nigerian Television, August 1960;

Night of the Hunted, Western Nigerian Television, November 1961.

RADIO: *Camwood on the Leaves*, Nigerian Broadcasting Corporation, September 1960;

The Tortoise, Nigerian Broadcasting Corporation, December 1960;

Broke-Time Bar [series], WNBS, Lagos, 1961;

The Detainee, BBC African Service, 5 September 1965;

The Swamp Dwellers, BBC African Service, 3 August 1969;

Die Still, Rev'd Dr. Godspeak!, BBC African Service, 12 December 1982;

A Scourge of Hyacinths, BBC Radio 4, 8 July 1991.

RECORDING: *Unlimited Liability Company*, Ife, Nigeria, Ewuro Productions, July 1983.

OTHER: Frances Ademola, ed., *Reflections: Nigerian Prose and Verse*, includes Soyinka's essay "Salutations to the Gut"; poems; and *The Exiles*, part of his trilogy "The House of Banigeji" (Lagos: African Universities Press, 1962);

"Telephone Conversation," in *A Book of African Verse*, edited by John Reed and Clive Wake (London: Heinemann, 1964), pp. 80–81;

D. O. Fagunwa, *The Forest of a Thousand Daemons: A Hunter's Saga*, translated by Soyinka (London:

Nelson, 1968; Atlantic Heights, N.J.: Humanities, 1969);

"The Writer in a Modern African State," in *The Writer in Modern Africa: African-Scandinavian Writers' Conference, Stockholm, 1967* (Uppsala, Sweden: Scandinavian Institute of African Studies, 1968), pp. 14–36;

"Modern Negro-African Theatre," in *Colloquium on Negro Art* (Paris: Présence Africaine, 1968), pp. 495–504;

"The Fourth Stage: Through the Mysteries of Ogun to the Origin of Yoruba Tragedy," in *The Morality of Art*, edited by D. W. Jefferson (London: Routledge, 1969);

The Bacchae of Euripides: A Communion Rite, adapted by Soyinka (London: Eyre Methuen, 1973; New York: Norton, 1974);

James Gibbs, *Study Aid to Kongi's Harvest*, prefatory letter by Soyinka (London: Collings, 1973);

"Theatre and the Emergence of the Nigerian Film Industry," in *The Development and Growth of the Film Industry in Nigeria*, edited by A. E. Opubor and O. E. Nwuneli (New York: Third Press, 1974);

John Wakeman, ed., *World Authors 1950–1970: A Companion Volume to Twentieth-Century Authors*, includes an autobiographical statement by Soyinka (New York: Wilson, 1975);

Poems of Black Africa, edited, with an introduction and selected poems, by Soyinka (London: Secker & Warburg, 1975; New York: Hill & Wang, 1975);

"Aesthetic Illusions," in *Reading Black: Essays in the Criticism of African, Caribbean, and Black American Literature*, edited by Houston A. Baker, Jr. (Ithaca, N.Y.: Cornell University African Studies and Research Center, 1976);

"Drama and the African World View," in *Exile and Tradition: Studies in African and Caribbean Literature*, edited by Rowland Smith (New York: Africana, 1976);

Abdias do Nascimento, *Racial Democracy in Brazil: Myth or Reality*, foreword by Soyinka (Ibadan: Sketch, 1977);

"Morality and Aesthetics in the Ritual Archetype," in *Colloque sur littérature et esthétique négro-africaine*, edited by Christopher Dailly (Abidjan, Ivory Coast & Dakar, Senegal: Nouvelles Editions Africaines, 1979);

"The Man Who Was Absent," in *And They Finally Killed Him: Speeches and Poems at a Memorial Rally for Walter Rodney (1942–80)*, edited by Femi Falana and others (Ife, Nigeria: Positive Review, 1980);

"Cross-Currents: The 'New African' After Cultural Encounters," in *Writers in East-West Encounter: New Cultural Bearings*, edited by Guy Amirthanayagam (London: Macmillan, 1982);

"The African World and the Eurocultural Debate," in *Africa Under Colonial Domination*, edited by A. Adu Boahen (Paris: UNESCO, 1985);

"Ethics, ideology and the Critic," in *Criticism and Ideology: Second African Writers' Conference, Stockholm, 1986* (Uppsala, Sweden: Scandinavian Institute of African Studies, 1988), pp. 26–51.

SELECTED PERIODICAL PUBLICATIONS– UNCOLLECTED:

POETRY

"One Tree that Made a Forest," *Guardian* (Lagos), 10 June 1987.

FICTION

"Keffi's Birthday Treat," *Nigerian Radio Times* (July 1954): 15–16;

"Madame Etienne's Establishment," *Gryphon* (March 1957): 11–22;

"A Tale of Two Cities," *Gryphon* (Autumn 1957): 16–22;

"Egbe's Sworn Enemy," *Geste*, 5 (21 April 1960): 22–26.

NONFICTION

"An Open Letter to the Western Obas," *Daily Times* (Lagos), 10 November 1966;

"Let's Think about the Aftermath of This War," *Daily Sketch* (Ibadan), 4 August 1967, p. 8;

"The Scholar in African Society," *Nigerian Herald*, 31 February 1977 and 2 March 1977;

"1979: Year of the Road," *Daily Sketch* (Ibadan), 1 January 1979, pp. 5, 13–14;

"The Wasted Generation – the Real Wasters," *Guardian* (Lagos), August 1982;

"Shakespeare and the Living Dramatist," *Shakespeare Survey*, 36 (1983);

"Ethics and Aesthetics of Chichidodo," *Guardian* (Lagos), 7 December 1985, p. 9;

"Religion and Human Rights," *Index on Censorship*, 17 (May 1988);

"Power and Creative Strategies," *Index on Censorship*, 17 (August 1988);

"Nobel Lecture," *Black American Literature Forum*, 22 (Fall 1988): 429–448;

"A Time of Transition" and "Beyond the Berlin Wall," *Transition* (New York): new series 51 (1991): 4–5; 6–25;

"The New Driver's Licence: Rights and Responsibilities," *Guardian* (Lagos), 10 April 1991, p. 28;

Amiri Baraka, Soyinka, Charles Davis of Yale University, and Derek Walcott (photograph: the Guardian, Lagos, Nigeria)

"No, This Is Not a Job for the Boys," *Vanguard* (Lagos), 24 April 1991, p. 6;

"Why I Cannot Support Obasanjo," *Sunday Champion* (Lagos), 2 June 1991.

Until he became, in October 1986, the first black African writer to be awarded the Nobel Prize for Literature, Wole Soyinka was probably best known within his own country, Nigeria, as a political activist with a fierce commitment to individual liberty and human rights. His involvement over the previous quarter of a century had alerted his compatriots to the shortcomings of those in power and with responsibilities. For some younger Nigerians and for those outside the educational system, he had become particularly well known because of his efforts to reduce the number of accidents on the nation's roads. Many people were, of course, aware of his varied and impressive achievements as a writer: he had many enthusiastic and discriminating admirers, and he exerted a major influence on younger generations of creative Nigerians. He also had his critics. Some of those on the Left considered him irresponsible and ideologically suspect, and some nationalists and "decolonizers" condemned him for allowing Western models to influence his writing. Soyinka insisted that his receiving the

Nobel Prize should be seen as an award to the continent of Africa as a whole, but some regarded it as an indication, or as a further indication, of Soyinka's appeal to a European audience.

Soyinka's distinction as a writer, particularly as a playwright and poet, had also become apparent to many Africans outside Nigeria who had encountered his work on the stage or in the classroom. His writings had been featured extensively on course syllabi – evidence of endeavors to come to terms with African experiences – and African academics had examined his work from a variety of angles. Beyond the educational system, some had become aware of his interest in Pan-Africanist issues, his firmly held conviction that African intellectuals should be concerned about developments in the continent, particularly in sub-Saharan Africa.

His being awarded various honors and his plays being favorably received in Europe and the United States reflect Soyinka's standing among academics and theater people on other continents. His work embodies a profound knowledge of the European intellectual tradition as well as a deep awareness of Yoruba attitudes and aesthetics. The Swedish Academy described him as "a writer who in a wide cultural perspective and with poetic overtones fashions the drama of existence." More than any other single award, the Nobel Prize elevated Soyinka to a position of international prominence from which he could make his voice heard on social and political issues, and it provided him with opportunities to realize new creative projects. The award came after a period of five years during which Soyinka had produced some intense political dramas and a book of childhood memories, *Aké* (1981), which had made an impact on many who might never have read his poetry or seen his plays. *Aké* brought him wide recognition but also, from those who take a different stand on social and political issues, criticism.

Akinwande Oluwole Soyinka was born in Abeokuta, in Western Nigeria, on 13 July 1934; he was the second child and eldest son of Samuel Ayodele (Ayo) and Grace Eniola Soyinka. His father, dubbed "Essay" in *Aké*, was principal of St. Peter's Primary School, and his mother, nicknamed "Wild Christian" in *Aké*, was a teacher and became involved in agitation against the *Alake*, the local officeholder through whom the British ruled. Ayo Soyinka's hometown, an ancestral base with which he maintained links throughout his life, was Isara, in the Ijebu part of Yoruba-speaking Western Nigeria. Wole Soyinka spent holidays there during his childhood and thus came in contact with a relatively isolated community, one that had managed to keep British colonial influences at arm's length. Abeokuta, by contrast, was a refugee settlement, founded during the 1830s by a variety of mostly Egba groups fleeing southward before aggressors from the north. The town retained considerable political independence for decades; only after World War I did it become part of the British colony of Nigeria. But it was open to religious and economic influences. Beginning in the 1840s Christian missions established churches and schools there, and it gradually became an important trading center for the region. Abeokuta, particularly in its religious and commercial life, provided an example of creative syncretism that deeply impressed the young Soyinka. His mother was a member of one of the most distinguished families in the town. She was closely related to I. O. Ransome-Kuti, pioneering headmaster of Abeokuta Grammar School, whose wife, Funmilayo, played a decisive role in local and national politics. For the young Soyinka, the Ransome-Kuti family exemplified creative endeavor and political action.

At age eleven Soyinka left Abeokuta for Ibadan, where he completed his secondary education at the well-equipped Government College. After a brief period working as a clerk in Lagos, he returned to Ibadan, this time to the recently established University College to begin undergraduate courses. In 1954, at the end of his second year, he was awarded a scholarship to study English literature in the United Kingdom and took a place at the University of Leeds. He was awarded a B.A. in 1957 and started work on an M.A. He then moved to London, where he was encouraged by the directors at the Royal Court Theatre and gained valuable practical experience. He has since continued to move between universities and theaters, using the relative security of academia to work on creative challenges, always remaining his own man, resisting temptations to compromise and resolutely refusing to remain silent in the face of tyranny.

On 1 January 1960 Soyinka returned to Ibadan to accept a research post at University College and to contribute to the development of West African drama. Two years later he was made a lecturer at the newly founded University College of Ife, and then, after a break, he was promoted to a senior lectureship at the University of Lagos. In 1967 he was appointed director of the School of Drama at the University of Ibadan but was soon arrested and imprisoned for his political activity during the Nigerian civil war. After his release in 1969 he spent some time at Ibadan before leaving the country for visiting professorships, at Churchill College, Cambridge (1972–1973); at the University of Sheffield (1973–1974); and then at the Institute of African Studies, part of the University of Ghana. He returned to Nigeria, to a professorship at the University of Ife, in 1976 and remained there, with numerous absences to attend conferences, deliver papers, and direct plays, until 1985. During the mid and late 1980s he held visiting professorships at some American universities, including Yale and Cornell, and continued to find and make time to write, direct, and contribute to conferences and workshops in Nigeria and elsewhere.

His pattern of employment shows Soyinka moving between the classroom and the theater, his position and attitude often affected by the tumultuous political developments in Nigeria and black Africa during the last thirty years. These developments have included the nationalist movements' agitation for independence; the tensions in the Western Region of Nigeria during the early 1960s, which resulted in the imposition of a state of emergency; the corruption and rigging that characterized the Nigerian elections of 1964; the rise and fall of Kwame Nkrumah in Ghana; the January 1966 coup in Nigeria and the countercoup that followed; the massacres of Igbos in the Northern Region and the drift toward the secession of Biafra and civil war; Idi Amin's and Macias Nguema's reigns of terror in Uganda and Equatorial Guinea; the scandals of the Second Nigerian Republic; the repressive tone of the Buhari regime, which followed the coup of December 1983; and the restrictive elements that, in the late 1980s, crept into the Babangida regime.

Soyinka has returned again and again to particular themes and areas of interest in his work. These have included the responsibilities of the individual, the vigorous influence of the past on contemporary events, and the value of making a willing sacrifice. He has also campaigned against individuals and groups who have betrayed the trust placed in them and abused the privileges of office.

As a schoolboy, clerk, and student in Nigeria, Soyinka wrote poetry, short stories, and brief plays. He prepared sketches for production in school and pioneered Nigerian radio drama. At Leeds he deepened and broadened his awareness of Western literary and theatrical traditions and responded to the challenges of teachers such as George Wilson Knight and Arnold Kettle. He wrote witty, subversive short stories that attacked British insensitivity and ignorance about Africa, he campaigned against the South African policy of apartheid, and he gained valuable experience working as a reporter, interviewer, and presenter for the BBC during the late 1950s.

Toward the end of his time at Leeds, probably in 1957 and 1958, he wrote *The Swamp Dwellers* (in *Three Plays*, 1963), a drama triggered by reports of the extent of Nigeria's reserves of oil. The play was produced in London (1958) and Ibadan (1959) and stimulated debates, which still continue, about Soyinka's intentions as a playwright: should he be regarded primarily as a poetic or a political dramatist? Is he most interested in conveying mood, in exploring the effectiveness of ritual sacrifice, or in motivating the masses to improve their conditions? Is he writing for intimate "art" theaters or for his fellow countrymen? *The Swamp Dwellers* works through contrasts and juxtapositions but shows an uncertainty that marks it as an apprentice work, an interesting failure that carries too clearly the marks of Soyinka's reading in his "World Drama" class at Leeds.

The Lion and the Jewel, from the same period (produced in 1959, published in 1963), is part of a dialogue with the European tradition of comedy and with Eurocentric views of Africa—specifically with Joyce Cary's novel *Mister Johnson* (1939). Set in a village called Ilujinle, the play presents the clash between the seventy-two-year-old Bale Baroka and

the young schoolmaster, Lakunle, for the village belle, Sidi. Intrigue and fine—and merely bombastic—speeches are combined with elaborate passages of mime and dance. The wily Baroka completely outmaneuvers his opponent, and by so doing he challenges preconceptions, not least preconceptions about elderly people. Although demanding numerous skills from the performers, the play has been successfully produced in schools and colleges in Africa, Europe, and America, and it is among Soyinka's best-known works. The 1966–1967 production at the Royal Court Theatre in London was a landmark in the recognition of Soyinka as a significant English-language dramatist. Some of those who have responded to productions and those who have written about the text have been confused by the openness that is a feature of much of Soyinka's stagecraft, and they have been uncertain how to interpret this relatively straightforward play. Many have jumped to the conclusion that Baroka "represents tradition" and that Soyinka is being reactionary in allowing him to win Sidi. Closer examination within the context of Soyinka's ideas indicates that Baroka is a discriminating syncretist taking what he considers useful from outsiders and combining it with the virtues and privileges in the indigenous culture. Lakunle, the challenger, has considerable vitality and some creativity, but he is, by contrast, undiscriminating and infatuated with foreign novelties. While in some respects a challenge to European ideas about Africa and about the role played by Europeans in Africa – there is a revealing episode in which a venal white surveyor appears – the play is a contribution to the debate that preoccupied many Nigerians in the years preceding independence, about how imported and indigenous elements were to be "married" in the new, independent nation. An important element in Soyinka's creative and intellectual makeup derives from the debates among African intellectuals during the 1950s; his writing frequently reflects an awareness of tradition and a flair for incorporating foreign ideas. There remains something of Baroka in Soyinka, and he continues to find inspiration in controversy.

In London during 1958 and 1959 Soyinka made contact with the BBC and wrote scripts for both the domestic and overseas services. He also did some part-time teaching in London day schools. An evening of political, semi–improvised drama in the tradition of the Living Newspaper, presented at the Royal Court's Theatre Upstairs during 1959, provided Soyinka with an opportunity to sing songs he had composed. One, with the refrain "Long Time, Bwana," articulated, in an easily accessible folk idiom, the resentment of an exploited African worker. Soyinka's considerable musical talents include composition, guitar playing, and singing, and the interweaving of musical with dramatic elements is a distinctive feature of his work. He has explored the capacity of music and song to make an impact on popular audiences and has found his songwriting abilities particularly valuable in attempting to communicate political opinions to mass audiences.

In November 1959 Soyinka directed an evening of his own work at the Theatre Upstairs. The first half of the program consisted of poetry and extracts from "A Dance of the African Forest" (unpublished); the second was an antiracist play, *The Invention* (also unpublished). By the time he mounted the production, Soyinka had already started publishing poems in Nigerian publications, and his range as a poet went far beyond the dramatic monologue: he was experimenting with a variety of poetic styles. The program contained some poems that are now familiar, including "Telephone Conversation" (in *A Book of African Verse*, 1964) and "Alagemo," which appears as a prefatory poem to the published version of *The Road* (1965). The program also included a few Yoruba folk songs and Negro spirituals, which helped to define the parameters within which Soyinka was seeking his voice as a poet. Some of Soyinka's poetry is densely textured, highly allusive, convoluted, even verbose, but to argue – as some do – as if all his poetry is in this style is to miss the variety of his output. Of the poems recited or sung at the Royal Court in 1959, only "Deserted Markets" and "Abiku" are in his first published collection of verse, *Idanre & Other Poems* (1967) – a succinct comment on the scope of the collection and a warning to those tempted to generalize on the basis of the thin volumes of poetry Soyinka has published in London and New York.

The Invention, a heavy-handed attack on racist notions, is set in South Africa after a nuclear explosion has turned everyone a pasty gray color. South African scientists have been commissioned to produce a means of finding out who had been "Bantu," "Coloured," and "White" before the mutation. The thin story line, which appears to owe certain elements to Hans Christian Andersen's 1837 fairy tale "The Emperor's New Clothes," does not adequately sustain the satire, which includes American, British, and South African bigots among its targets, and Soyinka has not included the play in any collections. He takes his role as a writer seriously and tries to fulfill many functions in this play and others. From time to time he uses his pen to attack specific targets, usually by exposing them to ridicule, in

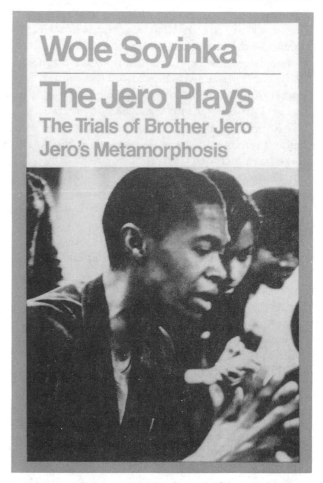

Dust jacket for the comedies for which Soyinka created the popular Nigerian character Jero to convey his political and social commentary

the hope that he will sway the wavering and stiffen the resolve of the committed. He has long felt passionately about South Africa and is acutely aware of the problems faced by the outsider who wants to write about conditions in that country.

Toward the end of his stay in England, Soyinka submitted a research proposal to the Rockefeller Foundation. He drew attention to what he considered the major issues confronting the African dramatist who endeavored to combine the "strong aesthetic awareness of traditional art" with dramatic conventions developed elsewhere. He anticipated the fusion of "the idiom beneath traditional drama" with other idioms, and he referred in passing to Japanese No theater and commended Bertolt Brecht as "the truly modern dramatist who has perpetuated the morality/parable as a dramatic form." There is evidence in Soyinka's interviews, critical writing, and plays that he has consciously endeavored to combine African, particularly Yoruba, forms with the European tradition of dialogue drama. He has published critical and theoretical writing, some of it clear and direct, some obscure, which provides a theoretical justification for his own experiments, has expressed an admiration for elements in Brecht's work on several occasions, and has drawn on his poems and plays for ideas and conventions. In *Opera Wonyosi* (performed, 1977; published, 1981) Soyinka used *The Threepenny Opera* (1929; translated, 1964) as the basis for an attack on the vices of his country and his continent.

His proposal was accepted by the foundation, and Soyinka returned, with his research grant, to Nigeria in 1960, the year in which the country became independent. He immediately threw himself into the creative activities of the country, particularly those in Lagos and Ibadan and those associated with University College and the Nigerian Broadcasting Service. He gave radio talks, acted in a production of Bertolt Brecht's *Good Woman of Setzuan* (1943; translated, 1948), published poetry, performed at concerts organized by the American Society for African Culture (AMSAC), and became secretary of the Committee of Writers for Individual Liberty (CWIL). He also wrote plays for radio, television, and the stage. As was expected of him by his Rockefeller sponsors and University College, Ibadan, he undertook research into West African drama, but writing it up was not given priority.

The Trials of Brother Jero (performed, 1960; published in *Three Plays*), his best-known work of this period, was written, or rewritten, at short notice, in response to a request for a play that could be performed in a converted dining hall in Ibadan. Drawing on his observation of the separatist Christian churches of Nigeria, on Ijebu folk narratives, and on theatrical conventions exploited by Brecht, Soyinka put together a vital and vigorous comedy, which contains a stark warning to a country on the eve of independence and a more general message about gullibility and false leaders. The negative reactions of those critics who regarded the play as an attack on Christianity have not endured. Indeed, because separatist sects are familiar throughout the continent and because the theatrical idioms employed are acceptable and exciting, the play has become a favorite with school, college, and community-center audiences throughout anglophone Africa. Productions in London and New York, sometimes with additional, topical references, have shown that the appeal of the play extends far beyond the continent of its birth. Aware of the vitality of the central character, and of the advantages of using a popular figure in order to make a series of social and political comments, Soyinka has written

at least one other play in which Jero is featured, *Jero's Metamorphosis* (published in *The Jero Plays*, 1973; performed, 1974).

The approach of independence made Nigerians particularly self-conscious, keenly aware of the possibilities for growth and change offered by the change of status. Soyinka presented two other plays to his countrymen in 1960: a radio play entitled *Camwood on the Leaves* (published in 1973); and a national drama, *A Dance of the Forests* (published in 1963), partly a reworking of "A Dance of the African Forest."

Soyinka has described *Camwood on the Leaves* as an attempt to use "the idiom of the masquerade in auditory terms." Set in a community like that in which Soyinka grew up, in which conflicts between Christian groups and followers of *Egungun* (native-religion) processions could divide families, the play explores the relationship between the Reverend Erinjobi and his son Isola. The drama unfolds with masterly control and important local details, accompanied by the effective use of the singing of the dirge "Agbe." In the closing moments Isola kills, or "sacrifices," his father, and the dirge wells up. The play can be seen as a rite of passage, with implications for a nation at a time of transition. It can also be regarded as an essay in tragedy: a dramatic statement of particular importance to those, mostly European, observers who had denied the existence of an African sense of tragedy. *Camwood* contains several of the ingredients found in German playwright Frank Wedekind's *Awakening of Spring* (1891; translated, 1909), notably the repercussions of a youthful pregnancy, but the perspective of the community presented in Soyinka's play is distinctively and challengingly different. After being broadcast during September 1960, *Camwood* lay neglected for many years. Often disregarded by those writing on Soyinka, it deserves consideration particularly for the way it uses sound, for its evocation of a divided community, and for the manner in which it establishes a dialogue between two traditions. Soyinka's own interest in the play led to its publication in 1973 and his decision to stage it at the National Theatre in Lagos in March 1982.

As the similarities between the titles suggest, *A Dance of the Forests* is closely linked with "A Dance of the African Forest," extracts from which formed part of Soyinka's Royal Court evening. But whereas the London production was directed at the racist regime in South Africa, the latter play is directed at Nigeria; indeed, it draws on encounters with the politicians who were about to inherit power from the British. This "independence" play shows an awareness of the capacity of leaders to exploit those they lead, and it warns that euphoria at a change in national status "should," in the playwright's words, "be tempered by the reality of the eternal history of oppression." A major theme in the play concerns the difficulties involved in making "new beginnings," but there is much more. The cast list includes human beings and supernatural entities; the action incorporates rites, masques, a flashback, and a series of dances; there are also references to a variety of European dramas. Not surprisingly Soyinka encountered numerous difficulties in mounting the production. Some of these were the result of extraneous factors (some members of the cast lived in Lagos, some in Ibadan; official support was reduced when the local implications of the play became apparent); others grew out of the text and the demands it made on the cast. As a result certain elements in the original text had to be abandoned – as the existence of alternative endings in various versions makes clear. *A Dance* remains extraordinarily ambitious, a young man's endeavor, full of themes that were to be more effectively worked out in his later writing.

Reviews of the premiere indicate that members of the first audiences were bewildered. Soyinka has claimed that it was the culturally alienated – the sort of people who wrote reviews – who found the play difficult, and he has maintained that "ordinary" members of the audience, the cooks and cleaners who allowed themselves to respond to the unfolding of the stage images without intellectualizing, returned to watch the production night after night. Since publication of the play, critical debate has continued about its meaning and significance. The play can be seen as an attempt to combine Yoruba traditions of festival drama with European traditions of dialogue drama, and the themes of expiation and purification are, with Soyinka's grim warning about the "recurrent cycle of stupidities," central. In a world in which envy and wickedness are often dominant, the possibility of establishing harmony may, Soyinka suggests, come from a recognition of past failures, from suffering, and from a willingness to assert oneself in a responsible manner on behalf of the community.

A Dance reveals Soyinka's ambition and the range of dramatic sources, both African and European, which he can draw on in his creative endeavors. The history of the first production shows the limitations, both human and political, which sometimes have restrained him. The critical response indicates the haste with which some critics reject him and the seriousness with which others take him.

There has been speculative comment about the Nigerian reception of Soyinka's plays in performance. Text-based criticism has often failed to appreciate the delight Nigerian audiences take in watching Soyinka's plays, and this situation predisposes one to give some weight to Soyinka's observation about "ordinary" members of the audience.

Twelve years after his independence-year production of *A Dance*, Soyinka directed extracts from the play in Paris, and reports suggest that he brought to the production a strong hand, establishing a firm sense of ritual and carefully controlled, stylized effects. Since he is an accomplished and experienced director, there is a sense in which his plays exist most authoritatively when he directs them.

Confronting the challenges posed by directing *A Dance* in 1960 did not sap Soyinka's creative energies, and the early 1960s continued to be a time of exceptional productivity. He wrote for television and radio and undertook research into West African drama. Two of his television plays reveal the tremendous range of his writing: *My Father's Burden* (August 1960) is a naturalistic drama in which issues of ethnic differences, corruption, and, once again, the possibility of breaking with the past provide central interests in a play set among the bourgeoisie of Lagos. *Night of the Hunted*, the first part of a projected trilogy titled "The House of Banigeji," was telecast during November 1961. An extract from the trilogy had appeared in the 1959 Royal Court performance, and portions of the second part, titled *The Exiles*, was published in the anthology *Reflections* (1962). It shows how the curse of a dying mother is fulfilled despite efforts to evade the curse by flight from Nigeria to London. Written in a variety of styles, "The House of Banigeji" was on Soyinka's desk for a long time and, perhaps, never reached a form that satisfied him. Furthermore, the conditions under which he worked at the Nigerian Television studio at Ibadan were frustrating: for instance, the transmission of *My Father's Burden* was delayed by an hour due to a power cut, and as a result some members of the potential audience missed it. The importance of the plays for television is that they show a young dramatist anxious to exploit every available means of communicating with his fellow countrymen. "The House of Banigeji" is, in fact, a potentially important text that should be rescued from near oblivion.

During 1961 Soyinka was committed to writing scripts for a weekly radio comedy series, *Broke-Time Bar*, which ran for many months and was a cross between a situation comedy and a soap opera.

Eventually Soyinka's desire to introduce what he called "astringent political comment" into the series brought him into conflict with administrators and politicians; he then stopped working on the program, which came to an end. The scripts indicate Soyinka's skill at putting together popular comedies and at creating variations on mistaken identities and farcical confusions. *Broke-Time Bar* provided Soyinka with a means of communication and with additional income; it also enabled him to bring together and keep together a group of young people who wanted to become professional actors. *A Dance* had been put on by "The 1960 Masks," largely made up from the professional classes. Soyinka wanted to go further and to encourage younger people who could give more time to acting. To his end he formed the Orisun Theatre company, a major effort in the campaign to sustain a reliable group of actors and an effort that was encouraged by *Broke-Time Bar*.

During 1960 and 1961, as a Rockefeller research fellow, Soyinka was in a rather unusual position within the structure of University College, Ibadan; he was a postgraduate student at a time when University College was made up almost entirely of undergraduates or members of staff. The grant provided him with considerable freedom, and he was entitled to a Land Rover and a mileage allowance. During his time as a researcher Soyinka observed rituals and performances in Nigeria, Ghana, and the Ivory Coast, and he attended conferences in Europe and the United States. He also spent some time in libraries reading old issues of *Nigeria Magazine* and *Nigerian Field*, he kept abreast of the work Ulli Beier was publishing on Yoruba festivals, and he thought about the essential ingredients of African, and more precisely Yoruba, theater.

Within Soyinka there has always been a tension between the academic and the man of the theater, the critic and the creator, the analyst and the writer. Despite excursions into academic, critical, and analytical writing, he is basically and most importantly a creative writer, and his conduct as a research student indicates his own recognition of his aptitudes. It was expected that he would write a book based on his research, but the book does not seem to have been completed. He did, however, gather material for a paper and for subsequent writing. The paper, titled "The African Approach to Drama," was delivered at a UNESCO-sponsored conference on African culture held at Ibadan during December 1960 and was an artist's manifesto, which, in some lights, sounded like a research paper. He dispensed with the formalities of academic papers but drew on reading and observation, and on an essentially comparative approach. Soyinka is constantly seeking and finding parallels, both within and outside the field of African drama; he feels similarities and is sensitive to affinities with other traditions of drama. He was, in the paper, more concerned to state a position than to argue a case. "Dramaturgically," Soyinka asserted, "the African is an instinctively metaphorical artist, eschewing the plain historical restatement for a symbolic ritual." Much of the paper was personal, idiosyncratic, and impressionistic; it ultimately said more about his approach to drama than about "the African approach to drama."

In his plays, among other concerns, he is particularly interested in symbolic ritual. The play that appears to owe most to Soyinka's period as a research student, one that is worth more than any monograph on West African drama that he might have written, is *The Strong Breed* (published in *Three Plays*; performed, 1966). It contrasts two purification rituals, one highly stylized, the other comparatively unsophisticated. Soyinka seems to borrow structural features from Eugene O'Neill's *Emperor Jones* (1920) in order to explore the conduct of Eman, a member of "the strong breed," one of those who bear the burdens of the community. The chronological sequence of events is scrambled and can be confusing, but the dramatic contrasts, the oppressive mood, and the challenge to Eman's will that Soyinka establishes help to make this a compelling drama. Though short, *The Strong Breed* stands near the center of his achievement as a dramatist, clarifying ideas about sacrifice that had been obscure in *A Dance*, employing ritual for dramatic effect, exploring the position of the individual, and continuing a dialogue with Christianity and with the Western theatrical tradition.

During the early 1960s Soyinka prepared an abbreviated version of *The Strong Breed*, and that version formed part of the film *Culture in Transition* (1964). The play has since been produced professionally in New York (1967) and London (1968), has been translated into French, has been produced by Nigerian students, and has attracted amateur groups in several anglophone African countries. Its appeal is not nearly as immediate as *The Trials of Brother Jero*, but it remains an invaluable introduction to serious themes in Soyinka's work.

Soyinka combined his writing with his other contributions to the vigorous development of Nigerian cultural life that characterized the early 1960s. He shared in enterprises with other Nigerian literary figures of his generation, such as Chinua

Achebe, J. P. Clark, and Christopher Okigbo, and with some of them he attended the Writers' Conference held at Makerere, Uganda, during June 1962. There he criticized negritude (though not for the first time), advocating that African writers accept their African background and feel free to respond to experiences originating outside the continent. He expressed this attitude by reportedly saying, "The tiger does not proclaim his tigritude, he pounces." Some critics have demanded that African writers should strive to eliminate non-African images and influences from their work and have taken Soyinka to task for this attitude. His debate with nationalists, chauvinists, and "decolonizers" – whom Soyinka sometimes calls "Neo-Tarzanists" or "throwback activists" – continues.

In 1962 Soyinka began his career as a university lecturer at University College, Ife. But the following year he resigned, disgusted at the weakness shown by the authorities of the college in the face of political pressure. He has never been averse to making the most of a potentially dramatic situation – some regard him as impetuous – and has always been prepared to put his principles above his well-being. The struggle for power between Nigerian political parties and their leaders during the early 1960s led to the erosion of academic freedom and provided a test of his commitment to human rights. Temporarily cut off from any base at a university, Soyinka worked with amateur and professional theater groups to bring together a season of plays in English and Yoruba. He began producing plays he thought were particularly relevant to his contemporaries, and he cultivated links with the vigorous Yoruba traveling theater companies. He had been interested in these companies for some years, supported their efforts in various ways, and drew inspiration from the skills and styles they cultivated.

The political and human tensions Soyinka had drawn attention to in his plays of 1960 – such as the gullibility of the people, the hypocrisy of leaders, and the difficulties involved in making a new beginning – became increasingly apparent. Eventually the federal government found an excuse to declare a state of emergency in the Western Region. To Soyinka and other Nigerian intellectuals, the country appeared to be following the trend set elsewhere in Africa toward repression, a one-party state, and dictatorship.

During 1965 Soyinka took a post as senior lecturer in English at the University of Lagos. His being hired was probably based on recognition of his creative rather than his scholarly achievements. In Lagos he watched the challenges to democratic

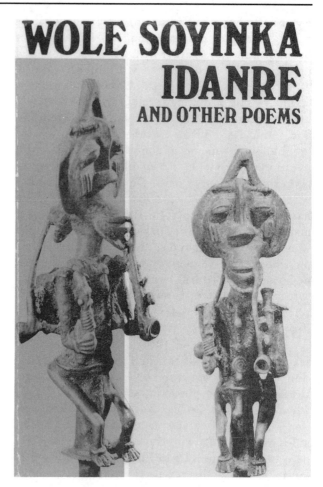

Dust jacket for Soyinka's first poetry collection. In the long title poem he intermingles Yoruba myths with mid-twentieth-century events.

institutions grow stronger, and, because of censorship, he experienced difficulties in communicating his ideas. With the 1960 Masks, Orisun Theatre, and Yemi Lijadu he gave his genius for satire full rein in working on a series of revues: *The Republican* (1963), *The (New) Republican* (1964), and *Before the Blackout* (1965; published circa 1972). Through them he attacked a variety of targets, including opportunist politicians, corrupt timeservers, and cynical manipulators, exposing clearly identifiable individuals to ridicule and providing a commentary on the state of the nation since independence. Some of the more literary sketches from the revues were subsequently published under the title *Before the Blackout* (probably in 1965, though the book is not dated). They reveal Soyinka's skills as a songwriter and satirist as well as his confidence that the writer can sway the audience. His strategy in the revues was to identify and pillory individuals who in his opinion had behaved irresponsibly. Critics from the Left have sometimes challenged this approach, regarding it as focusing on symptoms and neglecting causes, but Soyinka has changed little over the years. Given the vigor of the Marxist school of criticism in Nigeria and the wide distribution of other Marxists, it seems probable that this debate, like that over negritude, will continue.

The year 1965 was also marked by the publication of Soyinka's first novel, *The Interpreters*; the first public reading by him of his long major poem *Idanre*; the premiere of *The Road* at the Theatre Royal Stratford East in London; and the opening of *Kongi's Harvest* at Independence Hall in Lagos. During October the rigged elections in Western Nigeria caused despair among intellectuals and were followed by the arrest and trial of Soyinka on the charge of holding up a radio station and stealing two tapes. He was eventually acquitted.

Soyinka has described *The Interpreters*, which he must have worked on for an extended period during the early 1960s, as "an attempt to capture a particular moment in the lives of a generation which was trying to find its feet after Independence." The novel has a complex structure and dense passages of descriptive prose, which have alienated some readers and some critics. The structure may indeed be disconcerting, but it is also intriguing, especially when one understands that narrative in Soyinka's creative world is only one way in which a piece of work can be held together. He has always maintained his right to communicate with different groups at different times, to write adaptations of Yoruba folk songs in Yoruba, and to arrange a pattern of interrelated events for those, perhaps a far-flung elite, who respond to a challenging work of literature. *The Interpreters* marked an authoritative move into a genre new to Soyinka; and it quickly established itself as a classic of African writing. The novel's momentum is sustained by the detailed portrayal of life in Lagos and Ibadan, particularly among the academic community, and by the vigorous satire at the expense of Nigerian newspapers.

Composed, apparently, within a period of twenty-four hours, *Idanre* is a mythological poem on a scale and on themes for which little in Soyinka's previous output had prepared readers. During the early 1960s he had continued his experiments with verse, and his works, often concerning gyres or cycles of history, had become increasingly assured. He carried over from Yoruba usage a delight in the manipulation of word, image, and idiom that sometimes pleases but other times becomes bombastic and anarchic. He is a mythopoet for whom Yoruba and other myths provide a means of coming to terms with and communicating experiences. In *Idanre* he works particularly on stories associated with the Yoruba mythological figures Ogun, Atunda, Sango, and Oya, and the Idanre Hills, within a tradition that, he argues, is resilient and syncretistic, a tradition in which new experiences are easily incorporated within an old framework. To illustrate the context in which he writes, Soyinka says in his notes to the volume that a statue of Sango, god of lightning, stands outside the offices of the Nigerian electricity supply company, and Ogun, the daring pioneer who made a road through a swamp that had divided gods from men, is regarded as "the primal motor mechanic." Ogun, compounded of opposites, powerful, Promethean, daring, and dangerous to know, is Soyinka's patron deity.

Soyinka read *Idanre* at the Royal Court Theatre during the Commonwealth Arts Festival, in September 1965. *The Road*, though not an official Nigerian entry in the festival, was given a professional production that same month at the Theater Royal Stratford East to coincide with the festival. Actors from a variety of backgrounds took part, and Soyinka contributed advice. The critics were divided in their response: several were taken aback by the mixture of the satirical and the spiritual, by the buried story line, and by the use of Yoruba rituals; but there was a widespread feeling that the production was stimulating and theatrically diverting. A few critics were of the opinion that Soyinka had made a major contribution to English-language theater. Literary critics, including Eldred D. Jones and Gerald Moore, have subsequently written of the published text (1965), and some have become embroiled in trying to explain the meaning of particular passages. Soyinka himself has drawn attention to the origin of the play in his interest in investigations into the transition from life to death, the groping to define the essence of death. He has also said that the play was originally conceived as a film.

The Road is profoundly influenced by a Yoruba sense of the continuity between life and death and of the limits on human knowledge of the universe. Songs and rituals constantly break through the surface of the drama and draw attention to this Yoruba dimension. But in other respects *The Road* is the product of Nigerian experiences during the middle of the twentieth century, and it reflects the roles played by drugs, criminals, corrupt policemen, and unscrupulous politicians. Some of Soyinka's critics have commented on the obscurity and complexity of this play, but others — notably some on the Left, including Biodun Jeyifo — have responded favorably to his treatment of economic and social issues.

While in London to take part in the Commonwealth Arts Festival, Soyinka played Konu in a BBC radio play he had been commissioned to write, *The Detainee* (unpublished). Set in a prison in a recently independent African country, it reflects the profound concern with which African intellectuals viewed the developments that had followed independence in many African countries. The imaginary state in which *The Detainee* is set bears resemblances to Ghana, which Soyinka knew firsthand and which, under the leadership of Nkrumah, had carried many of the hopes of the continent. The introduction of repressive, antidemocratic measures had marked the end of Nkrumah's honeymoon with African intellectuals, and in *The Detainee* Soyinka set out to show that the reality of independence had fallen short of the dream. The playwright's prognostications had been proved right: the hopes that accompanied independence had been proved false. Independence was not a horn of plenty but a Pandora's box full of political monsters and diseases.

Kongi's Harvest (performed, 1965; published, 1967), also draws on contemporary political developments; it combines particular and topical allusions with comments applicable to various countries. The play was apparently inspired by Hastings Banda, president of Malawi, saying that he wanted a particular opponent brought to him dead or alive. Other African leaders alluded to include Nigerian politicians and, more controversially, Nkrumah. But perennial Soyinkan concerns, such as his interests in the possibility of change and in the conflict between the forces of life and the forces of death, lie at the heart of the play. The 1965 production in Lagos seems to have emphasized certain links between the megalomaniac Kongi, autocratic ruler of Ismaland, and Nkrumah. The play is built, in a manner characteristic of Soyinka, around an interrupted ritual, in this case the ritual associated with the harvest of yams, and casts Kongi as a barren, hate-filled tyrant determined to usurp the right of traditional ruler Oba Danlola to receive "the first fruit" of the new crop. Danlola resists the political pressure from the new head of state and supports the vital challenge to Kongi launched by the characters Daodu and Segi. Daodu, an educated farmer and Danlola's heir, and Segi, the mysterious female owner of a nightclub and the organizer of a women's group, arrange for Kongi to be shot during the New Yam Festival, but their plan goes awry when the assassin is killed. Segi then improvises a ceremonial dance in which Kongi is presented with the assassin's head, a gesture showing that Kongi is a harvester of death. At least part 2 ends this way in

Wole Soyinka (photograph by George Hallett)

the printed version of the play; in his productions Soyinka has experimented with a variety of stage actions at this point. And he has on occasion omitted the final section of the published version, "Hangover," in which three of the characters respond to the public humiliation of the despot.

Some critics have condemned the play for what they regard as its disrespectful portrait of Nkrumah, others for Soyinka's failure to clarify the narrative line. (What exactly are Daodu and Segi planning?) Soyinka has also been accused of other crimes with an ideological dimension, of mystification, of selecting an elitist hero (Daodu) rather than a man of the people, and of adding yet another seductive "superwoman" (Segi) to his list of female stereotypes.

Shortly after returning to Nigeria from the Commonwealth Arts Festival, Soyinka was tried for holding up a radio station and stealing tapes. The trial grew out of an incident in which an intruder, angry at the way regional elections had been conducted and the way S. L. Akintola had been declared the winner, entered the radio station at Ibadan and, at gun point, forced the acting head of programs to remove Akintola's taped victory address and substitute a tape the intruder had brought with him. According to an observer sent to cover the trial for Amnesty International, the intruder's tape began, "This is the Voice of Free Nigeria"and went on to advise Akintola and his followers to "quit the country." The opening sentences of the intruder's tape had been broadcast before a vigilant employee of the broadcasting service interrupted transmission. The Nigerian police declared Soyinka a wanted man, and in due course he gave himself up, was denied bail, and, with legal help, defended himself against the charges. The courtroom exchanges and other events – Soyinka went on hunger strike at one point – guaranteed extensive newspaper coverage and placed the playwright firmly at the center of the national stage. Eventually, on the grounds that there were material contradictions in the evidence against him, he was acquitted in December 1965 and carried shoulder-high from the court.

Soyinka is a political activist as well as a writer: he regards it as his duty to take a part in influencing the direction taken by Nigeria. He articulated his commitment to political action in his seminal address to the First African-Scandinavian Writers' Conference, held at Stockholm during 1967. Toward the end of his paper ("The Writer in a Modern African State") he declared, "The artist has always functioned in African society as the record of the mores and experience of his society *and* as the voice of vision in his own time." Over the years Soyinka has taken various roles in national life, and, in statements, papers, and essays, he has contributed to the debate about the role of the writer. The full story of the radio-station holdup has not yet been told, and Soyinka has been reluctant to comment on the judge's verdict.

The months between Soyinka's acquittal on the charge of holding up the radio station and his rearrest during August 1967, in connection with, among other things, an open letter he wrote about the Nigerian civil war, were momentous ones for Nigeria. There was a coup by radical and progressive officers who had the support of many Nigerian intellectuals, but the coup was subsequently presented to the nation as having been masterminded by a particular ethnic faction. It was followed by a countercoup launched by conservative forces, which brought Yakubu Gowon to power.

During 1966 Soyinka revised his production of *Kongi's Harvest* and went with it to Dakar, Senegal, for the Festival of Negro Arts. There he was awarded a prize for *The Road*, gave a paper (on Nigerian theater) titled "A Study in Tyranny and Individual Survival," and sat on a panel concerned with African film. But his doubts about the philosophy that provided theoretical justification for the festival – negritude – remained. Subsequently, over

a period of several years, he explored differences and common ground in conversations with Léopold Sedar Senghor.

During this period he directed plays by local and foreign playwrights and channeled a considerable amount of creative energy into poetry. In 1966 he celebrated the "First Rite of the Harmattan Solstice" with a small, mimeographed (unpublished) collection of his verse, some of which may have been composed some years before. The titles suggest that some of these were written in Yoruba and in the form of Yoruba *oriki* (poems of praise). During the latter part of 1966 Soyinka's poetry became more directly focused on events in Nigeria. In *Idanre & Other Poems* he subtitled one section "October '66" and included in it poems that embody responses to scenes of violence and reports of massacres, which he places in a wider context. For example, in "Harvest of Hate," meditating on the way the current situation had arisen, he writes:

Now pay we forfeit on old abdications
The child dares flames his fathers lit
And in the briefness of too bright flares
Shrivels a heritage of blighted futures[.]

The relatively private response to events represented by the majority of the poems in the collection was complemented by outspoken contributions by Soyinka to the press. Public controversy was nothing new to him; he had reveled in the brisk exchanges of student politics and taken part in debates during his undergraduate days. Starting shortly after his return to his native land, he had written to the press on a variety of issues, including the quality of the first festival organized by AMSAC, the hazards encountered on Nigerian roads, the state of emergency, the need to adapt African dances for the stage, Ahmadu Bello's *My Life* (1962) and the way Soyinka's review of it (*Daily Express*, Lagos, 17 November 1962) was edited, preventive detention, and the sentencing of five northern women to one year in prison and eighty strokes of the lash for "insulting behavior." His poem "For Segun Awolowo," in memory of the son of a leading Western Region politician, also appeared in the press; though complex and metaphysical, it was widely appreciated and later collected as "In Memory of Segun Awolowo" in *Idanre & Other Poems*.

During November 1966, following the massacres of Igbos and the announcements that a group of *obas* (Yoruba traditional rulers) was about to set out on a nationwide peace mission, Soyinka wrote "An Open Letter to the Western Obas" (*Daily Times*, Lagos). He made it clear that he regarded the peace mission as a purposeless charade, a confusionist tactic that would try to cover with words the wounds that only actions could heal. He coupled his criticism of the *obas* with an attack on members of the Yoruba community in Zaria for the "un-Yoruba" manner in which they had expressed their thanks for being protected during disturbances. One of the *obas* responded in the same newspaper by saying that "Soyinka is a carbon-copy of Shakespeare. He is rather the modern Shakespeare of our time and he is entitled to his opinion." Another said venomously and with the confidence that comes with age in some communities, "Soyinka is not seriously wishing to help the country. Being a small boy he could be childish in ideas." In the correspondence columns of the newspaper during the days that followed the publication of the open letter, there were more critics than supporters of Soyinka's position.

Undaunted by the reaction to his first open letter, Soyinka wrote again during August 1967. At this stage the times were even tenser, and his style was appropriately more acerbic. By 4 August, when the letter appeared, Biafra had seceded from Nigeria, there were "Igbos Must Go" demonstrations in Lagos, rumors were circulating that Igbos were planning to blow up the city, and the *Sunday Sketch* newspaper had reported the capture of the city of Nsukka. Official accounts, however, were still talking of the conflict as a "police action." Soyinka's 4 August 1967 article "Let's Think of the Aftermath of This War," was an appeal for a truce and a demand for plain speaking. It was also an attack on those he regarded as exploiting the confusion and chaos: "the now familiar brigade of professional congratulators, opportunists, patriots and other sordid racketeers who are riding high into positions of influence on the wave of hysteria and tribal hatred." Soyinka was detained shortly after the letter was published and just after he had made a visit to Biafra and spoken to leaders there. Accusations were made against him. Although he spent twenty-seven months in prison, he was never charged, and, it seems, he was victimized because he raised his voice in the interests of peace and diplomacy.

Soyinka has described his experience of detention in his prison notes, *The Man Died* (1972). This book should not be regarded as a comprehensive, factual account of the entire period Soyinka spent in prison but as a celebration of a creative response to detention. It contains thoughts about the nature of tragedy; poems; tributes to the resilience of fellow prisoners; and grotesque, amusing, poignant descriptions of people and events. There are also some word sketches of the artist as a political prisoner.

While Soyinka was in prison, *Idanre & Other Poems* and *The Forest of a Thousand Daemons: A Hunter's Saga*, his 1968 translation of D. O. Fagunwa's *Ogboju Ode Ninu Igbo Irunmale* (1950), were published. Work on the translation had been in progress for several years and indicated Soyinka's anxiety to make a distinguished Yoruba novel accessible to a wider readership. As a translator Soyinka is concerned with communicating the spirit of the original rather than with producing a faithfully literal version, and the book provides a focus for his ideas about language and the issues raised by translation.

Shortly before his arrest Soyinka had dispatched the essay "The Fourth Stage: Through the Mysteries of Ogun to the Origin of Yoruba Tragedy" to D. W. Jefferson, who was editing a festschrift in honor of George Wilson Knight (*The Morality of Art*, 1969). It is not clear when this essay was composed or whether it was written with Jefferson's collection in mind. Although sometimes tending toward an affectionate parody of Wilson Knight's style, it provides considerable insight into the principles on which Soyinka has constructed his tragedies, principles that exploit the common ground between African and European experience. Central to Soyinka's thinking about tragedy is the ritual root of the form and a selection of myths associated with Ogun, particularly the stories of how he built a road to link men and gods, and how, confused and drunk, he killed many of his friends and supporters. Soyinka maintains that Ogun worshipers reenact the deity's crossing of the "transitional gulf." In this essay, as elsewhere, Soyinka can be seen establishing his ideas in the course of a dialogue or a debate and finding, within the traditions of the Yoruba people, elements that echo his deeply held feelings. He recognizes, for example, that creative and destructive impulses are closely allied and are found together in the truly creative.

After his release from detention Soyinka returned to the University of Ibadan as director of the School of Drama and took over a production of *Kongi's Harvest*, which was in rehearsal. He gave the production an antimilitary slant, and those who had previously recognized Nkrumah in Kongi now saw a portrait of the head of the Nigerian military junta, Gowon. In a program note Soyinka emphasized that the play was about a condition, "Kongism," rather than about an individual. He maintained that "there are a thousand and more forms of Kongism – from the crude and blasphemous to the subtle and sanctimonious."

During the early months of 1970 Soyinka

worked on and completed a film version of the play. He "opened out" the text, reshaped the plot, and provided opportunities for spectacular shots of Abeokuta and of Olumo Rock, which rises above the town. He played the role of Kongi himself, communicating an acute sense of spiritual exhaustion and occasionally calling to mind President Mobutu Sese Seko of Zaire. Soyinka had long been interested in film as an art form and as a means of communication, but he was unhappy with the version of the film that was released. He went so far as to dissociate himself from it, describing his performance as Kongi as "the extent of [his] participation." The film never made as deep an impact as the American and Nigerian backers, Calpenny-Omega, hoped it would, but, despite dismissive comments to the contrary, it is technically acceptable. Thematically it is generally faithful to Soyinka's scenario: the final image (of Segi's father becoming a dictator) is not quite what Soyinka seems to have had in mind, but the implication, that Kongism has not been dethroned and will not easily be overthrown, comes across.

By July 1970 the shooting of the film had finished and Soyinka had obtained support from the University of Ibadan for proposals to establish a performing company attached to the university and to upgrade the School of Drama to a Department of Theatre Arts. Along with some of those who were to become deeply involved in the company and the department, he responded to an invitation from the Eugene O'Neill Memorial Theatre Center at Waterford, Connecticut, to stay at the center and work on a bitter, sardonic play he had thought about and perhaps partly scripted while in prison, *Madmen and Specialists* (performed, 1970; published, 1971). In the excellent working conditions provided at the center, Soyinka wrote with a freedom that had rarely if ever been possible in Nigeria: passages were rewritten overnight, roles were expanded or reduced, sections were cut, and new material was added. Soyinka seems to have used the play as a means of "exorcising" his civil-war experiences, and it has been described by Abiola Irele as embodying "a passionate and consuming obsession with the problem of evil." However, the play is not entirely bleak. Humor breaks through from time to time, although it is often grim or "sick": smiles tend to come through clenched teeth. After putting on the play at the center and in some predominantly black neighborhoods in the United States, the group returned to Nigeria, where a revised version was staged during March 1971.

The invitation from America provided evi-

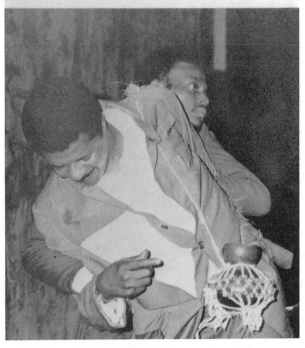

Dust jacket for the play Soyinka conceived during his imprisonment in Nigeria (1967-1969) and completed in 1970 at the Eugene O'Neill Memorial Theatre Center in Waterford, Connecticut

dence of the growth of Soyinka's international reputation, not only as a writer but increasingly as a director. Over the years Soyinka has built up a company of reliable, versatile performers who are in tune with the kind of theater he wants to create, and he was able to draw them together at Waterford, to alter his scripts in rehearsal to accommodate particular talents, and to cope with cast changes. The character Si Bero, for example, was originally a mother figure, not a sister figure, in *Madmen*, the alteration being necessitated by a change of actress.

After the Nigerian production of *Madmen* and on the eve of the release of the film of *Kongi's Harvest*, Soyinka left Nigeria for what he intended to be a "brief exile" in Europe. He was away, in fact, for five years, during which time he resigned from his post at Ibadan and wrote, published, or prepared for publication an impressive list of books: *A Shuttle in the Crypt* (1972), *The Man Died* (1972), his adaptation *The Bacchae of Euripides* (1973), *The Jero Plays* (1973), *Season of Anomy* (1973), *Poems of Black Africa* (edited by Soyinka, 1975), *Death and the King's Horseman* (1975), and *Myth, Literature and the African World* (1976). He also acted in Joan Littlewood's May 1971 Paris production of Conor Cruise O'Brien's *Murderous Angels* (published in 1969). The latter part of Soyinka's exile was spent in Ghana, where he edited the journal *Transition* and was a prime mover in the formation of the Union of Writers of the African Peoples (UWAP).

The energy that went into this extraordinary creativity was released by the experiences of the Nigerian civil war, by the circumstances of his exile, and by his continued, but distanced, contact with Nigeria. *A Shuttle in the Crypt*, a volume of poetry, is a "map of the course trodden by the [poet's] mind" during his imprisonment. One of the most controversial features of the collection is the extent to which he draws on Western modes and archetypes, particularly in the section that includes the creative interaction of the prisoner with such figures as Hamlet, Joseph, Ulysses, and Gulliver. Some critics have argued that the tribulations of incarceration drove Soyinka back to his foreign sources of inspiration, others that the imprisonment represented an abyss into which the poet, like Ogun, descended and in which, again like Ogun, he triumphed by asserting himself.

The Man Died carried Soyinka's fame and opinions far beyond the literary circles that reacted to *A Shuttle*: it was read as a contribution to Nigerian studies, widely reviewed, and much discussed. Apparently it was conceived as two books and can be seen as an unusual combination of a hard-hitting political exposé and a prison memoir, with poetry and literary thoughts. Soyinka wrote part of the book to straighten the record regarding the background to his imprisonment, but other elements in it reveal the range of his interests and the variety of his concerns. Central to the political aspect of the book is the reference to the so-called Third Force, which Soyinka, apparently, supported. The significance of this group has not yet been adequately indicated. Indeed historians and political scientists who have written about the civil war have generally found little or no space for discussion of the group, its political philosophy, its modus operandi, or its impact. Soyinka boldly – or rashly – "named names" in the book, and Rex Collings, a London publisher and friend, took some risk in publishing it. Sales in Nigeria were not as high as had been hoped, partly because of the distribution problems of the book trade in that country, partly because

booksellers were discouraged from stocking it. Some years later another effort to keep the book from the Nigerian reading public was successful when Femi Okunnu, one of those named, sued the African publisher, the University of Lagos Press, resulting in an order to withdraw all copies from the shops. By that time, however, *The Man Died* had become an established part of the literature on the Nigerian civil war. (The court case was eventually settled many years later, and Soyinka was ordered to pay a small amount in damages.) Soyinka's book is provocative and couched in characteristically strong, sometimes hyperbolic, terms. Though these words are not out of place in the hectic badinage that is the current coin of much Nigerian public debate, they seem self-indulgent when encountered beyond the nation's boundaries. The title, incidentally, is taken from a telegram concerning the fate of an innocent man at the hands of the agents of the new rulers of Nigeria. It also calls to mind Soyinka's conviction that "the man dies" in all who keep silent in the face of tyranny.

Season of Anomy, Soyinka's second novel, takes central concerns from *The Interpreters* and selects a new moment at which to consider the choices confronting those working for change. Fast moving, readable, and mythological – links are established with the myths of Orpheus and Euridice – the novel presents claims of a harmonious community (Aiyero), the appeal of a cold-blooded assassin (Isola Demakin), and the responses of the artist/media man (Ofeyi). Some critics have objected to what they consider the chauvinistic presentation of the major female character, to the use of a Greek mythological source, and to the lushness of some of the writing. Others have tended to downplay the forceful evocation of the brutality of civil war and the intellectual debate about the responsibility of the individual.

Soyinka spent most of 1972 in Europe, and during the academic year 1973–1974 he held a fellowship at Churchill College, Cambridge. While there he delivered a series of lectures subsequently published under the title *Myth, Literature and the African World*. They combine lucid criticism of specific texts with discussions that reveal the scope of Soyinka's acquaintance with literary and theatrical traditions and his search for an idiosyncratic perspective. The lectures were given in the anthropology department, a fact that provides an insight into the authorities' attitudes toward African studies and reveals that the struggle to have African creativity recognized had yet to be won in certain contexts. The existence of these contexts explains the polemical nature of some of Soyinka's arguments in his lectures and his attempts to articulate ideas about existence, drama, and morality.

While at Cambridge, Soyinka returned to an episode suggested to him in about 1960 as suitable material for a drama: the interrupted ritual suicide of the king's horseman at Oyo during the mid 1940s. Soyinka was able to write the play quickly, and it was given a group reading at Cambridge. Initially titled "Death and the D. O.," it was published as *Death and the King's Horseman*, and in 1976, after Soyinka had returned to Nigeria, it was given its premiere. Three years later, in 1979, Soyinka directed a production at the Goodman Theater in Chicago, and the play was subsequently staged at the John F. Kennedy Center for the Performing Arts in Washington, D.C. American interest in the play has remained high, and during 1986 Soyinka directed a production in one of the theaters at the Lincoln Center in New York.

Response to the first Nigerian production and to the published version tended in Nigeria to be dominated by the feeling that the concern with the "feudal" values of the court at Oyo is irrelevant and that tensions between the classes should have been presented. In America the reaction has been more encouraging. Despite difficulties in drawing the performances he required from his American casts, Soyinka has found that his presentation of an African society and of the issues confronting it was widely acceptable. The decision to transfer the first American production to Washington, D.C., for example, indicated the feeling of influential individuals that the play deserved a wider and more cosmopolitan audience than it had in Chicago. In his "Author's Note" to the book, Soyinka writes about the importance of the play's "threnodic essence" and the need to avoid the "reductionist tendency" to analyze it in terms of a "clash of cultures." Despite this note, the play does confront issues raised by the interaction of the Yoruba worldview with the prejudices cultivated at the outposts of the British Empire. The movement of the horseman, Elesin, toward death and his failure to commit suicide at the appropriate time provide considerable dramatic interest and a sharper dramatic focus than the metaphysical dimension.

Death and the King's Horseman combines powerful dramatic verse and some impressive characterization with a structure that incorporates contrast and juxtaposition. It explores the complexities of situations, ambiguities, and uncertainties in human relations and refuses to opt for the easy rhetoric of the anticolonial struggle. Some have praised the play as

Caricature of Soyinka by Obe Ess

a penetrating examination of responsibilities and as a worthwhile examination of the notion of honor. Others have drawn attention to the way in which Soyinka "re-creates" Olunde, Elesin's son, who kills himself to salvage his family's reputation. Unlike the figure in the original sources, Olunde is presented as a medical student who is foreign educated: yet another of Soyinka's elitist heroes, a recruit to the ranks of the lonely saviors. This line of criticism frequently fails to take into account the almost inevitable concentration on individual characters in those dramas that are aimed at affecting the emotions of the audience.

While in exile Soyinka fulfilled a commission from the National Theatre in London to prepare an adaptation of *The Bacchae* by Euripides. He had first worked on an adaptation of this play, which he regarded as a flawed masterpiece, while an undergraduate at Ibadan, and his mature work drew on his long acquaintance with the text, as well as on his thinking about the nature of Ogun. He also incorporated ideas from his reading – some of it Marxist analysis – about the social and economic conditions that provided a background to the play. In Soyinka's version Pentheus emerges as a "colonial" figure obsessed with "order"; and Dionysus, "the god of the people," as an Ogun figure. Those familiar with his earlier plays recognized Soyinka's characteristic emphasis on cultural coincidences, on the need for a willing sacrifice, and on the renewal that comes through ritual death, while those who knew *Idanre* and "The Fourth Stage" drew attention to the extent to which the new version repeated Soyinka's earlier ideas about Ogun.

The British National Theatre entrusted the production of Soyinka's *The Bacchae of Euripides* to a young director, Roland Joffe, who has since made a reputation as a film director. A distinguished cast was assembled, and the 1973 premiere production was widely, though not always favorably, reviewed. It was suggested in some quarters – and this seems to have been Soyinka's opinion – that Joffe's production was out of sympathy with basic elements in the adaptation and that the performers were ill-equipped to cope with the demands made on them. *The Bacchae of Euripides* presented by the National Theatre did not mark, as some had hoped it would, the arrival of Soyinka in a major London theater. But the text provides an opportunity to observe the points of convergence and separation between the Greek original and the Nigerian adaptation, and a comparison brings out important aspects of Soyinka's abilities and sensibilities.

While in Europe, Soyinka remained in touch with events in Nigeria, with the result that some of his work from this period is a contribution to the debate about Nigerian issues. In the middle of 1972 a member of the Gowon junta was given the task of clearing the prophets and leaders of separatist sects from Bar Beach, the fictional home of Soyinka's Brother Jero, near Lagos. Soyinka seems to have already entertained thoughts of bringing Jero back onto the stage – a play titled "The Exodus of Brother Jero" had been announced at one point but not completed. The junta's clearance scheme, together with the spate of public executions carried out in a panic response to an increase in armed robberies in the country, provided a situation around which Soyinka could work a play. He called the new drama *Jero's Metamorphosis* (produced in 1974 and published in *The Jero Plays*). It combines broad comedy, at the expense of recognizable types, with a clever, subversive attack on the Nigerian military regime. In the course of the play Jero, alert, subtle, and manipulative, uses blackmail and his wits to bargain his way into a powerful position. He becomes the leader of the Church of the Apostolic Salvation Army and obtains a "spiritual monopoly" in the National Execution Amphitheatre, which is to be built on Bar Beach once the prophets have been

removed. Soyinka sent copies of the play to people he thought might direct it and clearly hoped for a Nigerian production, but apparently there wasn't one until the middle of 1981, by which time the soldiers were safely, if temporarily, back in their barracks. One of the reviews of that production was headlined "Corruption Glorified in *Jero's Metamorphosis*"–a perverse response, which shows that even the straightforward Jero plays can be misunderstood.

While following Nigerian affairs with great intensity and responding to specific episodes, Soyinka in exile was also able to cultivate his sense of the experiences that unite the African continent. There is every indication that he welcomed the task of editing a volume of poems from black Africa for Secker and Warburg, a volume that runs to 378 pages and includes his introduction and about 240 poems, 9 of them by Soyinka. The collection differs from earlier anthologies of African verse and makes a Pan-Africanist point by arranging the poems according to theme rather than by the nationality of the poet. One intriguing feature is to be found in the biographical notes at the end of the volume: Soyinka has indicated the towns in which most of the contributors were born, but he writes discreetly, or perhaps secretively, that he himself was born simply "in Nigeria."

This major collection, the result of wide reading and careful selection, shows the points at which black African experiences in different parts of the continent touch, and it brings together traditional verse with the work of several generations of writers. In the introduction Soyinka confronts the issue of outside influences on African poets and argues that in poetry, as in fields of major technological development, there has obviously been outside influence, which is not necessarily bad. He makes the point in relation to freedom fighters: "To recommend, on the one hand, that the embattled general or the liberation fighter seek the most sophisticated weaponry from Europe, America or China, while, on the other, that the poet must totally expunge from his consciousness all knowledge of a foreign tradition in his own craft, is an absurdity." In these lines it is possible to hear, once again, distant echoes of Soyinka's exchanges over negritude and his debates with those who demand "the decolonization of African literature." Much of his writing over the years has been given an edge, and made more difficult to follow, by being part of a debate or a contribution to a series of debates.

After leaving Cambridge, Soyinka took the post of editor of *Transition*, a magazine devoted to

"Culture and the African Creative Scene," which had been founded in 1961 and had been edited in Kampala, Uganda, by Rajat Neogy. But with the rise and tyranny of Idi Amin, Uganda could no longer provide a base for either Neogy or a publication devoted to freedom. Soyinka was guest editor for volume 46 (1974), and in an editorial he struck a distinctive note, carrying over concerns apparent in *Death and the King's Horseman*:

> Peoples who have experienced the humiliation of imperial attitudes on their own soil must recognise that any pretence towards decolonisation is a gesture of betrayal as long as vestiges of such attitudes remain on the liberated soil. Attitudes are directly related to values. The African people, minus such national leaders as are hopelessly seduced by their own image of the black colonial governor, must know that the values of the outgoing imperial powers must be replaced by an ethnically appropriate system of values and social structure, if the work of true liberation is to be completed.

Soyinka's policy pushed forward the cause of liberation by focusing on the positive achievements in Guinea-Bissau and of Amilcar Cabral and then by boldly exposing tyranny and failure in Ethiopia and Uganda. Volume 46 of *Transition* also featured an article on the 1973 famine in Ethiopia, and a subsequent issue documented the extent of the bloodshed caused by Amin. On the literary side Soyinka published an article by some of his severest critics, Chinweizu, Onwuchewka Jemie, and Ihechukwu Madubuike, and he replied to them in a typically spirited article titled "Neo-Tarzanism: The Poetics of Pseudo-Traditionalism" (in *Art, Dialogue and Outrage*, 1988).

With volume 50 Soyinka sought to reflect the new direction in which he was taking *Transition* by changing the name to *Ch'Indaba*, an invocation composed of " 'Indaba' – the Great Assembly, Council, Colloque (Matabele) and 'Cha' – to dawn (Swahili)." But his efforts were to no avail: stories linking the American Central Intelligence Agency with associations and congresses for cultural freedom began to appear in other publications, and financial support for *Transition* was seen to have come from a partisan American source. Attempts were made to find alternative funding, but these were unsuccessful; *Transition/Ch'Indaba* died. One of the last issues printed a preliminary "Declaration of African Writers." Dated March 1975, it looked forward to the inaugural meeting of UWAP, scheduled to take place during 1975. Soyinka had been an active member of a campaigning writers' group in Nigeria during the early 1960s and had carried on his interest in creating a writers' organization that would fight for

Cover of a Lagos magazine featuring an article on Soyinka

human rights and promote the development of literature. He took a leading role in the formation of UWAP and was elected secretary-general at the inaugural meeting. The extent of the union's activities have not been fully documented, but Soyinka wrote, spoke, and organized functions in the name of the union during the years that followed. For instance, he wrote an open letter (*Daily Times*, Lagos, 9 December 1978) to Senghor objecting to the banning of the film *Ceddo*, and he wrote to Daniel Arap Moi demanding the release of the imprisoned Ngugi wa Thiong'o. Soyinka organized a press conference at the time of the Second Black and African Festival of Arts and Culture (FESTAC), and he spoke at a public meeting called to celebrate the removal of Amin. UWAP came into existence because of Soyinka's vision, passion, enthusiasm, and energy.

In December 1975 Soyinka, speaking on behalf of the Cabralist Movement for African Alternatives, welcomed the stand taken on Angola by Murtala Mohammed, who had overthrown Gowon during the previous July. The new junta provided a leadership under which Soyinka, for all his dislike of military rule, felt he could live and work. He returned to Nigeria and in January 1976 took a professorship at the University of Ife. In certain respects he began to work within the establishment. Soyinka enjoyed a few days of Mohammed's brief but, for many, golden reign: in February the leader was shot dead during an attempted putsch. He was succeeded by the uncharismatic Olusegun Obasanjo.

When, on 3 March, Samora Machel put Mozambique on a war footing against Rhodesia, Soyinka celebrated by writing a major poem, *Ogun Abibimañ* (1976), which runs to twenty-two pages and is dedicated to the dead and maimed of Soweto. The poem, which brings together the gods Ogun and Shaka, ends with Ogun in the ascendant. However, the fact that Machel subsequently signed the Nkomati Accord, a nonaggression pact with South Africa, was viewed by Soyinka as a betrayal.

During December 1976 Soyinka produced *Death and the King's Horseman* at the University of Ife, but the play seems to have been out of tune with the times. The Nigeria to which Soyinka had returned was a country in which the rich had become richer and the poor poorer than before, in which the economy had been distorted by the oil-boom years, and in which the voice of the Left was louder and more articulate than ever before. The arts festival FESTAC, which took place early in 1977, provided Soyinka with many insights into the extent to which corruption and inefficiency had come to characterize his native land. Hoping that something could be salvaged from the occasion, he became involved in the organization of the festival, but he eventually resigned, frustrated and angry. It had become clear that the "cultural jamboree" was being run for the benefit of contractors and business people, rather than for artists or performers; the festival was not for those interested in the contribution the arts could make to the nation or the continent. Although he resigned from his official festival post, Soyinka did not boycott the celebrations entirely: he delivered a paper at the Colloquium on Black Civilization and Education, which constituted one of the less spectacular, less extravagant, and more productive aspects of the festival. In "The Scholar in African Society," Soyinka injected notes of controversy and idealism into his speech, alluding to diplomatic dramas and stressing the social obligations of the academic community. He defined the black scholar as "a historicized machine for chewing up the carcase of knowledge to regurgitate mortar for social reconstruction," and he addressed himself to the vexed question of a language for the continent. After reviewing the debate up to 1977, he asked the assembly whether it joined him "in calling upon [African] governments to commence the teaching of Kiswahili

in all the schools on this continent." No answer is recorded. It seems that plans to adopt Kiswahili as the continental language remain pious resolutions.

During 1976 Soyinka used Brecht's *Threepenny Opera* as a basis for *Opera Wonyosi*, literally "The Fool Buys *Wonyosi*" – *wonyosi* being a particularly expensive lace very popular with wealthy Nigerians. In some respects the work (performed, 1977; published, 1981) can be seen as a response to those who had condemned *Death and the King's Horseman* as well as a reaction to the brutalized society to which Soyinka had returned. The Nigerian version of the story follows Brecht, and therefore to some extent John Gay's *Beggar's Opera* (1728), but Soyinka added new characters and sequences, and gave the work a distinctively African and Nigerian flavor. Soyinka's script contains allusions to continental and local scandals – for example, the outrageous extravagance of Jean-Bedel Bokassa's coronation and the mysterious deaths associated with the marble deposits at Igbetti. Some of these atrocities are attacked in effective musical sequences or in memorable songs. The play might seem to be the kind of production the Left would have welcomed, and to some extent they did: it was vigorous and accessible theater. But, in the words of Biodun Jeyifo (in a review collected in *The Truthful Lie*, 1985), it fell short of what was desired because it lacked "a solid class perspective." This absence was to be expected in view of the indebtedness to an early Brecht script and in view of Soyinka's rejection of a perspective based on class as providing the answer to all questions about human behavior. His response to Jeyifo's criticism, an important document in Soyinka's encounters with the Left, is to be found at the beginning of the Collings edition of the play. But his most recent creative work, particularly his agitprop theater, his popular, satirical music, and his ventures into filmmaking, must also be taken into account when describing his response to such criticism.

It was planned that *Opera Wonyosi* would move on from Ife, where it premiered, to the National Theatre in Lagos, but the production was deemed unsuitable, and the invitation was withdrawn. The scale of the piece meant that it could not easily be accommodated in other venues. Determined to avoid similar frustrations and in order to communicate with the general public, Soyinka created his next productions in an agitprop style. He wrote *Home to Roost* and *Big Game Safari*, known collectively as *Before the Blow-Out* (performed in 1978; unpublished), which provide a commentary on current affairs, particularly on the preparations being made

Soyinka receiving the Nobel Prize for Literature, December 1986 (photograph by Lasse Hedberg;
Pressens Bild AB, Stockholm)

for a return to civilian rule. These sketches, which are suitable for performance in almost any open space and require few properties, follow the careers of some of the characters introduced in *Opera Wonyosi* as they return to Nigeria to fight for their place at the "table of delights" that would be laid for the politicians successful in the forthcoming elections. The opportunists were getting ready for "the blow-out." The sketches, performed by a new group, the Guerrilla Theatre Unit of the University of Ife, reveal that Soyinka still had something to learn about using performance arts to make an impact on his countrymen. They are written in English, and although many of the effects created are easily appreciated, some of the humor assumes a fairly advanced knowledge of the language. Their importance resides in what they reveal of Soyinka's moving toward popular, political theater.

During 1978, while working with the Guerrilla Theatre Unit, Soyinka also directed *The Biko Inquest*, a version of the eponymous proceedings in a South African court that had been edited by Jon Blair and Norman Fenton, and a major indictment of the South African police state. Soyinka designed

an effective set for the production and stepped in at an advanced stage in the rehearsals to avert possible disaster by taking over a major role. The production was subsequently televised and taken to New York for a festival in 1980 – evidence of Soyinka's desire to use the media to take his theater to a large audience and to broaden the experience of those working with him.

Soyinka's concern about his country and his continent did not only find expression in theatrical activities. He had long been distressed by the number of people killed on Nigerian roads and by the appalling risks taken by those who travel by road. In a 1 January 1979 newspaper article he asked that 1979 be designated "The Year of the Road," and he became an active campaigner for road safety, putting forward proposals and accepting certain responsibilities. This activity might seem meekly virtuous and thoroughly uncontroversial, but, in the context of the cross between a racetrack and a battleground that Nigerian roads sometimes resemble, it was no easy undertaking. Unroadworthy vehicles; unlicensed drivers; reckless nihilists behind steering wheels; irresponsible, inept, ill-equipped, and inefficient road-maintenance engineers; and profit margins that depend on high speeds, low maintenance costs, and overloaded trucks make Nigerian roads a formidable challenge. Soyinka has put vast resources of energy into patrolling roads, writing about roads, and framing proposals to make the roads of Nigeria safer. He has composed leaflets and, at one point, was said to be working on a road-safety film, applying his talents and skills in an effective manner. In handling officers and the press, Soyinka's conduct has been high-handed on occasion and has attracted criticism from inside and outside the Road Safety Corps.

In the period immediately before the October 1979 Nigerian elections, Soyinka was in Chicago working on the production of *Death and the King's Horseman* for the Goodman Theatre, but he returned home from time to time and followed what was happening closely. As a result of the elections, or rather as a result of a particular reading of the provisions of the constitution, Shehu Shagari became president of the Second Republic of Nigeria. It was a new beginning, ending thirteen years of military rule in a nation that had not yet been independent for twenty years. But the very announcement of Shagari's victory provided serious grounds for concern. In Oyo State, within which both Ibadan and Ife are situated, Bola Ige, a member of the Unity party of Nigeria and an old friend of Soyinka, was elected governor. Soyinka accepted from him the chairmanship of the Oyo State Road Safety Corps and threw himself into its crusade. He also worked closely with Tunji Aboyade, the vice-chancellor of the University of Ife and another companion of long standing.

In December 1980 Soyinka delivered his inaugural lecture, a professorial obligation. Like much that he had written before, it is stimulating and exciting but shows more of the creative writer than of the academic. Titled "The Critic and Society: Barthes, Leftocracy and Other Mythologies" (collected in *Art, Dialogue and Outrage*), it regurgitates Roland Barthes's concepts so as to make them unrecognizable – merely a starting point for an inquiry. The critics whose works are examined are predominantly those of the Nigerian Left, but Soyinka also comments scathingly on some European and American critics.

In 1981 Soyinka was a visiting professor at Yale University, which had already awarded him an honorary doctorate. It was anticipated that he would direct a new work, *A Play of Giants*, subtitled "A Fantasia on an Aminian Theme," but other commitments prevented the immediate realization of this project. The play, which was eventually published and performed in 1984, is partly a specific campaign against Amin, who had begun his reign of terror in Uganda during February 1971, and partly the presentation of a more general concern with responsible leadership in Africa. It is a ferocious attack on a selection of the tyrants who had taken power in Africa: Macias Nguema, Amin, Bokassa, and Seko. Some of those, from the Eastern and Western blocs, who interfere in African affairs are attacked, and the gullibility of those who are manipulated is exposed. The drama, set in the "Bugaran Embassy" in New York, shares some qualities with plays by Jean Genet and is somewhat static, more concerned with making satirical points than with maintaining dramatic momentum. It ends with Kamini, the Amin figure, turning the firepower with which he had been supplied by the world powers (and which he had smuggled into the embassy in diplomatic bags) on the United Nations building. *A Play of Giants* recalls *The Invention* in being a political drama first presented to a non-Nigerian audience by a non-Nigerian cast and in being so bitter that the attack sometimes proves wearisome. It is iconoclastic theater, nonnaturalistic, grotesque, reminiscent of Alfred Jarry's *Ubu Roi* (1896), and linked at many points with the lives of the powerful tyrants who had emerged in Africa. Indeed, power and its exercise have long fascinated Soyinka, and *Giants* is just one in a series of his works that examine the theme.

Soyinka began writing his autobiography in Ghana during his time as editor of *Transition* and had encouragement from publisher Rex Collings. The story of his first eleven years was completed at the beginning of the 1980s and published under the title *Aké: The Years of Childhood*. It is a dramatist's autobiography, filled with vividly realized characters, neatly shaped episodes, and effective dialogue. The mature Soyinka was clearly prepared to fill out specific recollections and produced an entertaining book with a wealth of information about the families and communities that nurtured him. The apparent totality of the recall should not mislead the reader into regarding the book as the final, authoritative account of Soyinka's childhood: *Aké* reveals a dramatist's recognition of the need to simplify and highlight, fueled by the desire to capture in writing the characteristics of a disappearing culture. The impact of the autobiography in Nigeria has not been as great as might have been expected because of problems of distribution and, until the paperback was issued, of cost. Some of the most important Nigerian writing on *Aké* has been from a particular angle, concerned, for example, with Soyinka's ver-

Wole Soyinka (photograph: Daily Sketch, *Ibadan, Nigeria)*

sion of political developments in Abeokuta or his presentation of women. In the United Kingdom the book was widely and favorably reviewed, but it made a much greater impact in the United States, where it found an enthusiastic readership and drew the author and his resilient African world to the attention of a new public.

During 1982 Soyinka worked, once again, in a variety of contexts. For instance, in January he launched *Aké* at Abeokuta, using the occasion to attack Shagari's government and draw attention to the political violence and injustice apparent in the country; during March and April he staged his early radio play, *Camwood on the Leaves,* at the National Theatre in Lagos; in the middle of the year he delivered his paper "Shakespeare and the Living Dramatist" at a conference held in Stratford-upon-Avon; he also fulfilled a commission to write a radio play for the BBC (*Die Still, Rev'd Dr. Godspeak!*). These and other engagements showed Soyinka to be a full-fledged international figure with a deep involvement in Nigerian affairs and a commitment to a wide variety of practical, academic, social, and creative projects.

Die Still was further developed and, under the title *Requiem for a Futurologist,* widely toured within Nigeria in 1982 and 1983 and was published in 1985. Drawing inspiration from a text by Jonathan Swift about an almanac maker, John Partridge, the play mingles satire and social comment with metaphysical speculation. While not vintage Soyinka, *Requiem* provides evidence of Soyinka's continued concerns and creativity. It was toured with a series of sketches, titled *Priority Projects,* which made a considerable impact: they used spectacle, simple dialogue, pungent lyrics, and effective music to draw attention to the corruption, mismanagement, and hypocrisy in Nigeria. Soyinka released the songs that made a major contribution to *Priority Projects* on a long-playing record, together with a *chanson à clefs* titled *Unlimited Liability Company.* This song was a witty and telling attack on the widely discredited government Shagari headed. The record was sold, sung, and danced to in the weeks before the national elections of August 1983. In those states that opposed Shagari, the record was broadcast, reached a large section of the population, and seems to have become an anthem of the opposition.

Millions voted against Shagari, and many were convinced that Shagari had been voted out. However, he was declared the winner – a sequence of events that recalled for many the 1965 elections. Soyinka's reaction was to head for a microphone: he flew to London and gave an interview to the BBC in which he described the background to the elections, the way the Western press had been manipulated, and the distortions apparent in the official version of the results. The interview was broadcast by the BBC to Europe and Africa and was heard by millions. Shagari's second term was short, ended by the coup that brought Mohammed Buhari to power. Soyinka was initially prepared to give this new military regime a chance to prove its worth, but he quickly became disillusioned; he was distressed by its intolerance of opposition and its repressive tendencies, and he began saying so.

On 13 July 1984 Soyinka celebrated his fiftieth birthday. A symposium was held at Ife, providing opportunities for colleagues, friends, and critics to assess his achievements as a dramatist, novelist, poet, filmmaker, political activist, and social commentator. The Left was well represented, asking whether Soyinka was progressive or reactionary, urging a move toward greater "audience consciousness" and a "transparency which is simple but delicate," drawing attention to his penchant for histrionics, and requiring that as an artist he should go "beyond the rot." The celebrations included a showing of a rough-cut version of Soyinka's *Blues for a Prodigal* (released in 1985), a film designed initially to expose the violence and corruption that characterized the Shagari government. *Blues* is, however, something of a disappointment: it slides occasionally below B-movie standards, searching for an idiom in which narrative and political comment can be effectively brought together. There are also technical weaknesses, which may be the result of the small budget and of having to shoot part of the film under the occasionally vigilant eye of antagonistic political opponents. Soyinka, like some of the others working in film in Nigeria, is still seeking to come to terms with the cinema; he is aware of the enormous potential of film as a means of communication and is anxious to develop a characteristic approach to the medium but troubled by problems of finance and technical support.

When, at the beginning of 1985, Soyinka attempted to screen *Blues* in Lagos, the print was seized by officers of the National Security Organization; Buhari was not prepared to allow the showing of a film directed primarily at the regime he had toppled. During the following months Soyinka attacked the Buhari regime on several counts, particularly for Decree 20, which meant "death by retroaction" for some criminals held in prison; for the "deafness" of the leaders; and for the detention of columnist/educationist Tai Solarin. On 17 June, Soyinka, mobile as ever, was in London, where he spoke at the Institute of Contemporary Art on "Climates of Terror," a topic that enabled him to draw together apparently disparate ideas and experiences and to challenge, provoke, and entertain his audience. (The paper was later published in *Art, Dialogue and Outrage*.) In the question-and-answer session that followed, he spoke about the Nigerian situation and about the future: "The dam must burst . . . a people like ours cannot be held down."

During early August, Soyinka severed some of his links with the University of Ife. A special program of poetry, music, drama, and several farewell speeches revealed the esteem in which he was held. He designed the house he intended to build at Abeokuta, and during the years that followed, he devoted time and energy to the construction of what he regarded as a center for creative people rather than as a home. The end of August 1985 saw yet another coup in Nigeria. Led by Maj. Gen. Ibrahim Babangida, who had been involved in planning previous coups, the coup showed that the dam had not burst, but a sluice gate had been opened. In September, Soyinka combined approval of the first few steps taken by the new regime with advice to the new junta about the dangers that might come from the indiscriminate release of political detainees.

His departure from Ife, assumption of academic responsibilities at Cornell University, and work on a production, in French, of *Jero's Metamorphosis* with a theater group in Martinique reflected the shift in focus of part of his life. One effect of the move was to bring him to even greater international prominence. During the year following his resignation he was president of the International Theatre Institute, was runner-up (to Max Frisch) for the Neustadt International Prize for Literature, was awarded the Mattei Prize for Humanities, and was elected a corresponding member of the East German Academy of Arts and Letters. He also became an honorary member of the American Institute of Arts and Letters.

Soyinka's career in the mid 1980s exhibited familiar ingredients: there were national and international concerns and academic and creative projects. But the proportions altered somewhat since he was no longer attached to a Nigerian university and since, in 1986, he was elected president of the International Theatre Institute. His election was in recognition of his achievements as a widely produced playwright. Based part of the year at Cornell University, he fulfilled various ITI obligations, lecturing and taking responsibilities connected with an international theater festival held in Baltimore, where there were Russian objections to the presentation of *Animal Farm* by the British National Theatre. Tested in the fire of Nigerian politics, and experienced in the diplomatic moves that go into the smooth running of African arts festivals, Soyinka found himself caught up in the tensions of the cold war. In the same year, moving confidently where Nigerian affairs were concerned and speaking boldly on familiar issues, he joined with Chinua Achebe and J. P. Clark in petitioning Babangida to spare the life of Maj. Gen. Mamman Vatsa, a poet/soldier accused of plotting a coup. Their approach was unsuccessful. A month later Soyinka delivered a provocative paper, "Ethics, Ideology and the Critic," at the Second Stockholm Conference for African Writers.

The announcement that he had been awarded the 1986 Nobel Prize for Literature came on 16 October. The citation described Soyinka as "a writer who in a wide cultural perspective and with poetic overtones fashions the drama of existence." Soyinka expressed the opinion that the prize was not an award for himself "but to all the others who [had] laid the basis and were the source from which [he] could draw. It is," he observed, "the African world which can now be recognised." Soyinka was informed about the award in France when he flew in from the United States en route to a drama festival at Limoges. After giving the world press the quotes it needed for the story about the first black African to win the Nobel Prize for Literature, he cut short his visit to Europe and returned to Nigeria. Minutes after his arrival he was informed that the military leader had made him a "Commander of the Federal Republic."

In the months following the award of the Nobel Prize, Soyinka directed *Death and the King's Horseman* in New York and gave readings, lectures, and interviews. He also wrote what he described as "scraps of poetry . . . chapters of this . . . sketches of that" and accepted a commission from the Royal Shakespeare Company in London to prepare a script of *The Blacks* by Genet for their autumn 1987 season. He never completed the script to his own satisfaction, and the production never took place.

In May 1987 he read poems at the Albert Hall about Muhammed Ali, Master Sergeant Doe of Liberia, and Nelson Mandela. The reading came just after the death of Nigerian politician Obafemi

Awolowo, and Soyinka responded by composing for Awolowo a tribute in verse titled "One Tree that Made a Forest," published in the *Guardian* (Lagos), 10 June 1987.

The year 1988 saw the publication of a collection of Soyinka's essays, *Art, Dialogue and Outrage*, and a volume of poetry, *Mandela's Earth*. A sequel to *Aké*, titled *Isara*, was published the following year. The essays brought together the familiar with the previously unpublished, the most striking being those written in outrage, angry contributions to debates that show Soyinka's passionate concern. In the poems, written with supreme self-confidence, Soyinka comments on experiences in America and responds to the villains and heroes of Africa. The poems about the Mandelas and poems that evoke Nigeria are the most moving and powerful. The final note of the final poem in the collection brings together powerful images of fire and rain, which run through many African cultures, and, in the final stage, Soyinka marries "earth to heaven."

Isara explores the world in which Soyinka's father, Ayodele, grew up. Throughout the novel runs the conviction that, though the earlier generation had limited opportunities, it responded to the challenges posed by a changing world with considerable determination and praiseworthy resourcefulness. Inevitably there are parallels with Soyinka's own generation, a group he has described as "wasted." Although set in the past, his readable, fluent novel engages the modern reader.

Much of Soyinka's work since *Isara* has been an attempt to salvage something of value from the failed hopes of the heirs of the colonialists, and the tone of his writing over the last few years is often desperate. Regarding Nigeria's roads, the playwright continued his campaign to try to reduce the terrible death toll, for example, by putting vast resources of creative energy into a program to replace existing driver's licenses with "new national laminated" documents. This step might appear to be a relatively straightforward exercise in many societies, but, despite training schemes, the distribution of free booklets, and a huge publicity onslaught, the program was thrown off course at almost every turn in Nigeria. Corruption, opportunism, ineptitude, inefficiency, and the willingness of Nigerians to allow themselves to be imposed upon triumphed again and again. In a newspaper article, "The New Driver's Licence," Soyinka wrote: "I would be frankly ill at ease with myself if I failed to call the attention of the public to its own laziness, its continuing abdication of basic rights to official crooks, thugs, touts and other adventurist scum of society who prey upon the public's civic shortcomings, even where the crucial interests of [the] public are involved."

It may seem strange to see a poet and a Nobel Prize winner using his command of language to address his community in such abusive terms on such a mundane subject as that of driver's licenses. But the passage is, in a sense, typical of Soyinka – the school principal's son, the poet/policeman, the "angry old man." Campaigning for road safety was a means through which he attempted to improve his society in a very practical and down-to-earth manner. From the words just quoted it is clear that, in some respects, he found it a desperately frustrating experience. After an extended period during which a successor was sought, he eventually relinquished the chairmanship of the Governing Council of the Federal Road Safety Commission at the end of 1991. His resignation did not, however, mean an end to his involvement with road safety or with other attempts to improve the quality of life in Nigeria and reduce corruption. In August of 1991 he came out in favor of "Reparations" – a movement to ensure that the account left open by the slave trade was settled. Soyinka's solution, given in an address to an April 1992 internationl conference held in Washington, D.C., involved a distinctive twist: a writing-off of the debts to international bodies and banks owed by African nations. "Let all debts be," he said, "not forgiven but – simply annulled."

A more obviously creative response to some aspects of the spiritual, financial, and social malaise he diagnosed in Nigeria came in *Before the Deluge*, a satirical revue, the successor to *Before the Blackout* and *Before the Blow-out*. Staged in October 1991 with the help of musicians, actors, and directors who had worked with Soyinka over the years, the revue included attacks on the gutter press, the conditions in Nigerian prisons, the head of state (Babangida), and the violent solutions offered for urban housing problems.

This engagement with social issues, and the determination to continue defying the encroaching tentacles of corruption and compromise, can also be seen in his published dramatic texts from this period. In July 1991 the BBC broadcast Soyinka's play *A Scourge of Hyacinths*, and in June 1992 Soyinka directed *From Zia, with Love* at a festival in Siena, Italy. Both were published in the same volume in 1992, and a comparison shows that they are two versions of the same play. The first is for a radio audience with limited knowledge of the intricacies of Nigerian politics. The second, more expansive, exploits the particular possibilities of live theater, includes songs, and contains a stinging indictment of Nigerian society – particularly the involvement of the business and military communities in drug transactions.

The central dilemma in both plays concerns Miguel Domingo, who is accused of a crime that has retroactively become a capital offense. Such retroactive legislation was put on the statute books during the 1980s and predictably enraged Soyinka's sense of justice. In these plays he is searching for a dramatic vehicle to convey his outrage.

The drug plot is tied in with an increase in drug-related offenses during the 1980s, which led to the arrest of many Nigerian women who were being used to carry drugs into Europe and North America. Investigations within Nigeria linked local drug barons with the highest officials, and this situation is also explored. The hyacinths in the title of the first play are a dominant image in both texts and refer to the water hyacinths that have spread uncontrollably in certain African waters. Soyinka makes them a symbol of the military who are in power in so much of the continent, and of the "official crooks, thugs, touts and other adventurist scum." Nigeria has become a place in which it is difficult to do anything in a straightforward manner: inefficiency and corruption are widespread, an appeal to the public good rarely gets a wholehearted response. Bureaucratic arteries are clogged like the waters full of hyacinths.

In both plays, but particularly in the stage version, the desire to embody the struggle of the man of principle is confused because of Soyinka's compulsion to comment on current events. He seems to be looking for vehicles to carry the concerns of Soyinka the social critic, but that which finds convenient expression in a revue sketch or a newspaper article is not always suitable for a play.

The theater has not been the only means Soyinka has employed to communicate during the early 1990s. For example, during 1992 he not only directed *From Zia*, he also traveled to Britain, where *The Road* received its second London production, and to Washington, D.C., where he addressed the international conference on finance with his speech called "Culture, Memory and Development." Back in Nigeria he broadcast, wrote for the press, and organized various projects. Toward the end of March he launched the African Democratic League, with the stated aim of concerning "itself with state crimes against individuals," and which set 1995 as a "reasonable date" for establishment of "the total democratic process on the continent." At a time when Nigeria was beginning to get caught up in election fever and when local parties were being formed, Soyinka, the maverick supporter of human rights, took a nonpartisan stance, embodying his commitment to multiparty democracy and thereby establishing a platform from which he could comment on events.

In all this restless activity there is much that recalls Forest Head, the deity who guided the humans into the forest in Soyinka's *A Dance of the Forests* in the hope of "torturing awareness" from them. In a speech that shows his awareness of the futility of his attempts and also his compulsion to undertake them, Head says, "The fooleries of beings whom I have fashioned closer to me weary and distress me. Yet I must persist, knowing that nothing is ever altered. My secret burden — to pierce the encrustations of soul-deadening habit, and bare the mirror of original nakedness — knowing full well, it is all futility." More than thirty years after writing that, and after speaking the words in the premiere production, Soyinka is still engaged in the same task. While remaining true to basic principles, he uses his talents, and the prominence his fame has brought him, to address his chosen constituency.

His own attempts to make a way through the "water hyacinths" that seem destined to strangle society has a parallel, which he is well aware of, in the journey of his patron deity, Ogun, who made a path through the primordial waste. Ogun labored in order to bring gods and humankind together, to marry earth to heaven; Soyinka's self-appointed task is similarly confrontational and reconciling.

Versatile, restless, always on the move, Soyinka remains true to Ogun, while asserting himself and moving confidently into new areas of creative endeavor. He is a major black African playwright, a poet and novelist of distinction, a critic of significance, and a political activist who has responded with eloquence and courage to the developments in Nigeria during the last thirty years.

Interviews:

John Agetua, *When the Man Died: Views, Reviews and Interview on Wole Soyinka's Controversial Book* (Benin City, Nigeria: Agetua, 1972), pp. 31–46;

Dennis Duerden and Cosmo Pieterse, eds., *African Writers Talking: A Collection of Radio Interviews* (London: Heinemann, 1972; New York: Africana, 1972), pp. 169–180;

Biodun Jeyifo, "A *Transition* Interview," *Transition*, 42 (1973): 62–64;

Henry Louis Gates, Jr., "An Interview with Wole Soyinka," *Black World*, 24 (August 1975): 30–48;

Karen L. Morell, ed., *In Person: Achebe, Awoonor and Soyinka at the University of Washington* (Seattle: Institute of Comparative and Foreign Area Studies, University of Washington, 1975), pp. 89–130;

Art Borreca, "Idi Amin Was the Supreme Actor," *Theater*, 16 (Spring 1985): 32–37;

Chuck Mike, *Soyinka as Director* (Ife, Nigeria: Department of Literature in English, University of Ife, 1986);

Jane Wilkinson, *Talking with African Writers* (London: Currey, 1992), pp. 90–108.

Bibliographies:

Malcolm Page, *Wole Soyinka: Bibliography, Biography, Playography* (London: Theatre Quarterly Publications, 1979);

B. Okpu, *Wole Soyinka: A Bibliography* (Lagos: Libriservice, 1984);

James Gibbs, Ketu H. Katrak, and Henry Louis Gates, Jr., *Wole Soyinka: A Bibliography of Primary and Secondary Sources* (Westport, Conn.: Greenwood, 1986).

References:

Dapo Adelugba, *Wole Soyinka: A Birthday Letter, and Other Essays* (Ibadan: Department of Theatre Arts, University of Ibadan, 1984);

Adelugba, ed., *Before Our Very Eyes: Tribute to Wole Soyinka* (Ibadan: Spectrum, 1987);

Aderemi Bamikunle, *Introduction to Soyinka's Poetry: Analysis of A Shuttle in the Crypt* (Zaria, Nigeria: Ahmadu Bello University Press, 1991);

Viktor Aleksandrovich Beilis, *Wole Soyinka* (Moscow: Nauka, 1977);

Rita Böttcher-Wöbcke, *Komik, Ironie und Satire im dramatischen Werk von Wole Soyinka* (Hamburg: Buske, 1976);

Chinweizu, Onwuchekwa Jemie, and Ihechukwu Madubuike, *Toward the Decolonization of African Literature* (Enugu, Nigeria: Fourth Dimension, 1980; Washington, D.C.: Howard University Press, 1983; London: Routledge & Kegan Paul, 1985), pp. 163–238;

Greta M. K. Coger, *Index of Subjects, Proverbs, and Themes in the Writings of Wole Soyinka* (Westport, Conn.: Greenwood, 1988);

Jean-Pierre Durix, ed. *Commonwealth Essays and Studies*, special issue on *A Dance of the Forests*, 13 (Spring 1991);

Romanus N. Egudu, *Modern African Poetry and the African Predicament* (London: Macmillan, 1978;

New York: Barnes & Noble, 1978), pp. 104–124;

Michael Etherton, *The Development of African Drama* (London: Hutchinson, 1982), pp. 242–284;

Robert Fraser, *West African Poetry: A Critical History* (Cambridge: Cambridge University Press, 1986), pp. 231–250, 265–270, 295–300;

Shatto Arthur Gakwandi, *The Novel and Contemporary Experience in Africa* (London: Heinemann, 1977; New York: Africana, 1977), pp. 66–86;

Etienne Galle, *L'Homme vivant de Wole Soyinka* (Paris: Silex, 1977);

James Gibbs, *Wole Soyinka* (London & Basingstoke: Macmillan, 1986; New York: Grove, 1986);

Gibbs, ed., *Critical Perspectives on Wole Soyinka* (Washington, D.C.: Three Continents, 1980; London: Heinemann, 1981);

Ken Goodwin, *Understanding African Poetry: A Study of Ten African Poets* (London: Heinemann, 1982);

M. Radhamani Gopalakrishnan, *At Ogun's Feet: Wole Soyinka the Playwright* (Tirupati, India: Sri Venkateswara University, 1986);

Anthony Graham-White, *The Drama of Black Africa* (New York: French, 1974);

Edde M. Iji, *Three Radical Dramatists: Brecht, Artaud, Soyinka* (Lagos: Kraft, 1991);

Iji, *Understanding Brecht and Soyinka: A Study in Antiheroism* (Lagos: Kraft, 1991);

Abiola Irele, *The African Experience in Literature and Ideology* (London: Heinemann, 1981);

Biodun Jeyifo, *The Truthful Lie: Essays in the Sociology of African Literature* (London: New Beacon, 1985), pp. 11–45;

Eldred D. Jones, *Wole Soyinka* (New York: Twayne, 1973); also published as *The Writing of Wole Soyinka* (London: Heinemann, 1973; revised edition, London: Currey, 1988);

Denise Kakou-Koné, *Shakespeare et Soyinka: Le Théâtre du monde* (Abidjan, Ivory Coast: Nouvelles Editions Africaines, 1988);

Ketu Katrak, *Wole Soyinka and Modern Tragedy: A Study of Dramatic Theory and Practice* (Westport, Conn.: Greenwood, 1986);

Stephan Larsen, *A Writer and His Gods: A Study of the Importance of Yoruba Myths and Religious Ideas to the Writing of Wole Soyinka* (Stockholm: University of Stockholm, Department of the History of Literature, 1983);

Charles R. Larson, *The Emergence of African Fiction* (Bloomington: Indiana University Press, 1971);

Margaret Laurence, *Long Drums and Cannons: Nigerian Dramatists and Novelists, 1952–1966* (London: Macmillan, 1968; New York: Praeger, 1969);

Bernth Lindfors and Gibbs, eds., *Research on Wole Soyinka* (Trenton, N.J.: Africa World, 1992);

Michèle Lurdos, *Côté cour, côté savane: Le Théâtre de Wole Soyinka* (Nancy, France: Presses Universitaires de Nancy, 1990);

Obi Maduakor, *Wole Soyinka: An Introduction to His Writing* (New York & London: Garland, 1986);

Gerald Moore, *Wole Soyinka* (London: Evans, 1971; New York: Africana, 1971);

Oyin Ogunba, *The Movement of Transition: A Study of the Plays of Wole Soyinka* (Ibadan: Ibadan University Press, 1975);

Ogunba and Abiola Irele, eds., *Theatre in Africa* (Ibadan: Ibadan University Press, 1978), pp. 151–175;

Yemi Ogunbiyi, ed., *Drama and Theatre in Nigeria: A Critical Source Book* (Lagos: Nigeria Magazine, 1981);

M. Rajeshwar, *The Intellectual and Society in the Novels of Wole Soyinka* (New Delhi: Prestige, 1990);

Alain Ricard, *Theatre and Nationalism: Wole Soyinka and LeRoi Jones* (Ife, Nigeria: University of Ife Press, 1983);

Ricard, *Wole Soyinka ou l'ambition démocratique* (Paris: Silex, 1988);

Adrian A. Roscoe, *Mother Is Gold: A Study in West African Literature* (London: Cambridge University Press, 1971), pp. 48–63, 219–252;

Wiveca Sotto, *The Rounded Rite: A Study of Wole Soyinka's Play, The Bacchae of Euripides* (Lund, Sweden: C. W. K. Gleerup, 1985);

Nyong Udoeyop, *Three Nigerian Poets: A Critical Study of the Poetry of Soyinka, Clark and Okigbo* (Ibadan: Ibadan University Press, 1973), pp. 19–59, 147–157;

Derek Wright, *Wole Soyinka Revisited* (New York: Twayne, 1993).

Taban lo Liyong

(1939? –)

Peter Nazareth
University of Iowa

BOOKS: *The Last Word: Cultural Synthesism* (Nairobi: East African Publishing House, 1969);

Fixions, & Other Stories (London: Heinemann, 1969);

Meditations in Limbo (Nairobi: Equatorial Publishers, 1970); revised and enlarged as *Meditations of Taban lo Liyong* (London: Collings, 1978);

Eating Chiefs: Lwo Culture from Lolwe to Malkal (London: Heinemann, 1970);

Frantz Fanon's Uneven Ribs, with Poems, More and More (London: Heinemann, 1971);

The Uniformed Man (Nairobi: East African Literature Bureau, 1971);

Another Nigger Dead (London: Heinemann, 1972);

Thirteen Offensives Against Our Enemies (Nairobi: East African Literature Bureau, 1973);

Ballads of Underdevelopment (Kampala: East African Literature Bureau, 1976);

Another Last Word (Nairobi: Heinemann Kenya, 1990);

Culture Is Rutan (Nairobi: Longman Kenya, 1991).

OTHER: *Popular Culture of East Africa: Oral Literature*, edited by Taban (Nairobi: Longman Kenya, 1972).

Taban lo Liyong is one of the liveliest figures on the African literary scene. His works are so unconventional in form and style that few critics know what to make of him or how to respond appropriately to the stimulation his writings provide. Some applaud, others condemn, but all admit that he is a highly original writer, with an extravagant style matching his extravagant personality.

Even the facts of Taban's life are controversial. He wrote to his friend Lennard Okola from the University of Iowa in 1967, "I feel satisfied when I say I am from Uganda, and decided that I was born in 1939 – there being no record of when I was born." In 1984 Lee Nichols of the Voice of America said that Taban was born circa 1938 and "told this writer his birthplace was the village of Kajo Kaji, southern Sudan; other East African literary scholars

believe he may have been born in northern Uganda; in any case he was brought up in Uganda from early childhood." Taban told Peter Nazareth that he was born in Uganda of immigrant Sudanese parents. The difficulty may derive from the European partition of Africa, which did not take account of ethnic groupings. Or it may be that Taban invents the facts as he goes along. He is generally considered to be a Ugandan writer, but he is now living in Sudan and says in *Cuture Is Rutan* (1991), "I am not a Ugandan."

Taban attended local schools and wrote his first substantial story in 1955. He then studied at the Government Teacher Training College in Kyambogo, Uganda, and National Teachers College in Kampala. He continued his higher education in the United States at Knoxville College in Tennessee, the University of North Carolina, Georgetown University, Howard University, and the University of Iowa. He obtained his B.A. with a major in literature and a minor in journalism at Howard University in 1966 and his M.F.A. at Iowa in 1968. He was the first African to be accepted by the Creative Writing Program there, popularly known as the Writers' Workshop, then under the directorship of Paul Engle. While Taban was at Iowa, Engle left the workshop to found the International Writing Program, which was to bring thirty to forty published writers from all over the world for each session; Taban was informally associated with this program, too. His M.F.A. thesis, "The Education of Taban lo Liyong and Other Stories," was supervised by William Cotter Murray, an Irish novelist who has said he felt empathy toward Taban because both of them were colonials who had grown up in a village; thus Murray was able to appreciate Taban's writing and to let him go his own way while other colleagues were frequently mystified by his writing. The thesis contains many characteristics of Taban's published work, including the heterogeneity of the style and subject matter.

Taban staked his literary claim with his well-

Taban lo Liyong (photograph: The Standard Limited, Nairobi, Kenya)

known prose lament on East Africa's literary barrenness, published in 1965 in *Transition*, the influential journal edited by Rajat Neogy in Kampala. The lament was later collected in *The Last Word* (1969), Taban's first book. He told Bernth Lindfors that he used to spend a lot of time reading African and African-American books in the Moorland Library of Howard University and found few books written by East Africans, "so I started writing this lament about East Africa's literary barrenness." Regardless of its origins, the point is that, just as the colonial explorers had described the land as virgin territory, thus preparing it for conquest by the European colonizers, Taban surveyed it for literary reconquest:

> I sing a song to Thee, Oh Country. It is a song to thy poetic mountains. A song dedicated to thy symphonic valleys and prosaic lakes which hold fast the people. This is a song of lamentations, do you hear? It is a song worthy of thy modern-music waterfalls. Waterfalls worthy of the inspiration of odes to a passing beauty in face of the overflowing civilization-nursing and time-defying natural streams.

Taban went further than just being a surveyor – he was summoning up African energies to begin the massive task:

> We go hunting. And we hunt elephants, *simbas, kifaroos*, zebras, giraffes, impalas, gazelles. But Hemingway writes a safari. Conrad and Kurtz and Congo trading companies and civil civilizing missions. Sir Rider Haggard and Gagool and King Solomon's mines. Who will turn the record over and give us the music on the reverse side? Have we no Nigerian forests for a Tutuola journey? Is our traditional life blown and gone west by a strong eastern wind? Yet there is a harmattan in Nigeria. We squatted too long to form and preserve Ibo societies of Achebe's specialization.

Taban returned to Uganda in 1968 but, to his surprise, was unable to get a teaching job at Makerere University, perhaps because it was still under British domination. Asked by Lindfors whether he thought his education and experience in the United States had made his writing different from that of other East Africans, Taban replied, "I was not brought up on the Makerere syllabus, the Anglocentric syllabus which graduates of places like Makerere, Ibadan, and Legon went through. I had a more liberal education in America, and of course I

Dust jacket for the 1978 London edition of Taban's third book, which his friend Chris L. Wanjala called "a sequence of reflections . . . thrown on the paper haphazardly"

started off by studying political science and sociology rather than literature. I think I devoured more books within my three years of study there than I could have done had I been at Makerere concentrating on the set textbooks." Indeed Taban claimed that reading Mark Twain's *Huckleberry Finn* (1884) in New York during the summer of 1963 got him interested in literature again. Taban went to Kenya, where he worked at the University of Nairobi, first doing research at the Institute of African Studies – his *Eating Chiefs* (1970) coming out of this experience – and then being appointed lecturer in the English department, which he and Ngugi wa Thiong'o were instrumental in abolishing and replacing with what they called the Department of Literature. Taban was productive, preparing and publishing eight books and editing one, *Popular Culture of East Africa: Oral Literature* (1972), before leaving Kenya

in 1975. The material for four of these books was typed out and completed at Howard University and the University of Iowa, but almost all the other things he published were written in Nairobi. He was so prolific, he told Lindfors, because he was concerned, together with some other writers, "with producing material that would fertilize the East African literary scene." He feels he was successful: "perhaps part of the reason why there are so many more writers now in East Africa is that some of them noticed that two or three people were actually inundating the market, and they said to one another 'Look, if so-and-so can do it, why not us?'"

Prolific he may be, but Taban does not stick to one genre or to one ideological position in any book; his poetry is frequently proselike, and his prose tends to include thoughts that appear to be random rather than parts of developed arguments.

His volumes consist of stories, essays, folktales, poems, prose poems, aphorisms, one-liners, one-worders, call-and-response patterns, and straight-man/comic-man dialogues. But most of his critics tend to overlook his forms and to go instead to his ideas. "He is a person deeply suspect because of his alien and uncongenial ideas," says K. L. Goodwin, who continues, "African poets in English are often expected to develop political ideas within a fairly narrow band of liberal or left-wing orthodoxy, whereas Taban conforms to no expectations, not even his own. . . . He never loses the sense of being a jester, an entertainer, and the fabulation that flows from this role sometimes serves to veil his own true feelings or beliefs in a confusing swirl of contrary ironic indicators. Deep emotion is beyond him in poetry; it is hard to imagine any reader being moved to grief or ecstasy by his work."

There seem to be six Tabans: the singer; the jester, humorist, and language-juggler; the egoist; the legislator, who speaks in two voices, that of the Fanonist socialist and that of the antisocialist; the brainwashed colonial, who bemoans the fact that he is black; and the folklorist, sympathetic to communal values. Taban himself asks in his "Seven Meditations" (in *Meditations in Limbo*, 1970) whether there is any center to his fragmented selves. Taban is a transitional figure who bears no responsibility toward what he was yesterday or what he will be tomorrow. What he does in his writing is deliberately to break what he calls (after Immanuel Kant) "categorical imperatives," linking together the apparently irreconcilable because these diverse elements unite in his being. Taban's personalities are relevant to his writing. Thus his work is full of material from his own experience: his relationship to his wife, his sexual episodes, and so on. Although he once appeared to praise Plato for his large vision of humanity, in fact Taban now considers the Platonic vision of humanity and art to be the enemy. For Plato, only content is fluid while form is permanent; whereas, for Taban, both are fragmented.

Taban's most complete work of art is his *Meditations in Limbo*, to which are thematically connected *The Uniformed Man* (1971) – a kind of afterword – and *Meditations of Taban lo Liyong* (1978), the expanded and updated version. *Meditations in Limbo* is a novel in the form of an antinovel, with Taban as protagonist and his father (symbolically paired with Plato) as antagonist. The book begins, as does his M.F.A. thesis at Iowa, as follows:

The fictional "seemingly true," derives its valid existence from the universal "seemingly true." The univer-

sally true is protean in its essence and in its changeful nature. As such the seemingly true has to try to catch (attempt to register) as much of the changing change as it can; trying to match shape with shape, change with change, pose with pose. Today (1967) our observation of Proteus tells us that he has feigned fragmentation. So fragments we are to produce.

One of the few early critics to have partially understood Taban is his Nairobi colleague Chris L. Wanjala, who did not realize that *Meditations in Limbo* was an antinovel, calling it "merely a sequence of reflections the author makes about his own life, thrown on the paper haphazardly." Wanjala goes on to say, "it is experimental, unlike most African writing, breaking the tradition of straightforward narrative." Taban's ultimate aim was to reach out through cultural synthesis and create a new person. But Taban has not yet succeeded in creating this new individual: all is a process of transition. This continuing process of transition causes problems for critics who tend to have fixed concepts of personality, of ideological beliefs held by individuals, and also of genres in art. "Taban lo Liyong is an exciting avant-garde writer who refuses to be tied to any traditional literary models," says F. Odun Balogun in *Tradition and Modernity in the African Short Story* (1991).

After Taban left Nairobi in the mid 1970s, he went on to teach literature at the University of Papua, New Guinea. During his time there he published two books, *Ballads of Underdevelopment* (1976) and *Meditations of Taban lo Liyong*, both of which had been completed in Kenya. He returned to Sudan in 1978, where he has worked at the University of Juba as director of public relations and then as senior lecturer in the College of Education.

Another Last Word (1990), a collection of essays originally published in the 1970s and 1980s, is profound, provocative, humorous, sarcastic, relaxed, anti-ideological, anticolonial, antineocolonial, antinegritude, antistereotype, and antifailure – the work of a gadfly. "I regard this book as an essay in establishing an African base for all our endeavors," Taban says. He wants people to think, not to mythify. He attacks the notion most writers have that their country needs them: "Some of us are needed, that's true. Some of us are also feared and hated. For others of us nobody really cares." He attacks African intellectuals for their irresponsibility: "When the coups came through the barrels of the guns, we danced like little children for a day and cried thereafter. African so-called intellectual servants have been the blindest creatures amongst their peers in the world." A price must be paid for the blindness — exile, so that distance can put things in perspective and help design better alternatives for the future. *Another Last Word* contains old steps, but the dance is new.

Taban continues to write in his provocative manner. "Culture is *rutan*," he says, explaining that, in Juban Arabic, "*rutan* means *vernacular*, the languages of the original peoples of Sudan." *Culture Is Rutan* is Taban's literary homecoming. "With a name like mine, Lo, or Liyong, or Liong or Liang," he says, "I am justified in claiming Chinese ancestry." Taban may be a Jungian trickster, but he has brought fresh perspectives to African literature and has inspired and helped younger writers.

Interview:

Bernth Lindfors, ed., *Mazumgumzo: Interviews with East African Writers, Publishers, Editors and Scholars* (Athens: Ohio University Center for International Studies, 1980), pp. 46–62.

References:

Kofi Awoonor, "Voyager and the Earth," *New Letters*, 40 (Autumn 1973): 85–93;

F. Odun Balogun, "Characteristics of Absurdist African Literature: Taban lo Liyong's *Fixions* — A Study in the Absurd," *African Studies Review*, 27 (1984): 41–55;

Balogun, *Tradition and Modernity in the African Short Story* (New York, Westport, Conn. & London: Greenwood, 1991);

Ezenwa-Ohaeto, "Black Consciousness in East and South African Poetry: Unity and Divergence in the Poetry of Taban lo Liyong and Sipho Sepamla," *Présence Africaine*, 140 (1986): 10–24;

K. L. Goodwin, *Understanding African Poetry* (London: Heinemann, 1972);

Elizabeth Knight, "Taban lo Liyong's Narrative Art," *African Literature Today*, 12 (1982): 104–117;

Peter Nazareth, "Bibliyongraphy, or Six Tabans in Search of an Author," in *The Writing of East and Central Africa*, edited by G. D. Killam (Nairobi: Heinemann, 1984);

Lee Nichols, *African Writers at the Microphone* (Washington, D.C.: Three Continents, 1984);

Reinhard Sander, "An East African Yankee," *East Africa Journal*, 9 (July 1972): 27–35;

Frank Schulze, "Taban lo Liyong's Short Stories: A Western Form of Art?," *World Literature Written in English*, 26 (Autumn 1986): 228–235;

Chris L. Wanjala, "The Tabanic Genre," in his *Standpoints on African Literature* (Nairobi, Kampala & Dar es Salaam: East African Literature Bureau, 1973).

Amos Tutuola

(1920 –)

Bernth Lindfors
University of Texas at Austin

BOOKS: *The Palm-Wine Drinkard and His Dead Palm-Wine Tapster in the Deads' Town* (London: Faber & Faber, 1952; New York: Grove, 1953);

My Life in the Bush of Ghosts (London: Faber & Faber, 1954; New York: Grove, 1954);

Simbi and the Satyr of the Dark Jungle (London: Faber & Faber, 1955; San Francisco: City Lights, 1988);

The Brave African Huntress (London: Faber & Faber, 1958; New York: Grove, 1958);

Feather Woman of the Jungle (London: Faber & Faber, 1962; San Francisco: City Lights, 1988);

Ajaiyi and His Inherited Poverty (London: Faber & Faber, 1967);

The Witch-Herbalist of the Remote Town (London & Boston: Faber & Faber, 1981);

The Wild Hunter in the Bush of the Ghosts (Washington, D.C.: Three Continents, 1982; revised, 1989);

Pauper, Brawler, and Slanderer (London & Boston: Faber & Faber, 1987);

The Village Witch Doctor & Other Stories (London & Boston: Faber & Faber, 1990).

OTHER: *Yoruba Folktales*, compiled and translated by Tutuola (Ibadan: Ibadan University Press, 1986).

Amos Tutuola is one of the great eccentrics in African literature. Born to Charles (a cocoa farmer) and Esther Aina Tutuola in Abeokuta, Western Nigeria, in 1920, educated no more than six years in missionary primary schools, trained as a coppersmith during World War II, and employed as a messenger and storeroom clerk throughout most of his adult life, he appears to be the kind of man least likely to win an international reputation as an author. Indeed, considering his cultural background, minimal education, and lack of literary sophistication, it is surprising that he began writing at all and even more astonishing that he chose to write in English rather than in Yoruba, his native tongue. His works are crudely constructed, severely restricted

Amos Tutuola (photograph by Bernth Lindfors)

in narrative range, and marred by gauche grammatical blunders; yet aided by a remarkably vigorous imagination, he has been able to turn some of these liabilities into great assets, thereby transcending his own natural limitations as an inexperienced man of letters. Like the heroes in his stories, Tutuola seems amply blessed with both genius and good luck.

He began his literary career almost by accident. In fact, if postwar demobilization in Nigeria had not thrown him out of work as a coppersmith in the Royal Air Force (RAF) and if his own subsequent efforts to establish a blacksmith shop had not failed, he probably never would have turned to writing. In 1947 he married Alake Victoria, and they later had several children. Only after he had taken a job as a messenger in the Labour Department in Lagos in 1948, a position that left him with plenty of free time on his hands, did he begin to write on pieces of scrap paper the English versions of the stories he claims to have heard old people tell in Yoruba. He did not originally intend to publish these jottings; he was merely trying to relieve his boredom by occupying his time in a profitable manner.

But after he had been engaged in this writing pastime awhile, something must have urged him to put these stories into a longer narrative sequence and to seek publication abroad. In the late 1940s he wrote to Focal Press, an English publisher of photography books, asking if they would care to consider a manuscript about spirits in the Nigerian bush that was illustrated by photographs of the spirits. The director of the press, amused by the offer, replied that he would indeed be interested in looking at such a manuscript. Several months later Tutuola's first long narrative, *The Wild Hunter in the Bush of the Ghosts* (eventually published in 1982), arrived in London wrapped in brown paper, rolled up like a magazine, and bound with twine. The sixteen photographic negatives accompanying the seventy-six-page handwritten manuscript turned out to be snapshots of hand-drawn sketches of spirits featured in the story. A reputable publisher of technical books on photography obviously could not print such a tale, but the director of Focal Press, impressed by the amount of labor that had gone into writing out the story in longhand, felt that Tutuola deserved some compensation for his efforts and therefore bought the manuscript for a nominal sum. He had absolutely no intention of publishing it and believed no other publisher in London would seriously consider bringing out such a book. He himself was interested in it only as a curiosity and conversation piece.

Reading the book today, one wonders whether Tutuola's unusual literary career would have been quite the same if *The Wild Hunter in the Bush of the Ghosts* had been his first published book. In most respects it closely resembles his later books, but it also contains a few idiosyncrasies. Like the others, it is an episodic adventure story told in the first person by a hero who has been forced to undertake a long, hazardous journey in a spirit-infested wilderness. As he wanders from one village to another in this ghostly forest seeking a way home, he encounters strange creatures and experiences extreme deprivations, tortures, and other ordeals that test his mettle and ingenuity. Fortunately a generous legacy of protective medicine (in this case the juju of his father, a famous hunter and magician) enables him to survive any ordeal he fails to avoid through cunning or chance. After decades of such exploits, which include visits to both heaven and hell, the Wild Hunter finally returns to the human world and offers his people the benefits of his knowledge of other realms.

The story is divided neatly into seven parts, the opening chapter being the narrator's recollection of his father's life story as told to him the night before the father died: the old man had also been transported to the bush of ghosts many years earlier when he had been swallowed by a one-legged ghost while hunting big game, but he had suffered only six months of colorful horrors before managing to escape. The narrator begins his own autobiography in the next chapter, which opens with a brief account of his father's death, followed by a detailed description of how he himself was drawn ineluctably into the "First Town of the Ghosts in the Bush of the Ghosts." After a succession of misadventures involving tree ghosts, dead-smelling ghosts, and equestrian ghosts, he succeeds in slipping out of town only to be captured again early in the next chapter by a short, stout, taper-headed, hungry ghost who conveys him to the subterranean Second Town of the Ghosts. So it goes, chapter by chapter, town by town, with the narrator facing in each episode two or three major threats on his life and numerous petty harassments until he reaches the Fourth Town, where he is sheltered in a Salvation Army church run by a saintly South African ghost named Victoria Juliana. This woman had died prematurely at age twelve, more than twenty years earlier than predestined, so she has been biding her time before ascension into heaven by performing good works. She had even started a school for illiterate young ghosts, a school she persuades the Wild Hunter to attend. He does so well in his studies that eventually he is appointed headmaster, a position he surrenders after her ascension, when the pupils begin to act unruly.

From there he moves on to the Fifth Town, the abode of the Devil; it is pictured as a well-organized ministate with a huge standing army, an efficient engineering department that controls the fuel supply for all four subdivisions of hell, a correspondence section in the Devil's office that employs eighteen thousand clerks, and an employment exchange

PAGE I   PART Ⅴ   (3I)

The 4ᵗʰ Town of Ghosts

When I left the river which I met the old woman,
I began to roam about in this bush, but when
I was tired, I saw a log of wood, and I sat on it, and started
to think, when I thought writing myself that these
ghosts could not do me harm again, then I
got up from the log of wood that I sat on,
and began to walk about, it was not more than
two hours, before I saw an orange tree which was
far away to me, then I was going towards it,
but before I could reach there, I saw a creature
who was crocodile-like, he was half crocodile and
half man, and he was plucking the oranges and
swallowing them. But immediately I saw him there,
I wanted to fire at him, but before I could fire
at him, there I saw him coming towards me,
when this man was very near me, I saw that one
of his eyes was brass, his left arm was lead,
and his right foot was copper.

When the man saw that I held a gun, he turned into
fire, and running towards me, but when I
saw that he changed into fire and coming to me, then
I took one of the medicine given to me by the old
woman who sat near the river, then I used it, and
at the same time, I turned into a heavy rain
and quenched the fire, then after I have quenched the fire
the man then changed into a big snake which was
114 feet long and 7 feet diameter. then I myself
turned into a long and thick stick, and I began to
beat the snake, but when I nearly kill
him, he turned into a big tree, then I myself
turned into an ax, and I began to cut this tree,
but when it was nearly to fall down, he changed into a
very thick smoke, and covered me so that, I could hardly
breathe, then I myself changed to a strong breeze

72

Page from the manuscript for The Wild Hunter in the Bush of the Ghosts, *which Tutuola wrote in the late 1940s but did not publish until 1982 (by permission of Amos Tutuola)* office that keeps extensive records on all sinners, both human and ghostly. Tutuola's vision of hell as a vast bureaucracy is one of the most entertaining conceptions in the whole story – something no doubt inspired by the government offices in Lagos with which his job brought him into regular contact. In this comically Kafkaesque underworld there is even a Labour Headquarters run by a commissioner named "Death," who is "the Devil's Cousin."

The final stop for the Wild Hunter is heaven, which, despite its "Glorious Technicolors" and busy orchestras, is a mild letdown for the reader after the hilarious vibrancy of hell. Though the Wild Hunter is still a living human being, he gains admission to heaven through the intervention of his old friend and mentor Victoria Juliana, who gives him a grand tour of the facilities before arranging his split-second return trip to Earth. Then, just before bringing his story to an appropriate moral conclusion, the Wild Hunter pauses briefly for a commercial: he announces that he will transmit written messages via Victoria Juliana to any dead person in heaven the reader may wish to contact, if the reader will be careful to print the name of the person or persons clearly in capital letters on the back of an envelope containing the message and enclose this envelope in another along with a five-shilling postal order or money order to cover expenses. The second envelope should be addressed to:

> THE "WILD-HUNTER"
> c/o AMOS TUTUOLA
> 35, VAUGHAN STREET
> EBUTTE-METTA (LAGOS) NIGERIA.

The Wild Hunter had made a similar offer just after leaving hell. Any reader who wanted to find out if his or her name was included in the Devil's records office (thereby indicating that the person was classified a sinner and would ultimately wind up in hell) could follow the same procedure, addressing the inserted envelope to:

> His Majesty's the King of the Hell,
> 17896, Woe Lane,
> 5th Town of Ghosts,
> Bush of Ghosts,
> Hell,

and mailing the entire packet and five-shilling fee to the same address in Ebutte-Metta.

Anyone familiar with Tutuola's other works will recognize in this synopsis some features that place *The Wild Hunter in the Bush of the Ghosts* in the same distinctive narrative tradition. First there is the monomythic, cyclical structure of the story, involving a departure, an initiation, and a return. Then there is the loosely coordinated internal structure, the result of a concatenation of discrete fictive units strung together in an almost random order on the lifeline of a fabulous hero. The hero is a composite of the most popular folktale protagonists – hunter, magician, trickster, superman, and culture hero – and some of the adventures he relates closely resemble episodes in well-known Yoruba yarns (for example, a half-bodied ghost, similar to the half-bodied child found not only in folktales but also in Tutuola's *The Palm-Wine Drinkard* [1952], torments the Wild Hunter before he gets to the Fifth Town of Ghosts). Moreover, certain motifs, such as the facile shifting of bodily shapes, the contests between rival magicians, and the encounters with monsters, mutants, and multiform ghosts, clearly derive from oral tradition. The story is a collage of borrowed materials put together in an eclectic manner by a resourceful raconteur working well within the conventions governing oral storytelling.

Yet there are signs of literary influences, too. The narrative frame – a hunter's memoirs prefaced by a brief biography of the hunter's father – appears to have been inspired by D. O. Fagunwa's *Ogboju ode ninu igbo irunmale* (1938), which uses the same device. Indeed, the title of Tutuola's story is close to Fagunwa's "The Brave Hunter in the Forest of Four Hundred Spirits" (a literal translation of *Ogboju ode*), suggesting a strong kindred relationship between the texts, possibly bordering on plagiarism. In any case, no one could deny that they belong to the same family of letters.

Certainly there are striking similarities in some of the events recounted. For instance, in the course of fighting with a fierce ghost in the First Town of Ghosts, Tutuola's Wild Hunter breaks his cutlass on his adversary's body and the ghost calmly repairs it and returns it to him so they can resume their battle; Fagunwa's Akara-Ogun is offered the same strange courtesy in his duel with Agbako, a monster he meets in his first sojourn to Irunmale. Next the Wild Hunter is victimized by a ghost who mounts and rides him as a horse; so is Akara-Ogun. Both books tell of encounters with one-legged ghosts, four-headed ghosts, ghosts who want to learn how to cook, and ghosts with major social and psychological problems. Furthermore, there are suggestive resemblances between parts of Tutuola's story and parts of Fagunwa's second novel, *Igbo Olodumare*, published in 1948, apparently the year Tutuola began writing. Such a plethora of motific parallels, added to the structural similarities, establishes beyond doubt that Fagunwa had an important formative influence on Tutuola's mode of writing. Both writers made extensive use of the techniques and materials of indigenous oral lore, but Tutuola appears to have learned from Fagunwa how to transmute this oral art into written art.

And Fagunwa was not his only teacher. Tutuola had also read John Bunyan's *Pilgrim's Progress* (two volumes, 1678, 1684) and *The Arabian Nights*, classic adventure stories fabricated out of a chain of old tales loosely linked together. Events in Bunyan's narrative, such as Christian's fight with the monster Apollyon; Christian's scalings of the Hill Difficulty and the Delectable Mountains; and his visits to Vanity Fair, Doubting Castle, the Palace Beautiful, and the Celestial City may have served as distant models for some of the Wild Hunter's peripatetic adventures. Certainly there is the same element of restless questing, with the pilgrim either struggling against fearsome adversaries or learning the ways of God, the Devil, and humankind through discussions with helpful advisers. At one point even the Wild Hunter turns evangelist when he meets a ghost named Woe, who had been expelled from heaven for bad behavior and punished in hell for sixty-five years before being rusticated to the Third Town of Ghosts to live for eternity among the "wild beasts, poisonous snakes and scorpions": "After the ghost related his story like that, I was very sorry for him, and I advised him that if he could change his bad character, the God Almighty may take you away from these punishments, but he said immediately, that he could not change his bad character . . . and he said he was waiting for more punishments from God." When the Wild Hunter offers this ghost a drink of water to slake his thirst, the ghost consumes no more than two drops before being transformed into a little hill near the way to heaven. The Wild Hunter decides to write the ghost's name on the hill "for . . . bad ghosts to see whenever they would pass, and as a remembrance."

This vignette illustrates one point of difference between *The Wild Hunter in the Bush of the Ghosts* and the books Tutuola later wrote: missionary Christianity is a major theme in Tutuola's earliest writing. Although this theme was to resurface in some of his later works — as in the well-known episode in *My Life in the Bush of Ghosts* (1954) in which the narrator meets his dead cousin who has established in the Tenth Town of Ghosts a successful Methodist church with more than a thousand provincial branches over which he presides as bishop at annual synod meetings — Ulli Beier was right to

Caricature of Tutuola by Obe Ess

note that Tutuola is not the Christian moralist that Fagunwa was. Nevertheless, Tutuola started from a position much closer to Fagunwa spiritually than has hitherto been recognized. They both began as didactic writers combining Christian theology with traditional Yoruba moral wisdom, but Tutuola, after initially following Fagunwa's example in Africanizing Bunyan, returned to more indigenous sources of artistic inspiration and wrote less-homiletic secular sagas.

Another exceptional feature of *The Wild Hunter in the Bush of the Ghosts* is what might be termed its autobiographical content. Tutuola had attended a Salvation Army school, had served briefly in a branch of the military service, and was working in a government office in Lagos while writing this story. It is not surprising, then, to find him inserting in his narrative fairly elaborate descriptions of Victoria Juliana's school, the Devil's army, and the crowded offices of hell. He was obviously using his own first-hand experience of such places as the basis for his fantasies. The story may thus be said to have a greater fidelity to actual circumstances and scenes in terrestrial life than is usually the case in Tutuola's fiction: readers are still in an imaginary garden, but it appears to have some freakishly real toads in it.

Yet it must be admitted that *The Wild Hunter in the Bush of the Ghosts* is neither Tutuola's most interesting narrative nor his most accomplished. Crudities abound, and there are moments when spectacularly outlandish happenings are robbed of imaginative intensity by colorless narration. The tale is obviously the work of a novice writer, in this case an apprentice craftsman with no formal training. Had it been published earlier, it would not have generated the same excitement among readers overseas as did his next narrative, a bizarre yarn with the improbable title *The Palm-Wine Drinkard and His Dead Palm-Wine Tapster in the Deads' Town.*

Tutuola was lucky to get this second story published and luckier still that it happened to become a commercial success. Tutuola had originally submitted the manuscript to Lutterworth Press, a missionary publisher for the United Society for Christian Literature, in response to an advertisement in a Nigerian magazine listing books Lutterworth had published by African authors. Two of the editors at Lutterworth were intrigued by the story and passed it on first to an educational publisher, Thomas Nelson and Sons, who rejected it outright, and then to Faber and Faber, who had the courage to publish it in May 1952. The book might have sunk rapidly into obscurity had it not been enthusiastically reviewed a few weeks later by Dylan Thomas in the *Observer* (6 July 1952). Within a year Grove Press published an American edition, which won similar acclaim, and neither edition has gone out of print. By 1978 more than ninety thousand copies of *The Palm-Wine Drinkard* had been sold.

In Nigeria, however, Tutuola's writing did not get such a friendly reception. Educated Nigerians were shocked to learn that a book written in substandard English by a lowly Lagos messenger was being lionized abroad, and they were contemptuous of Tutuola's efforts when they saw that he had borrowed heavily from both oral tradition and the works of Fagunwa. Some Yoruba readers went so far as to say he had plagiarized from these sources, creating nothing startlingly new or original in the process and often mangling the best of the material he forged. To them he was not a naive, native genius endowed with a protean imagination but rather a bungling literary burglar with no imagination at all.

The book that sparked such controversy was summarized by Thomas as a "brief, thronged, grisly and bewitching story, or series of stories . . . about the journey of an expert and devoted palmwine drinkard through a nightmare of indescribable adventures, all simply and carefully described, in the spirit-bristling bush. From the age of ten he drank 225 kegs a day, and wished to do nothing else; he knew what was good for him, it was just what the witch-doctor ordered. But when his tapster fell from a tree and died, and as, naturally, he himself 'did not satisfy with water as with palm-wine,' he set out to search for the tapster in Deads' Town."

The Palm-Wine Drinkard is pure fantasy, a voyage of the imagination into a never-never land of magic, marvels, and monsters. But the beings and doings in this fantasy world are not entirely unfamiliar. The journey to the land of the dead, the abnormal conception, the monstrous child, the enormous drinking capacity, the all-providing magical object, the tree spirits, the personifications, the fabulous monsters — these are standard materials of oral tradition, the stuff of which folktales are made.

The drinker himself appears at first to be an unpromising hero. He has, after all, done nothing but drink palm wine all his life. But once he starts on his journey to Deads' Town, his extraordinary cleverness and unusual powers of endurance enable him to circumvent or survive numerous misadventures. He carries with him a substantial supply of juju so he can transform himself at will whenever he gets into a tight corner. However, even though he is part trickster, part magician, and part superman, he cannot overcome every adversary or extricate himself from every difficult situation; supernatural helpers have to come to his assistance from time to time. Eventually he finds his tapster in Deads' Town but cannot persuade him to reenter the world of the "alives." The drinker and his wife leave Deads' Town and, several adventures later, arrive home only to discover that their people are starving. Heaven and Land have had a bitter quarrel, and Heaven has refused to send rain to Land. The ensuing drought and famine have killed millions. The drinker springs into action and in a short time manages to feed the remaining multitudes, settle the cosmic dispute, end the drought and famine, and restore the world to normal functioning order. The unpromising hero, who had set out on his quest with limited powers and purely selfish ambitions, becomes in the end a miracle worker, the savior and benefactor of all humankind. He changes, in other words, from a typical folktale hero into a typical epic hero. Such a change does not take him outside the stream of oral tradition.

Many of the folktales Tutuola uses in *The*

drinkard

I was a palm-wine ~~drinkard~~ since I was a boy of ten years of age, I had no other work more than to drink palm-wine in my life. In those days we did not know other money, except COWRIES, so that everything was very cheap, and my father was the richest man in our town.

My father got eight children and I was the eldest among them, all of the rest were hard workers, but I myself was an expert palm-wine drinkard, I was drinking palm-wine from morning till night and from night till morning. By that time I could not drink ordinary water at all except palm-wine.

But when my father noticed that I could not do any work more than to drink, he engaged an expert palm-wine tapster for me; he had no other work more than to tap palm-wine every day.

So my father gave me a palm-tree farm which was nine miles square and it contained 560,000 palm-trees, and this palm-wine tapster was tapping one hundred and fifty kegs of palm-wine every morning, but before 2 o'clock p. m., I would have drunk all of it, after that he would go and tap another 75 kegs in the evening which I would be drinking till morning. So my friends were uncountable by that time and they were drinking palm-wine with me from morning till a late hour in the night. But when my palm-wine tapster completed the period of 15 years that he was tapping the palm-wine for me, then my father died suddenly. and when it was the 6th month that my father had died, the tapster went to th

Page from the manuscript for The Palm-Wine Drinkard and His Dead Palm-Wine Tapster in the Deads' Town *(by permission of Amos Tutuola; Harry Ransom Humanities Research Center, University of Texas at Austin)*

Palm-Wine Drinkard exist in Yoruba oral tradition. Any sizable collection of Yoruba tales will yield parallels, and some of Tutuola's most striking episodes can be found in more than one collection. For example, the celebrated passage in which a "beautiful complete gentleman" lures a lady deep into the forest and then dismembers himself, returning the hired parts of his body to their owners and paying rent until he is reduced to a humming skull, appears in at least seven different versions in Yoruba folktale collections. There are almost as many texts of the incident of the all-providing magical object, which produces first an abundance of food and later an abundance of whips. Many other tales and motifs in Tutuola's book — the quarrel between heaven and earth, the carrying of a sacrifice to heaven, the tiny creature that makes newly cleared fields sprout weeds, the enfant terrible, and the magical transformations — can be documented as traditional among the Yoruba. Some cannot be so documented, but Adeboye Babalola, a prominent Yoruba scholar, writes in "Yoruba Folktales" (*Black Orpheus*, 1965) that "the Yoruba are lovers of the marvellous, the awe-inspiring, the weird, the eerie. It is a small minority of [Yoruba] folk-tales that concern human beings only. The great majority of the tales feature human beings, animals behaving like humans, and often also superhuman beings: demons, ogres, deities." Further confirmation of Tutuola's debt to Yoruba oral tradition comes from Yoruba critics who insist that his stories are well known.

The tales are known not only in Yorubaland but throughout West Africa. The distinguished anthropologist Melville J. Herskovits remarks in his introduction to *Dahomean Narrative*, a 1958 collection of folktales from Dahomey (now the republic of Benin), that "it will be instructive for one who reads the narratives in this volume to go to Tutuola's books with the motifs and orientations of the tales given here in mind. He will find them all." Though this is certainly an overstatement, it serves to emphasize the fact that folktales known to the Yoruba are known to other West African peoples as well. Tutuola's tale of the self-dismembering "complete gentleman," for example, has been found not only among the Fon but also among the Igbo and Ibibio of Nigeria and the Krio of Sierra Leone. According to critic Jack Berry, the tale of the magical food-and-whips producer is widely distributed in West Africa, as are tales of ogres and other supernatural beings. Alice Werner, in her 1964 study of African mythology, reports that stories of people who have penetrated into the world of ghosts and returned "are not uncommon" and that shape-shifting transformations are not only present in many folktales but also "are believed in as actual occurrences at the present day." Thus *The Palm-Wine Drinkard*, a lineal descendant of Yoruba oral tradition, hails from a large extended family of West African oral traditions.

What has been said about *The Palm-Wine Drinkard* also applies to Tutuola's other books, for his method and content have not changed much over the years. The quest pattern basic to his fiction has already been described; though Tutuola varies this pattern from book to book, he never abandons it entirely. He never chooses a totally different pattern. One suspects that his roots in oral tradition run so deep that he knows of no other way to compose book-length fiction.

Nevertheless, minor changes in Tutuola's writing are worth noting, for they reveal that though Tutuola has not moved any great distance from where he was in 1948, when he began writing *The Palm-Wine Drinkard*, he has not been standing still all these years. His most radical departure from the quest pattern is in *My Life in the Bush of Ghosts*, which opens with its narrator/hero, a boy of seven, being maltreated and abandoned by his stepmothers, separated from his older brother, and left to wander in the bush during a tribal war. Frightened by the sounds of gunfire and unable to distinguish between bad and good, he enters the Bush of Ghosts and spends the next twenty-four years wandering in an African spirit world replete with towns, kings, civic ceremonies, festivals, law courts, and even his cousin's Methodist church. He has experiences both harrowing and happy, and at one point he considers taking up permanent residence in the Tenth Town of Ghosts with his dead cousin, but he cannot bring himself to do it because he keeps longing to return to his earthly home. In this respect he resembles the protagonist of *The Wild Hunter in the Bush of the Ghosts*. And like the deus ex machina that appears at the end of that story, eventually a "Television-handed ghostess" turns up and helps the young man to escape so that he is reunited with his mother and brother and begins to lead a more normal life.

Obviously the hero's journey cannot really be termed a quest. Harold R. Collins describes it as a "West African Odyssey," and Gerald Moore sees it as "a kind of extended Initiation or 'rite of passage' ... or Purgatory [in which the] initiation of the boy-hero is not sought, but is imposed upon him as the price of his development into full understanding." Both of these interpretations are apt, but they presuppose a degree of premeditation, of careful organization and methodical development, which cannot be found in the story. Again the plot consists of a string of loosely connected episodes in a random sequence. There is a distinct beginning and distinct end, but the middle is a muddle, confirming the improvisatory nature of Tutuola's art. He moves from one episode to another not by calculation but by chance. And when he gets to the end of the chain, when all conflicts are resolved and his hero returns to a state of equilibrium, as most folktale heroes do, Tutuola rounds off the narrative with a moral: "This is what hatred did." The moral reminds the reader that the hero's sufferings and misfortunes can be blamed on his stepmothers, who rejected him twenty-four years before. Tutuola thus ends his story in typical folktale fashion by using it to teach a lesson about human behavior.

In his *Simbi and the Satyr of the Dark Jungle* (1955) Tutuola returns to the quest pattern. Beautiful Simbi, an only child who has never known poverty and punishment, desires to set out on a journey "to know and experience their difficulties." Her mother and others warn her not to, but she feels she must. Toward the end of the story, she is fed up with poverty and punishment. She has been kidnapped, sold into slavery, beaten, starved, almost beheaded, set afloat on a river in a sealed coffin, carried off by an eagle, imprisoned in a tree trunk, half-swallowed by a boa constrictor, attacked by a satyr, shrunk and put in a bottle, bombarded by a stone-carrying phoenix, and petrified into a rock. Fortunately she is a talented girl who can sing well enough to wake the dead, and she gets plenty of assistance from girlfriends, gods, and a friendly gnome, so that in the end she manages to return home to her mother. Then, "having rested for some days, she was going from house to house . . . warning all the children that it was a great mistake to a girl who did not obey her parents." Simbi, too, has a lesson to teach.

Although it resembles Tutuola's other books in matter and manner, *Simbi and the Satyr of the Dark Jungle* marks a new stage in his development as a writer, for it displays definite signs of formal literary influence. It was the first of his published works to be divided into numbered chapters, each encompassing a major adventure, and the only one to be written in the third-person point of view. Moore has noted that it contains far more dialogue and more frequent adverbial "stage directions" than the earlier books. Furthermore, there are creatures such as goblins, imps, a gnome, phoenix, nymph, and satyr whose names, at least, derive from European mythology. And one passage closely resembles an epi-

sode in a Yoruba novel by Fagunwa. Tutuola must have been doing some reading between 22 July 1952 and 26 November 1954, the respective dates on which *My Life in the Bush of Ghosts* and *Simbi and the Satyr of the Dark Jungle* were submitted for publication, but when Eric Larrabee interviewed him (for the article "Palm-Wine Drinkard Searches for a Tapster," *Reporter*, 12 May 1953), Tutuola owned no books and did not think of himself as an author. After *My Life in the Bush of Ghosts* was published, Tutuola decided to attend evening classes to improve himself. Reading was no doubt a part of his program for self-improvement. When Larrabee offered to send him books, Tutuola requested *A Survey of Economic Education*, published by the Brookings Institution, Aldous Huxley's *The Devils of Loudun* (1952), and "some other books which contain stories like that of the P.W.D. [*The Palm-Wine Drinkard*] which are written by either West Africans, White men or Negroes, etc." Larrabee recalls that, of the other books sent, "the two he seemed most to enjoy were Joyce Cary's *Mr. Johnson* [1939] and Edith Hamilton's *Mythology* [1942], which he said contained stories similar to those he had heard as a child" (*Chicago Review*, 1956). Not surprisingly there are traces of literary influence in *Simbi and the Satyr of the Dark Jungle*. Tutuola was becoming conscious of himself as an author, was reading more widely, and was trying hard to improve his writing. He could still tell only one kind of story, but should the traditional wellspring ever fail to provide him with sufficient material, he could now turn to other sources for inspiration.

Tutuola succeeded in improving the structure of his narratives considerably. They began to be organized into more neatly demarcated chapters. In *The Brave African Huntress* (1958) and *Ajaiyi and His Inherited Poverty* (1967), he adopted the practice of citing one or more proverbs at the head of a chapter and then using the action in that chapter to illustrate the proverbs. In *Feather Woman of the Jungle* (1962), his most stylized work, he created an *Arabian Nights* structure by having a seventy-six-year-old chief entertain villagers every night for ten nights with accounts of his past adventures. Both of these narrative techniques must have entered literature from oral tradition. If Tutuola picked them up from his reading, as appears likely, he is to be commended for selecting those that suited his material perfectly. Using such techniques he could remain a raconteur and àt the same time could link and unify his tales more effectively.

The tales were still woven into the familiar quest pattern. Adebisi, the heroine in *The Brave Afri-*

can Huntress, ventures into the dangerous Jungle of the Pigmies to rescue her four brothers. The chief in *Feather Woman of the Jungle* sets out on a series of hazardous journeys in quest of treasure and adventure. Ajaiyi in *Ajaiyi and His Inherited Poverty* simply wants to get out of debt and is willing to go to the Creator, the God of Iron, the Devil, and assorted witches, witch doctors, and wizards to ask for help. Each of the adventurers, after a succession of ups and downs, achieves his or her objective.

As for the tales themselves, Tutuola appears to have continued to rely more heavily on traditional Yoruba material than on non-Yoruba material. In *The Brave African Huntress* there are references to "elves, genii, goblins, demons, imps, gnomes," and a "cyclops-like creature," but the actual monsters encountered and the adventures undergone resemble those in Tutuola's earlier books. The episode in which Adebisi cuts the hair of the king of Ibembe Town and discovers he has horns has been cited by critics as a possible example of European or Indian influence because it resembles the story of King Midas and the Ass's Ears, but Tutuola, in a letter to Collins, stated: "The king who has horns is in the traditional story of my town." In published Yoruba folktale collections, one can easily find parallels to other tales and motifs, such as Adebisi's palace adventure in Bachelors' Town in *The Brave African Huntress*; the three dogs that rescue their master from woodchoppers, the journey to the underwater kingdom, and the town where people consume only water in *Feather Woman of the Jungle*; and the dead rats that come alive, the person who hides in the pupil of a blacksmith's eye, and the quarrel between lenders in *Ajaiyi and His Inherited Poverty*. Moreover, these books are packed with Yoruba deities, towns, customs, superstitions, and proverbs. Tutuola, despite his reading and increased sophistication, apparently chose to remain a teller of Yoruba tales.

There was a fourteen-year gap between publication of *Ajaiyi and His Inherited Poverty* and Tutuola's next long narrative, *The Witch-Herbalist of the Remote Town* (1981), but the hiatus does not appear to have had any measurable impact, positive or negative, on his chosen mode of storytelling. The later narrative is another rambling, episodic adventure tale, the quest this time being for medicine to cure a woman's barrenness. The brave hunter who undertakes the hazardous journey to obtain this boon from an expert witch-herbalist meets many curious creatures along his way, but eventually his persistence and ingenuity pay off. He gets the medicine, sips some of it on his return to stave off hun-

Dust jacket for Tutuola's first published book, which Dylan Thomas characterized as "brief, thronged, grisly and bewitching"

ger, and then gives the rest to his wife, who promptly becomes pregnant. However, so does he, and he must undergo further trials and torments before being cured.

Tutuola's next new book, published five years later, is a different sort of venture, a small collection of short traditional tales rather than a long, consecutive story fabricated out of a concatenation of fictive motifs, some traditional, some not. *Yoruba Folktales* (1986) is significant as Tutuola's first attempt at pure narrative preservation; his other works could be described as exercises in impure narrative perversion. In *Yoruba Folktales* he must remain to a large extent faithful to his sources, for these stories are presented as being the communal literary property of his people. He cannot claim to have invented such narratives; he is merely passing them along to others in written form and in a foreign language. If he takes any liberties with texts, they must be small liberties, the sort that any storyteller might take when relating to a well-known tale. Moral essences must stay more or less the same. In transcribing such narratives, most of them stories told throughout West Africa, Tutuola remains true to tradition but occasionally appears to add some zaniness to spice up characterization and plot.

The only major change in Tutuola's storytelling style that readers are likely to notice – and some possibly deplore – is sociolinguistic in nature: in *Yoruba Folktales* there are hardly any of the grammatical blunders and stylistic infelicities that one associates with Tutuola's earlier works. The idiom that Dylan Thomas characterized as "young English" is gone almost without a trace. The reason is not difficult to discern: the book was aimed by its publisher at primary-school classrooms, and one cannot address a school audience in Nigeria in a fractured foreign tongue. Textbook English has to be correct English; otherwise the textbook will not be approved for school use. In the case of *Yoruba Folktales*, an American professor, the late Robert Wren, was responsible for purifying and refining Tutuola's language. His works have always been edited to some degree by his publishers, but *Yoruba Folktales* may mark the first time one has been edited to such an advanced degree that no naive Tutuolaisms survive.

However, for those who may have missed Tutuola's authentic narrative voice, another book soon followed that had all the defining characteristics of the genre he had made distinctively his own. *Pauper, Brawler, and Slanderer* (1987) tells of the peripatetic adventures of three characters – two men and a woman (Brawler, the wife of Pauper) – who, rejected by their parents and expelled from their town, create havoc wherever they go, often getting into amusing scrapes with one another as well as with more-ordinary mortals. In the end they stand before the Creator in the Land of Judgement and are transformed into smoky whirlwinds that blow to every corner of the earth; and "to these days they are still roaming about invisibly on earth and yet they continue to trouble the people."

Tutuola's *The Village Witch Doctor & Other Stories* (1990) comprises a dozen of Tutuola's short stories, some of which had been published previously in magazines or broadcast on radio. It is a diverse collection, not anchored to the life story of a single character or single group of characters, so it more closely resembles *Yoruba Folktales* than it does any of his other works. Tutuola also had further help from Wren, so the English is a bit smoother than usual. But the same buoyant imagination is in evidence, the same fascination with comically grotesque fan-

tasy worlds. Tutuola, after more than forty years of writing, remains a very resourceful raconteur.

A few critics, seeking to demonstrate how Tutuola improves upon the material he borrows, have contrasted passages in his books with analogous folktales. This type of argument, no matter how well documented, is not very persuasive because the critic cannot prove that the particular folktale text chosen for comparison is the version of the tale that Tutuola knew. Perhaps Tutuola had heard a different version, perhaps even a better version than he himself was able to tell. Eldred Jones makes the mistake of assuming that the Yoruba tale on which Tutuola based his account of the self-dismembering "complete gentleman" in *The Palm-Wine Drinkard* is very similar to the Krio version of this tale. Jones therefore credits Tutuola with the invention of several striking details, which, though absent from the Krio version, are quite common in published Yoruba texts of the tale. Even a critic familiar with all the published Yoruba versions would not be able to draw a firm line between borrowed and invented details in Tutuola's redaction. Without knowing exactly what and from where Tutuola borrowed, it is impossible to know how much he contributed to the stories he tells.

Critics who search for literary influences on Tutuola's writing are on safer ground insofar as texts are concerned. Bunyan is again a case in point. The episode in which Death shows the palm-wine drinker the bones of former victims appears to be modeled on a scene in *The Pilgrim's Progress* in which Christian meets the Giant Despair in Doubting Castle. Several towns the drinker and other Tutuolan heroes visit bear a distinct resemblance to Vanity Fair. And the monsters often seem to belong to the same subspecies as Bunyan's Apollyon, who was "clothed with scales, like a fish. . . . had wings like a dragon, feet like a bear, and out of his belly came fire and smoke, and his mouth was as the mouth of a lion." However, unlike *The Pilgrim's Progress*, Tutuola's narratives are not religious allegories. They have been influenced far more by Yoruba oral tradition than by the Bible. Bunyan may have been instructive in teaching Tutuola how to put an extended quest tale together, but Bunyan did not convert him to Christianity. In substance and spirit Tutuola remains a thoroughly African storyteller. Only in *The Wild Hunter in the Bush of the Ghosts* does Bunyan appear to have left a religious imprint on Tutuola's narrative strategy.

Fagunwa, though, is the crucial literary influence on Tutuola. Between 1948 and 1951, the years in which Tutuola began his writing career, Fa-

Amos Tutuola (photograph: Nigerian Tribune, *Ibadan)*

gunwa published at least nine books, including a new edition of his first work of fiction, *Ogboju ode ninu igbo irunmale.* Tutuola, who had read this book at school, must have been aware of Fagunwa's extraordinary outburst of literary activity in these postwar years. Indeed it is conceivable that Tutuola got both the idea of writing stories and the idea of submitting them for publication from seeing Fagunwa's works in print. Yet there are sufficient differences between the two writers to show that Tutuola is not merely translating Fagunwa and that Tutuola is always sensitive to the demands of his own narrative. Such differences also suggest that, even when he follows Fagunwa most faithfully, he does so from memory rather than from a printed text, that, instead of actually plagiarizing, he vividly re-creates what he best remembers from Fagunwa's books, knitting the spirit if not the substance of the most suitable material into the loose fibers of his own yarn.

Because Fagunwa occasionally makes use of material from Yoruba oral tradition, it is not always easy to tell when Tutuola is borrowing from Fagunwa and when from folktales. For example, both writers use motifs such as the "juju-compass," which helps travelers find their way; the hall of

singing birds, which turns out to be a trap; the fierce gatekeeper who must be overcome in combat; and the deer-woman who marries a hunter. Tutuola's handling of these motifs may owe more to Yoruba oral tradition than to Fagunwa. Tutuola seems closest to Fagunwa when Fagunwa is closest to oral tradition. Fagunwa's books were among those that taught Tutuola how to weave various old stories into a flexible narrative pattern that could be stretched into a book. Fagunwa's contribution to Tutuola should perhaps be measured more in terms of overall structure and descriptive technique than in terms of content. Tutuola followed Fagunwa's lead and traveled in the same direction, but he did not always walk in Fagunwa's tracks.

Tutuola has never pretended that his stories were original creations: he has admitted in interviews and letters that he borrowed extensively from Yoruba oral tradition and always enjoyed reading works by Fagunwa, Bunyan, and other writers who made imaginative use of folktales and stories of fabulous adventure. Any storyteller building up his repertoire of tales probably would have done the same. In oral art what matters most is not uniqueness of invention but adroitness of performance. A storyteller is judged not by his capacity for fabricating new stories but by his ability to tell old, well-known tales in an entertaining manner. This fact may explain why Tutuola looted the treasury of ready-made fictions he found around him. He was creatively exploiting his cultural heritage, not robbing it.

Yet some of his early critics maintained that his work was an unprincipled act of piracy, especially since Tutuola was writing in English for a foreign audience rather than in Yoruba for his own people. What made it worse, they said, was that he was an inept craftsman who could not match Fagunwa as a storyteller and could not write in proper English. According to some critics Tutuola's barbarous verbal behavior was giving readers overseas a poor opinion of Africans.

One can understand the virulence of this reaction if one remembers that Tutuola's first books appeared at a time when Africans were trying to prove to the outside world that they were ready to manage their own political affairs. The colonial era was coming to an end, and educated Africans, in their eagerness for national independence, were becoming acutely conscious of their image abroad. They wanted to give an appearance of modernity, maturity, competence, and sophistication, but the naive fantasies of Tutuola projected just the opposite image. Moore has suggested that Tutuola aroused the antipathy of some of his countrymen by reminding them of a world from which they wanted to escape. To such readers Tutuola was a disgrace, a setback, and a national calamity.

But, to readers in Europe and America, Tutuola was an exotic delight. The critic for the *New Yorker* went so far as to say, "One catches a glimpse of the very beginning of literature, that moment when writing at last seizes and pins down the myths and legends of an analphabetic culture." In a similar vein V. S. Pritchett (*New Statesman and Nation*, 6 March 1954) claimed that *My Life in the Bush of Ghosts* "discernibly expresses the unconscious of a race and even moments of the nightmare element of our own unconsciousness.... Tutuola's voice is like the beginning of man on earth." The image-conscious Nigerians apparently had good reason to worry.

What fascinated many non-African readers of Tutuola was his style. Pritchett characterized it as "a loose, talking prose"; Dylan Thomas called it "young English." To native speakers of English, Tutuola's splintered style was an amusing novelty; to educated Nigerians who had spent years honing and polishing their English, it was a schoolboy's abomination.

Tutuola's later books were not as enthusiastically received in England and America as his first two. Reviewers complained that Tutuola's writing began to seem repetitive and deliberately childish rather than pleasingly childlike. Since Faber and Faber no longer took pains to cleanse his manuscripts of their grossest linguistic impurities, he appeared more inarticulate, more splintery, at times almost unintelligible. Clearly Tutuola's novelty had worn off, and the pendulum of critical opinion had begun to reverse its direction. Later it was to swing back to a more neutral position.

In Nigeria, on the other hand, the pendulum had started to swing in a decidedly more positive direction shortly after independence. In the early 1960s *The Palm-Wine Drinkard* was adapted for presentation on the stage as a Yoruba opera, and performances in Nigeria and at various drama festivals abroad were extremely well received. In the late 1960s and early 1970s a few Nigerian critics began serious reassessments of Tutuola's works, studying them with great care. In more recent years there has been a tendency, particularly among established Nigerian writers, toward a greater acceptance of Tutuola. More is being written about him and his works today than at any time in the past, the consensus of opinion being that, though he is not a typical author, he is far too important a phenomenon to be overlooked.

His importance resides not only in his eccentricities but also in his affinities with two established traditions of creative expression. His works unite oral and written art, bridging folk narratives on the one hand with precursors of the novel (such as *The Pilgrim's Progress*) on the other. Tutuola could be called the link between preliterate and literate man, for his creativity is firmly rooted in the cultural heritage of both. One sees in his works how two disparate systems of expressive conventions can be joined in a productive synthesis. Tutuola's writings will no doubt continue to interest readers for some time to come because they are a fascinating amalgam of old and new, indigenous and foreign, and oral and written materials. Tutuola, despite obvious limitations, is one of the most remarkably successful syncretists in African literature.

Though he has mostly resided in Ibadan and Ago-Odo, Nigeria, he has also traveled around Africa, Europe, and the United States. In 1979 he was a visiting research fellow at the University of Ife (Nigeria), and in 1983 he was an associate in the International Writing Program at the University of Iowa. He has also worked for the Nigerian Broadcasting Corporation. He is now retired.

Interviews:

Lewis Nkosi, "Conversation with Amos Tutuola," *Africa Report*, 9, no. 7 (1964): 11;

Kole Omotoso, "Interview with Amos Tutuola," *Afriscope*, 4, no. 1 (1974): 62, 64;

John Agetua, ed., *Interviews with Six Nigerian Writers* (Benin City, Nigeria: Agetua, 1976), pp. 5–8;

Ad'Obe Obe, "An Encounter with Amos Tutuola," *West Africa* (14 May 1984): 1022–1023;

Edward A. Gargan, "From a Nigerian Pen, Yoruba Tales," *New York Times*, 23 February 1986, p. 18.

References:

A. Afolayan, "Language and Sources of Amos Tutuola," in *Perspectives on African Literature*, edited by Christopher Heywood (London: Heinemann, 1971; New York: Africana, 1971), pp. 49–63;

Fred Akporobaro, "Narrative Form and Style in the Novels of Amos Tutuola," in *Studies in the African Novel*, edited by Samuel O. Asein and Albert O. Ashaolu (Ibadan: Ibadan University Press, 1986), pp. 101–112;

Sunday O. Anozie, "Amos Tutuola: Littérature et folklore ou le problème de la synthèse," *Cahiers d'Etudes Africaines*, 10 (1970): 335–351;

Robert P. Armstrong, "The Narrative and Intensive Continuity: *The Palm-Wine Drinkard*," *Research in African Literatures*, 1 (1970): 9–34;

O. A. Asagba, "The Folktale Structure in Amos Tutuola's *The Palm-Wine Drinkard*," *Lore and Language*, 4, no. 1 (1985): 31–39;

Ulli Beier, "Fagunwa, a Yoruba Novelist," *Black Orpheus*, 17 (1965): 51–56;

Viktor Beilis, "Ghosts, People, and Books of Yorubaland," *Research in African Literatures*, 18 (1987): 447–457;

Catherine E. Belvaude, *Amos Tutuola et l'univers du conte africain* (Paris: L'Harmattan, 1989);

Jack Berry, *Spoken Art in Africa* (London: School of Oriental and African Studies, University of London, 1961);

Eckhard Breitinger, "Images of Illness and Cultural Values in the Writings of Amos Tutuola," in *Health and Development in Africa*, edited by Peter Oberender, Hans Jochen Diesfeld, and Wolfgang Gitter (Frankfurt: Lang, 1983), pp. 64–73;

Henry M. Chakava, "Amos Tutuola: The Unselfconscious Eccentric," *Busara*, 3, no. 3 (1971): 50–57;

John Coates, "The Inward Journey of a Palm-Wine Drinkard," *African Literature Today*, 11 (1980): 122–129;

Harold R. Collins, *Amos Tutuola* (New York: Twayne, 1969);

Collins, "Founding a New National Literature: The Ghost Novels of Amos Tutuola," *Critique*, 4, no. 1 (1960–1961): 17–28;

Collins, "A Theory of Creative Mistakes and the Mistaking Style of Amos Tutuola," *World Literature Written in English*, 13 (November 1974): 155–171;

D. Coussy, "Deux romanciers yorubas: Amos Tutuola et Wole Soyinka," *L'Afrique Littéraire et Artistique*, 67 (1983): 111–132;

O. R. Dathorne, "Amos Tutuola: The Nightmare of the Tribe," in *Introduction to Nigerian Literature*, edited by Bruce King (Lagos: University of Lagos / London: Evans, 1971), pp. 64–76;

Michele Dussutour-Hammer, *Amos Tutuola: Tradition orale et écriture de conte* (Paris: Présence Africaine, 1976);

Paul Edwards, "The Farm and the Wilderness in Tutuola's *The Palm-Wine Drinkard*," *Journal of Commonwealth Literature*, 9, no. 1 (1974): 57–65;

Arlene A. Elder, "Paul Carter Harrison and Amos Tutuola: The Vitality of the African Continuum," *World Literature Written in English*, 28 (Autumn 1988): 171–178;

William R. Ferris, Jr., "Folklore and the African Novelist: Achebe and Tutuola," *Journal of American Folklore*, 86 (1973): 25–36;

Melville J. Herskovits and Frances S. Herskovits, *Dahomean Narrative: A Cross-Cultural Analysis* (Evanston, Ill.: Northwestern University Press, 1958);

Abiola Irele, "Tradition and the Yoruba Writer: D. O. Fagunwa, Amos Tutuola and Wole Soyinka," *Odu*, 11 (1975): 75–100;

Eldred Jones, "Amos Tutuola – *The Palm-Wine Drinkard*: Fourteen Years On," *Bulletin of the Association for African Literature in English*, 4 (1966): 24–30;

Vladimír Klíma, "Tutuola's Inspiration," *Archiv Orientalni*, 35 (1967): 556–562;

Eric Larrabee, "Amos Tutuola: A Problem in Translation," *Chicago Review*, 10 (1956): 40–44;

Larrabee, "Palm-Wine Drinkard Searches for a Tapster," *Reporter* (12 May 1953): 37–39;

Charles R. Larson, *The Emergence of African Fiction* (Bloomington: Indiana University Press, 1972);

Bernth Lindfors, "Amos Tutuola and D. O. Fagunwa," *Journal of Commonwealth Literature*, 9 (1970): 57–65;

Lindfors, "Amos Tutuola: Debts and Assets," *Cahiers d'Etudes Africaines*, 10 (1970): 306–334;

Lindfors, "Amos Tutuola's Earliest Long Narrative," *Journal of Commonwealth Literature*, 16, no. 1 (1981): 45–55;

Lindfors, "Amos Tutuola's Search for a Publisher," *Journal of Commonwealth Literature*, 17, no. 1 (1982): 90–106;

Lindfors, *Folklore in Nigerian Literature* (New York: Africana, 1973);

Lindfors, "Tutuola's Latest Stories," in *Short Fiction in the New Literatures in English*, edited by Jacqueline Bardolph (Nice: Faculté des Lettres & Sciences Humaines de Nice, 1989), pp. 271–276;

Lindfors, ed., *Critical Perspectives on Amos Tutuola* (Washington, D.C.: Three Continents, 1975; London: Heinemann, 1980);

Gerald Moore, "Amos Tutuola: A Nigerian Visionary," *Black Orpheus*, 1 (1957): 27–35;

Jamile Morsiani, *Da Tutuola a Rotimi: Una letteratura africana in lingua inglese* (Abano Terme, Italy: Piovan, 1983);

Emmanuel Obiechina, "Amos Tutuola and the Oral Tradition," *Présence Africaine*, 65 (1968): 85–106;

'Molara Ogundipe-Leslie, "*The Palm-Wine Drinkard*: A Reassessment of Amos Tutuola," *Présence Africaine*, 71 (1969): 99–108;

Ogundipe-Leslie, "Ten Years of Tutuola Studies, 1966–1976," *African Perspectives*, 1 (1977): 67–76;

Chikwenye Okonjo Ogunyemi, "The Africanness of *The Conjure Woman* and *Feather Woman of the Jungle*," *Ariel*, 8, no. 2 (1977): 17–30;

Sydney E. Onyeberechi, "Myth, Magic and Appetite in Amos Tutuola's *The Palm-Wine Drinkard*," *MAWA Review*, 4, no. 1 (1989): 22–26;

Eustace Palmer, "Twenty-Five Years of Amos Tutuola," *International Fiction Review*, 5 (1978): 15–24;

Richard Priebe, *Myth, Realism and the West African Writer* (Trenton, N.J.: Africa World, 1988);

Joseph Swann, "Disrupted Worlds: Knowledge and Encounter in Amos Tutuola's *The Palm-Wine Drinkard* and Chinua Achebe's *Arrow of God*," in *Studies in Commonwealth Literature*, edited by Eckhard Breitinger and Reinhard Sander (Tübingen, Germany: Narr, 1985);

Taban lo Liyong, "Tutuola, Son of Zinjanthropus," *Busara*, 1, no. 1 (1968): 3–8;

Alice Werner, "African Mythology," in *The Mythology of All Races*, edited by John Arnott MacCulloch (New York: Cooper Square, 1964), pp. 118–121.

Books for Further Reading

Achebe, Chinua. *Morning Yet on Creation Day: Essays*. London: Heinemann, 1975; enlarged edition, Garden City, N.Y.: Anchor/Doubleday, 1975.

Awoonor, Kofi. *The Breast of the Earth: A Survey of the History, Culture and Literature of Africa South of the Sahara*. Garden City, N.Y.: Anchor, 1975.

Barthold, Bonnie J. *Black Time: Fiction of Africa, the Caribbean and the United States*. New Haven: Yale University Press, 1981.

Baugh, Edward. *West Indian Poetry 1900-1970: A Study in Cultural Decolonisation*. Kingston, Jamaica: Savacou, 1971.

Baugh, ed. *Critics on Caribbean Literature*. London: Allen & Unwin / New York: St. Martin's Press, 1978.

Bjornson, Richard. *The African Quest for Freedom and Identity: Cameroonian Writing and the National Experience*. Bloomington & Indianapolis: Indiana University Press, 1991.

Brown, Lloyd W. *West Indian Poetry*. Boston: Twayne, 1978.

Brown. *Women Writers in Black Africa*. Westport, Conn. & London: Greenwood, 1981.

Cartey, Wilfred G. *Whispers from a Continent*. New York: Random House, 1969.

Cartey. *Whispers from the Caribbean*. Los Angeles: Center for Afro-American Studies, University of California, 1991.

Chinweizu, Onwuchekwa Jemie, and Ihechukwu Madubuike. *Toward the Decolonization of African Literature*. Washington, D.C.: Howard University Press, 1983.

Cudjoe, Selwyn R. *Resistance and Caribbean Literature*. Athens: Ohio University Press, 1980.

Cudjoe, ed. *Caribbean Women Writers*. Wellesley, Mass.: Calaloux, 1990.

Dance, Daryl C., ed. *Fifty Caribbean Writers: A Bio-Bibliographical Critical Sourcebook*. New York, Westport, Conn. & London: Greenwood, 1986.

Davies, Carole Boyce, and Anne Adams Graves, eds. *Ngambika: Studies of Women in African Literature*. Trenton, N.J.: Africa World, 1986.

Davies and Elaine Savory Fido, eds. *Out of the Kumbla: Caribbean Women and Literature*. Trenton, N.J.: Africa World, 1990.

Etherton, Michael. *The Development of African Drama*. London: Hutchinson, 1982.

Fraser, Robert. *West African Poetry: A Critical History*. Cambridge: Cambridge University Press, 1986.

Gérard, Albert, ed. *European-Language Writing in Sub-Saharan Africa*. Budapest: Akadémiai Kiadó, 1986.

Gikandi, Simon. *Writing in Limbo: Modernism and Caribbean Literature.* Ithaca, N.Y. & London: Cornell University Press, 1992.

Gilkes, Michael. *The West Indian Novel.* Boston: Twayne, 1981.

Goodwin, Ken. *Understanding African Poetry: A Study of Ten Poets.* London: Heinemann, 1982.

Griffiths, Gareth. *A Double Exile: African and West Indian Writing Between Two Cultures.* London: Boyars, 1978.

Harris, Wilson. *Tradition, the Writer and Society: Critical Essays.* London & Port of Spain: New Beacon, 1967.

Irele, Abiola. *The African Experience in Literature and Ideology.* London & Exeter, N.H.: Heinemann, 1981.

James, Louis, ed. *The Islands in Between: Essays on West Indian Literature.* London: Oxford University Press, 1968.

JanMohamed, Abdul. *Manichean Aesthetics: The Politics of Literature in Colonial Africa.* Amherst: University of Massachusetts Press, 1983.

Jonas, Joyce. *Anancy in the Great House: Ways of Reading West Indian Fiction.* New York, Westport, Conn. & London: Greenwood, 1990.

King, Bruce, ed. *West Indian Literature.* London: Macmillan, 1979.

Lamming, George. *The Pleasures of Exile.* London: Joseph, 1960.

Larson, Charles R. *The Emergence of African Fiction,* revised edition. Bloomington: Indiana University Press, 1972.

Moore, Gerald. *The Chosen Tongue.* London: Longmans, 1969.

Ngara, Emmanuel. *Stylistic Criticism and the African Novel: A Study of the Influence of Marxism on African Writing.* London & Hanover, N.H.: Heinemann, 1985.

Ngugi wa Thiong'o. *Decolonising the Mind: The Politics of Language in African Literature.* London: Currey / Portsmouth, N.H.: Heinemann, 1986.

Ngugi. *Homecoming: Essays on African and Caribbean Literature, Culture and Politics.* London: Heinemann, 1972.

Ngugi. *Writers in Politics.* London & Exeter, N.H.: Heinemann, 1981.

Obiechina, Emmanuel. *Culture, Tradition and Society in the West African Novel.* Cambridge: Cambridge University Press, 1975.

Omotoso, Kole. *The Theatrical into Theatre: A Study of the Drama and Theatre of the English-Speaking Caribbean.* London: New Beacon, 1982.

Palmer, Eustace. *The Growth of the African Novel.* London & Exeter, N.H.: Heinemann, 1979.

Ramchand, Kenneth. *An Introduction to the Study of West Indian Literature.* Sunbury-on-Thames, U.K. & Kingston, Jamaica: Nelson Caribbean, 1976.

Ramchand. *The West Indian Novel and Its Background.* London: Faber & Faber, 1970.

Soyinka, Wole. *Art, Dialogue and Outrage: Essays on Literature and Culture*. Ibadan: New Horn, 1988.

Soyinka. *Myth, Literature and the African World*. Cambridge: Cambridge University Press, 1976.

Taylor, Patrick. *The Narrative of Liberation: Perspectives on Afro-Caribbean Literature, Popular Culture, and Politics*. Ithaca, N.Y.: Cornell University Press, 1989.

Van Sertima, Ivan. *Caribbean Writers: Critical Essays*. London & Port of Spain: New Beacon, 1968.

Wauthier, Claude. *The Literature and Thought of Modern Africa*. Translated by Shirley Kay. London: Heinemann, 1978.

Webb, Barbara J. *Myth and History in Caribbean Fiction: Alejo Carpentier, Wilson Harris, and Edouard Glissant*. Amherst: University of Massachusetts Press, 1992.

Contributors

Joel Adedeji..*Irvington, New Jersey*
David Attwell ....*University of Natal, Pietermaritzburg*
F. Odun Balogun...*Delaware State College*
Jacqueline Bardolph ....*University of Nice*
Ursula A. Barnett .... *Surbiton, Surrey, England*
Harold Barratt.....................................*University College of Cape Breton*
Brenda F. Berrian ....*University of Pittsburgh*
Anthony Boxill..*University of New Brunswick*
Kamau Brathwaite...*New York University*
Laurence A. Breiner...*Boston University*
David Bunn ....*University of the Western Cape*
Michael G. Cooke ....*Yale University*
Al Creighton.. *University of Guyana*
James Gibbs ....*Bristol, England*
Simon Gikandi ....*University of Michigan*
Ketu H. Katrak ....*University of Massachusetts – Amherst*
Bruce King..*University of Guelph*
Omari H. Kokole....................................*State University of New York at Binghamton*
Bernth Lindfors ....*University of Texas at Austin*
Cecily Lockett....................................*Rand Africaans University, Johannesburg*
David Maughan-Brown..*University of Natal, Pietermaritzburg*
Peter Nazareth...*University of Iowa*
Donatus Ibe Nwoga ....*University of Nigeria, Nsukka*
Sandra Pouchet Paquet ....*University of Miami*
Victor J. Ramraj..*University of Calgary*
Sandra L. Richards ....*Northwestern University*
Reinhard Sander...*Amherst College*
John Thieme..*University of Hull*
Chezia Thompson-Cager ....*Smith College*
Martin Trump..*University of South Africa*
Gay Wilentz ....*East Carolina University*
Brian P. Willan ....*Cambridge, England*

Cumulative Index

Dictionary of Literary Biography, Volumes 1-125
Dictionary of Literary Biography Yearbook, 1980-1991
Dictionary of Literary Biography Documentary Series, Volumes 1-10

Cumulative Index

DLB before number: *Dictionary of Literary Biography*, Volumes 1-125
Y before number: *Dictionary of Literary Biography Yearbook*, 1980-1991
DS before number: *Dictionary of Literary Biography Documentary Series*, Volumes 1-10

A

Abbey Press DLB-49

The Abbey Theatre and Irish Drama, 1900-1945 ...... DLB-10

Abbot, Willis J. 1863-1934 .... DLB-29

Abbott, Jacob 1803-1879 .... DLB-1

Abbott, Lyman 1835-1922 .... DLB-79

Abbott, Robert S. 1868-1940 .... DLB-29, 91

Abelard, Peter circa 1079-1142 .... DLB-115

Abelard-Schuman DLB-46

Abell, Arunah S. 1806-1888 .... DLB-43

Abercrombie, Lascelles 1881-1938 .... DLB-19

Aberdeen University Press Limited DLB-106

Abrahams, Peter 1919- DLB-117

Abrams, M. H. 1912- DLB-67

Abse, Dannie 1923- DLB-27

Academy Chicago Publishers DLB-46

Ace Books DLB-46

Achebe, Chinua 1930- DLB-117

Achtenberg, Herbert 1938- DLB-124

Ackerman, Diane 1948- DLB-120

Acorn, Milton 1923-1986 .... DLB-53

Acosta, Oscar Zeta 1935?- DLB-82

Actors Theatre of Louisville DLB-7

Adair, James 1709?-1783? DLB-30

Adam, Graeme Mercer 1839-1912 .... DLB-99

Adame, Leonard 1947- DLB-82

Adamic, Louis 1898-1951 .... DLB-9

Adams, Alice 1926- Y-86

Adams, Brooks 1848-1927 .... DLB-47

Adams, Charles Francis, Jr. 1835-1915 .... DLB-47

Adams, Douglas 1952- Y-83

Adams, Franklin P. 1881-1960 .... DLB-29

Adams, Henry 1838-1918 .... DLB-12, 47

Adams, Herbert Baxter 1850-1901 .... DLB-47

Adams, J. S. and C. [publishing house] DLB-49

Adams, James Truslow 1878-1949 .... DLB-17

Adams, John 1735-1826 .... DLB-31

Adams, John Quincy 1767-1848 .... DLB-37

Adams, Léonie 1899-1988 .... DLB-48

Adams, Levi 1802-1832 .... DLB-99

Adams, Samuel 1722-1803 .... DLB-31, 43

Adams, William Taylor 1822-1897 .... DLB-42

Adamson, Sir John 1867-1950 .... DLB-98

Adcock, Betty 1938- DLB-105

Adcock, Betty, Certain Gifts DLB-105

Adcock, Fleur 1934- DLB-40

Addison, Joseph 1672-1719 .... DLB-101

Ade, George 1866-1944 .... DLB-11, 25

Adeler, Max (see Clark, Charles Heber)

Advance Publishing Company DLB-49

AE 1867-1935 .... DLB-19

Aesthetic Poetry (1873), by Walter Pater DLB-35

Afro-American Literary Critics:
    An Introduction DLB-33

Agassiz, Jean Louis Rodolphe 1807-1873 .... DLB-1

Agee, James 1909-1955 .... DLB-2, 26

The Agee Legacy: A Conference at
    the University of Tennessee
    at Knoxville Y-89

Ai 1947- DLB-120

Aichinger, Ilse 1921- DLB-85

Aidoo, Ama Ata 1942- DLB-117

Aiken, Conrad 1889-1973 .... DLB-9, 45, 102

Ainsworth, William Harrison 1805-1882 ....DLB-21

Aitken, Robert [publishing house] DLB-49

Akenside, Mark 1721-1770 ....DLB-109

Akins, Zoe 1886-1958 ....DLB-26

Alain-Fournier 1886-1914 ....DLB-65

Alarcon, Francisco X. 1954- DLB-122

Alba, Nanina 1915-1968 ....DLB-41

Albee, Edward 1928- DLB-7

Albert the Great circa 1200-1280 ....DLB-115

Alberti, Rafael 1902- DLB-108

Alcott, Amos Bronson 1799-1888 ....DLB-1

Alcott, Louisa May 1832-1888 .... DLB-1, 42, 79

Alcott, William Andrus 1798-1859 ....DLB-1

Alden, Henry Mills 1836-1919 ....DLB-79

Alden, Isabella 1841-1930 ....DLB-42

Alden, John B. [publishing house] DLB-49

Alden, Beardsley and Company DLB-49

Aldington, Richard 1892-1962 .... DLB-20, 36, 100

Aldis, Dorothy 1896-1966 ....DLB-22

Aldiss, Brian W. 1925- DLB-14

Aldrich, Thomas Bailey 1836-1907 .... DLB-42, 71, 74, 79

Alegría, Ciro 1909-1967 ....DLB-113

Aleixandre, Vicente 1898-1984 ....DLB-108

Aleramo, Sibilla 1876-1960 ....DLB-114

Alexander, Charles 1868-1923 ....DLB-91

Alexander, Charles Wesley [publishing house] DLB-49

Alexander, James 1691-1756 ....DLB-24

Alexander, Lloyd 1924- DLB-52

Alexander, Sir William, Earl of Stirling 1577?-1640 ...DLB-121

Alger, Horatio, Jr. 1832-1899 ....DLB-42

Algonquin Books of Chapel Hill DLB-46

Algren, Nelson 1909-1981 .... DLB-9; Y-81, 82

Allan, Andrew 1907-1974 ....DLB-88

Allan, Ted 1916- DLB-68

Allbeury, Ted 1917- DLB-87

Alldritt, Keith 1935- DLB-14

Allen, Ethan 1738-1789 ....DLB-31

Allen, Gay Wilson 1903- DLB-103

Allen, George 1808-1876 ....DLB-59

Allen, George [publishing house] DLB-106

Allen, George, and Unwin Limited DLB-112

Allen, Grant 1848-1899 .... DLB-70, 92

Allen, Henry W. 1912- Y-85

Allen, Hervey 1889-1949 .... DLB-9, 45

Allen, James 1739-1808 ....DLB-31

Allen, James Lane 1849-1925 ....DLB-71

Allen, Jay Presson 1922- DLB-26

Allen, John, and Company DLB-49

Allen, Samuel W. 1917- DLB-41

Allen, Woody 1935- DLB-44

Alline, Henry 1748-1784 ....DLB-99

Allingham, Margery 1904-1966 ....DLB-77

Allingham, William 1824-1889 ....DLB-35

Allison, W. L. [publishing house] DLB-49

Allott, Kenneth 1912-1973 ....DLB-20

Allston, Washington 1779-1843 ....DLB-1

Alonzo, Dámaso 1898-1990 ....DLB-108

Alsop, George 1636-post 1673 ....DLB-24

Alsop, Richard 1761-1815 ....DLB-37

Altemus, Henry, and Company DLB-49

Altenberg, Peter 1885-1919 ....DLB-81

Altolaguirre, Manuel 1905-1959 ....DLB-108

Aluko, T. M. 1918- DLB-117

Alurista 1947- DLB-82

Alvarez, A. 1929- DLB-14, 40

Amadi, Elechi 1934- DLB-117

Amado, Jorge 1912- DLB-113

Ambler, Eric 1909- DLB-77

America: or, a Poem on the Settlement of the British Colonies (1780?), by Timothy Dwight DLB-37

American Conservatory Theatre DLB-7

American Fiction and the 1930s DLB-9

American Humor: A Historical Survey
East and Northeast
South and Southwest
Midwest
West DLB-11

American News Company DLB-49

The American Poets' Corner: The First Three Years (1983-1986) Y-86

American Publishing Company DLB-49

American Stationers' Company DLB-49

American Sunday-School Union DLB-49

American Temperance Union DLB-49

American Tract Society DLB-49

The American Writers Congress (9-12 October 1981) Y-81

The American Writers Congress: A Report on Continuing Business Y-81

Ames, Fisher 1758-1808 ....DLB-37

Ames, Mary Clemmer 1831-1884 ....DLB-23

Amini, Johari M. 1935- DLB-41

Amis, Kingsley 1922- DLB-15, 27, 100

Amis, Martin 1949- DLB-14

Ammons, A. R. 1926- DLB-5

Amory, Thomas 1691?-1788 ....DLB-39

Anaya, Rudolfo A. 1937- DLB-82

Andersch, Alfred 1914-1980 ....DLB-69

Anderson, Margaret 1886-1973 ....DLB-4, 91

Anderson, Maxwell 1888-1959 ....DLB-7

Anderson, Patrick 1915-1979 ....DLB-68

Anderson, Paul Y. 1893-1938 ....DLB-29

Anderson, Poul 1926- DLB-8

Anderson, Robert 1917- DLB-7

Anderson, Sherwood 1876-1941 ......DLB-4, 9, 86; DS-1

Andreas-Salomé, Lou 1861-1937 ....DLB-66

Andres, Stefan 1906-1970 ....DLB-69

Andrews, Charles M. 1863-1943 ....DLB-17

Andrews, Miles Peter ?-1814 ....DLB-89

Andrian, Leopold von 1875-1951 ....DLB-81

Andrieux, Louis (see Aragon, Louis)

Andrus, Silas, and Son DLB-49

Angell, James Burrill 1829-1916 ....DLB-64

Angelou, Maya 1928- DLB-38

Angers, Félicité (see Conan, Laure)

The "Angry Young Men" DLB-15

Angus and Robertson (UK) Limited DLB-112

Anhalt, Edward 1914- DLB-26

Anners, Henry F. [publishing house] DLB-49

Anselm of Canterbury 1033-1109 ....DLB-115

Anthony, Michael 1932- DLB-125

Anthony, Piers 1934- DLB-8

Anthony Burgess's *99 Novels*: An Opinion Poll Y-84

Antin, Mary 1881-1949 ....Y-84

Antschel, Paul (see Celan, Paul)

Anzaldúa, Gloria 1942- DLB-122

Apodaca, Rudy S. 1939- DLB-82

Appleton, D., and Company DLB-49

Appleton-Century-Crofts DLB-46

Applewhite, James 1935- DLB-105

Apple-wood Books DLB-46

Aquin, Hubert 1929-1977 ....DLB-53

Aquinas, Thomas 1224 or 1225-1274 ....DLB-115

Aragon, Louis 1897-1982 ....DLB-72

Arbor House Publishing Company DLB-46

Arbuthnot, John 1667-1735 ....DLB-101

Arcadia House DLB-46

Arce, Julio G. (see Ulica, Jorge)

Archer, William 1856-1924 ....DLB-10

Arden, John 1930- DLB-13

Arden of Faversham DLB-62

Ardis Publishers Y-89

Arellano, Juan Estevan 1947- DLB-122

The Arena Publishing Company DLB-49

Arena Stage DLB-7

Arensberg, Ann 1937- Y-82

Arguedas, José María 1911-1969 ....DLB-113

Arias, Ron 1941- DLB-82

Arland, Marcel 1899-1986 ....DLB-72

Arlen, Michael 1895-1956 ....DLB-36, 77

Armah, Ayi Kwei 1939- DLB-117

Armed Services Editions DLB-46

Arndt, Ernst Moritz 1769-1860 ....DLB-90

Arnim, Achim von 1781-1831 ....DLB-90

Arnim, Bettina von 1785-1859 ....DLB-90

Arno Press DLB-46

Arnold, Edwin 1832-1904 ....DLB-35

Arnold, Matthew 1822-1888 ....DLB-32, 57

Arnold, Thomas 1795-1842 ....DLB-55

Arnold, Edward [publishing house] DLB-112

Arnow, Harriette Simpson 1908-1986 ....DLB-6

Arp, Bill (see Smith, Charles Henry)

Arreola, Juan José 1918- DLB-113

Arrowsmith, J. W. [publishing house] DLB-106

Arthur, Timothy Shay 1809-1885 .... DLB-3, 42, 79

Artmann, H. C. 1921- DLB-85

Arvin, Newton 1900-1963 ....DLB-103

As I See It, by Carolyn Cassady DLB-16

Asch, Nathan 1902-1964 ....DLB-4, 28

Ash, John 1948- DLB-40

Ashbery, John 1927- DLB-5; Y-81

Ashendene Press DLB-112

Asher, Sandy 1942- Y-83

Ashton, Winifred (see Dane, Clemence)

Asimov, Isaac 1920-1992 ....DLB-8

Asselin, Olivar 1874-1937 ....DLB-92

Asturias, Miguel Angel 1899-1974 ....DLB-113

Atheneum Publishers DLB-46

Atherton, Gertrude 1857-1948 ....DLB-9, 78

Athlone Press DLB-112

Atkins, Josiah circa 1755-1781 ....DLB-31

Atkins, Russell 1926- DLB-41

The Atlantic Monthly Press DLB-46

Attaway, William 1911-1986 ....DLB-76

Atwood, Margaret 1939- DLB-53

Aubert, Alvin 1930- DLB-41

Aubert de Gaspé, Phillipe-Ignace-François
    1814-1841 ....DLB-99

Aubert de Gaspé, Phillipe-Joseph 1786-1871 ....DLB-99

Aubin, Napoléon 1812-1890 ....DLB-99

Aubin, Penelope 1685-circa 1731 ....DLB-39

Aubrey-Fletcher, Henry Lancelot (see Wade, Henry)

Auchincloss, Louis 1917- DLB-2; Y-80

Auden, W. H. 1907-1973 .... DLB-10, 20

Audio Art in America: A Personal Memoir Y-85

Auernheimer, Raoul 1876-1948 ....DLB-81

Augustine 354-430 ....DLB-115

Austen, Jane 1775-1817 ....DLB-116

Austin, Alfred 1835-1913 ....DLB-35

Austin, Mary 1868-1934 .... DLB-9, 78

Austin, William 1778-1841 ....DLB-74

The Author's Apology for His Book
    (1684), by John Bunyan DLB-39

An Author's Response, by Ronald Sukenick Y-82

Authors and Newspapers Association DLB-46

Authors' Publishing Company DLB-49

Avalon Books DLB-46

Avendaño, Fausto 1941- DLB-82

Averroës 1126-1198 ....DLB-115

Avicenna 980-1037 ....DLB-115

Avison, Margaret 1918- DLB-53

Avon Books DLB-46

Awoonor, Kofi 1935- DLB-117

Ayckbourn, Alan 1939- DLB-13

Aymé, Marcel 1902-1967 ....DLB-72

Aytoun, Sir Robert 1570-1638 ....DLB-121

Aytoun, William Edmondstoune 1813-1865 ....DLB-32

B

B. V. (see Thomson, James)

Babbitt, Irving 1865-1933 ....DLB-63

Babbitt, Natalie 1932- DLB-52

Babcock, John [publishing house] DLB-49

Baca, Jimmy Santiago 1952- DLB-122

Bache, Benjamin Franklin 1769-1798 ....DLB-43

Bachmann, Ingeborg 1926-1973 ....DLB-85

Bacon, Delia 1811-1859 ....DLB-1

Bacon, Roger circa 1214/1220-1292 ....DLB-115

Bacon, Thomas circa 1700-1768 ....DLB-31

Badger, Richard G., and Company DLB-49

Bage, Robert 1728-1801 ....DLB-39

Bagehot, Walter 1826-1877 ....DLB-55

Bagley, Desmond 1923-1983 ....DLB-87

Bagnold, Enid 1889-1981 ....DLB-13

Bahr, Hermann 1863-1934 ....DLB-81, 118

Bailey, Alfred Goldsworthy 1905- DLB-68

Bailey, Francis [publishing house] DLB-49

Bailey, H. C. 1878-1961 ....DLB-77

Bailey, Jacob 1731-1808 ....DLB-99

Bailey, Paul 1937- DLB-14

Bailey, Philip James 1816-1902 ....DLB-32

Baillargeon, Pierre 1916-1967 ....DLB-88

Baillie, Hugh 1890-1966 ....DLB-29

Baillie, Joanna 1762-1851 ....DLB-93

Bailyn, Bernard 1922- DLB-17

Bainbridge, Beryl 1933- DLB-14

Baird, Irene 1901-1981 ....DLB-68

Baker, Carlos 1909-1987 ....DLB-103

Baker, David 1954- DLB-120

Baker, Herschel C. 1914-1990 ....DLB-111

Baker, Houston A., Jr. 1943- DLB-67

Baker, Walter H., Company
("Baker's Plays") DLB-49

The Baker and Taylor Company DLB-49

Balaban, John 1943- DLB-120

Bald, Wambly 1902- DLB-4

Balderston, John 1889-1954 ....DLB-26

Baldwin, James 1924-1987 ....DLB-2, 7, 33; Y-87

Baldwin, Joseph Glover 1815-1864 ....DLB-3, 11

Ballantine Books DLB-46

Ballard, J. G. 1930- DLB-14

Ballou, Maturin Murray 1820-1895 ....DLB-79

Ballou, Robert O. [publishing house] DLB-46

Balzac, Honoré de 1799-1855 ....DLB-119

Bambara, Toni Cade 1939- DLB-38

Bancroft, A. L., and Company DLB-49

Bancroft, George 1800-1891 ....DLB-1, 30, 59

Bancroft, Hubert Howe 1832-1918 ....DLB-47

Bangs, John Kendrick 1862-1922 ....DLB-11, 79

Banim, John 1798-1842 ....DLB-116

Banks, John circa 1653-1706 ....DLB-80

Bantam Books DLB-46

Banville, John 1945- DLB-14

Baraka, Amiri 1934- DLB-5, 7, 16, 38; DS-8

Barbauld, Anna Laetitia 1743-1825 ....DLB-107, 109

Barbeau, Marius 1883-1969 ....DLB-92

Barber, John Warner 1798-1885 ....DLB-30

Barbey d'Aurevilly, Jules-Amédée 1808-1889 ....DLB-119

Barbour, Ralph Henry 1870-1944 ....DLB-22

Barbusse, Henri 1873-1935 ....DLB-65

Barclay, E. E., and Company DLB-49

Bardeen, C. W. [publishing house] DLB-49

Baring, Maurice 1874-1945 ....DLB-34

Barker, A. L. 1918- DLB-14

Barker, George 1913-1991 ....DLB-20

Barker, Harley Granville 1877-1946 ....DLB-10

Barker, Howard 1946- DLB-13

Barker, James Nelson 1784-1858 ....DLB-37

Barker, Jane 1652-1727? DLB-39

Barker, Arthur, Limited DLB-112

Barks, Coleman 1937- DLB-5

Barlach, Ernst 1870-1938 . . . . DLB-56, 118

Barlow, Joel 1754-1812 . . . . DLB-37

Barnard, John 1681-1770 . . . . DLB-24

Barnes, A. S., and Company DLB-49

Barnes, Djuna 1892-1982 . . . . DLB-4, 9, 45

Barnes, Margaret Ayer 1886-1967 . . . . DLB-9

Barnes, Peter 1931- DLB-13

Barnes, William 1801-1886 . . . . DLB-32

Barnes and Noble Books DLB-46

Barney, Natalie 1876-1972 . . . . DLB-4

Baron, Richard W., Publishing Company DLB-46

Barr, Robert 1850-1912 . . . . DLB-70, 92

Barrax, Gerald William 1933- DLB-41, 120

Barrès, Maurice 1862-1923 . . . . DLB-123 `

Barrett, Eaton Stannard 1786-1820 . . . . DLB-116

Barrie, James M. 1860-1937 . . . . DLB-10

Barrie and Jenkins DLB-112

Barrio, Raymond 1921- DLB-82

Barrios, Gregg 1945- DLB-122

Barry, Philip 1896-1949 . . . . DLB-7

Barry, Robertine (see Françoise)

Barse and Hopkins DLB-46

Barstow, Stan 1928- DLB-14

Barth, John 1930- DLB-2

Barthelme, Donald 1931-1989 . . . . DLB-2; Y-80, 89

Barthelme, Frederick 1943- Y-85

Bartlett, John 1820-1905 . . . . DLB-1

Bartol, Cyrus Augustus 1813-1900 . . . . DLB-1

Barton, Bernard 1784-1849 . . . . DLB-96

Bartram, John 1699-1777 . . . . DLB-31

Bartram, William 1739-1823 . . . . DLB-37

Basic Books DLB-46

Bass, T. J. 1932- Y-81

Basse, William circa 1583-1653 . . . . DLB-121

Bassett, John Spencer 1867-1928 . . . . DLB-17

Bassler, Thomas Joseph (see Bass, T. J.)

Bate, Walter Jackson 1918- DLB-67, 103

Bates, Katharine Lee 1859-1929 . . . . DLB-71

Batsford, B. T. [publishing house] DLB-106

Bauer, Wolfgang 1941- DLB-124

Baum, L. Frank 1856-1919 . . . . DLB-22

Baum, Vicki 1888-1960 . . . . DLB-85

Baumbach, Jonathan 1933- Y-80

Bawden, Nina 1925- DLB-14

Bax, Clifford 1886-1962 . . . . DLB-10, 100

Bayer, Eleanor (see Perry, Eleanor)

Bayer, Konrad 1932-1964 . . . . DLB-85

Bazin, Hervé 1911- DLB-83

Beach, Sylvia 1887-1962 . . . . DLB-4

Beacon Press DLB-49

Beadle and Adams DLB-49

Beagle, Peter S. 1939- Y-80

Beal, M. F. 1937- Y-81

Beale, Howard K. 1899-1959 . . . . DLB-17

Beard, Charles A. 1874-1948 . . . . DLB-17

A Beat Chronology: The First Twenty-five
     Years, 1944-1969 . . . . DLB-16

Beattie, Ann 1947- Y-82

Beattie, James 1735-1803 . . . . DLB-109

Beauchemin, Nérée 1850-1931 . . . . DLB-92

Beauchemin, Yves 1941- DLB-60

Beaugrand, Honoré 1848-1906 . . . . DLB-99

Beaulieu, Victor-Lévy 1945- DLB-53

Beaumont, Francis circa 1584-1616
     and Fletcher, John 1579-1625 . . . . DLB-58

Beaumont, Sir John 1583?-1627 . . . . DLB-121

Beauvoir, Simone de 1908-1986 . . . . DLB-72; Y-86

Becher, Ulrich 1910- DLB-69

Becker, Carl 1873-1945 . . . . DLB-17

Becker, Jurek 1937- DLB-75

Becker, Jurgen 1932- DLB-75

Beckett, Samuel 1906-1989 ....DLB-13, 15, Y-90

Beckford, William 1760-1844 ....DLB-39

Beckham, Barry 1944- DLB-33

Beddoes, Thomas Lovell 1803-1849 ....DLB-96

Beecher, Catharine Esther 1800-1878 ....DLB-1

Beecher, Henry Ward 1813-1887 ....DLB-3, 43

Beer, George L. 1872-1920 ....DLB-47

Beer, Patricia 1919- DLB-40

Beerbohm, Max 1872-1956 ....DLB-34, 100

Beer-Hofmann, Richard 1866-1945 ....DLB-81

Beers, Henry A. 1847-1926 ....DLB-71

Beeton, S. O. [publishing house] DLB-106

Bégon, Elisabeth 1696-1755 ....DLB-99

Behan, Brendan 1923-1964 ....DLB-13

Behn, Aphra 1640?-1689 ....DLB-39, 80

Behn, Harry 1898-1973 ....DLB-61

Behrman, S. N. 1893-1973 ....DLB-7, 44

Belaney, Archibald Stansfeld (see Grey Owl)

Belasco, David 1853-1931 ....DLB-7

Belford, Clarke and Company DLB-49

Belitt, Ben 1911- DLB-5

Belknap, Jeremy 1744-1798 ....DLB-30, 37

Bell, Clive 1881-1964 ....DS-10

Bell, James Madison 1826-1902 ....DLB-50

Bell, Marvin 1937- DLB-5

Bell, Millicent 1919- DLB-111

Bell, Vanessa 1879-1961 ....DS-10

Bell, George, and Sons DLB-106

Bell, Robert [publishing house] DLB-49

Bellamy, Edward 1850-1898 ....DLB-12

Bellamy, Joseph 1719-1790 ....DLB-31

La Belle Assemblée 1806-1837 ....DLB-110

Belloc, Hilaire 1870-1953 ....DLB-19, 100

Bellow, Saul 1915- DLB-2, 28; Y-82; DS-3

Belmont Productions DLB-46

Bemelmans, Ludwig 1898-1962 ....DLB-22

Bemis, Samuel Flagg 1891-1973 ....DLB-17

Bemrose, William [publishing house] DLB-106

Benchley, Robert 1889-1945 ....DLB-11

Benedetti, Mario 1920- DLB-113

Benedictus, David 1938- DLB-14

Benedikt, Michael 1935- DLB-5

Benét, Stephen Vincent 1898-1943 ....DLB-4, 48, 102

Benét, William Rose 1886-1950 ....DLB-45

Benford, Gregory 1941- Y-82

Benjamin, Park 1809-1864 ....DLB-3, 59, 73

Benn, Gottfried 1886-1956 ....DLB-56

Benn Brothers Limited DLB-106

Bennett, Arnold 1867-1931 ....DLB-10, 34, 98

Bennett, Charles 1899- DLB-44

Bennett, Gwendolyn 1902- DLB-51

Bennett, Hal 1930- DLB-33

Bennett, James Gordon 1795-1872 ....DLB-43

Bennett, James Gordon, Jr. 1841-1918 ....DLB-23

Bennett, John 1865-1956 ....DLB-42

Bennett, Louise 1919- DLB-117

Benoit, Jacques 1941- DLB-60

Benson, A. C. 1862-1925 ....DLB-98

Benson, Jackson J. 1930- DLB-111

Benson, Stella 1892-1933 ....DLB-36

Bentham, Jeremy 1748-1832 ....DLB-107

Bentley, E. C. 1875-1956 ....DLB-70

Bentley, Richard [publishing house] DLB-106

Benton, Robert 1932- and Newman,
    David 1937- DLB-44

Benziger Brothers DLB-49

Beresford, Anne 1929- DLB-40

Beresford-Howe, Constance 1922- DLB-88

Berford, R. G., Company DLB-49

Berg, Stephen 1934- DLB-5

Bergengruen, Werner 1892-1964 ....DLB-56

Berger, John 1926- DLB-14

Berger, Meyer 1898-1959 ....DLB-29

Berger, Thomas 1924- DLB-2; Y-80

Berkeley, Anthony 1893-1971 ....DLB-77

Berkeley, George 1685-1753 .... DLB-31, 101

The Berkley Publishing Corporation DLB-46

Bernal, Vicente J. 1888-1915 ....DLB-82

Bernanos, Georges 1888-1948 ....DLB-72

Bernard, Harry 1898-1979 ....DLB-92

Bernard, John 1756-1828 ....DLB-37

Bernard of Chartres circa 1060-1124? DLB-115

Bernhard, Thomas 1931-1989 .... DLB-85, 124

Berrigan, Daniel 1921- DLB-5

Berrigan, Ted 1934-1983 ....DLB-5

Berry, Wendell 1934- DLB-5, 6

Berryman, John 1914-1972 ....DLB-48

Bersianik, Louky 1930- DLB-60

Berton, Pierre 1920- DLB-68

Bessette, Gerard 1920- DLB-53

Bessie, Alvah 1904-1985 ....DLB-26

Bester, Alfred 1913- DLB-8

The Bestseller Lists: An Assessment Y-84

Betjeman, John 1906-1984 ....DLB-20; Y-84

Betts, Doris 1932- Y-82

Beveridge, Albert J. 1862-1927 ....DLB-17

Beverley, Robert circa 1673-1722 ....DLB-24, 30

Beyle, Marie-Henri (see Stendhal)

Bibaud, Adèle 1854-1941 ....DLB-92

Bibaud, Michel 1782-1857 ....DLB-99

Bibliographical and Textual Scholarship
    Since World War II Y-89

The Bicentennial of James Fenimore Cooper:
    An International Celebration Y-89

Bichsel, Peter 1935- DLB-75

Bickerstaff, Isaac John 1733-circa 1808 ....DLB-89

Biddle, Drexel [publishing house] DLB-49

Bidwell, Walter Hilliard 1798-1881 ....DLB-79

Bienek, Horst 1930- DLB-75

Bierbaum, Otto Julius 1865-1910 ....DLB-66

Bierce, Ambrose 1842-1914? DLB-11, 12, 23, 71, 74

Bigelow, William F. 1879-1966 ....DLB-91

Biggle, Lloyd, Jr. 1923- DLB-8

Biglow, Hosea (see Lowell, James Russell)

Billinger, Richard 1890-1965 ....DLB-124

Billings, Josh (see Shaw, Henry Wheeler)

Binding, Rudolf G. 1867-1938 ....DLB-66

Bingham, Caleb 1757-1817 ....DLB-42

Binyon, Laurence 1869-1943 ....DLB-19

Biographical Documents I Y-84

Biographical Documents II Y-85

Bioren, John [publishing house] DLB-49

Bioy Casares, Adolfo 1914- DLB-113

Bird, William 1888-1963 ....DLB-4

Birney, Earle 1904- DLB-88

Birrell, Augustine 1850-1933 ....DLB-98

Bishop, Elizabeth 1911-1979 ....DLB-5

Bishop, John Peale 1892-1944 .... DLB-4, 9, 45

Bissett, Bill 1939- DLB-53

Black, David (D. M.) 1941- DLB-40

Black, Winifred 1863-1936 ....DLB-25

Black, Walter J. [publishing house] DLB-46

The Black Aesthetic: Background DS-8

The Black Arts Movement, by Larry Neal DLB-38

Black Theaters and Theater Organizations in
    America, 1961-1982: A Research List DLB-38

Black Theatre: A Forum [excerpts] DLB-38

Blackamore, Arthur 1679-? DLB-24, 39

Blackburn, Alexander L. 1929- Y-85

Blackburn, Paul 1926-1971 .... DLB-16; Y-81

Blackburn, Thomas 1916-1977 ....DLB-27

Blackmore, R. D. 1825-1900 ....DLB-18

Blackmur, R. P. 1904-1965 ....DLB-63

Blackwell, Basil, Publisher DLB-106

Blackwood, Caroline 1931- DLB-14

Blackwood's Edinburgh Magazine 1817-1980 ....DLB-110

Blair, Eric Arthur (see Orwell, George)

Blair, Francis Preston 1791-1876 ....DLB-43

Blair, James circa 1655-1743 ....DLB-24

Blair, John Durburrow 1759-1823 ....DLB-37

Blais, Marie-Claire 1939- DLB-53

Blaise, Clark 1940- DLB-53

Blake, Nicholas 1904-1972 ....DLB-77
(see Day Lewis, C.)

Blake, William 1757-1827 ....DLB-93

The Blakiston Company DLB-49

Blanchot, Maurice 1907- DLB-72

Blanckenburg, Christian Friedrich von
1744-1796 ....DLB-94

Bledsoe, Albert Taylor 1809-1877 ....DLB-3, 79

Blelock and Company DLB-49

Blennerhassett, Margaret Agnew 1773-1842 ....DLB-99

Bles, Geoffrey [publishing house] DLB-112

Blish, James 1921-1975 ....DLB-8

Bliss, E., and E. White [publishing house] DLB-49

Bloch, Robert 1917- DLB-44

Block, Rudolph (see Lessing, Bruno)

Blondal, Patricia 1926-1959 ....DLB-88

Bloom, Harold 1930- DLB-67

Bloomer, Amelia 1818-1894 ....DLB-79

Bloomfield, Robert 1766-1823 ....DLB-93

Bloomsbury Group abDS-10

Blotner, Joseph 1923- DLB-111

Bloy, Léon 1846-1917 ....DLB-123

Blume, Judy 1938- DLB-52

Blunck, Hans Friedrich 1888-1961 ....DLB-66

Blunden, Edmund 1896-1974 ....DLB-20, 100

Blunt, Wilfrid Scawen 1840-1922 ....DLB-19

Bly, Nellie (see Cochrane, Elizabeth)

Bly, Robert 1926- DLB-5

Boaden, James 1762-1839 ....DLB-89

The Bobbs-Merrill Archive at the
Lilly Library, Indiana University Y-90

The Bobbs-Merrill Company DLB-46

Bobrowski, Johannes 1917-1965 ....DLB-75

Bodenheim, Maxwell 1892-1954 ....DLB-9, 45

Bodkin, M. McDonnell 1850-1933 ....DLB-70

Bodley Head DLB-112

Bodmer, Johann Jakob 1698-1783 ....DLB-97

Bodmershof, Imma von 1895-1982 ....DLB-85

Bodsworth, Fred 1918- DLB-68

Boehm, Sydney 1908- DLB-44

Boer, Charles 1939- DLB-5

Boethius circa 480-circa 524 ....DLB-115

Boethius of Dacia circa 1240-? DLB-115

Bogan, Louise 1897-1970 ....DLB-45

Bogarde, Dirk 1921- DLB-14

Bogue, David [publishing house] DLB-106

Bohn, H. G. [publishing house] DLB-106

Boie, Heinrich Christian 1744-1806 ....DLB-94

Bok, Edward W. 1863-1930 ....DLB-91

Boland, Eavan 1944- DLB-40

Bolingbroke, Henry St. John, Viscount
1678-1751 ....DLB-101

Böll, Heinrich 1917-1985 ....Y-85, DLB-69

Bolling, Robert 1738-1775 ....DLB-31

Bolt, Carol 1941- DLB-60

Bolt, Robert 1924- DLB-13

Bolton, Herbert E. 1870-1953 ....DLB-17

Bonaventura DLB-90

Bonaventure circa 1217-1274 ....DLB-115

Bond, Edward 1934- DLB-13

Boni, Albert and Charles [publishing house] DLB-46

Boni and Liveright DLB-46

Robert Bonner's Sons DLB-49

Bontemps, Arna 1902-1973 ....DLB-48, 51

The Book League of America DLB-46

Book Reviewing in America: I Y-87

Book Reviewing in America: II Y-88

Book Reviewing in America: III Y-89

Book Reviewing in America: IV Y-90

Book Reviewing in America: V Y-91

Book Supply Company DLB-49

The Booker Prize
    Address by Anthony Thwaite, Chairman
    of the Booker Prize Judges
    Comments from Former Booker Prize
    Winners Y-86

Boorstin, Daniel J. 1914- DLB-17

Booth, Mary L. 1831-1889 . . . . .DLB-79

Booth, Philip 1925- Y-82

Booth, Wayne C. 1921- DLB-67

Borchardt, Rudolf 1877-1945 .DLB-66

Borchert, Wolfgang 1921-1947 . . . . DLB-69, 124

Borel, Pétrus 1809-1859 . . . . .DLB-119

Borges, Jorge Luis 1899-1986 . . . . .DLB-113; Y-86

Börne, Ludwig 1786-1837 . . . . .DLB-90

Borrow, George 1803-1881 . . . . .DLB-21, 55

Bosco, Henri 1888-1976 . . . . .DLB-72

Bosco, Monique 1927- DLB-53

Boswell, James 1740-1795 . . . . .DLB-104

Botta, Anne C. Lynch 1815-1891 . . . . .DLB-3

Bottomley, Gordon 1874-1948 . . . . .DLB-10

Bottoms, David 1949- DLB-120; Y-83

Bottrall, Ronald 1906- DLB-20

Boucher, Anthony 1911-1968 . . . . .DLB-8

Boucher, Jonathan 1738-1804 . . . . .DLB-31

Boucher de Boucherville, George 1814-1894 . . . . .DLB-99

Boudreau, Daniel (see Coste, Donat)

Bourassa, Napoéon 1827-1916 . . . . .DLB-99

Bourget, Paul 1852-1935 . . . . .DLB-123

Bourinot, John George 1837-1902 . . . . .DLB-99

Bourjaily, Vance Nye 1922- DLB-2

Bourne, Edward Gaylord 1860-1908 . . . . .DLB-47

Bourne, Randolph 1886-1918 . . . . .DLB-63

Bousono, Carlos 1923- DLB-108

Bousquet, Joë 1897-1950 . . . . .DLB-72

Bova, Ben 1932- Y-81

Bovard, Oliver K. 1872-1945 . . . . .DLB-25

Bove, Emmanuel 1898-1945 .DLB-72

Bowen, Elizabeth 1899-1973 .DLB-15

Bowen, Francis 1811-1890 . . . . DLB-1, 59

Bowen, John 1924- DLB-13

Bowen-Merrill Company DLB-49

Bowering, George 1935- DLB-53

Bowers, Claude G. 1878-1958 . . . . .DLB-17

Bowers, Edgar 1924- DLB-5

Bowers, Fredson Thayer 1905-1991 . . . . Y-91

Bowles, Paul 1910- DLB-5, 6

Bowles, Samuel III 1826-1878 . . . . .DLB-43

Bowles, William Lisles 1762-1850 . . . . .DLB-93

Bowman, Louise Morey 1882-1944 . . . . .DLB-68

Boyd, James 1888-1944 . . . . .DLB-9

Boyd, John 1919- DLB-8

Boyd, Thomas 1898-1935 . . . . .DLB-9

Boyesen, Hjalmar Hjorth 1848-1895 . . . . DLB-12, 71

Boyle, Kay 1902- DLB-4, 9, 48, 86

Boyle, Roger, Earl of Orrery 1621-1679 . . . . .DLB-80

Boyle, T. Coraghessan 1948- Y-86

Brackenbury, Alison 1953- DLB-40

Brackenridge, Hugh Henry 1748-1816 . . . . DLB-11, 37

Brackett, Charles 1892-1969 . . . . .DLB-26

Brackett, Leigh 1915-1978 . . . . DLB-8, 26

Bradburn, John [publishing house] DLB-49

Bradbury, Malcolm 1932- .DLB-14

Bradbury, Ray 1920- DLB-2, 8

Bradbury and Evans DLB-106

Braddon, Mary Elizabeth 1835-1915 . . . . DLB-18, 70

Bradford, Andrew 1686-1742 . . . . DLB-43, 73

Bradford, Gamaliel 1863-1932 . . . . .DLB-17

Bradford, John 1749-1830 . . . . .DLB-43

Bradford, Roark 1896-1948 .DLB-86

Bradford, William 1590-1657 . . . . DLB-24, 30

Bradford, William III 1719-1791 . . . . DLB-43, 73

Bradlaugh, Charles 1833-1891 ....DLB-57

Bradley, David 1950- DLB-33

Bradley, Marion Zimmer 1930- DLB-8

Bradley, William Aspenwall 1878-1939 ....DLB-4

Bradley, Ira, and Company DLB-49

Bradley, J. W., and Company DLB-49

Bradstreet, Anne 1612 or 1613-1672 ....DLB-24

Bradwardine, Thomas circa 1295-1349 ....DLB-115

Brady, Frank 1924-1986 ....DLB-111

Brady, Frederic A. [publishing house] DLB-49

Bragg, Melvyn 1939- DLB-14

Brainard, Charles H. [publishing house] DLB-49

Braine, John 1922-1986 ....DLB-15; Y-86

Braithwaite, William Stanley 1878-1962 ....DLB-50, 54

Braker, Ulrich 1735-1798 ....DLB-94

Bramah, Ernest 1868-1942 ....DLB-70

Branagan, Thomas 1774-1843 ....DLB-37

Branch, William Blackwell 1927- DLB-76

Branden Press DLB-46

Brathwaite, Edward Kamau 1930- DLB-125

Brault, Jacques 1933- DLB-53

Braun, Volker 1939- DLB-75

Brautigan, Richard 1935-1984 ....DLB-2, 5; Y-80, 84

Braxton, Joanne M. 1950- DLB-41

Bray, Anne Eliza 1790-1883 ....DLB-116

Bray, Thomas 1656-1730 ....DLB-24

Braziller, George [publishing house] DLB-46

The Bread Loaf Writers' Conference 1983 ....Y-84

The Break-Up of the Novel (1922),
    by John Middleton Murry DLB-36

Breasted, James Henry 1865-1935 ....DLB-47

Brecht, Bertolt 1898-1956 ....DLB-56, 124

Bredel, Willi 1901-1964 ....DLB-56

Breitinger, Johann Jakob 1701-1776 ....DLB-97

Bremser, Bonnie 1939- DLB-16

Bremser, Ray 1934- DLB-16

Brentano, Bernard von 1901-1964 ....DLB-56

Brentano, Clemens 1778-1842 ....DLB-90

Brentano's DLB-49

Brenton, Howard 1942- DLB-13

Breton, Andre 1896-1966 ....DLB-65

Brewer, Warren and Putnam DLB-46

Brewster, Elizabeth 1922- DLB-60

Bridgers, Sue Ellen 1942- DLB-52

Bridges, Robert 1844-1930 ....DLB-19, 98

Bridie, James 1888-1951 ....DLB-10

Briggs, Charles Frederick 1804-1877 ....DLB-3

Brighouse, Harold 1882-1958 ....DLB-10

Brimmer, B. J., Company DLB-46

Brinnin, John Malcolm 1916- DLB-48

Brisbane, Albert 1809-1890 ....DLB-3

Brisbane, Arthur 1864-1936 ....DLB-25

British Academy DLB-112

The British Library and the Regular Readers' Group Y-91

The British Critic 1793-1843 ....DLB-110

*The British Review and London
    Critical Journal* 1811-1825 ....DLB-110

Brito, Aristeo 1942- DLB-122

Broadway Publishing Company DLB-46

Broch, Hermann 1886-1951 ....DLB-85, 124

Brochu, Andre 1942- DLB-53

Brock, Edwin 1927- DLB-40

Brod, Max 1884-1968 ....DLB-81

Brodhead, John R. 1814-1873 ....DLB-30

Brome, Richard circa 1590-1652 ....DLB-58

Bromfield, Louis 1896-1956 ....DLB-4, 9, 86

Broner, E. M. 1930- DLB-28

Bronnen, Arnolt 1895-1959 ....DLB-124

Bronte, Anne 1820-1849 ....DLB-21

Bronte, Charlotte 1816-1855 ....DLB-21

Bronte, Emily 1818-1848 ....DLB-21, 32

Brooke, Frances 1724-1789 ....DLB-39, 99

Brooke, Henry 1703?-1783 ....DLB-39

Brooke, Rupert 1887-1915 ....DLB-19

Brooker, Bertram 1888-1955 ....DLB-88

Brooke-Rose, Christine 1926- DLB-14

Brookner, Anita 1928- Y-87

Brooks, Charles Timothy 1813-1883 ....DLB-1

Brooks, Cleanth 1906- DLB-63

Brooks, Gwendolyn 1917- DLB-5, 76

Brooks, Jeremy 1926- DLB-14

Brooks, Mel 1926- DLB-26

Brooks, Noah 1830-1903 ....DLB-42

Brooks, Richard 1912- DLB-44

Brooks, Van Wyck 1886-1963 .... DLB-45, 63, 103

Brophy, Brigid 1929- DLB-14

Brossard, Chandler 1922- DLB-16

Brossard, Nicole 1943- DLB-53

Brother Antoninus (see Everson, William)

Brougham and Vaux, Henry Peter
 Brougham, Baron 1778-1868 ....DLB-110

Brougham, John 1810-1880 ....DLB-11

Broughton, James 1913- DLB-5

Broughton, Rhoda 1840-1920 ....DLB-18

Broun, Heywood 1888-1939 ....DLB-29

Brown, Alice 1856-1948 ....DLB-78

Brown, Bob 1886-1959 ....DLB-4, 45

Brown, Cecil 1943- DLB-33

Brown, Charles Brockden 1771-1810 .... DLB-37, 59, 73

Brown, Christy 1932-1981 ....DLB-14

Brown, Dee 1908- Y-80

Brown, Frank London 1927-1962 ....DLB-76

Brown, Fredric 1906-1972 ....DLB-8

Brown, George Mackay 1921- DLB-14, 27

Brown, Harry 1917-1986 ....DLB-26

Brown, Marcia 1918- DLB-61

Brown, Margaret Wise 1910-1952 ....DLB-22

Brown, Morna Doris (see Ferrars, Elizabeth)

Brown, Oliver Madox 1855-1874 ....DLB-21

Brown, Sterling 1901-1989 .... DLB-48, 51, 63

Brown, T. E. 1830-1897 ....DLB-35

Brown, William Hill 1765-1793 ....DLB-37

Brown, William Wells 1814-1884 .... DLB-3, 50

Browne, Charles Farrar 1834-1867 ....DLB-11

Browne, Francis Fisher 1843-1913 ....DLB-79

Browne, Michael Dennis 1940- DLB-40

Browne, William, of Tavistock 1590-1645 ....DLB-121

Browne, Wynyard 1911-1964 ....DLB-13

Browne and Nolan DLB-106

Brownell, W. C. 1851-1928 ....DLB-71

Browning, Elizabeth Barrett 1806-1861 ....DLB-32

Browning, Robert 1812-1889 ....DLB-32

Brownjohn, Allan 1931- DLB-40

Brownson, Orestes Augustus 1803-1876 .... DLB-1, 59, 73

Bruccoli, Matthew J. 1931- DLB-103

Bruce, Charles 1906-1971 ....DLB-68

Bruce, Leo 1903-1979 ....DLB-77

Bruce, Philip Alexander 1856-1933 ....DLB-47

Bruce Humphries [publishing house] DLB-46

Bruce-Novoa, Juan 1944- DLB-82

Bruckman, Clyde 1894-1955 ....DLB-26

Bruckner, Ferdinand 1891-1958 ....DLB-118

Brundage, John Herbert (see Herbert, John)

Brutus, Dennis 1924- DLB-117

Bryant, William Cullen 1794-1878 .... DLB-3, 43, 59

Brydges, Sir Samuel Egerton 1762-1837 ....DLB-107

Buchan, John 1875-1940 .... DLB-34, 70

Buchanan, Robert 1841-1901 .... DLB-18, 35

Buchman, Sidney 1902-1975 ....DLB-26

Buck, Pearl S. 1892-1973 .... DLB-9, 102

Bucke, Charles 1781-1846 ....DLB-110

Bucke, Richard Maurice 1837-1902 ....DLB-99

Buckingham, Joseph Tinker 1779-1861 and
 Buckingham, Edwin 1810-1833 ....DLB-73

Buckler, Ernest 1908-1984 ....DLB-68

Buckley, William F., Jr. 1925- Y-80

Buckminster, Joseph Stevens 1784-1812 ....DLB-37

Buckner, Robert 1906- DLB-26

Budd, Thomas ?-1698 ....DLB-24

Budrys, A. J. 1931- DLB-8

Buechner, Frederick 1926- Y-80

Buell, John 1927- DLB-53

Buffum, Job [publishing house] DLB-49

Bugnet, Georges 1879-1981 ....DLB-92

Buies, Arthur 1840-1901 ....DLB-99

Bukowski, Charles 1920- DLB-5

Bullins, Ed 1935- DLB-7, 38

Bulwer-Lytton, Edward (also Edward Bulwer)
    1803-1873 ....DLB-21

Bumpus, Jerry 1937- Y-81

Bunce and Brother DLB-49

Bunner, H. C. 1855-1896 ....DLB-78, 79

Bunting, Basil 1900-1985 ....DLB-20

Bunyan, John 1628-1688 ....DLB-39

Burch, Robert 1925- DLB-52

Burciaga, José Antonio 1940- DLB-82

Bürger, Gottfried August 1747-1794 ....DLB-94

Burgess, Anthony 1917- DLB-14

Burgess, Gelett 1866-1951 ....DLB-11

Burgess, John W. 1844-1931 ....DLB-47

Burgess, Thornton W. 1874-1965 ....DLB-22

Burgess, Stringer and Company DLB-49

Burk, John Daly circa 1772-1808 ....DLB-37

Burke, Edmund 1729?-1797 ....DLB-104

Burke, Kenneth 1897- DLB-45, 63

Burlingame, Edward Livermore 1848-1922 ....DLB-79

Burnet, Gilbert 1643-1715 ....DLB-101

Burnett, Frances Hodgson 1849-1924 ....DLB-42

Burnett, W. R. 1899-1982 ....DLB-9

Burney, Fanny 1752-1840 ....DLB-39

Burns, Alan 1929- DLB-14

Burns, John Horne 1916-1953 ....Y-85

Burns, Robert 1759-1796 ....DLB-109

Burns and Oates DLB-106

Burnshaw, Stanley 1906- DLB-48

Burr, C. Chauncey 1815?-1883 ....DLB-79

Burroughs, Edgar Rice 1875-1950 ....DLB-8

Burroughs, John 1837-1921 ....DLB-64

Burroughs, Margaret T. G. 1917- DLB-41

Burroughs, William S., Jr. 1947-1981 ....DLB-16

Burroughs, William Seward 1914-
    ....DLB-2, 8, 16; Y-81

Burroway, Janet 1936- DLB-6

Burt, Maxwell S. 1882-1954 ....DLB-86

Burt, A. L., and Company DLB-49

Burton, Miles (see Rhode, John)

Burton, Richard F. 1821-1890 ....DLB-55

Burton, Virginia Lee 1909-1968 ....DLB-22

Burton, William Evans 1804-1860 ....DLB-73

Burwell, Adam Hood 1790-1849 ....DLB-99

Bury, Lady Charlotte 1775-1861 ....DLB-116

Busch, Frederick 1941- DLB-6

Busch, Niven 1903-1991 ....DLB-44

Bussieres, Arthur de 1877-1913 ....DLB-92

Butler, Juan 1942-1981 ....DLB-53

Butler, Octavia E. 1947- DLB-33

Butler, Samuel 1613-1680 ....DLB-101

Butler, Samuel 1835-1902 ....DLB-18, 57

Butler, E. H., and Company DLB-49

Butor, Michel 1926- DLB-83

Butterworth, Hezekiah 1839-1905 ....DLB-42

Buttitta, Ignazio 1899- DLB-114

Byars, Betsy 1928- DLB-52

Byatt, A. S. 1936- DLB-14

Byles, Mather 1707-1788 ....DLB-24

Bynner, Witter 1881-1968 ....DLB-54

Byrd, William II 1674-1744 ....DLB-24

Byrne, John Keyes (see Leonard, Hugh)

Byron, George Gordon, Lord 1788-1824 ....DLB-96, 110

C

Caballero Bonald, José Manuel 1926- DLB-108

Cabell, James Branch 1879-1958 ....DLB-9, 78

Cabeza de Baca, Manuel 1853-1915 ....DLB-122

Cabeza de Baca Gilbert, Fabiola 1898- DLB-122

Cable, George Washington 1844-1925 ....DLB-12, 74

Cabrera Infante, Guillermo 1929- DLB-113

Cady, Edwin H. 1917- DLB-103

Cahan, Abraham 1860-1951 .... DLB-9, 25, 28

Cain, George 1943- DLB-33

Calder, John (Publishers), Limited DLB-112

Caldwell, Ben 1937- DLB-38

Caldwell, Erskine 1903-1987 ....DLB-9, 86

Caldwell, H. M., Company DLB-49

Calhoun, John C. 1782-1850 ....DLB-3

Calisher, Hortense 1911- DLB-2

A Call to Letters and an Invitation
  to the Electric Chair,
  by Siegfried Mandel DLB-75

Callaghan, Morley 1903-1990 ....DLB-68

Callaloo Y-87

Calmer, Edgar 1907- DLB-4

Calverley, C. S. 1831-1884 ....DLB-35

Calvert, George Henry 1803-1889 ....DLB-1, 64

Cambridge Press DLB-49

Cameron, Eleanor 1912- DLB-52

Cameron, George Frederick
  1854-1885 ....DLB-99

Cameron, William Bleasdell 1862-1951 ....DLB-99

Camm, John 1718-1778 ....DLB-31

Campana, Dino 1885-1932 ....DLB-114

Campbell, Gabrielle Margaret Vere
  (see Shearing, Joseph)

Campbell, James Edwin 1867-1896 ....DLB-50

Campbell, John 1653-1728 ....DLB-43

Campbell, John W., Jr. 1910-1971 ....DLB-8

Campbell, Roy 1901-1957 ....DLB-20

Campbell, Thomas 1777-1844 ....DLB-93

Campbell, William Wilfred 1858-1918 ....DLB-92

Campion, Thomas 1567-1620 ....DLB-58

Camus, Albert 1913-1960 ....DLB-72

Canby, Henry Seidel 1878-1961 ....DLB-91

Candelaria, Cordelia 1943- DLB-82

Candelaria, Nash 1928- DLB-82

Candour in English Fiction (1890),
  by Thomas Hardy DLB-18

Canetti, Elias 1905- DLB-85, 124

Cannan, Gilbert 1884-1955 ....DLB-10

Cannell, Kathleen 1891-1974 ....DLB-4

Cannell, Skipwith 1887-1957 ....DLB-45

Cantwell, Robert 1908-1978 ....DLB-9

Cape, Jonathan, and Harrison Smith
  [publishing house] DLB-46

Cape, Jonathan, Limited DLB-112

Capen, Joseph 1658-1725 ....DLB-24

Capote, Truman 1924-1984 .... DLB-2; Y-80, 84

Cardarelli, Vincenzo 1887-1959 ....DLB-114

Cardenas, Reyes 1948- DLB-122

Cardinal, Marie 1929- DLB-83

Carey, Henry circa 1687-1689-1743 ....DLB-84

Carey, Mathew 1760-1839 .... DLB-37, 73

Carey and Hart DLB-49

Carey, M., and Company DLB-49

Carlell, Lodowick 1602-1675 ....DLB-58

Carleton, G. W. [publishing house] DLB-49

Carlile, Richard 1790-1843 ....DLB-110

Carlyle, Jane Welsh 1801-1866 ....DLB-55

Carlyle, Thomas 1795-1881 ....DLB-55

Carman, Bliss 1861-1929 ....DLB-92

Carnero, Guillermo 1947- DLB-108

Carossa, Hans 1878-1956 ....DLB-66

Carpenter, Stephen Cullen ?-1820? DLB-73

Carpentier, Alejo 1904-1980 ....DLB-113

Carr, Emily 1871-1945 ....DLB-68

Carr, Virginia Spencer 1929- DLB-111

Carrier, Roch 1937- DLB-53

Carrillo, Adolfo 1855-1926 ....DLB-122

Carroll, Gladys Hasty 1904- DLB-9

Carroll, John 1735-1815 .... DLB-37

Carroll, John 1809-1884 .... DLB-99

Carroll, Lewis 1832-1898 .... DLB-18

Carroll, Paul 1927- DLB-16

Carroll, Paul Vincent 1900-1968 .... DLB-10

Carroll and Graf Publishers DLB-46

Carruth, Hayden 1921- DLB-5

Carryl, Charles E. 1841-1920 .... DLB-42

Carswell, Catherine 1879-1946 .... DLB-36

Carter, Angela 1940- DLB-14

Carter, Elizabeth 1717-1806 .... DLB-109

Carter, Henry (see Leslie, Frank)

Carter, Landon 1710-1778 .... DLB-31

Carter, Lin 1930- Y-81

Carter, Martin 1927- DLB-117

Carter and Hendee DLB-49

Carter, Robert, and Brothers DLB-49

Caruthers, William Alexander 1802-1846 .... DLB-3

Carver, Jonathan 1710-1780 .... DLB-31

Carver, Raymond 1938-1988 .... Y-84, 88

Cary, Joyce 1888-1957 .... DLB-15, 100

Casey, Juanita 1925- DLB-14

Casey, Michael 1947- DLB-5

Cassady, Carolyn 1923- DLB-16

Cassady, Neal 1926-1968 .... DLB-16

Cassell and Company DLB-106

Cassell Publishing Company DLB-49

Cassill, R. V. 1919- DLB-6

Cassity, Turner 1929- DLB-105

Castellano, Olivia 1944- DLB-122

Castellanos, Rosario 1925-1974 .... DLB-113

Castillo, Ana 1953- DLB-122

Castlemon, Harry (see Fosdick, Charles Austin)

Caswall, Edward 1814-1878 .... DLB-32

Catacalos, Rosemary 1944- DLB-122

Cather, Willa 1873-1947 .... DLB-9, 54, 78; DS-1

Catherwood, Mary Hartwell 1847-1902 .... DLB-78

Catton, Bruce 1899-1978 .... DLB-17

Causley, Charles 1917- DLB-27

Caute, David 1936- DLB-14

Cawein, Madison 1865-1914 .... DLB-54

The Caxton Printers, Limited DLB-46

Cayrol, Jean 1911- DLB-83

Celan, Paul 1920-1970 .... DLB-69

Celaya, Gabriel 1911-1991 .... DLB-108

Céline, Louis-Ferdinand 1894-1961 .... DLB-72

Center for Bibliographical Studies and Research at the University of California, Riverside Y-91

Center for the Book Research Y-84

Centlivre, Susanna 1669?-1723 .... DLB-84

The Century Company DLB-49

Cervantes, Lorna Dee 1954- DLB-82

Chacón, Eusebio 1869-1948 .... DLB-82

Chacón, Felipe Maximiliano 1873-? DLB-82

Challans, Eileen Mary (see Renault, Mary)

Chalmers, George 1742-1825 .... DLB-30

Chamberlain, Samuel S. 1851-1916 .... DLB-25

Chamberland, Paul 1939- DLB-60

Chamberlin, William Henry 1897-1969 .... DLB-29

Chambers, Charles Haddon 1860-1921 .... DLB-10

Chambers, W. and R. [publishing house] DLB-106

Chamisso, Albert von 1781-1838 .... DLB-90

Champfleury 1821-1889 .... DLB-119

Chandler, Harry 1864-1944 .... DLB-29

Chandler, Raymond 1888-1959 .... DS-6

Channing, Edward 1856-1931 .... DLB-17

Channing, Edward Tyrrell 1790-1856 .... DLB-1, 59

Channing, William Ellery 1780-1842 .... DLB-1, 59

Channing, William Ellery, II 1817-1901 .... DLB-1

Channing, William Henry 1810-1884 .... DLB-1, 59

Chaplin, Charlie 1889-1977 .... DLB-44

Chapman, George 1559 or 1560 - 1634 .... DLB-62, 121

Chapman, John DLB-106

Chapman, William 1850-1917 .... DLB-99

Chapman and Hall DLB-106

Chappell, Fred 1936- DLB-6, 105

Chappell, Fred, A Detail in a Poem DLB-105

Charbonneau, Jean 1875-1960 .... DLB-92

Charbonneau, Robert 1911-1967 .... DLB-68

Charles, Gerda 1914- DLB-14

Charles, William [publishing house] DLB-49

The Charles Wood Affair:
    A Playwright Revived Y-83

Charlotte Forten: Pages from her Diary DLB-50

Charteris, Leslie 1907- DLB-77

Charyn, Jerome 1937- Y-83

Chase, Borden 1900-1971 .... DLB-26

Chase, Edna Woolman 1877-1957 .... DLB-91

Chase-Riboud, Barbara 1936- DLB-33

Chateaubriand, François-René de 1768-1848 .... DLB-119

Chatterton, Thomas 1752-1770 .... DLB-109

Chatto and Windus DLB-106

Chauncy, Charles 1705-1787 .... DLB-24

Chauveau, Pierre-Joseph-Olivier 1820-1890 .... DLB-99

Chávez, Denise 1948- DLB-122

Chávez, Fray Angélico 1910- DLB-82

Chayefsky, Paddy 1923-1981 .... DLB-7, 44; Y-81

Cheever, Ezekiel 1615-1708 .... DLB-24

Cheever, George Barrell 1807-1890 .... DLB-59

Cheever, John 1912-1982 .... DLB-2, 102; Y-80, 82

Cheever, Susan 1943- Y-82

Chelsea House DLB-46

Cheney, Ednah Dow (Littlehale) 1824-1904 .... DLB-1

Cheney, Harriet Vaughn 1796-1889 .... DLB-99

Cherry, Kelly 1940 .... Y-83

Cherryh, C. J. 1942- Y-80

Chesnutt, Charles Waddell 1858-1932 .... DLB-12, 50, 78

Chester, George Randolph 1869-1924 .... DLB-78

Chesterfield, Philip Dormer Stanhope,
    Fourth Earl of 1694-1773 .... DLB-104

Chesterton, G. K. 1874-1936 .... DLB-10, 19, 34, 70, 98

Cheyney, Edward P. 1861-1947 .... DLB-47

Chicano History DLB-82

Chicano Language DLB-82

Child, Francis James 1825-1896 .... DLB-1, 64

Child, Lydia Maria 1802-1880 .... DLB-1, 74

Child, Philip 1898-1978 .... DLB-68

Childers, Erskine 1870-1922 .... DLB-70

Children's Book Awards and Prizes DLB-61

Childress, Alice 1920- DLB-7, 38

Childs, George W. 1829-1894 .... DLB-23

Chilton Book Company DLB-46

Chittenden, Hiram Martin 1858-1917 .... DLB-47

Chivers, Thomas Holley 1809-1858 .... DLB-3

Chopin, Kate 1850-1904 .... DLB-12, 78

Chopin, Rene 1885-1953 .... DLB-92

Choquette, Adrienne 1915-1973 .... DLB-68

Choquette, Robert 1905- DLB-68

The Christian Publishing Company DLB-49

Christie, Agatha 1890-1976 .... DLB-13, 77

Church, Benjamin 1734-1778 .... DLB-31

Church, Francis Pharcellus 1839-1906 .... DLB-79

Church, William Conant 1836-1917 .... DLB-79

Churchill, Caryl 1938- DLB-13

Churchill, Charles 1731-1764 .... DLB-109

Churchill, Sir Winston 1874-1965 .... DLB-100

Churton, E., and Company DLB-106

Chute, Marchette 1909- DLB-103

Ciardi, John 1916-1986 .... DLB-5; Y-86

Cibber, Colley 1671-1757 .... DLB-84

Cirese, Eugenio 1884-1955 .... DLB-114

Cisneros, Sandra 1954- DLB-122

City Lights Books DLB-46

Cixous, Hélène 1937- DLB-83

Clampitt, Amy 1920- DLB-105

Clapper, Raymond 1892-1944 ....DLB-29

Clare, John 1793-1864 ....DLB-55, 96

Clarendon, Edward Hyde, Earl of
    1609-1674 ....DLB-101

Clark, Alfred Alexander Gordon (see Hare, Cyril)

Clark, Ann Nolan 1896- DLB-52

Clark, Catherine Anthony 1892-1977 ....DLB-68

Clark, Charles Heber 1841-1915 ....DLB-11

Clark, Davis Wasgatt 1812-1871 ....DLB-79

Clark, Eleanor 1913- DLB-6

Clark, J. P. 1935- DLB-117

Clark, Lewis Gaylord 1808-1873 ....DLB-3, 64, 73

Clark, Walter Van Tilburg 1909-1971 ....DLB-9

Clark, C. M., Publishing Company DLB-46

Clarke, Austin 1896-1974 ....DLB-10, 20

Clarke, Austin C. 1934- DLB-53, 125

Clarke, Gillian 1937- DLB-40

Clarke, James Freeman 1810-1888 ....DLB-1, 59

Clarke, Rebecca Sophia 1833-1906 ....DLB-42

Clarke, Robert, and Company DLB-49

Claudius, Matthias 1740-1815 ....DLB-97

Clausen, Andy 1943- DLB-16

Claxton, Remsen and Haffelfinger DLB-49

Clay, Cassius Marcellus 1810-1903 ....DLB-43

Cleary, Beverly 1916- DLB-52

Cleaver, Vera 1919-   and
    Cleaver, Bill 1920-1981 ....DLB-52

Cleland, John 1710-1789 ....DLB-39

Clemens, Samuel Langhorne
    1835-1910 ....DLB-11, 12, 23, 64, 74

Clement, Hal 1922- DLB-8

Clemo, Jack 1916- DLB-27

Clifford, James L. 1901-1978 ....DLB-103

Clifton, Lucille 1936- DLB-5, 41

Clode, Edward J. [publishing house] DLB-46

Clough, Arthur Hugh 1819-1861 ....DLB-32

Cloutier, Cécile 1930- DLB-60

Clutton-Brock, Arthur 1868-1924 ....DLB-98

Coates, Robert M. 1897-1973 ....DLB-4, 9, 102

Coatsworth, Elizabeth 1893- DLB-22

Cobb, Charles E., Jr. 1943- DLB-41

Cobb, Frank I. 1869-1923 ....DLB-25

Cobb, Irvin S. 1876-1944 ....DLB-11, 25, 86

Cobbett, William 1763-1835 ....DLB-43, 107

Cochran, Thomas C. 1902- DLB-17

Cochrane, Elizabeth 1867-1922 ....DLB-25

Cockerill, John A. 1845-1896 ....DLB-23

Cocteau, Jean 1889-1963 ....DLB-65

Coderre, Emile (see Jean Narrache)

Coffee, Lenore J. 1900?-1984 ....DLB-44

Coffin, Robert P. Tristram 1892-1955 ....DLB-45

Cogswell, Fred 1917- DLB-60

Cogswell, Mason Fitch 1761-1830 ....DLB-37

Cohen, Arthur A. 1928-1986 ....DLB-28

Cohen, Leonard 1934- DLB-53

Cohen, Matt 1942- DLB-53

Colden, Cadwallader 1688-1776 ....DLB-24, 30

Cole, Barry 1936- DLB-14

Colegate, Isabel 1931- DLB-14

Coleman, Emily Holmes 1899-1974 ....DLB-4

Coleridge, Hartley 1796-1849 ....DLB-96

Coleridge, Mary 1861-1907 ....DLB-19, 98

Coleridge, Samuel Taylor 1772-1834 ....DLB-93, 107

Colette 1873-1954 ....DLB-65

Colette, Sidonie Gabrielle (see Colette)

Collier, John 1901-1980 ....DLB-77

Collier, Mary 1690-1762 ....DLB-95

Collier, Robert J. 1876-1918 ....DLB-91

Collier, P. F. [publishing house] DLB-49

Collin and Small DLB-49

Collins, Mortimer 1827-1876 ....DLB-21, 35

Collins, Wilkie 1824-1889 ....DLB-18, 70

Collins, William 1721-1759 ....DLB-109

Collins, Isaac [publishing house] DLB-49

Collyer, Mary 1716?-1763? DLB-39

Colman, Benjamin 1673-1747 ....DLB-24

Colman, George, the Elder
    1732-1794 ....DLB-89

Colman, George, the Younger 1762-1836 ....DLB-89

Colman, S. [publishing house] DLB-49

Colombo, John Robert 1936- DLB-53

Colter, Cyrus 1910- DLB-33

Colum, Padraic 1881-1972 ....DLB-19

Colwin, Laurie 1944- Y-80

Comden, Betty 1919- and Green,
    Adolph 1918- DLB-44

Comi, Girolamo 1890-1968 ....DLB-114

The Comic Tradition Continued
    [in the British Novel] DLB-15

Commager, Henry Steele 1902- DLB-17

The Commercialization of the Image of
    Revolt, by Kenneth Rexroth DLB-16

Community and Commentators: Black
    Theatre and Its Critics DLB-38

Compton-Burnett, Ivy 1884?-1969 ....DLB-36

Conan, Laure 1845-1924 ....DLB-99

Conde, Carmen 1901- DLB-108

Conference on Modern Biography Y-85

Congreve, William 1670-1729 ....DLB-39, 84

Conkey, W. B., Company DLB-49

Connell, Evan S., Jr. 1924- DLB-2; Y-81

Connelly, Marc 1890-1980 ....DLB-7; Y-80

Connolly, Cyril 1903-1974 ....DLB-98

Connolly, James B. 1868-1957 ....DLB-78

Connor, Ralph 1860-1937 ....DLB-92

Connor, Tony 1930- DLB-40

Conquest, Robert 1917- DLB-27

Conrad, Joseph 1857-1924 .... DLB-10, 34, 98

Conrad, John, and Company DLB-49

Conroy, Jack 1899-1990 .... Y-81

Conroy, Pat 1945- DLB-6

The Consolidation of Opinion: Critical
    Responses to the Modernists DLB-36

Constable and Company Limited DLB-112

Constant, Benjamin 1767-1830 ....DLB-119

Constant de Rebecque, Henri-Benjamin de
    (see Constant, Benjamin)

Constantine, David 1944- DLB-40

Constantin-Weyer, Maurice 1881-1964 ....DLB-92

Contempo Caravan: Kites in a Windstorm Y-85

A Contemporary Flourescence of Chicano
    Literature Y-84

The Continental Publishing Company DLB-49

A Conversation with Chaim Potok Y-84

Conversations with Publishers I: An Interview
    with Patrick O'Connor Y-84

Conversations with Rare Book Dealers I: An
    Interview with Glenn Horowitz Y-90

The Conversion of an Unpolitical Man,
    by W. H. Bruford DLB-66

Conway, Moncure Daniel 1832-1907 ....DLB-1

Cook, Ebenezer circa 1667-circa 1732 ....DLB-24

Cook, Michael 1933- DLB-53

Cook, David C., Publishing Company DLB-49

Cooke, George Willis 1848-1923 ....DLB-71

Cooke, Increase, and Company DLB-49

Cooke, John Esten 1830-1886 ....DLB-3

Cooke, Philip Pendleton 1816-1850 .... DLB-3, 59

Cooke, Rose Terry 1827-1892 .... DLB-12, 74

Coolbrith, Ina 1841-1928 ....DLB-54

Cooley, Peter 1940- DLB-105

Cooley, Peter, Into the Mirror DLB-105

Coolidge, George [publishing house] DLB-49

Coolidge, Susan (see Woolsey, Sarah Chauncy)

Cooper, Giles 1918-1966 ....DLB-13

Cooper, James Fenimore 1789-1851 ....DLB-3

Cooper, Kent 1880-1965 ....DLB-29

Coover, Robert 1932- DLB-2; Y-81

Copeland and Day DLB-49

Coppel, Alfred 1921- Y-83

Coppola, Francis Ford 1939- DLB-44

Corazzini, Sergio 1886-1907 ....DLB-114

Corbett, Richard 1582-1635 ....DLB-121

Corcoran, Barbara 1911- DLB-52

Corelli, Marie 1855-1924 ....DLB-34

Corle, Edwin 1906-1956 ....Y-85

Corman, Cid 1924- DLB-5

Cormier, Robert 1925- DLB-52

Corn, Alfred 1943- DLB-120; Y-80

Cornish, Sam 1935- DLB-41

Cornwall, Barry (see Procter, Bryan Waller)

Cornwell, David John Moore (see le Carre, John)

Corpi, Lucha 1945- DLB-82

Corrington, John William 1932- DLB-6

Corrothers, James D. 1869-1917 ....DLB-50

Corso, Gregory 1930- DLB-5, 16

Cortazar, Julio 1914-1984 ....DLB-113

Cortez, Jayne 1936- DLB-41

Corvo, Baron (see Rolfe, Frederick William)

Cory, William Johnson 1823-1892 ....DLB-35

Cosmopolitan Book Corporation DLB-46

Costain, Thomas B. 1885-1965 ....DLB-9

Coste, Donat 1912-1957 ....DLB-88

Cota-Cárdenas, Margarita 1941- DLB-122

Cotter, Joseph Seamon, Sr. 1861-1949 ....DLB-50

Cotter, Joseph Seamon, Jr. 1895-1919 ....DLB-50

Cotton, John 1584-1652 ....DLB-24

Coulter, John 1888-1980 ....DLB-68

Cournos, John 1881-1966 ....DLB-54

Coventry, Francis 1725-1754 ....DLB-39

Coverly, N. [publishing house] DLB-49

Covici-Friede DLB-46

Coward, Noel 1899-1973 ....DLB-10

Coward, McCann and Geoghegan DLB-46

Cowles, Gardner 1861-1946 ....DLB-29

Cowley, Hannah 1743-1809 ....DLB-89

Cowley, Malcolm 1898-1989 ....DLB-4, 48; Y-81, 89

Cowper, William 1731-1800 ....DLB-104, 109

Cox, A. B. (see Berkeley, Anthony)

Cox, Palmer 1840-1924 ....DLB-42

Coxe, Louis 1918- DLB-5

Coxe, Tench 1755-1824 ....DLB-37

Cozzens, James Gould 1903-1978 ....DLB-9; Y-84; DS-2

Crabbe, George 1754-1832 ....DLB-93

Craddock, Charles Egbert (see Murfree, Mary N.)

Cradock, Thomas 1718-1770 ....DLB-31

Craig, Daniel H. 1811-1895 ....DLB-43

Craik, Dinah Maria 1826-1887 ....DLB-35

Cranch, Christopher Pearse 1813-1892 ....DLB-1, 42

Crane, Hart 1899-1932 ....DLB-4, 48

Crane, R. S. 1886-1967 ....DLB-63

Crane, Stephen 1871-1900 ....DLB-12, 54, 78

Crapsey, Adelaide 1878-1914 ....DLB-54

Craven, Avery 1885-1980 ....DLB-17

Crawford, Charles 1752-circa 1815 ....DLB-31

Crawford, F. Marion 1854-1909 ....DLB-71

Crawford, Isabel Valancy 1850-1887 ....DLB-92

Crawley, Alan 1887-1975 ....DLB-68

Crayon, Geoffrey (see Irving, Washington)

Creasey, John 1908-1973 ....DLB-77

Creative Age Press DLB-46

Creel, George 1876-1953 ....DLB-25

Creeley, Robert 1926- DLB-5, 16

Creelman, James 1859-1915 ....DLB-23

Cregan, David 1931- DLB-13

Creighton, Donald Grant 1902-1979 ....DLB-88

Cremazie, Octave 1827-1879 ....DLB-99

Crémer, Victoriano 1909?- DLB-108

Crescas, Hasdai circa 1340-1412? DLB-115

Cresset Press DLB-112

Crèvecoeur, Michel Guillaume Jean de 1735-1813 .....DLB-37

Crews, Harry 1935- DLB-6

Crichton, Michael 1942- Y-81

A Crisis of Culture: The Changing Role
of Religion in the New Republic DLB-37

Crispin, Edmund 1921-1978 ....DLB-87

Cristofer, Michael 1946- DLB-7

"The Critic as Artist" (1891), by Oscar Wilde DLB-57

Criticism In Relation To Novels (1863),
by G. H. Lewes DLB-21

Crockett, David (Davy) 1786-1836 ....DLB-3, 11

Croft-Cooke, Rupert (see Bruce, Leo)

Crofts, Freeman Wills 1879-1957 ....DLB-77

Croker, John Wilson 1780-1857 ....DLB-110

Croly, Herbert 1869-1930 ....DLB-91

Croly, Jane Cunningham 1829-1901 ....DLB-23

Crosby, Caresse 1892-1970 ....DLB-48

Crosby, Caresse 1892-1970 and Crosby,
Harry 1898-1929 ....DLB-4

Crosby, Harry 1898-1929 ....DLB-48

Crossley-Holland, Kevin 1941- DLB-40

Crothers, Rachel 1878-1958 ....DLB-7

Crowell, Thomas Y., Company DLB-49

Crowley, John 1942- Y-82

Crowley, Mart 1935- DLB-7

Crown Publishers DLB-46

Crowne, John 1641-1712 ....DLB-80

Crowninshield, Frank 1872-1947 ....DLB-91

Croy, Homer 1883-1965 ....DLB-4

Crumley, James 1939- Y-84

Cruz, Victor Hernández 1949- DLB-41

Csokor, Franz Theodor 1885-1969 ....DLB-81

Cuala Press DLB-112

Cullen, Countee 1903-1946 ....DLB-4, 48, 51

Culler, Jonathan D. 1944- DLB-67

The Cult of Biography
Excerpts from the Second Folio Debate:
"Biographies are generally a disease of
English Literature"Germaine Greer,
Victoria Glendinning, Auberon Waugh,
and Richard Holmes Y-86

Cumberland, Richard 1732-1811 ....DLB-89

Cummings, E. E. 1894-1962 ....DLB-4, 48

Cummings, Ray 1887-1957 ....DLB-8

Cummings and Hilliard DLB-49

Cummins, Maria Susanna 1827-1866 ....DLB-42

Cundall, Joseph [publishing house] DLB-106

Cuney, Waring 1906-1976 ....DLB-51

Cuney-Hare, Maude 1874-1936 ....DLB-52

Cunningham, Allan 1784-1842 ....DLB-116

Cunningham, J. V. 1911- DLB-5

Cunningham, Peter F. [publishing house] DLB-49

Cuomo, George 1929- Y-80

Cupples and Leon DLB-46

Cupples, Upham and Company DLB-49

Cuppy, Will 1884-1949 ....DLB-11

Currie, Mary Montgomerie Lamb Singleton,
Lady Currie (see Fane, Violet)

Curti, Merle E. 1897- DLB-17

Curtis, Cyrus H. K. 1850-1933 ....DLB-91

Curtis, George William 1824-1892 ....DLB-1, 43

Curzon, Sarah Anne 1833-1898 ....DLB-99

D

D. M. Thomas: The Plagiarism Controversy Y-82

Dabit, Eugene 1898-1936 ....DLB-65

Daborne, Robert circa 1580-1628 ....DLB-58

Dacey, Philip 1939- DLB-105

Dacey, Philip, Eyes Across Centuries:
Contemporary Poetry and "That
Vision Thing" DLB-105

Daggett, Rollin M. 1831-1901 ....DLB-79

Dahlberg, Edward 1900-1977 ....DLB-48

Dale, Peter 1938- DLB-40

Dall, Caroline Wells (Healey) 1822-1912 ....DLB-1

Dallas, E. S. 1828-1879 ....DLB-55

The Dallas Theater Center DLB-7

D'Alton, Louis 1900-1951 ....DLB-10

Daly, T. A. 1871-1948 ....DLB-11

Damon, S. Foster 1893-1971 ....DLB-45

Damrell, William S. [publishing house] DLB-49

Dana, Charles A. 1819-1897 ....DLB-3, 23

Dana, Richard Henry, Jr. 1815-1882 ....DLB-1

Dandridge, Ray Garfield DLB-51

Dane, Clemence 1887-1965 ....DLB-10

Danforth, John 1660-1730 ....DLB-24

Danforth, Samuel I 1626-1674 ....DLB-24

Danforth, Samuel II 1666-1727 ....DLB-24

Dangerous Years: London Theater,
    1939-1945 ....DLB-10

Daniel, John M. 1825-1865 ....DLB-43

Daniel, Samuel 1562 or 1563-1619 ....DLB-62

Daniel Press DLB-106

Daniells, Roy 1902-1979 ....DLB-68

Daniels, Jim 1956- DLB-120

Daniels, Josephus 1862-1948 ....DLB-29

Danner, Margaret Esse 1915- DLB-41

Dantin, Louis 1865-1945 ....DLB-92

Darley, George 1795-1846 ....DLB-96

Darwin, Charles 1809-1882 ....DLB-57

Darwin, Erasmus 1731-1802 ....DLB-93

Daryush, Elizabeth 1887-1977 ....DLB-20

Dashwood, Edmée Elizabeth Monica
    de la Pasture (see Delafield, E. M.)

Daudet, Alphonse 1840-1897 ....DLB-123

d'Aulaire, Edgar Parin 1898- and
    d'Aulaire, Ingri 1904- DLB-22

Davenant, Sir William 1606-1668 ....DLB-58

Davenport, Robert ?-? DLB-58

Daves, Delmer 1904-1977 ....DLB-26

Davey, Frank 1940- DLB-53

Davies, John, of Hereford 1565?-1618 ....DLB-121

Davies, Peter, Limited DLB-112

Davidson, Avram 1923- DLB-8

Davidson, Donald 1893-1968 ....DLB-45

Davidson, John 1857-1909 ....DLB-19

Davidson, Lionel 1922- DLB-14

Davie, Donald 1922- DLB-27

Davies, Robertson 1913- DLB-68

Davies, Samuel 1723-1761 ....DLB-31

Davies, W. H. 1871-1940 ....DLB-19

Daviot, Gordon 1896?-1952 ....DLB-10
    (see also Tey, Josephine)

Davis, Charles A. 1795-1867 ....DLB-11

Davis, Clyde Brion 1894-1962 ....DLB-9

Davis, Dick 1945- DLB-40

Davis, Frank Marshall 1905-? DLB-51

Davis, H. L. 1894-1960 ....DLB-9

Davis, John 1774-1854 ....DLB-37

Davis, Margaret Thomson 1926- DLB-14

Davis, Ossie 1917- DLB-7, 38

Davis, Rebecca Harding 1831-1910 ....DLB-74

Davis, Richard Harding
    1864-1916 ....DLB-12, 23, 78, 79

Davis, Samuel Cole 1764-1809 ....DLB-37

Davison, Peter 1928- DLB-5

Davys, Mary 1674-1732 ....DLB-39

DAW Books DLB-46

Dawson, William 1704-1752 ....DLB-31

Day, Benjamin Henry 1810-1889 ....DLB-43

Day, Clarence 1874-1935 ....DLB-11

Day, Dorothy 1897-1980 ....DLB-29

Day, Frank Parker 1881-1950 ....DLB-92

Day, John circa 1574-circa 1640 ....DLB-62

Day, The John, Company DLB-46

Day Lewis, C. 1904-1972 ....DLB-15, 20
    (see also Blake, Nicholas)

Day, Mahlon [publishing house] DLB-49

Day, Thomas 1748-1789 ....DLB-39

Deacon, William Arthur 1890-1977 ....DLB-68

Deal, Borden 1922-1985 ....DLB-6

de Angeli, Marguerite 1889-1987 ....DLB-22

De Bow, James Dunwoody Brownson
 1820-1867 ....DLB-3, 79

de Bruyn, Günter 1926- DLB-75

de Camp, L. Sprague 1907- DLB-8

The Decay of Lying (1889),
 by Oscar Wilde [excerpt] DLB-18

Dedication, *Ferdinand Count Fathom* (1753),
 by Tobias Smollett DLB-39

Dedication, *Lasselia* (1723), by Eliza
 Haywood [excerpt] DLB-39

Dedication, *The History of Pompey the
 Little (1751),* by Francis Coventry DLB-39

Dedication, *The Wanderer* (1814),
 by Fanny Burney DLB-39

Defense of *Amelia* (1752), by Henry Fielding DLB-39

Defoe, Daniel 1660-1731 .... DLB-39, 95, 101

de Fontaine, Felix Gregory 1834-1896 ....DLB-43

De Forest, John William 1826-1906 ....DLB-12

DeFrees, Madeline 1919- DLB-105

DeFrees, Madeline, The Poet's Kaleidoscope:
 The Element of Surprise in the Making
 of the Poem DLB-105

de Graff, Robert 1895-1981 ....Y-81

de Graft, Joe 1924-1978 ....DLB-117

Deighton, Len 1929- DLB-87

DeJong, Meindert 1906-1991 ....DLB-52

Dekker, Thomas circa 1572-1632 ....DLB-62

Delacorte, Jr., George T. 1894-1991 ....DLB-91

Delafield, E. M. 1890-1943 ....DLB-34

Delahaye, Guy 1888-1969 ....DLB-92

de la Mare, Walter 1873-1956 ....DLB-19

Deland, Margaret 1857-1945 ....DLB-78

Delaney, Shelagh 1939- DLB-13

Delany, Martin Robinson 1812-1885 ....DLB-50

Delany, Samuel R. 1942- DLB-8, 33

de la Roche, Mazo 1879-1961 ....DLB-68

Delbanco, Nicholas 1942- DLB-6

De León, Nephtal 1945- DLB-82

Delgado, Abelardo Barrientos 1931- DLB-82

De Libero, Libero 1906-1981 ....DLB-114

DeLillo, Don 1936- DLB-6

de Lisser H. G. 1878-1944 ....DLB-117

Dell, Floyd 1887-1969 ....DLB-9

Dell Publishing Company DLB-46

delle Grazie, Marie Eugene 1864-1931 ....DLB-81

del Rey, Lester 1915- DLB-8

Del Vecchio, John M. 1947- DS-9

de Man, Paul 1919-1983 ....DLB-67

Demby, William 1922- DLB-33

Deming, Philander 1829-1915 ....DLB-74

Demorest, William Jennings 1822-1895 ....DLB-79

Denham, Sir John 1615-1669 ....DLB-58

Denison, Merrill 1893-1975 ....DLB-92

Denison, T. S., and Company DLB-49

Dennie, Joseph 1768-1812 .... DLB-37, 43, 59, 73

Dennis, John 1658-1734 ....DLB-101

Dennis, Nigel 1912-1989 .... DLB-13, 15

Dent, Tom 1932- DLB-38

Dent, J. M., and Sons DLB-112

Denton, Daniel circa 1626-1703 ....DLB-24

DePaola, Tomie 1934- DLB-61

De Quincey, Thomas 1785-1859 ....DLB-110

Derby, George Horatio 1823-1861 ....DLB-11

Derby, J. C., and Company DLB-49

Derby and Miller DLB-49

Derleth, August 1909-1971 ....DLB-9

The Derrydale Press DLB-46

Desaulniers, Gonsalve 1863-1934 ....DLB-92

Desbiens, Jean-Paul 1927- DLB-53

des Forêts, Louis-Rene 1918- DLB-83

DesRochers, Alfred 1901-1978 .... DLB-68

Desrosiers, Léo-Paul 1896-1967 .... DLB-68

Destouches, Louis-Ferdinand (see Celine, Louis-Ferdinand)

De Tabley, Lord 1835-1895 .... DLB-35

Deutsch, Babette 1895-1982 .... DLB-45

Deutsch, André, Limited DLB-112

Deveaux, Alexis 1948- DLB-38

The Development of Lighting in the Staging
   of Drama, 1900-1945 [in Great Britain] DLB-10

de Vere, Aubrey 1814-1902 .... DLB-35

The Devin-Adair Company DLB-46

De Voto, Bernard 1897-1955 .... DLB-9

De Vries, Peter 1910- DLB-6; Y-82

Dewdney, Christopher 1951- DLB-60

Dewdney, Selwyn 1909-1979 .... DLB-68

DeWitt, Robert M., Publisher DLB-49

DeWolfe, Fiske and Company DLB-49

Dexter, Colin 1930- DLB-87

de Young, M. H. 1849-1925 .... DLB-25

The Dial Press DLB-46

Diamond, I. A. L. 1920-1988 .... DLB-26

Di Cicco, Pier Giorgio 1949- DLB-60

Dick, Philip K. 1928- DLB-8

Dick and Fitzgerald DLB-49

Dickens, Charles 1812-1870 .... DLB-21, 55, 70

Dickey, James 1923- DLB-5; Y-82; DS-7

Dickey, William 1928- DLB-5

Dickinson, Emily 1830-1886 .... DLB-1

Dickinson, John 1732-1808 .... DLB-31

Dickinson, Jonathan 1688-1747 .... DLB-24

Dickinson, Patric 1914- DLB-27

Dickinson, Peter 1927- DLB-87

Dicks, John [publishing house] DLB-106

Dickson, Gordon R. 1923- DLB-8

Didion, Joan 1934- DLB-2; Y-81, 86

Di Donato, Pietro 1911- DLB-9

Dillard, Annie 1945- Y-80

Dillard, R. H. W. 1937- DLB-5

Dillingham, Charles T., Company DLB-49

The G. W. Dillingham Company DLB-49

Dintenfass, Mark 1941- Y-84

Diogenes, Jr. (see Brougham, John)

DiPrima, Diane 1934- DLB-5, 16

Disch, Thomas M. 1940- DLB-8

Disney, Walt 1901-1966 .... DLB-22

Disraeli, Benjamin 1804-1881 .... DLB-21, 55

D'Israeli, Isaac 1766-1848 .... DLB-107

Ditzen, Rudolf (see Fallada, Hans)

Dix, Dorothea Lynde 1802-1887 .... DLB-1

Dix, Dorothy (see Gilmer, Elizabeth Meriwether)

Dix, Edwards and Company DLB-49

Dixon, Paige (see Corcoran, Barbara)

Dixon, Richard Watson 1833-1900 .... DLB-19

Dobell, Sydney 1824-1874 .... DLB-32

Döblin, Alfred 1878-1957 .... DLB-66

Dobson, Austin 1840-1921 .... DLB-35

Doctorow, E. L. 1931- DLB-2, 28; Y-80

Dodd, William E. 1869-1940 .... DLB-17

Dodd, Mead and Company DLB-49

Doderer, Heimito von 1896-1968 .... DLB-85

Dodge, Mary Mapes 1831?-1905 .... DLB-42, 79

Dodge, B. W., and Company DLB-46

Dodge Publishing Company DLB-49

Dodgson, Charles Lutwidge (see Carroll, Lewis)

Dodsley, Robert 1703-1764 .... DLB-95

Dodson, Owen 1914-1983 .... DLB-76

Doesticks, Q. K. Philander, P. B. (see Thomson, Mortimer)

Domínguez, Sylvia Maida 1935- DLB-122

Donahoe, Patrick [publishing house] DLB-49

Donald, David H. 1920- DLB-17

Donaldson, Scott 1928- DLB-111

Donleavy, J. P. 1926- DLB-6

Donnadieu, Marguerite (see Duras, Marguerite)

Donne, John 1572-1631 .... DLB-121

Donnelley, R. R., and Sons Company DLB-49

Donnelly, Ignatius 1831-1901 .... DLB-12

Donohue and Henneberry DLB-49

Donoso, José 1924- DLB-113

Doolady, M. [publishing house] DLB-49

Dooley, Ebon (see Ebon)

Doolittle, Hilda 1886-1961 .... DLB-4, 45

Dor, Milo 1923- DLB-85

Doran, George H., Company DLB-46

Dorgelés, Roland 1886-1973 .... DLB-65

Dorn, Edward 1929- DLB-5

Dorr, Rheta Childe 1866-1948 .... DLB-25

Dorst, Tankred 1925- DLB-75, 124

Dos Passos, John 1896-1970 .... DLB-4, 9; DS-1

Doubleday and Company DLB-49

Dougall, Lily 1858-1923 .... DLB-92

Doughty, Charles M. 1843-1926 .... DLB-19, 57

Douglas, Keith 1920-1944 .... DLB-27

Douglas, Norman 1868-1952 .... DLB-34

Douglass, Frederick 1817?-1895 .... DLB-1, 43, 50, 79

Douglass, William circa 1691-1752 .... DLB-24

Dove, Rita 1952- DLB-120

Dover Publications DLB-46

Doves Press DLB-112

Dowden, Edward 1843-1913 .... DLB-35

Downes, Gwladys 1915- DLB-88

Downing, J., Major (see Davis, Charles A.)

Downing, Major Jack (see Smith, Seba)

Dowson, Ernest 1867-1900 .... DLB-19

Doxey, William [publishing house] DLB-49

Doyle, Sir Arthur Conan 1859-1930 .... DLB-18, 70

Doyle, Kirby 1932- DLB-16

Drabble, Margaret 1939- DLB-14

Drach, Albert 1902- DLB-85

The Dramatic Publishing Company DLB-49

Dramatists Play Service DLB-46

Draper, John W. 1811-1882 .... DLB-30

Draper, Lyman C. 1815-1891 .... DLB-30

Drayton, Michael 1563-1631 .... DLB-121

Dreiser, Theodore 1871-1945 .... DLB-9, 12, 102; DS-1

Drewitz, Ingeborg 1923-1986 .... DLB-75

Drieu La Rochelle, Pierre 1893-1945 .... DLB-72

Drinkwater, John 1882-1937 .... DLB-10, 19

The Drue Heinz Literature Prize
     Excerpt from "Excerpts from a Report
        of the Commission," in David
        Bosworth's *The Death of Descartes*
     An Interview with David Bosworth Y-82

Drummond, William Henry 1854-1907 .... DLB-92

Drummond, William, of Hawthornden
     1585-1649 .... DLB-121

Dryden, John 1631-1700 .... DLB-80, 101

Duane, William 1760-1835 .... DLB-43

Dubé, Marcel 1930- DLB-53

Dubé, Rodolphe (see Hertel, Francois)

Dubie, Norman 1945- DLB-120

Du Bois, W. E. B. 1868-1963 .... DLB-47, 50, 91

Du Bois, William Pène 1916- DLB-61

Ducharme, Réjean 1941- DLB-60

Duck, Stephen 1705?-1756 .... DLB-95

Duckworth, Gerald, and Company Limited DLB-112

Dudek, Louis 1918- DLB-88

Duell, Sloan and Pearce DLB-46

Duffield and Green DLB-46

Duffy, Maureen 1933- DLB-14

Dugan, Alan 1923- DLB-5

Dugas, Marcel 1883-1947 .... DLB-92

Dugdale, William [publishing house] DLB-106

Duhamel, Georges 1884-1966 .... DLB-65

Dujardin, Edouard 1861-1949 .... DLB-123

Dukes, Ashley 1885-1959 .... DLB-10

Dumas, Alexandre, *père* 1802-1870 .... DLB-119

Dumas, Henry 1934-1968 .... DLB-41

Dunbar, Paul Laurence 1872-1906 .... DLB-50, 54, 78

Duncan, Norman 1871-1916 .... DLB-92

Duncan, Robert 1919-1988 .... DLB-5, 16

Duncan, Ronald 1914-1982 .... DLB-13

Duncan, Sara Jeannette 1861-1922 .... DLB-92

Dunigan, Edward, and Brother DLB-49

Dunlap, John 1747-1812 .... DLB-43

Dunlap, William 1766-1839 .... DLB-30, 37, 59

Dunn, Douglas 1942- DLB-40

Dunn, Stephen 1939- DLB-105

Dunn, Stephen,
    The Good, The Not So Good DLB-105

Dunne, Finley Peter 1867-1936 .... DLB-11, 23

Dunne, John Gregory 1932- Y-80

Dunne, Philip 1908- DLB-26

Dunning, Ralph Cheever 1878-1930 .... DLB-4

Dunning, William A. 1857-1922 .... DLB-17

Duns Scotus, John circa 1266-1308 .... DLB-115

Dunsany, Edward John Moreton Drax
    Plunkett, Lord 1878-1957 .... DLB-10, 77

Dupin, Amantine-Aurore-Lucile (see Sand, George)

Durand, Lucile (see Bersianik, Louky)

Duranty, Walter 1884-1957 .... DLB-29

Duras, Marguerite 1914- DLB-83

Durfey, Thomas 1653-1723 .... DLB-80

Durrell, Lawrence 1912-1990 .... DLB-15, 27; Y-90

Durrell, William [publishing house] DLB-49

Durrenmatt, Friedrich 1921-1990 .... DLB-69, 124

Dutton, E. P., and Company DLB-49

Duvoisin, Roger 1904-1980 .... DLB-61

Duyckinck, Evert Augustus 1816-1878 .... DLB-3, 64

Duyckinck, George L. 1823-1863 .... DLB-3

Duyckinck and Company DLB-49

Dwight, John Sullivan 1813-1893 .... DLB-1

Dwight, Timothy 1752-1817 .... DLB-37

Dyer, Charles 1928- DLB-13

Dyer, George 1755-1841 .... DLB-93

Dyer, John 1699-1757 .... DLB-95

Dylan, Bob 1941- DLB-16

E

Eager, Edward 1911-1964 .... DLB-22

Earle, James H., and Company DLB-49

Early American Book Illustration,
    by Sinclair Hamilton DLB-49

Eastlake, William 1917- DLB-6

Eastman, Carol ?- DLB-44

Eastman, Max 1883-1969 .... DLB-91

Eberhart, Richard 1904- DLB-48

Ebner, Jeannie 1918- DLB-85

Ebner-Eschenbach, Marie von 1830-1916 .... DLB-81

Ebon 1942- DLB-41

Ecco Press DLB-46

Eckhart, Meister circa 1260-circa 1328 .... DLB-115

The Eclectic Review 1805-1868 .... DLB-110

Edel, Leon 1907- DLB-103

Edes, Benjamin 1732-1803 .... DLB-43

Edgar, David 1948- DLB-13

Edgeworth, Maria 1768-1849 .... DLB-116

The Edinburgh Review 1802-1929 .... DLB-110

Edinburgh University Press DLB-112

The Editor Publishing Company DLB-49

Edmonds, Randolph 1900- DLB-51

Edmonds, Walter D. 1903- DLB-9

Edschmid, Kasimir 1890-1966 .... DLB-56

Edwards, Jonathan 1703-1758 .... DLB-24

Edwards, Jonathan, Jr. 1745-1801 .... DLB-37

Edwards, Junius 1929- DLB-33

Edwards, Richard 1524-1566 .... DLB-62

Effinger, George Alec 1947- DLB-8

Eggleston, Edward 1837-1902 .... DLB-12

Eggleston, Wilfred 1901-1986 .... DLB-92

Ehrenstein, Albert 1886-1950 .... DLB-81

Ehrhart, W. D. 1948- DS-9

Eich, Günter 1907-1972 .... DLB-69, 124

Eichendorff, Joseph Freiherr von 1788-1857 ....DLB-90

1873 Publishers' Catalogues DLB-49

Eighteenth-Century Aesthetic Theories DLB-31

Eighteenth-Century Philosophical Background DLB-31

Eigner, Larry 1927- DLB-5

Eisenreich, Herbert 1925-1986 ....DLB-85

Eisner, Kurt 1867-1919 ....DLB-66

Eklund, Gordon 1945- Y-83

Ekwensi, Cyprian 1921- DLB-117

Elder, Lonne III 1931- DLB-7, 38, 44

Elder, Paul, and Company DLB-49

Elements of Rhetoric (1828; revised, 1846),
by Richard Whately [excerpt] DLB-57

Elie, Robert 1915-1973 ....DLB-88

Eliot, George 1819-1880 .... DLB-21, 35, 55

Eliot, John 1604-1690 ....DLB-24

Eliot, T. S. 1888-1965 .... DLB-7, 10, 45, 63

Elizondo, Sergio 1930- DLB-82

Elkin, Stanley 1930- DLB-2, 28; Y-80

Elles, Dora Amy (see Wentworth, Patricia)

Ellet, Elizabeth F. 1818?-1877 ....DLB-30

Elliot, Ebenezer 1781-1849 ....DLB-96

Elliott, George 1923- DLB-68

Elliott, Janice 1931- DLB-14

Elliott, William 1788-1863 ....DLB-3

Elliott, Thomes and Talbot DLB-49

Ellis, Edward S. 1840-1916 ....DLB-42

Ellis, Frederick Staridge [publishing house] DLB-106

The George H. Ellis Company DLB-49

Ellison, Harlan 1934- DLB-8

Ellison, Ralph 1914- DLB-2, 76

Ellmann, Richard 1918-1987 ....DLB-103; Y-87

The Elmer Holmes Bobst Awards in Arts and Letters Y-87

Emanuel, James Andrew 1921- DLB-41

Emecheta, Buchi 1944- DLB-117

The Emergence of Black Women Writers DS-8

Emerson, Ralph Waldo 1803-1882 .... DLB-1, 59, 73

Emerson, William 1769-1811 ....DLB-37

Empson, William 1906-1984 ....DLB-20

The End of English Stage Censorship,
1945-1968 ....DLB-13

Ende, Michael 1929- DLB-75

Engel, Marian 1933-1985 ....DLB-53

Engle, Paul 1908- DLB-48

English Composition and Rhetoric (1866),
by Alexander Bain [excerpt] DLB-57

The English Renaissance of Art (1908),
by Oscar Wilde DLB-35

Enright, D. J. 1920- DLB-27

Enright, Elizabeth 1909-1968 ....DLB-22

L'Envoi (1882), by Oscar Wilde DLB-35

Epps, Bernard 1936- DLB-53

Epstein, Julius 1909- and
Epstein, Philip 1909-1952 ....DLB-26

Equiano, Olaudah circa 1745-1797 .... DLB-37, 50

Eragny Press DLB-112

Erichsen-Brown, Gwethalyn Graham
(see Graham, Gwethalyn)

Eriugena, John Scottus circa 810-877 ....DLB-115

Ernst, Paul 1866-1933 .... DLB-66, 118

Erskine, John 1879-1951 .... DLB-9, 102

Ervine, St. John Greer 1883-1971 ....DLB-10

Eschenburg, Johann Joachim 1743-1820 ....DLB-97

Eshleman, Clayton 1935- DLB-5

Ess Ess Publishing Company DLB-49

Essay on Chatterton (1842), by Robert Browning DLB-32

Essex House Press DLB-112

Estes, Eleanor 1906-1988 ....DLB-22

Estes and Lauriat DLB-49

Etherege, George 1636-circa 1692 ....DLB-80

Ets, Marie Hall 1893- DLB-22

Etter, David 1928- DLB-105

Eudora Welty: Eye of the Storyteller Y-87

Eugene O'Neill Memorial Theater Center DLB-7

Eugene O'Neill's Letters: A Review Y-88

Evans, Donald 1884-1921 ....DLB-54

Evans, George Henry 1805-1856 ....DLB-43

Evans, Hubert 1892-1986 ....DLB-92

Evans, M., and Company DLB-46

Evans, Mari 1923- DLB-41

Evans, Mary Ann (see Eliot, George)

Evans, Nathaniel 1742-1767 ....DLB-31

Evans, Sebastian 1830-1909 ....DLB-35

Everett, Alexander Hill 1790-1847 ....DLB-59

Everett, Edward 1794-1865 ....DLB-1, 59

Everson, R. G. 1903- DLB-88

Everson, William 1912- DLB-5, 16

Every Man His Own Poet; or, The
    Inspired Singer's Recipe Book (1877),
    by W. H. Mallock DLB-35

Ewart, Gavin 1916- DLB-40

Ewing, Juliana Horatia 1841-1885 ....DLB-21

The Examiner 1808-1881 ....DLB-110

Exley, Frederick 1929- Y-81

Experiment in the Novel (1929),
    by John D. Beresford DLB-36

Eyre and Spottiswoode DLB-106

F

"F. Scott Fitzgerald: St. Paul's Native Son
    and Distinguished American Writer":
    University of Minnesota Conference,
    29-31 October 1982 ....Y-82

Faber, Frederick William 1814-1863 ....DLB-32

Faber and Faber Limited DLB-112

Faccio, Rena (see Aleramo, Sibilla)

Fair, Ronald L. 1932- DLB-33

Fairfax, Beatrice (see Manning, Marie)

Fairlie, Gerard 1899-1983 ....DLB-77

Fallada, Hans 1893-1947 ....DLB-56

Fancher, Betsy 1928- Y-83

Fane, Violet 1843-1905 ....DLB-35

Fanfrolico Press DLB-112

Fantasy Press Publishers DLB-46

Fante, John 1909-1983 ....Y-83

Al-Farabi circa 870-950 ....DLB-115

Farah, Nurridin 1945- DLB-125

Farber, Norma 1909-1984 ....DLB-61

Farigoule, Louis (see Romains, Jules)

Farley, Walter 1920-1989 ....DLB-22

Farmer, Philip José 1918- DLB-8

Farquhar, George circa 1677-1707 ....DLB-84

Farquharson, Martha (see Finley, Martha)

Farrar and Rinehart DLB-46

Farrar, Straus and Giroux DLB-46

Farrell, James T. 1904-1979 ....DLB-4, 9, 86; DS-2

Farrell, J. G. 1935-1979 ....DLB-14

Fast, Howard 1914- DLB-9

Faulkner, William 1897-1962
    ....DLB-9, 11, 44, 102; DS-2; Y-86

Fauset, Jessie Redmon 1882-1961 ....DLB-51

Faust, Irvin 1924- DLB-2, 28; Y-80

Fawcett Books DLB-46

Fearing, Kenneth 1902-1961 ....DLB-9

Federal Writers' Project DLB-46

Federman, Raymond 1928- Y-80

Feiffer, Jules 1929- DLB-7, 44

Feinberg, Charles E. 1899-1988 ....Y-88

Feinstein, Elaine 1930- DLB-14, 40

Felipe, Léon 1884-1968 ....DLB-108

Fell, Frederick, Publishers DLB-46

Fels, Ludwig 1946- DLB-75

Felton, Cornelius Conway 1807-1862 ....DLB-1

Fennario, David 1947- DLB-60

Fenno, John 1751-1798 ....DLB-43

Fenno, R. F., and Company DLB-49

Fenton, James 1949- DLB-40

Ferber, Edna 1885-1968 ....DLB-9, 28, 86

Ferdinand, Vallery III (see Salaam, Kalamu ya)

Ferguson, Sir Samuel 1810-1886 ....DLB-32

Ferguson, William Scott 1875-1954 ....DLB-47

Fergusson, Robert 1750-1774 ....DLB-109

Ferland, Albert 1872-1943 ....DLB-92

Ferlinghetti, Lawrence 1919- DLB-5, 16

Fern, Fanny (see Parton, Sara Payson Willis)

Ferrars, Elizabeth 1907- DLB-87

Ferret, E., and Company DLB-49

Ferrier, Susan 1782-1854 ....DLB-116

Ferrini, Vincent 1913- DLB-48

Ferron, Jacques 1921-1985 ....DLB-60

Ferron, Madeleine 1922- DLB-53

Fetridge and Company DLB-49

Feuchtwanger, Lion 1884-1958 ....DLB-66

Fichte, Johann Gottlieb 1762-1814 ....DLB-90

Ficke, Arthur Davison 1883-1945 ....DLB-54

Fiction Best-Sellers, 1910-1945 ....DLB-9

Fiction into Film, 1928-1975: A List of Movies
    Based on the Works of Authors in
    British Novelists, 1930-1959 ....DLB-15

Fiedler, Leslie A. 1917- DLB-28, 67

Field, Edward 1924- DLB-105

Field, Edward, The Poetry File DLB-105

Field, Eugene 1850-1895 ....DLB-23, 42

Field, Nathan 1587-1619 or 1620 ....DLB-58

Field, Rachel 1894-1942 ....DLB-9, 22

A Field Guide to Recent Schools of American Poetry Y-86

Fielding, Henry 1707-1754 .... DLB-39, 84, 101

Fielding, Sarah 1710-1768 ....DLB-39

Fields, James Thomas 1817-1881 ....DLB-1

Fields, Julia 1938- DLB-41

Fields, W. C. 1880-1946 ....DLB-44

Fields, Osgood and Company DLB-49

Fifty Penguin Years Y-85

Figes, Eva 1932- DLB-14

Figuera, Angela 1902-1984 ....DLB-108

Filson, John circa 1753-1788 ....DLB-37

Finch, Anne, Countess of Winchilsea 1661-1720 ......DLB-95

Finch, Robert 1900- DLB-88

Findley, Timothy 1930- DLB-53

Finlay, Ian Hamilton 1925- DLB-40

Finley, Martha 1828-1909 ....DLB-42

Finney, Jack 1911- DLB-8

Finney, Walter Braden (see Finney, Jack)

Firbank, Ronald 1886-1926 ....DLB-36

Firmin, Giles 1615-1697 ....DLB-24

First Edition Library/Collectors' Reprints, Inc. Y-91

First Strauss "Livings" Awarded to Cynthia
        Ozick and Raymond Carver
    An Interview with Cynthia Ozick
    An Interview with Raymond Carver Y-83

Fischer, Karoline Auguste Fernandine 1764-1842 ......DLB-94

Fish, Stanley 1938- DLB-67

Fishacre, Richard 1205-1248 ....DLB-115

Fisher, Clay (see Allen, Henry W.)

Fisher, Dorothy Canfield 1879-1958 .... DLB-9, 102

Fisher, Leonard Everett 1924- DLB-61

Fisher, Roy 1930- DLB-40

Fisher, Rudolph 1897-1934 .... DLB-51, 102

Fisher, Sydney George 1856-1927 ....DLB-47

Fisher, Vardis 1895-1968 ....DLB-9

Fiske, John 1608-1677 ....DLB-24

Fiske, John 1842-1901 .... DLB-47, 64

Fitch, Thomas circa 1700-1774 ....DLB-31

Fitch, William Clyde 1865-1909 ....DLB-7

FitzGerald, Edward 1809-1883 ....DLB-32

Fitzgerald, F. Scott 1896-1940 ....DLB-4, 9, 86; Y-81; DS-1

Fitzgerald, Penelope 1916- DLB-14

Fitzgerald, Robert 1910-1985 ....Y-80

Fitzgerald, Thomas 1819-1891 ....DLB-23

Fitzgerald, Zelda Sayre 1900-1948 ....Y-84

Fitzhugh, Louise 1928-1974 ....DLB-52

Fitzhugh, William circa 1651-1701 ....DLB-24

Flanagan, Thomas 1923- Y-80

Flanner, Hildegarde 1899-1987 ....DLB-48

Flanner, Janet 1892-1978 ....DLB-4

Flaubert, Gustave 1821-1880 ....DLB-119

Flavin, Martin 1883-1967 ....DLB-9

Flecker, James Elroy 1884-1915 ....DLB-10, 19

Fleeson, Doris 1901-1970 ....DLB-29

Fleißer, Marieluise 1901-1974 ....DLB-56, 124

Fleming, Ian 1908-1964 ....DLB-87

The Fleshly School of Poetry and Other
    Phenomena of the Day (1872), by Robert
    Buchanan DLB-35

The Fleshly School of Poetry: Mr. D. G.
    Rossetti (1871), by Thomas Maitland
    (Robert Buchanan) DLB-35

Fletcher, Giles, the younger 1585 or 1586 - 1623 .....DLB-121

Fletcher, J. S. 1863-1935 ....DLB-70

Fletcher, John (see Beaumont, Francis)

Fletcher, John Gould 1886-1950 ....DLB-4, 45

Fletcher, Phineas 1582-1650 ....DLB-121

Flieg, Helmut (see Heym, Stefan)

Flint, F. S. 1885-1960 ....DLB-19

Flint, Timothy 1780-1840 ....DLB-734

Folio Society DLB-112

Follen, Eliza Lee (Cabot) 1787-1860 ....DLB-1

Follett, Ken 1949- Y-81, DLB-87

Follett Publishing Company DLB-46

Folsom, John West [publishing house] DLB-49

Foote, Horton 1916- DLB-26

Foote, Samuel 1721-1777 ....DLB-89

Foote, Shelby 1916- DLB-2, 17

Forbes, Calvin 1945- DLB-41

Forbes, Ester 1891-1967 ....DLB-22

Forbes and Company DLB-49

Force, Peter 1790-1868 ....DLB-30

Forche, Carolyn 1950- DLB-5

Ford, Charles Henri 1913- DLB-4, 48

Ford, Corey 1902-1969 ....DLB-11

Ford, Ford Madox 1873-1939 ....DLB-34, 98

Ford, J. B., and Company DLB-49

Ford, Jesse Hill 1928- DLB-6

Ford, John 1586-? DLB-58

Ford, R. A. D. 1915- DLB-88

Ford, Worthington C. 1858-1941 ....DLB-47

Fords, Howard, and Hulbert DLB-49

Foreman, Carl 1914-1984 ....DLB-26

Forester, Frank (see Herbert, Henry William)

Fornés, María Irene 1930- DLB-7

Forrest, Leon 1937- DLB-33

Forster, E. M. 1879-1970 ....DLB-34, 98; DS-10

Forster, Georg 1754-1794 ....DLB-94

Forsyth, Frederick 1938- DLB-87

Forten, Charlotte L. 1837-1914 ....DLB-50

Fortune, T. Thomas 1856-1928 ....DLB-23

Fosdick, Charles Austin 1842-1915 ....DLB-42

Foster, Genevieve 1893-1979 ....DLB-61

Foster, Hannah Webster 1758-1840 ....DLB-37

Foster, John 1648-1681 ....DLB-24

Foster, Michael 1904-1956 ....DLB-9

Fouqué, Caroline de la Motte 1774-1831 ....DLB-90

Fouqué, Friedrich de la Motte 1777-1843 ....DLB-90

Four Essays on the Beat Generation,
    by John Clellon Holmes DLB-16

Four Seas Company DLB-46

Four Winds Press DLB-46

Fournier, Henri Alban (see Alain-Fournier)

Fowler and Wells Company DLB-49

Fowles, John 1926- DLB-14

Fox, John, Jr. 1862 or 1863-1919 ....DLB-9

Fox, Paula 1923- DLB-52

Fox, Richard K. [publishing house] DLB-49

Fox, Richard Kyle 1846-1922 ....DLB-79

Fox, William Price 1926- DLB-2; Y-81

Fraenkel, Michael 1896-1957 ....DLB-4

France, Anatole 1844-1924 ....DLB-123

France, Richard 1938- DLB-7

Francis, C. S. [publishing house] DLB-49

Francis, Convers 1795-1863 ....DLB-1

Francis, Dick 1920- DLB-87

Francis, Jeffrey, Lord 1773-1850 ....DLB-107

François 1863-1910 ....DLB-92

Francke, Kuno 1855-1930 ....DLB-71

Frank, Bruno 1887-1945 ....DLB-118

Frank, Leonhard 1882-1961 ....DLB-56, 118

Frank, Melvin (see Panama, Norman)

Frank, Waldo 1889-1967 ....DLB-9, 63

Franken, Rose 1895?-1988 ....Y-84

Franklin, Benjamin 1706-1790 ....DLB-24, 43, 73

Franklin, James 1697-1735 ....DLB-43

Franklin Library DLB-46

Frantz, Ralph Jules 1902-1979 ....DLB-4

Fraser, G. S. 1915-1980 ....DLB-27

Frayn, Michael 1933- DLB-13, 14

Frederic, Harold 1856-1898 ....DLB-12, 23

Freeling, Nicolas 1927- DLB-87

Freeman, Douglas Southall 1886-1953 ....DLB-17

Freeman, Legh Richmond 1842-1915 ....DLB-23

Freeman, Mary E. Wilkins 1852-1930 ....DLB-12, 78

Freeman, R. Austin 1862-1943 ....DLB-70

French, Alice 1850-1934 ....DLB-74

French, David 1939- DLB-53

French, James [publishing house] DLB-49

French, Samuel [publishing house] DLB-49

Samuel French, Limited DLB-106

Freneau, Philip 1752-1832 ....DLB-37, 43

Fried, Erich 1921-1988 ....DLB-85

Friedman, Bruce Jay 1930- DLB-2, 28

Friel, Brian 1929- DLB-13

Friend, Krebs 1895?-1967? DLB-4

Fries, Fritz Rudolf 1935- DLB-75

Fringe and Alternative Theater in Great Britain DLB-13

Frisch, Max 1911-1991 ....DLB-69, 124

Frischmuth, Barbara 1941- DLB-85

Fritz, Jean 1915- DLB-52

Fromentin, Eugene 1820-1876 ....DLB-123

Frost, Robert 1874-1963 ....DLB-54; DS-7

Frothingham, Octavius Brooks 1822-1895 ....DLB-1

Froude, James Anthony 1818-1894 ....DLB-18, 57

Fry, Christopher 1907- DLB-13

Fry, Roger 1866-1934 ....DS-10

Frye, Northrop 1912-1991 ....DLB-67, 68

Fuchs, Daniel 1909- DLB-9, 26, 28

Fuentes, Carlos 1928- DLB-113

Fuertas, Gloria 1918- DLB-108

The Fugitives and the Agrarians: The First Exhibition ... Y-85

Fuller, Charles H., Jr. 1939- DLB-38

Fuller, Henry Blake 1857-1929 ....DLB-12

Fuller, John 1937- DLB-40

Fuller, Roy 1912-1991 ....DLB-15, 20

Fuller, Samuel 1912- DLB-26

Fuller, Sarah Margaret, Marchesa
    D'Ossoli 1810-1850 ....DLB-1, 59, 73

Fulton, Len 1934- Y-86

Fulton, Robin 1937- DLB-40

Furman, Laura 1945- Y-86

Furness, Horace Howard 1833-1912 ....DLB-64

Furness, William Henry 1802-1896 ....DLB-1

Furthman, Jules 1888-1966 ....DLB-26

The Future of the Novel (1899), by Henry James DLB-18

G

The G. Ross Roy Scottish Poetry
    Collection at the University of
    South Carolina Y-89

Gaddis, William 1922- DLB-2

Gág, Wanda 1893-1946 ....DLB-22

Gagnon, Madeleine 1938- DLB-60

Gaine, Hugh 1726-1807 ....DLB-43

Gaine, Hugh [publishing house] DLB-49

Gaines, Ernest J. 1933- DLB-2, 33; Y-80

Gaiser, Gerd 1908-1976 ....DLB-69

Galarza, Ernesto 1905-1984 ....DLB-122

Galaxy Science Fiction Novels DLB-46

Gale, Zona 1874-1938 ....DLB-9, 78

Gallagher, Tess 1943- DLB-120

Gallagher, William Davis 1808-1894 ....DLB-73

Gallant, Mavis 1922- DLB-53

Gallico, Paul 1897-1976 ....DLB-9

Galsworthy, John 1867-1933 ....DLB-10, 34, 98

Galt, John 1779-1839 ....DLB-99, 116

Galvin, Brendan 1938- DLB-5

Gambit DLB-46

Gamboa, Reymundo 1948- DLB-122

Gammer Gurton's Needle DLB-62

Gannett, Frank E. 1876-1957 ....DLB-29

García, Lionel G. 1935- DLB-82

García Lorca, Federico 1898-1936 ....DLB-108

García Marquez, Gabriel 1928- DLB-113

Gardam, Jane 1928- DLB-14

Garden, Alexander circa 1685-1756 ....DLB-31

Gardner, John 1933-1982 ....DLB-2; Y-82

Garis, Howard R. 1873-1962 ....DLB-22

Garland, Hamlin 1860-1940 ....DLB-12, 71, 78

Garneau, Francis-Xavier 1809-1866 ....DLB-99

Garneau, Hector de Saint-Denys 1912-1943 ....DLB-88

Garneau, Michel 1939- DLB-53

Garner, Hugh 1913-1979 ....DLB-68

Garnett, David 1892-1981 ....DLB-34

Garraty, John A. 1920- DLB-17

Garrett, George 1929- DLB-2, 5; Y-83

Garrick, David 1717-1779 ....DLB-84

Garrison, William Lloyd 1805-1879 ....DLB-1, 43

Garth, Samuel 1661-1719 ....DLB-95

Garve, Andrew 1908- DLB-87

Gary, Romain 1914-1980 ....DLB-83

Gascoyne, David 1916- DLB-20

Gaskell, Elizabeth Cleghorn 1810-1865 ....DLB-21

Gaspey, Thomas 1788-1871 ....DLB-116

Gass, William Howard 1924- DLB-2

Gates, Doris 1901- DLB-22

Gates, Henry Louis, Jr. 1950- DLB-67

Gates, Lewis E. 1860-1924 ....DLB-71

Gatto, Alfonso 1909-1976 ....DLB-114

Gautier, Théophile 1811-1872 ....DLB-119

Gauvreau, Claude 1925-1971 ....DLB-88

Gay, Ebenezer 1696-1787 ....DLB-24

Gay, John 1685-1732 ....DLB-84, 95

The Gay Science (1866), by E. S. Dallas [excerpt] DLB-21

Gayarré, Charles E. A. 1805-1895 ....DLB-30

Gaylord, Charles [publishing house] DLB-49

Geddes, Gary 1940- DLB-60

Geddes, Virgil 1897- DLB-4

Geis, Bernard, Associates DLB-46

Geisel, Theodor Seuss 1904-1991 ....DLB-61; Y-91

Gelb, Arthur 1924- DLB-103

Gelb, Barbara 1926- DLB-103

Gelber, Jack 1932- DLB-7

Gelinas, Gratien 1909- DLB-88

Gellert, Christian Füerchtegott 1715-1769 ....DLB-97

Gellhorn, Martha 1908- Y-82

Gems, Pam 1925- DLB-13

A General Idea of the College of Mirania (1753),
    by William Smith [excerpts] DLB-31

Genet, Jean 1910-1986 ....DLB-72; Y-86

Genevoix, Maurice 1890-1980 ....DLB-65

Genovese, Eugene D. 1930- DLB-17

Gent, Peter 1942-   Y-82

George, Henry 1839-1897 ....DLB-23

George, Jean Craighead 1919- DLB-52

Gerhardie, William 1895-1977 ....DLB-36

Gérin-Lajoie, Antoine 1824-1882 ....DLB-99

German Drama from Naturalism
　　to Fascism: 1889-1933 ....DLB-118

German Radio Play, The DLB-124

German Transformation from the Baroque
　　to the Enlightenment, The DLB-97

Germanophilism, by Hans Kohn DLB-66

Gernsback, Hugo 1884-1967 ....DLB-8

Gerould, Katharine Fullerton 1879-1944 ....DLB-78

Gerrish, Samuel [publishing house] DLB-49

Gerrold, David 1944- DLB-8

Gersonides 1288-1344 ....DLB-115

Gerstenberg, Heinrich Wilhelm von 1737-1823 ....DLB-97

Geßner, Salomon 1730-1788 ....DLB-97

Geston, Mark S. 1946- DLB-8

Al-Ghazali 1058-1111 ....DLB-115

Gibbon, Edward 1737-1794 ....DLB-104

Gibbon, John Murray 1875-1952 ....DLB-92

Gibbon, Lewis Grassic (see Mitchell, James Leslie)

Gibbons, Floyd 1887-1939 ....DLB-25

Gibbons, Reginald 1947- DLB-120

Gibbons, William ?-? DLB-73

Gibson, Graeme 1934- DLB-53

Gibson, Margaret 1944- DLB-120

Gibson, Wilfrid 1878-1962 ....DLB-19

Gibson, William 1914- DLB-7

Gide, André 1869-1951 ....DLB-65

Giguère, Diane 1937- DLB-53

Giguère, Roland 1929- DLB-60

Gil de Biedma, Jaime 1929-1990 ....DLB-108

Gilbert, Anthony 1899-1973 ....DLB-77

Gilbert, Michael 1912- DLB-87

Gilbert, Sandra M. 1936- DLB-120

Gilder, Jeannette L. 1849-1916 ....DLB-79

Gilder, Richard Watson 1844-1909 ....DLB-64, 79

Gildersleeve, Basil 1831-1924 ....DLB-71

Giles, Henry 1809-1882 ....DLB-64

Giles of Rome circa 1243-1316 ....DLB-115

Gill, Eric 1882-1940 ....DLB-98

Gill, William F., Company DLB-49

Gillespie, A. Lincoln, Jr. 1895-1950 ....DLB-4

Gilliam, Florence ?-? DLB-4

Gilliatt, Penelope 1932- DLB-14

Gillott, Jacky 1939-1980 ....DLB-14

Gilman, Caroline H. 1794-1888 ....DLB-3, 73

Gilman, W. and J. [publishing house] DLB-49

Gilmer, Elizabeth Meriwether 1861-1951 ....DLB-29

Gilmer, Francis Walker 1790-1826 ....DLB-37

Gilroy, Frank D. 1925- DLB-7

Ginsberg, Allen 1926- DLB-5, 16

Ginzkey, Franz Karl 1871-1963 ....DLB-81

Gioia, Dana 1950- DLB-120

Giono, Jean 1895-1970 ....DLB-72

Giotti, Virgilio 1885-1957 ....DLB-114

Giovanni, Nikki 1943- DLB-5, 41

Gipson, Lawrence Henry 1880-1971 ....DLB-17

Girard, Rodolphe 1879-1956 ....DLB-92

Giraudoux, Jean 1882-1944 ....DLB-65

Gissing, George 1857-1903 ....DLB-18

Gladstone, William Ewart 1809-1898 ....DLB-57

Glaeser, Ernst 1902-1963 ....DLB-69

Glanville, Brian 1931- DLB-15

Glapthorne, Henry 1610-1643? DLB-58

Glasgow, Ellen 1873-1945 ....DLB-9, 12

Glaspell, Susan 1876-1948 ....DLB-7, 9, 78

Glass, Montague 1877-1934 ....DLB-11

Glassco, John 1909-1981 ....DLB-68

Glauser, Friedrich 1896-1938 ....DLB-56

F. Gleason's Publishing Hall DLB-49

Gleim, Johann Wilhelm Ludwig 1719-1803 ....DLB-97

Glover, Richard 1712-1785 ....DLB-95

Glück, Louise 1943- DLB-5

Gobineau, Joseph-Arthur de 1816-1882 ....DLB-123

Godbout, Jacques 1933- DLB-53

Goddard, Morrill 1865-1937 ....DLB-25

Goddard, William 1740-1817 ....DLB-43

Godey, Louis A. 1804-1878 ....DLB-73

Godey and McMichael DLB-49

Godfrey, Dave 1938- DLB-60

Godfrey, Thomas 1736-1763 ....DLB-31

Godine, David R., Publisher DLB-46

Godkin, E. L. 1831-1902 ....DLB-79

Godwin, Gail 1937- DLB-6

Godwin, Parke 1816-1904 ....DLB-3, 64

Godwin, William 1756-1836 ....DLB-39, 104

Goering, Reinhard 1887-1936 ....DLB-118

Goes, Albrecht 1908- DLB-69

Goethe, Johann Wolfgang von 1749-1832 ....DLB-94

Goetz, Curt 1888-1960 ....DLB-124

Goffe, Thomas circa 1592-1629 ....DLB-58

Goffstein, M. B. 1940- DLB-61

Gogarty, Oliver St. John 1878-1957 ....DLB-15, 19

Goines, Donald 1937-1974 ....DLB-33

Gold, Herbert 1924- DLB-2; Y-81

Gold, Michael 1893-1967 ....DLB-9, 28

Goldbarth, Albert 1948- DLB-120

Goldberg, Dick 1947- DLB-7

Golden Cockerel Press DLB-112

Golding, William 1911- DLB-15, 100

Goldman, William 1931- DLB-44

Goldsmith, Oliver 1730 or 1731-1774 .... DLB-39, 89, 104

Goldsmith, Oliver 1794-1861 ....DLB-99

Goldsmith Publishing Company DLB-46

Gollancz, Victor, Limited DLB-112

Gómez-Quiñones, Juan 1942- DLB-122

Gomme, Laurence James [publishing house] DLB-46

Goncourt, Edmond de 1822-1896 ....DLB-123

Goncourt, Jules de 1830-1870 ....DLB-123

Gonzales, Rodolfo "Corky" 1928- DLB-122

González, Angel 1925- DLB-108

Gonzalez, Genaro 1949- DLB-122

Gonzalez, Ray 1952- DLB-122

González de Mireles, Jovita 1899-1983 ....DLB-122

González-T., César A. 1931- DLB-82

The Goodman Theatre DLB-7

Goodrich, Frances 1891-1984 and
  Hackett, Albert 1900- DLB-26

Goodrich, S. G. [publishing house] DLB-49

Goodrich, Samuel Griswold 1793-1860 .... DLB-1, 42, 73

Goodspeed, C. E., and Company DLB-49

Goodwin, Stephen 1943- Y-82

Gookin, Daniel 1612-1687 ....DLB-24

Gordon, Caroline 1895-1981 .... DLB-4, 9, 102; Y-81

Gordon, Giles 1940- DLB-14

Gordon, Mary 1949- DLB-6; Y-81

Gordone, Charles 1925- DLB-7

Gore, Catherine 1800-1861 ....DLB-116

Gorey, Edward 1925- DLB-61

Görres, Joseph 1776-1848 ....DLB-90

Gosse, Edmund 1849-1928 ....DLB-57

Gotlieb, Phyllis 1926- DLB-88

Gottsched, Johann Christoph 1700-1766 ....DLB-97

Götz, Johann Nikolaus 1721-1781 ....DLB-97

Gould, Wallace 1882-1940 ....DLB-54

Govoni, Corrado 1884-1965 ....DLB-114

Goyen, William 1915-1983 ....DLB-2; Y-83

Gozzano, Guido 1883-1916 ....DLB-114

Gracq, Julien 1910- DLB-83

Grady, Henry W. 1850-1889 ....DLB-23

Graf, Oskar Maria 1894-1967 ....DLB-56

Graham, George Rex 1813-1894 ....DLB-73

Graham, Gwethalyn 1913-1965 ....DLB-88

Graham, Jorie 1951- DLB-120

Graham, Lorenz 1902-1989 ....DLB-76

Graham, R. B. Cunninghame 1852-1936 ....DLB-98

Graham, Shirley 1896-1977 ....DLB-76

Graham, W. S. 1918- DLB-20

Graham, William H. [publishing house] DLB-49

Graham, Winston 1910- DLB-77

Grahame, Kenneth 1859-1932 ....DLB-34

Grainger, Martin Allerdale 1874-1941 ....DLB-92

Gramatky, Hardie 1907-1979 ....DLB-22

Grandbois, Alain 1900-1975 ....DLB-92

Granich, Irwin (see Gold, Michael)

Grant, Duncan 1885-1978 ....DS-10

Grant, George 1918-1988 ....DLB-88

Grant, George Monro 1835-1902 ....DLB-99

Grant, Harry J. 1881-1963 ....DLB-29

Grant, James Edward 1905-1966 ....DLB-26

Grass, Günter 1927- DLB-75, 124

Grasty, Charles H. 1863-1924 ....DLB-25

Grau, Shirley Ann 1929- DLB-2

Graves, John 1920- Y-83

Graves, Richard 1715-1804 ....DLB-39

Graves, Robert 1895-1985 ....DLB-20, 100; Y-85

Gray, Asa 1810-1888 ....DLB-1

Gray, David 1838-1861 ....DLB-32

Gray, Simon 1936- DLB-13

Gray, Thomas 1716-1771 ....DLB-109

Grayson, William J. 1788-1863 ....DLB-3, 64

The Great War and the Theater, 1914-1918
    [Great Britain] DLB-10

Greeley, Horace 1811-1872 ....DLB-3, 43

Green, Adolph (see Comden, Betty)

Green, Duff 1791-1875 ....DLB-43

Green, Gerald 1922- DLB-28

Green, Henry 1905-1973 ....DLB-15

Green, Jonas 1712-1767 ....DLB-31

Green, Joseph 1706-1780 ....DLB-31

Green, Julien 1900- DLB-4, 72

Green, Paul 1894-1981 ....DLB-7, 9; Y-81

Green, T. and S. [publishing house] DLB-49

Green, Timothy [publishing house] DLB-49

Greenberg: Publisher DLB-46

Green Tiger Press DLB-46

Greene, Asa 1789-1838 ....DLB-11

Greene, Benjamin H. [publishing house] DLB-49

Greene, Graham 1904-1991 ...DLB-13, 15, 77, 100; Y-85, Y-91

Greene, Robert 1558-1592 ....DLB-62

Greenhow, Robert 1800-1854 ....DLB-30

Greenough, Horatio 1805-1852 ....DLB-1

Greenwell, Dora 1821-1882 ....DLB-35

Greenwillow Books DLB-46

Greenwood, Grace (see Lippincott, Sara Jane Clarke)

Greenwood, Walter 1903-1974 ....DLB-10

Greer, Ben 1948- DLB-6

Greg, W. R. 1809-1881 ....DLB-55

Gregg Press DLB-46

Gregory, Isabella Augusta
    Persse, Lady 1852-1932 ....DLB-10

Gregory, Horace 1898-1982 ....DLB-48

Gregory of Rimini circa 1300-1358 ....DLB-115

Gregynog Press DLB-112

Grenfell, Wilfred Thomason 1865-1940 ....DLB-92

Greve, Felix Paul (see Grove, Frederick Philip)

Greville, Fulke, First Lord Brooke 1554-1628 ....DLB-62

Grey, Zane 1872-1939 ....DLB-9

Grey Owl 1888-1938 ....DLB-92

Grey Walls Press DLB-112

Grier, Eldon 1917- DLB-88

Grieve, C. M. (see MacDiarmid, Hugh)

Griffith, Elizabeth 1727?-1793 ....DLB-39, 89

Griffiths, Trevor 1935- DLB-13

Griggs, S. C., and Company DLB-49

Griggs, Sutton Elbert 1872-1930 ....DLB-50

Grignon, Claude-Henri 1894-1976 ....DLB-68

Grigson, Geoffrey 1905- DLB-27

Grimké, Angelina Weld 1880-1958 ....DLB-50, 54

Grimm, Hans 1875-1959 ....DLB-66

Grimm, Jacob 1785-1863 ....DLB-90

Grimm, Wilhelm 1786-1859 ....DLB-90

Griswold, Rufus Wilmot 1815-1857 ....DLB-3, 59

Gross, Milt 1895-1953 ....DLB-11

Grosset and Dunlap DLB-49

Grossman Publishers DLB-46

Grosseteste, Robert circa 1160-1253 ....DLB-115

Grosvenor, Gilbert H. 1875-1966 ....DLB-91

Groulx, Lionel 1878-1967 ....DLB-68

Grove, Frederick Philip 1879-1949 ....DLB-92

Grove Press DLB-46

Grubb, Davis 1919-1980 ....DLB-6

Gruelle, Johnny 1880-1938 ....DLB-22

Guare, John 1938- DLB-7

Guest, Barbara 1920- DLB-5

Guèvremont, Germaine 1893-1968 ....DLB-68

Guillén, Jorge 1893-1984 ....DLB-108

Guilloux, Louis 1899-1980 ....DLB-72

Guiney, Louise Imogen 1861-1920 ....DLB-54

Guiterman, Arthur 1871-1943 ....DLB-11

Günderrode, Caroline von 1780-1806 ....DLB-90

Gunn, Bill 1934-1989 ....DLB-38

Gunn, James E. 1923- DLB-8

Gunn, Neil M. 1891-1973 ....DLB-15

Gunn, Thom 1929- DLB-27

Gunnars, Kristjana 1948- DLB-60

Gurik, Robert 1932- DLB-60

Gustafson, Ralph 1909- DLB-88

Gütersloh, Albert Paris 1887-1973 ....DLB-81

Guthrie, A. B., Jr. 1901- DLB-6

Guthrie, Ramon 1896-1973 ....DLB-4

The Guthrie Theater DLB-7

Guy, Ray 1939- DLB-60

Guy, Rosa 1925- DLB-33

Gwynne, Erskine 1898-1948 ....DLB-4

Gyles, John 1680-1755 ....DLB-99

Gysin, Brion 1916- DLB-16

H

H. D. (see Doolittle, Hilda)

Hacker, Marilyn 1942- DLB-120

Hackett, Albert (see Goodrich, Frances)

Hacks, Peter 1928- DLB-124

Hadas, Rachel 1948- DLB-120

Hadden, Briton 1898-1929 ....DLB-91

Hagelstange, Rudolf 1912-1984 ....DLB-69

Haggard, H. Rider 1856-1925 ....DLB-70

Haig-Brown, Roderick 1908-1976 ....DLB-88

Haight, Gordon S. 1901-1985 ....DLB-103

Hailey, Arthur 1920- DLB-88; Y-82

Haines, John 1924- DLB-5

Hake, Thomas Gordon 1809-1895 ....DLB-32

Halbe, Max 1865-1944 ....DLB-118

Haldeman, Joe 1943- DLB-8

Haldeman-Julius Company DLB-46

Hale, E. J., and Son DLB-49

Hale, Edward Everett 1822-1909 ....DLB-1, 42, 74

Hale, Leo Thomas (see Ebon)

Hale, Lucretia Peabody 1820-1900 ....DLB-42

Hale, Nancy 1908-1988 ....DLB-86; Y-80, 88

Hale, Sarah Josepha (Buell) 1788-1879 ....DLB-1, 42, 73

Haley, Alex 1921-1992 ....DLB-38

Haliburton, Thomas Chandler 1796-1865 ....DLB-11, 99

Hall, Donald 1928- DLB-5

Hall, James 1793-1868 ....DLB-73, 74

Hall, Joseph 1574-1656 ....DLB-121

Hall, Samuel [publishing house] DLB-49

Hallam, Arthur Henry 1811-1833 ....DLB-32

Halleck, Fitz-Greene 1790-1867 ....DLB-3

Hallmark Editions DLB-46

Halper, Albert 1904-1984 ....DLB-9

Halperin, John William 1941- DLB-111

Halstead, Murat 1829-1908 ....DLB-23

Hamann, Johann Georg 1730-1788 ....DLB-97

Hamburger, Michael 1924- DLB-27

Hamilton, Alexander 1712-1756 ....DLB-31

Hamilton, Alexander 1755?-1804 ....DLB-37

Hamilton, Cicely 1872-1952 ....DLB-10

Hamilton, Edmond 1904-1977 ....DLB-8

Hamilton, Elizabeth 1758-1816 ....DLB-116

Hamilton, Gail (see Corcoran, Barbara)

Hamilton, Ian 1938- DLB-40

Hamilton, Patrick 1904-1962 ....DLB-10

Hamilton, Virginia 1936- DLB-33, 52

Hamilton, Hamish, Limited DLB-112

Hammett, Dashiell 1894-1961 .... DS-6

Dashiell Hammett: An Appeal in *TAC* Y-91

Hammon, Jupiter 1711-died between
        1790 and 1806 ....DLB-31, 50

Hammond, John ?-1663 ....DLB-24

Hamner, Earl 1923- DLB-6

Hampton, Christopher 1946- DLB-13

Handel-Mazzetti, Enrica von 1871-1955 ....DLB-81

Handke, Peter 1942- DLB-85, 124

Handlin, Oscar 1915- DLB-17

Hankin, St. John 1869-1909 ....DLB-10

Hanley, Clifford 1922- DLB-14

Hannah, Barry 1942- DLB-6

Hannay, James 1827-1873 ....DLB-21

Hansberry, Lorraine 1930-1965 ....DLB-7, 38

Hapgood, Norman 1868-1937 ....DLB-91

Harcourt Brace Jovanovich DLB-46

Hardenberg, Friedrich von (see Novalis)

Harding, Walter 1917- DLB-111

Hardwick, Elizabeth 1916- DLB-6

Hardy, Thomas 1840-1928 ....DLB-18, 19

Hare, Cyril 1900-1958 ....DLB-77

Hare, David 1947- DLB-13

Hargrove, Marion 1919- DLB-11

Harjo, Joy 1951- DLB-120

Harlow, Robert 1923- DLB-60

Harness, Charles L. 1915- DLB-8

Harper, Fletcher 1806-1877 ....DLB-79

Harper, Frances Ellen Watkins 1825-1911 ....DLB-50

Harper, Michael S. 1938- DLB-41

Harper and Brothers DLB-49

Harrap, George G., and Company Limited DLB-112

Harris, Benjamin ?-circa 1720 .... DLB-42, 43

Harris, Christie 1907- DLB-88

Harris, George Washington 1814-1869 .... DLB-3, 11

Harris, Joel Chandler 1848-1908 ....DLB-11, 23, 42, 78, 91

Harris, Mark 1922- DLB-2; Y-80

Harris, Wilson 1921- DLB-117

Harrison, Charles Yale 1898-1954 ....DLB-68

Harrison, Frederic 1831-1923 ....DLB-57

Harrison, Harry 1925- DLB-8

Harrison, James P., Company DLB-49

Harrison, Jim 1937- Y-82

Harrison, Paul Carter 1936- DLB-38

Harrison, Susan Frances 1859-1935 ....DLB-99

Harrison, Tony 1937- DLB-40

Harrisse, Henry 1829-1910 ....DLB-47

Harsent, David 1942- DLB-40

Hart, Albert Bushnell 1854-1943 ....DLB-17

Hart, Julia Catherine 1796-1867 ....DLB-99

Hart, Moss 1904-1961 ....DLB-7

Hart, Oliver 1723-1795 ....DLB-31

Hart-Davis, Rupert, Limited DLB-112

Harte, Bret 1836-1902 ....DLB-12, 64, 74, 79

Hartlaub, Felix 1913-1945 ....DLB-56

Hartlebon, Otto Erich 1864-1905 ....DLB-118

Hartley, L. P. 1895-1972 ....DLB-15

Hartley, Marsden 1877-1943 ....DLB-54

Hartling, Peter 1933- DLB-75

Hartman, Geoffrey H. 1929- DLB-67

Hartmann, Sadakichi 1867-1944 ....DLB-54

Harvey, Jean-Charles 1891-1967 ....DLB-88

Harvill Press Limited DLB-112

Harwood, Lee 1939- DLB-40

Harwood, Ronald 1934- DLB-13

Haskins, Charles Homer 1870-1937 ....DLB-47

Hass, Robert 1941- DLB-105

The Hatch-Billops Collection DLB-76

Hathaway, William 1944- DLB-120

Hauff, Wilhelm 1802-1827 ....DLB-90

A Haughty and Proud Generation (1922),
    by Ford Madox Hueffer DLB-36

Hauptmann, Carl 1858-1921 ....DLB-66, 118

Hauptmann, Gerhart 1862-1946 ....DLB-66, 118

Hauser, Marianne 1910- Y-83

Hawker, Robert Stephen 1803-1875 ....DLB-32

Hawkes, John 1925- DLB-2, 7; Y-80

Hawkins, Sir John 1719 or 1721-1789 ....DLB-104

Hawkins, Walter Everette 1883-? DLB-50

Hawthorne, Nathaniel 1804-1864 ....DLB-1, 74

Hay, John 1838-1905 ....DLB-12, 47

Hayden, Robert 1913-1980 ....DLB-5, 76

Haydon, Benjamin Robert 1786-1846 ....DLB-110

Hayes, John Michael 1919- DLB-26

Hayley, William 1745-1820 ....DLB-93

Hayman, Robert 1575-1629 ....DLB-99

Hayne, Paul Hamilton 1830-1886 ....DLB-3, 64, 79

Haywood, Eliza 1693?-1756 ....DLB-39

Hazard, Willis P. [publishing house] DLB-49

Hazlitt, William 1778-1830 ....DLB-110

Hazzard, Shirley 1931- Y-82

Head, Bessie 1937-1986 ....DLB-117

Headley, Joel T. 1813-1897 ....DLB-30

Heaney, Seamus 1939- DLB-40

Heard, Nathan C. 1936- DLB-33

Hearn, Lafcadio 1850-1904 ....DLB-12, 78

Hearne, John 1926- DLB-117

Hearne, Samuel 1745-1792 ....DLB-99

Hearst, William Randolph 1863-1951 ....DLB-25

Heath, Catherine 1924- DLB-14

Heath, Roy A. K. 1926- DLB-117

Heath-Stubbs, John 1918- DLB-27

Heavysege, Charles 1816-1876 ....DLB-99

Hebel, Johann Peter 1760-1826 ....DLB-90

Hébert, Anne 1916- DLB-68

Hébert, Jacques 1923- DLB-53

Hecht, Anthony 1923- DLB-5

Hecht, Ben 1894-1964 ....DLB-7, 9, 25, 26, 28, 86

Hecker, Isaac Thomas 1819-1888 ....DLB-1

Hedge, Frederic Henry 1805-1890 ....DLB-1, 59

Hegel, Georg Wilhelm Friedrich 1770-1831 ....DLB-90

Heidish, Marcy 1947- Y-82

Heidsenbüttel 1921- DLB-75

Hein, Christoph 1944- DLB-124

Heine, Heinrich 1797-1856 ....DLB-90

Heinemann, Larry 1944- DS-9

Heinemann, William, Limited DLB-112

Heinlein, Robert A. 1907- DLB-8

Heinrich, Willi 1920- DLB-75

Heinse, Wilhelm 1746-1803 ....DLB-94

Heller, Joseph 1923- DLB-2, 28; Y-80

Hellman, Lillian 1906-1984 ....DLB-7; Y-84

Helprin, Mark 1947- Y-85

Helwig, David 1938- DLB-60

Hemans, Felicia 1793-1835 ....DLB-96

Hemingway, Ernest 1899-1961
          ....DLB-4, 9, 102; Y-81, 87; DS-1

Hemingway: Twenty-Five Years Later Y-85

Hémon, Louis 1880-1913 ....DLB-92

Hemphill, Paul 1936- Y-87

Hénault, Gilles 1920- DLB-88

Henchman, Daniel 1689-1761 ....DLB-24

Henderson, Alice Corbin 1881-1949 ....DLB-54

Henderson, Archibald 1877-1963 ....DLB-103

Henderson, David 1942- DLB-41

Henderson, George Wylie 1904- DLB-51

Henderson, Zenna 1917- DLB-8

Henisch, Peter 1943- DLB-85

Henley, Beth 1952- Y-86

Henley, William Ernest 1849-1903 ....DLB-19

Henry, Alexander 1739-1824 ....DLB-99

Henry, Buck 1930- DLB-26

Henry, Marguerite 1902- DLB-22

Henry, O. (see Porter, William Sydney)

Henry, Robert Selph 1889-1970 ....DLB-17

Henry, Will (see Allen, Henry W.)

Henschke, Alfred (see Klabund)

Henry of Ghent circa 1217-1229 - 1293 ....DLB-115

Hensley, Sophie Almon 1866-1946 ....DLB-99

Henty, G. A. 1832-1902 ....DLB-18

Hentz, Caroline Lee 1800-1856 ....DLB-3

Herbert, Alan Patrick 1890-1971 ....DLB-10

Herbert, Edward, Lord, of Cherbury
    1583-1648 ....DLB-121

Herbert, Frank 1920-1986 ....DLB-8

Herbert, Henry William 1807-1858 ....DLB-3, 73

Herbert, John 1926- DLB-53

Herbst, Josephine 1892-1969 ....DLB-9

Herburger, Gunter 1932- DLB-75, 124

Hercules, Frank E. M. 1917- DLB-33

Herder, B., Book Company DLB-49

Herder, Johann Gottfried 1744-1803 ....DLB-97

Hergesheimer, Joseph 1880-1954 ....DLB-9, 102

Heritage Press DLB-46

Hermes, Johann Timotheus 1738-1821 ....DLB-97

Hermlin, Stephan 1915- DLB-69

Hernández, Alfonso C. 1938- DLB-122

Hernández, Ines 1947- DLB-122

Hernton, Calvin C. 1932- DLB-38

"The Hero as Man of Letters: Johnson,
    Rousseau, Burns" (1841), by Thomas
    Carlyle [excerpt] DLB-57

The Hero as Poet. Dante; Shakspeare (1841),
    by Thomas Carlyle DLB-32

Herrera, Juan Felipe 1948- DLB-122

Herrick, E. R., and Company DLB-49

Herrick, Robert 1868-1938 ....DLB-9, 12, 78

Herrick, William 1915- Y-83

Herrmann, John 1900-1959 ....DLB-4

Hersey, John 1914- DLB-6

Hertel, François 1905-1985 ....DLB-68

Hervé-Bazin, Jean Pierre Marie (see Bazin, Hervé)

Hervey, John, Lord 1696-1743 ....DLB-101

Herzog, Emile Salomon Wilhelm (see Maurois, André)

Hesse, Hermann 1877-1962 ....DLB-66

Hewat, Alexander circa 1743-circa 1824 ....DLB-30

Hewitt, John 1907- DLB-27

Hewlett, Maurice 1861-1923 ....DLB-34

Heyen, William 1940- DLB-5

Heyer, Georgette 1902-1974 ....DLB-77

Heym, Stefan 1913- DLB-69

Heytesbury, William circa 1310-1372 or 1373 ....DLB-115

Heyward, Dorothy 1890-1961 and
    Heyward, DuBose 1885-1940 ....DLB-7

Heyward, DuBose 1885-1940 ....DLB-7, 9, 45

Heywood, Thomas 1573 or 1574-1641 ....DLB-62

Hickman, William Albert 1877-1957 ....DLB-92

Hidalgo, José Luis 1919-1947 ....DLB-108

Hiebert, Paul 1892-1987 ....DLB-68

Hierro, José 1922- DLB-108

Higgins, Aidan 1927- DLB-14

Higgins, Colin 1941-1988 ....DLB-26

Higgins, George V. 1939- DLB-2; Y-81

Higginson, Thomas Wentworth 1823-1911 ....DLB-1, 64

Highwater, Jamake 1942?- DLB-52; Y-85

Hildesheimer, Wolfgang 1916-1991 ....DLB-69, 124

Hildreth, Richard 1807-1865 ....DLB-1, 30, 59

Hill, Aaron 1685-1750 ....DLB-84

Hill, Geoffrey 1932- DLB-40

Hill, George M., Company DLB-49

Hill, "Sir" John 1714?-1775 ....DLB-39

Hill, Lawrence, and Company, Publishers DLB-46

Hill, Leslie 1880-1960 .... DLB-51

Hill, Susan 1942- DLB-14

Hill, Walter 1942- DLB-44

Hill and Wang DLB-46

Hillberry, Conrad 1928- DLB-120

Hilliard, Gray and Company DLB-49

Hillyer, Robert 1895-1961 .... DLB-54

Hilton, James 1900-1954 .... DLB-34, 77

Hilton and Company DLB-49

Himes, Chester 1909-1984 .... DLB-2, 76

Hine, Daryl 1936- DLB-60

Hinojosa-Smith, Rolando 1929- DLB-82

Hippel, Theodor Gottlieb von 1741-1796 .... DLB-97

The History of the Adventures of Joseph Andrews
        (1742), by Henry Fielding [excerpt] DLB-39

Hirsch, E. D., Jr. 1928- DLB-67

Hirsch, Edward 1950- DLB-120

Hoagland, Edward 1932- DLB-6

Hoagland, Everett H. III 1942- DLB-41

Hoban, Russell 1925- DLB-52

Hobsbaum, Philip 1932- DLB-40

Hobson, Laura Z. 1900- DLB-28

Hochhuth, Rolf 1931- DLB-124

Hochman, Sandra 1936- DLB-5

Hodder and Stoughton, Limited DLB-106

Hodgins, Jack 1938- DLB-60

Hodgman, Helen 1945- DLB-14

Hodgson, Ralph 1871-1962 .... DLB-19

Hodgson, William Hope 1877-1918 .... DLB-70

Hoffenstein, Samuel 1890-1947 .... DLB-11

Hoffman, Charles Fenno 1806-1884 .... DLB-3

Hoffman, Daniel 1923- DLB-5

Hoffmann, E. T. A. 1776-1822 .... DLB-90

Hofmann, Michael 1957- DLB-40

Hofmannsthal, Hugo von 1874-1929 .... DLB-81, 118

Hofstadter, Richard 1916-1970 .... DLB-17

Hogan, Desmond 1950- DLB-14

Hogan and Thompson DLB-49

Hogarth Press DLB-112

Hogg, James 1770-1835 .... DLB-93, 116

Hohl, Ludwig 1904-1980 .... DLB-56

Holbrook, David 1923- DLB-14, 40

Holcroft, Thomas 1745-1809 .... DLB-39, 89

Holden, Jonathan 1941- DLB-105

Holden, Jonathan, Contemporary
        Verse Story-telling DLB-105

Holden, Molly 1927-1981 .... DLB-40

Hölderlin, Friedrich 1770-1843 .... DLB-90

Holiday House DLB-46

Holland, Norman N. 1927- DLB-67

Hollander, John 1929- DLB-5

Holley, Marietta 1836-1926 .... DLB-11

Hollingsworth, Margaret 1940- DLB-60

Hollo, Anselm 1934- DLB-40

Holloway, Emory 1885-1977 .... DLB-103

Holloway, John 1920- DLB-27

Holloway House Publishing Company DLB-46

Holme, Constance 1880-1955 .... DLB-34

Holmes, Abraham S. 1821?-1908 .... DLB-99

Holmes, John Clellon 1926-1988 .... DLB-16

Holmes, Oliver Wendell 1809-1894 .... DLB-1

Holst, Hermann E. von 1841-1904 .... DLB-47

Holt, Henry, and Company DLB-49

Holt, John 1721-1784 .... DLB-43

Holt, Rinehart and Winston DLB-46

Holthusen, Hans Egon 1913- DLB-69

Hölty, Ludwig Christoph Heinrich 1748-1776 .... DLB-94

Holz, Arno 1863-1929 .... DLB-118

Home, Henry, Lord Kames (see Kames, Henry Home, Lord)

Home, John 1722-1808 .... DLB-84

Home Publishing Company DLB-49

Home, William Douglas 1912- DLB-13

Homes, Geoffrey (see Mainwaring, Daniel)

Honan, Park 1928- DLB-111

Hone, William 1780-1842 ....DLB-110

Hongo, Garrett Kaoru 1951- DLB-120

Honig, Edwin 1919- DLB-5

Hood, Hugh 1928- DLB-53

Hood, Thomas 1799-1845 ....DLB-96

Hook, Theodore 1788-1841 ....DLB-116

Hooker, Jeremy 1941- DLB-40

Hooker, Thomas 1586-1647 ....DLB-24

Hooper, Johnson Jones 1815-1862 ....DLB-3, 11

Hopkins, Gerard Manley 1844-1889 ....DLB-35, 57

Hopkins, John H., and Son DLB-46

Hopkins, Lemuel 1750-1801 ....DLB-37

Hopkins, Pauline Elizabeth 1859-1930 ....DLB-50

Hopkins, Samuel 1721-1803 ....DLB-31

Hopkinson, Francis 1737-1791 ....DLB-31

Horgan, Paul 1903- DLB-102; Y-85

Horizon Press DLB-46

Horne, Frank 1899-1974 ....DLB-51

Horne, Richard Henry (Hengist) 1802 or 1803-1884 ...DLB-32

Hornung, E. W. 1866-1921 ....DLB-70

Horovitz, Israel 1939- DLB-7

Horton, George Moses 1797?-1883? DLB-50

Horváth, Ödön von 1901-1938 .... DLB-85, 124

Horwood, Harold 1923- DLB-60

Hosford, E. and E. [publishing house] DLB-49

Hoskyns, John 1566-1638 ....DLB-121

Hotchkiss and Company DLB-49

Hough, Emerson 1857-1923 ....DLB-9

Houghton Mifflin Company DLB-49

Houghton, Stanley 1881-1913 ....DLB-10

Household, Geoffrey 1900-1988 ....DLB-87

Housman, A. E. 1859-1936 ....DLB-19

Housman, Laurence 1865-1959 ....DLB-10

Houwald, Ernst von 1778-1845 ....DLB-90

Hovey, Richard 1864-1900 ....DLB-54

Howard, Donald R. 1927-1987 ....DLB-111

Howard, Maureen 1930- Y-83

Howard, Richard 1929- DLB-5

Howard, Roy W. 1883-1964 ....DLB-29

Howard, Sidney 1891-1939 .... DLB-7, 26

Howe, E. W. 1853-1937 .... DLB-12, 25

Howe, Henry 1816-1893 ....DLB-30

Howe, Irving 1920- DLB-67

Howe, Joseph 1804-1873 ....DLB-99

Howe, Julia Ward 1819-1910 ....DLB-1

Howe, Susan 1937- DLB-120

Howell, Clark, Sr. 1863-1936 ....DLB-25

Howell, Evan P. 1839-1905 ....DLB-23

Howell, Soskin and Company DLB-46

Howells, William Dean 1837-1920 .... DLB-12, 64, 74, 79

Howitt, William 1792-1879 and
    Howitt, Mary 1799-1888 ....DLB-110

Hoyem, Andrew 1935- DLB-5

de Hoyos, Angela 1940- DLB-82

Hoyt, Henry [publishing house] DLB-49

Hubbard, Elbert 1856-1915 ....DLB-91

Hubbard, Kin 1868-1930 ....DLB-11

Hubbard, William circa 1621-1704 ....DLB-24

Huber, Therese 1764-1829 ....DLB-90

Huch, Friedrich 1873-1913 ....DLB-66

Huch, Ricarda 1864-1947 ....DLB-66

Huck at 100: How Old Is Huckleberry Finn? Y-85

Hudgins, Andrew 1951- DLB-120

Hudson, Henry Norman 1814-1886 ....DLB-64

Hudson, W. H. 1841-1922 ....DLB-98

Hudson and Goodwin DLB-49

Huebsch, B. W. [publishing house] DLB-46

Hughes, David 1930- DLB-14

Hughes, John 1677-1720 ....DLB-84

Hughes, Langston 1902-1967 ....DLB-4, 7, 48, 51, 86

Hughes, Richard 1900-1976 ....DLB-15

Hughes, Ted 1930- DLB-40

Hughes, Thomas 1822-1896 ....DLB-18

Hugo, Richard 1923-1982 ....DLB-5

Hugo, Victor 1802-1885 ....DLB-119

Hugo Awards and Nebula Awards DLB-8

Hull, Richard 1896-1973 ....DLB-77

Hulme, T. E. 1883-1917 ....DLB-19

Humboldt, Alexander von 1769-1859 ....DLB-90

Humboldt, Wilhelm von 1767-1835 ....DLB-90

Hume, David 1711-1776 ....DLB-104

Hume, Fergus 1859-1932 ....DLB-70

Hummer, T. R. 1950- DLB-120

Humorous Book Illustration DLB-11

Humphrey, William 1924- DLB-6

Humphreys, David 1752-1818 ....DLB-37

Humphreys, Emyr 1919- DLB-15

Huncke, Herbert 1915- DLB-16

Huneker, James Gibbons 1857-1921 ....DLB-71

Hunt, Irene 1907- DLB-52

Hunt, Leigh 1784-1859 ....DLB-96, 110

Hunt, William Gibbes 1791-1833 ....DLB-73

Hunter, Evan 1926- Y-82

Hunter, Jim 1939- DLB-14

Hunter, Kristin 1931- DLB-33

Hunter, N. C. 1908-1971 ....DLB-10

Hunter-Duvar, John 1821-1899 ....DLB-99

Hurd and Houghton DLB-49

Hurst, Fannie 1889-1968 ....DLB-86

Hurst and Blackett DLB-106

Hurst and Company DLB-49

Hurston, Zora Neale 1901?-1960 ....DLB-51, 86

Husson, Jules-François-Félix (see Champfleury)

Huston, John 1906-1987 ....DLB-26

Hutcheson, Francis 1694-1746 ....DLB-31

Hutchinson, Thomas 1711-1780 ....DLB-30, 31

Hutchinson and Company (Publishers) Limited DLB-112

Hutton, Richard Holt 1826-1897 ....DLB-57

Huxley, Aldous 1894-1963 ....DLB-36, 100

Huxley, Elspeth Josceline 1907- DLB-77

Huxley, T. H. 1825-1895 ....DLB-57

Huyghue, Douglas Smith 1816-1891 ....DLB-99

Huysmans, Joris-Karl 1848-1907 ....DLB-123

Hyman, Trina Schart 1939- DLB-61

I

Ibn Bajja circa 1077-1138 ....DLB-115

Ibn Gabirol, Solomon circa 1021-circa 1058 ....DLB-115

The Iconography of Science-Fiction Art DLB-8

Iffland, August Wilhelm 1759-1814 ....DLB-94

Ignatow, David 1914- DLB-5

Iles, Francis (see Berkeley, Anthony)

Imbs, Bravig 1904-1946 ....DLB-4

Inchbald, Elizabeth 1753-1821 ....DLB-39, 89

Inge, William 1913-1973 ....DLB-7

Ingelow, Jean 1820-1897 ....DLB-35

The Ingersoll Prizes Y-84

Ingraham, Joseph Holt 1809-1860 ....DLB-3

Inman, John 1805-1850 ....DLB-73

Innerhofer, Franz 1944- DLB-85

Innis, Harold Adams 1894-1952 ....DLB-88

Innis, Mary Quayle 1899-1972 ....DLB-88

International Publishers Company DLB-46

An Interview with James Ellroy Y-91

An Interview with George Greenfield, Literary Agent Y-91

An Interview with Russell Hoban Y-90

An Interview with Tom Jenks Y-86

An Interview with Peter S. Prescott Y-86

An Interview with David Rabe Y-91

Introduction to Paul Laurence Dunbar,
    Lyrics of Lowly Life (1896),
    by William Dean Howells DLB-50

Introductory Essay: *Letters of Percy Bysshe
    Shelley* (1852), by Robert Browning DLB-32

Introductory Letters from the Second Edition
of *Pamela* (1741), by Samuel Richardson DLB-39

Irving, John 1942- DLB-6; Y-82

Irving, Washington 1783-1859 ......DLB-3, 11, 30, 59, 73, 74

Irwin, Grace 1907- DLB-68

Irwin, Will 1873-1948 ....DLB-25

Isherwood, Christopher 1904-1986 ....DLB-15; Y-86

The Island Trees Case: A Symposium on School
Library Censorship
An Interview with Judith Krug
An Interview with Phyllis Schlafly
An Interview with Edward B. Jenkinson
An Interview with Lamarr Mooneyham
An Interview with Harriet Bernstein Y-82

Islas, Arturo 1938-1991 ....DLB-122

Ivers, M. J., and Company DLB-49

J

Jackmon, Marvin E. (see Marvin X)

Jackson, Angela 1951- DLB-41

Jackson, Helen Hunt 1830-1885 ....DLB-42, 47

Jackson, Holbrook 1874-1948 ....DLB-98

Jackson, Laura Riding 1901-1991 ....DLB-48

Jackson, Shirley 1919-1965 ....DLB-6

Jacob, Piers Anthony Dillingham (see Anthony, Piers)

Jacobi, Friedrich Heinrich 1743-1819 ....DLB-94

Jacobi, Johann Georg 1740-1841 ....DLB-97

Jacobs, George W., and Company DLB-49

Jacobson, Dan 1929- DLB-14

Jahier, Piero 1884-1966 ....DLB-114

Jahnn, Hans Henny 1894-1959 .... DLB-56, 124

Jakes, John 1932- Y-83

James, C. L. R. 1901-1989 ....DLB-125

James, George P. R. 1801-1860 ....DLB-116

James, Henry 1843-1916 .... DLB-12, 71, 74

James, John circa 1633-1729 ....DLB-24

James Joyce Centenary: Dublin, 1982 ....Y-82

James Joyce Conference Y-85

James, P. D. 1920- DLB-87

James, U. P. [publishing house] DLB-49

Jameson, Anna 1794-1860 ....DLB-99

Jameson, Fredric 1934- DLB-67

Jameson, J. Franklin 1859-1937 ....DLB-17

Jameson, Storm 1891-1986 ....DLB-36

Jaramillo, Cleofas M. 1878-1956 ....DLB-122

Jarman, Mark 1952- DLB-120

Jarrell, Randall 1914-1965 .... DLB-48, 52

Jarrold and Sons DLB-106

Jasmin, Claude 1930- DLB-60

Jay, John 1745-1829 ....DLB-31

Jefferies, Richard 1848-1887 ....DLB-98

Jeffers, Lance 1919-1985 ....DLB-41

Jeffers, Robinson 1887-1962 ....DLB-45

Jefferson, Thomas 1743-1826 ....DLB-31

Jelinek, Elfriede 1946- DLB-85

Jellicoe, Ann 1927- DLB-13

Jenkins, Robin 1912- DLB-14

Jenkins, William Fitzgerald (see Leinster, Murray)

Jenkins, Herbert, Limited DLB-112

Jennings, Elizabeth 1926- DLB-27

Jens, Walter 1923- DLB-69

Jensen, Merrill 1905-1980 ....DLB-17

Jephson, Robert 1736-1803 ....DLB-89

Jerome, Jerome K. 1859-1927 .... DLB-10, 34

Jerome, Judson 1927-1991 ....DLB-105

Jerome, Judson, Reflections: After a Tornado DLB-105

Jesse, F. Tennyson 1888-1958 ....DLB-77

Jewett, John P., and Company DLB-49

Jewett, Sarah Orne 1849-1909 .... DLB-12, 74

The Jewish Publication Society DLB-49

Jewitt, John Rodgers 1783-1821 ....DLB-99

Jewsbury, Geraldine 1812-1880 ....DLB-21

Joans, Ted 1928- DLB-16, 41

John of Dumbleton circa 1310-circa 1349 ....DLB-115

John Edward Bruce: Three Documents DLB-50

John O'Hara's Pottsville Journalism Y-88

John Steinbeck Research Center Y-85

John Webster: The Melbourne Manuscript Y-86

Johnson, B. S. 1933-1973 ....DLB-14, 40

Johnson, Benjamin [publishing house] DLB-49

Johnson, Benjamin, Jacob, and
    Robert [publishing house] DLB-49

Johnson, Charles 1679-1748 ....DLB-84

Johnson, Charles R. 1948- DLB-33

Johnson, Charles S. 1893-1956 ....DLB-51, 91

Johnson, Denis 1949- DLB-120

Johnson, Diane 1934- Y-80

Johnson, Edgar 1901- DLB-103

Johnson, Edward 1598-1672 ....DLB-24

Johnson, Fenton 1888-1958 ....DLB-45, 50

Johnson, Georgia Douglas 1886-1966 ....DLB-51

Johnson, Gerald W. 1890-1980 ....DLB-29

Johnson, Helene 1907- DLB-51

Johnson, Jacob, and Company DLB-49

Johnson, James Weldon 1871-1938 ....DLB-51

Johnson, Lionel 1867-1902 ....DLB-19

Johnson, Nunnally 1897-1977 ....DLB-26

Johnson, Owen 1878-1952Y Y-87

Johnson, Pamela Hansford 1912- DLB-15

Johnson, Pauline 1861-1913 ....DLB-92

Johnson, Samuel 1696-1772 ....DLB-24

Johnson, Samuel 1709-1784 ....DLB-39, 95, 104

Johnson, Samuel 1822-1882 ....DLB-1

Johnson, Uwe 1934-1984 ....DLB-75

Johnston, Annie Fellows 1863-1931 ....DLB-42

Johnston, Basil H. 1929- DLB-60

Johnston, Denis 1901-1984 ....DLB-10

Johnston, George 1913- DLB-88

Johnston, Jennifer 1930- DLB-14

Johnston, Mary 1870-1936 ....DLB-9

Johnston, Richard Malcolm 1822-1898 ....DLB-74

Johnstone, Charles 1719?-1800? DLB-39

Johst, Hanns 1890-1978 ....DLB-124

Jolas, Eugene 1894-1952 ....DLB-4, 45

Jones, Alice C. 1853-1933 ....DLB-92

Jones, Charles C., Jr. 1831-1893 ....DLB-30

Jones, D. G. 1929- DLB-53

Jones, David 1895-1974 ....DLB-20, 100

Jones, Ebenezer 1820-1860 ....DLB-32

Jones, Ernest 1819-1868 ....DLB-32

Jones, Gayl 1949- DLB-33

Jones, Glyn 1905- DLB-15

Jones, Gwyn 1907- DLB-15

Jones, Henry Arthur 1851-1929 ....DLB-10

Jones, Hugh circa 1692-1760 ....DLB-24

Jones, James 1921-1977 ....DLB-2

Jones, LeRoi (see Baraka, Amiri)

Jones, Lewis 1897-1939 ....DLB-15

Jones, Major Joseph (see Thompson, William Tappan)

Jones, Preston 1936-1979 ....DLB-7

Jones, Rodney 1950- DLB-120

Jones, Sir William 1746-1794 ....DLB-109

Jones, William Alfred 1817-1900 ....DLB-59

Jones's Publishing House DLB-49

Jong, Erica 1942- DLB-2, 5, 28

Jonke, Gert F. 1946- DLB-85

Jonson, Ben 1572?-1637 ....DLB-62, 121

Jordan, June 1936- DLB-38

Joseph, Jenny 1932- DLB-40

Joseph, Michael, Limited DLB-112

Josephson, Matthew 1899-1978 ....DLB-4

Josiah Allen's Wife (see Holley, Marietta)

Josipovici, Gabriel 1940- DLB-14

Josselyn, John ?-1675 ....DLB-24

Joudry, Patricia 1921- DLB-88

Joyaux, Philippe (see Sollers, Philippe)

Joyce, Adrien (see Eastman, Carol)

Joyce, James 1882-1941 .... DLB-10, 19, 36

Judd, Orange, Publishing Company DLB-49

Judd, Sylvester 1813-1853 .... DLB-1

June, Jennie (see Croly, Jane Cunningham)

Jung, Franz 1888-1963 .... DLB-118

Jünger, Ernst 1895- DLB-56

Jung-Stilling, Johann Heinrich 1740-1817 .... DLB-94

Justice, Donald 1925- Y-83

K

Kacew, Romain (see Gary, Romain)

Kafka, Franz 1883-1924 .... DLB-81

Kaiser, Georg 1878-1945 .... DLB-124

Kalechofsky, Roberta 1931- DLB-28

Kaler, James Otis 1848-1912 .... DLB-12

Kames, Henry Home, Lord 1696-1782 .... DLB-31, 104

Kandel, Lenore 1932- DLB-16

Kanin, Garson 1912- DLB-7

Kant, Hermann 1926- DLB-75

Kant, Immanuel 1724-1804 .... DLB-94

Kantor, Mackinlay 1904-1977 .... DLB-9, 102

Kaplan, Fred 1937- DLB-111

Kaplan, Johanna 1942- DLB-28

Kaplan, Justin 1925- DLB-111

Karsch, Anna Louisa 1722-1791 .... DLB-97

Kasack, Hermann 1896-1966 .... DLB-69

Kaschnitz, Marie Luise 1901-1974 .... DLB-69

Kästner, Erich 1899-1974 .... DLB-56

Kattan, Naim 1928- DLB-53

Katz, Steve 1935- Y-83

Kauffman, Janet 1945- Y-86

Kaufman, Bob 1925- DLB-16, 41

Kaufman, George S. 1889-1961 .... DLB-7

Kavanagh, Patrick 1904-1967 .... DLB-15, 20

Kavanagh, P. J. 1931- DLB-40

Kaye-Smith, Sheila 1887-1956 .... DLB-36

Kazin, Alfred 1915- DLB-67

Keane, John B. 1928- DLB-13

Keating, H. R. F. 1926- DLB-87

Keats, Ezra Jack 1916-1983 .... DLB-61

Keats, John 1795-1821 .... DLB-96, 110

Keble, John 1792-1866 .... DLB-32, 55

Keeble, John 1944- Y-83

Keeffe, Barrie 1945- DLB-13

Keeley, James 1867-1934 .... DLB-25

W. B. Keen, Cooke and Company DLB-49

Keillor, Garrison 1942- Y-87

Keith, Marian 1874?-1961 .... DLB-92

Keller, Gary D. 1943- DLB-82

Kelley, Edith Summers 1884-1956 .... DLB-9

Kelley, William Melvin 1937- DLB-33

Kellogg, Ansel Nash 1832-1886 .... DLB-23

Kellogg, Steven 1941- DLB-61

Kelly, George 1887-1974 .... DLB-7

Kelly, Hugh 1739-1777 .... DLB-89

Kelly, Piet and Company DLB-49

Kelly, Robert 1935- DLB-5

Kelmscott Press DLB-112

Kemble, Fanny 1809-1893 .... DLB-32

Kemelman, Harry 1908- DLB-28

Kempowski, Walter 1929- DLB-75

Kendall, Claude [publishing company] DLB-46

Kendell, George 1809-1867 .... DLB-43

Kenedy, P. J., and Sons DLB-49

Kennedy, Adrienne 1931- DLB-38

Kennedy, John Pendleton 1795-1870 .... DLB-3

Kennedy, Leo 1907- DLB-88

Kennedy, Margaret 1896-1967 .... DLB-36

Kennedy, Richard S. 1920- DLB-111

Kennedy, William 1928- Y-85

Kennedy, X. J. 1929- DLB-5

Kennelly, Brendan 1936- DLB-40

Kenner, Hugh 1923- DLB-67

Kennerley, Mitchell [publishing house] DLB-46

Kent, Frank R. 1877-1958 ....DLB-29

Kenyon, Jane 1947- DLB-120

Keppler and Schwartzmann DLB-49

Kerner, Justinus 1776-1862 ....DLB-90

Kerouac, Jack 1922-1969 .... DLB-2, 16; DS-3

Kerouac, Jan 1952- DLB-16

Kerr, Charles H., and Company DLB-49

Kerr, Orpheus C. (see Newell, Robert Henry)

Kesey, Ken 1935- DLB-2, 16

Kessel, Joseph 1898-1979 ....DLB-72

Kessel, Martin 1901- DLB-56

Kesten, Hermann 1900- DLB-56

Keun, Irmgard 1905-1982 ....DLB-69

Key and Biddle DLB-49

Keynes, John Maynard 1883-1946 .... DS-10

Keyserling, Eduard von 1855-1918 ....DLB-66

Khan, Ismith 1925- DLB-125

Kidd, Adam 1802?-1831 ....DLB-99

Kidd, William [publishing house] DLB-106

Kiely, Benedict 1919- DLB-15

Kiggins and Kellogg DLB-49

Kiley, Jed 1889-1962 ....DLB-4

Killens, John Oliver 1916- DLB-33

Killigrew, Thomas 1612-1683 ....DLB-58

Kilmer, Joyce 1886-1918 ....DLB-45

Kilwardby, Robert circa 1215-1279 ....DLB-115

King, Clarence 1842-1901 ....DLB-12

King, Florence 1936 ....Y-85

King, Francis 1923- DLB-15

King, Grace 1852-1932 ....DLB-12, 78

King, Solomon [publishing house] DLB-49

King, Stephen 1947- Y-80

King, Woodie, Jr. 1937- DLB-38

Kinglake, Alexander William 1809-1891 ....DLB-55

Kingsley, Charles 1819-1875 ....DLB-21, 32

Kingsley, Henry 1830-1876 ....DLB-21

Kingsley, Sidney 1906- DLB-7

Kingston, Maxine Hong 1940- Y-80

Kinnell, Galway 1927- DLB-5; Y-87

Kinsella, Thomas 1928- DLB-27

Kipling, Rudyard 1865-1936 ....DLB-19, 34

Kipphardt, Heinar 1922-1982 ....DLB-124

Kirby, William 1817-1906 ....DLB-99

Kirk, John Foster 1824-1904 ....DLB-79

Kirkconnell, Watson 1895-1977 ....DLB-68

Kirkland, Caroline M. 1801-1864 .... DLB-3, 73, 74

Kirkland, Joseph 1830-1893 ....DLB-12

Kirkup, James 1918- DLB-27

Kirouac, Conrad (see Marie-Victorin, Frère)

Kirsch, Sarah 1935- DLB-75

Kirst, Hans Hellmut 1914-1989 ....DLB-69

Kitchin, C. H. B. 1895-1967 ....DLB-77

Kizer, Carolyn 1925- DLB-5

Klabund 1890-1928 ....DLB-66

Klappert, Peter 1942- DLB-5

Klass, Philip (see Tenn, William)

Klein, A. M. 1909-1972 ....DLB-68

Kleist, Ewald von 1715-1759 ....DLB-97

Kleist, Heinrich von 1777-1811 ....DLB-90

Klinger, Friedrich Maximilian 1752-1831 ....DLB-94

Klopstock, Friedrich Gottlieb 1724-1803 ....DLB-97

Klopstock, Meta 1728-1758 ....DLB-97

Kluge, Alexander 1932- DLB-75

Knapp, Joseph Palmer 1864-1951 ....DLB-91

Knapp, Samuel Lorenzo 1783-1838 ....DLB-59

Knickerbocker, Diedrich (see Irving, Washington)

Knigge, Adolph Franz Friedrich Ludwig,
    Freiherr von 1752-1796 ....DLB-94

Knight, Damon 1922- DLB-8

Knight, Etheridge 1931- DLB-41

Knight, John S. 1894-1981 ....DLB-29

Cumulative Index

Knight, Sarah Kemble 1666-1727 . . . . DLB-24

Knight, Charles, and Company DLB-106

Knister, Raymond 1899-1932 . . . . DLB-68

Knoblock, Edward 1874-1945 . . . . DLB-10

Knopf, Alfred A. 1892-1984 . . . . Y-84

Knopf, Alfred A. [publishing house] DLB-46

Knowles, John 1926- DLB-6

Knox, Frank 1874-1944 . . . . DLB-29

Knox, John Armoy 1850-1906 . . . . DLB-23

Knox, Ronald Arbuthnott 1888-1957 . . . . DLB-77

Kober, Arthur 1900-1975 . . . . DLB-11

Koch, Howard 1902- DLB-26

Koch, Kenneth 1925- DLB-5

Koenigsberg, Moses 1879-1945 . . . . DLB-25

Koeppen, Wolfgang 1906- DLB-69

Körner, Theodor 1791-1813 . . . . DLB-90

Koertge, Ronald 1940- DLB-105

Koestler, Arthur 1905-1983 . . . . Y-83

Kokoschka, Oskar 1886-1980 . . . . DLB-124

Kolb, Annette 1870-1967 . . . . DLB-66

Kolbenheyer, Erwin Guido 1878-1962 . . . . DLB-66, 124

Kolleritsch, Alfred 1931- DLB-85

Kolodny, Annette 1941- DLB-67

Komroff, Manuel 1890-1974 . . . . DLB-4

Komunyakaa, Yusef 1947- DLB-120

Konigsburg, E. L. 1930- DLB-52

Kooser, Ted 1939- DLB-105

Kopit, Arthur 1937- DLB-7

Kops, Bernard 1926?- DLB-13

Kornbluth, C. M. 1923-1958 . . . . DLB-8

Kornfeld, Paul 1889-1942 . . . . DLB-118

Kosinski, Jerzy 1933-1991 . . . . DLB-2; Y-82

Kotzebue, August von 1761-1819 . . . . DLB-94

Kraf, Elaine 1946- Y-81

Krasna, Norman 1909-1984 . . . . DLB-26

Kraus, Karl 1874-1936 . . . . DLB-118

Krauss, Ruth 1911- DLB-52

Kreisel, Henry 1922- DLB-88

Kreuder, Ernst 1903-1972 . . . . DLB-69

Kreymborg, Alfred 1883-1966 . . . . DLB-4, 54

Krieger, Murray 1923- DLB-67

Krim, Seymour 1922-1989 . . . . DLB-16

Krock, Arthur 1886-1974 . . . . DLB-29

Kroetsch, Robert 1927- DLB-53

Krutch, Joseph Wood 1893-1970 . . . . DLB-63

Kubin, Alfred 1877-1959 . . . . DLB-81

Kubrick, Stanley 1928- DLB-26

Kumin, Maxine 1925- DLB-5

Kunene, Mazisi 1930- DLB-117

Kunnert, Gunter 1929- DLB-75

Kunitz, Stanley 1905- DLB-48

Kunjufu, Johari M. (see Amini, Johari M.)

Kunze, Reiner 1933- DLB-75

Kupferberg, Tuli 1923- DLB-16

Kurz, Isolde 1853-1944 . . . . DLB-66

Kusenberg, Kurt 1904-1983 . . . . DLB-69

Kuttner, Henry 1915-1958 . . . . DLB-8

Kyd, Thomas 1558-1594 . . . . DLB-62

Kyger, Joanne 1934- DLB-16

Kyne, Peter B. 1880-1957 . . . . DLB-78

L

L. E. L. (see Landon, Letitia Elizabeth)

Laberge, Albert 1871-1960 . . . . DLB-68

Laberge, Marie 1950- DLB-60

Lacombe, Patrice (see Trullier-Lacombe, Joseph Patrice)

Lacretelle, Jacques de 1888-1985 . . . . DLB-65

Ladd, Joseph Brown 1764-1786 . . . . DLB-37

La Farge, Oliver 1901-1963 . . . . DLB-9

Lafferty, R. A. 1914- DLB-8

La Guma, Alex 1925-1985 . . . . DLB-117

Lahaise, Guillaume (see Delahaye, Guy)

Lahontan, Louis-Armand de Lom d'Arce, Baron de
1666-1715? DLB-99

Laird, Carobeth 1895- Y-82

Laird and Lee DLB-49

Lalonde, Michèle 1937- DLB-60

Lamantia, Philip 1927- DLB-16

Lamb, Charles 1775-1834 ....DLB-93, 107

Lamb, Lady Caroline 1785-1828 ....DLB-116

Lambert, Betty 1933-1983 ....DLB-60

Lamming, George 1927- DLB-125

L'Amour, Louis 1908?- Y-80

Lampman, Archibald 1861-1899 ....DLB-92

Lamson, Wolffe and Company DLB-49

Lancer Books DLB-46

Landesman, Jay 1919- and
Landesman, Fran 1927- DLB-16

Landon, Letitia Elizabeth 1802-1838 ....DLB-96

Landor, William Savage 1775-1864 ....DLB-93, 107

Landry, Napoléon-P. 1884-1956 ....DLB-92

Lane, Charles 1800-1870 ....DLB-1

The John Lane Company DLB-49

Lane, Laurence W. 1890-1967 ....DLB-91

Lane, M. Travis 1934- DLB-60

Lane, Patrick 1939- DLB-53

Lane, Pinkie Gordon 1923- DLB-41

Laney, Al 1896- DLB-4

Lang, Andrew 1844-1912 ....DLB-98

Langevin, André 1927- DLB-60

Langgässer, Elisabeth 1899-1950 ....DLB-69

Langhorne, John 1735-1779 ....DLB-109

Langton, Anna 1804-1893 ....DLB-99

Lanham, Edwin 1904-1979 ....DLB-4

Lanier, Sidney 1842-1881 ....DLB-64

Lanyer, Aemilia 1569-1645 ....DLB-121

Lapointe, Gatien 1931-1983 ....DLB-88

Lapointe, Paul-Marie 1929- DLB-88

Lardner, Ring 1885-1933 ....DLB-11, 25, 86

Lardner, Ring, Jr. 1915- DLB-26

Lardner 100: Ring Lardner
Centennial Symposium Y-85

Larkin, Philip 1922-1985 ....DLB-27

La Roche, Sophie von 1730-1807 ....DLB-94

La Rocque, Gilbert 1943-1984 ....DLB-60

Laroque de Roquebrune, Robert (see Roquebrune, Robert de)

Larrick, Nancy 1910- DLB-61

Larsen, Nella 1893-1964 ....DLB-51

Lasker-Schüler, Else 1869-1945 ....DLB-66, 124

Lasnier, Rina 1915- DLB-88

Lathrop, Dorothy P. 1891-1980 ....DLB-22

Lathrop, George Parsons 1851-1898 ....DLB-71

Lathrop, John, Jr. 1772-1820 ....DLB-37

Latimore, Jewel Christine McLawler (see Amini, Johari M.)

Laughlin, James 1914- DLB-48

Laumer, Keith 1925- DLB-8

Laurence, Margaret 1926-1987 ....DLB-53

Laurents, Arthur 1918- DLB-26

Laurie, Annie (see Black, Winifred)

Laut, Agnes Christiana 1871-1936 ....DLB-92

Lavater, Johann Kaspar 1741-1801 ....DLB-97

Lavin, Mary 1912- DLB-15

Lawless, Anthony (see MacDonald, Philip)

Lawrence, David 1888-1973 ....DLB-29

Lawrence, D. H. 1885-1930 ....DLB-10, 19, 36, 98

Lawson, John ?-1711 ....DLB-24

Lawson, Robert 1892-1957 ....DLB-22

Lawson, Victor F. 1850-1925 ....DLB-25

Layton, Irving 1912- DLB-88

Lea, Henry Charles 1825-1909 ....DLB-47

Lea, Sydney 1942- DLB-120

Lea, Tom 1907- DLB-6

Leacock, John 1729-1802 ....DLB-31

Leacock, Stephen 1869-1944 ....DLB-92

Leadenhall Press DLB-106

Leapor, Mary 1722-1746 ....DLB-109

Lear, Edward 1812-1888 . . . . DLB-32

Leary, Timothy 1920- DLB-16

Leary, W. A., and Company DLB-49

Léautaud, Paul 1872-1956 . . . . DLB-65

Leavitt and Allen DLB-49

le Carré, John 1931- DLB-87

Lécavelé, Roland (see Dorgeles, Roland)

Lechlitner, Ruth 1901- DLB-48

Leclerc, Félix 1914- DLB-60

Le Clézio, J. M. G. 1940- DLB-83

Lectures on Rhetoric and Belles Lettres (1783),
    by Hugh Blair [excerpts] DLB-31

Leder, Rudolf (see Hermlin, Stephan)

Lederer, Charles 1910-1976 . . . . DLB-26

Ledwidge, Francis 1887-1917 . . . . DLB-20

Lee, Dennis 1939- DLB-53

Lee, Don L. (see Madhubuti, Haki R.)

Lee, George W. 1894-1976 . . . . DLB-51

Lee, Harper 1926- DLB-6

Lee, Harriet (1757-1851) and
    Lee, Sophia (1750-1824) DLB-39

Lee, Laurie 1914- DLB-27

Lee, Nathaniel circa 1645 - 1692 . . . . DLB-80

Lee, Vernon 1856-1935 . . . . DLB-57

Lee and Shepard DLB-49

Le Fanu, Joseph Sheridan 1814-1873 . . . . DLB-21, 70

Leffland, Ella 1931- Y-84

le Fort, Gertrud von 1876-1971 . . . . DLB-66

Le Gallienne, Richard 1866-1947 . . . . DLB-4

Legaré, Hugh Swinton 1797-1843 . . . . DLB-3, 59, 73

Legaré, James M. 1823-1859 . . . . DLB-3

Léger, Antoine-J. 1880-1950 . . . . DLB-88

Le Guin, Ursula K. 1929- DLB-8, 52

Lehman, Ernest 1920- DLB-44

Lehmann, John 1907- DLB-27, 100

Lehmann, John, Limited DLB-112

Lehmann, Rosamond 1901-1990 . . . . DLB-15

Lehmann, Wilhelm 1882-1968 . . . . DLB-56

Leiber, Fritz 1910- DLB-8

Leicester University Press DLB-112

Leinster, Murray 1896-1975 . . . . DLB-8

Leisewitz, Johann Anton 1752-1806 . . . . DLB-94

Leitch, Maurice 1933- DLB-14

Leithauser, Brad 1943- DLB-120

Leland, Charles G. 1824-1903 . . . . DLB-11

Lemay, Pamphile 1837-1918 . . . . DLB-99

Lemelin, Roger 1919- DLB-88

Le Moine, James MacPherson 1825-1912 . . . . DLB-99

Le Moyne, Jean 1913- DLB-88

L'Engle, Madeleine 1918- DLB-52

Lennart, Isobel 1915-1971 . . . . DLB-44

Lennox, Charlotte 1729 or 1730-1804 . . . . DLB-39

Lenski, Lois 1893-1974 . . . . DLB-22

Lenz, Hermann 1913- DLB-69

Lenz, J. M. R. 1751-1792 . . . . DLB-94

Lenz, Siegfried 1926- DLB-75

Leonard, Hugh 1926- DLB-13

Leonard, William Ellery 1876-1944 . . . . DLB-54

Leonowens, Anna 1834-1914 . . . . DLB-99

LePan, Douglas 1914- DLB-88

Leprohon, Rosanna Eleanor 1829-1879 . . . . DLB-99

Le Queux, William 1864-1927 . . . . DLB-70

Lerner, Max 1902- DLB-29

Lernet-Holenia, Alexander 1897-1976 . . . . DLB-85

Le Rossignol, James 1866-1969 . . . . DLB-92

Lescarbot, Marc circa 1570-1642 . . . . DLB-99

LeSieg, Theo. (see Geisel, Theodor Seuss)

Leslie, Frank 1821-1880 . . . . DLB-43, 79

The Frank Leslie Publishing House DLB-49

Lesperance, John 1835?-1891 . . . . DLB-99

Lessing, Bruno 1870-1940 . . . . DLB-28

Lessing, Doris 1919- DLB-15; Y-85

Lessing, Gotthold Ephraim 1729-1781 . . . . DLB-97

LeSeur, William Dawson 1840-1917 ....DLB-92

Lettau, Reinhard 1929- DLB-75

Letter to [Samuel] Richardson on *Clarissa*
   (1748), by Henry Fielding DLB-39

Lever, Charles 1806-1872 ....DLB-21

Levertov, Denise 1923- DLB-5

Levi, Peter 1931- DLB-40

Levien, Sonya 1888-1960 ....DLB-44

Levin, Meyer 1905-1981 ....DLB-9, 28; Y-81

Levine, Norman 1923- DLB-88

Levine, Philip 1928- DLB-5

Levis, Larry 1946- DLB-120

Levy, Benn Wolfe 1900-1973 ....DLB-13; Y-81

Lewes, George Henry 1817-1878 ....DLB-55

Lewis, Alfred H. 1857-1914 ....DLB-25

Lewis, Alun 1915-1944 ....DLB-20

Lewis, C. Day (see Day Lewis, C.)

Lewis, Charles B. 1842-1924 ....DLB-11

Lewis, C. S. 1898-1963 ....DLB-15, 100

Lewis, Henry Clay 1825-1850 ....DLB-3

Lewis, Janet 1899- Y-87

Lewis, Matthew Gregory 1775-1818 ....DLB-39

Lewis, R. W. B. 1917- DLB-111

Lewis, Richard circa 1700-1734 ....DLB-24

Lewis, Sinclair 1885-1951 ....DLB-9, 102; DS-1

Lewis, Wyndham 1882-1957 ....DLB-15

Lewisohn, Ludwig 1882-1955 ....DLB-4, 9, 28, 102

Lezama Lima, José 1910-1976 ....DLB-113

The Library of America DLB-46

The Licensing Act of 1737 ....DLB-84

Lichtenberg, Georg Christoph 1742-1799 ....DLB-94

Liebling, A. J. 1904-1963 ....DLB-4

Lieutenant Murray (see Ballou, Maturin Murray)

Lighthall, William Douw 1857-1954 ....DLB-92

Lilar, Françoise (see Mallet-Joris, Françoise)

Lillo, George 1691-1739 ....DLB-84

Lilly, Wait and Company DLB-49

Limited Editions Club DLB-46

Lincoln and Edmands DLB-49

Lindsay, Jack 1900- Y-84

Lindsay, Vachel 1879-1931 ....DLB-54

Linebarger, Paul Myron Anthony (see Smith, Cordwainer)

Link, Arthur S. 1920- DLB-17

Linn, John Blair 1777-1804 ....DLB-37

Linton, Eliza Lynn 1822-1898 ....DLB-18

Linton, William James 1812-1897 ....DLB-32

Lion Books DLB-46

Lionni, Leo 1910- DLB-61

Lippincott, J. B., Company DLB-49

Lippincott, Sara Jane Clarke 1823-1904 ....DLB-43

Lippmann, Walter 1889-1974 ....DLB-29

Lipton, Lawrence 1898-1975 ....DLB-16

Liscow, Christian Ludwig 1701-1760 ....DLB-97

Lispector, Clarice 1925-1977 ....DLB-113

The Literary Chronicle and Weekly Review 1819-1828 ....DLB-110

Literary Documents: William Faulkner
   and the People-to-People Program Y-86

Literary Documents II: *Library Journal*
   Statements and Questionnaires from
   First Novelists Y-87

Literary Effects of World War II
   [British novel] DLB-15

Literary Prizes [British] DLB-15

Literary Research Archives: The Humanities
   Research Center, University of Texas Y-82

Literary Research Archives II: Berg
   Collection of English and American Literature
   of the New York Public Library Y-83

Literary Research Archives III:
   The Lilly Library Y-84

Literary Research Archives IV:
   The John Carter Brown Library Y-85

Literary Research Archives V:
   Kent State Special Collections Y-86

Literary Research Archives VI: The Modern
   Literary Manuscripts Collection in the
   Special Collections of the Washington
   University Libraries Y-87

Literary Research Archives VII:
   The University of Virginia Libraries Y-91

"Literary Style" (1857), by William
   Forsyth [excerpt] DLB-57

Literatura Chicanesca: The View From Without DLB-82

Literature at Nurse, or Circulating Morals (1885),
   by George Moore DLB-18

Littell, Eliakim 1797-1870 ....DLB-79

Littell, Robert S. 1831-1896 ....DLB-79

Little, Brown and Company DLB-49

Littlewood, Joan 1914- DLB-13

Lively, Penelope 1933- DLB-14

Liverpool University Press DLB-112

Livesay, Dorothy 1909- DLB-68

Livesay, Florence Randal 1874-1953 ....DLB-92

Livings, Henry 1929- DLB-13

Livingston, Anne Howe 1763-1841 ....DLB-37

Livingston, Myra Cohn 1926- DLB-61

Livingston, William 1723-1790 ....DLB-31

Liyong, Taban lo (see Taban lo Liyong)

Lizarraga, Sylvia S. 1925- DLB-82

Llewellyn, Richard 1906-1983 ....DLB-15

Lloyd, Edward [publishing house] DLB-106

Lobel, Arnold 1933- DLB-61

Lochridge, Betsy Hopkins (see Fancher, Betsy)

Locke, David Ross 1833-1888 ....DLB-11, 23

Locke, John 1632-1704 ....DLB-31, 101

Locke, Richard Adams 1800-1871 ....DLB-43

Locker-Lampson, Frederick 1821-1895 ....DLB-35

Lockhart, John Gibson 1794-1854 .... DLB-110, 116

Lockridge, Ross, Jr. 1914-1948 .... Y-80

Locrine and *Selimus* DLB-62

Lodge, David 1935- DLB-14

Lodge, George Cabot 1873-1909 ....DLB-54

Lodge, Henry Cabot 1850-1924 ....DLB-47

Loeb, Harold 1891-1974 ....DLB-4

Logan, James 1674-1751 ....DLB-24

Logan, John 1923- DLB-5

Logan, William 1950- DLB-120

Logue, Christopher 1926- DLB-27

London, Jack 1876-1916 .... DLB-8, 12, 78

The London Magazine 1820-1829 ....DLB-110

Long, H., and Brother DLB-49

Long, Haniel 1888-1956 ....DLB-45

Longfellow, Henry Wadsworth 1807-1882 .... DLB-1, 59

Longfellow, Samuel 1819-1892 ....DLB-1

Longley, Michael 1939- DLB-40

Longmans, Green and Company DLB-49

Longmore, George 1793?-1867 ....DLB-99

Longstreet, Augustus Baldwin 1790-1870 ...... DLB-3, 11, 74

Longworth, D. [publishing house] DLB-49

Lonsdale, Frederick 1881-1954 ....DLB-10

A Look at the Contemporary Black Theatre
   Movement DLB-38

Loos, Anita 1893-1981 .... DLB-11, 26; Y-81

Lopate, Phillip 1943- Y-80

López, Diana (see Isabella, Ros)

Loranger, Jean-Aubert 1896-1942 ....DLB-92

Lorca, Federico García 1898-1936 ....DLB-108

The Lord Chamberlain's Office and Stage
   Censorship in England DLB-10

Lord, John Keast 1818-1872 ....DLB-99

Lorde, Audre 1934- DLB-41

Lorimer, George Horace 1867-1939 ....DLB-91

Loring, A. K. [publishing house] DLB-49

Loring and Mussey DLB-46

Lossing, Benson J. 1813-1891 ....DLB-30

Lothar, Ernst 1890-1974 ....DLB-81

Lothrop, D., and Company DLB-49

Lothrop, Harriet M. 1844-1924 ....DLB-42

Loti, Pierre 1850-1923 ....DLB-123

The Lounger, no. 20 (1785), by Henry
   Mackenzie DLB-39

Lounsbury, Thomas R. 1838-1915 ....DLB-71

Louÿs, Pierre 1870-1925 ....DLB-123

Lovelace, Earl 1935- DLB-125

Lovell, John W., Company DLB-49

Lovell, Coryell and Company DLB-49

Lovesey, Peter 1936- DLB-87

Lovingood, Sut (see Harris, George Washington)

Low, Samuel 1765-? DLB-37

Lowell, Amy 1874-1925 ....DLB-54

Lowell, James Russell 1819-1891 ....DLB-1, 11, 64, 79

Lowell, Robert 1917-1977 ....DLB-5

Lowenfels, Walter 1897-1976 ....DLB-4

Lowndes, Marie Belloc 1868-1947 ....DLB-70

Lowry, Lois 1937- DLB-52

Lowry, Malcolm 1909-1957 ....DLB-15

Lowther, Pat 1935-1975 ....DLB-53

Loy, Mina 1882-1966 ....DLB-4, 54

Lozeau, Albert 1878-1924 ....DLB-92

Lucas, E. V. 1868-1938 ....DLB-98

Lucas, Fielding, Jr. [publishing house] DLB-49

Luce, Henry R. 1898-1967 ....DLB-91

Luce, John W., and Company DLB-46

Lucie-Smith, Edward 1933- DLB-40

Lucini, Gian Pietro 1867-1914 ....DLB-114

Ludlum, Robert 1927- Y-82

Ludvigson, Susan 1942- DLB-120

Ludwig, Jack 1922- DLB-60

Luera, Yolanda 1953- DLB-122

Luke, Peter 1919- DLB-13

The F. M. Lupton Publishing Company DLB-49

Lurie, Alison 1926- DLB-2

Lyall, Gavin 1932- DLB-87

Lyly, John circa 1554-1606 ....DLB-62

Lynd, Robert 1879-1949 ....DLB-98

Lyon, Matthew 1749-1822 ....DLB-43

Lytle, Andrew 1902- DLB-6

Lytton, Edward (see Bulwer-Lytton, Edward)

Lytton, Edward Robert Bulwer 1831-1891 ....DLB-32

M

Maass, Joachim 1901-1972 ....DLB-69

Mabie, Hamilton Wright 1845-1916 ....DLB-71

Mac A'Ghobhainn, Iain (see Smith, Iain Crichton)

MacArthur, Charles 1895-1956 ....DLB-7, 25, 44

Macaulay, Catherine 1731-1791 ....DLB-104

Macaulay, David 1945- DLB-61

Macaulay, Rose 1881-1958 ....DLB-36

Macaulay, Thomas Babington 1800-1859 ....DLB-32, 55

Macaulay Company DLB-46

MacBeth, George 1932- DLB-40

Macbeth, Madge 1880-1965 ....DLB-92

MacCaig, Norman 1910- DLB-27

MacDiarmid, Hugh 1892-1978 ....DLB-20

MacDonald, Cynthia 1928- DLB-105

MacDonald, George 1824-1905 ....DLB-18

MacDonald, John D. 1916-1986 ....DLB-8; Y-86

MacDonald, Philip 1899?-1980 ....DLB-77

Macdonald, Ross (see Millar, Kenneth)

MacDonald, Wilson 1880-1967 ....DLB-92

Macdonald and Company (Publishers) DLB-112

MacEwen, Gwendolyn 1941- DLB-53

Macfadden, Bernarr 1868-1955 ....DLB-25, 91

MacGregor, Mary Esther (see Keith, Marian)

Machado, Antonio 1875-1939 ....DLB-108

Machado, Manuel 1874-1947 ....DLB-108

Machar, Agnes Maule 1837-1927 ....DLB-92

Machen, Arthur Llewelyn Jones 1863-1947 ....DLB-36

MacInnes, Colin 1914-1976 ....DLB-14

MacInnes, Helen 1907-1985 ....DLB-87

Mack, Maynard 1909- DLB-111

MacKaye, Percy 1875-1956 ....DLB-54

Macken, Walter 1915-1967 ....DLB-13

Mackenzie, Alexander 1763-1820 ....DLB-99

Mackenzie, Compton 1883-1972 .... DLB-34, 100

Mackenzie, Henry 1745-1831 .... DLB-39

Mackey, William Wellington 1937- DLB-38

Mackintosh, Elizabeth (see Tey, Josephine)

Macklin, Charles 1699-1797 .... DLB-89

MacLean, Katherine Anne 1925- DLB-8

MacLeish, Archibald 1892-1982 .... DLB-4, 7, 45; Y-82

MacLennan, Hugh 1907-1990 .... DLB-68

MacLeod, Alistair 1936- DLB-60

Macleod, Norman 1906-1985 .... DLB-4

Macmillan and Company DLB-106

The Macmillan Company DLB-49

MacNamara, Brinsley 1890-1963 .... DLB-10

MacNeice, Louis 1907-1963 .... DLB-10, 20

MacPhail, Andrew 1864-1938 .... DLB-92

Macpherson, James 1736-1796 .... DLB-109

Macpherson, Jay 1931- DLB-53

Macpherson, Jeanie 1884-1946 .... DLB-44

Macrae Smith Company DLB-46

Macrone, John [publishing house] DLB-106

MacShane, Frank 1927- DLB-111

Macy-Masius DLB-46

Madden, David 1933- DLB-6

Maddow, Ben 1909- DLB-44

Madgett, Naomi Long 1923- DLB-76

Madhubuti, Haki R. 1942- DLB-5, 41; DS-8

Madison, James 1751-1836 .... DLB-37

Maginn, William 1794-1842 .... DLB-110

Mahan, Alfred Thayer 1840-1914 .... DLB-47

Maheux-Forcier, Louise 1929- DLB-60

Mahin, John Lee 1902-1984 .... DLB-44

Mahon, Derek 1941- DLB-40

Mailer, Norman 1923- DLB-2, 16, 28; Y-80, 83; DS-3

Maillet, Adrienne 1885-1963 .... DLB-68

Maimonides, Moses 1138-1204 .... DLB-115

Maillet, Antonine 1929- DLB-60

Main Selections of the Book-of-the-Month Club,
    1926-1945 .... DLB-9

Main Trends in Twentieth-Century Book Clubs DLB-46

Mainwaring, Daniel 1902-1977 .... DLB-44

Mair, Charles 1838-1927 .... DLB-99

Mais, Roger 1905-1955 .... DLB-125

Major, Andre 1942- DLB-60

Major, Clarence 1936- DLB-33

Major, Kevin 1949- DLB-60

Major Books DLB-46

Makemie, Francis circa 1658-1708 .... DLB-24

The Making of a People, by J. M. Ritchie DLB-66

Malamud, Bernard 1914-1986 .... DLB-2, 28; Y-80, 86

Malleson, Lucy Beatrice (see Gilbert, Anthony)

Mallet-Joris, Françoise 1930- DLB-83

Mallock, W. H. 1849-1923 .... DLB-18, 57

Malone, Dumas 1892-1986 .... DLB-17

Malraux, André 1901-1976 .... DLB-72

Malthus, Thomas Robert 1766-1834 .... DLB-107

Maltz, Albert 1908-1985 .... DLB-102

Malzberg, Barry N. 1939- DLB-8

Mamet, David 1947- DLB-7

Manchester University Press DLB-112

Mandel, Eli 1922- DLB-53

Mandeville, Bernard 1670-1733 .... DLB-101

Mandiargues, André Pieyre de 1909- DLB-83

Manfred, Frederick 1912- DLB-6

Mangan, Sherry 1904-1961 .... DLB-4

Mankiewicz, Herman 1897-1953 .... DLB-26

Mankiewicz, Joseph L. 1909- DLB-44

Mankowitz, Wolf 1924- DLB-15

Manley, Delarivière 1672?-1724 .... DLB-39, 80

Mann, Abby 1927- DLB-44

Mann, Heinrich 1871-1950 .... DLB-66, 118

Mann, Horace 1796-1859 .... DLB-1

Mann, Klaus 1906-1949 .... DLB-56

Mann, Thomas 1875-1955 .... DLB-66

Manning, Marie 1873?-1945 ....DLB-29

Manning and Loring DLB-49

Mano, D. Keith 1942- DLB-6

Manor Books DLB-46

March, William 1893-1954 ....DLB-9, 86

Marchand, Leslie A. 1900- DLB-103

Marchessault, Jovette 1938- DLB-60

Marcus, Frank 1928- DLB-13

Marek, Richard, Books DLB-46

Mares, E. A. 1938- DLB-122

Mariani, Paul 1940- DLB-111

Marie-Victorin, Frère 1885-1944 ....DLB-92

Marinetti, Filippo Tommaso 1876-1944 ....DLB-114

Marion, Frances 1886-1973 ....DLB-44

Marius, Richard C. 1933- Y-85

The Mark Taper Forum DLB-7

Markfield, Wallace 1926- DLB-2, 28

Markham, Edwin 1852-1940 ....DLB-54

Markle, Fletcher 1921-1991 ....DLB-68; Y-91

Marlatt, Daphne 1942- DLB-60

Marlowe, Christopher 1564-1593 ....DLB-62

Marlyn, John 1912- DLB-88

Marmion, Shakerley 1603-1639 ....DLB-58

Marquand, John P. 1893-1960 ....DLB-9, 102

Marqués, René 1919-1979 ....DLB-113

Marquis, Don 1878-1937 ....DLB-11, 25

Marriott, Anne 1913- DLB-68

Marryat, Frederick 1792-1848 ....DLB-21

Marsh, George Perkins 1801-1882 ....DLB-1, 64

Marsh, James 1794-1842 ....DLB-1, 59

Marsh, Capen, Lyon and Webb DLB-49

Marsh, Ngaio 1899-1982 ....DLB-77

Marshall, Edison 1894-1967 ....DLB-102

Marshall, Edward 1932- DLB-16

Marshall, James 1942- DLB-61

Marshall, Joyce 1913- DLB-88

Marshall, Paule 1929- DLB-33

Marshall, Tom 1938- DLB-60

Marsilius of Padua circa 1275-circa 1342 ....DLB-115

Marston, John 1576-1634 ....DLB-58

Marston, Philip Bourke 1850-1887 ....DLB-35

Martens, Kurt 1870-1945 ....DLB-66

Martien, William S. [publishing house] DLB-49

Martin, Abe (see Hubbard, Kin)

Martin, Charles 1942- DLB-120

Martin, Claire 1914- DLB-60

Martin, Jay 1935- DLB-111

Martin du Gard, Roger 1881-1958 ....DLB-65

Martineau, Harriet 1802-1876 ....DLB-21, 55

Martínez, Eliud 1935- DLB-122

Martínez, Max 1943- DLB-82

Martyn, Edward 1859-1923 ....DLB-10

Marvin X 1944- DLB-38

Marzials, Theo 1850-1920 ....DLB-35

Masefield, John 1878-1967 ....DLB-10, 19

Mason, A. E. W. 1865-1948 ....DLB-70

Mason, Bobbie Ann 1940- Y-87

Mason Brothers DLB-49

Massey, Gerald 1828-1907 ....DLB-32

Massinger, Philip 1583-1640 ....DLB-58

Masters, Edgar Lee 1868-1950 ....DLB-54

Mather, Cotton 1663-1728 ....DLB-24, 30

Mather, Increase 1639-1723 ....DLB-24

Mather, Richard 1596-1669 ....DLB-24

Matheson, Richard 1926- DLB-8, 44

Matheus, John F. 1887- DLB-51

Mathews, Cornelius 1817?-1889 ....DLB-3, 64

Mathews, Elkin [publishing house] DLB-112

Mathias, Roland 1915- DLB-27

Mathis, June 1892-1927 ....DLB-44

Mathis, Sharon Bell 1937- DLB-33

Matthews, Brander 1852-1929 ....DLB-71, 78

Matthews, Jack 1925- DLB-6

Matthews, William 1942- DLB-5

Matthiessen, F. O. 1902-1950 ....DLB-63

Matthiessen, Peter 1927- DLB-6

Maugham, W. Somerset 1874-1965 ......DLB-10, 36, 77, 100

Maupassant, Guy de 1850-1893 ....DLB-123

Mauriac, Claude 1914- DLB-83

Mauriac, Francois 1885-1970 ....DLB-65

Maurice, Frederick Denison 1805-1872 ....DLB-55

Maurois, André 1885-1967 ....DLB-65

Maury, James 1718-1769 ....DLB-31

Mavor, Elizabeth 1927- DLB-14

Mavor, Osborne Henry (see Bridie, James)

Maxwell, H. [publishing house] DLB-49

Maxwell, John [publishing house] DLB-106

Maxwell, William 1908- Y-80

May, Elaine 1932- DLB-44

May, Thomas 1595 or 1596-1650 ....DLB-58

Mayer, Mercer 1943- DLB-61

Mayer, O. B. 1818-1891 ....DLB-3

Mayes, Wendell 1919- DLB-26

Mayfield, Julian 1928-1984 ....DLB-33; Y-84

Mayhew, Henry 1812-1887 ....DLB-18, 55

Mayhew, Jonathan 1720-1766 ....DLB-31

Mayne, Seymour 1944- DLB-60

Mayor, Flora Macdonald 1872-1932 ....DLB-36

Mayrocker, Friederike 1924- DLB-85

Mazrui, Ali A. 1933- DLB-125

Mazursky, Paul 1930- DLB-44

McAlmon, Robert 1896-1956 ....DLB-4, 45

McArthur, Peter 1866-1924 ....DLB-92

McBride, Robert M., and Company DLB-46

McCaffrey, Anne 1926- DLB-8

McCarthy, Cormac 1933- DLB-6

McCarthy, Mary 1912-1989 ....DLB-2; Y-81

McCay, Winsor 1871-1934 ....DLB-22

McClatchy, C. K. 1858-1936 ....DLB-25

McClellan, George Marion 1860-1934 ....DLB-50

McCloskey, Robert 1914- DLB-22

McClung, Nellie Letitia 1873-1951 ....DLB-92

McClure, Joanna 1930- DLB-16

McClure, Michael 1932- DLB-16

McClure, Phillips and Company DLB-46

McClure, S. S. 1857-1949 ....DLB-91

McClurg, A. C., and Company DLB-49

McCluskey, John A., Jr. 1944- DLB-33

McCollum, Michael A. 1946 .... Y-87

McConnell, William C. 1917- DLB-88

McCord, David 1897- DLB-61

McCorkle, Jill 1958- Y-87

McCorkle, Samuel Eusebius 1746-1811 ....DLB-37

McCormick, Anne O'Hare 1880-1954 ....DLB-29

McCormick, Robert R. 1880-1955 ....DLB-29

McCourt, Edward 1907-1972 ....DLB-88

McCoy, Horace 1897-1955 ....DLB-9

McCrae, John 1872-1918 ....DLB-92

McCullagh, Joseph B. 1842-1896 ....DLB-23

McCullers, Carson 1917-1967 .... DLB-2, 7

McCulloch, Thomas 1776-1843 ....DLB-99

McDonald, Forrest 1927- DLB-17

McDonald, Walter 1934- DLB-105, DS-9

McDonald, Walter, Getting Started:
    Accepting the Regions You Own—
    or Which Own You DLB-105

McDougall, Colin 1917-1984 ....DLB-68

McDowell, Obolensky DLB-46

McEwan, Ian 1948- DLB-14

McFadden, David 1940- DLB-60

McFarlane, Leslie 1902-1977 ....DLB-88

McGahern, John 1934- DLB-14

McGee, Thomas D'Arcy 1825-1868 ....DLB-99

McGeehan, W. O. 1879-1933 ....DLB-25

McGill, Ralph 1898-1969 ....DLB-29

McGinley, Phyllis 1905-1978 ....DLB-11, 48

McGirt, James E. 1874-1930 ....DLB-50

McGlashan and Gill DLB-106

McGough, Roger 1937- DLB-40

McGraw-Hill DLB-46

McGuane, Thomas 1939- DLB-2; Y-80

McGuckian, Medbh 1950- DLB-40

McGuffey, William Holmes 1800-1873 ....DLB-42

McIlvanney, William 1936- DLB-14

McIlwraith, Jean Newton 1859-1938 ....DLB-92

McIntyre, James 1827-1906 ....DLB-99

McIntyre, O. O. 1884-1938 ....DLB-25

McKay, Claude 1889-1948 .... DLB-4, 45, 51, 117

The David McKay Company DLB-49

McKean, William V. 1820-1903 ....DLB-23

McKinley, Robin 1952- DLB-52

McLachlan, Alexander 1818-1896 ....DLB-99

McLaren, Floris Clark 1904-1978 ....DLB-68

McLaverty, Michael 1907- DLB-15

McLean, John R. 1848-1916 ....DLB-23

McLean, William L. 1852-1931 ....DLB-25

McLennan, William 1856-1904 ....DLB-92

McLoughlin Brothers DLB-49

McLuhan, Marshall 1911-1980 ....DLB-88

McMaster, John Bach 1852-1932 ....DLB-47

McMurtry, Larry 1936- DLB-2; Y-80, 87

McNally, Terrence 1939- DLB-7

McNeil, Florence 1937- DLB-60

McNeile, Herman Cyril 1888-1937 ....DLB-77

McPherson, James Alan 1943- DLB-38

McPherson, Sandra 1943- Y-86

McWhirter, George 1939- DLB-60

Mead, Matthew 1924- DLB-40

Mead, Taylor ?- DLB-16

Medill, Joseph 1823-1899 ....DLB-43

Medoff, Mark 1940- DLB-7

Meek, Alexander Beaufort 1814-1865 ....DLB-3

Meeke, Mary ?-1816? DLB-116

Meinke, Peter 1932- DLB-5

Mejia Vallejo, Manuel 1923- DLB-113

Melançon, Robert 1947- DLB-60

Mell, Max 1882-1971 ....DLB-81, 124

Mellow, James R. 1926- DLB-111

Meltzer, David 1937- DLB-16

Meltzer, Milton 1915- DLB-61

Melville, Herman 1819-1891 ....DLB-3, 74

Memoirs of Life and Literature (1920),
    by W. H. Mallock [excerpt] DLB-57

Mencken, H. L. 1880-1956 .... DLB-11, 29, 63

Mendelssohn, Moses 1729-1786 ....DLB-97

Méndez M., Miguel 1930- DLB-82

Mercer, Cecil William (see Yates, Dornford)

Mercer, David 1928-1980 ....DLB-13

Mercer, John 1704-1768 ....DLB-31

Meredith, George 1828-1909 .... DLB-18, 35, 57

Meredith, Owen (see Lytton, Edward Robert Bulwer)

Meredith, William 1919- DLB-5

Mérimée, Prosper 1803-1870 ....DLB-119

Merivale, John Herman 1779-1844 ....DLB-96

Meriwether, Louise 1923- DLB-33

Merlin Press DLB-112

Merriam, Eve 1916- DLB-61

The Merriam Company DLB-49

Merrill, James 1926- DLB-5; Y-85

Merrill and Baker DLB-49

The Mershon Company DLB-49

Merton, Thomas 1915-1968 ....DLB-48; Y-81

Merwin, W. S. 1927- DLB-5

Messner, Julian [publishing house] DLB-46

Metcalf, J. [publishing house] DLB-49

Metcalf, John 1938- DLB-60

The Methodist Book Concern DLB-49

Methuen and Company DLB-112

Mew, Charlotte 1869-1928 . . . . .DLB-19

Mewshaw, Michael 1943- Y-80

Meyer, E. Y. 1946- DLB-75

Meyer, Eugene 1875-1959 . . . . .DLB-29

Meyers, Jeffrey 1939- DLB-111

Meynell, Alice 1847-1922 . . . . .DLB-19, 98

Meyrink, Gustav 1868-1932 .DLB-81

Micheaux, Oscar 1884-1951 .DLB-50

Micheline, Jack 1929- DLB-16

Michener, James A. 1907?- .DLB-6

Micklejohn, George circa 1717-1818 . . . . .DLB-31

Middle Hill Press DLB-106

Middleton, Christopher 1926- DLB-40

Middleton, Stanley 1919- .DLB-14

Middleton, Thomas 1580-1627 . . . . .DLB-58

Miegel, Agnes 1879-1964 . . . . .DLB-56

Miles, Josephine 1911-1985 . . . . .DLB-48

Milius, John 1944- DLB-44

Mill, James 1773-1836 . . . . .DLB-107

Mill, John Stuart 1806-1873 . . . . .DLB-55

Millar, Kenneth 1915-1983 . . . . .DLB-2; Y-83; DS-6

Millay, Edna St. Vincent 1892-1950 . . . . .DLB-45

Miller, Arthur 1915- DLB-7

Miller, Caroline 1903- DLB-9

Miller, Eugene Ethelbert 1950- DLB-41

Miller, Heather Ross 1939- DLB-120

Miller, Henry 1891-1980 . . . . .DLB-4, 9; Y-80

Miller, J. Hillis 1928- .DLB-67

Miller, James [publishing house] DLB-49

Miller, Jason 1939- DLB-7

Miller, May 1899- DLB-41

Miller, Perry 1905-1963 . . . . .DLB-17, 63

Miller, Walter M., Jr. 1923- DLB-8

Miller, Webb 1892-1940 . . . . .DLB-29

Millhauser, Steven 1943- .DLB-2

Millican, Arthenia J. Bates 1920- DLB-38

Mills and Boon DLB-112

Milman, Henry Hart 1796-1868 . . . . .DLB-96

Milne, A. A. 1882-1956 . . . . .DLB-10, 77, 100

Milner, Ron 1938- DLB-38

Milner, William [publishing house] DLB-106

Milnes, Richard Monckton (Lord Houghton)
1809-1885 . . . . .DLB-32

Minor Poets of the Earlier Seventeenth Century DLB-121

Minton, Balch and Company DLB-46

Mirbeau, Octave 1848-1917 . . . . .DLB-123

Miron, Gaston 1928- DLB-60

Mitchel, Jonathan 1624-1668 . . . . .DLB-24

Mitchell, Adrian 1932- DLB-40

Mitchell, Donald Grant 1822-1908 . . . . .DLB-1

Mitchell, Gladys 1901-1983 . . . . .DLB-77

Mitchell, James Leslie 1901-1935 . . . . .DLB-15

Mitchell, John (see Slater, Patrick)

Mitchell, John Ames 1845-1918 . . . . .DLB-79

Mitchell, Julian 1935- DLB-14

Mitchell, Ken 1940- DLB-60

Mitchell, Langdon 1862-1935 . . . . .DLB-7

Mitchell, Loften 1919- DLB-38

Mitchell, Margaret 1900-1949 . . . . .DLB-9

Mitchell, W. O. 1914- DLB-88

Mitford, Mary Russell 1787-1855 . . . . .DLB-110, 116

Mittelholzer, Edgar 1909-1965 . . . . .DLB-117

Mitterer, Erika 1906- DLB-85

Mitterer, Felix 1948- DLB-124

Mizener, Arthur 1907-1988 . . . . .DLB-103

Modern Age Books DLB-46

"Modern English Prose" (1876),
by George Saintsbury DLB-57

The Modern Language Association of America
Celebrates Its Centennial Y-84

The Modern Library DLB-46

Modern NovelistsGreat and Small (1855), by
Margaret Oliphant DLB-21

"Modern Style" (1857), by Cockburn
    Thomson [excerpt] DLB-57

The Modernists (1932), by Joseph Warren Beach DLB-36

Modiano, Patrick 1945- DLB-83

Moffat, Yard and Company DLB-46

Monkhouse, Allan 1858-1936 ....DLB-10

Monro, Harold 1879-1932 ....DLB-19

Monroe, Harriet 1860-1936 ....DLB-54, 91

Monsarrat, Nicholas 1910-1979 ....DLB-15

Montale, Eugenio 1896-1981 ....DLB-114

Montagu, Lady Mary Wortley 1689-1762 ....DLB-95, 101

Montague, John 1929- DLB-40

Montgomery, James 1771-1854 ....DLB-93

Montgomery, John 1919- DLB-16

Montgomery, Lucy Maud 1874-1942 ....DLB-92

Montgomery, Marion 1925- DLB-6

Montgomery, Robert Bruce (see Crispin, Edmund)

Montherlant, Henry de 1896-1972 ....DLB-72

The Monthly Review 1749-1844 ....DLB-110

Montigny, Louvigny de 1876-1955 ....DLB-92

Montoya, José 1932- DLB-122

Moodie, John Wedderburn Dunbar 1797-1869 ....DLB-99

Moodie, Susanna 1803-1885 ....DLB-99

Moody, Joshua circa 1633-1697 ....DLB-24

Moody, William Vaughn 1869-1910 ....DLB-7, 54

Moorcock, Michael 1939- DLB-14

Moore, Catherine L. 1911- DLB-8

Moore, Clement Clarke 1779-1863 ....DLB-42

Moore, Dora Mavor 1888-1979 ....DLB-92

Moore, George 1852-1933 ....DLB-10, 18, 57

Moore, Marianne 1887-1972 ....DLB-45; DS-7

Moore, Mavor 1919- DLB-88

Moore, Richard 1927- DLB-105

Moore, Richard, The No Self, the Little Self, and
    the Poets DLB-105

Moore, T. Sturge 1870-1944 ....DLB-19

Moore, Thomas 1779-1852 ....DLB-96

Moore, Ward 1903-1978 ....DLB-8

Moore, Wilstach, Keys and Company DLB-49

The Moorland-Spingarn Research Center DLB-76

Moraga, Cherríe 1952- DLB-82

Morales, Alejandro 1944- DLB-82

Morales, Rafael 1919- DLB-108

More, Hannah 1745-1833 ....DLB-107, 109, 116

Moreno, Dorinda 1939- DLB-122

Morency, Pierre 1942- DLB-60

Moretti, Marino 1885-1979 ....DLB-114

Morgan, Berry 1919- DLB-6

Morgan, Charles 1894-1958 ....DLB-34, 100

Morgan, Edmund S. 1916- DLB-17

Morgan, Edwin 1920- DLB-27

Morgan, Robert 1944- DLB-120

Morgan, Sydney Owenson, Lady 1776?-1859 ....DLB-116

Morgner, Irmtraud 1933- DLB-75

Morier, James Justinian 1782 or 1783?-1849 ....DLB-116

Morin, Paul 1889-1963 ....DLB-92

Morison, Samuel Eliot 1887-1976 ....DLB-17

Moritz, Karl Philipp 1756-1793 ....DLB-94

Morley, Christopher 1890-1957 ....DLB-9

Morley, John 1838-1923 ....DLB-57

Morris, George Pope 1802-1864 ....DLB-73

Morris, Lewis 1833-1907 ....DLB-35

Morris, Richard B. 1904-1989 ....DLB-17

Morris, William 1834-1896 ....DLB-18, 35, 57

Morris, Willie 1934- Y-80

Morris, Wright 1910- DLB-2; Y-81

Morrison, Arthur 1863-1945 ....DLB-70

Morrison, Charles Clayton 1874-1966 ....DLB-91

Morrison, Toni 1931- DLB-6, 33; Y-81

Morrow, William, and Company DLB-46

Morse, James Herbert 1841-1923 ....DLB-71

Morse, Jedidiah 1761-1826 ....DLB-37

Morse, John T., Jr. 1840-1937 ....DLB-47

Mortimer, John 1923- DLB-13

Morton, Carlos 1942- DLB-122

Morton, John P., and Company DLB-49

Morton, Nathaniel 1613-1685 ....DLB-24

Morton, Sarah Wentworth 1759-1846 ....DLB-37

Morton, Thomas circa 1579-circa 1647 ....DLB-24

Möser, Justus 1720-1794 ....DLB-97

Mosley, Nicholas 1923- DLB-14

Moss, Arthur 1889-1969 ....DLB-4

Moss, Howard 1922- DLB-5

Moss, Thylias 1954- DLB-120

The Most Powerful Book Review in America
[*New York Times Book Review*] Y-82

Motion, Andrew 1952- DLB-40

Motley, John Lothrop 1814-1877 .... DLB-1, 30, 59

Motley, Willard 1909-1965 ....DLB-76

Motteux, Peter Anthony 1663-1718 ....DLB-80

Mottram, R. H. 1883-1971 ....DLB-36

Mouré, Erin 1955- DLB-60

Movies from Books, 1920-1974 ....DLB-9

Mowat, Farley 1921- DLB-68

Mowbray, A. R., and Company, Limited DLB-106

Mowrer, Edgar Ansel 1892-1977 ....DLB-29

Mowrer, Paul Scott 1887-1971 ....DLB-29

Moxon, Edward [publishing house] DLB-106

Mphahlele, Es'kia (Ezekiel) 1919- DLB-125

Mtshali, Oswald Mbuyiseni 1940- DLB-125

Mucedorus.....................................DLB-62

Mueller, Lisel 1924- DLB-105

Muhajir, El (see Marvin X)

Muhajir, Nazzam Al Fitnah (see Marvin X)

Muir, Edwin 1887-1959 .... DLB-20, 100

Muir, Helen 1937- DLB-14

Mukherjee, Bharati 1940- DLB-60

Muldoon, Paul 1951- DLB-40

Müller, Friedrich (see Muller, Maler)

Müller, Heiner 1929- DLB-124

Müller, Maler 1749-1825 ....DLB-94

Müller, Wilhelm 1794-1827 ....DLB-90

Mumford, Lewis 1895-1990 ....DLB-63

Munby, Arthur Joseph 1828-1910 ....DLB-35

Munday, Anthony 1560-1633 ....DLB-62

Munford, Robert circa 1737-1783 ....DLB-31

Munonye, John 1929- DLB-117

Munro, Alice 1931- DLB-53

Munro, George [publishing house] DLB-49

Munro, H. H. 1870-1916 ....DLB-34

Munro, Norman L. [publishing house] DLB-49

Munroe, James, and Company DLB-49

Munroe, Kirk 1850-1930 ....DLB-42

Munroe and Francis DLB-49

Munsell, Joel [publishing house] DLB-49

Munsey, Frank A. 1854-1925 .... DLB-25, 91

Munsey, Frank A., and Company DLB-49

Murdoch, Iris 1919- DLB-14

Murfree, Mary N. 1850-1922 .... DLB-12, 74

Murger, Henry 1822-1861 ....DLB-119

Murger, Louis-Henri (see Murger, Henry)

Muro, Amado 1915-1971 ....DLB-82

Murphy, Arthur 1727-1805 ....DLB-89

Murphy, Beatrice M. 1908- DLB-76

Murphy, Emily 1868-1933 ....DLB-99

Murphy, John, and Company DLB-49

Murphy, Richard 1927- DLB-40

Murray, Albert L. 1916- DLB-38

Murray, Gilbert 1866-1957 ....DLB-10

Murray, Judith Sargent 1751-1820 ....DLB-37

Murray, Pauli 1910-1985 ....DLB-41

Musäus, Johann Karl August 1735-1787 ....DLB-97

Muschg, Adolf 1934- DLB-75

Musil, Robert 1880-1942 .... DLB-81, 124

Mussey, Benjamin B., and Company DLB-49

Mwangi, Meja 1948- DLB-125

Myers, Gustavus 1872-1942 ....DLB-47

Myers, L. H. 1881-1944 ....DLB-15

Myers, Walter Dean 1937- DLB-33

N

Nabbes, Thomas circa 1605-1641 ....DLB-58

Nabl, Franz 1883-1974 ....DLB-81

Nabokov, Vladimir 1899-1977 ...... DLB-2; Y-80, Y-91; DS-3

Nabokov Festival at Cornell Y-83

The Vladimir Nabokov Archive
      in the Berg Collection Y-91

Nafis and Cornish DLB-49

Naipaul, Shiva 1945-1985 ....Y-85

Naipaul, V. S. 1932- DLB-125; Y-85

Nancrede, Joseph [publishing house] DLB-49

Narrache, Jean 1893-1970 ....DLB-92

Nasby, Petroleum Vesuvius (see Locke, David Ross)

Nash, Ogden 1902-1971 ....DLB-11

Nash, Eveleigh [publishing house] DLB-112

Nast, Conde 1873-1942 ....DLB-91

Nathan, Robert 1894-1985 ....DLB-9

The National Jewish Book Awards Y-85

The National Theatre and the Royal Shakespeare
      Company: The National Companies DLB-13

Naughton, Bill 1910- DLB-13

Neagoe, Peter 1881-1960 ....DLB-4

Neal, John 1793-1876 ....DLB-1, 59

Neal, Joseph C. 1807-1847 ....DLB-11

Neal, Larry 1937-1981 ....DLB-38

The Neale Publishing Company DLB-49

Neely, F. Tennyson [publishing house] DLB-49

Negri, Ada 1870-1945 ....DLB-114

"The Negro as a Writer," by
      G. M. McClellan DLB-50

"Negro Poets and Their Poetry," by
      Wallace Thurman DLB-50

Neihardt, John G. 1881-1973 ....DLB-9, 54

Nelligan, Emile 1879-1941 ....DLB-92

Nelson, Alice Moore Dunbar 1875-1935 ....DLB-50

Nelson, Thomas, and Sons [U.S.] DLB-49

Nelson, Thomas, and Sons [U.K.] DLB-106

Nelson, William 1908-1978 ....DLB-103

Nelson, William Rockhill 1841-1915 ....DLB-23

Nemerov, Howard 1920-1991 ....DLB-5, 6; Y-83

Ness, Evaline 1911-1986 ....DLB-61

Neugeboren, Jay 1938- DLB-28

Neumann, Alfred 1895-1952 ....DLB-56

Nevins, Allan 1890-1971 ....DLB-17

The New American Library DLB-46

New Approaches to Biography: Challenges
      from Critical Theory, USC Conference
      on Literary Studies, 1990 ....Y-90

New Directions Publishing Corporation DLB-46

A New Edition of *Huck Finn* Y-85

New Forces at Work in the American Theatre:
      1915-1925 ....DLB-7

New Literary Periodicals: A Report for 1987 ....Y-87

New Literary Periodicals: A Report for 1988 ....Y-88

New Literary Periodicals: A Report for 1989 ....Y-89

New Literary Periodicals: A Report for 1990 ....Y-90

New Literary Periodicals: A Report for 1991 ....Y-91

The New Monthly Magazine 1814-1884 ....DLB-110

The New *Ulysses* Y-84

The New Variorum Shakespeare Y-85

A New Voice: The Center for the Book's First
      Five Years Y-83

The New Wave [Science Fiction] DLB-8

Newbolt, Henry 1862-1938 ....DLB-19

Newbound, Bernard Slade (see Slade, Bernard)

Newby, P. H. 1918- DLB-15

Newby, Thomas Cautley [publishing house] DLB-106

Newcomb, Charles King 1820-1894 ....DLB-1

Newell, Peter 1862-1924 ....DLB-42

Newell, Robert Henry 1836-1901 ....DLB-11

Newman, David (see Benton, Robert)

Newman, Frances 1883-1928 . . . . Y-80

Newman, John Henry 1801-1890 . . . . DLB-18, 32, 55

Newman, Mark [publishing house] DLB-49

Newnes, George, Limited DLB-112

Newsome, Effie Lee 1885-1979 . . . . DLB-76

Newspaper Syndication of American Humor DLB-11

Ngugi wa Thiong'o 1938- DLB-125

Nichol, B. P. 1944- DLB-53

Nicholas of Cusa 1401-1464 . . . . DLB-115

Nichols, Dudley 1895-1960 . . . . DLB-26

Nichols, John 1940- Y-82

Nichols, Mary Sargeant (Neal) Gove 1810-1884 . . . . . . .DLB-1

Nichols, Peter 1927- DLB-13

Nichols, Roy F. 1896-1973 . . . . DLB-17

Nichols, Ruth 1948- DLB-60

Nicolson, Harold 1886-1968 . . . . DLB-100

Nicholson, Norman 1914- DLB-27

Ní Chuilleanáin, Eiléan 1942- DLB-40

Nicol, Eric 1919- DLB-68

Nicolai, Friedrich 1733-1811 . . . . DLB-97

Nicolay, John G. 1832-1901 and
    Hay, John 1838-1905 . . . . DLB-47

Niebuhr, Reinhold 1892-1971 . . . . DLB-17

Niedecker, Lorine 1903-1970 . . . . DLB-48

Nieman, Lucius W. 1857-1935 . . . . DLB-25

Niggli, Josefina 1910- Y-80

Niles, Hezekiah 1777-1839 . . . . DLB-43

Nims, John Frederick 1913- DLB-5

Nin, Anaïs 1903-1977 . . . . .DLB-2, 4

1985: The Year of the Mystery:
    A Symposium Y-85

Nissenson, Hugh 1933- DLB-28

Niven, Frederick John 1878-1944 . . . . DLB-92

Niven, Larry 1938- DLB-8

Nizan, Paul 1905-1940 . . . . DLB-72

Nobel Peace Prize
    The 1986 Nobel Peace Prize
        Nobel Lecture 1986: Hope, Despair
            and Memory
        Tributes from Abraham Bernstein,
            Norman Lamm, and John R. Silber Y-86

The Nobel Prize and Literary Politics Y-86

Nobel Prize in Literature
    The 1982 Nobel Prize in Literature
        Announcement by the Swedish Academy of the Nobel
            Prize
        Nobel Lecture 1982: The Solitude of Latin America
        Excerpt from One Hundred Years of Solitude
        The Magical World of Macondo
        A Tribute to Gabriel Garca Marquez Y-82
    The 1983 Nobel Prize in Literature
        Announcement by the Swedish Academy
        Nobel Lecture 1983
        The Stature of William Golding Y-83
    The 1984 Nobel Prize in Literature
        Announcement by the Swedish Academy
        Jaroslav Seifert Through the Eyes of the
        English-Speaking Reader
        Three Poems by Jaroslav Seifert Y-84
    The 1985 Nobel Prize in Literature
        Announcement by the Swedish Academy
        Nobel Lecture 1985 . . . . Y-85
    The 1986 Nobel Prize in Literature
        Nobel Lecture 1986: This Past Must Address
        Its Present Y-86
    The 1987 Nobel Prize in Literature
        Nobel Lecture 1987 . . . . Y-87
    The 1988 Nobel Prize in Literature
        Nobel Lecture 1988 . . . . Y-88
    The 1989 Nobel Prize in Literature
        Nobel Lecture 1989 . . . . Y-89
    The 1990 Nobel Prize in Literature
        Nobel Lecture 1990 . . . . Y-90
    The 1991 Nobel Prize in Literature
        Nobel Lecture 1991 . . . . Y-91

Nodier, Charles 1780-1844 . . . . DLB-119

Noel, Roden 1834-1894 . . . . DLB-35

Nolan, William F. 1928- DLB-8

Noland, C. F. M. 1810?-1858 . . . . DLB-11

Nonesuch Press DLB-112

Noonday Press DLB-46

Noone, John 1936- DLB-14

Nordhoff, Charles 1887-1947 . . . . DLB-9

Norman, Charles 1904- DLB-111

Norman, Marsha 1947- Y-84

Norris, Charles G. 1881-1945 ....DLB-9

Norris, Frank 1870-1902 ....DLB-12

Norris, Leslie 1921- DLB-27

Norse, Harold 1916- DLB-16

North Point Press DLB-46

Nortje, Arthur 1942-1970 ....DLB-125

Norton, Alice Mary (see Norton, Andre)

Norton, Andre 1912- DLB-8, 52

Norton, Andrews 1786-1853 ....DLB-1

Norton, Caroline 1808-1877 ....DLB-21

Norton, Charles Eliot 1827-1908 ....DLB-1, 64

Norton, John 1606-1663 ....DLB-24

Norton, Thomas (see Sackville, Thomas)

Norton, W. W., and Company DLB-46

Norwood, Robert 1874-1932 ....DLB-92

Nossack, Hans Erich 1901-1977 ....DLB-69

A Note on Technique (1926), by Elizabeth
    A. Drew [excerpts] DLB-36

Nourse, Alan E. 1928- DLB-8

Novalis 1772-1801 ....DLB-90

Novaro, Mario 1868-1944 ....DLB-114

The Novel in [Robert Browning's] "The Ring
    and the Book" (1912), by Henry James DLB-32

The Novel of Impressionism,
    by Jethro Bithell DLB-66

Novel-Reading: *The Works of Charles Dickens,
The Works of W. Makepeace Thackeray* (1879),
    by Anthony Trollope DLB-21

The Novels of Dorothy Richardson (1918), by
    May Sinclair DLB-36

Novels with a Purpose (1864), by Justin M'Carthy DLB-21

Noventa, Giacomo 1898-1960 ....DLB-114

Nowlan, Alden 1933-1983 ....DLB-53

Noyes, Alfred 1880-1958 ....DLB-20

Noyes, Crosby S. 1825-1908 ....DLB-23

Noyes, Nicholas 1647-1717 ....DLB-24

Noyes, Theodore W. 1858-1946 ....DLB-29

Nugent, Frank 1908-1965 ....DLB-44

Nutt, David [publishing house] DLB-106

Nwapa, Flora 1931- DLB-125

Nye, Edgar Wilson (Bill) 1850-1896 ....DLB-11, 23

Nye, Naomi Shihab 1952- DLB-120

Nye, Robert 1939- DLB-14

O

Oakes, Urian circa 1631-1681 ....DLB-24

Oates, Joyce Carol 1938- DLB-2, 5; Y-81

Oberholtzer, Ellis Paxson 1868-1936 ....DLB-47

O'Brien, Edna 1932- DLB-14

O'Brien, Fitz-James 1828-1862 ....DLB-74

O'Brien, Kate 1897-1974 ....DLB-15

O'Brien, Tim 1946- Y-80, DS-9

O'Casey, Sean 1880-1964 ....DLB-10

Ochs, Adolph S. 1858-1935 ....DLB-25

O'Connor, Flannery 1925-1964 ....DLB-2; Y-80

Octopus Publishing Group DLB-112

Odell, Jonathan 1737-1818 ....DLB-31, 99

O'Dell, Scott 1903-1989 ....DLB-52

Odets, Clifford 1906-1963 ....DLB-7, 26

Odhams Press Limited DLB-112

O'Donnell, Peter 1920- DLB-87

O'Faolain, Julia 1932- DLB-14

O'Faolain, Sean 1900- DLB-15

Off Broadway and Off-Off-Broadway DLB-7

Off-Loop Theatres DLB-7

Offord, Carl Ruthven 1910- DLB-76

O'Flaherty, Liam 1896-1984 ....DLB-36; Y-84

Ogilvie, J. S., and Company DLB-49

Ogot, Grace 1930- DLB-125

O'Grady, Desmond 1935- DLB-40

O'Hagan, Howard 1902-1982 ....DLB-68

O'Hara, Frank 1926-1966 ....DLB-5, 16

O'Hara, John 1905-1970 ....DLB-9, 86; DS-2

Okara, Christopher 1930-1967 ....DLB-125

O'Keeffe, John 1747-1833 ....DLB-89

Okigbo, Christopher 1930-1967 ....DLB-125

Okot p'Bitek 1931-1982 ....DLB-125

Olaudah Equiano and Unfinished Journeys:
The Slave-Narrative Tradition and
Twentieth-Century Continuities, by
Paul Edwards and Pauline T. Wangman DLB-117

Old Franklin Publishing House DLB-49

Older, Fremont 1856-1935 ....DLB-25

Olds, Sharon 1942- DLB-120

Oliphant, Laurence 1829?-1888 ....DLB-18

Oliphant, Margaret 1828-1897 ....DLB-18

Oliver, Chad 1928- DLB-8

Oliver, Mary 1935- DLB-5

Ollier, Claude 1922- DLB-83

Olsen, Tillie 1913?- DLB-28; Y-80

Olson, Charles 1910-1970 ....DLB-5, 16

Olson, Elder 1909- DLB-48, 63

Omotoso, Kole 1943- DLB-125

On Art in Fiction (1838), by Edward Bulwer DLB-21

On Learning to Write Y-88

On Some of the Characteristics of Modern
Poetry and On the Lyrical Poems of Alfred
Tennyson (1831), by Arthur Henry
Hallam DLB-32

"On Style in English Prose" (1898), by Frederic
Harrison DLB-57

"On Style in Literature: Its Technical Elements"
(1885), by Robert Louis Stevenson DLB-57

"On the Writing of Essays" (1862),
by Alexander Smith DLB-57

Ondaatje, Michael 1943- DLB-60

O'Neill, Eugene 1888-1953 ....DLB-7

Onetti, Juan Carlos 1909- DLB-113

Onofri, Arturo 1885-1928 ....DLB-114

Opie, Amelia 1769-1853 ....DLB-116

Oppen, George 1908-1984 ....DLB-5

Oppenheim, E. Phillips 1866-1946 ....DLB-70

Oppenheim, James 1882-1932 ....DLB-28

Oppenheimer, Joel 1930- DLB-5

Optic, Oliver (see Adams, William Taylor)

Orczy, Emma, Baroness 1865-1947 ....DLB-70

Orlovitz, Gil 1918-1973 ....DLB-2, 5

Orlovsky, Peter 1933- DLB-16

Ormond, John 1923- DLB-27

Ornitz, Samuel 1890-1957 ....DLB-28, 44

Ortiz, Simon 1941- DLB-120

Orton, Joe 1933-1967 ....DLB-13

Orwell, George 1903-1950 ....DLB-15, 98

The Orwell Year Y-84

Osbey, Brenda Marie 1957- DLB-120

Osbon, B. S. 1827-1912 ....DLB-43

Osborne, John 1929- DLB-13

Osgood, Herbert L. 1855-1918 ....DLB-47

Osgood, James R., and Company DLB-49

Osgood, McIlvaine and Company DLB-112

O'Shaughnessy, Arthur 1844-1881 ....DLB-35

O'Shea, Patrick [publishing house] DLB-49

Osofisan, Femi 1946- DLB-125

Ostenso, Martha 1900-1963 ....DLB-92

Ostriker, Alicia 1937- DLB-120

Oswald, Eleazer 1755-1795 ....DLB-43

Otero, Miguel Antonio 1859-1944 ....DLB-82

Otis, James (see Kaler, James Otis)

Otis, James, Jr. 1725-1783 ....DLB-31

Otis, Broaders and Company DLB-49

Ottendorfer, Oswald 1826-1900 ....DLB-23

Otway, Thomas 1652-1685 ....DLB-80

Ouellette, Fernand 1930- DLB-60

Ouida 1839-1908 ....DLB-18

Outing Publishing Company DLB-46

Outlaw Days, by Joyce Johnson DLB-16

The Overlook Press DLB-46

Overview of U.S. Book Publishing, 1910-1945 ....DLB-9

Owen, Guy 1925- DLB-5

Owen, John 1564-1622 ....DLB-121

Owen, John [publishing house] DLB-49

Owen, Robert 1771-1858 ....DLB-107

Owen, Wilfred 1893-1918 ....DLB-20

Owen, Peter, Limited DLB-112

Owsley, Frank L. 1890-1956 ....DLB-17

Ozick, Cynthia 1928- DLB-28; Y-82

P

Pacey, Desmond 1917-1975 ....DLB-88

Pack, Robert 1929- DLB-5

Packaging Papa: *The Garden of Eden* Y-86

Padell Publishing Company DLB-46

Padgett, Ron 1942- DLB-5

Padilla, Ernesto Chavez 1944- DLB-122

Page, L. C., and Company DLB-49

Page, P. K. 1916- DLB-68

Page, Thomas Nelson 1853-1922 ....DLB-12, 78

Page, Walter Hines 1855-1918 ....DLB-71, 91

Paget, Violet (see Lee, Vernon)

Pain, Philip ?-circa 1666 ....DLB-24

Paine, Robert Treat, Jr. 1773-1811 ....DLB-37

Paine, Thomas 1737-1809 ....DLB-31, 43, 73

Palazzeschi, Aldo 1885-1974 ....DLB-114

Paley, Grace 1922- DLB-28

Palfrey, John Gorham 1796-1881 ....DLB-1, 30

Palgrave, Francis Turner 1824-1897 ....DLB-35

Paltock, Robert 1697-1767 ....DLB-39

Pan Books Limited DLB-112

Panamaa, Norman 1914- and
    Frank, Melvin 1913-1988 ....DLB-26

Panero, Leopoldo 1909-1962 ....DLB-108

Pangborn, Edgar 1909-1976 ....DLB-8

"Panic Among the Philistines": A Postscript,
    An Interview with Bryan Griffin Y-81

Panneton, Philippe (see Ringuet)

Panshin, Alexei 1940- DLB-8

Pansy (see Alden, Isabella)

Pantheon Books DLB-46

Paperback Library DLB-46

Paperback Science Fiction DLB-8

Paquet, Alfons 1881-1944 ....DLB-66

Paradis, Suzanne 1936- DLB-53

Parents' Magazine Press DLB-46

Parisian Theater, Fall 1984: Toward
    A New Baroque Y-85

Parizeau, Alice 1930- DLB-60

Parke, John 1754-1789 ....DLB-31

Parker, Dorothy 1893-1967 ....DLB-11, 45, 86

Parker, Gilbert 1860-1932 ....DLB-99

Parker, James 1714-1770 ....DLB-43

Parker, Theodore 1810-1860 ....DLB-1

Parker, William Riley 1906-1968 ....DLB-103

Parker, J. H. [publishing house] DLB-106

Parker, John [publishing house] DLB-106

Parkman, Francis, Jr. 1823-1893 ....DLB-1, 30

Parks, Gordon 1912- DLB-33

Parks, William 1698-1750 ....DLB-43

Parks, William [publishing house] DLB-49

Parley, Peter (see Goodrich, Samuel Griswold)

Parnell, Thomas 1679-1718 ....DLB-95

Parrington, Vernon L. 1871-1929 ....DLB-17, 63

Partridge, S. W., and Company DLB-106

Parton, James 1822-1891 ....DLB-30

Parton, Sara Payson Willis 1811-1872 ....DLB-43, 74

Pastan, Linda 1932- DLB-5

Pastorius, Francis Daniel 1651-circa 1720 ....DLB-24

Patchen, Kenneth 1911-1972 ....DLB-16, 48

Pater, Walter 1839-1894 ....DLB-57

Paterson, Katherine 1932- DLB-52

Patmore, Coventry 1823-1896 ....DLB-35, 98

Paton, Joseph Noel 1821-1901 ....DLB-35

Patrick, John 1906- DLB-7

Pattee, Fred Lewis 1863-1950 ....DLB-71

Pattern and Paradigm: History as
    Design, by Judith Ryan DLB-75

Patterson, Eleanor Medill 1881-1948 ....DLB-29

Patterson, Joseph Medill 1879-1946 ....DLB-29

Pattillo, Henry 1726-1801 ....DLB-37

Paul, Elliot 1891-1958 ....DLB-4

Paul, Jean (see Richter, Johann Paul Friedrich)

Paul, Kegan, Trench, Trubner and Company
    Limited DLB-106

Paul, Peter, Book Company DLB-49

Paul, Stanley, and Company Limited DLB-112

Paulding, James Kirke 1778-1860 .... DLB-3, 59, 74

Paulin, Tom 1949- DLB-40

Pauper, Peter, Press DLB-46

Paxton, John 1911-1985 ....DLB-44

Payn, James 1830-1898 ....DLB-18

Payne, John 1842-1916 ....DLB-35

Payne, John Howard 1791-1852 ....DLB-37

Payson and Clarke DLB-46

Peabody, Elizabeth Palmer 1804-1894 ....DLB-1

Peabody, Elizabeth Palmer [publishing house] DLB-49

Peabody, Oliver William Bourn 1799-1848 ....DLB-59

Peachtree Publishers, Limited DLB-46

Peacock, Molly 1947- DLB-120

Peacock, Thomas Love 1785-1866 .... DLB-96, 116

Pead, Deuel ?-1727 ....DLB-24

Peake, Mervyn 1911-1968 ....DLB-15

Pear Tree Press DLB-112

Pearson, H. B. [publishing house] DLB-49

Peck, George W. 1840-1916 ....DLB-23, 42

Peck, H. C., and Theo. Bliss [publishing house] DLB-49

Peck, Harry Thurston 1856-1914 ....DLB-71, 91

Peele, George 1556-1596 ....DLB-62

Pellegrini and Cudahy DLB-46

Pelletier, Aimé (see Vac, Bertrand)

Pemberton, Sir Max 1863-1950 ....DLB-70

Penguin Books [U.S.] DLB-46

Penguin Books [U.K.] DLB-112

Penn Publishing Company DLB-49

Penn, William 1644-1718 ....DLB-24

Penna, Sandro 1906-1977 ....DLB-114

Penner, Jonathan 1940- Y-83

Pennington, Lee 1939- Y-82

Pepys, Samuel 1633-1703 ....DLB-101

Percy, Thomas 1729-1811 ....DLB-104

Percy, Walker 1916-1990 .... DLB-2; Y-80, 90

Perec, Georges 1936-1982 ....DLB-83

Perelman, S. J. 1904-1979 .... DLB-11, 44

Perez, Raymundo "Tigre" 1946- DLB-122

Periodicals of the Beat Generation DLB-16

Perkins, Eugene 1932- DLB-41

Perkoff, Stuart Z. 1930-1974 ....DLB-16

Perley, Moses Henry 1804-1862 ....DLB-99

Permabooks DLB-46

Perry, Bliss 1860-1954 ....DLB-71

Perry, Eleanor 1915-1981 ....DLB-44

"Personal Style" (1890), by John Addington
    Symonds DLB-57

Perutz, Leo 1882-1957 ....DLB-81

Pestalozzi, Johann Heinrich 1746-1827 ....DLB-94

Peter, Laurence J. 1919-1990 ....DLB-53

Peter of Spain circa 1205-1277 ....DLB-115

Peterkin, Julia 1880-1961 ....DLB-9

Peters, Lenrie 1932- DLB-117

Peters, Robert 1924- DLB-105

Peters, Robert, Foreword to Ludwig of Bavaria DLB-105

Petersham, Maud 1889-1971 and
    Petersham, Miska 1888-1960 ....DLB-22

Peterson, Charles Jacobs 1819-1887 ....DLB-79

Peterson, Len 1917- DLB-88

Peterson, Louis 1922- DLB-76

Peterson, T. B., and Brothers DLB-49

Petitclair, Pierre 1813-1860 .... DLB-99

Petry, Ann 1908- DLB-76

Phaidon Press Limited DLB-112

Pharr, Robert Deane 1916-1989 .... DLB-33

Phelps, Elizabeth Stuart 1844-1911 .... DLB-74

Philippe, Charles-Louis 1874-1909 .... DLB-65

Philips, John 1676-1708 .... DLB-95

Phillips, David Graham 1867-1911 .... DLB-9, 12

Phillips, Jayne Anne 1952- Y-80

Phillips, Robert 1938- DLB-105

Phillips, Robert, Finding, Losing,
    Reclaiming: A Note on My Poems DLB-105

Phillips, Stephen 1864-1915 .... DLB-10

Phillips, Ulrich B. 1877-1934 .... DLB-17

Phillips, Willard 1784-1873 .... DLB-59

Phillips, Sampson and Company DLB-49

Phillpotts, Eden 1862-1960 .... DLB-10, 70

Philosophical Library DLB-46

"The Philosophy of Style" (1852), by
    Herbert Spencer DLB-57

Phinney, Elihu [publishing house] DLB-49

Phoenix, John (see Derby, George Horatio)

PHYLON (Fourth Quarter, 1950),
    The Negro in Literature:
    The Current Scene DLB-76

Piccolo, Lucio 1903-1969 .... DLB-114

Pickard, Tom 1946- DLB-40

Pickering, William [publishing house] DLB-106

Pickthall, Marjorie 1883-1922 .... DLB-92

Pictorial Printing Company DLB-49

Piercy, Marge 1936- DLB-120

Pike, Albert 1809-1891 .... DLB-74

Pilon, Jean-Guy 1930- DLB-60

Pinckney, Josephine 1895-1957 .... DLB-6

Pindar, Peter (see Wolcot, John)

Pinero, Arthur Wing 1855-1934 .... DLB-10

Pinget, Robert 1919- DLB-83

Pinnacle Books DLB-46

Pinsky, Robert 1940- Y-82

Pinter, Harold 1930- DLB-13

Piontek, Heinz 1925- DLB-75

Piozzi, Hester Lynch [Thrale] 1741-1821 .... DLB-104

Piper, H. Beam 1904-1964 .... DLB-8

Piper, Watty DLB-22

Pisar, Samuel 1929- Y-83

Pitkin, Timothy 1766-1847 .... DLB-30

The Pitt Poetry Series: Poetry Publishing Today Y-85

Pitter, Ruth 1897- DLB-20

Pix, Mary 1666-1709 .... DLB-80

Plaatje, Sol T. 1876-1932 .... DLB-125

The Place of Realism in Fiction (1895), by
    George Gissing DLB-18

Plante, David 1940- Y-83

Platen, August von 1796-1835 .... DLB-90

Plath, Sylvia 1932-1963 .... DLB-5, 6

Platt and Munk Company DLB-46

Playboy Press DLB-46

Plays, Playwrights, and Playgoers DLB-84

Playwrights and Professors, by Tom Stoppard DLB-13

Playwrights on the Theater DLB-80

Plenzdorf, Ulrich 1934- DLB-75

Plessen, Elizabeth 1944- DLB-75

Plievier, Theodor 1892-1955 .... DLB-69

Plomer, William 1903-1973 .... DLB-20

Plumly, Stanley 1939- DLB-5

Plumpp, Sterling D. 1940- DLB-41

Plunkett, James 1920- DLB-14

Plymell, Charles 1935- DLB-16

Pocket Books DLB-46

Poe, Edgar Allan 1809-1849 .... DLB-3, 59, 73, 74

Poe, James 1921-1980 .... DLB-44

The Poet Laureate of the United States
    Statements from Former Consultants
    in Poetry Y-86

Pohl, Frederik 1919- DLB-8

Poirier, Louis (see Gracq, Julien)

Polanyi, Michael 1891-1976 ....DLB-100

Poliakoff, Stephen 1952- DLB-13

Polidori, John William 1795-1821 ....DLB-116

Polite, Carlene Hatcher 1932- DLB-33

Pollard, Edward A. 1832-1872 ....DLB-30

Pollard, Percival 1869-1911 ....DLB-71

Pollard and Moss DLB-49

Pollock, Sharon 1936- DLB-60

Polonsky, Abraham 1910- DLB-26

Ponce, Mary Helen 1938- DLB-122

Ponce-Montoya, Juanita 1949- DLB-122

Poniatowski, Elena 1933- DLB-113

Poole, Ernest 1880-1950 ....DLB-9

Poore, Benjamin Perley 1820-1887 ....DLB-23

Pope, Alexander 1688-1744 .... DLB-95, 101

Popular Library DLB-46

Porlock, Martin (see MacDonald, Philip)

Porpoise Press DLB-112

Porter, Anna Maria 1780-1832 ....DLB-116

Porter, Eleanor H. 1868-1920 ....DLB-9

Porter, Henry ?-? DLB-62

Porter, Jane 1776-1850 ....DLB-116

Porter, Katherine Anne 1890-1980 .... DLB-4, 9, 102; Y-80

Porter, Peter 1929- DLB-40

Porter, William Sydney 1862-1910 .... DLB-12, 78, 79

Porter, William T. 1809-1858 ....DLB-3, 43

Porter and Coates DLB-49

Portis, Charles 1933- DLB-6

Poston, Ted 1906-1974 ....DLB-51

Postscript to [the Third Edition of] *Clarissa*
    (1751), by Samuel Richardson DLB-39

Potok, Chaim 1929- DLB-28; Y-84

Potter, David M. 1910-1971 ....DLB-17

Potter, John E., and Company DLB-49

Pottle, Frederick A. 1897-1987 ....DLB-103; Y-87

Poulin, Jacques 1937- DLB-60

Pound, Ezra 1885-1972 .... DLB-4, 45, 63

Powell, Anthony 1905- DLB-15

Pownall, David 1938- DLB-14

Powys, John Cowper 1872-1963 ....DLB-15

Powys, Llewelyn 1884-1939 ....DLB-98

Powys, T. F. 1875-1953 ....DLB-36

The Practice of Biography: An Interview with
    Stanley Weintraub Y-82

The Practice of Biography II: An Interview with
    B. L. Reid Y-83

The Practice of Biography III: An Interview with
    Humphrey Carpenter Y-84

The Practice of Biography IV: An Interview with
    William Manchester Y-85

The Practice of Biography V: An Interview with
    Justin Kaplan Y-86

The Practice of Biography VI: An Interview with
    David Herbert Donald Y-87

Praed, Winthrop Mackworth 1802-1839 ....DLB-96

Praeger Publishers DLB-46

Pratt, E. J. 1882-1964 ....DLB-92

Pratt, Samuel Jackson 1749-1814 ....DLB-39

Preface to *Alwyn* (1780), by Thomas
    Holcroft DLB-39

Preface to *Colonel Jack* (1722), by Daniel
    Defoe DLB-39

Preface to *Evelina* (1778), by Fanny Burney DLB-39

Preface to *Ferdinand Count Fathom* (1753), by
    Tobias Smollett DLB-39

Preface to *Incognita* (1692), by William
    Congreve DLB-39

Preface to *Joseph Andrews* (1742), by
    Henry Fielding DLB-39

Preface to *Moll Flanders* (1722), by Daniel Defoe DLB-39

Preface to *Poems* (1853), by Matthew Arnold DLB-32

Preface to *Robinson Crusoe* (1719), by Daniel Defoe DLB-39

Preface to *Roderick Random* (1748), by Tobias
    Smollett DLB-39

Preface to *Roxana* (1724), by Daniel Defoe DLB-39

Preface to *St. Leon* (1799), by William Godwin DLB-39

Preface to Sarah Fielding's *Familiar Letters* (1747), by Henry Fielding [excerpt] DLB-39

Preface to Sarah Fielding's *The Adventures of David Simple* (1744), by Henry Fielding DLB-39

Preface to *The Cry* (1754), by Sarah Fielding DLB-39

Preface to *The Delicate Distress* (1769), by Elizabeth Griffin DLB-39

Preface to *The Disguis'd Prince* (1733), by Eliza Haywood [excerpt] DLB-39

Preface to *The Farther Adventures of Robinson Crusoe (1719)*, by Daniel Defoe DLB-39

Preface to the First Edition of *Pamela* (1740), by Samuel Richardson DLB-39

Preface to the First Edition of *The Castle of Otranto (1764)*, by Horace Walpole DLB-39

Preface to *The History of Romances* (1715), by Pierre Daniel Huet [excerpts] DLB-39

Preface to *The Life of Charlotta du Pont* (1723), by Penelope Aubin DLB-39

Preface to *The Old English Baron* (1778), by Clara Reeve DLB-39

Preface to the Second Edition of *The Castle of Otranto (1765)*, by Horace Walpole DLB-39

Preface to *The Secret History, of Queen Zarah, and the Zarazians (1705), by* Delariviere Manley DLB-39

Preface to the Third Edition of *Clarissa* (1751), by Samuel Richardson [excerpt] DLB-39

Preface to *The Works of Mrs. Davys* (1725), by Mary Davys DLB-39

Preface to Volume 1 of *Clarissa* (1747), by Samuel Richardson DLB-39

Preface to Volume 3 of *Clarissa* (1748), by Samuel Richardson DLB-39

Préfontaine, Yves 1937- DLB-53

Prelutsky, Jack 1940- DLB-61

Premisses, by Michael Hamburger DLB-66

Prentice, George D. 1802-1870 ....DLB-43

Prentice-Hall DLB-46

Prescott, William Hickling 1796-1859 ....DLB-1, 30, 59

The Present State of the English Novel (1892), by George Saintsbury DLB-18

Preston, Thomas 1537-1598 ....DLB-62

Price, Reynolds 1933- DLB-2

Price, Richard 1949- Y-81

Priest, Christopher 1943- DLB-14

Priestley, J. B. 1894-1984 ....DLB-10, 34, 77, 100; Y-84

Prime, Benjamin Young 1733-1791 ....DLB-31

Prince, F. T. 1912- DLB-20

Prince, Thomas 1687-1758 ....DLB-24

The Principles of Success in Literature (1865), by George Henry Lewes [excerpt] DLB-57

Prior, Matthew 1664-1721 ....DLB-95

Pritchard, William H. 1932- DLB-111

Pritchett, V. S. 1900- DLB-15

Procter, Adelaide Anne 1825-1864 ....DLB-32

Procter, Bryan Waller 1787-1874 ....DLB-96

The Profession of Authorship: Scribblers for Bread Y-89

The Progress of Romance (1785), by Clara Reeve [excerpt] DLB-39

Prokosch, Frederic 1906-1989 ....DLB-48

The Proletarian Novel DLB-9

Propper, Dan 1937- DLB-16

The Prospect of Peace (1778), by Joel Barlow DLB-37

Proud, Robert 1728-1813 ....DLB-30

Proust, Marcel 1871-1922 ....DLB-65

Prynne, J. H. 1936- DLB-40

Przybyszewski, Stanislaw 1868-1927 ....DLB-66

Pseudo-Dionysius the Areopagite floruit circa 500 ....DLB-115

The Public Lending Right in America Statement by Sen. Charles McC. Mathias, Jr.

  PLR and the Meaning of Literary Property Statements on PLR by American Writers Y-83

The Public Lending Right in the United Kingdom Public Lending Right: The First Year in the United Kingdom Y-83

The Publication of English Renaissance Plays DLB-62

Publications and Social Movements [Transcendentalism] DLB-1

Publishers and Agents: The Columbia Connection Y-87

Publishing Fiction at LSU Press Y-87

Pugin, A. Welby 1812-1852 .... DLB-55

Puig, Manuel 1932-1990 .... DLB-113

Pulitzer, Joseph 1847-1911 .... DLB-23

Pulitzer, Joseph, Jr. 1885-1955 .... DLB-29

Pulitzer Prizes for the Novel, 1917-1945 .... DLB-9

Purdy, Al 1918- DLB-88

Purdy, James 1923- DLB-2

Pusey, Edward Bouverie 1800-1882 .... DLB-55

Putnam, George Palmer 1814-1872 .... DLB-3, 79

Putnam, Samuel 1892-1950 .... DLB-4

G. P. Putnam's Sons [U.S.] DLB-49

G. P. Putnam's Sons [U.K.] DLB-106

Puzo, Mario 1920- DLB-6

Pyle, Ernie 1900-1945 .... DLB-29

Pyle, Howard 1853-1911 .... DLB-42

Pym, Barbara 1913-1980 .... DLB-14; Y-87

Pynchon, Thomas 1937- DLB-2

Pyramid Books DLB-46

Pyrnelle, Louise-Clarke 1850-1907 .... DLB-42

Q

Quad, M. (see Lewis, Charles B.)

The Quarterly Review 1809-1967 .... DLB-110

Quasimodo, Salvatore 1901-1968 .... DLB-114

The Queen City Publishing House DLB-49

Queneau, Raymond 1903-1976 .... DLB-72

Quesnel, Joseph 1746-1809 .... DLB-99

The Question of American Copyright
  in the Nineteenth Century
    Headnote
    Preface, by George Haven Putnam
    The Evolution of Copyright, by Brander Matthews
    Summary of Copyright Legislation in the
      United States, by R. R. Bowker
    Analysis of the Provisions of the Copyright
      Law of 1891, by George Haven Putnam
    The Contest for International Copyright,
      by George Haven Putnam
    Cheap Books and Good Books,
      by Brander Matthews DLB-49

Quin, Ann 1936-1973 .... DLB-14

Quincy, Samuel, of Georgia ?-? DLB-31

Quincy, Samuel, of Massachusetts 1734-1789 .... DLB-31

Quinn, Anthony 1915- DLB-122

Quintana, Leroy V. 1944- DLB-82

Quintana, Miguel de 1671-1748
  A Forerunner of Chicano Literature DLB-122

Quist, Harlin, Books DLB-46

Quoirez, Françoise (see Sagan, Francçise)

R

Rabe, David 1940- DLB-7

Rachilde 1860-1953 .... DLB-123

Radcliffe, Ann 1764-1823 .... DLB-39

Raddall, Thomas 1903- DLB-68

Radiguet, Raymond 1903-1923 .... DLB-65

Radványi, Netty Reiling (see Seghers, Anna)

Raimund, Ferdinand Jakob 1790-1836 .... DLB-90

Raine, Craig 1944- DLB-40

Raine, Kathleen 1908- DLB-20

Ralph, Julian 1853-1903 .... DLB-23

Ralph Waldo Emerson in 1982 .... Y-82

Rambler, no. 4 (1750), by Samuel Johnson
  [excerpt] DLB-39

Ramée, Marie Louise de la (see Ouida)

Ramke, Bin 1947- DLB-120

Ramler, Karl Wilhelm 1725-1798 .... DLB-97

Rampersad, Arnold 1941- DLB-111

Ramsay, Allan 1684 or 1685-1758 ....DLB-95

Ramsay, David 1749-1815 ....DLB-30

Ranck, Katherine Quintana 1942- DLB-122

Rand, Avery and Company DLB-49

Rand McNally and Company DLB-49

Randall, Dudley 1914- DLB-41

Randall, Henry S. 1811-1876 ....DLB-30

Randall, James G. 1881-1953 ....DLB-17

The Randall Jarrell Symposium: A Small
   Collection of Randall Jarrells
     Excerpts From Papers Delivered at
      the Randall Jarrell Symposium Y-86

Randolph, A. Philip 1889-1979 ....DLB-91

Randolph, Anson D. F. [publishing house] DLB-49

Randolph, Thomas 1605-1635 ....DLB-58

Random House DLB-46

Ranlet, Henry [publishing house] DLB-49

Ransom, John Crowe 1888-1974 ....DLB-45, 63

Raphael, Frederic 1931- DLB-14

Raphaelson, Samson 1896-1983 ....DLB-44

Raskin, Ellen 1928-1984 ....DLB-52

Rattigan, Terence 1911-1977 ....DLB-13

Rawlings, Marjorie Kinnan 1896-1953 ....DLB-9, 22, 102

Raworth, Tom 1938- DLB-40

Ray, David 1932- DLB-5

Ray, Gordon N. 1915-1986 ....DLB-103

Ray, Henrietta Cordelia 1849-1916 ....DLB-50

Raymond, Henry J. 1820-1869 ....DLB-43, 79

Raymond Chandler Centenary Tributes
   from Michael Avallone, James Elroy, Joe Gores,
   and William F. Nolan Y-88

Reach, Angus 1821-1856 ....DLB-70

Read, Herbert 1893-1968 ....DLB-20

Read, Opie 1852-1939 ....DLB-23

Read, Piers Paul 1941- DLB-14

Reade, Charles 1814-1884 ....DLB-21

Reader's Digest Condensed Books DLB-46

Reading, Peter 1946- DLB-40

Reaney, James 1926- DLB-68

Rèbora, Clemente 1885-1957 ....DLB-114

Rechy, John 1934- DLB-122; Y-82

The Recovery of Literature: Criticism in the 1990s:
   A Symposium Y-91

Redding, J. Saunders 1906-1988 ....DLB-63, 76

Redfield, J. S. [publishing house] DLB-49

Redgrove, Peter 1932- DLB-40

Redmon, Anne 1943- Y-86

Redmond, Eugene B. 1937- DLB-41

Redpath, James [publishing house] DLB-49

Reed, Henry 1808-1854 ....DLB-59

Reed, Henry 1914- DLB-27

Reed, Ishmael 1938- DLB-2, 5, 33; DS-8

Reed, Sampson 1800-1880 ....DLB-1

Reedy, William Marion 1862-1920 ....DLB-91

Reese, Lizette Woodworth 1856-1935 ....DLB-54

Reese, Thomas 1742-1796 ....DLB-37

Reeve, Clara 1729-1807 ....DLB-39

Reeves, John 1926- DLB-88

Regnery, Henry, Company DLB-46

Rehberg, Hans 1901-1963 ....DLB-124

Rehfisch, Hans Josè 1891-1960 ....DLB-124

Reid, Alastair 1926- DLB-27

Reid, B. L. 1918-1990 ....DLB-111

Reid, Christopher 1949- DLB-40

Reid, Helen Rogers 1882-1970 ....DLB-29

Reid, James ?-? DLB-31

Reid, Mayne 1818-1883 ....DLB-21

Reid, Thomas 1710-1796 ....DLB-31

Reid, V. S. (Vic) 1913-1987 ....DLB-125

Reid, Whitelaw 1837-1912 ....DLB-23

Reilly and Lee Publishing Company DLB-46

Reimann, Brigitte 1933-1973 ....DLB-75

Reisch, Walter 1903-1983 ....DLB-44

Remarque, Erich Maria 1898-1970 ....DLB-56

"Re-meeting of Old Friends": The Jack Kerouac
Conference Y-82

Remington, Frederic 1861-1909 ....DLB-12

Renaud, Jacques 1943- DLB-60

Renault, Mary 1905-1983 .... Y-83

Rendell, Ruth 1930- DLB-87

Representative Men and Women: A Historical
Perspective on the British Novel, 1930-1960 ....DLB-15

(Re-)Publishing Orwel Y-86

Reuter, Gabriele 1859-1941 ....DLB-66

Revell, Fleming H., Company DLB-49

Reventlow, Franziska Gräfin zu 1871-1918 ....DLB-66

Review of Reviews Office DLB-112

Review of [Samuel Richardson's] Clarissa (1748), by Henry
Fielding DLB-39

The Revolt (1937), by Mary Colum [excerpts] DLB-36

Rexroth, Kenneth 1905-1982 .... DLB-16, 48; Y-82

Rey, H. A. 1898-1977 ....DLB-22

Reynal and Hitchcock DLB-46

Reynolds, G. W. M. 1814-1879 ....DLB-21

Reynolds, John Hamilton 1794-1852 ....DLB-96

Reynolds, Mack 1917- DLB-8

Reynolds, Sir Joshua 1723-1792 ....DLB-104

Reznikoff, Charles 1894-1976 ....DLB-28, 45

"Rhetoric" (1828; revised, 1859), by Thomas de
Quincey [excerpt] DLB-57

Rhett, Robert Barnwell 1800-1876 ....DLB-43

Rhode, John 1884-1964 ....DLB-77

Rhodes, James Ford 1848-1927 ....DLB-47

Rhys, Jean 1890-1979 .... DLB-36, 117

Ricardo, David 1772-1823 ....DLB-107

Ricardou, Jean 1932- DLB-83

Rice, Elmer 1892-1967 ....DLB-4, 7

Rice, Grantland 1880-1954 ....DLB-29

Rich, Adrienne 1929- DLB-5, 67

Richards, David Adams 1950- DLB-53

Richards, George circa 1760-1814 ....DLB-37

Richards, I. A. 1893-1979 ....DLB-27

Richards, Laura E. 1850-1943 ....DLB-42

Richards, William Carey 1818-1892 ....DLB-73

Richards, Grant [publishing house] DLB-112

Richardson, Charles F. 1851-1913 ....DLB-71

Richardson, Dorothy M. 1873-1957 ....DLB-36

Richardson, Jack 1935- DLB-7

Richardson, John 1796-1852 ....DLB-99

Richardson, Samuel 1689-1761 ....DLB-39

Richardson, Willis 1889-1977 ....DLB-51

Richler, Mordecai 1931- DLB-53

Richter, Conrad 1890-1968 ....DLB-9

Richter, Hans Werner 1908- DLB-69

Richter, Johann Paul Friedrich 1763-1825 ....DLB-94

Rickerby, Joseph [publishing house] DLB-106

Rickword, Edgell 1898-1982 ....DLB-20

Riddell, John (see Ford, Corey)

Ridge, Lola 1873-1941 ....DLB-54

Riding, Laura (see Jackson, Laura Riding)

Ridler, Anne 1912- DLB-27

Ridruego, Dionisio 1912-1975 ....DLB-108

Riel, Louis 1844-1885 ....DLB-99

Riffaterre, Michael 1924- DLB-67

Riis, Jacob 1849-1914 ....DLB-23

Riker, John C. [publishing house] DLB-49

Riley, John 1938-1978 ....DLB-40

Rilke, Rainer Maria 1875-1926 ....DLB-81

Rinehart and Company DLB-46

Ringuet 1895-1960 ....DLB-68

Ringwood, Gwen Pharis 1910-1984 ....DLB-88

Rinser, Luise 1911- DLB-69

Ríos, Alberto 1952- DLB-122

Ríos, Isabella 1948- DLB-82

Ripley, Arthur 1895-1961 ....DLB-44

Ripley, George 1802-1880 .... DLB-1, 64, 73

The Rising Glory of America: Three Poems DLB-37

The Rising Glory of America: Written in 1771
   (1786), by Hugh Henry Brackenridge and
   Philip Freneau DLB-37

Riskin, Robert 1897-1955 ....DLB-26

Risse, Heinz 1898- DLB-69

Ritchie, Anna Mowatt 1819-1870 ....DLB-3

Ritchie, Anne Thackeray 1837-1919 ....DLB-18

Ritchie, Thomas 1778-1854 ....DLB-43

Rites of Passage [on William Saroyan] Y-83

The Ritz Paris Hemingway Award Y-85

Rivard, Adjutor 1868-1945 ....DLB-92

Rive, Richard 1931-1989 ....DLB-125

Rivera, Marina 1942- DLB-122

Rivera, Tomás 1935-1984 ....DLB-82

Rivers, Conrad Kent 1933-1968 ....DLB-41

Riverside Press DLB-49

Rivington, James circa 1724-1802 ....DLB-43

Rivkin, Allen 1903-1990 ....DLB-26

Roa Bastos, Augusto 1917- DLB-113

Robbe-Grillet, Alain 1922- DLB-83

Robbins, Tom 1936- Y-80

Roberts, Charles G. D. 1860-1943 ....DLB-92

Roberts, Dorothy 1906- DLB-88

Roberts, Elizabeth Madox 1881-1941 ....DLB-9, 54, 102

Roberts, Kenneth 1885-1957 ....DLB-9

Roberts Brothers DLB-49

Robertson, A. M., and Company DLB-49

Robertson, William 1721-1793 ....DLB-104

Robinson, Casey 1903-1979 ....DLB-44

Robinson, Edwin Arlington 1869-1935 ....DLB-54

Robinson, Henry Crabb 1775-1867 ....DLB-107

Robinson, James Harvey 1863-1936 ....DLB-47

Robinson, Lennox 1886-1958 ....DLB-10

Robinson, Mabel Louise 1874-1962 ....DLB-22

Robinson, Therese 1797-1870 ....DLB-59

Roblès, Emmanuel 1914- DLB-83

Roccatagliata Ceccardi, Ceccardo 1871-1919 ....DLB-114

Rodgers, Carolyn M. 1945- DLB-41

Rodgers, W. R. 1909-1969 ....DLB-20

Rodriguez, Richard 1944- DLB-82

Roethke, Theodore 1908-1963 ....DLB-5

Rogers, Pattiann 1940- DLB-105

Rogers, Samuel 1763-1855 ....DLB-93

Rogers, Will 1879-1935 ....DLB-11

Rohmer, Sax 1883-1959 ....DLB-70

Roiphe, Anne 1935- Y-80

Rojas, Arnold R. 1896-1988 ....DLB-82

Rolfe, Frederick William 1860-1913 ....DLB-34

Rolland, Romain 1866-1944 ....DLB-65

Rolvaag, O. E. 1876-1931 ....DLB-9

Romains, Jules 1885-1972 ....DLB-65

Roman, A., and Company DLB-49

Romano, Octavio 1923- DLB-122

Romero, Leo 1950- DLB-122

Romero, Lin 1947- DLB-122

Romero, Orlando 1945- DLB-82

Roosevelt, Theodore 1858-1919 ....DLB-47

Root, Waverley 1903-1982 ....DLB-4

Root, William Pitt 1941- DLB-120

Roquebrune, Robert de 1889-1978 ....DLB-68

Rosa, João Guimarães 1908-1967 ....DLB-113

Rose, Reginald 1920- DLB-26

Rosei, Peter 1946- DLB-85

Rosen, Norma 1925- DLB-28

Rosenberg, Isaac 1890-1918 ....DLB-20

Rosenfeld, Isaac 1918-1956 ....DLB-28

Rosenthal, M. L. 1917- DLB-5

Ross, Leonard Q. (see Rosten, Leo)

Ross, Sinclair 1908- DLB-88

Ross, W. W. E. 1894-1966 ....DLB-88

Rossen, Robert 1908-1966 ....DLB-26

Rossetti, Christina 1830-1894 ....DLB-35

Rossetti, Dante Gabriel 1828-1882 ....DLB-35

Rossner, Judith 1935- DLB-6

Rosten, Leo 1908- DLB-11

Bertram Rota and His Bookshop Y-91

Roth, Gerhard 1942- DLB-85, 124

Roth, Henry 1906?- DLB-28

Roth, Joseph 1894-1939 ....DLB-85

Roth, Philip 1933- DLB-2, 28; Y-82

Rothenberg, Jerome 1931- DLB-5

Rotimi, Ola 1938- DLB-125

Routhier, Adolphe-Basile 1839-1920 ....DLB-99

Routier, Simone 1901-1987 ....DLB-88

Routledge, George, and Sons DLB-106

Rowe, Elizabeth Singer 1674-1737 ....DLB-39, 95

Rowe, Nicholas 1674-1718 ....DLB-84

Rowlands, Samuel circa 1570-1630 ....DLB-121

Rowlandson, Mary circa 1635-circa 1678 ....DLB-24

Rowley, William circa 1585-1626 ....DLB-58

Rowson, Susanna Haswell circa 1762-1824 ....DLB-37

Roy, Camille 1870-1943 ....DLB-92

Roy, Gabrielle 1909-1983 ....DLB-68

Roy, Jules 1907- DLB-83

The Royal Court Theatre and the English
    Stage Company DLB-13

The Royal Court Theatre and the New Drama DLB-10

The Royal Shakespeare Company at the Swan Y-88

Royall, Anne 1769-1854 ....DLB-43

The Roycroft Printing Shop DLB-49

Ruark, Gibbons 1941- DLB-120

Rubens, Bernice 1928- DLB-14

Rudd and Carleton DLB-49

Rudkin, David 1936- DLB-13

Ruffin, Josephine St. Pierre 1842-1924 ....DLB-79

Ruggles, Henry Joseph 1813-1906 ....DLB-64

Rukeyser, Muriel 1913-1980 ....DLB-48

Rule, Jane 1931- DLB-60

Rulfo, Juan 1918-1986 ....DLB-113

Rumaker, Michael 1932- DLB-16

Rumens, Carol 1944- DLB-40

Runyon, Damon 1880-1946 ....DLB-11, 86

Rush, Benjamin 1746-1813 ....DLB-37

Rusk, Ralph L. 1888-1962 ....DLB-103

Ruskin, John 1819-1900 ....DLB-55

Russ, Joanna 1937- DLB-8

Russell, B. B., and Company DLB-49

Russell, Benjamin 1761-1845 ....DLB-43

Russell, Bertrand 1872-1970 ....DLB-100

Russell, Charles Edward 1860-1941 ....DLB-25

Russell, George William (see AE)

Russell, R. H., and Son DLB-49

Rutherford, Mark 1831-1913 ....DLB-18

Ryan, Michael 1946- Y-82

Ryan, Oscar 1904- DLB-68

Ryga, George 1932- DLB-60

Rymer, Thomas 1643?-1713 ....DLB-101

Ryskind, Morrie 1895-1985 ....DLB-26

S

The Saalfield Publishing Company DLB-46

Saba, Umberto 1883-1957 ....DLB-114

Saberhagen, Fred 1930- DLB-8

Sackler, Howard 1929-1982 ....DLB-7

Sackville, Thomas 1536-1608
    and Norton, Thomas 1532-1584 ....DLB-62

Sackville-West, V. 1892-1962 ....DLB-34

Sadlier, D. and J., and Company DLB-49

Sadlier, Mary Anne 1820-1903 ....DLB-99

Sadoff, Ira 1945- DLB-120

Saffin, John circa 1626-1710 ....DLB-24

Sagan, Françoise 1935- DLB-83

Sage, Robert 1899-1962 ....DLB-4

Sagel, Jim 1947- DLB-82

Sahagún, Carlos 1938- DLB-108

Sahkomaapii, Piitai (see Highwater, Jamake)

Sahl, Hans 1902- DLB-69

Said, Edward W. 1935- DLB-67

Saiko, George 1892-1962 ....DLB-85

St. Dominic's Press DLB-112

Saint-Exupéry, Antoine de 1900-1944 ....DLB-72

St. Johns, Adela Rogers 1894-1988 ....DLB-29

St. Martin's Press DLB-46

St. Omer, Garth 1931- DLB-117

Saint Pierre, Michel de 1916-1987 ....DLB-83

Saintsbury, George 1845-1933 ....DLB-57

Saki (see Munro, H. H.)

Salaam, Kalamu ya 1947- DLB-38

Salas, Floyd 1931- DLB-82

Sálaz-Marquez, Rubén 1935- DLB-122

Salemson, Harold J. 1910-1988 ....DLB-4

Salinas, Luis Omar 1937- DLB-82

Salinger, J. D. 1919- DLB-2, 102

Salkey, Andrew 1928- DLB-125

Salt, Waldo 1914- DLB-44

Salter, Mary Jo 1954- DLB-120

Salustri, Carlo Alberto (see Trilussa)

Salverson, Laura Goodman 1890-1970 ....DLB-92

Sampson, Richard Henry (see Hull, Richard)

Samuels, Ernest 1903- DLB-111

Sanborn, Franklin Benjamin 1831-1917 ....DLB-1

Sánchez, Philomeno "Phil" 1917- DLB-122

Sánchez, Ricardo 1941- DLB-82

Sanchez, Sonia 1934- DLB-41; DS-8

Sand, George 1804-1876 ....DLB-119

Sandburg, Carl 1878-1967 ....DLB-17, 54

Sanders, Ed 1939- DLB-16

Sandoz, Mari 1896-1966 ....DLB-9

Sandwell, B. K. 1876-1954 ....DLB-92

Sandys, George 1578-1644 ....DLB-24, 121

Sangster, Charles 1822-1893 ....DLB-99

Santayana, George 1863-1952 ....DLB-54, 71

Santiago, Danny 1911-1988 ....DLB-122

Santmyer, Helen Hooven 1895-1986 ....Y-84

Sapir, Edward 1884-1939 ....DLB-92

Sapper (see McNeile, Herman Cyril)

Sarduy, Severo 1937- DLB-113

Sargent, Pamela 1948- DLB-8

Saroyan, William 1908-1981 ....DLB-7, 9, 86; Y-81

Sarraute, Nathalie 1900- DLB-83

Sarrazin, Albertine 1937-1967 ....DLB-83

Sarton, May 1912- DLB-48; Y-81

Sartre, Jean-Paul 1905-1980 ....DLB-72

Sassoon, Siegfried 1886-1967 ....DLB-20

Saturday Review Press DLB-46

Saunders, James 1925- DLB-13

Saunders, John Monk 1897-1940 ....DLB-26

Saunders, Margaret Marshall 1861-1947 ....DLB-92

Saunders and Otley DLB-106

Savage, James 1784-1873 ....DLB-30

Savage, Marmion W. 1803?-1872 ....DLB-21

Savage, Richard 1697?-1743 ....DLB-95

Savard, Félix-Antoine 1896-1982 ....DLB-68

Sawyer, Ruth 1880-1970 ....DLB-22

Sayers, Dorothy L. 1893-1957 ....DLB-10, 36, 77, 100

Sayles, John Thomas 1950- DLB-44

Sbarbaro, Camillo 1888-1967 ....DLB-114

Scannell, Vernon 1922- DLB-27

Scarry, Richard 1919- DLB-61

Schaeffer, Albrecht 1885-1950 ....DLB-66

Schaeffer, Susan Fromberg 1941- DLB-28

Schaper, Edzard 1908-1984 ....DLB-69

Scharf, J. Thomas 1843-1898 ....DLB-47

Schelling, Friedrich Wilhelm Joseph von 1775-1854 ...DLB-90

Schickele, René 1883-1940 ....DLB-66

Schiller, Friedrich 1759-1805 ....DLB-94

Schlaf, Johannes 1862-1941 ....DLB-118

Schlegel, August Wilhelm 1767-1845 ....DLB-94

Schlegel, Dorothea 1763-1839 ....DLB-90

Schlegel, Friedrich 1772-1829 ....DLB-90

Schleiermacher, Friedrich 1768-1834 ....DLB-90

Schlesinger, Arthur M., Jr. 1917- DLB-17

Schlumberger, Jean 1877-1968 ....DLB-65

Schmid, Eduard Hermann Wilhelm (see Edschmid, Kasimir)

Schmidt, Arno 1914-1979 ....DLB-69

Schmidt, Michael 1947- DLB-40

Schmidtbonn, Wilhelm August 1876-1952 ....DLB-118

Schmitz, James H. 1911- DLB-8

Schnackenberg, Gjertrud 1953- DLB-120

Schnitzler, Arthur 1862-1931 .... DLB-81, 118

Schnurre, Wolfdietrich 1920- DLB-69

Schocken Books DLB-46

Schönbeck, Virgilio (see Giotti, Virgilio)

Schönherr, Karl 1867-1943 ....DLB-118

Scholartis Press DLB-112

The Schomburg Center for Research
   in Black Culture DLB-76

Schopenhauer, Arthur 1788-1860 ....DLB-90

Schopenhauer, Johanna 1766-1838 ....DLB-90

Schorer, Mark 1908-1977 ....DLB-103

Schouler, James 1839-1920 ....DLB-47

Schrader, Paul 1946- DLB-44

Schreiner, Olive 1855-1920 ....DLB-18

Schroeder, Andreas 1946- DLB-53

Schubart, Christian Friedrich Daniel 1739-1791 ....DLB-97

Schubert, Gotthilf Heinrich 1780-1860 ....DLB-90

Schulberg, Budd 1914- DLB-6, 26, 28; Y-81

Schulte, F. J., and Company DLB-49

Schurz, Carl 1829-1906 ....DLB-23

Schuyler, George S. 1895-1977 ....DLB-29, 51

Schuyler, James 1923-1991 ....DLB-5

Schwartz, Delmore 1913-1966 ....DLB-28, 48

Schwartz, Jonathan 1938- Y-82

Schwob, Marcel 1867-1905 ....DLB-123

Science Fantasy DLB-8

Science-Fiction Fandom and Conventions DLB-8

Science-Fiction Fanzines: The Time Binders DLB-8

Science-Fiction Films DLB-8

Science Fiction Writers of America and the
   Nebula Awards DLB-8

Scott, Dennis 1939-1991 ....DLB-125

Scott, Dixon 1881-1915 ....DLB-98

Scott, Duncan Campbell 1862-1947 ....DLB-92

Scott, Evelyn 1893-1963 .... DLB-9, 48

Scott, F. R. 1899-1985 ....DLB-88

Scott, Frederick George 1861-1944 ....DLB-92

Scott, Harvey W. 1838-1910 ....DLB-23

Scott, Paul 1920-1978 ....DLB-14

Scott, Sarah 1723-1795 ....DLB-39

Scott, Tom 1918- DLB-27

Scott, Sir Walter 1771-1832 .... DLB-93, 107, 116

Scott, William Bell 1811-1890 ....DLB-32

Scott, Walter, Publishing Company Limited DLB-112

Scott, William R. [publishing house] DLB-46

Scott-Heron, Gil 1949- DLB-41

Charles Scribner's Sons DLB-49

Scripps, E. W. 1854-1926 ....DLB-25

Scudder, Horace Elisha 1838-1902 .... DLB-42, 71

Scudder, Vida Dutton 1861-1954 ....DLB-71

Scupham, Peter 1933- DLB-40

Seabrook, William 1886-1945 ....DLB-4

Seabury, Samuel 1729-1796 ....DLB-31

Sears, Edward I. 1819?-1876 ....DLB-79

Sears Publishing Company DLB-46

Seaton, George 1911-1979 ....DLB-44

Seaton, William Winston 1785-1866 ....DLB-43

Secker, Martin, and Warburg Limited DLB-112

Secker, Martin [publishing house] DLB-112

Sedgwick, Arthur George 1844-1915 ....DLB-64

Sedgwick, Catharine Maria 1789-1867 .... DLB-1, 74

Sedgwick, Ellery 1872-1930 ....DLB-91

Seeger, Alan 1888-1916 ....DLB-45

Seers, Eugene (see Dantin, Louis)

Segal, Erich 1937- Y-86

Seghers, Anna 1900-1983 ....DLB-69

Seid, Ruth (see Sinclair, Jo)

Seidel, Frederick Lewis 1936- Y-84

Seidel, Ina 1885-1974 ....DLB-56

Seizin Press DLB-112

Séjour, Victor 1817-1874 ....DLB-50

Séjour Marcou et Ferrand, Juan Victor (see Séjour, Victor)

Selby, Hubert, Jr. 1928- DLB-2

Selden, George 1929-1989 ....DLB-52

Selected English-Language Little Magazines and Newspapers [France, 1920-1939] DLB-4

Selected Humorous Magazines (1820-1950) DLB-11

Selected Science-Fiction Magazines and Anthologies DLB-8

Seligman, Edwin R. A. 1861-1939 ....DLB-47

Seltzer, Chester E. (see Muro, Amado)

Seltzer, Thomas [publishing house] DLB-46

Selvon, Sam 1923- DLB-125

Senancour, Etienne de 1770-1846 ....DLB-119

Sendak, Maurice 1928- DLB-61

Senécal, Eva 1905- DLB-92

Sensation Novels (1863), by H. L. Manse DLB-21

Seredy, Kate 1899-1975 ....DLB-22

Serling, Rod 1924-1975 ....DLB-26

Serote, Mongane Wally 1944- DLB-125

Serrano, Nina 1934- DLB-122

Service, Robert 1874-1958 ....DLB-92

Seth, Vikram 1952- DLB-120

Seton, Ernest Thompson 1860-1942 ....DLB-92

Settle, Mary Lee 1918- DLB-6

Seume, Johann Gottfried 1763-1810 ....DLB-94

Seuss, Dr. (see Geisel, Theodor Seuss)

Sewall, Joseph 1688-1769 ....DLB-24

Sewall, Richard B. 1908- DLB-111

Sewell, Samuel 1652-1730 ....DLB-24

Sex, Class, Politics, and Religion [in the British Novel, 1930-1959] DLB-15

Sexton, Anne 1928-1974 ....DLB-5

Shaara, Michael 1929-1988 ....Y-83

Shadwell, Thomas 1641?-1692 ....DLB-80

Shaffer, Anthony 1926- DLB-13

Shaffer, Peter 1926- DLB-13

Shaftesbury, Anthony Ashley Cooper, Third Earl of 1671-1713 ....DLB-101

Shairp, Mordaunt 1887-1939 ....DLB-10

Shakespeare, William 1564-1616 ....DLB-62

Shakespeare Head Press DLB-112

Shange, Ntozake 1948- DLB-38

Shapiro, Karl 1913- DLB-48

Sharon Publications DLB-46

Sharpe, Tom 1928- DLB-14

Shaw, Albert 1857-1947 ....DLB-91

Shaw, Bernard 1856-1950 ....DLB-10, 57

Shaw, Henry Wheeler 1818-1885 ....DLB-11

Shaw, Irwin 1913-1984 ....DLB-6, 102; Y-84

Shaw, Robert 1927-1978 ....DLB-13, 14

Shaw, Robert B. 1947- DLB-120

Shay, Frank [publishing house] DLB-46

Shea, John Gilmary 1824-1892 ....DLB-30

Sheaffer, Louis 1912- DLB-103

Shearing, Joseph 1886-1952 ....DLB-70

Shebbeare, John 1709-1788 ....DLB-39

Sheckley, Robert 1928- DLB-8

Shedd, William G. T. 1820-1894 ....DLB-64

Sheed, Wilfred 1930- DLB-6

Sheed and Ward [U.S.] DLB-46

Sheed and Ward Limited [U.K.] DLB-112

Sheldon, Alice B. (see Tiptree, James, Jr.)

Sheldon, Edward 1886-1946 ....DLB-7

Sheldon and Company DLB-49

Shelley, Mary Wollstonecraft 1797-1851 ....DLB-110, 116

Shelley, Percy Bysshe 1792-1822 ....DLB-96, 110

Shenstone, William 1714-1763 .... DLB-95

Shepard, Sam 1943- DLB-7

Shepard, Thomas I 1604 or 1605-1649 .... DLB-24

Shepard, Thomas II 1635-1677 .... DLB-24

Shepard, Clark and Brown DLB-49

Sheridan, Frances 1724-1766 .... DLB-39, 84

Sheridan, Richard Brinsley 1751-1816 .... DLB-89

Sherman, Francis 1871-1926 .... DLB-92

Sherriff, R. C. 1896-1975 .... DLB-10

Sherwood, Robert 1896-1955 .... DLB-7, 26

Shiels, George 1886-1949 .... DLB-10

Shillaber, B.[enjamin] P.[enhallow] 1814-1890 ...... DLB-1, 11

Shine, Ted 1931- DLB-38

Ship, Reuben 1915-1975 .... DLB-88

Shirer, William L. 1904- DLB-4

Shirley, James 1596-1666 .... DLB-58

Shockley, Ann Allen 1927- DLB-33

Shorthouse, Joseph Henry 1834-1903 .... DLB-18

Showalter, Elaine 1941- DLB-67

Shulevitz, Uri 1935- DLB-61

Shulman, Max 1919-1988 .... DLB-11

Shute, Henry A. 1856-1943 .... DLB-9

Shuttle, Penelope 1947- DLB-14, 40

Sidgwick and Jackson Limited DLB-112

Sidney, Margaret (see Lothrop, Harriet M.)

Sidney's Press DLB-49

Siegfried Loraine Sassoon: A Centenary Essay
    Tributes from Vivien F. Clarke and
    Michael Thorpe Y-86l

Sierra, Rubén 1946- DLB-122

Sierra Club Books DLB-49

Siger of Brabant circa 1240-circa 1284 .... DLB-115

Sigourney, Lydia Howard (Huntley)
    1791-1865 .... DLB-1, 42, 73

Silkin, Jon 1930- DLB-27

Silliphant, Stirling 1918- DLB-26

Sillitoe, Alan 1928- DLB-14

Silman, Roberta 1934- DLB-28

Silva, Beverly 1930- DLB-122

Silverberg, Robert 1935- DLB-8

Silverman, Kenneth 1936- DLB-111

Simak, Clifford D. 1904-1988 .... DLB-8

Simcoe, Elizabeth 1762-1850 .... DLB-99

Simcox, George Augustus 1841-1905 .... DLB-35

Sime, Jessie Georgina 1868-1958 .... DLB-92

Simenon, Georges 1903-1989 .... DLB-72; Y-89

Simic, Charles 1938- DLB-105

Simic, Charles, Images and "Images" DLB-105

Simmel, Johannes Mario 1924- DLB-69

Simmons, Ernest J. 1903-1972 .... DLB-103

Simmons, Herbert Alfred 1930- DLB-33

Simmons, James 1933- DLB-40

Simms, William Gilmore 1806-1870 .... DLB-3, 30, 59, 73

Simms and M'Intyre DLB-106

Simon, Claude 1913- DLB-83

Simon, Neil 1927- DLB-7

Simon and Schuster DLB-46

Simons, Katherine Drayton Mayrant 1890-1969 .... Y-83

Simpson, Helen 1897-1940 .... DLB-77

Simpson, Louis 1923- DLB-5

Simpson, N. F. 1919- DLB-13

Sims, George 1923- DLB-87

Sims, George R. 1847-1922 .... DLB-35, 70

Sinclair, Andrew 1935- DLB-14

Sinclair, Bertrand William 1881-1972 .... DLB-92

Sinclair, Jo 1913- DLB-28

Sinclair Lewis Centennial Conference Y-85

Sinclair, Lister 1921- DLB-88

Sinclair, May 1863-1946 .... DLB-36

Sinclair, Upton 1878-1968 .... DLB-9

Sinclair, Upton [publishing house] DLB-46

Singer, Isaac Bashevis 1904-1991 .... DLB-6, 28, 52; Y-91

Singmaster, Elsie 1879-1958 .... DLB-9

Sinisgalli, Leonardo 1908-1981 . . . . DLB-114

Siodmak, Curt 1902- DLB-44

Sissman, L. E. 1928-1976 . . . . DLB-5

Sisson, C. H. 1914- DLB-27

Sitwell, Edith 1887-1964 . . . . DLB-20

Sitwell, Osbert 1892-1969 . . . . DLB-100

Skeffington, William [publishing house] DLB-106

Skelton, Robin 1925- DLB-27, 53

Skinner, Constance Lindsay 1877-1939 . . . . DLB-92

Skinner, John Stuart 1788-1851 . . . . DLB-73

Skipsey, Joseph 1832-1903 . . . . DLB-35

Slade, Bernard 1930- DLB-53

Slater, Patrick 1880-1951 . . . . DLB-68

Slavitt, David 1935- DLB-5, 6

Sleigh, Burrows Willcocks Arthur 1821-1869 . . . . DLB-99

A Slender Thread of Hope: The Kennedy
    Center Black Theatre Project DLB-38

Slesinger, Tess 1905-1945 . . . . DLB-102

Slick, Sam (see Haliburton, Thomas Chandler)

Sloane, William, Associates DLB-46

Small, Maynard and Company DLB-49

Small Presses in Great Britain and Ireland,
    1960-1985 . . . . DLB-40

Small Presses I: Jargon Society Y-84

Small Presses II: The Spirit That Moves Us Press Y-85

Small Presses III: Pushcart Press Y-87

Smart, Christopher 1722-1771 . . . . DLB-109

Smart, Elizabeth 1913-1986 . . . . DLB-88

Smiles, Samuel 1812-1904 . . . . DLB-55

Smith, A. J. M. 1902-1980 . . . . DLB-88

Smith, Adam 1723-1790 . . . . DLB-104

Smith, Alexander 1829-1867 . . . . DLB-32, 55

Smith, Betty 1896-1972 . . . . Y-82

Smith, Carol Sturm 1938- Y-81

Smith, Charles Henry 1826-1903 . . . . DLB-11

Smith, Charlotte 1749-1806 . . . . DLB-39, 109

Smith, Cordwainer 1913-1966 . . . . DLB-8

Smith, Dave 1942- DLB-5

Smith, Dodie 1896- DLB-10

Smith, Doris Buchanan 1934- DLB-52

Smith, E. E. 1890-1965 . . . . DLB-8

Smith, Elihu Hubbard 1771-1798 . . . . DLB-37

Smith, Elizabeth Oakes (Prince) 1806-1893 . . . . DLB-1

Smith, George O. 1911-1981 . . . . DLB-8

Smith, Goldwin 1823-1910 . . . . DLB-99

Smith, H. Allen 1907-1976 . . . . DLB-11, 29

Smith, Harrison, and Robert Haas
    [publishing house] DLB-46

Smith, Horatio (Horace) 1779-1849 . . . . DLB-116

Smith, Horatio (Horace) 1779-1849 and
    James Smith 1775-1839 . . . . DLB-96

Smith, Iain Chrichton 1928- DLB-40

Smith, J. Allen 1860-1924 . . . . DLB-47

Smith, J. Stilman, and Company DLB-49

Smith, John 1580-1631 . . . . DLB-24, 30

Smith, Josiah 1704-1781 . . . . DLB-24

Smith, Ken 1938- DLB-40

Smith, Lee 1944- Y-83

Smith, Logan Pearsall 1865-1946 . . . . DLB-98

Smith, Mark 1935- Y-82

Smith, Michael 1698-circa 1771 . . . . DLB-31

Smith, Red 1905-1982 . . . . DLB-29

Smith, Roswell 1829-1892 . . . . DLB-79

Smith, Samuel Harrison 1772-1845 . . . . DLB-43

Smith, Samuel Stanhope 1751-1819 . . . . DLB-37

Smith, Seba 1792-1868 . . . . DLB-1, 11

Smith, Stevie 1902-1971 . . . . DLB-20

Smith, Sydney 1771-1845 . . . . DLB-107

Smith, Sydney Goodsir 1915-1975 . . . . DLB-27

Smith, W. B., and Company DLB-49

Smith, W. H., and Son DLB-106

Smith, William 1727-1803 . . . . DLB-31

Smith, William 1728-1793 . . . . DLB-30

Smith, William Gardner 1927-1974 . . . . DLB-76

Smith, William Jay 1918- DLB-5

Smithers, Leonard [publishing house] DLB-112

Smollett, Tobias 1721-1771 .... DLB-39, 104

Snellings, Rolland (see Touré, Askia Muhammad)Snodgrass,
  W. D. 1926- DLB-5

Snow, C. P. 1905-1980 ....DLB-15, 77

Snyder, Gary 1930- DLB-5, 16

Sobiloff, Hy 1912-1970 ....DLB-48

The Society for Textual Scholarship and *TEXT* Y-87

Soffici, Ardengo 1879-1964 ....DLB-114

Solano, Solita 1888-1975 ....DLB-4

Sollers, Philippe 1936- DLB-83

Solmi, Sergio 1899-1981 ....DLB-114

Solomon, Carl 1928- DLB-16

Solway, David 1941- DLB-53

Solzhenitsyn and America Y-85

Sontag, Susan 1933- DLB-2, 67

Sorrentino, Gilbert 1929- DLB-5; Y-80

Sorge, Reinhard Johannes 1892-1916 ....DLB-118

Sotheby, William 1757-1833 ....DLB-93

Soto, Gary 1952- DLB-82

Sources for the Study of Tudor and Stuart Drama DLB-62

Souster, Raymond 1921- DLB-88

Southerland, Ellease 1943- DLB-33

Southern, Terry 1924- DLB-2

Southern Writers Between the Wars DLB-9

Southerne, Thomas 1659-1746 ....DLB-80

Southey, Caroline Anne Bowles 1786-1854 ....DLB-116

Southey, Robert 1774-1843 .... DLB-93, 107

Soyfer, Jura 1912-1939 ....DLB-124

Soyinka, Wole 1934- DLB-125

Spacks, Barry 1931- DLB-105

Spark, Muriel 1918- DLB-15

Sparks, Jared 1789-1866 ....DLB-1, 30

Sparshott, Francis 1926- DLB-60

Späth, Gerold 1939- DLB-75

The Spectator 1828- DLB-110

Spellman, A. B. 1935- DLB-41

Spencer, Anne 1882-1975 ....DLB-51, 54

Spencer, Elizabeth 1921- DLB-6

Spencer, Herbert 1820-1903 ....DLB-57

Spencer, Scott 1945- Y-86

Spender, J. A. 1862-1942 ....DLB-98

Spender, Stephen 1909- DLB-20

Sperr, Martin 1944- DLB-124

Spicer, Jack 1925-1965 ....DLB-5, 16

Spielberg, Peter 1929- Y-81

Spier, Peter 1927- DLB-61

Spinrad, Norman 1940- DLB-8

Spires, Elizabeth 1952- DLB-120

Spofford, Harriet Prescott 1835-1921 ....DLB-74

Squibob (see Derby, George Horatio)

Staël, Germaine de 1766-1817 ....DLB-119

Stael-Holstein, Anne-Louise Germaine de
  (see Stael, Germaine de)

Stafford, Jean 1915-1979 ....DLB-2

Stafford, William 1914- DLB-5

Stage Censorship: "The Rejected Statement"
  (1911), by Bernard Shaw [excerpts] DLB-10

Stallings, Laurence 1894-1968 ....DLB-7, 44

Stallworthy, Jon 1935- DLB-40

Stampp, Kenneth M. 1912- DLB-17

Stanford, Ann 1916- DLB-5

Stanton, Elizabeth Cady 1815-1902 ....DLB-79

Stanton, Frank L. 1857-1927 ....DLB-25

Stanton, Maura 1946- DLB-120

Stapledon, Olaf 1886-1950 ....DLB-15

Star Spangled Banner Office DLB-49

Starkweather, David 1935- DLB-7

Statements on the Art of Poetry DLB-54

Stead, Robert J. C. 1880-1959 ....DLB-92

Steadman, Mark 1930- DLB-6

The Stealthy School of Criticism (1871), by
  Dante Gabriel Rossetti DLB-35

Stearns, Harold E. 1891-1943 ....DLB-4

Stedman, Edmund Clarence 1833-1908 ....DLB-64

Steegmuller, Francis 1906- DLB-111

Steele, Max 1922- Y-80

Steele, Richard 1672-1729 ....DLB-84, 101

Steele, Timothy 1948- DLB-120

Steele, Wilbur Daniel 1886-1970 ....DLB-86

Steere, Richard circa 1643-1721 ....DLB-24

Stegner, Wallace 1909- DLB-9

Stehr, Hermann 1864-1940 ....DLB-66

Steig, William 1907- DLB-61

Stein, Gertrude 1874-1946 ....DLB-4, 54, 86

Stein, Leo 1872-1947 ....DLB-4

Stein and Day Publishers DLB-46

Steinbeck, John 1902-1968 .... DLB-7, 9; DS-2

Steiner, George 1929- DLB-67

Stendhal 1783-1842 ....DLB-119

Stephen Crane: A Revaluation Virginia
    Tech Conference, 1989 ....Y-89

Stephen, Leslie 1832-1904 ....DLB-57

Stephens, Alexander H. 1812-1883 ....DLB-47

Stephens, Ann 1810-1886 ....DLB-3, 73

Stephens, Charles Asbury 1844?-1931 ....DLB-42

Stephens, James 1882?-1950 ....DLB-19

Sterling, George 1869-1926 ....DLB-54

Sterling, James 1701-1763 ....DLB-24

Sterling, John 1806-1844 ....DLB-116

Stern, Gerald 1925- DLB-105

Stern, Madeleine B. 1912- DLB-111

Stern, Gerald, Living in Ruin DLB-105

Stern, Richard 1928- Y-87

Stern, Stewart 1922- DLB-26

Sterne, Laurence 1713-1768 ....DLB-39

Sternheim, Carl 1878-1942 ....DLB-56, 118

Stevens, Wallace 1879-1955 ....DLB-54

Stevenson, Anne 1933- DLB-40

Stevenson, Robert Louis 1850-1894 ....DLB-18, 57

Stewart, Donald Ogden 1894-1980 .... DLB-4, 11, 26

Stewart, Dugald 1753-1828 ....DLB-31

Stewart, George, Jr. 1848-1906 ....DLB-99

Stewart, George R. 1895-1980 ....DLB-8

Stewart and Kidd Company DLB-46

Stewart, Randall 1896-1964 ....DLB-103

Stickney, Trumbull 1874-1904 ....DLB-54

Stiles, Ezra 1727-1795 ....DLB-31

Still, James 1906- DLB-9

Stith, William 1707-1755 ....DLB-31

Stock, Elliot [publishing house] DLB-106

Stockton, Frank R. 1834-1902 ....DLB-42, 74

Stoddard, Ashbel [publishing house] DLB-49

Stoddard, Richard Henry 1825-1903 ....DLB-3, 64

Stoddard, Solomon 1643-1729 ....DLB-24

Stoker, Bram 1847-1912 ....DLB-36, 70

Stokes, Frederick A., Company DLB-49

Stokes, Thomas L. 1898-1958 ....DLB-29

Stokesbury, Leon 1945- DLB-120

Stolberg, Christian Graf zu 1748-1821 ....DLB-94

Stolberg, Friedrich Leopold Graf zu 1750-1819 ....DLB-94

Stone, Herbert S., and Company DLB-49

Stone, Lucy 1818-1893 ....DLB-79

Stone, Melville 1848-1929 ....DLB-25

Stone, Ruth 1915- DLB-105

Stone, Samuel 1602-1663 ....DLB-24

Stone and Kimball DLB-49

Stoppard, Tom 1937- DLB-13; Y-85

Storey, Anthony 1928- DLB-14

Storey, David 1933- DLB-13, 14

Story, Thomas circa 1670-1742 ....DLB-31

Story, William Wetmore 1819-1895 ....DLB-1

Storytelling: A Contemporary Renaissance Y-84

Stoughton, William 1631-1701 ....DLB-24

Stowe, Harriet Beecher 1811-1896 .... DLB-1, 12, 42, 74

Stowe, Leland 1899- DLB-29

Strachey, Lytton 1880-1932 .... DS-10

Strand, Mark 1934- DLB-5

Strahan and Company DLB-106

Stratemeyer, Edward 1862-1930 ....DLB-42

Stratton and Barnard DLB-49

Straub, Peter 1943- Y-84

Strauß, Botho 1944- DLB-124

Street, Cecil John Charles (see Rhode, John)

Street and Smith DLB-49

Streeter, Edward 1891-1976 ....DLB-11

Stribling, T. S. 1881-1965 ....DLB-9

Strickland, Samuel 1804-1867 ....DLB-99

Stringer and Townsend DLB-49

Stringer, Arthur 1874-1950 ....DLB-92

Strittmatter, Erwin 1912- DLB-69

Strother, David Hunter 1816-1888 ....DLB-3

Strouse, Jean 1945- DLB-111

Stuart, Dabney 1937- DLB-105

Stuart, Dabney, Knots into Webs: Some Autobiographical
        Sources DLB-105

Stuart, Jesse 1906-1984 .... DLB-9, 48, 102; Y-84

Stuart, Lyle [publishing house] DLB-46

Stubbs, Harry Clement (see Clement, Hal)

Studio DLB-112

The Study of Poetry (1880), by Matthew Arnold DLB-35

Sturgeon, Theodore 1918-1985 ....DLB-8; Y-85

Sturges, Preston 1898-1959 ....DLB-26

"Style" (1840; revised, 1859), by Thomas
        de Quincey [excerpt] DLB-57

"Style" (1888), by Walter Pater DLB-57

Style (1897), by Walter Raleigh [excerpt] DLB-57

"Style" (1877), by T. H. Wright [excerpt] DLB-57

"Le Style c'est l'homme" (1892), by W. H. Mallock ...DLB-57

Styron, William 1925- DLB-2; Y-80

Suárez, Mario 1925- DLB-82

Such, Peter 1939- DLB-60

Suckling, Sir John 1609-1642 ....DLB-58

Suckow, Ruth 1892-1960 .... DLB-9, 102

Sudermann, Hermann 1857-1928 ....DLB-118

Sue, Eugène 1804-1857 ....DLB-119

Sue, Marie-Joseph (see Sue, Eugène)

Suggs, Simon (see Hooper, Johnson Jones)

Sukenick, Ronald 1932- Y-81

Suknaski, Andrew 1942- DLB-53

Sullivan, Alan 1868-1947 ....DLB-92

Sullivan, C. Gardner 1886-1965 ....DLB-26

Sullivan, Frank 1892-1976 ....DLB-11

Sulte, Benjamin 1841-1923 ....DLB-99

Sulzer, Johann Georg 1720-1779 ....DLB-97

Summers, Hollis 1916- DLB-6

Sumner, Henry A. [publishing house] DLB-49

Surtees, Robert Smith 1803-1864 ....DLB-21

A Survey of Poetry Anthologies, 1879-1960 ....DLB-54

Surveys of the Year's Biography
    A Transit of Poets and Others: American
            Biography in 1982 ....Y-82
        The Year in Literary Biography Y-83
        The Year in Literary Biography Y-84
        The Year in Literary Biography Y-85
        The Year in Literary Biography Y-86
        The Year in Literary Biography Y-87
        The Year in Literary Biography Y-88
        The Year in Literary Biography Y-89, Y-90, Y-91
    Surveys of the Year's Book Publishing
        The Year in Book Publishing Y-86
    Surveys of the Year's Drama
        The Year in Drama Y-82
        The Year in Drama Y-83
        The Year in Drama Y-84
        The Year in Drama Y-85
        The Year in Drama Y-87
        The Year in Drama Y-88
        The Year in Drama Y-89, Y-90, Y-91
    Surveys of the Year's Fiction
        The Year's Work in Fiction: A Survey Y-82
        The Year in Fiction: A Biased View Y-83
        The Year in Fiction Y-84
        The Year in Fiction Y-85
        The Year in Fiction Y-86
        The Year in the Novel Y-87
        The Year in Short Stories Y-87
        The Year in the Novel Y-88, Y-90, Y-91
        The Year in Short Stories Y-88, Y-90, Y-91

The Year in Fiction Y-89
Surveys of the Year's Poetry
    The Year's Work in American Poetry Y-82
       The Year in Poetry Y-83
       The Year in Poetry Y-84
       The Year in Poetry Y-85
       The Year in Poetry Y-86
       The Year in Poetry Y-87
       The Year in Poetry Y-88
       The Year in Poetry Y-89

Sutherland, Efua Theodora 1924- DLB-117

Sutherland, John 1919-1956 .... DLB-68

Sutro, Alfred 1863-1933 .... DLB-10

Swados, Harvey 1920-1972 .... DLB-2

Swain, Charles 1801-1874 .... DLB-32

Swallow Press DLB-46

Swan Sonnenschein Limited DLB-106

Swanberg, W. A. 1907- DLB-103

Swenson, May 1919-1989 .... DLB-5

Swerling, Jo 1897- DLB-44

Swift, Jonathan 1667-1745 .... DLB-39, 95, 101

Swinburne, A. C. 1837-1909 .... DLB-35, 57

Swineshead, Richard floruit circa 1350 .... DLB-115

Swinnerton, Frank 1884-1982 .... DLB-34

Swisshelm, Jane Grey 1815-1884 .... DLB-43

Swope, Herbert Bayard 1882-1958 .... DLB-25

Swords, T. and J., and Company DLB-49

Swords, Thomas 1763-1843 and
    Swords, James ?-1844 .... DLB-73

Sylvester, Josuah 1562 or 1563 - 1618 .... DLB-121

Symonds, John Addington 1840-1893 .... DLB-57

Symons, Arthur 1865-1945 .... DLB-19, 57

Symons, Julian 1912- DLB-87

Symons, Scott 1933- DLB-53

Synge, John Millington 1871-1909 .... DLB-10, 19

T

Taban lo Liyong 1939?- DLB-125

Taché, Joseph-Charles 1820-1894 .... DLB-99

Tafolla, Carmen 1951- DLB-82

Taggard, Genevieve 1894-1948 .... DLB-45

Tagger, Theodor (see Bruckner, Ferdinand)

Tait, J. Selwin, and Sons DLB-49

Tait's Edinburgh Magazine 1832-1861 .... DLB-110

The Takarazaka Revue Company Y-91

Talvj or Talvi (see Robinson, Therese)

Taradash, Daniel 1913- DLB-44

Tarbell, Ida M. 1857-1944 .... DLB-47

Tardivel, Jules-Paul 1851-1905 .... DLB-99

Tarkington, Booth 1869-1946 .... DLB-9, 102

Tashlin, Frank 1913-1972 .... DLB-44

Tate, Allen 1899-1979 .... DLB-4, 45, 63

Tate, James 1943- DLB-5

Tate, Nahum circa 1652-1715 .... DLB-80

Taylor, Bayard 1825-1878 .... DLB-3

Taylor, Bert Leston 1866-1921 .... DLB-25

Taylor, Charles H. 1846-1921 .... DLB-25

Taylor, Edward circa 1642-1729 .... DLB-24

Taylor, Henry 1942- DLB-5

Taylor, Sir Henry 1800-1886 .... DLB-32

Taylor, John 1577 or 1578 - 1653 .... DLB-121

Taylor, Mildred D. ?- DLB-52

Taylor, Peter 1917- Y-81

Taylor, William, and Company DLB-49

Taylor-Made Shakespeare? Or Is
    "Shall I Die?" the Long-Lost Text
    of Bottom's Dream? Y-85

Teasdale, Sara 1884-1933 .... DLB-45

The Tea-Table (1725), by Eliza Haywood [excerpt] DLB-39

Telles, Lygia Fagundes 1924- DLB-113

Temple, Sir William 1628-1699 .... DLB-101

Tenn, William 1919- DLB-8

Tennant, Emma 1937- DLB-14

Tenney, Tabitha Gilman 1762-1837 .... DLB-37

Tennyson, Alfred 1809-1892 .... DLB-32

Tennyson, Frederick 1807-1898 .... DLB-32

Terhune, Albert Payson 1872-1942 .... DLB-9

Terry, Megan 1932- DLB-7

Terson, Peter 1932- DLB-13

Tesich, Steve 1943- Y-83

Tessa, Delio 1886-1939 ....DLB-114

Tey, Josephine 1896?-1952 ....DLB-77

Thacher, James 1754-1844 ....DLB-37

Thackeray, William Makepeace 1811-1863 ....DLB-21, 55

Thames and Hudson Limited DLB-112

Thanet, Octave (see French, Alice)

The Theater in Shakespeare's Time DLB-62

The Theatre Guild DLB-7

Thelwall, John 1764-1834 ....DLB-93

Theriault, Yves 1915-1983 ....DLB-88

Thério, Adrien 1925- DLB-53

Theroux, Paul 1941- DLB-2

Thibaudeau, Colleen 1925- DLB-88

Thielen, Benedict 1903-1965 ....DLB-102

Thiong'o Ngugi wa (see Ngugi wa Thiong'o)

Thoma, Ludwig 1867-1921 ....DLB-66

Thoma, Richard 1902- DLB-4

Thomas, Audrey 1935- DLB-60

Thomas, D. M. 1935- DLB-40

Thomas, Dylan 1914-1953 ....DLB-13, 20

Thomas, Edward 1878-1917 ....DLB-19, 98

Thomas, Gwyn 1913-1981 ....DLB-15

Thomas, Isaiah 1750-1831 ....DLB-43, 73

Thomas, Isaiah [publishing house] DLB-49

Thomas, John 1900-1932 ....DLB-4

Thomas, Joyce Carol 1938- DLB-33

Thomas, Lorenzo 1944- DLB-41

Thomas, R. S. 1915- DLB-27

Thompson, David 1770-1857 ....DLB-99

Thompson, Dorothy 1893-1961 ....DLB-29

Thompson, Francis 1859-1907 ....DLB-19

Thompson, George Selden (see Selden, George)

Thompson, John 1938-1976 ....DLB-60

Thompson, John R. 1823-1873 ....DLB-3, 73

Thompson, Lawrance 1906-1973 ....DLB-103

Thompson, Maurice 1844-1901 ....DLB-71, 74

Thompson, Ruth Plumly 1891-1976 ....DLB-22

Thompson, Thomas Phillips 1843-1933 ....DLB-99

Thompson, William Tappan 1812-1882 ....DLB-3, 11

Thomson, Edward William 1849-1924 ....DLB-92

Thomson, James 1700-1748 ....DLB-95

Thomson, James 1834-1882 ....DLB-35

Thomson, Mortimer 1831-1875 ....DLB-11

Thoreau, Henry David 1817-1862 ....DLB-1

Thorpe, Thomas Bangs 1815-1878 ....DLB-3, 11

Thoughts on Poetry and Its Varieties (1833),
     by John Stuart Mill DLB-32

Thrale, Hester Lynch (see Piozzi, Hester Lynch [Thrale])

Thümmel, Moritz August von 1738-1817 ....DLB-97

Thurber, James 1894-1961 ....DLB-4, 11, 22, 102

Thurman, Wallace 1902-1934 ....DLB-51

Thwaite, Anthony 1930- DLB-40

Thwaites, Reuben Gold 1853-1913 ....DLB-47

Ticknor, George 1791-1871 ....DLB-1, 59

Ticknor and Fields DLB-49

Ticknor and Fields (revived) DLB-46

Tieck, Ludwig 1773-1853 ....DLB-90

Tietjens, Eunice 1884-1944 ....DLB-54

Tilt, Charles [publishing house] DLB-106

Tilton, J. E., and Company DLB-49

Time and Western Man (1927), by Wyndham
     Lewis [excerpts] DLB-36

Time-Life Books DLB-46

Times Books DLB-46

Timothy, Peter circa 1725-1782 ....DLB-43

Timrod, Henry 1828-1867 ....DLB-3

Tinsley Brothers DLB-106

Tiptree, James, Jr. 1915- DLB-8

Titus, Edward William 1870-1952 ....DLB-4

Toklas, Alice B. 1877-1967 ....DLB-4

Tolkien, J. R. R. 1892-1973 . . . . .DLB-15

Toller, Ernst 1893-1939 . . . . .DLB-124

Tollet, Elizabeth 1694-1754 . . . . .DLB-95

Tolson, Melvin B. 1898-1966 . . . . .DLB-48, 76

Tom Jones (1749), by Henry Fielding [excerpt] DLB-39

Tomlinson, Charles 1927- .DLB-40

Tomlinson, H. M. 1873-1958 . . . . .DLB-36, 100

Tompkins, Abel [publishing house] DLB-49

Tompson, Benjamin 1642-1714 . . . . .DLB-24

Tonks, Rosemary 1932- DLB-14

Toole, John Kennedy 1937?-1969 . . . . .Y-81

Toomer, Jean 1894-1967 .DLB-45, 51

Tor Books DLB-46

Torberg, Friedrich 1908-1979 . . . . .DLB-85

Torrence, Ridgely 1874-1950 . . . . .DLB-54

Torres-Metzger, Joseph V. 1933- DLB-122

Toth, Susan Allen 1940- Y-86

Tough-Guy Literature DLB-9

Touré, Askia Muhammad 1938- DLB-41

Tourgée, Albion W. 1838-1905 . . . . .DLB-79

Tourneur, Cyril circa 1580-1626 . . . . .DLB-58

Tournier, Michel 1924- .DLB-83

Tousey, Frank [publishing house] DLB-49

Tower Publications DLB-46

Towne, Benjamin circa 1740-1793 . . . . .DLB-43

Towne, Robert 1936- DLB-44

Townshend, Aurelian by 1583 - circa 1651 . . . . .DLB-121

Tracy, Honor 1913- DLB-15

Traill, Catharine Parr 1802-1899 . . . . .DLB-99

Train, Arthur 1875-1945 . . . . .DLB-86

The Transatlantic Publishing Company DLB-49

Transcendentalists, American DS-5

Translators of the Twelfth Century: Literary Issues
    Raised and Impact Created DLB-115

Traven, B. 1882? or 1890?-1969? DLB-9, 56

Travers, Ben 1886-1980 . . . . .DLB-10

Trejo, Ernesto 1950- DLB-122

Trelawny, Edward John 1792-1881 . . . . .DLB-110, 116

Tremain, Rose 1943- DLB-14

Tremblay, Michel 1942- DLB-60

Trends in Twentieth-Century
    Mass Market Publishing .DLB-46

Trent, William P. 1862-1939 . . . . .DLB-47

Trescot, William Henry 1822-1898 . . . . .DLB-30

Trevor, William 1928- DLB-14

Trilling, Lionel 1905-1975 . . . . .DLB-28, 63

Trilussa 1871-1950 . . . . .DLB-114

Triolet, Elsa 1896-1970 . . . . .DLB-72

Tripp, John 1927- DLB-40

Trocchi, Alexander 1925- DLB-15

Trollope, Anthony 1815-1882 . . . . .DLB-21, 57

Trollope, Frances 1779-1863 . . . . .DLB-21

Troop, Elizabeth 1931- DLB-14

Trotter, Catharine 1679-1749 . . . . .DLB-84

Trotti, Lamar 1898-1952 . . . . .DLB-44

Trottier, Pierre 1925- DLB-60

Troupe, Quincy Thomas, Jr. 1943- DLB-41

Trow, John F., and Company DLB-49

Truillier-Lacombe, Joseph-Patrice 1807-1863 . . . . .DLB-99

Trumbo, Dalton 1905-1976 . . . . .DLB-26

Trumbull, Benjamin 1735-1820 . . . . .DLB-30

Trumbull, John 1750-1831 .DLB-31

T. S. Eliot Centennial Y-88

Tucholsky, Kurt 1890-1935 . . . . .DLB-56

Tucker, George 1775-1861 . . . . .DLB-3, 30

Tucker, Nathaniel Beverley 1784-1851 . . . . .DLB-3

Tucker, St. George 1752-1827 . . . . .DLB-37

Tuckerman, Henry Theodore 1813-1871 . . . . .DLB-64

Tunis, John R. 1889-1975 .DLB-22

Tuohy, Frank 1925- DLB-14

Tupper, Martin F. 1810-1889 . . . . .DLB-32

Turbyfill, Mark 1896- DLB-45

Turco, Lewis 1934- Y-84

Turnbull, Andrew 1921-1970 . . . . .DLB-103

Turnbull, Gael 1928- DLB-40

Turner, Arlin 1909-1980 ....DLB-103

Turner, Charles (Tennyson) 1808-1879 ....DLB-32

Turner, Frederick 1943- DLB-40

Turner, Frederick Jackson 1861-1932 ....DLB-17

Turner, Joseph Addison 1826-1868 ....DLB-79

Turpin, Waters Edward 1910-1968 ....DLB-51

Turrini, Peter 1944- DLB-124

Tutuola, Amos 1920- DLB-125

Twain, Mark (see Clemens, Samuel Langhorne)

The 'Twenties and Berlin, by Alex Natan DLB-66

Tyler, Anne 1941- DLB-6; Y-82

Tyler, Moses Coit 1835-1900 ....DLB-47, 64

Tyler, Royall 1757-1826 ....DLB-37

Tylor, Edward Burnett 1832-1917 ....DLB-57

U

Udall, Nicholas 1504-1556 ....DLB-62

Uhland, Ludwig 1787-1862 ....DLB-90

Uhse, Bodo 1904-1963 ....DLB-69

Ulibarrí, Sabine R. 1919- DLB-82

Ulica, Jorge 1870-1926 ....DLB-82

Unamuno, Miguel de 1864-1936 ....DLB-108

Under the Microscope (1872), by A. C. Swinburne DLB-35

Unger, Friederike Helene 1741-1813 ....DLB-94

Ungaretti, Giuseppe 1888-1970 ....DLB-114

United States Book Company DLB-49

Universal Publishing and Distributing Corporation DLB-46

The University of Iowa Writers'
   Workshop Golden Jubilee Y-86

University of Wales Press DLB-112

"The Unknown Public" (1858), by
   Wilkie Collins [excerpt] DLB-57

Unruh, Fritz von 1885-1970 .... DLB-56, 118

Unwin, T. Fisher [publishing house] DLB-106

Upchurch, Boyd B. (see Boyd, John)

Updike, John 1932- DLB-2, 5; Y-80, 82; DS-3

Upton, Charles 1948- DLB-16

Upward, Allen 1863-1926 ....DLB-36

Urista, Alberto Baltazar (see Alurista) Urzidil, Johannes
   1896-1976 ....DLB-85

The Uses of Facsimile Y-90

Uslar Pietri, Arturo 1906- DLB-113

Ustinov, Peter 1921- DLB-13

Uz, Johann Peter 1720-1796 ....DLB-97

V

Vac, Bertrand 1914- DLB-88

Vail, Laurence 1891-1968 ....DLB-4

Vailland, Roger 1907-1965 ....DLB-83

Vajda, Ernest 1887-1954 ....DLB-44

Valdés, Gina 1943- DLB-122

Valdez, Luis Miguel 1940- DLB-122

Valente, José Angel 1929- DLB-108

Valenzuela, Luisa 1938- DLB-113

Valgardson, W. D. 1939- DLB-60

Valle, Vctor Manuel 1950- DLB-122

Vallejo, Armando 1949- DLB-122

Valles, Julès 1832-1885 ....DLB-123

Vallette, Marguerite Eymery (see Rachilde)

Valverde, José María 1926- DLB-108

Van Allsburg, Chris 1949- DLB-61

Van Anda, Carr 1864-1945 ....DLB-25

Vanbrugh, Sir John 1664-1726 ....DLB-80

Vance, Jack 1916?- DLB-8

Van Doren, Mark 1894-1972 ....DLB-45

van Druten, John 1901-1957 ....DLB-10

Van Duyn, Mona 1921- DLB-5

Van Dyke, Henry 1852-1933 ....DLB-71

Van Dyke, Henry 1928- DLB-33

Vane, Sutton 1888-1963 ....DLB-10

Vanguard Press DLB-46

van Itallie, Jean-Claude 1936- DLB-7

Vann, Robert L. 1879-1940 .... DLB-29

Van Rensselaer, Mariana Griswold 1851-1934 .... DLB-47

Van Rensselaer, Mrs. Schuyler (see Van
    Rensselaer, Mariana Griswold)

Van Vechten, Carl 1880-1964 .... DLB-4, 9

van Vogt, A. E. 1912- DLB-8

Varley, John 1947- Y-81

Varnhagen von Ense, Karl August 1785-1858 .... DLB-90

Varnhagen von Ense, Rahel 1771-1833 .... DLB-90

Vassa, Gustavus (see Equiano, Olaudah)

Vega, Janine Pommy 1942- DLB-16

Veiller, Anthony 1903-1965 .... DLB-44

Velásquez-Trevino, Gloria 1949- DLB-122

Venegas, Daniel ?-? DLB-82

Verne, Jules 1828-1905 .... DLB-123

Verplanck, Gulian C. 1786-1870 .... DLB-59

Very, Jones 1813-1880 .... DLB-1

Vian, Boris 1920-1959 .... DLB-72

Vickers, Roy 1888?-1965 .... DLB-77

Victoria 1819-1901 .... DLB-55

Victoria Press DLB-106

Vidal, Gore 1925- DLB-6

Viebig, Clara 1860-1952 .... DLB-66

Viereck, George Sylvester 1884-1962 .... DLB-54

Viereck, Peter 1916- DLB-5

Viets, Roger 1738-1811 .... DLB-99

Viewpoint: Politics and Performance, by David
    Edgar DLB-13

Vigil-Piñon, Evangelina 1949- DLB-122

Vigneault, Gilles 1928- DLB-60

Vigny, Alfred de 1797-1863 .... DLB-119

Vigolo, Giorgio 1894-1983 .... DLB-114

The Viking Press DLB-46

Villanueva, Alma Luz 1944- DLB-122

Villanueva, Tino 1941- DLB-82

Villard, Henry 1835-1900 .... DLB-23

Villard, Oswald Garrison 1872-1949 .... DLB-25, 91

Villarreal, José Antonio 1924- DLB-82

Villegas de Magnón, Leonor 1876-1955 .... DLB-122

Villemaire, Yolande 1949- DLB-60

Villiers de l'Isle-Adam, Jean-Marie
    Mathias Philippe-Auguste, Comte de 1838-1889 ... DLB-123

Villiers, George, Second Duke
    of Buckingham 1628-1687 .... DLB-80

Vine Press DLB-112

Viorst, Judith ?- DLB-52

Viramontes, Helena María 1954- DLB-122

Vivanco, Luis Felipe 1907-1975 .... DLB-108

Vizetelly and Company DLB-106

Voaden, Herman 1903- DLB-88

Voigt, Ellen Bryant 1943- DLB-120

Volkoff, Vladimir 1932- DLB-83

Volland, P. F., Company DLB-46

von der Grün, Max 1926- DLB-75

Vonnegut, Kurt 1922- DLB-2, 8; Y-80; DS-3

Voß, Johann Heinrich 1751-1826 .... DLB-90

Vroman, Mary Elizabeth circa 1924-1967 .... DLB-33

W

Wackenroder, Wilhelm Heinrich 1773-1798 .... DLB-90

Waddington, Miriam 1917- DLB-68

Wade, Henry 1887-1969 .... DLB-77

Wagenknecht, Edward 1900- DLB-103

Wagner, Heinrich Leopold 1747-1779 .... DLB-94

Wagoner, David 1926- DLB-5

Wah, Fred 1939- DLB-60

Waiblinger, Wilhelm 1804-1830 .... DLB-90

Wain, John 1925- DLB-15, 27

Wainwright, Jeffrey 1944- DLB-40

Waite, Peirce and Company DLB-49

Wakoski, Diane 1937- DLB-5

Walck, Henry Z. DLB-46

Walcott, Derek 1930- DLB-117; Y-81

Waldman, Anne 1945- DLB-16

Walker, Alice 1944- DLB-6, 33

Walker, George F. 1947- DLB-60

Walker, Joseph A. 1935- DLB-38

Walker, Margaret 1915- DLB-76

Walker, Ted 1934- DLB-40

Walker and Company DLB-49

Walker, Evans and Cogswell Company DLB-49

Walker, John Brisben 1847-1931 ....DLB-79

Wallace, Edgar 1875-1932 ....DLB-70

Wallant, Edward Lewis 1926-1962 ....DLB-2, 28

Walpole, Horace 1717-1797 .... DLB-39, 104

Walpole, Hugh 1884-1941 ....DLB-34

Walrond, Eric 1898-1966 ....DLB-51

Walser, Martin 1927- DLB-75, 124

Walser, Robert 1878-1956 ....DLB-66

Walsh, Ernest 1895-1926 ....DLB-4, 45

Walsh, Robert 1784-1859 ....DLB-59

Wambaugh, Joseph 1937- DLB-6; Y-83

Waniek, Marilyn Nelson 1946- DLB-120

Warburton, William 1698-1779 ....DLB-104

Ward, Aileen 1919- DLB-111

Ward, Artemus (see Browne, Charles Farrar)

Ward, Arthur Henry Sarsfield (see Rohmer, Sax)

Ward, Douglas Turner 1930- DLB-7, 38

Ward, Lynd 1905-1985 ....DLB-22

Ward, Lock and Company DLB-106

Ward, Mrs. Humphry 1851-1920 ....DLB-18

Ward, Nathaniel circa 1578-1652 ....DLB-24

Ward, Theodore 1902-1983 ....DLB-76

Wardle, Ralph 1909-1988 ....DLB-103

Ware, William 1797-1852 ....DLB-1

Warne, Frederick, and Company [U.S.] DLB-49

Warne, Frederick, and Company [U.K.] DLB-106

Warner, Charles Dudley 1829-1900 ....DLB-64

Warner, Rex 1905- DLB-15

Warner, Susan Bogert 1819-1885 .... DLB-3, 42

Warner, Sylvia Townsend 1893-1978 ....DLB-34

Warner Books DLB-46

Warr, Bertram 1917-1943 ....DLB-88

Warren, John Byrne Leicester (see De Tabley, Lord)

Warren, Lella 1899-1982 ....Y-83

Warren, Mercy Otis 1728-1814 ....DLB-31

Warren, Robert Penn 1905-1989 .... DLB-2, 48; Y-80, 89

Warton, Joseph 1722-1800 .... DLB-104, 109

Warton, Thomas 1728-1790 .... DLB-104, 109

Washington, George 1732-1799 ....DLB-31

Wassermann, Jakob 1873-1934 ....DLB-66

Wasson, David Atwood 1823-1887 ....DLB-1

Waterhouse, Keith 1929- DLB-13, 15

Waterman, Andrew 1940- DLB-40

Waters, Frank 1902- Y-86

Waters, Michael 1949- DLB-120

Watkins, Tobias 1780-1855 ....DLB-73

Watkins, Vernon 1906-1967 ....DLB-20

Watmough, David 1926- DLB-53

Watson, James Wreford (see Wreford, James)

Watson, Sheila 1909- DLB-60

Watson, Wilfred 1911- DLB-60

Watt, W. J., and Company DLB-46

Watterson, Henry 1840-1921 ....DLB-25

Watts, Alan 1915-1973 ....DLB-16

Watts, Franklin [publishing house] DLB-46

Watts, Isaac 1674-1748 ....DLB-95

Waugh, Auberon 1939- DLB-14

Waugh, Evelyn 1903-1966 ....DLB-15

Way and Williams DLB-49

Wayman, Tom 1945- DLB-53

Weatherly, Tom 1942- DLB-41

Weaver, Robert 1921- DLB-88

Webb, Frank J. ?-? DLB-50

Webb, James Watson 1802-1884 ....DLB-43

Webb, Mary 1881-1927 .... DLB-34

Webb, Phyllis 1927- DLB-53

Webb, Walter Prescott 1888-1963 .... DLB-17

Webster, Augusta 1837-1894 .... DLB-35

Webster, Charles L., and Company DLB-49

Webster, John 1579 or 1580-1634? DLB-58

Webster, Noah 1758-1843 .... DLB-1, 37, 42, 43, 73

Wedekind, Frank 1864-1918 .... DLB-118

Weems, Mason Locke 1759-1825 .... DLB-30, 37, 42

Weidenfeld and Nicolson DLB-112

Weidman, Jerome 1913- DLB-28

Weigl, Bruce 1949- DLB-120

Weinbaum, Stanley Grauman 1902-1935 .... DLB-8

Weintraub, Stanley 1929- DLB-111

Weisenborn, Gunther 1902-1969 .... DLB-69, 124

Weiß, Ernst 1882-1940 .... DLB-81

Weiss, John 1818-1879 .... DLB-1

Weiss, Peter 1916-1982 .... DLB-69, 124

Weiss, Theodore 1916- DLB-5

Weisse, Christian Felix 1726-1804 .... DLB-97

Welch, Lew 1926-1971? DLB-16

Weldon, Fay 1931- DLB-14

Wellek, René 1903- DLB-63

Wells, Carolyn 1862-1942 .... DLB-11

Wells, Charles Jeremiah circa 1800-1879 .... DLB-32

Wells, H. G. 1866-1946 .... DLB-34, 70

Wells, Robert 1947- DLB-40

Wells-Barnett, Ida B. 1862-1931 .... DLB-23

Welty, Eudora 1909- DLB-2, 102; Y-87

Wendell, Barrett 1855-1921 .... DLB-71

Wentworth, Patricia 1878-1961 .... DLB-77

Werfel, Franz 1890-1945 .... DLB-81, 124

The Werner Company DLB-49

Werner, Zacharias 1768-1823 .... DLB-94

Wersba, Barbara 1932- DLB-52

Wescott, Glenway 1901- DLB-4, 9, 102

Wesker, Arnold 1932- DLB-13

Wesley, Charles 1707-1788 .... DLB-95

Wesley, John 1703-1791 .... DLB-104

Wesley, Richard 1945- DLB-38

Wessels, A., and Company DLB-46

West, Anthony 1914-1988 .... DLB-15

West, Dorothy 1907- DLB-76

West, Jessamyn 1902-1984 .... DLB-6; Y-84

West, Mae 1892-1980 .... DLB-44

West, Nathanael 1903-1940 .... DLB-4, 9, 28

West, Paul 1930- DLB-14

West, Rebecca 1892-1983 .... DLB-36; Y-83

West and Johnson DLB-49

Western Publishing Company DLB-46

The Westminster Review 1824-1914 .... DLB-110

Wetherald, Agnes Ethelwyn 1857-1940 .... DLB-99

Wetherell, Elizabeth (see Warner, Susan Bogert)

Wetzel, Friedrich Gottlob 1779-1819 .... DLB-90

Wezel, Johann Karl 1747-1819 .... DLB-94

Whalen, Philip 1923- DLB-16

Whalley, George 1915-1983 .... DLB-88

Wharton, Edith 1862-1937 .... DLB-4, 9, 12, 78

Wharton, William 1920s?- Y-80

What's Really Wrong With Bestseller Lists Y-84

Wheatley, Dennis Yates 1897-1977 .... DLB-77

Wheatley, Phillis circa 1754-1784 .... DLB-31, 50

Wheeler, Charles Stearns 1816-1843 .... DLB-1

Wheeler, Monroe 1900-1988 .... DLB-4

Wheelock, John Hall 1886-1978 .... DLB-45

Wheelwright, John circa 1592-1679 .... DLB-24

Wheelwright, J. B. 1897-1940 .... DLB-45

Whetstone, Colonel Pete (see Noland, C. F. M.)

Whicher, Stephen E. 1915-1961 .... DLB-111

Whipple, Edwin Percy 1819-1886 .... DLB-1, 64

Whitaker, Alexander 1585-1617 .... DLB-24

Whitaker, Daniel K. 1801-1881 .... DLB-73

Whitcher, Frances Miriam 1814-1852 ....DLB-11

White, Andrew 1579-1656 ....DLB-24

White, Andrew Dickson 1832-1918 ....DLB-47

White, E. B. 1899-1985 ....DLB-11, 22

White, Edgar B. 1947- DLB-38

White, Ethel Lina 1887-1944 ....DLB-77

White, Henry Kirke 1785-1806 ....DLB-96

White, Horace 1834-1916 ....DLB-23

White, Phyllis Dorothy James (see James, P. D.)

White, Richard Grant 1821-1885 ....DLB-64

White, Walter 1893-1955 ....DLB-51

White, William, and Company DLB-49

White, William Allen 1868-1944 ....DLB-9, 25

White, William Anthony Parker (see Boucher, Anthony)

White, William Hale (see Rutherford, Mark)

Whitechurch, Victor L. 1868-1933 ....DLB-70

Whitehead, Alfred North 1861-1947 ....DLB-100

Whitehead, James 1936- Y-81

Whitehead, William 1715-1785 ....DLB-84, 109

Whitfield, James Monroe 1822-1871 ....DLB-50

Whiting, John 1917-1963 ....DLB-13

Whiting, Samuel 1597-1679 ....DLB-24

Whitlock, Brand 1869-1934 ....DLB-12

Whitman, Albert, and Company DLB-46

Whitman, Albery Allson 1851-1901 ....DLB-50

Whitman, Alden 1913-1990 ....Y-91

Whitman, Sarah Helen (Power) 1803-1878 ....DLB-1

Whitman, Walt 1819-1892 ....DLB-3, 64

Whitman Publishing Company DLB-46

Whittemore, Reed 1919- DLB-5

Whittier, John Greenleaf 1807-1892 ....DLB-1

Whittlesey House DLB-46

Wideman, John Edgar 1941- DLB-33

Wiebe, Rudy 1934- DLB-60

Wiechert, Ernst 1887-1950 ....DLB-56

Wied, Martina 1882-1957 ....DLB-85

Wieland, Christoph Martin 1733-1813 ....DLB-97

Wieners, John 1934- DLB-16

Wier, Ester 1910- DLB-52

Wiesel, Elie 1928- DLB-83; Y-87

Wiggin, Kate Douglas 1856-1923 ....DLB-42

Wigglesworth, Michael 1631-1705 ....DLB-24

Wilbur, Richard 1921- DLB-5

Wild, Peter 1940- DLB-5

Wilde, Oscar 1854-1900 ....DLB-10, 19, 34, 57

Wilde, Richard Henry 1789-1847 ....DLB-3, 59

Wilde, W. A., Company DLB-49

Wilder, Billy 1906- DLB-26

Wilder, Laura Ingalls 1867-1957 ....DLB-22

Wilder, Thornton 1897-1975 ....DLB-4, 7, 9

Wildgans, Anton 1881-1932 ....DLB-118

Wiley, Bell Irvin 1906-1980 ....DLB-17

Wiley, John, and Sons DLB-49

Wilhelm, Kate 1928- DLB-8

Wilkes, George 1817-1885 ....DLB-79

Wilkinson, Anne 1910-1961 ....DLB-88

Wilkinson, Sylvia 1940- Y-86

Wilkinson, William Cleaver 1833-1920 ....DLB-71

Willard, L. [publishing house] DLB-49

Willard, Nancy 1936- DLB-5, 52

Willard, Samuel 1640-1707 ....DLB-24

William of Auvergne 1190-1249 ....DLB-115

William of Conches circa 1090-circa 1154 ....DLB-115

William of Ockham circa 1285-1347 ....DLB-115

William of Ockham 1200 / 1205-1266 / 1271 ....DLB-115

Williams, A., and Company DLB-49

Williams, Ben Ames 1889-1953 ....DLB-102

Williams, C. K. 1936- DLB-5

Williams, Chancellor 1905- DLB-76

Williams, Charles 1886-1945 ....DLB-100

Williams, Denis 1923- DLB-117

Williams, Emlyn 1905- DLB-10, 77

Williams, Garth 1912- DLB-22

Williams, George Washington 1849-1891 ....DLB-47

Williams, Heathcote 1941- DLB-13

Williams, Hugo 1942- DLB-40

Williams, Isaac 1802-1865 ....DLB-32

Williams, Joan 1928- DLB-6

Williams, John A. 1925- DLB-2, 33

Williams, John E. 1922- DLB-6

Williams, Jonathan 1929- DLB-5

Williams, Miller 1930- DLB-105

Williams, Raymond 1921- DLB-14

Williams, Roger circa 1603-1683 ....DLB-24

Williams, Samm-Art 1946- DLB-38

Williams, Sherley Anne 1944- DLB-41

Williams, T. Harry 1909-1979 ....DLB-17

Williams, Tennessee 1911-1983 ....DLB-7; Y-83; DS-4

Williams, Valentine 1883-1946 ....DLB-77

Williams, William Appleman 1921- DLB-17

Williams, William Carlos 1883-1963 ....DLB-4, 16, 54, 86

Williams, Wirt 1921- DLB-6

Williams Brothers DLB-49

Williamson, Jack 1908- DLB-8

Willingham, Calder Baynard, Jr. 1922- DLB-2, 44

Willis, Nathaniel Parker 1806-1867 ....DLB-3, 59, 73, 74

Wilmer, Clive 1945- DLB-40

Wilson, A. N. 1950- DLB-14

Wilson, Angus 1913-1991 ....DLB-15

Wilson, Arthur 1595-1652 ....DLB-58

Wilson, Augusta Jane Evans 1835-1909 ....DLB-42

Wilson, Colin 1931- DLB-14

Wilson, Edmund 1895-1972 ....DLB-63

Wilson, Ethel 1888-1980 ....DLB-68

Wilson, Harriet E. Adams 1828?-1863? DLB-50

Wilson, Harry Leon 1867-1939 ....DLB-9

Wilson, John 1588-1667 ....DLB-24

Wilson, John 1785-1854 ....DLB-110

Wilson, Lanford 1937- DLB-7

Wilson, Margaret 1882-1973 ....DLB-9

Wilson, Michael 1914-1978 ....DLB-44

Wilson, Woodrow 1856-1924 ....DLB-47

Wimsatt, William K., Jr. 1907-1975 ....DLB-63

Winchell, Walter 1897-1972 ....DLB-29

Winchester, J. [publishing house] DLB-49

Winckelmann, Johann Joachim 1717-1768 ....DLB-97

Windham, Donald 1920- DLB-6

Wingate, Allan [publishing house] DLB-112

Winsloe, Christa 1888-1944 ....DLB-124

Winsor, Justin 1831-1897 ....DLB-47

John C. Winston Company DLB-49

Winters, Yvor 1900-1968 ....DLB-48

Winthrop, John 1588-1649 ....DLB-24, 30

Winthrop, John, Jr. 1606-1676 ....DLB-24

Wirt, William 1772-1834 ....DLB-37

Wise, John 1652-1725 ....DLB-24

Wiseman, Adele 1928- DLB-88

Wishart and Company DLB-112

Wisner, George 1812-1849 ....DLB-43

Wister, Owen 1860-1938 ....DLB-9, 78

Wither, George 1588-1667 ....DLB-121

Witherspoon, John 1723-1794 ....DLB-31

Withrow, William Henry 1839-1908 ....DLB-99

Wittig, Monique 1935- DLB-83

Wodehouse, P. G. 1881-1975 ....DLB-34

Wohmann, Gabriele 1932- DLB-75

Woiwode, Larry 1941- DLB-6

Wolcot, John 1738-1819 ....DLB-109

Wolcott, Roger 1679-1767 ....DLB-24

Wolf, Christa 1929- DLB-75

Wolf, Friedrich 1888-1953 ....DLB-124

Wolfe, Gene 1931- DLB-8

Wolfe, Thomas 1900-1938 ....DLB-9, 102; Y-85; DS-2

Wollstonecraft, Mary 1759-1797 ....DLB-39, 104

Wondratschek, Wolf 1943- DLB-75

Wood, Benjamin 1820-1900 ....DLB-23

Wood, Charles 1932- DLB-13

Wood, Mrs. Henry 1814-1887 ....DLB-18

Wood, Joanna E. 1867-1927 ....DLB-92

Wood, Samuel [publishing house] DLB-49

Wood, William ?-? DLB-24

Woodberry, George Edward 1855-1930 .... DLB-71, 103

Woodbridge, Benjamin 1622-1684 ....DLB-24

Woodcock, George 1912- DLB-88

Woodhull, Victoria C. 1838-1927 ....DLB-79

Woodmason, Charles circa 1720-? DLB-31

Woodress, Jr., James Leslie 1916- DLB-111

Woodson, Carter G. 1875-1950 ....DLB-17

Woodward, C. Vann 1908- DLB-17

Woolf, David (see Maddow, Ben)

Woolf, Leonard 1880-1969 .... DLB-100; DS-10

Woolf, Virginia 1882-1941 .... DLB-36, 100; DS-10

Woollcott, Alexander 1887-1943 ....DLB-29

Woolman, John 1720-1772 ....DLB-31

Woolner, Thomas 1825-1892 ....DLB-35

Woolsey, Sarah Chauncy 1835-1905 ....DLB-42

Woolson, Constance Fenimore 1840-1894 ....DLB-12, 74

Worcester, Joseph Emerson 1784-1865 ....DLB-1

Wordsworth, Dorothy 1771-1855 ....DLB-107

Wordsworth, Elizabeth 1840-1932 ....DLB-98

Wordsworth, William 1770-1850 .... DLB-93, 107

The Works of the Rev. John Witherspoon
      (1800-1801) [excerpts] DLB-31

A World Chronology of Important Science
      Fiction Works (1818-1979) DLB-8

World Publishing Company DLB-46

Worthington, R., and Company DLB-49

Wotton, Sir Henry 1568-1639 ....DLB-121

Wouk, Herman 1915- Y-82

Wreford, James 1915- DLB-88

Wright, C. D. 1949- DLB-120

Wright, Charles 1935- Y-82

Wright, Charles Stevenson 1932- DLB-33

Wright, Frances 1795-1852 ....DLB-73

Wright, Harold Bell 1872-1944 ....DLB-9

Wright, James 1927-1980 ....DLB-5

Wright, Jay 1935- DLB-41

Wright, Louis B. 1899-1984 ....DLB-17

Wright, Richard 1908-1960 .... DLB-76, 102; DS-2

Wright, Richard B. 1937- DLB-53

Wright, Sarah Elizabeth 1928- DLB-33

Writers and Politics: 1871-1918,
      by Ronald Gray DLB-66

Writers' Forum Y-85

Writing for the Theatre, by Harold Pinter DLB-13

Wroth, Lady Mary 1587-1653 ....DLB-121

Wycherley, William 1641-1715 ....DLB-80

Wylie, Elinor 1885-1928 ....DLB-9, 45

Wylie, Philip 1902-1971 ....DLB-9

Y

Yates, Dornford 1885-1960 ....DLB-77

Yates, J. Michael 1938- DLB-60

Yates, Richard 1926- DLB-2; Y-81

Yearsley, Ann 1753-1806 ....DLB-109

Yeats, William Butler 1865-1939 .... DLB-10, 19, 98

Yep, Laurence 1948- DLB-52

Yerby, Frank 1916-1991 ....DLB-76

Yezierska, Anzia 1885-1970 ....DLB-28

Yolen, Jane 1939- DLB-52

Yonge, Charlotte Mary 1823-1901 ....DLB-18

A Yorkshire Tragedy DLB-58

Yoseloff, Thomas [publishing house] DLB-46

Young, Al 1939- DLB-33

Young, Edward 1683-1765 ....DLB-95

Young, Stark 1881-1963 .... DLB-9, 102

Young, Waldeman 1880-1938 .... DLB-26

Young, William [publishing house] DLB-49

Yourcenar, Marguerite 1903-1987 .... DLB-72; Y-88

"You've Never Had It So Good," Gusted by "Winds of Change": British Fiction in the 1950s, 1960s, and After DLB-14

Z

Zachariä, Friedrich Wilhelm 1726-1777 .... DLB-97

Zamora, Bernice 1938- DLB-82

Zand, Herbert 1923-1970 .... DLB-85

Zangwill, Israel 1864-1926 .... DLB-10

Zapata Olivella, Manuel 1920- DLB-113

Zebra Books DLB-46

Zebrowski, George 1945- DLB-8

Zech, Paul 1881-1946 .... DLB-56

Zeidner, Lisa 1955- DLB-120

Zelazny, Roger 1937- DLB-8

Zenger, John Peter 1697-1746 .... DLB-24, 43

Zieber, G. B., and Company DLB-49

Zieroth, Dale 1946- DLB-60

Zimmer, Paul 1934- DLB-5

Zindel, Paul 1936- DLB-7, 52

Zola, Emile 1840-1902 .... DLB-123

Zolotow, Charlotte 1915- DLB-52

Zschokke, Heinrich 1771-1848 .... DLB-94

Zubly, John Joachim 1724-1781 .... DLB-31

Zu-Bolton II, Ahmos 1936- DLB-41

Zuckmayer, Carl 1896-1977 .... DLB-56, 124

Zukofsky, Louis 1904-1978 .... DLB-5

zur Mühlen, Hermynia 1883-1951 .... DLB-56

Zweig, Arnold 1887-1968 .... DLB-66

Zweig, Stefan 1881-1942 .... DLB-81, 118

ISBN 0-8103-5384-9

90000

9 780810 354845